Munich & Bavaria

Andrea Schulte-Peevers
Jeremy Gray, Catherine Le Nevez

Contents

Franconia
p183

Eastern Bavaria
p157

Allgäu-Bavarian
Swabia p247

Munich
p51

Salzburg &
Upper Bavaria p113

Destination Munich & Bavaria

Bavaria is a land every bit as bewitching as in the movie of your imagination. Perhaps the opening scene has you strolling through a medieval town laced with narrow, meandering lanes, their cobblestones worn smooth by centuries of carriages, horses' hooves and leather soles. Or possibly you're driving along an undulating country road, heading for a whimsical fantasy castle dreamed up by a noble, lonely and tragic king.

The plot may next hurtle you skyward into the big-shouldered Alps, carved into rugged glory by glaciers and the elements. Trails weave through an enchanted Hänsel-&-Gretel forest. Well-groomed cows graze lazily in high-mountain pastures, the clanging of their heavy bells echoing across the valley. In the distance you spot the onion-domed church in a hamlet where traditions have changed little for centuries. Cut!

You're in Munich now, a grand metropolis, at once radiantly old-world and joyfully modern. You're drinking in palaces where powder-wigged gents once waltzed with their silken-gowned ladies. Then it's on to museums filled with an Aladdin's cave worth of treasures. And the beer halls beckon, of course. A waitress slams down an enormous mug of foamy nectar before you. Ah, Bavarian beer. It's the best in the world, some say. And they're right.

The next scenes may have you schussing down powdered slopes or wandering the halls of castles redolent of intrigue and betrayal. You could join lustily in song and dance at a festival or head to a concert hall to be swept away by the celestial music of Mozart.

Bavaria is all that and then some. And no matter how your 'movie' ends, you'll know that you and this enchanted land have delivered an Oscar-worthy performance.

City

ESBIN ANDERSON PHOTOGRAPHY

Catch a bird's-eye view of the historic Altstadt (old town) in Munich (p63)

OTHER HIGHLIGHTS

- The Oktoberfest (p88) is the world's largest beer party and deluges the city with thousands of visitors every year.
- Munich's trio of Pinakothek museums (p70) has one of the world's greatest collections of European art.
- Visit Munich's artsy Schwabing district (p72), home to the main university and hip bars and cafés.

On a hot afternoon, there's nothing better than downing a cold beer in a Munich beer garden (p97)

WAYNE WALTON

Explore the neo-Gothic Neues Rathaus (New Town Hall) and discover the delightful glockenspiel (p64)

THOMA

MICHELLE LEWIS

Climb every mountain and cast your gaze over Salzburg from the heights of Festung Hohensalzburg (p117), Salzburg

MICHELLE LEWIS

Delight in the glorious baroque cloak of the Romanesque Stiftskirche St Peter (p120), Salzburg

Travel beautiful, old-world Salzburg (p125) in a romantic horse-drawn carriage

MARK HONAN

Country

The Altes Rathaus (Old Town Hall; p200), on a little
island in the Regnitz, is Bamberg's most photographed building

Local colour and tradition (p26) abounds
in picturesque regional Bavaria

Stroll the maze of lanes in the walled city
of Rothenburg ob der Tauber (p229)

OTHER HIGHLIGHTS

- The Tölzer Land (p134) is a pastiche of crystal-
  clear lakes, snow-covered mountains and
  convivial towns.

- Tour the Romantic Road (p12), Germany's most
  famous touring route, which winds for 350km
  from Würzburg to Füssen.

- Schloss Neuschwanstein (p261), Ludwig II's
  fairytale palace, was the inspiration for the
  castle in Disney's *Sleeping Beauty*.

DAVID PEEVERS

Walhalla (p166), a neoclassical temple overlooking the Danube, is a shrine to Germany's greatest poets, thinkers and scientists

MICHELLE LEWIS

Enjoy fabulous Alpine views from the Eagle's Nest (p148), a birthday gift to Adolf Hitler

The Danube, Ilz and Inn Rivers converge at Passau (p169), a delightful town with baroque flair

WAYNE WALTON

Outdoors

ANDREW LUBRAN

Lush, mountain paths await the keen walker in the many forests of Bavaria (p42)

Watch your step as you make your way through the 'Magic Forest' in the Zauberwald (p150).

GARETH McCORMACK

Embark on an adrenaline-fuelled two-wheeled adventure in Bavaria (p39)

MARTIN

OTHER HIGHLIGHTS

- Meet some of the animal inhabitants while wandering the trails through the Bavarian Forest (p175).
- Glide past craggy cliffs on a boat ride through the dramatic Danube Gorge (p166) near Regensburg.
- Live like a German and soak it up at a spa – visit the historic spa towns of Bad Reichenhall (p144) and Bad Tölz (p134).

Getting Started

Bavaria has an extremely well organised tourism infrastructure. Anyone from backpackers to families to jet-setters will find their needs and expectations met. Room and travel reservations are a good idea during peak season (July and August and around major holidays), but otherwise you can keep your advance planning to a minimum.

WHEN TO GO

Bavaria is a great place to visit year-round, but most people arrive between May and September when sunny skies and warm temperatures are most likely. This is the best time for hiking, cycling, water sports and other outdoor pursuits, for hanging out in beer gardens and outdoor cafés, and for partying at festivals or alfresco events.

See Climate Charts on p277 for more information.

The shoulder seasons (March to May and October) bring fewer tourists and often surprisingly pleasant weather. Spring, when flowers and fruit trees are in bloom, is a lovely time to visit, as is autumn when trees are cloaked in a rainbow of colours.

In winter, skies tend to be gloomy, daylight hours short and temperatures low. With the exception of winter sports, activities during these months are likely to focus more on culture and city life. Expect reduced opening times or seasonal closures at museums and other sightseeing venues. Many smaller lodging establishments, especially in rural areas, close down from November to early December. The ski season usually starts in early to mid-December, moves into full swing after New Year and winds down sometime in March.

For related information, see Holidays (p279).

COSTS & MONEY

Outside major cities such as Munich and Nuremberg, Bavaria can be quite a bargain. In most regions you can live comfortably on about €100 a day; double that and you'll be living it up. For mere survival you'll need to budget from €40 to €50, but you'll be camping or sleeping in hostels, preparing your own meals or eating snack food, and limiting your entertainment.

Comfortable midrange accommodation starts at about €80 for a double room with breakfast in the cities, and €50 in the countryside. Many hotels and hostels have special 'family rooms' with three or four beds, or they can supply sleeping cots for a small fee. Families can also take advantage of discounts offered by most sightseeing venues and tour operators. For more information on travelling with children, see p276.

DON'T LEAVE HOME WITHOUT...

- Valid travel insurance (p279)
- Running shoes to burn off all that beer
- A cholesterol meter (all that meat!)
- Booking accommodation when travelling in summer (p274)
- An umbrella and rainproof shoes, and clothing for those days when the sun is a no-show
- Nerves of steel for driving on autobahns
- This book and an open mind

Itineraries
CLASSIC ROUTES

THE ROMANTIC ROAD

One week / 350km

Kick off your adventure in **Würzburg** (p216), a lively city shaped by wine, bishops and architecture. From here it's south through the Tauber Valley where **Bad Mergentheim** (p226), headquarters of the Teutonic Knights, **Weikersheim** (p228) with its Schloss (palace), and **Creglingen** (p228), famous for the Riemenschneider altar, all merit a stop. Top billing goes to **Rothenburg ob der Tauber** (p229), whose medieval looks and charming lanes make for an irresistible sightseeing cocktail. Plunge on via tiny **Feuchtwangen** (p235) to **Dinkelsbühl** (p236) and **Nördlingen** (p256); which are encircled by ancient town walls. Further south, magnificent **Harburg** (p257), a story-book medieval castle, lords over the valley. Continue via **Donauwörth** (p258) to energetic **Augsburg** (p248), the largest city on the Romantic Road. Many churches line this route, but the one packing the biggest punch is the **Wieskirche** (p259), a composition of truly heavenly proportions. Next is what many consider the crowning glory of the Romantic Road: **Schloss Neuschwanstein** (p261), the 'fairy-tale' castle and embodiment of both the genius and tragedy of its creator, King Ludwig II.

Germany's most popular holiday route, the Romantic Road is a spectacular ribbon of riches, myth and legend. It meanders through some of the finest in culture, history and nature Bavaria has to offer. Most people follow the north–south order outlined here but vice versa works just as well.

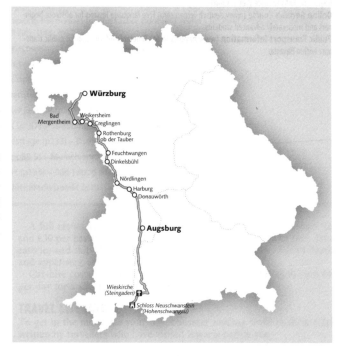

THE BEST OF BAVARIA   Two to three weeks / 1000km

Munich (p51), Bavaria's capital, is the starting point of this loop route. Allow at least three days to tour the city's palaces, museums and churches and to absorb its unique mix of cosmopolitan flair and earthy *Gemütlichkeit* (cosiness). Heading east, make a stop at the Chiemsee, a vast lake where **Schloss Herrenchiemsee** (p139) – King Ludwig II's version of Versailles – is the top-flight attraction. Next up is sophisticated **Salzburg** (p114), across the Austrian border. Mozart's birth town is an achingly beautiful place that also had a starring role in the famous musical *The Sound of Music*. From here, the mountains, lakes and intriguing, if dark, history of **Berchtesgadener Land** (p146) make for a dramatic side trip. Otherwise plough on northward to postcard-pretty **Passau** (p169), an Italianate city perched at the confluence of three rivers. Further north beckons **Regensburg** (p158), a lively university town with a nearly impeccably preserved medieval core. Bustling **Nuremberg** (p184), meanwhile, is another major draw, and not only for Third Reich history buffs. Continue north to **Bamberg** (p198), famous for its excellent breweries and pristine Altstadt (old town), a Unesco World Heritage site. West of here, **Würzburg** (p216) also got the Unesco nod for its famous baroque Residenz. It's also the gateway to the **Franconian Wine Country** (p223) as well as the Romantic Road, where major stops include **Rothenburg ob der Tauber** (p229) and **Augsburg** (p248). For details, see The Romantic Road itinerary opposite. From Augsburg it's a quick drive back to Munich.

Bavaria is packed with jaw-dropping scenery, fanciful palaces and cities dripping in history, as you will discover on this grand loop route. It can be 'done' in two weeks but adding a few more will allow you to immerse yourself more deeply in this great region and its bevy of treats, treasures and temptations.

TAILORED TRIPS

BAVARIAN BREW

Beer is to Bavaria what tea is to Britain and wine to France – a national drink or, as some may say, an obsession. Those who worship at the altar of hops may want to consider a pilgrimage to these fine places for a personal in-depth study. Even if you can't make it to the Oktoberfest (see the boxed text on pp88-9) in Munich, you can still enjoy brews by the city's six local beermeisters in a boisterous beer hall, including the (in)famous **Hofbräuhaus** (p97), or a convivial beer garden. Monasteries have produced some fine quality brews since medieval times and

today's monks of **Kloster Andechs** (p107), south of Munich, and **Kloster Weltenburg** (p166), near **Regensburg** (itself no slouch in the beer department; p158) do their utmost to uphold the tradition. North of here, Franconia is especially famous for the foamy stuff, as detailed in the boxed text on p196. Those with an academic bent should steer towards the brewery museums in **Bayreuth** (p206) and **Kulmbach** (p211). The latter is as famous for its unique *Eisbock* (iced beer) as nearby **Bamberg** (p198) is for its equally distinctive *Rauchbier* (smoked beer). But no matter where you're headed, you'll never be far from a mug of amber ale.

FAIRY-TALE FANTASIES

Once upon a time, Bavaria was an enchanted land ruled by bishops, princes and other feudal lords. Each of them resided in a splendid Schloss or *Burg* (castle) that today offer a good look at the lifestyles of the rich and powerful of yore. No-one conjured more romantic visions than madcap King Ludwig II, whose **Schloss Neuschwanstein** (p261) is Bavaria's most visited tourist attraction. Other Ludwig fantasies, such as **Schloss Linderhof** (p132), **Schloss Herrenchiemsee** (p139) and the remote **Jagdschloss Schachen** (p128), are equally as impressive. In Munich, **Schloss Nymphenburg** (p81), a huge confection backed by sprawling gardens, is an elegant presence.

In the same vein, though much smaller, is the lesser-known **Schloss Weikersheim** (p228) on the Romantic Road. A good place to fancy yourself a knight in shining armour (or perhaps a damsel in distress) is the medieval **Harburg** (p257), also along this famous holiday road. In the Middle Ages castles were of course not only residences but had defensive purposes, a fact that leaps into focus at the fortified **Veste Coburg** (p214), overlooking its namesake town. Commanding an equally impressive hilltop setting is **Festung Hohensalzburg** (p117), one of Europe's largest fortresses.

The Authors

ANDREA SCHULTE-PEEVERS   Coordinating Author, Eastern Bavaria

Andrea grew up in northern Germany thinking that Bavarians, with their dirndls, lederhosen and accent, were, well, kinda cute. But when sent on assignment to research this guide's 1st edition (then called *Bavaria*), she found that they're also pretty cool. So she was more than happy to return to the land of 'beemers', beer and *Bratwurst* (sausage), for a quick but joyous romp around Eastern Bavaria. Andrea now makes her home in Los Angeles with her husband David and cat, Mep the Fierce. She has worked on about two dozen other LP guides, including *Germany* and *Berlin*.

My Bavaria

While I love Munich, the Alps and Neuschwanstein as much as anybody – how could one not? – the places in Bavaria that intrigue me most are those that take me away from the tourist hordes. In springtime, I could imagine few lovelier regions to explore than the gentle Naturpark Altmühltal (p237), either on a leisurely bicycle tour or paddling a canoe. In summer, French-flavoured Lindau (p268) on Lake Constance beckons with swimming, sailing, windsurfing and other watery delights. Medieval Regensburg (p158) is a charismatic spot for soaking up the final rays of summer, while in snowy winters, the skiing is excellent in the Bavarian Forest (p175), far from the madding crowd of the Alpine resorts. The beer, of course, is delicious any time of the year.

JEREMY GRAY   The Culture, Munich, Salzburg & Upper Bavaria

Jeremy worked on the Munich, Salzburg & Upper Bavaria and the Culture chapters of this book. A lifelong fan of Bavarian *Lebensqualität* (lifestyle), not to mention tasty *Leberkäs* (meatloaf), Jeremy has written extensively about southern Germany and jumped at the chance to go back. Previously, he penned the 1st edition of Lonely Planet's *Munich* and contributed to its *Germany* guide. Jeremy lives in Berlin.

CATHERINE LE NEVEZ   Franconia, Allgäu-Bavarian Swabia

An Aussie, Catherine first roadtripped in Europe at age four, when she made her initial German foray. This assignment was a somewhat wilder ride, in an über-complicated hire car that was supplied without an instruction manual or winter tyres, leading to some heart-stopping slides down snowy slopes, among other (mis)adventures. Despite this, she's enchanted by the Romantic Road and surrounding regions, and by the kind-hearted and fun-loving people she met along the way. Catherine recently completed her Doctorate of Creative Arts in Writing, while on the road in far-flung locations.

Snapshot

Life's pretty good in Bavaria these days. While the rest of Germany is mired in an economic malaise not seen since the end of WWII, the country's southernmost state is sitting pretty with an unemployment rate almost 4% below the national average of 10.3% (at the time of writing) and an enviable growth rate of nearly 30% over the past 10 years. Its gross domestic product now surpasses that of Belgium, Switzerland or Sweden. And this is a single German state!

The engines driving this economic powerhouse are not only traditional manufacturers such as Audi, BMW and electronics giant Siemens; Bavaria has also taken leading roles in high-tech fields, including aviation, aeronautics, computers, medical technology and pharmaceutical research. An openness toward innovation and adaptability, a favourable business climate and a highly qualified workforce are all factors playing a role in this success story.

FAST FACTS

Area: 70,550 sq km

Population: 12,397,000

Number of pigs: 3,731,000

GDP: €371 billion

Per capita income: €2462 per month (blue-collar), €3470 per month (white-collar)

Unemployment rate: 6.5%

Hotel beds: 558,000

Kilometres of autobahn: 2299

Passenger cars: 7.1 million

Museums: 1100

And the good news doesn't stop there: Bavaria has the lowest air pollution levels in Germany (albeit thanks to relying primarily on nuclear power, see p38). Its popularity with tourists – both domestic and foreign – is unflagging due to its stunning scenery and *Gemütlichkeit* (cosiness), and even its birth rate beats the national average.

Education is another area where Bavaria scores relatively high grades. While German students as a whole did poorly in a recent international study comparing academic performance, Bavaria found itself near the top of the class. Experts credit this overachiever status to higher and more efficient spending programmes and tougher educational standards in general. And apparently the introduction, a few years ago, of special German courses for immigrant children also contributed to the good report card.

The Bavarian state government, helmed by Prime Minister Edmund Stoiber of the conservative Christian Social Union (CSU) since 1993, considers language proficiency a key component to the integration of foreigners into Bavarian society, currently a hotly debated issue in the media and at dinner tables. Non-Germans make up 10% of the state's population, the vast majority of them Turks. Although largely long-term residents, many still live in social, intellectual and, in some cities, physical ghettos, where they're either unwilling or unable to assimilate fully and instead cling to their own traditions and values.

If Stoiber has his way, this situation is about to change. His party recently included a plank in its platform stipulating that foreigners who refuse to integrate risk a cut in their welfare payments. The Bavarian state parliament also passed a law prohibiting female Muslim teachers from wearing headscarves in public schools. It remains to be seen if any of these measures are just ham-fisted token gestures pandering to right-wing voters or serious attempts at addressing the complex and sensitive problems facing multicultural societies in Bavaria and beyond.

History

Wedged against the magnificent Alps, Bavaria is Germany's largest and southernmost state, as well as one of the oldest in Europe with origins in the 6th century. Today's territory unites three distinct tribes: the Bajuwaren (Bavarians), the Franken (Franconians) and the Schwaben (Swabians). Each developed quite separately until united by Napoleon as the Kingdom of Bavaria in 1806. Although never at the centre of power, Bavaria was still a key player in continental politics for centuries. Governed by the same family, the Wittelsbachs, for over 700 years, it was able to form a distinct culture that continues to shape its image and identity to this day.

ORIGINS

The earliest inhabitants of today's Bavarian territory were probably Celts, who proved to be an easy pushover for the Romans who began barrelling across the Alps in the 1st century AD. The invaders founded the province of Raetia, whose main settlements included Augusta Vindelicorum (Augsburg, p248), Ratisbona (Regensburg, p158) and Boiodurum (Passau, p169). The Limes, a fortified Roman wall, ran right through today's Naturpark Altmühltal (p237) in Franconia. By the 5th century the tables were turned on the Romans by marauding eastern Germanic tribes pushing up the Danube valley in search of new *Lebensraum* (living space).

The precise origin of the Bavarian tribe is obscure, but it's widely assumed that it coalesced from the remaining Romans, the newcomers from the east and the original Celtic population. The name 'Bajuwaren', which roughly translates as 'men of Baia', can be traced to a tribe hailing from Boiohaemum (Bohemia) in today's Czech Republic.

The Franken began forming in the 3rd century AD from several western Germanic tribes who settled along the central and lower Rhine River, on the border with the Roman Empire. The Schwaben, meanwhile, are a subtribe of the population group of the Alemannen (Alemannic tribes) who inhabited the southwestern corner of Germany from the 2nd century AD. In the 3rd century, they expanded their territory eastward by battling the Romans, eventually pushing as far east as the Lech River, which today still forms the boundary between Swabia and Upper Bavaria.

BAVARIA & THE FRANKISH EMPIRE

Members of the Agilofingian dynasty formed the first Bavarian duchy in the 6th century, with Garibald I (r 555–91) being the first known duke. The region's main power players of the day, however, were the Franks, led by the Merovingian clan, who repeatedly tried to meddle in Bavaria's affairs. Despite such adversity, the duchy managed to consolidate its power, primarily through strategic marriages, eventually controlling a vast region extending as far as Carinthia in today's Austria.

This didn't sit too well with the Franks, where a leadership change had put the ambitious Carolingians into pole position. In the 8th century, they set out to bring the region's renegade duchies under their control,

On Bavaria's state crest the old Bavarians are represented by a blue panther and a golden lion, the Franconians by a red-and-white rake and the Swabians by three black lions.

555	8th century
First Bavarian duchy founded under Garibald I of the Agilofingian dynasty	Christianisation takes hold as roving missionaries found bishoprics and monasteries

first crushing Swabia in 744, then defeating Duke Tassilo of Bavaria in 788. This spelled an end to Bavarian and Swabian independence as they now became absorbed into the powerful Frankenreich (Frankish empire).

In 843, the Treaty of Verdun divided this Reich into two kingdoms: Westfranken (western Frankish empire, the future France) and Ostfranken (eastern Frankish empire, the future Germany), with Bavaria belonging to the latter, along with Swabia, Franconia and Saxony. Regensburg (p158) emerged as a centre of the kingdom, especially after Emperor Arnulf of Carinthia made it his main royal residence in the late 9th century.

EARLY CHRISTIANITY

Meanwhile, another mighty force had muscled its way across the land: Christianity. While Bavaria's Agilofingians had adopted the faith early on, most people remained pagan until a league of Irish, Anglo-Saxon and Franconian missionaries began spreading the gospel in the 7th century. Christianity quickly took root and by 739 there were bishoprics in Regensburg, Passau, Freising (p105) and Salzburg (p114). This was accompanied by the founding of monasteries, mostly of the Benedictine variety, such as those in Ottobeuren (p267), Benediktbeuern (p136) and Weltenburg (p166).

Friedrich Heer's *Holy Roman Empire* details the events, intrigues and conflicts of the political construct that shaped European history for more than 1000 years.

BAVARIA & THE HOLY ROMAN EMPIRE

Ostfranken's stature reached new heights when one of its kings Otto I, a Saxon, was crowned Kaiser (emperor) by the pope in 962, which marked the beginning of the so-called Holy Roman Empire, a major force in European history until 1806.

The title *Kaiser* (emperor) is a direct derivation of the Roman word 'Caesar'.

Otto's promotion did not make it any easier for the Bavarian dukes to assert their independent streak. Throughout the 9th and 10th centuries, changing fortunes saw Bavaria variously governed by its own duke, by king-appointed vassals or directly by the emperor. Stability finally arrived when the Welf dynasty came to power in 1070; it ruled Bavaria for five generations and, along with the Hohenstaufen (Staufians) of Swabia, became one of the most powerful families in Central Europe.

The Welfs' rule finally came to an end after Duke Heinrich der Löwe (Henry the Lion), who founded Munich (p51) in 1158, showed himself a tad too ambitious and was thus stripped of his titles and power by Emperor Friedrich Barbarossa in 1180. Later that year, the emperor appointed Otto von Wittelsbach, a distant relative of his, as the new Bavarian duke. It was a momentous decision, for the Wittelsbach family would remain in charge of the duchy and later the kingdom for an unprecedented seven centuries, until 1918.

GROWING PAINS

Over the next generations, the Wittelsbachs put their energies towards expanding Bavarian territory – and with it their sphere of influence – through purchase, marriage, exchange and war. The acquisition of the Palatinate, an area along the Rhine River northwest of present-day boundaries, was a good start back in 1214, but the family's fortunes peaked when one of their

962	1158
Otto I crowned Kaiser by the pope, marking the beginning of the Holy Roman Empire	Duke Heinrich der Löwe (Henry the Lion) founds Munich

own, Ludwig the Bavarian, became Holy Roman emperor in 1328. As the first Wittelsbach on the imperial throne, Ludwig used his exalted position to bring various territories, including the March of Brandenburg (around Berlin), the Tyrol (part of today's Austria) and several Dutch provinces under Bavarian control.

In subsequent centuries, however, the Wittelsbachs' might was weakened, not by quarrels with other factions but by an old-fashioned law of inheritance. If a ruler had more than one son, upon his death the brothers either had to rule all of Bavaria together or carve it up between them. This system became so ludicrous that, at one time, there were four separate sub-duchies: Bavaria-Straubing, Bavaria-Landshut, Bavaria-Ingolstadt and Bavaria-Munich. In 1506 Duke Albrecht IV (nicknamed 'the Wise'; r 1460–1508) finally put an end to the nonsense by introducing the 'law of primogeniture' by which the first-born son got the entire lot. A 'wise' decision indeed.

Franconia and Swabia, meanwhile, remained a hotchpotch of fiefdoms owned and governed either by secular rulers, counts, dukes, margraves etc or clerical lords (the prince-bishops). The most powerful prince-bishops sat in Würzburg (p216), but Bamberg (p198) and Eichstätt (p238) were also controlled in this fashion. Some cities managed to break from local rule and become so-called 'free imperial cities', directly beholden only to the Kaiser. Nuremberg (p184) as well as Augsburg (p248) were important free imperial cities, but smaller ones, including Rothenburg ob der Tauber (p229), Dinkelsbühl (p236), Nördlingen (p256) and Kaufbeuren (p267) also achieved this quasi-autonomous status.

The world's first pocket watch, the so-called Nuremberg Egg, was invented in 1510 by locksmith Peter Henlein.

RELIGIOUS STRIFE

In 1517, in the eastern German university town of Wittenberg, the monk and theology professor Martin Luther sparked the Reformation with his 95 theses that condemned the Roman Catholic Church's practice of selling indulgences to exonerate sins. The following year, Church authorities ordered Luther to Augsburg demanding that he repudiate his theses, which he refused. Despite the Church's attempt to quash the reformer, his teachings resonated in large parts of the Reich, especially in Franconia and Swabia. Supporters included Margrave Georg von Ansbach-Kulmbach and several free imperial cities including, ironically, Augsburg. In the duchy of Bavaria, by contrast, the Reformation was ultimately a flop.

Albrecht the Wise's son, Wilhelm IV (r 1508–50) had initially been sympathetic to Luther's teachings but feared that a reformed faith would undermine his authority. He clamped down on anyone embracing Protestantism and encouraged the Jesuits to establish their headquarters at the university of Ingolstadt. But neither he nor Emperor Karl V could squeeze the Reformation genie back in the bottle. The Peace of Augsburg in 1555 gave each local ruler the right to determine the religion of his principality and essentially put the Catholic and Lutheran churches more or less on equal footing.

But the religious issue simply would not die, leading first to the Counter-Reformation before escalating into the Thirty Years' War (1618–48), which brought widespread starvation and left Europe's soil drenched with the

Highroad to the Stake: A Tale of Witchcraft, by Michael Kunze, is a haunting account of the life, arrest, torture and execution of an entire family of paupers in 16th century Bavaria.

738 years of Wittelsbach reign begin with Otto von Wittelsbach's appointment as duke of Bavaria by Emperor Friedrich Barbarossa | Peace of Augsburg allows princes to decide which religion to adopt in their principality

blood of millions. During the conflict, Bavaria's Duke Maximilian I (r 1598–1651) fought firmly on the side of Catholic Emperor Ferdinand II. His loyalty paid off handsomely in 1623 when the Kaiser elevated Bavaria to an electorate (ie giving it a say in the election of future emperors), making Maximilian *Kurfürst* (prince elector) and tacking the region north of Regensburg (the Upper Palatinate) onto his territory.

The war finally came to an end with the Peace of Westphalia in 1648, but the Reich was ravaged and splintered into more than 300 states and about 1000 smaller territories. The once mighty Holy Roman Empire had turned into a nominal, essentially impotent entity.

POLITICAL AMBITIONS

The Thirty Years' War made France the dominant power in Europe. Meanwhile Bavaria lay largely in shambles, leaving Maximilian's son and successor, Ferdinand Maria (r 1651–79), to repair the damage while keeping Bavaria out of conflict. His son, however, Maximilian II Emanuel (r 1679–1726), was a man of great ambition and poor judgment.

In the 1680s, he bravely fought for the Habsburg Kaiser in the battles against the Turks that spelled the end of the Ottoman Empire. Much to his dismay, his allegiance did not lead to the rewards (land, titles, power) he had expected. So he tried again, this time switching sides and fighting with France against Austria in the War of the Spanish Succession (1701–14). This didn't go so well either. The conflict ended in a disastrous Franco-Bavarian loss and a 10-year occupation of Bavaria by Habsburg troops. Not only had Maximilian II Emanuel failed to achieve his personal goals, his flip-flop policies had also seriously weakened Bavaria's position.

His son, Karl Albrecht (r 1726–45), was determined to avenge his father's double humiliation and initially seemed to have better luck. Through some fancy political manoeuvring, he managed to take advantage of the confusion caused by the Austrian War of Succession and, with the backing of Prussia and France, was crowned Emperor Karl VII in 1742. His triumph, however, would be short-lived as Bavaria was quickly reoccupied by Austrian troops. Upon Karl Albrecht's death in 1745, his son Maximilian III Joseph (r 1745–77) was forced forever to renounce the Wittelsbach's claims to the imperial crown.

Until the arrival of Maximilian III Joseph the progressive ideas of the Enlightenment that had swept through other parts of Europe in the early 18th century had largely been ignored in Bavaria. Not busy waging war like his father and grandfather, he focused on reforming the legal system, founded the Bavarian Academy of Sciences and made school compulsory till the age of 16.

During secularisation in the early 19th century, even the monk on Munich's coat of arms was banished (it re-appeared in 1835, as did many monasteries).

BIRTH OF A KINGDOM

Modern Bavaria, more or less as we know it today, was established in the early 19th century thanks to a ferocious little Corsican named Napoleon. At the onset of the Napoleonic wars (1799–1815), Bavaria initially found itself again on the losing side against France. Tired of war and demonstrating a pragmatic streak at the urging of his powerful minister Maximilian Graf von Montgelas, Kurfürst Maximilian IV Joseph

1618–48	1810
Thirty Years' War brings murder, starvation and disease, decimating Europe's population from 21 million to 13.5 million	Ludwig I's wedding to Princess Therese von Sachsen-Hildburghausen launches the tradition of the annual Munich Oktoberfest

(r 1799–1825) decided to put his territory under Napoleon's protection. This would turn out to be smart move that ultimately paved the way to modern Bavarian statehood.

In 1803, after victories over Austria and Prussia, Napoleon set about remapping much of Europe. Bavaria fared rather well, nearly doubling its size by receiving control over the territories of Franconia and Swabia. In 1806 Napoleon created the kingdom of Bavaria, which was helmed by his new best friend who now called himself King Maximilian I Joseph.

Napoleon didn't know it, but Bavaria's alliance with France was only strategic and ultimately short-lived. Already in 1813, with the French ruler's fortunes waning, Montgelas shrewdly threw the new kingdom's support against him and behind Austria and Prussia. Napoleon's defeat led to the Congress of Vienna (1814–15), in which the victorious allies again reshaped European boundaries. Thanks to this time being on the winning side, Bavaria got to keep most of the territory it had obtained with Napoleon's help.

Meanwhile, Montgelas worked feverishly to forge a united state from the mosaic of 'core Bavaria', Franconia and Swabia. He did so largely by introducing sweeping political, administrative and social changes, including the secularisation of the monasteries. The reforms ultimately led to Bavaria's first constitution in 1808, which was based on rights of freedom, equality and property and the promise of representative government. Ten years later Bavaria got its first *Landtag* (two-chamber parliament).

Germany's first stamp was issued in Bavaria in November 1849 and was called the *Schwarze Einser* (Black Penny).

LUDWIG I

Under Maximilian I Joseph's son, Ludwig I (r 1825–48), Bavaria became an artistic and cultural centre that drew many prominent painters, poets and philosophers to Munich. Much of Bavaria's finest neoclassical architecture was built on his watch, including the Glyptothek (p69) and Propyläen (p69) on Munich's Königsplatz, and the monumental Befreiungshalle (p166) and Walhalla (p166), both on the Danube. The king was also keen on new technology and heavily supported the idea of a nationwide railway. The first, short line, which ran from Nuremberg to Fürth, opened during his reign in 1835.

Although initially a strong supporter of Bavaria's constitution, revolutionary rumblings in other parts of Europe coaxed out Ludwig's reactionary streak. An arch-Catholic, he restored the monasteries, introduced press censorship and authorised arrests of students, journalists and university professors whom he judged to be subversive. Bavaria was turning restrictive, even as French and American democratic ideas flourished elsewhere in Germany.

Bruce Seymour's *Lola Montez: A Life* is a highly entertaining and comprehensive romp through the life of Bavaria's ultimate courtesan whose affair with Ludwig I changed the course of history.

In the end, it wasn't politics but his libido that brought on Ludwig's downfall. The king made no secret of his passion for beautiful women, even commissioning a series of portraits of stunning females for his Schönheitengalerie (Gallery of Beauties) in Munich's Schloss Nymphenburg (p81). Most of his affairs were kept out of the public eye but eventually the king met a dancer named Lola Montez (see the boxed text, p22). Their affair had disastrous consequences.

On 22 March 1848 Ludwig abdicated in favour of his son, Maximilian II (r 1848–64) who finally put into place many of the progressive reforms

1835	1886
First railway starts operating between Nuremberg and Fürth	Ludwig II drowns under mysterious circumstances in Lake Starnberg

Ludwig II of Bavaria: The Swan King by Christopher McIntosh tries to unravel the mysteries surrounding the fairy-tale king without shying away from such controversial issues as his alleged homosexuality and madness.

anchored in the constitution but ignored by his father, such as the abolition of censorship and the right to assemble.

LUDWIG II

Maximilian II's son Ludwig II (r 1864–86) took the reins of power at the tender age of 18 and continued passing a wealth of progressive measures, including welfare for the poor, liberalised marriage law and free trade. Unfortunately for the young king, lasting peace would be harder to come by.

Bound by his alliances and pressured by his cabinet, Ludwig found himself at war on the Austrian side against Prussia in 1866. Defeat came quickly and brought grave consequences. Prussia demanded that Ludwig give up supreme command over Bavarian troops in wartime. Four years later, this concession forced Bavaria to fight with Prussia against France in the Franco-German War of 1870–71, this time on the victorious side.

This war was the final piece in Prussian Prime Minister Otto von Bismarck's grand plan to create a vast, unified Germany. It soon became clear

---

LOLA MONTEZ, FEMME FATALE   *Jeremy Gray*

A whip-toting dominatrix and seductress of royalty, Lola Montez (1818–61) showed the prim Victorians what sex scandals were all about. Born as Eliza Gilbert in Limerick, Ireland, to a young British army officer and a 13-year-old Creole chorus girl, Lola claimed to be the illegitimate daughter of poet Lord Byron (or, depending on her mood, of a matador). When her actual father died of cholera in India, her mother remarried and then shipped the seven-year-old Eliza off to Scotland. During her time in Scotland she was occasionally seen running stark-naked through the streets. She then finished her schooling in Paris and after an unsuccessful stab at acting, she reinvented herself as the Spanish dancer, Lola Montez.

She couldn't dance either but her beauty fascinated men, who fell at her feet – sometimes under the lash of her ever-present riding crop. One time she fired her pistol at a lover who'd performed poorly, but he managed to escape with his trousers about his knees.

Those succumbing to her charms included the tsar of Russia, who paid her 1000 roubles for a 'private audience', novelist Alexandre Dumas and composer Franz Liszt. Liszt eventually tired of Lola's incendiary temper, locked his sleeping mistress in their hotel room, and fled – leaving a deposit for the furniture Lola would demolish when she awoke.

When fired by a Munich theatre manager, Lola took her appeal to the court of Ludwig I himself. As the tale goes, Ludwig asked casually whether her lovely figure was a work of nature or art. The direct gal she was, Lola seized a pair of scissors and slit open the front of her dress, leaving the ageing monarch to judge for himself. Predictably, she was rehired (and the manager sacked).

The king fell head over heels for Lola, giving her a huge allowance, a lavish palace and even the doubtful title of Countess of Landsfeld. Her ladyship virtually began running the country, too, and when Munich students rioted during the 1848 revolution, Lola had Ludwig shut down the university. This was too much for the townsfolk, who joined the students in revolt. Ludwig was forced to abdicate and soon Lola was chased out of town.

Lola cancanned her way around the world; her increasingly lurid show was very popular with Californian gold miners. Next came a book of 'beauty secrets' and a lecture tour featuring topics such as 'Heroines of History and Strong-Minded Women'. She shed her Spanish identity, but in doing so Lola – who had long publicly denied any link to her alter ego, Eliza – became a schizophrenic wreck. She spent her final two years as a pauper in New York, shuffling through the streets muttering to herself, before dying of pneumonia and a stroke at age 43.

1918	1923
Wittelsbach dynasty is overthrown and a free state of Bavaria declared	Hitler's failed putsch attempt lands him in jail where he writes his hate-driven manifesto *Mein Kampf*

that Bavaria's absorption into the newly forming German Reich was inevitable. Bowing to the public mood, his ministers' advice, and pressure from Berlin, Ludwig officially expressed support for the Prussian king, Wilhelm I, to become emperor of a united Germany that included Bavaria – but not without negotiating generous regular stipends for himself.

The loss of Bavarian sovereignty killed Ludwig's enthusiasm for his royal responsibilities. The exalted, almost sacred, view he held of the office was out of place in a society increasingly ruled by industry and the bourgeoisie. Ludwig had become a misfit, an anachronism. The *Zeitgeist* (spirit) of the late 19th century had overtaken him.

Disillusioned, the king retreated to the Bavarian Alps and focused his energies on building his versions of paradise on earth: the castles of Neuschwanstein (p261), Linderhof (p132), and Herrenchiemsee (p139). Declared mentally unfit after a dubious psychological exam in 1886, Ludwig was dethroned and taken to Schloss Berg on Lake Starnberg (p105). Here, he mysteriously drowned a few days later.

His brother Otto, a certified nut case, was unable to take the throne, so his uncle Luitpold (r 1886–1912) took charge as prince regent. He became one of Bavaria's most popular rulers. His motto 'the people's will is the highest law' revealed a refreshing lack of absolutist ambition. During Luitpold's reign, Bavaria shared in Germany's overall growth and progress and the arts and sciences flourished more than ever before.

WWI & THE RISE OF THE NAZIS

During WWI, the last Bavarian king, Ludwig III (r 1912–18), sided fervently with Prussia, much to the chagrin of his people, especially as the war brought widespread death and suffering both on and off the battlefields. When Kurt Eisner, the leader of the German Independent Socialist Party, proclaimed the monarchy dead during a political rally, few people came to the king's defence. With Ludwig III's abdication in 1918, Bavaria entered a new chapter in history as the Freistaat Bayern (Free State of Bavaria).

In the early 1920s, though, Munich remained a political tinderbox. Political turmoil and infighting – along with runaway inflation and economic collapse – created fertile ground for right-wing splinter groups. One of them was the Nationalsozialistische Arbeiterpartei (NSDAP), led by a failed Austrian artist – Adolf Hitler. In an ambitious bid to topple the left-leaning national government, Hitler led his supporters in a revolt on 8 November 1923 in Munich (the so-called Bierhallenputsch; Beer Hall Putsch). For a brief while, the daring move seemed a success, but the following day the state government disbanded the Nazi troops marching on the Feldherrnhalle in Munich. The NSDAP was banned and Hitler arrested and sentenced to five years in the Landsberg jail, west of Munich. Here he began work on *Mein Kampf* (My Struggle), dictated in extended ramblings to his secretary Rudolf Hess. Incredibly, Hitler was released after only six months, in 1924, on grounds of 'good behaviour'.

There were few signs of the 'Roaring Twenties' in Munich, which sank into a cultural stupor. Experimental or racy works were banned, and artists and musicians left town in droves for Berlin. Thomas Mann, one of the few leading writers who remained in Munich until 1933, condemned the city, in a 1926 speech, as 'notorious', 'anti-Semitic' and a 'stronghold of reaction'.

Hitler hand-picked Leni Riefenstahl to direct *Triumph of the Will*, a documentary about the 1934 Nazi Party Rally in Nuremberg, which is considered an innovative, if controversial, classic. So is *Olympia*, filmed two years later.

Hitler called his government the 'Third Reich' because he thought of the Holy Roman Empire and Bismarck's German empire as the first and second Reichs, respectively.

Success, a novel by Lion Feuchtwanger, is set in Munich in the early 1920s, a period of great political and economic instability that led to the rise of Hitler and the Nazis.

1933	1943
Hitler takes power over Germany	Members of the Nazi resistance group, Die Weisse Rose, are executed in Munich

THE NAZI YEARS

Hitler's *Mein Kampf* sold over nine million copies in 1925, its first year of publication.

After Hitler took power of Germany in January 1933, Bavaria lost its political independence but was also assigned a special status. Munich was declared the 'Capital of the Movement' and Nuremberg became the site of the Nazi party's mass rallies. In 1935 the party brass met to pass the Nuremberg Laws, which ushered in the systematic repression of the Jews. In Dachau (p109), north of Munich, Germany's first concentration camp was built in 1933. In addition, many Nazi honchos hailed from Bavaria, including *Sturmabteilung* (SA) chief Ernst Röhm (later killed by Hitler), Heinrich Himmler, Hermann Göring and Franconia's *Gauleiter* (regional chief), Julius Streicher. Hitler himself was born just across the border, in Austria's Braunau. The Alpine resort of Berchtesgaden (p146) served as the southern party headquarters. And the Winter Olympic Games of 1936 took place in Garmisch-Partenkirchen (p125). The Nazis enjoyed great support in Bavaria, but there were also a few voices of dissent, most famously the Munich-based Die Weisse Rose (The White Rose) resistance group (see the boxed text, p74).

Popular Opinion and Political Dissent in the Third Reich, Bavaria, 1933–1945, by noted historian Ian Kershaw, looks at how Bavarians reacted to Nazi policy and ideology before and after the dictator's rise to power.

In 1938 Hitler's troops were welcomed into Austria. The same year, foreign powers, in an attempt to avoid another war, continued their policy of appeasement by essentially handing Hitler control over large portions of Czechoslovakia in the Munich Agreement. It didn't work. On 1 September 1939, Nazi troops marched into Poland kicking off the bloody nightmare of WWII, which left millions dead and countless cities in ruins.

MODERN BAVARIA

After WWII, Bavaria was occupied by American troops whose military command regulated all aspects of public life, appointed officials and dismissed hundreds of former NSDAP members from public service. Only a year after the last shots had been fired, Bavarians held elections for state parliament. The Christlich-Soziale Union (CSU; Christian Social Union) won an absolute majority, a dominant status it has since held with few interruptions. One of the most memorable party leaders was Franz-Josef Strauss, a controversial, scandal-plagued but also immensely powerful figure, who served in a variety of ministerial offices before becoming *Ministerpräsident* (minister-president) in 1978, a position he held until his death in 1988.

Although solidly part of modern Germany, Bavaria still asserts the independent streak that's characterised it throughout history. In 1949 it was the only German state not to ratify the German constitution because, for its taste, it put unacceptable limitations on state powers. Bavaria did, however, agree to honour and abide by the constitution and has done so to this day.

Michael Verhoeven's *The White Rose* tells the tragic story of the Munich-based Nazi resistance group. A remake by Angelica Huston is to begin production in 2005.

Bavaria's economic postwar recovery has been impressive, as it transformed itself from an essentially agrarian society into a progressive and modern state. The upturn was partly fuelled by a workforce provided by the influx of nearly two million ethnic Germans who had been expelled from the Sudetenland by the Czech government. Many settled in entire new suburbs, such as Neugablonz in Kaufbeuren (p268).

In 1972 Bavaria showed off its prosperity, friendliness and cutting-edge architecture during the Olympic Games, although the event will

1957	1970
Munich's population reaches one million, one year before its 800th anniversary	Nationalpark Bayerischer Wald becomes Germany's first national park

forever be overshadowed by the so-called Munich Massacre, a deadly terrorist attack on Israeli athletes.

Bavaria may be thoroughly integrated within the German political construct, but its people take great pride in their 'otherness'. Its history, traditions, attitudes, political priorities and culture are, in many ways, quite different from the rest of Germany. They are uniquely Bavarian.

1972	2005
Munich hosts the 20th modern Olympic Games	Cardinal Joseph Ratzinger from Marktl am Inn, Upper Bavaria is elected Pope Benedict XVI

The Culture

REGIONAL IDENTITY

For music-lovers Bavaria remains the land of Wagner, for romantics it's the touchstone of lavish castles. But for most Bavarians, the defining element in their self-image is local tradition – penetrating, embracing and family-oriented. The government splashes out millions every year on *Heimatpflege* (heritage preservation), and Bavarian culture is taught in every school. In this proud Free State – Bavaria sets itself apart from other German states by having a special legal status – culture is even safeguarded by the constitution.

Bavarians take their roots very seriously. Many families belong to *Heimatverbände* (heritage associations), music or folkloric groups. These associations celebrate their history in colourful festivals, such as the Landshut Wedding (see the boxed text on p180) or the Rothenburger Reichsstadttage. And they dress in folkloric garments called *Tracht* (costumed dress). The costumes recall Bavaria's past as an agrarian society, and even today Bavaria produces a quarter of all the milk and a fifth of all the grain in Germany.

But this sprawling *Land* (state) is no provincial backwater. Since the end of WWII, Bavaria has transformed itself from a farming state into a powerhouse of high-tech industries, filmmaking and financial services. Fancy BMW roadsters are now as common around the region as frothy heads of beer. A popular slogan coined by the tourist authority calls Bavaria the land of 'lederhosen and laptops', conjuring up images of farmers and computer scientists happily working hand in virtual hand.

Access to old trade routes gives Bavaria a whiff of Mediterranean flair, even north of the chilly Alps. The effect on the Bavarian character? Try an easygoing outlook tempered with a Germanic respect for law and order. Patriotic feeling runs high, and any hint of an affront and the wagons are circled, at least until the next party.

LIFESTYLE

The wearing of Bavarian *Tracht* is cultivated alongside regular modern garb. Men wear a country shirt and decorated *Janker* (jacket), lederhosen with flowery suspenders, and a felt hat garnished with chamois hair and ornamental pins, bells and trinkets. For women there's the dirndl – usually a skirt with a low-cut bodice, petticoat, blouse and apron.

It's not just a show for the tourists, but something the locals truly value. The costumes are worn widely on Sunday, and in Munich during Oktoberfest. Some people wear modern designer *Tracht* for the occasion, which miffs the traditionalists.

Bavarians dress conservatively but that needn't mean formally. When in business mode, or at social events such as opera and theatre performances, you'll probably feel more comfortable if slightly dressed up. But fancy clothes are a must to get into Munich's nightclubs.

Shaking hands is common among both men and women, as is a hug or a kiss on the cheek, especially among young people. When making a phone call, start by giving your name (eg 'Smith, Grüss Gott'). Not doing so is considered impolite.

Importance is placed on the formal 'Sie' form of address, especially in business situations. Among younger people and in social settings, though, people are much more relaxed about using 'Sie' and 'Du'. See the Language chapter (p294) for more information.

In parts of Bavaria, country folk tie small baskets of wild strawberries to the horns of their cattle as an offering to elves, who help produce healthy calves and an abundance of milk.

While Ludwig II's fairy-tale castle, Neuschwanstein, was being built in the 1870s, people were already drinking soft drinks in the USA.

On the whole, Bavarians are not prudish. Nude bathing and mixed saunas are commonplace. Nude-bathing areas are marked FKK, or form spontaneously in certain areas on beaches or the shores of lakes.

POPULATION

Bavaria is Germany's second most populous state with around 12.4 million inhabitants. The population density is lower here than in Germany's industrial heartland, and some rural settlements can have an isolated feel. The majority of inhabitants still live in small towns, with only about one-fifth living in cities of 100,000 or more. Munich is the third-largest city in Germany, after Berlin and Hamburg.

The population was originally made up of three distinct historical 'tribes': the Altbayern ('old' Bavarians), the Franconians and the Swabians. There is a fourth tribe of foreigners who arrived after WWII, especially from the Czech Sudentenland. Although it may seem anachronistic to outsiders, these groups still identify strongly with their heritage.

Every 10th resident is of non-German origin, but in cosmopolitan Munich it's about one in five. Ethnic groups, particularly from Turkey and eastern Europe, are concentrated in larger cities such as Munich or Nuremberg.

The religious make-up of the population changed after WWII, with a heavy influx of Protestants. The vast majority of Bavarians are still Catholic but substantial numbers of Lutherans can be found in Munich, Augsburg and other cities.

SPORT
Football

Mention *Fussball* (football, soccer) in Bavaria and passions will flare. The local heroes, Munich's FC Bayern, have dominated the national league for the past two decades. The team has been German national champion 18 times – most recently in 2003 – and has covered itself in international glory. Club president is the legendary Franz Beckenbauer, who led the German side to victory in both the World and European Cups, as a player and manager.

Munich's star soccer club FC Bayern is sometimes called 'FC Hollywood' because its players are the best paid in Germany.

Hopes are running high for a repeat victory at World Cup 2006, the final stages of which are to be played during June and July in 12 German cities, including Munich and Nuremberg. The mother of all football contests will kick off in Munich's sparkling new Allianz Arena, north of town. Shaped like a futuristic inner tube, the stadium has a transparent cover of diamond-shaped panels that can be individually lit to fantastic effect.

Munich's secondary team, TSV 1860 München, has played many seasons in the premier league as well. The only other Bavarian team in this class is the 1 FC Nürnberg, which has a spottier record.

The official site of the 2006 World Cup (being held in Germany) is www.fifaworldcup.com, in four soccer-loving languages.

Football season runs from September to June, with a winter break from Christmas to mid-February.

Skiing

Skiing is a major spectator sport with World Cup races held annually in several resorts, including Oberstdorf (p271), Reit im Winkl (p143) and Berchtesgaden (p146). Around New Year, Oberstdorf and Garmisch-Partenkirchen (p125) are the first two stops of the Vierschanzen-Tournee, the World Cup ski-jumping competition. Famous women champions from Bavaria include Rosi Mittermaier, a two-time Olympic gold medal winner in 1976, and more recently Martina Ertl and Hilde Gerg. In early

2005 Alois Vogl ended the men's drought by snagging the World Cup for slalom, the first victory in the event by a German male in 14 years.

MEDIA

The Bavarian media are a fairly independent bunch. The conservative Christian Social Union (CSU) helps to oversee the media but generally doesn't meddle. The state's combined TV and radio station, Bayerischer Rundfunk, is known for its quality documentaries and cultural fare, including numerous broadcasts of folk music.

There are several 'party' newspapers in Bavaria. The CSU has the *Bayern Kurier* and the *Münchener Merkur*. Although the papers claim not to be directly affiliated with any single party, the editorial lines do tend towards one end of the political spectrum. Readers who seek a more left-leaning approach should grab the *Süddeutsche Zeitung*.

Munich bills itself as Germany's 'media centre' but this boils down to the TV and film industry (p29). The multimedia sector is booming, but most of its firms are small newcomers.

In Anna Rosmus' Against the Stream: Growing Up Where Hitler Used to Live, a teenage girl writes an essay and uncovers shocking crimes in prewar Passau

ARTS
Literature

Many renowned German writers and poets, more than you may think, lived at least part of their lives in Bavaria. Landmark novelists of the 18th and early 19th centuries include Jean Paul, who wrote Romantic novels with a whimsical edge. There's a museum devoted to his work in Bayreuth (p207). ETA Hoffmann is known for bizarre tales such as *Mademoiselle de Scudérie*, which is considered a forerunner of the modern mystery (see p201).

The golden age of Bavarian literature, however, began in the second half of the 19th century. Munich writers began to flaunt the stuffy conventions of their predecessors in favour of a realistic, political tone. Their vanguard was *Simplicissimus,* a satirical magazine whose cover bore a trademark red bulldog. Some of its barbs were aimed at Emperor Wilhelm II, who ordered a round of censorship that sent some writers to jail. One of them was Frank Wedekind, who wrote the coming-of-age tale *Frühlings Erwachen* (Spring Awakening; 1891).

Thomas Mann's Herr und Hund (A Man and His Dog) gives charming insight into a mongrel's mind as he accompanies his master, Mann, on walks through the English Garden.

Catholic Bavaria has produced few Jewish writers of note. A giant exception is Jakob Wassermann, a popular novelist of the early 20th century. Many of his works grapple with Jewish identity, and were later banned by the Nazis. But Wassermann is actually better known for his sentimental take on Kaspar Hauser (see the boxed text on p194).

Though born in northern Germany, Thomas Mann spent about 40 years of his life in Munich where he wrote a pile of acclaimed works and also picked up a Nobel prize. His Bavarian gems include the short story *Gladius Dei* (1902), a clever parody of Munich's pretensions to being the Florence of Bavaria.

Oskar Maria Graf's books, suffused with wry humour and the deepest Bavarian dialect, are a delight if you read German or can find a rare translation. His novel *Wir sind Gefangene* (We are Prisoners) captures the sense of disillusionment and confusion that many Germans felt between the world wars. Bavaria's greatest playwright of international stature was the ever abrasive Bertolt Brecht (see the boxed text on p254). After WWII, writers throughout Germany either dropped out of sight ('inner exile' was the favoured term) or, as Hans Carossa and Ernst Wiechert did, attempted some kind of political and intellectual renewal.

Herbert Rosendorfer's Briefe in die chinesische Vergangenheit (Letters Back to Ancient China) is a fantastical story of how a 10th-century mandarin time travels to Munich in the 1980s, told as a series of thoughtful letters to a friend back home.

Today's leading literary lights are an eclectic bunch, writing in a range of genres that defy labels. Herbert Rosendorfer, a former Munich judge, has

---

THE HEIMATFILM

Bavaria's gorgeous landscape helped spawn a new film genre in the 1930s. The so-called *Heimatfilm* (homeland film) reached its zenith during the 1950s and helped spread many of today's clichés about Bavaria.

Most *Heimatfilms* show a world at peace with itself, focusing on basic themes such as love, family and the joys of village life. An interloper, such as a priest, creates some kind of conflict for the main characters – perhaps a milkmaid and her boyfriend or a poacher fighting local laws – who then invoke traditional values to solve the problem. Stories are set in the mountains of Austria, Bavaria or Switzerland, with predictable plots and schmaltzy film scores.

Hundreds of these films were made but you'll be pressed to find them in any language but German. An updated version is the TV film *Bergpfarrer* (Mountain Pastor; 2004), which is set in the Bavarian village of Aschau.

---

a long list of credits including a legal satire, a critique of the Thirty Years' War and travel guides for the German automobile association, ADAC. Anna Rosmus has turned her investigation of the history of the Third Reich in Passau, her birthplace, into several best-selling novels.

Cinema & TV

Marlene Dietrich may have been born in Berlin (and shot to fame with Berlin's legendary Babelsberg Studios), but veteran German director Joseph Vilsmaier's biopic *Marlene* was filmed in a Munich studio.

Continental Europe's largest film studio, Bavaria Film's 3000-sq-metre space forms the hub of the German film stronghold at Munich's Geiselgasteig. It may lack the glamour of Hollywood, but Munich now produces more for the airwaves than any other German city, edging out Berlin, Cologne and Hamburg. The city lures top producers with arguably the best shooting conditions in the land.

Munich is no newcomer to the film biz. During the 1970s a generation of hot young directors cut their teeth here, including Rainer Werner Fassbinder, Werner Herzog and Wim Wenders. But the real breakthrough came with Wolfgang Petersen's *Das Boot,* the epic submarine drama. Much of the elaborate set has been preserved at Bavaria Filmpark (p83). Many made-for-TV films, detective series such as *Polizeiruf 110* and popular soaps such as *Marienhof* are still produced at the Geiselgasteig today.

At the centre of the web is Germany's second-wealthiest film-and-TV fund, FilmFernsehFonds Bayern (FFF). The FFF pumps as much as €35 million per year into the industry, and many top 10 German pics are shot and produced in Bavaria.

Music
EARLY MUSIC
The Church ran the arts scene in medieval Germany, including music. The *Lied* (song) started off as a standard marching tune, or a tune to celebrate victory or work. But soon this was split into *Volkslieder* (folk songs) and *Kunstlieder* (artistic songs). The latter were religious, allowing the clerics to monitor the content.

In the Middle Ages the court became the chief musical stage. Their minstrels had a form of song called the *Minnesang,* from the German word for love songs. These love ballads, which had Moorish origins, praised the women of the court and were often performed by knights. The most famous of *Minnesangers* was Walther von der Vogelweide, whose Würzburg grave is still honoured with flowers.

The Bavarian state TV fund website www .fff-bayern.de has a bewildering number of links to every corner of the film industry.

Werner Herzog's *The Enigma of Kaspar Hauser* (1995) probes a mystery that has puzzled German society for nearly two centuries: was the dungeon boy a prince, and who wanted him dead?

Suspense master Alfred Hitchcock made his first film, *The Pleasure Garden,* in 1925 with funds collected in Munich.

Around the 15th century the musical troubadour became a feature of everyday life. To become a *Meistersinger* (master singer) a performer had to pass a test and bring something new to melody and lyric. One famous *Meistersinger* Hans Sachs was later the subject of a Richard Wagner opera *Die Meistersinger von Nürnberg*.

RENAISSANCE & BAROQUE PERIODS

Germany lingered in the Gothic period long after Italy had experienced re-birth, and organ-led church music continued until the 16th century. One of the most versatile composers of the late Renaissance was Orlandi di Lasso, a Belgium-born talent who became a singer at the Munich court before being promoted to director of the court orchestra. His body of about 2000 compositions ranged from church masses and motets (polyphonic sacred songs) to madrigals (love poems set to music) and French chansons.

The baroque period introduced Nuremberg-born composer and organist Johann Pachelbel, who is renowned for his harmonious fugues, organ chorales and toccatas. From 1695 onward he was chief organist in the St Sebalduskirche (p187) in Nuremberg.

ROMANTICISM

The French Revolution had a loosening effect on classical forms, and artists in Germany followed suit. The cultural budgets of the new Bavarian kingdom attracted the likes of Franz Liszt, a Hungarian-born pianist and composer noted for his innovative approach to scales in piano music. The father-in-law of Richard Wagner, Liszt died in Bayreuth while attending the Richard Wagner Festival.

Luchino Visconti's *Ludwig* (1973) is a four-hour costume drama that charts, to the strains of Wagner, the king's mental decline in the fabulous palaces he built.

Richard Wagner was the most influential German composer of the 19th century. He balanced all the components of operatic form to produce the *Gesamtkunstwerk* (complete work of art). Strongly influenced by Beethoven and Mozart, he's most famous for his operas, many of which dealt with mythological themes (eg the *Lohengrin* or *Tristan und Isolde*). He was also an infamous anti-Semite, which made him popular with the Nazis. For more about Wagner see the boxed text on p209.

THE 20TH CENTURY

As the scores for symphonies became more complex, not the least thanks to Wagner, Bavarian composers hastened to join in. Munich-born Richard Strauss created some famous symphonies including *Don Juan* and *Macbeth*, but he later focused on operas, including the successful *Der Rosenkavalier* (The Knight of the Rose).

Also born in Munich, composer Carl Orff achieved lasting fame with just one work: his life-embracing cantata *Carmina Burana* (see the boxed text on p137). Simple harmonies, rhythms and hypnotic repetition are some of his hallmarks.

TRADITIONAL VOLKSMUSIK

No other musical genre is as closely associated with Bavaria as *Volksmusik* (folk music). Every village has its own proud brass band and the state government puts serious euros into preserving this traditional music. It's most common in the Alpine regions, but Franconia and Swabia also have their own brand of *Volksmusik*.

MODERN VOLKSMUSIK

In the 1970s and '80s, a new style of *Volksmusik* emerged on the small stages of Munich, such as the Fraunhofer pub. Performers gave the folklore concept a political edge, freed it from conservative ideology and fused it with folk music from other countries such as Ireland and Ghana. Among the pioneers was the Biermösl Blosn, a band known for its satirical and provocative songs. Other groups include the Fraunhofer Saitenmusik, Rudi Zapf and the Guglhupfa.

More recently, the scene has created bizarre crossovers of *Volksmusik* with pop, rock, punk, hip-hop and techno in what some have termed 'New Alpine Wave'. Look for the folk rockers Hundsbuam Miserablige, avant-garde folk artist Haindling, Hubert von Goisern and the hardcore folk punk band Attwenger.

> Check out http://aib .de/volksmusik, a guide to the cutting edge of new Bavarian *Volksmusik*. It's in German only but full of links to major artists and their tour schedules.

OPERA & CLASSICAL MUSIC

Fans of opera and classical music will find a fertile scene in Bavaria. Opera aficionados can get their fill with the world-class Bayerische Staatsoper, which performs at the Nationaltheater in Munich; Nuremberg and Regensburg have their own productions. But the granddaddy of German opera festivals is the Richard Wagner Festival in Bayreuth (p209). *Der Ring des Nibelungen* (The Ring of Nibelungen), which premiered at the first festival in 1876, is a four-opera marathon of gods, humans and dwarfs that draws on themes from Nordic and German myths. Festival director Wolfgang Wagner, the grandson of the composer, has been trying to shake up the event, which had been seen as increasingly staid. The 2004 festival included a flamboyant and controversial production of *Parsifal*, whose bizarre African costumes reflected a recent trip to Namibia by its maverick director, Christoph Schlingensief.

Munich has the most famous orchestras, including the Münchener Philharmoniker (conducted by Zubin Mehta) and the Symphonieorchester des Bayerischen Rundfunks. A concert by the Bamberger Symphoniker (p204) in Bamberg is also a special treat.

Painting & Sculpture
EARLY WORKS

The two major art forms between the 9th and 13th centuries were frescoes and manuscript illumination. The oldest frescoes in Bavaria are in the crypt of the Benedictine Abbey of St Mang (p262) in Füssen. Stained glass emerged in around 1100 and the 'Prophets' Windows' in Augsburg's Dom (cathedral; p251) are the earliest in Central Europe.

GOTHIC PERIOD

Portraiture and altar painting appeared in Bavaria in around 1300. A number of such works were commissioned by the Wittelsbachs, the Bavarian ruling family, but most are believed to be lost or destroyed. Late panel works that did survive include those by Polish artist Jan Polack who is regarded as Munich's most important late-Gothic painter.

Two sculptors of this period stand out. One is Erasmus Grasser, whose masterpieces include the St Peter altar in the St Peterskirche in Munich (p64) and the Morris Dancers in the Munich Stadtmuseum (p68). The other is Veit Stoss, a Franconian who imbued his sculptures with dramatic realism. In 1503 Stoss spent a stint in jail for forgery but restored his reputation with the Bamberger Altar in Bamberg's Dom (p201), his crowning achievement.

RENAISSANCE PERIOD

The Renaissance saw the rise of human elements in painting: religious figures were now depicted alongside mere mortals. The style arrived in Germany by the early 1500s, more than a century after surfacing in Italy. In Bavaria, the Nuremberg-born Albrecht Dürer became its main exponent. Dürer's influence on the Renaissance was so great, in fact, that the period is often called the *Dürerzeit* (Age of Dürer).

Dürer excelled as a painter and graphic artist. His subjects ranged from mythology to religion to animals, all in fantastic anatomical detail, natural perspective and vivid colours. Some of his work is displayed in Munich's Alte Pinakothek (p70), including his famous Christlike self-portrait.

Dürer influenced Lucas Cranach the Elder, a main artist of the Reformation. Cranach's approach to landscape painting grew out of the *Donauschule* (Danube School), an artistic movement based in Passau and Regensburg. The amazing details of these landscapes seethed with dark movement, making them the focal point of the painting rather than a mere backdrop.

The brightest star among Renaissance sculptors was Tilman Riemenschneider. His skills were formidable, allowing his stone to mimic wood and featuring compositions playing on light and shadow. Must-sees include the altars in the Jakobskirche (p231) in Rothenburg ob der Tauber and in the Hergottskirche (p228) in Creglingen, both on the Romantic Road.

BAROQUE & ROCOCO PERIODS

The sugary styles of these periods left their mark throughout Bavaria, especially in church art. Illusionary effects and contrast between light and shadow were typical features, and surfaces were often so ornate it's hard to know where to look. Two sets of brothers dominated the baroque period: Dominikus and Johann Baptist Zimmermann, who collaborated on the astounding Wieskirche (p259), and Cosmas Damian and Egid Quirin Asam.

Arguably the finest and most prolific rococo artists ever to work in Bavaria, the Asam brothers were of a generation of Germans educated in Rome in the Italian baroque tradition. Their father, Hans Georg, was a master fresco artist who transformed the Basilika St Benedikt (p136). Word of their supreme talent, along with the family's connections in the Benedictine order, meant the duo were always swamped with work. Cosmas was primarily a fresco painter while Egid excelled as an architect and a sculptor of stucco. The Asamkirche (p68) in Munich and the Basilika St Emmeram (p162) in Regensburg stand out among their most brilliant creations, although the complex weaving of style and decoration makes it difficult to spot their individual contributions.

Another outstanding sculptor of rococo was Johann Baptist Straub. His most stunning works were altars, where sculptures flowed elegantly into paintings via curtains and billowing clouds. Grand examples can be viewed in the Marienmünster (p108) in Diessen on the Ammersee, the monastery church in Andechs (p107) and the Klosterkirche St Anna (p78) in Munich.

The website www .kulturportal-bayern.de is your chaperone to Bavarian culture, including sections on fine arts, film, museums, traditions and much, much more.

THE 19TH CENTURY

This period was the heyday of Romanticism, the heart-on-your-sleeve school of art and literature that drew heavily on emotion and a dreamy idealism. Austrian-born Moritz von Schwind is noted for his moody scenes of German legends and fairy tales. His teacher Peter Cornelius was a follower of the Nazarenes, a group of religious painters who tapped the old masters for inspiration. His work can be seen in Munich's Ludwigskirche (p74). The Schack-Galerie (p79), also in Munich, is a great place to survey Romantic art.

Romanticism gradually gave way to the sharp edges of realism and, later on, the meticulous detail of naturalism. Artists in this genre include Wilhelm Leibl, who portrayed the lives of simple country folk. Look for his paintings in Munich's Städtische Galerie im Lenbachhaus (p70).

MUNICH SECESSION & JUGENDSTIL

During the 1890s a group of artists set about shaking up the Munich art establishment. About 100 of them split from Munich's *Künstler-gesellschaft* (Artists' Society), a traditionalist organisation led by portrait artist Franz von Lenbach.

Secessionists were fed up with the reactionary professors in the arts academies, who sought to stifle any new forms of expression. The idea was to paint everyday scenes out in the fresh air, rather than historical and religious subjects in the studio. In 1893 the Secessionists held their first international exposition.

The journal that promoted it, *Die Jugend,* lent its name to the new art, *Jugendstil* (Art Nouveau). *Jugendstil* was a new aesthetic that incorporated flowing lines from Japanese painting and the lacy, interwoven designs of William Morris. The style proved enormously popular, lasting until WWI. In Munich you can view some beautiful examples along Ainmillerstrasse (p73) in Schwabing. The houses themselves are stolid but adorned with a flowing ornamentation, often with fruit or flower motifs and sometimes the tender face of a young woman.

The website www .kulturportal-bayern.de is your chaperone to Bavarian culture, including sections on fine arts, film, museums, traditions and much, much more.

EXPRESSIONISM

German artists tried to find a purer, freer approach to painting through abstraction, vivid colours and expression. They embraced the new form with gusto, and produced the first German art in centuries to leave a mark outside the country. The trailblazers were artists of Der Blaue Reiter (The Blue Rider), a Murnau group of artists founded by Wassily Kandinsky and Franz Marc, and joined later by Paul Klee and Gabriele Münter.

A famous collection of German expressionists is displayed at the Buchheim Museum (p107) on Starnberger See (Lake Starnberg). Here the focus is on members of Die Brücke (The Bridge), another artists' group founded in 1905 in Dresden by four disgruntled architecture students: Ernst Ludwig Kirchner, Erich Heckel, Karl Schmidt-Rottluff and Fritz Bleyl.

NAZI ART

Hitler was no great fan of 20th-century painting unless it was his own. In 1937 the Nazis organised an exhibition of *Entartete Kunst* (Degenerate Art) in Munich's Deutsches Haus der Kunst (German House of Art), now simply called Haus der Kunst (see the boxed text on p75). Leading works of the day were displayed, but most were banned after the exhibition and the Nazis then sold them abroad to raise cash.

POST-1945

Germany's artistic scene was fragmented after WWII and the momentum for true revival came from elsewhere. Some respected artists did return to breathe life back into the cultural scene, but Munich and the rest of Bavaria were soon eclipsed by other German cities as centres of artistic renewal.

Works of avant-garde artists enjoy renown beyond Bavaria's borders. The whimsical horselike *Kentaurs* (centaurs) of Würzburg's Fritz Koenig, in the form of sketches, paper cutouts and sculptures, are a good example. From Ingolstadt, Alf Lechner is one of Germany's most sought-after sculptors, crafting his provocative objects in rolled steel.

One modern genre that has found major representation in Bavaria is concrete art, even if its artists are usually not Bavarians. Concrete art emerged in the 1950s and takes abstract art to its extreme, rejecting any natural form and using only planes and colours. The Museum für Konkrete Kunst (p244) in Ingolstadt and the Sammlung Ruppert at the Museum im Kulturspeicher (p219) in Würzburg both have excellent collections.

Theatre & Dance

Theatre in its various forms enjoys a wide following in Bavaria. Munich has the greatest variety of theatres, including a few English-language troupes. Other cities, including Nuremberg and Regensburg, also maintain their own ensembles whilst Bamberg has the ETA Hoffmann Theatre. Ludwig II's life story is the basis of a glitzy musical staged in a custom-built theatre in Füssen.

In the Alpine resort towns, you'll often find *Bauerntheater* (literally, 'peasant theatre'), which are usually silly and rustic tales performed in dialect by amateur or semiprofessional actors dressed in folkloric outfits. Even if you can't understand the lingo (and trust us, most non-Bavarians don't), you'll probably be able to follow the plot anyway and definitely get a good dose of local colour.

Another popular theatrical form is the *Kabarett*, a political and satirical entertainment featuring clever monologues and short skits. The Comödie Fürth and the Münchner Lach-und Schiessgesellschaft are two popular troupes.

Bavaria's longest-running drama is the *Passionsspiele* (Passion Play), which is performed at the Bavarian village of Oberammergau (p131) once every decade. Since the 17th century, local villagers have enacted the climax of the Gospels, Christ's Suffering, Crucifixion and Resurrection in a breathtaking, six-hour blend of opera, ritual and Hollywood epic. More than 2000 locals, or almost half the village, give more than 100 performances to half a million fans. The next shows are in 2010 – but don't wait till the last minute to buy tickets.

The ballet and contemporary dance scene is quite good in Munich under the auspices of the Bayerisches Staatsballett. The annual Tanzwerkstatt Europa showcases up-and-coming choreographers as well as established greats such as Charles Linehan.

Folk dance has a rich tradition throughout the region. Eastern Bavaria has the biggest repertoire, with 100-plus dances including the unique 'double dances', which feature a change in tempo. Costumed groups can be seen performing the heel-slapping *Schuhplattler* on stages closer to Munich, or even in the ballroom of the Löwenbräukeller (p98).

In 1950 the actress who was supposed to play the Virgin Mary in Oberammergau's Passion Play was dismissed for flirting with an American GI.

Environment

THE LAND

Bavaria sprawls over 70,550 sq km, making it bigger than Ireland, Portugal or Denmark. It is the largest and southernmost of Germany's 16 federal states and shares international borders with Austria in the south and the Czech Republic in the east.

In Bavaria nature has been as prolific and creative as Picasso was in his prime. The most dramatic region is the Bavarian Alps, a phalanx of craggy peaks created by tectonic uplift some 770 million years ago and chiselled and gouged by glaciers and erosion ever since. Several ranges stand sentinel above the rest of the land, including, west to east, the Allgäuer Alps, the Wetterstein/Karwendel Alps (with Germany's highest mountain, the Zugspitze at 2964m), and the Berchtesgadener Alps. Many peaks are well above 2000m.

North of here, the Alpine Foothills – a wedge of land between the Danube and the Alps – are a lush mosaic of moorland, rolling hills, farmland and pine forest dappled with dozens of glacial lakes, including the vast Chiemsee, Lake Starnberg and the Ammersee. The foothills are book-ended by Lake Constance in the west and the Inn and Salzach Rivers in the east.

The Bavarian Forest along the Czech border in eastern Bavaria is a classic *Mittelgebirge,* a midsize mountain range whose highest peak, the Grosse Arber (1456m), juts out like the tall kid in your class picture when you were nine. Much of it is blanketed by dark, dense forests that fade into the thinly populated Frankenwald and Fichtelgebirge areas further north.

Much of Franconia and Swabia are part of the Central Uplands, a complex patchwork of low ranges, rifts and deep meandering valleys that makes for a varied landscape. A Jurassic limestone range is responsible for various bizarre rock formations, such as those in the Franconian Switzerland region north of Nuremberg.

Bavaria is traversed by several major rivers, of which the Danube and the Main are the longest. The Inn and the Isar originate in the Alps and flow into the Danube, the former at Passau, the latter near Deggendorf on the edge of the Bavarian Forest.

Lonely Planet's *Walking in the Alps* has detailed descriptions of 47 walks, including several on the Bavarian side of this massive mountain range.

WILDLIFE

Spotting animals in their native habitat is a thrilling experience and Bavaria offers some promising opportunities for viewing wildlife, especially in its national and nature parks. Centuries of human impact have taken their toll, of course, causing many critters, including reptiles,

---

BAVARIAN WORLD HERITAGE SITES

For more information on World Heritage sites, visit Unesco's website: whc.unesco.org.

- Residenz and Hofgarten in Würzburg (Franconia; p218) – splendid art and opulence courtesy of the local prince-bishops.
- Wieskirche (Allgäu-Bavarian Swabia; p259) – richly decorated rococo pilgrimage church in the middle of a meadow.
- Altstadt (old town) of Bamberg (Franconia; p63) – immaculately preserved historic town centre.

ARRIVE PREPARED, LEAVE NO TRACE

If you are planning to roam around Bavarian forests, it's key that you do so responsibly. One thoughtless gesture – hiking off-trail through fragile soil, for example – can take years for nature to repair. Basic rule of thumb: do what you can to minimize your impact. Here's how:

■ Stick to established trails and camp sites

■ Leave plants where they belong

■ Don't litter

■ Observe wildlife, but do not approach or feed it

■ Make as little noise as possible

■ Use mountain bikes only on designated paths

■ Use public transport, where possible

---

beetles and butterflies, as well as plants, to limp onto the endangered species list.

Animals

The most common large forest mammal is the red deer, a quick-footed fellow with skinny legs supporting a chunky body. Males grow a magnificent set of antlers in the spring, only to discard them in the winter. Encounters with wild boar, a feral pig with a keen sense of smell but poor eyesight, are also possible. Keep your distance during mating season, though, when the tusk-sporting males develop a violent streak in their search for a suitable sow.

Beavers faced extinction in the 19th century thanks not only to being coveted for their precious pelts (beaver hats were all the rage) but also to being cooked up in strictly Catholic households each Friday because the good people considered them to be 'fish'. Reintroduced in the mid-1960s, beavers are thriving once again, especially along the Danube, between Ingolstadt and Kelheim, and its tributaries.

Lynxes actually died out in Germany in the 19th century but conservationists reintroduced about a dozen of them to the Bavarian Forest in the 1970s. Alas, poaching, accidents and migration brought numbers back down to virtually nil. In the '80s, Czech authorities released 17 lynxes in the Bohemian Forest and a small group of brave souls have since tried their luck again in the Bavarian Forest right across the border. The wildcat, another indigenous feline, has also returned to forest regions after nearly being hunted to extinction in the 1930s.

In the Alps, the alpine marmot, a sociable chap that looks like a fat squirrel, lives in burrows below the tree line, while the wild goat and the elusive chamois, a deerlike mammal, make their home in the upper mountains. The snow hare, whose fur is white in winter, is also a common Alpine denizen.

Bavarian skies are home to over 400 bird species, from white-backed woodpeckers and pygmy owls to sparrow hawks and black redstarts. The true king of the skies, though, is the golden eagle. If you're lucky, you might spot one patrolling the mountain peaks.

Plants

Despite environmental pressures, Bavarian forests remain beautiful places to escape the crowds. In fact, even most cities and towns have their own nearby *Stadtwald* (woods). Most forests are a potpourri of beech, oak,

---

Gustav Hegi's *Alpenflora* is an illustrated field guide (in German) to major alpine plant life in Bavaria, Austria and Switzerland.

Those interested in understanding the nature of German nature parks can download a comprehensive English-language document from www .naturparke.de.

birch, chestnut, lime, maple and ash that erupt into a kaleidoscope of colour in autumn. Up in the higher elevations, fir, pine, spruce and other conifers are more prevalent.

In spring, wildflowers – orchids, cyclamens, gentians, pulsatillas, Alpine roses, edelweiss and buttercups – blanket meadows and hillsides. Be sure to minimize your impact by always sticking to trails.

In summer, wild berries add splashes of colour to the forest. Many of them are perfectly edible, from blueberries to raspberries to blackberries. In late summer and early fall, mushroom hunters swarm the forests in search of *Pfifferling* (chanterelle) and other delicacies.

Bavaria's two national and 16 nature parks occupy about 30% of the state's total area.

NATIONAL & NATURE PARKS

Bavaria is home to Germany's oldest national park, the Nationalpark Bayerischer Wald, which was founded in 1970 and hugs the Czech border. There is only one more of Germany's 15 national parks in Bavaria and it's a good one: the Nationalpark Berchtesgaden on the Austrian border. Both parks have been relatively untouched by human impact and preserve places of outstanding natural beauty and rare geographical features. They also protect various species of wildlife and act as natural laboratories for researchers and scientists.

National parks enjoy a much higher degree of environmental protection than nature parks, which serve primarily as outdoor playgrounds. Don't picture them as traditional 'parks' either: these are sprawling rural landscapes crisscrossed by roads and dotted with villages. Logging and agricultural use is possible here, but done in a controlled and environ-

BAVARIAN NATIONAL & NATURE PARKS

Park	Features	Activities	Best time to visit	Page
Nationalpark Bayerischer Wald	mountain forest & upland moors (243 sq km); deer, hazel grouse, fox, otter, pygmy owl	hiking, mountain biking, cross-country skiing	year-round	p175
Nationalpark Berchtesgaden	lakes, mixed forest, cliffs, meadows (210 sq km); eagle, marmot, blue hare, salamander	hiking, skiing, wildlife watching	year-round	p146
Naturpark Altmühltal	mixed forest, streams, rock formations, Roman ruins (2962 sq km)	hiking, cycling, canoeing, kayaking, rock climbing, cross-country skiing, fossil digging	late spring to autumn	p237
Naturpark Bayerischer Wald	largest continuous forest in Germany, moorland, meadows, rolling hills (3077 sq km)	hiking, cycling, cross-country skiing, Nordic walking	May-Oct	p175
Naturpark Fränkische Schweiz	forest, valleys, caves (2346 sq km)	hiking, cycling, canoeing	late spring to autumn	p205
Naturpark Frankenwald	low mountains, dense coniferous forest, streams (1020 sq km)	hiking, cycling, mountain biking, cross-country skiing	spring, summer, autumn	p213
Naturpark Steigerwald	rolling hills, mixed forest, ponds, vineyards (1200 sq km)	hiking, cycling, swimming, canoeing	late spring to autumn	p204

mentally friendly fashion. See the table on p37 for an overview of the parks described in this book.

ENVIRONMENTAL ISSUES

Bavaria has an impressive environmental record that goes back to 1970 when it became the first German state to appoint a minister of the environment, some 16 years before such a position was created on the federal level. In 1984 the protection of nature was made part of the Bavarian state constitution.

Policy has largely focused on decreasing pollution and waste, investing in clean technologies and research into renewable energy sources, educating people and industry and cleaning up existing problems. A key goal is to lower greenhouse gas emissions in order to meet the requirements of the Kyoto Protocol.

The figures certainly look good: Bavarian carbon-dioxide levels are one-third below the national average. Detractors argue, however, that Bavaria has achieved such success only by selling its soul to the 'devil', in this case, nuclear power. Fully two-thirds of energy in Bavaria (vs 30% nationwide) is generated in this fashion. While nuclear power plants indeed eject less ozone-destroying gases than, say, coal power plants, there are of course incalculable potential risks, not to mention the thorny and as yet unsolved issue of nuclear-waste storage and disposal. For the time being at least, Bavarian politicians seem to feel that the benefits of nuclear energy – low cost, cleaner air, healthier forests – outweigh the risks. This approach, incidentally, puts the state at odds with federal policy by which all of Germany's 19 nuclear reactors will be phased out by 2020, a move that Bavaria obviously opposes.

Paradoxically, Bavaria is also a leader in the development and use of renewable energies, including hydroelectric, wind and solar energy. In fact photovoltaic power stations are sprouting all over the state. In April 2003 a huge plant generating electricity for 4500 people went into operation near Hernau, close to Regensburg, to be followed in 2005 by the even bigger Bavaria Solarpark. All in all, Bavaria generates about 7% of its energy through eco-friendly methods.

Another priority has been given to protecting natural spaces. Bavaria has two national parks, 16 nature parks and over 1200 protected nature areas totalling about 45,000 sq km. On the flip side, the extension of the Rhine-Main-Danube Canal between Bamberg and Kelheim has been severely detrimental to plant and animal habitats. Also see the boxed text on, p241.

The impact of humans on the environment is also felt throughout the Alpine region, where the mountains are becoming increasingly high tech. And it's not just the ever-expanding lift systems. Another problem is the beefed-up installation of snowmaking equipment, which is increasingly needed as the altitude at which there are reliable snow levels is now about 2000m due to global warming.

As are other Germans, Bavarians are big on recycling. Practically everyone separates their rubbish into biodegradable waste, recyclable paper, recyclable plastics and remaining waste. Most water bottles, beer and drink cans yield a returnable deposit of as much as €0.50 per container to encourage re-use.

For details about Bavaria's environment policy, check out the website of the Bavarian Environmental Protection Agency at www.bayern.de/lfu (partly in English).

Each Bavarian resident on average generates around 500kg of garbage per year.

Bavaria Outdoors

Bavaria lives up to its reputation as a splendid outdoor playground. Regardless of what kind of activity gets you off that couch, you'll be able to pursue it in this land of mountains and rivers, lakes and forests. Explore on your own or take advantage of local outfitters and tour operators, all eager to set you up.

CYCLING & MOUNTAIN BIKING

Bavaria is superb cycling territory, no matter whether you're off on a leisurely lakeside spin, an adrenaline-fuelled mountain exploration or a multiday hop from village to village.

Practically every town and region has a network of signposted bike routes. For short tours, staff at the local tourist offices can supply you with ideas, maps and advice. Most towns have some sort of bicycle-hire station (often at or near the train station) and outfitters are also listed throughout this book. Prices range from €10 to €25 per day or €40 to €90 per week, plus a deposit.

Mountain biking is especially popular in the Alpine region, including Ruhpolding and Reit im Winkl, in Chiemgau (p143), which host annual championships, but also around Garmisch-Partenkirchen (p125), Bad Reichenhall (p144) and Berchtesgaden (p146). Though lesser known, the Bayerischer Wald (p175) also has some good terrain.

With dozens of long-distance trails crisscrossing the state, Bavaria is tailor-made for *Radwandern* (bike touring). Routes are typically a combination of lightly travelled back roads, forest roads, and paved highways with dedicated bike lanes. Many routes traverse nature reserves, meander along rivers or venture into steep mountain terrain.

For inspiration, check out www.germany-tourism.de/biking in English, which provides an overview of available routes. For more detailed route descriptions German readers can consult www.bayerninfo.de, a website maintained by the Bavarian state government. Another German-language source is www.bayernbike.de, which has several dozen route guides available for free download (click on 'Roadbooks'), although so far only for Eastern Bavaria. *Radeln in Bayern* (www.galli-verlag.de) is a handy guide

---

TOP FIVE BIKE TOURING TRAILS

- **Altmühltal Radweg** (190km) Rothenburg ob der Tauber to Beilngries – this trail follows the Altmühl River through the Naturpark Altmühltal.

- **Bodensee–Königssee Radweg** (414km) Lindau to Berchtesgaden – this moderate route runs along the foot of the Alps with magnificent views of the mountains, charming lakes and forests.

- **Donauradweg** (434km) Neu-Ulm to Passau – a delightful, easy- to moderate-level riverside trip that travels along the Danube, one of Europe's great streams.

- **Nationalparkradweg** (88km) Zwiesel to Haidmühle – a moderate to strenuous mountain-bike route trailing through remote Nationalpark Bayerischer Wald with a dip across the border into the Czech Republic (bring your passport and check the visa requirements).

- **Romantic Road** (359km) Würzburg to Füssen – this easy to moderate trail is one of the nicest ways to explore Germany's most famous holiday route, although it can get busy.

SKIING & SNOWBOARDING

Modern lifts, trails from 'Sesame Street' to 'Death Wish', breathtaking scenery, cosy mountain huts, steaming mulled wine, hearty dinners by a crackling fireplace – all these are the hallmarks of a German skiing holiday.

The Bavarian Alps, only an hour's drive south of Munich, offer the best slopes and most reliable ski conditions. The most famous resort town here is, of course, Garmisch-Partenkirchen, which hosted the 1936 Olympic Games and is popular with the international set. Another major resort is Oberstdorf in the Allgäu, a picture-perfect mountain town that is largely car free. Like Garmisch it hosts the occasional world cup race, and both towns are also stops on the Vierschanzen-Tournee ski-jumping competition circuit.

There's also plenty of skiing and snowboarding to be done in the Bayerischer Wald where mountains may not soar as high as in the Alps but snow conditions are still surprisingly reliable. Smaller crowds and a more low-key atmosphere make this area especially well suited to families. The downhill action centres on the Grosser Arber mountain, while the Bretterschachten is a major draw for cross-country skiing aficionados, both are near the town of Bodenmais. The best cross-country skiing, though, is done in the Chiemgau, especially in Ruhpolding and Reit im Winkl, but many towns through southern Bavaria offer their own network of groomed tracks.

The skiing season generally runs from late November/early December to March, although this depends on specific elevations and weather conditions. Efficient snowmaking equipment ensures winter fun even in years when nature doesn't play along. All resorts have equipment-hire facilities. Rates for downhill gear start at about €10 per day, with discounts for longer rental periods. Cross-country equipment costs slightly less. Daily ski-lift passes start at around €17.

For more information, contact the Munich-based **Deutscher Skiverband** (German Skiing Association; ☎ 089-8579 0213; www.ski-online.de).

What follows is an overview of the best-known ski resorts in Bavaria. For additional details follow the cross-references to the destination chapters.

Garmisch-Partenkirchen

Germany's winter sports capital offers a superlative range of options for ski hounds, including 118km of downhill runs across five ski fields (Zugspitze, Alpspitze, Hausberg, Kreuzeck and Eckbauer) accessed by 30 cable cars and chairlifts. There are some runs for beginners, but intermediate or expert skiers will have more fun on this terrain. Snowboarders can get their adrenaline kick in a 120m long and 5m-high Superpipe or at the Kickerline with four straight jumps.

- Nearest town: Garmisch-Partenkirchen (p125)
- One-day adult lift ticket: Zugspitze €35, Classic Ski Area (Alpspitze, Hausberg, Kreuzeck) €29, Eckbauer €17
- Information: ☎ 08821-7970
- www.zugspitze.de

Oberstdorf

This resort town offers access to three ski areas, the Fellhorn/Kanzelwand cross-border terrain with Austria; the Nebelhorn, which boasts views of 400 peaks from the top as well as Germany's longest valley run (7.5km); and the compact Söllereck, which is ideal for families and less experienced skiers. Snowboarders can mix things up in two new Fun Parks.

- Nearest town: Oberstdorf (p271)
- One-day adult lift ticket: €33 (all areas)
- Information: Fellhorn/Kanzelwand ☎ 0700-555 33 888; Nebelhorn ☎ 0700-555 33 666; Söllereck ☎ 08322-987 56
- www.soellereckbahn.de in German & www.fellhorn.de in German

Winklmoos-Alm/Steinplatte
Small but choice, this is the top skiing area in the Chiemgau. It ranges in elevation from 1100m to 1900m and is famous for its reliable snow pack and sunny skies. The terrain is crisscrossed by 14 runs, the longest being 2.6km, with vertical drops up to 870m. Snowboarders have a half pipe to play in.

- Nearest town: Reit im Winkl (p143)
- One-day adult lift ticket: €33.50
- Information: ☎ 08640-80027
- www.winklmoosalm.com in German

Jenner-Königssee
The scenery, above the emerald depths of the Königssee, is truly breathtaking. This is the most demanding of the five ski fields in the Berchtesgadener Land with vertical drops up to 600m; the longest run is 3.1km.

- Nearest town: Berchtesgaden (p146)
- One-day adult lift ticket: €23.50
- Information: ☎ 08652-958 10
- www.jennerbahn.de in German

Götschen
Also in the Berchtesgadener Land, this compact ski field is set in a stunningly beautiful Alpine landscape. It enjoys a huge fan base among snowboarders and hosted the 2001 FIS Snowboarding World Cup. Twice a week pistes are illuminated for night skiing.

- Nearest town: Berchtesgaden (p146)
- One-day adult lift ticket: €20
- Information: ☎ 08652-7656
- www.goetschen.com in German

Grosser Arber
The highest mountain in the Bayerischer Wald (1456m), Grosser Arber has nine downhill runs, including the World Cup Slope for expert skiers, a snowboard park and access to 90km of cross-country skiing.

- Nearest town: Bodenmais (p178)
- One-day adult lift ticket: €22
- Information: ☎ 09925-941 40
- www.arber.de

Kranzberg
This smallish, family-friendly ski area offers superb views of the Karwendel and Wetterstein ranges. It has only 22km of pistes but some of them are above 2000m and the biggest vertical drop is 1340m. There's night skiing and a Kinderpark for children.

- Nearest town: Mittenwald (p130)
- One-day adult lift ticket: €20
- Information: ☎ 08823-1553
- www.skiparadies-kranzberg.de in German

with maps, elevation profiles and detailed route descriptions. It's in German and available at bookstores or directly from the publisher.

For a basic map of all routes, you can order the free *Bayernnetz für Radler* (Bavarian Cycling Network) from www.bayerninfo.de. For on-the-road navigating the best maps are those published by the national cycling organization **Allgemeiner Deutscher Fahrrad Club** (ADFC; www.adfc.de) and are available for about €7 in tourist offices, bookstores and from its website.

ADFC also operates a useful online directory called **Bett & Bike** (www.bett undbike.de) that lists hundreds of bicycle-friendly hotels, inns and hostels. Bookstores carry the printed version (€6.50).

For an overview of transporting your bike within Bavaria, see p287.

HIKING & WALKING

With scenery to die for, Bavaria is perfect for exploring on foot, even if you've got your heart set on rambling through romantic river valleys, peak-bagging in the Alps or a walk by the lake. Thousands of kilometres of trails travel through all regions, the nicest traversing the beautiful scenery of Bavaria's national and nature parks (p37).

Trails are usually well marked with signs or symbols, sometimes quaintly painted on tree trunks. To find a route matching your fitness level and time frame, talk to a park ranger or the staff at the local tourist offices, who can also supply you with maps and tips. Many also offer multiday 'hiking without luggage' packages that include accommodation and luggage transfer between hotels.

'the mellow Altmühl River meanders past steep cliffs, willow-fringed banks and little beaches'

KAYAKING, CANOEING & RAFTING

A placid paddle is a wonderful way to get to know Bavaria's beauty close-up and at leisure. The most popular area for this kind of pursuit is the Naturpark Altmühltal (p239), where the mellow Altmühl River meanders past steep cliffs, willow-fringed banks and little beaches. A similarly dreamy landscape awaits in the Fränkische Schweiz (p205). Here, the diminutive Wiesent River carves its course past villages, medieval castles and eroded rock faces. A good outfitter in this area is **Aktiv Reisen** (☎ 09196-998 566; www.aktiv-reisen.com). If you're up for a rollicking rafting trip, head to Lenggries (p137) at the foot of the Bavarian Alps for a wild ride on the Isar River, which gushes northward all the way to Munich.

MOUNTAINEERING

'Climb every mountain…' the Mother Superior belted out in the *Sound of Music*, and the Bavarian Alps – the centre of mountaineering in Germany – will give you plenty of opportunity to do just that. You can venture out on day treks or plan multiday clambers from hut to hut, as long as you keep in mind that hiking in the Alps is no walk in the park. You need to be in reasonable condition and come equipped with the right shoes, gear and topographic maps. Trails can be narrow, steep and have icy patches, even in summer. Some routes traverse difficult terrain along so-called *Klettersteige* (roughly translated as 'climbing ladders'), which essentially requires a form of rock climbing using pre-attached cables; you need a special harness, karabiners and a helmet.

Always check local weather conditions before setting out and take all precautions concerning clothing and provisions, and always let someone know where you're going. For more information about safety and how to deal with hypothermia, see p293.

In the Alps, Oberstdorf (p271), Garmisch-Partenkirchen (p125), Mittenwald (p130) and Berchtesgaden (p146) are good gateways to your mountain adventure. If it's your first time in the region, ask at the tourist offices about local outfitters offering instruction, equipment rental and guided tours. These are usually run by young, energetic and English-speaking folks with an infectious love for and deep knowledge of the mountains.

The **Deutscher Alpenverein** (DAV; German Alpine Club, ☎ 089-140 030; www.alpenverein .de in German; Von-Kahr-Strasse 2-4, Munich) is a good resource for information on hiking and mountaineering with local chapters in practically every Bavarian city and town. It also maintains numerous Alpine mountain huts, many of them open to the public, where you can spend the night and get a meal. These range from simple, remote shelters (category 1) to comfortable cabins suitable for multiday stays (category 2) to easy-access places geared primarily towards day-trippers (category 3). Nonmember rates vary from hut to hut but usually don't exceed €24 per night. Members pay about half price, get priority if space is tight, have access to cooking facilities and enjoy a number of other privileges. To become a member, you have to join a local chapter. Annual fees vary by chapter but are generally between €44 and €66.

Local DAV chapters also organise various courses (climbing, mountaineering etc) as well as guided treks, with which you can link up. Ask at the local tourist office.

The **Deutscher Wanderverband** (German Hiking Federation; ☎ 0561-938 730; www .wanderverband.de in German) co-publishes an excellent website filled with long-distance route descriptions, tips and maps at www.wanderbares-deutsch land.de, but it's in German only.

ROCK CLIMBING
There's rock climbing all over Bavaria, but rock hounds – from beginner to expert – are especially drawn to the Jurassic limestone formations in the Naturpark Altmühltal (p240) and the Fränkische Schweiz (p205), which have been chiselled by the elements for millions of years.

SPAS & SAUNAS
In spa towns and resort areas you'll find a growing number of sparkling water parks with several indoor and outdoor pools (often filled with thermal water from local mineral springs), Jacuzzis, surge channels, massage jets and waterfalls, multiple saunas plus a menu of pampering options, including massages. A few hours in one of these wellness oases is a great way to while away a rainy afternoon. Good spots include Königliche Kristall-Therme in Schwangau (p263), Alpamare in Bad Tölz (p135), Vita Alpina in Ruhpolding (p143), Prienavera in Prien on the Chiemsee (p140) and the brand new Rupertustherme in Bad Reichenhall (p145).

Germans love to sweat it out in the sauna, and most *Stadtbäder* (public baths) have sauna facilities, usually with fixed hours for men and women as well as mixed sessions. Prices start at around €6. Note that not a stitch of clothing is worn, so leave your modesty in the locker.

'Germans love to sweat it out in the sauna... leave your modesty in the locker.'

WATER SPORTS
Many of Bavaria's lakes and rivers are popular playgrounds for water-based pursuits. The Walchensee (p135) in the Tölzer Land enjoys peculiar wind conditions that make it a mecca for windsurfers, including the sport's elite. The Forggensee (p263) near the royal castles in the Allgäu also offers great surfing in lovely surroundings, as does Lake Constance (p268) to the west. Sailors will also feel at home on the latter as well as on Starnberger See (p105) and the Chiemsee (p139). Diving is a possibility in the Walchensee and Starnberger See, where water-skiing is also a popular pastime.

Food & Drink

Bavarian food is hearty, thigh-slapping fare that only gives a passing nod to the vegetable kingdom. Much of it is delicious and soul-sustaining but not so beneficial if you're watching your waistline or cholesterol. Occasionally you'll come across innovative chefs who've come up with creative new – and often lighter and healthier – spins on the old favourites. Although many traditional dishes can also be found on menus elsewhere in Germany, there are some culinary concoctions that are unique to Bavaria. Outside the cities you'll rarely see a non-German restaurant, except perhaps a pizzeria or Chinese eatery.

STAPLES & SPECIALITIES
Traditional Fare

No part of the pig is safe from the hands of Bavarian chefs. Its legs are turned into *Schweinshax'n*, its shoulder into *Schweineschäuferl*, its ribs into *Rippchen*, its tongue into *Züngerl* and its belly into *Wammerl*. If that's sounds too challenging, you can always stick to the tried-and-true *Hendl* (roast chicken) or sink your teeth into a *Fleischpflanzerl*, the Bavarian spin on the hamburger. Another favourite is *Leberkäs* (literally, 'liver cheese'), a savoury meatloaf that actually contains neither liver nor cheese. Another speciality is *Tellerfleisch* is slices of lean boiled beef served with horseradish or spicy mustard.

Fish features less commonly on menus, and if it does it's mostly freshwater species, such as *Zander* (pikeperch), *Forelle* (trout) and *Karpfen* (carp). Skewers of grilled mackerel, called *Steckerlfisch*, are hugely popular, especially at beer festivals and in beer gardens. For more typical beer-garden fare, see the boxed text on p99.

The main vegetable is, of course, the *Kartoffel* (potato), which can be served as *Salzkartoffeln* (boiled), *Bratkartoffeln* (fried), *Kartoffelpüree* (mashed) or shaped into *Knödel* (dumplings). Dumplings can also be *Semmelknödel* (made of bread) or *Leberknödel* (made of liver). Pickled cabbage is another common vegetable companion and comes as either sauerkraut (white) or *Rotkohl* and *Blaukraut* (red).

May is peak season for *Spargel* (white asparagus), which is classically paired with boiled potatoes, hollandaise sauce and sometimes *Schinken* (smoked or cooked ham). In spring, look for *Bärlauch*, a wild-growing garlic that is often turned into a delicious pesto sauce.

Originating in Swabia are *Maultaschen*, which are ravioli-like stuffed pasta pockets, and *Kässpätzle*, which is essentially the local version of macaroni and cheese.

As for dessert, *Dampfnudeln* are doughy sweet dumplings sprinkled with cinnamon or poppy seeds and drenched in custard sauce. Apple or plum strudel are tasty alternatives.

Bavarians like to 'pig out' and the numbers prove it: of the 60kg of meat consumed by the average resident each year, about two-thirds are pork. Oink!

Sausages

Bavarians love their wurst (sausage), which is traditionally served with *süsser Senf* (sweet mustard) alongside a dollop of sauerkraut or potato salad and a slice of bread.

Bavaria's flagship link is the *Weisswurst*, a veal sausage that's simmered in water and must be peeled before eating. Unlike local beers, *Weisswurst* has few friends beyond the Bavarian border, and some Germans still refer to that frontier as the '*Weisswurst* equator'.

In Eastern Bavaria and Franconia the mildly spicy *Bratwurst* rules. Nuremberg and Regensburg make the most famous versions: finger-sized links that are eaten by the half dozen or dozen. Other sausages you may encounter include *Blutwurst* (black pudding or blood sausage), the *Krakauer,* a paprika-spiced sausage of Polish origin, and the hot dog–like *Wiener.*

DRINKS
Beer

Bavarians have raised beermaking to a science, and not just since the passage of the *Reinheitsgebot* (Purity Law) in Ingolstadt in 1516. It stipulates that brewers may use only four ingredients – malt, yeast, hops and water – thus making it the world's first consumer protection law. All German beers adhere to this standard.

> In Bavaria beer is officially defined not as alcohol but as a staple food, just like bread.

Bavaria is among one of the most productive beer regions in the world. Almost exactly half of all German breweries, ie about 640, are in Bavaria, collectively producing over 23 million hectolitres. Yet the number belies the fact that not all is well in 'Beer-land'. A sharp drop in beer consumption in the past decade has forced many smaller breweries to close up shop, merge with others or be swallowed up by the big-boy brewers.

Still, for now, there are plenty left to keep up the tradition. Besides Munich, famous beer towns include Regensburg, Bamberg, Bayreuth and Kulmbach (see the itinerary on p14). Beer also takes centre stage at numerous festivals, most notably of course the Munich Oktoberfest (p88) but also at Straubing's Gäubodenfest (p167), the Erlanger Bergkirchweih (p195), the St Annafest in Forchheim (p196) and many others.

Beer aficionados face a bewildering choice of labels. The following is a small glossary of the most commonly encountered varieties. Note that most Bavarian beer has an alcohol content between 5% and 5.5%, although some can be as strong as 8%.

BEER GLOSSARY

Alkoholfreies Bier – nonalcoholic beer

Bockbier/Doppelbock – strong beer (*doppel* meaning even more so), either pale, amber or dark in colour with bittersweet flavour

Dampfbier – steam beer originating from Bayreuth, it's top-fermented and has a fruity flavour

Dunkles Lagerbier – *dunkles* (dark), a reddish-brown, full-bodied lager, malty and lightly hopped

Helles Lagerbier – *helles* (pale), a lightly hopped lager with strong malt aromas

Hofbräu – beer produced by a *Hof* (noble court)

Klosterbräu – beer produced by a monastery

Malzbier – sweet, aromatic, full-bodied malt beer

Märzen – full-bodied with strong malt aromas and traditionally brewed in March; today associated with Oktoberfest.

Pils – pilsener, a bottom-fermented lager with strong hop flavour

Rauchbier – dark beer with a fresh, spicy or 'smoky' flavour

Weissbier/Weizenbier – made with wheat instead of barley malt, comes as *Helles Weissbier* (pale), *Dunkles Weissbier* (dark), *Kristallweizen* (clear) and *Hefeweizen* (cloudy; with a layer of still-fermenting yeast on the bottom of the bottle)

If you want to go easy on the booze, order a sweetish *Radler,* which comes in half or full litres and mixes *Helles Lagerbier* and lemonade. A *Russe* (Russian) is generally a litre-sized concoction of *Helles Weissbier* and lemonade.

Wine

Bavaria's only wine-growing region is located in Franconia (p223) in and around Würzburg. Growers here produce some exceptional dry white wines, which are bottled in distinctive green flagons called *Bocksbeutel*. If *Silvaner* is the king of the grape here, then *Müller-Thurgau* is the prince and riesling, *Weissburgunder* (pinot grigio) and *Bacchus* the courtiers. The latter three thrive especially on the steep slopes flanking the Main River. Red wines play merely a supporting role. Nearly 80% of all wine produced is sold within the region.

For more information about German grape varieties, growing regions, wine festivals and courses, check out the pages of the German Wine Institute at www .deutscheweine.de.

Nonalcoholic Drinks

Tap water is fine to drink but asking for a glass at a restaurant will raise brows at best and may be refused altogether. Instead most people order *Mineralwasser* (mineral water) which usually comes loaded *mit Kohlensäure* (with bubbles). If you don't like this, ask for *stilles Wasser*. *Eiswürfel* (ice cubes) are usually served only on request.

Carbonated soft drinks are widely available, although the diet versions are not. You may find that familiar brands such as Pepsi or Coca-Cola have a slightly different flavour as they are reformulated to reflect German tastes. A popular and refreshing drink is *Apfelschorle*, which is apple juice mixed with sparkling mineral water.

Coffee is usually fresh, strong and served with condensed milk and sugar on the side. The bottomless cup has yet to hit Germany, but Italian-style latte macchiatos and cappuccinos are all the rage in fashionable cafés. Coffee usually comes in a *Tasse* (cup) or *Kännchen* (pot) and you should specify what you want when ordering. Except in better cafés, tea is usually a teabag in a glass or pot of hot water and served with a slice of lemon. If you want milk, ask for *Tee mit Milch*.

CELEBRATIONS

Major holidays are feast days and usually spent at home with family, gorging and guzzling way more than everyone knows is good for them. At Easter roast lamb is often the star of the show, while children, of course, go on egg hunts and devour chocolate bunnies. Easter is preceded by Lent, a period of fasting when sweet dishes such as *Rohrnudeln* (browned yeasty buns served with plum compote and vanilla sauce) are enjoyed and fish, especially carp, replaces meat in many households. Carp, served boiled, baked or fried, is also popular at Christmas time, although more people roast up a goose or a turkey as the main event. *Lebkuchen* (gingerbread) and *Spekulatius* (spicy cookies) are both sweet staples of Advent (the pre-Christmas season). Many families also bake their own Christmas cookies, often from recipes passed down through the generations. *Weihnachtsstollen*, a loaf-shaped fruit cake dusted with powdered sugar (a symbol of the baby Jesus in a nappy, believe it or not), is also popular. For drinks, *Glühwein* (spicy mulled wine), best consumed on a chilly evening at a Christmas market, is a favoured libation of the season.

WHERE TO EAT & DRINK

Restaurants are often formal places with uniformed servers, full menus, crisp white linen and high prices. A *Gaststätte* is generally a more relaxed and 'local' place to eat, with large menus, daily specials and perhaps a beer garden or terrace. Cafés tend to serve both coffee and alcohol as well as light meals, although ordering food is usually not obligatory. Beer halls are essentially large pubs serving hearty dishes that wash down well with the local brew. Once the last winter storms are gone, the action moves outdoors into the beer gardens, some of which let you bring your own picnic as long as you consume their drinks and don't sit at tables draped in tablecloths.

Most restaurants are open for lunch and dinner only, but more casual places tend to be open all day, serving a limited menu, often called *Brotzeit* (below), in the afternoon.

As a basic rule, if you like your cuisine to be authentic, avoid restaurants near major tourist attractions, on the main town square, in the *Ratskeller* (basement of the town hall) and those posting menus in multiple languages.

Quick Eats

German fast-food places are called *Imbiss* or *Schnellimbiss*. Kiosks selling sausages are ubiquitous and many bakeries serve sandwiches alongside their delicious pastries. A chain unique to Bavaria is Vinzenzmurr, a butcher-deli serving various hot and cold dishes. Nordsee is a popular chain of fish eateries that also sells fresh takeaway sandwiches. In the cities especially, the Turkish population has added the doner kebab to the snack repertoire. These are thin slivers of veal or chicken stuffed into a slightly toasted pitta alongside salad and vegetables and doused with garlicky yoghurt sauce. Vegetarians should try *Lahmacun,* a pancake-shaped bread stuffed with vegetables, drizzled with sauce and rolled up like a burrito. Pizza, sold by the slice, is also popular.

For an in-depth study of what's pouring at Munich's beer halls and gardens, Larry Hawthorne's *The Beer Drinker's Guide to Munich* is an indispensable tool that will take you far beyond the Hofbräuhaus.

VEGETARIANS & VEGANS

In the land of meat and potatoes, vegetarianism – let alone veganism – is still considered rather exotic. Most restaurant menus feature a few token 'vegetarian' dishes (usually veggie casseroles or dumplings with sauce), but some chefs don't see anything wrong with using chicken or beef stock in the preparation. Fish is also often considered a 'meatless' dish and salads may be dressed in mayonnaise and have eggs and ham mixed in with the lettuce and tomatoes. Indian, Thai, Vietnamese and other Asian eateries are your best bet for tofu- or vegetable-based mains.

EATING WITH KIDS

Dining with kids can be child's play as long as you avoid fancy restaurants and stick to *Gaststätten* and other less-formal eateries where (well-behaved) children are usually very welcome indeed. Many have special kids' dishes or even an entire children's menu; even those that don't can usually tailor a meal to your little one's taste. High chairs are ubiquitous. For more on travelling with children, see p276.

HABITS & CUSTOMS

Most Bavarians eat three meals a day. *Frühstück* (breakfast) is a hearty affair, usually consisting of various types of bread, cheese, cold cuts and

---

DOS & DON'TS

- If invited to someone's home, bring some flowers or a bottle of wine.
- After a dinner party, call the next day or send a thank-you note.
- At the start of a meal diners exchange a rousing *Guten Appetit!* (*bon appetit!*).
- Don't start eating until everyone has been served.
- *Prost!* (with beer) or *Zum Wohl!* (with wine) are typical drinking toasts.

jam and maybe a boiled egg. Hotel buffets usually also feature cereals, fruit and yoghurt.

Mittagessen (lunch) is the main meal of the day. Many restaurants tout lunch-time *Stammgericht* (specials) or a *Tagesmenü* (fixed lunch menu). *Abendbrot* (supper) at home is normally a simple meal served between 5pm and 7pm and doesn't usually involve cooked food. Going out to *Abendessen* (dinner) tends to be a relaxed and social event that starts between 7pm and 8pm and can easily last two or three hours. Restaurants are busiest on Friday to Sunday nights, when reservations are recommended.

Many Bavarians also indulge in a fourth meal, the *Brotzeit* (literally 'bread time'), typically an afternoon snack featuring bread with various cold cuts, cheeses or a pair of sausages. Many restaurants even have a special *Brotzeit* menu. Those with a sweet tooth may opt for *Kaffee und Kuchen* (coffee and cakes), served in cafés, instead.

> If you want to train your tummy for your trip to Bavaria, try any of the recipes – roast pork to liver dumplings – detailed on www.bavarian-online.de.

EAT YOUR WORDS

For additional pronunciation guidelines and other useful phrases see the Language chapter, p295.

Useful Phrases

I'd like to reserve a table.
Ich möchte einen Tisch reservieren.   ikh *merkh*·te *ai*·nen tish re·zer·*vee*·ren
Do you have a menu in English?
Haben Sie eine englische Speisekarte?   ha·ben zee *ai*·ne *eng*·li·she *shpai*·ze·kar·te?
What would you recommend?
Was empfehlen Sie?   vas emp·*fay*·len zee?
I'd like a local speciality.
Ich möchte etwas Typisches aus der Region.   ikh *merkh*·te *et*·vas *tü*·pi·shes ows dair re·*gyawn*
I'm a vegetarian.
Ich bin Vegetarier/Vegetarierin. (m/f)   ikh bin ve·ge·*tah*·ri·er/ve·ge·*tah*·ri·er·in
That was delicious!
Das war köstlich!   das var *kerst*·likh!
The bill, please.
Die Rechnung, bitte.   dee *rekh*·nung bi·te

Food Glossary

BASICS

Brot	brawt	bread
Butter	*bu*·ter	butter
Ei(er)	*ai*·(er)	egg
Käse	*kay*·ze	cheese
Milch	milkh	milk
Nudeln	*noo*·deln	noodles
Pfeffer	*pfe*·ffer	pepper
Reis	rais	rice
Salz	zalts	salt
Semmel	*tse*·mel	bread roll
Zucker	*tsu*·ker	sugar

MEAT & MEATY DISHES

Ente	*en*·te	duck
Fasan	fa·*zahn*	pheasant
Flammekuche	*fla*·me·koo·khen	Alsatian-style 'pizza' topped with cream and bacon
Fleischpflanzerl	*flaish*·pflan·tserl	meatballs

Gans	gans	goose
Hackfleisch	*hak*-flaish	chopped or minced meat
Herz	herts	heart
Hähnchen/Huhn	*hayn*-khen/hoon	chicken
Kalbfleisch	*kalp*-flaish	veal
Kalbsgeschnetzeltes	*kalps*-ge-shnet-tsel-tes	sautéed veal in cream sauce
Krustenbraten	*kroos*-ten-brah-ten	roast pork with crackling crust
Lammbraten	*lam*-brah-ten	roast lamb
Lammfleisch	*lam*-flaish	lamb
Lammkotelett	lam-ko-*let*	lamb chop
Leber	*lay*-ber	liver
Leberkäs	*lay*-ber-kay-ze	pork and beef meatloaf
Leberknödel	*lay*-ber-kner-del	chopped liver dumpling
Lende	*len*-de	loin
Niere	*nee*-re	kidney
Pressack	*pray*-sak	sausagelike spiced pork served sliced with bread
Pute	*pu*-te	turkey
Putenbrust	*pu*-ten-broost	turkey breast
Rehbraten	*ray*-brah-ten	roast venison
Rinderbraten	*rin*-de-brah-ten	roast beef
Rindfleisch	*rint*-flaish	beef
Roulade	roo-*lah*-de	thin-sliced beef rolled up and braised with spices
Sauerbraten	*zow*-er-brah-ten	beef marinated in vinegar, then braised
Saure Lungen	*zow*-re-*lung*-en	soup made with lungs marinated in vinegar
Saure Zipfel	*zow*-re-*tsee*-pfel	sausages boiled in vinegar and spices until blue
Schinken	*shing*-ken	ham
Schlachtteller/Schlachtplatte	*shlakh*-te-le/*shlakh*-pla-te	platter of various cold meats and sausages
Schweinefleisch	*shvai*-ne-flaish	pork
Spanferkel	*shpan*-fer-kel	suckling pig
Wachtel	*vakh*-tel	quail
Wild	vilt	game
Wildschwein	*vilt*-shvain	wild boar
Zunge/Züngerl	*tsung*-e/*tsoong*-erl	tongue

Fans of *Leberkäs* and *Schweinebraten* should pick up a copy of Olli Leeb's *Bavarian Cooking*, which serves up dozens of recipes with delicious sides of cooking history and cultural anecdotes.

FISH

Dorsch	dorsh	cod
Forelle	fo-*re*-le	trout
Garnele	gar-*nay*-le	prawn
Hering	*hay*-ring	herring
Karpfen	*karp*-fen	carp
Lachs	laks	salmon
Seezunge	see-*tsung*-e	sole

VEGETABLES & MEATLESS DISHES

Artischocke	ar-ti-*sho*-ke	artichoke
Auflauf	*owf*-lowf	casserole
Blumenkohl	*bloo*-men-kawl	cauliflower
Bohnen	*baw*-nen	beans
Gemüse	ge-*moo*-ze	vegetables

Gurke	*gur*·ke	cucumber; gherkin
Kartoffel	kar·*to*·fel	potato
Knoblauch	*knawp*·lowkh	garlic
Kohl	kawl	cabbage
Krautsalat	*krowt*·sa·lat	coleslaw
Linsen	*lin*·sen	lentils
Radieschen	ra·*dees*·khen	radish
Rosenkohl	*raw*·zen·kawl	Brussels sprouts
Rotkohl	*rawt*·kawl	red cabbage
Schupfnudeln	*shupf*·noo·deln	finger-shaped fried dumplings
Schwammerl	*shwam*·erl	mushroom
Spargel	*shpar*·gel	white asparagus
Zwiebel	*tswee*·bel	onion

FRUIT

Apfel	*ap*·fel	apple
Apfelsine	*ap*·fel·zee·ne	orange
Birne	*bir*·ne	pear
Dattel	*da*·tel	date
Erdbeere	*ert*·bair·re	strawberry
Feige	*fai*·ge	fig
Holunderbeere	*ho*·lund·er bair·re	elderberry
Kirsche	*kir*·she	cherry
Pfirsich	*pfir*·zikh	peach
Rote/Schwarze Johannisbeere	*ro*·te/*shvar* tse yo·*ha*·nis·bair re	red/blackcurrant
Weintraube	*vain*·trow·be	grape
Zitrone	tsi·*traw*·ne	lemon

Munich

HIGHLIGHTS

- **Green Oasis**
  Strolling the landscaped grounds of the Englischer Garten (p74), one of Europe's largest parks

- **Art Treasures**
  Admiring one of the world's finest Renaissance collections at the Alte Pinakothek (p70)

- **Delusions of Grandeur**
  Viewing the extravagant interiors and manicured gardens of Schloss Nymphenburg (p81)

- **Amazing Grace**
  Marvelling at the classic buildings on Königsplatz (p69) or in Schwabing's Art Nouveau district (p72)

- **Sports Mecca**
  Burning off the extra pounds at the Olympiapark (p75), site of the '72 Olympic Games

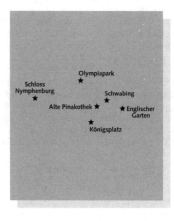

▪ AREA CODE: 089	▪ POP: 1.3 MILLION	▪ AREA: 310 SQ KM

Pulsing with prosperity and Bavarian *Gemütlichkeit* (cosiness), Munich loves to revel in its own contradictions. This sophisticated modern metropolis draws as much inspiration from *nouvelle cuisine* and Hugo Boss as sausages and thick leather shorts. Munich may be a high-minded fellow but pop a keg and he'll be out there tearing up the dance floor.

Polls of wistful Germans confirm Munich is the most popular place to live – and in a blink you'll see why. Balmy summer evenings at one of its streetside cafés make the city feel like a Florence or a Milan. Thrilling alpine landscapes, crystal-clear lakes and fairy-tale castles lie at its doorstep. It is a haven for all sorts of culture. And at Oktoberfest the entire planet converges to toast the town.

Parts of Germany may have fallen on hard times but Munich shakes it off like magic. A forest of construction cranes dots the landscape, planting high-tech office towers and sharp, eco-friendly residences where highways once stood.

Bavaria never grew much heavy industry, so Munich's centre retains a small-town feel. Global players such as Siemens and BMW hug the outskirts and their influence lends the city a cosmopolitan flair and a good chunk of its wealth. In the beer gardens you may hear more English than German, and almost as much Italian or Japanese.

Forget the Teutonic clichés about grim workaholics – Müncheners have plenty to smile about and any time of year the mood is infectious, be it during the tourist-packed summer or the cold stillness of a February afternoon.

HISTORY

It was the Benedictine monks, drawn by fertile farmland and the closeness to Catholic Italy, who settled in what is now Munich. The name comes from the medieval German *Munichen* (monks). The city was christened in 1158 under the rule of Heinrich der Löwe (Henry the Lion).

In 1240 the city passed to the house of Wittelsbach, which would run Munich (as well as Bavaria) until the 20th century. Munich prospered as a centre for the salt trade but was hit hard by the outbreak of plague in 1349. It was 150 years before the epidemic subsided and the Schäffler (coopers) began a ritualistic dance, performed every seven years, to remind people of their good fortune. The Schäfflertanz is reenacted daily by the little figures on the city's glocken-spiel (carillon) on Marienplatz.

By the early 19th century, furious monument building by successive kings gave Munich its wide Italian boulevards and the classical gems that line them. Culture and the arts flourished, but when Ludwig II ascended the throne his grandiose projects, his numerous lavish palaces for example, bankrupted the royal house and threatened the government. Ironically, they are the biggest money-spinners for the Bavarian tourism industry today.

Munich has seen many turbulent times but last century was particularly rough. The world wars starved the city, reduced it to ashes and killed hundreds of thousands. Reconstruction was largely finished when the city was awarded the 1972 Olympic Games, a celebration that ended in tragedy when 17 people were killed in a terrorist hostage-taking incident.

Today Munich wears a rich, self-assured reputation and is recognised for having the highest quality of life of any German city. It yearns for the status of a capital city, and its rivalry with a magnificent but struggling Berlin is seen by both sides as a 'still to come'.

ORIENTATION

The Hauptbahnhof (central train station) is less than 1km west of Marienplatz, the heart of the Altstadt, Munich's historic centre. To get there, walk east on Bayerstrasse to Karlsplatz, then take Neuhauser Strasse, which is Munich's main shopping street to Marienplatz.

North of Marienplatz is the Residenz (the former royal palace), packed with museums and theatres, and Odeonsplatz, home to the landmark Theatinerkirche. To the east of Marienplatz is the Platzl quarter, brimming with traditional pubs and restaurants such as the Hofbräuhaus. The hipper bars and venues are south of the square in the Gärtnerplatzviertel which, along with the Glockenbachviertel southwest of here, is also the centre of Munich's gay and lesbian scene. The Isar River flows through the eastern part of the city from south to north.

Munich is divided into various districts each with their own distinct character. Schwabing, north of the Altstadt, is home to Munich's university and a host of cafés and restaurants. It borders on Maxvorstadt, home to the Pinakothek museums. To the east sprawls the Englischer Garten (English Garden), one of Europe's largest city parks. North of Schwabing, the main attraction is the Olympiapark, site of the 1972 Olympic Games.

Just east of the Altstadt is Lehel, a peaceful quarter brimming with stylish Art Deco apartment houses and home to key museums along Prinzregentenstrasse. Across the Isar River lie the districts of Haidhausen, a trendy neighbourhood packed with pubs, and Bogenhausen, which is packed with old-money mansions.

South and west of the Altstadt and near the Hauptbahnhof is Ludwigsvorstadt, a half-seedy, half-lively area with shops, restaurants, cafés and cheap hotels. The Westend, further west, is a seat of the brewing industry but also bristles with renovated houses, hip cafés and wine bars. It adjoins the Theresienwiese, where the Oktoberfest is held.

Just further north of here is cosmopolitan Neuhausen, a more-residential area with plenty of good restaurants and pubs. Schloss Nymphenburg and its lovely gardens are a little further northwest. Munich's airport is 30km northeast of the city.

Maps

Falk's foldout concertina maps of Munich are the handiest to use. Allgemeiner Deutscher Automobil Club's (ADAC) large-format map is good but is tricky to use in tight spaces such as a car.

INFORMATION
Bookshops

Geobuch (Map pp56-7; ☎ 265 030; Rosental 6) Best travel bookshop in town.

Hugendubel (www.hugendubel.de) Karlsplatz (Map pp56-7; ☎ 484 484; Karlsplatz 11-12; ☼ 9.30am-8pm); Marienplatz (Map pp56-7; ☎ 484 484; Marienplatz 22; ☼ 9.30am-8pm) Well-respected national chain with comfy reading couches.

Hugendubel English bookshop (Map pp56-7; ☎ 484 484; Salvatorplatz 2)

Max&Milian (Map pp56-7; ☎ 260 3320; Ickstattstrasse 2; ☼ 10.30am-8pm Mon-Fri) Best-established gay bookshop.

Sussmann Presse + Buch (Map pp56-7; Hauptbahnhof) Major English-language publications and books for reading between train stops.

(Continued on page 62)

MUNICH IN...

Two Days

Start off your day with a yummy breakfast at **Café Voilá** (p96) in comfy Haidhausen, a perfect spot for people-watching. Visit the **Alte Pinakothek** (p70) and then take a stroll through the sprawling **Englischer Garten** (p74). Head in to the Altstadt and watch the glockenspiel do its thing on **Marienplatz** (p63). Treat yourself at Munich's fine Italian restaurant **Hippocampus** (p94), followed by a night at that design temple **Cortiina** (p90). Peruse the produce on **Viktualienmarkt** (p68) and linger over a cold one in a beer garden.

Four Days

Follow the two-day itinerary, then on your third day add an excursion to one of Ludwig's fantasy castles at **Neuschwanstein** (p261), **Linderhof** (p132) or **Herrenchiemsee** (p139). The next day visit swanky **Schloss Nymphenburg** (p81) and its folly-filled garden. Take in a classical concert at the **Gasteig** (p102), or a jazz gig at **Jazzclub Unterfahrt im Einstein** (p101). At night hop from bar to trendy bar in Schwabing's **Leopoldstrasse** (p99).

SIGHTS & ACTIVITIES   (pp83–4)
Münchener Tierpark Hellabrunn.... **1** D5
Schloss Blutenburg........................**2** B2

SLEEPING   (p92)
Campingplatz Nord-West..............**3** C1
Campingplatz Thalkirchen............**4** D6

DRINKING   (p100)
Kilombo...**5** E4

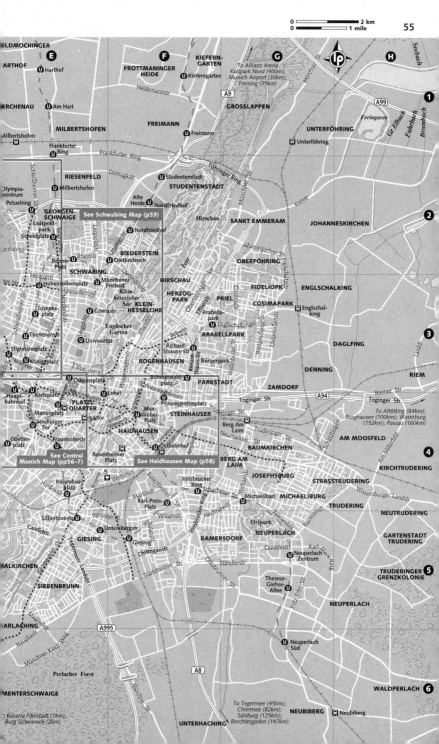

0   500 m
0   0.3 miles

Planetarium		(see 5)
Prinzregententheater	11	D2
St Annakirche	12	A1
St Nikolai & Lorettokapelle	13	B3
Schack-Galerie	14	B1
St-Johann-Baptist-Kirche	15	C3
Staatliches Museum für		
Völkerkunde	16	A2
SLEEPING		(p92)
Hotel Adria	17	A1
Opera-Garni	18	A2
Parkhotel in Lehel	19	A1
EATING		(pp93–7)
Café Voilà	20	C3
Creperie Bernard Bernard	21	B3
Diyar	22	C3
Hippocampus	23	D1
Käfer	24	C1
La Bretagne	25	B4
Rue des Halles	26	B3
Taverna Paros	27	C2
Unionsbräu Haidhausen	28	C2
Wirtshaus in der Au	29	A4
DRINKING		(pp97–100)
Dreigroschenkeller	30	A3
Julep's	31	D3
Lisboa Bar		(see 31)
Molly Malone's	32	B3
Nage & Sauge	33	A3
ENTERTAINMENT		(pp100–103)
Black Jump	34	D4
Jazzclub Unterfahrt im Einstein		(see 28)
Jazzy's	35	A3
Kleine Komödie am Max	K36	A3
Kultfabrik & Optimolwerke	37	D4
Kulturzentrum Gasteig	38	B3
Muffathalle	39	B3
Museum-Lichtspiele	40	A3
Philharmonie im Gasteig		(see 38)
SHOPPING		(pp103–4)
Auer Dult	41	A4

INFORMATION		
Stadtbücherei		(see 38)
SIGHTS & ACTIVITIES		(pp77–81)
Aktionsforum Praterinsel	1	B2
Alpines Museum	2	B2
Deutsches Museum	3	A3
Former Forum der Technik		(see 5)
Friedensengel	4	C1
IMAX Theatre	5	A3
Kartoffelmuseum	6	D4
Klosterkirche St Anna	7	A1
Kriechbaumhof	8	C3
Müllersches Volksbad	9	A3
Museum Villa Stuck	10	C1

0 | 500 m
0 | 0.3 miles

INFORMATION

Bayerische Staatsbibliothek	1 B6
Cyberice-C@fe	2 C3
Dresdner Bank	3 B4
Institut Français	4 B5
Stadtbücherei	5 B3
Universitätsbibliothek	6 B5
US Consulate	7 B6
Words' Worth Books	8 A5

SIGHTS & ACTIVITIES (pp72–5)

Akademie der Bildenden Künste	9 B5
Archäologische Staatssammlung	10 C6
Bayerisches Nationalmuseum	11 C6
Chinesischer Turm	12 C5
Denk Stätte	13 B6
Erlöserkirche	14 B3
Haus der Kunst	15 B6
Japanisches Teehaus	16 B6
Ludwigskirche	17 B5
Monopteros	18 C5
Schloss Suresne	19 C3
Seidlvilla	20 B4
Walking Man	21 B4

SLEEPING (p90)

Cosmopolitan Hotel	22 B4
Gästehaus Englischer Garten	23 C3
Mitwohnzentrale an der Uni	24 B5
München Park Hilton	25 D5
Pension Frank	26 A5

EATING (pp93–7)

Amalienstrasse	27 A5
Bobolovsky's	28 A5
Cohen's	29 A6
El Cortijo	30 C3
Friesische Teestube	31 A3
News Bar	32 A5
Nido	33 A5
Reiter Imbiss	34 B3
Sausalitos	35 A5
Wok Man	36 B3

DRINKING (pp97–100)

Alter Simpl	37 A5
Atzinger	38 A5
Brik	39 A5
Chinesischer Turm	(see 12)
Günther Murphy's Irish Tavern	40 B4
Hirschau	41 D3
Millennium	42 B4
News Café	43 B3
Roxy	44 B4
Seehaus	45 D3
Shamrock	46 B4

ENTERTAINMENT (pp100–103)

P1	47 B6
Titanic City	48 A4

See Western Munich Map (p60)

See Central Munich Map (pp56-7)

See Haidhausen Map (p58)

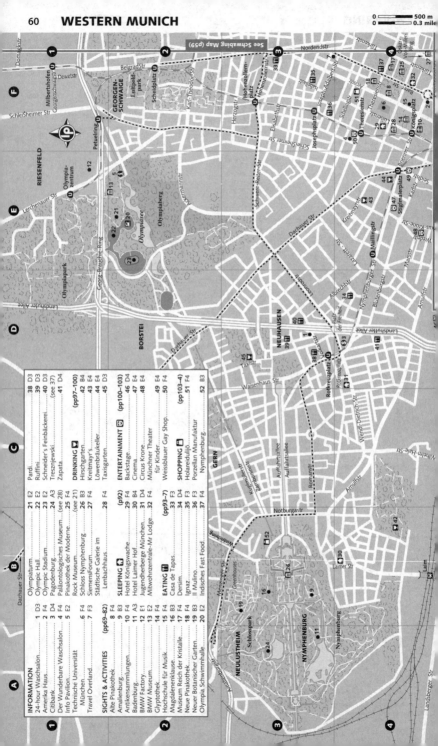

0 — 500 m
0 — 0.3 mile

INFORMATION
24-hour Waschsalon..................1 D3
Amerika Haus.............................2 F4
Citibank....................................3 D4
Der Wunderbare Waschsalon....4 F4
Info Pavilion..............................5 E2
Technische Universität
München.................................6 F4
Travel Overland........................7 F3

SIGHTS & ACTIVITIES (pp69–82)
Alte Pinakothek..........................8 F4
Amalienburg...............................9 B3
Antikensammlungen.................10 F4
Badenburg................................11 A3
BMW Factory............................12 E1
BMW Museum..........................13 E2
Glyptothek...............................14 F4
Hochschule für Musik...............15 F4
Magdalenenklause....................16 B3
Museum Reich der Kristalle......17 F4
Neue Pinakothek......................18 F4
Neuer Botanischer Garten........19 B3
Olympia Schwimmhalle.............20 E2
Olympiaturm.............................21 E2
Olympic Hall.............................22 F4
Olympic Stadium.......................23 E2
Pagodenburg............................24 A3
Paläontologisches Museum......25 F4
Pinakothek der Moderne.....(see 28)
Rock Museum...........................26 F4
Schloss Nymphenburg..............27 F3
SiemensForum...................(see 21)
Städtische Galerie im
Lenbachhaus.........................28 F4

SLEEPING (p92)
Hotel Königswache....................29 F4
Hotel Laimer Hof.......................30 B4
Jugendherberge München.........31 D4
Mitwohnzentrale-Mr Lodge.......32 F4

EATING (pp93–7)
Casa de Tapas...........................33 F3
Dersim......................................34 D4
Ignaz..35 F3
Il Mulino...................................36 F3
Indisches Fast Food..................37 F4

Pardi...38 D3
Ruffini......................................39 D3
Schneider's Feinbäckerei..........40 D3
Tresznjewski.....................(see 37)
Zapata......................................41 D4

DRINKING (pp97–100)
Hirschgarten............................42 B4
Kreitmayr's...............................43 F4
Löwenbräukeller.......................44 F4
Taxisgarten..............................45 D3

ENTERTAINMENT (pp100–103)
Backstage.................................46 D4
Cinema.....................................47 E4
Circus Krone.............................48 E4
Münchner Theater
für Kinder.............................49 E4
Weissblauer Gay Shop..............50 F4

SHOPPING (pp103–4)
Holareidulijö.............................51 F4
Porzellan Manufaktur
Nymphenburg.......................52 B3

See Schwabing Map (p59)

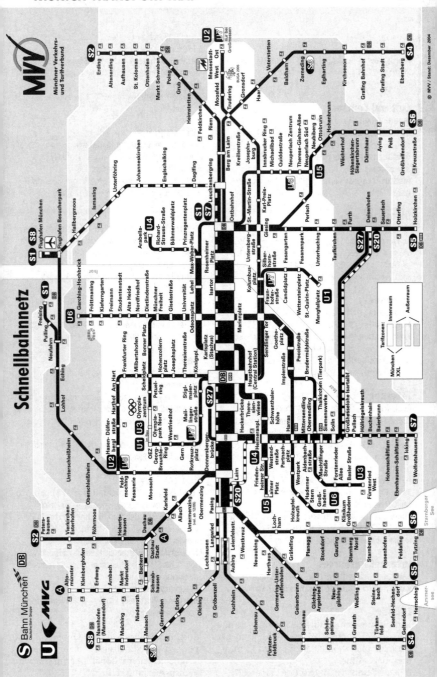

(Continued from page 53)

Words' Worth Books (Map p59; ☎ 280 9141; Schell-ingstrasse 21a) Gargantuan choice of English-language books.

Cultural Centres

Amerika Haus (Map p60; ☎ 552 5370; Karolinenplatz 3)
British Council Info Point (Map pp56-7; ☎ 2060 3310; Herzog-Heine-Strasse 7)
Goethe Institut (Map pp56-7; ☎ 551 9030; Sonnenstrasse 25)
Institut Français (Map p59; ☎ 286 6280; Kaulbach-strasse 13)

Discount Cards

Munich Welcome Card (1/3 days €6.50/16; 1-3-day card for up to 5 adults €11/23.50) This great little pass gives you unlimited public transport and big discounts on museums and attractions. On sale at tourist offices, hotels and travel agencies.

Emergency

Ambulance (☎ 192 22)
Fire brigade (☎ 112)
Police station (Map pp56-7; ☎ 110; Arnulfstrasse) On the north side of the Hauptbahnhof.
Rape Crisis Hotline (☎ 763 737; ☽ 10am-11pm Mon-Fri, 6pm-2am Sat & Sun)

Internet Access

Cyberice-C@fe (Map p59; ☎ 3407 6955; Feilitzsch-strasse 15; per 30/60 min €3/5; ☽ 10am-1am) In an ice-cream parlour near the Englischer Garten.
easyInternetCafe (Map pp56-7; Bahnhofplatz 1; per hr €1-3.80; ☽ 7.30am-11.45pm) This cyber meet-market has 600 terminals and demand-driven prices.
I-24 Center (Map pp56-7; ☎ 2070 2737; Im Tal 31; per 30min €1; ☽ 24hr) With extra services such as printing and CD burners.
Times Square Online Bistro (Map pp56-7; ☎ 5126 2600; Bayerstrasse 10a; per 5 min €0.50; ☽ 7am-1am) In the Hauptbahnhof, southern side.

Internet Resources

www.muenchen-tourist.de Munich's official website.
www.munichfound.de Munich's expat magazine.

Laundry

Laundrettes can be difficult to find in this town. Typical costs are about €2.50 to €4 per load, plus about €0.50 for 10 to 15 minutes' dryer time.
24-hour Waschsalon (Map p60; Landshuter Allee 77; ☽ 24hr)

City-SB Waschcenter (Map pp56-7; Paul-Heyse Strasse 21; ☽ 7am-11pm)
Der Wunderbare Waschsalon (Map p60; Theresien-strasse 134; ☽ 7am-11pm) The best laundrette close to the centre.
Schnell + Sauber (Map pp56-7; Klenzestrasse 18; ☽ 7am-11pm)

Left Luggage

Gepäckaufbewahrung (staffed storage room; ☎ 1308 6664; main hall, Hauptbahnhof; per piece daily €4; ☽ 8am-8pm Mon-Sat, 8am-6pm Sun)
Lockers (Hauptbahnhof main hall & opposite tracks 16, 24 & 28-36; per 24hr €2-4; ☽ 4am-12.30am)

Libraries

Bayerische Staatsbibliothek (Bavarian State Library; Map p59; ☎ 286 380; Ludwigstrasse 16; ☽ 9am-9pm Mon-Fri, 9am-5pm Sat) Has reading rooms with inter-national papers and mags.
Stadtbücherei Haidhausen (city library; Map p58; ☎ 4809 8316; Rosenheimer Strasse 5); Schwabing (Map p59; ☎ 336 013; Hohenzollernstrasse 16); Westend (Map pp56-7; ☎ 507 109; Schrenkstrasse 8)
Universitätsbibliothek (Map p59; ☎ 2180 2428; Geschwister-Scholl-Platz 1)

Media

Abendzeitung Light broadsheet that, despite the name, has a morning delivery.
Münchner Merkur The city's arch-conservative daily.
Süddeutsche Zeitung Widely read regional paper with a liberal streak. Monday's has a *New York Times* supple-ment in English.
tz Local daily similar to the saucy *Bild-Zeitung*, the biggest-selling tabloid in Europe.

Medical Services

The US and UK consulates (p278) can pro-vide lists of English-speaking doctors.
Bereitschaftsdienst der Münchner Ärzte (24-Hour Medical Services; Map pp56-7; ☎ 01805-191 212; Elisenhof) With English-speaking doctors.
Chirurgische Klinik (Hospital Emergency Room; Map pp56-7; ☎ 5160 2611; Nussbaumstrasse 20) For walk-in and emergency treatment.
Emergency Dentist (☎ 723 3093)
Emergency Pharmacy (☎ 594 475) Referrals to the nearest open pharmacy.

Most pharmacies will have employees who speak passable English, but there are several designated 'international' pharmacies with English-speaking staff:
Airport (☎ 9759 2950; Central Area, 3rd Fl)

Bahnhof-Apotheke (Map pp56-7; ☎ 555 830; Bahnhofplatz 7)
Ludwigs-Apotheke (Map pp56-7; ☎ 1894 0100; Neuhauser Strasse 11)

Money
American Express Neuhauser Strasse (Map pp56-7; ☎ 2289 1387; Neuhauser Strasse 47); Promenadeplatz (Map pp56-7; ☎ 2909 0145; Promenadeplatz 6)
Citibank (Map p59; Rotkreuzplatz)
Dresdner Bank (Map p59; Leopoldstrasse 37)
HypoVereinsbank (Map pp56-7; Marienplatz)
Postbank (Map pp56-7; Bahnhofplatz 1)
Reisebank (Map pp56-7; Hauptbahnhof; ✆ 7am-10pm)
EurAide's newsletter the *Inside Track* gets you a 50% reduction on commissions at this branch.
Sparkasse (Map pp56-7; Sparkassenstrasse 2)
Thomas Cook (Map pp56-7; ☎ 210 4900; Viktualien-markt 3)

Post
Post offices Altstadt (Map pp56-7; Residenzstrasse 2; ✆ 8am-6.30pm Mon-Fri, 9am-12.30pm Sat); Hauptbahn-hof (Map pp56-7; Bahnhofplatz 1; ✆ 7.30am-8pm Mon-Fri, 9am-4pm Sat) Poste restante at the Hauptbahnhof office is Postlagernd, Bahnhofplatz 1, 80074 Munich.

Telephone
There are public phones all over the city; most take phone cards that are available at post offices, newspaper stands and department stores. Some take credit cards too and others are coin-only, and a select few accept cards and coins.

Tourist Information
ADAC (Map pp56-7; ☎ 5491 7234; Sendlinger-Tor-Platz)
EurAide (Map pp56-7; ☎ 593 889; www.euraide.de; Room 3, track 11, Hauptbahnhof; ✆ 8am-12.30pm & 2-6pm May-Sep; 8am-noon & 2-5pm Oct-Apr) The office makes reservations, sells tickets for DB trains and a variety of tours, such as the 'Two Castles in a Day' tour to Neu-schwanstein and Hohenschwangau (p263) and finds rooms (€3 per booking). EurAide's free newsletter, the *Inside Track,* is packed with practical info about the city and surround-ings, and gives discounts on money changing (above).
Jugendinformationszentrum (Youth Information Centre; Map pp56-7; ☎ 5141 0660; www.jiz-muenchen.de in German; Paul-Heyse-Strasse 22; ✆ noon-6pm Mon-Fri, to 8pm Thu) A wide range of information for young visitors.
Tourist Office Hauptbahnhof (Map pp56-7; ☎ 2339 6500; Bahnhofplatz 2; ✆ 9am-8pm Mon-Sat, 10am-6pm Sun); Marienplatz (Map pp56-7; ☎ 2339 6500; Neues Rathaus; ✆ 10am-8pm Mon-Fri, 10am-4pm Sat) You can use the room-finding service for free or call ☎ 2339 6555.

Travel Agencies
EurAide (left) The best place to go with complicated rail-pass inquiries or to book train travel in Germany or elsewhere in Europe.
Atlas Reisen (Map pp56-7; ☎ 269 072; www.atlas-reisen.de in German; Kaufingerstrasse 1-5) In the Kaufhof department store.
Travel Overland (Map p60; ☎ 2727 6100; www.travel-overland.de in German; Barer Strasse 73)

Universities
Munich is home to about 84,000 students. The biggest universities are:
Ludwig-Maximilians-Universität München (Map p59; ☎ 218 00, foreign student inquiries ☎ 271 2642; www.dkfa.deGeschwister-Scholl-Platz 1) Runs German-language courses for foreigners throughout the year.
Technische Universität München (Map p60; ☎ 289 01; Arcisstrasse 21) One of Germany's top universities with renowned faculties of science, engineering and medicine.

DANGERS & ANNOYANCES
During Oktoberfest crime and staggering drunks are major problems, especially at the southern end of the Hauptbahnhof. It's no joke: drunks in a crowd trying to get home can get violent, and there are about 100 cases of assault every year. Leave early or stay very cautious, if not sober, yourself.

The *Föhn* is a weather-related phenom-enon known only in southern Germany. Static-charged wind from the south brings exquisite views clear to the Alps – and an area of dense pressure that bears down on the city. Asthmatics, rheumatics and hypo-chondriacs complain of headaches; other Müncheners claim that it simply makes them cranky.

SIGHTS
Munich's major sights are clustered around the Altstadt, with the main museum district near the Residenz. It will take another day or two to discover the delights of bohemian Schwabing, the sprawling Englischer Garten, and trendy Haidhausen to the east. North-west of the Altstadt you'll find cosmopolitan Neuhausen, the Olympiapark, and one of Munich's jewels – Schloss Nymphenburg.

Altstadt
MARIENPLATZ
Framed by a series of landmark buildings, Marienplatz is the beating heart of the Alt-stadt. It's a popular meeting place and a

lively outdoor stage for street artists, musicians and political demonstrations. At the centre of the square is the **Mariensäule** (Mary Column), erected in 1638 to celebrate the removal of Swedish forces. At the top is the golden figure of the Virgin Mary, carved in 1590 but later moved here from its original home in the Frauenkirche.

NEUES RATHAUS

The coal-blackened façade of the neo-Gothic **Neues Rathaus** (New Town Hall; 1867–1908) is festooned with gargoyles and statues, including, on the corner, a wonderful dragon climbing the turrets. Inside, six stately courtyards are used for festivals and events throughout the year. For a good view of the city you can climb to the top of the 85m-tall **tower** (adult/child €2/1; ☾ 9am-7pm Mon-Fri, 10am-7pm Sat & Sun). Those who take the staircase can peer into the corridors, which are decorated in colourful medieval style.

The highlight of the building is the **glockenspiel** (carillon), which has three levels; two portray the **Schäfflertanz** (p52) and the other the **Ritterturnier**, a knights' tournament held in 1568 to celebrate a royal marriage. The characters spring into action at 11am and noon (also at 5pm November to April). The night scene featuring the Münchener Kindl and Nachtwächter characters runs at 9pm.

ST PETERSKIRCHE

Opposite the Neues Rathaus, on the southern end of Marienplatz, is the **St Peterskirche** (Church of St Peter), Gothic in its core but with a flamboyant baroque interior. The magnificent high altar is by Erasmus Grasser (1517) and the eye-catching statues of the four church fathers by Egid Quirin Asam (1732). For spectacular views of the city, you can climb the rectangular 92m-tall **tower** (adult/child €1.50/0.30; ☾ 9am-6pm Mon-Sat, 10am-7pm Sun) – also known as 'Alter Peter' – via 297 steps. It draws smaller crowds than the Rathaus tower.

FISCHBRUNNEN

The **Fischbrunnen** (Fish Fountain) was used to keep river fish alive during medieval markets and later became the ceremonial dunking spot for butchers' apprentices. Local legend suggests that dipping an empty purse into the fountain on Ash Wednesday guarantees that it will always be full. Munich's mayor shows up every year with council officials to dip and hope for fuller city coffers.

ALTES RATHAUS

The Gothic Altes Rathaus (old town hall; 1474) was destroyed by lightning and bombs and was rebuilt in a plainer style after WWII. In its south tower is the city's **Spielzeugmuseum** (Toy Museum; ☎ 294 001; Alter Rathausturm; adult/child €3/1; ☾ 10am-5.30pm) with its huge collection of European and American toys. The bronze statue on the tower's southern side depicts Julia (as in Romeo and Juliet) and was a gift from Munich's sister city, Verona. Look out for the wind-powered sculpture by the entrance that releases pent-up energy by clanging and banging.

HEILIGGEISTKIRCHE

Just east of the Altes Rathaus, the **Heiliggeistkirche** (Church of the Holy Spirit; Im Tal 77; ☾ 7am-6pm) first appears almost economical in design until you look up to see the frescoes by Cosmas Damian Asam, completed during the interior revamp between 1727 and 1730. The high altar is about as old, and has more than its fair share of angels. The Marienaltar (1450) is one of the few leftovers from the original Gothic church.

Marienplatz to Max-Joseph-Platz

For many seasoned and mostly foreign drinkers, the **Hofbräuhaus** (p97) stands for fun in Munich. The locals may sneer but there's an undeniable, if touristy, charm about the place. This is Munich's most famous beer hall, ringing to the strains of an oompah band and crawling with visitors from its 10am opening time. But take a moment to consider the fabulous interior: right where waitresses come barrelling through holding eight or more tankards, gaze up at the vaulted ceiling to see the twirling flowers reminiscent of a medieval court. Delve further and you'll find the upstairs ballroom, the place where the National Socialist Party first met in a big way on 20 February 1920. You can peek inside if it's not booked for a function.

Northwest of here is the central courtyard of the **Alter Hof** (Burgstrasse 8), the oldest Wittelsbach residence. The royals moved in and out again in 1474, when their royal superrealm was completed at the Residenz. The bay window on the southern façade was nicknamed 'Monkey Tower'. Local lore has it that a monkey played here, in the bedroom of the infant king, Ludwig the Stern. One day a market pig attacked Ludwig's cradle, and the monkey grabbed the young royal and brought him to the safety of the window. It's a folk fantasy – at the time the window didn't even exist.

Exit the courtyard at its northern end and continue north on Hofgraben, past the former **Münzhof** (mint). This historic courtyard is remarkable for its three-storey arcades dating from 1567. An inscription on the western side of the building reads *Moneta Regis* (Money Rules).

MAX-JOSEPH-PLATZ

Just past the old mint is **Maximilianstrasse**, Munich's most glamorous shopping street. It adjoins **Max-Joseph-Platz**, home to some of Munich's most beloved buildings. Among them is the five-tiered **Nationaltheater** (☎ 2185 1920; Max-Joseph-Platz 2), home to the Bavarian State Opera, and the granddaddy of them all – the Residenz. The square's anchor is a statue of Bavarian **King Max I Joseph**, who proclaimed Germany's first constitution in 1818.

At the southern end of the square is the **old central post office** with a frescoed, very Italianate arcade. This was originally the town mansion of a local count. The place still dispatches mail; enter at the western side.

Residenz

On the north side of Max-Joseph-Platz looms the oldest section (1571) of the **Residenz**, the huge palace that housed Bavarian rulers from 1385 to 1918. Northern wings were added to create several interior courtyards, including the Emperor, Apothecary and Fountain courtyards and two smaller ones, Chapel and King's Tract. The museums here are among the jewels in Munich's cultural crown.

There are separate entrances to the various attractions inside the Residenz.

RESIDENZMUSEUM

The incomparable treasures of the Wittelsbach dynasty are displayed in a maze of roughly 130 rooms in the **Residenzmuseum** (Map pp56–7; ☎ 290 671; enter from Max-Joseph-Platz 3; adult/child under 18 €6/free; ☒ 9am–6pm, to 8pm Thu Apr–mid-Oct, 10am–4pm mid-Oct–March). The museum is so large that it's divided into two sections, one open in the morning, one in the afternoon. You can see it all on guided tours, or do it yourself with a copy of the excellent English-language guide (€3), which has room-by-room tours with photographs and explanations.

The enclosed **Grotto Court**, one of the first places you'll see when you enter, features the wonderful **Perseusbrunnen** (Perseus Fountain), with its namesake holding the dripping head of Medusa. Among the marble columns of the loggia you'll find a quirk of postwar Munich: a layer of common beach shells donated by holidaymakers in the 1950s, at the request of the curators. Next door is the famous **Antiquarium**, a lavishly ornamented barrel vault, smothered in frescoes and built to house the Wittelsbachs' huge antique collection.

The **Kurfürstenzimmer** (Elector's Rooms) contain some stunning Italian portraits and a passage lined with two dozen views of Italy, painted by romantic artist Carl Rottmann.

Other highlights include the **Ancestral Gallery**, with 121 portraits of the rulers of Bavaria ordered according to time, and as far as they were concerned, importance (note the larger paintings of Charlemagne and Ludwig the Bavarian). The **Schlachtensäle** (Battle Halls) show scenes from the Napoleonic campaigns, some of which Ludwig himself participated in, and Nibelungensäle trumpeting scenes from the medieval Nibelungen epic. François Cuvilliés' **Reiche Zimmer** (Rich Rooms) are a three-part extravaganza of exuberant rococo carried out by the top stucco and fresco artists of the day.

The **Porcelain Chambers** contain a massive selection of 18th-century porcelain hailing from Berlin, Meissen and Nymphenburg, while the **Asian Collections** feature assorted Chinese and Japanese lacquerware, tapestries, carpets, furniture and jewellery.

SCHATZKAMMER DER RESIDENZ

The Residenzmuseum entrance also leads to the **Schatzkammer der Residenz** (Residence Treasury; Map pp56–7; ☎ 290 671; enter from Max-Joseph-Platz 3; adult/child under 18 €6/free; ☒ 9am–6pm Mon–Wed & Fri–Sun, 9am–8pm Thu). It exhibits an Aladdin's cave worth of jewel-encrusted crowns, sceptres and royal accoutrements.

Included among the mind-boggling treasures are portable altars, the ruby jewellery of Queen Therese, amazing pocket watches, and 'exotic handicrafts' from Turkey, Iran, Mexico and India. It's well worth the entry price. The English-language guide to the collection is another €3.

ALTES RESIDENZTHEATER

The Residenz also harbours one of Europe's finest rococo theatres, the **Altes Residenztheater** (Old Residence Theatre; Map pp56-7; ☎ 290 671; enter from Residenzstrasse 1; adult/child under 18 €3/free; 🕑 9am-6pm Mon-Wed & Fri-Sun, to 8pm Thu). Also known as the Cuvilliés Theatre, it has a stunning interior designed by Belgian architect François Cuvilliés, once a court jester for the Wittelsbachs.

STAATLICHES MUSEUM ÄGYPTISCHER KUNST

Many German explorers in the Middle East brought back some excellent finds, and some made their way into the **Staatliches Museum Ägyptischer Kunst** (Egyptian Art Museum; Map pp56-7; ☎ 298 546; enter from Hofgartenstrasse 1; adult/child under 18 €2/1.50; 🕑 9am-5pm Wed-Fri, 9am-5pm & 7-9pm Tue, 10am-5pm Sat & Sun). The antiquities, monuments and statues shown here date from the Old, Middle and New Kingdoms (2670–1075 BC). Also on view is sculpture from ancient Nubia (present-day Sudan) and examples of Coptic art from Egypt.

Odeonsplatz

On Residenzstrasse there are two lions guarding the gates to the palace. Rubbing one of the lions' shields is said to bring you wealth. Residenzstrasse culminates in Odeonsplatz, the site of the so-called Beer Hall Putsch by the Nazis in 1923, which landed Hitler in jail.

Just north of here is the **Leuchtenberg-Palais** (Map pp56-7; ☎ 230 60; Odeonsplatz 4; 🕑 8am-5pm Mon-Fri), a stately town palace modelled after a Roman palazzo and today home of the Bavarian Finance Ministry. The western part of the square hosts other exclusive places such as the **Odeon**, a government office that was once a music and dance hall.

FELDHERRNHALLE

At the square's south end looms the **Feldherrnhalle** (Field Marshals' Hall; Map pp56-7; Odeonsplatz). Graced with huge Italianate arches, it was built in honour of the military leaders under the Wittelsbachs. Among its statues are represented several failed commanders including General Tilly, who surrendered Munich to the Swedes during the Thirty Years' War.

On 9 November 1923, police stopped Hitler's attempt – the so-called Beer Hall Putsch – to bring down the Weimar Republic right outside the Feldherrnhalle in a fierce skirmish that left 20 people, including 16 Nazis, dead. There's a little plaque in the pavement of the square's eastern side commemorating the police officers who perished in the incident.

Hitler was tried and sentenced to five years in jail, but ended up serving a mere nine months, which he used to pen *Mein Kampf*. After his rise to power in 1933, he required passers-by of the Feldherrnhalle to give the Hitler salute. Those who preferred not to salute circumvented the front via Viscardigasse, which came to be known as Dodger's Alley.

THEATINERKIRCHE

The mustard-yellow church at the square's west side is the **Theatinerkirche St Kajetan** (Map pp56-7; Theatinerstrasse 22), built between 1663 and 1690 to commemorate the birth of Prince Max Emanuel. The massive twin towers flanking a giant cupola are a landmark of Munich's skyline. Inside, the intensely ornate high dome stands above the **Fürstengruft** (royal crypt), which contains the remains of Wittelsbach family members.

HOFGARTEN

On the east side of Odeonsplatz, a neo-classical gate leads to the former **Hofgarten** (Royal Gardens), crisscrossed by lovely paths. To the left (north) of the entrance is the **Café Tambosi**, an exclusive street café usually chock-a-block with cashed up tourists. The entrance itself consists of **Klenze's Arcades**, bearing frescoes of Bavarian historical scenes and the Wittelsbachs.

Paths culminate in the centre at the **Hofgartentempel**, a striking octagonal pavilion honouring the Roman goddess Diana. In summer, it's a favourite spot for classical recitals. Impossible to overlook, east of the Hofgarten is the modern **Bayerische Staatskanzlei** (Map pp56-7; ☎ 216 50; Franz-Josef-Strauss-Ring 1), the Bavarian chancellery where the governor's office is located. The old-style cupola is the only remaining section of the ruined Army Museum that was left as a war memorial. It's known to Müncheners as the 'glass palace'.

On the northern side of the gardens is the **Deutsches Theatermuseum** (German Theatre Museum; Map pp56-7; ☎ 210 6910; Galeriestrasse 4a/6; admission free; ☻ 10am-4pm Tue-Sun). The museum's vast collection of stage sets, props, costumes, masks and theatre programmes thoroughly documents the history of the theatre in German-speaking countries. Three to five special exhibits, along with readings and other unique events, are organised each year.

Odeonsplatz to Karlsplatz

South of Odeonsplatz on Theatinerstrasse you'll find the eastern entrance of the **Fünf Höfe**, an exclusive shopping centre built around five courtyards. A perfect example of minimalist architecture (plenty of metal and glass), it's a maze of passageways lined by top-notch retailers. Also part of the complex is the **Kunsthalle der Hypo-Kulturstiftung** (Map pp56-7; ☎ 224 412; Theatinerstrasse 8; adult/child €8/7, half price Mon evenings; ☻ 10am-8pm), which has excellent rotating exhibitions ranging from antiquities to modern classics such as Monet, Chagall and Picasso.

FRAUENKIRCHE

The square Frauenplatz is dominated by the twin copper onion domes of Munich's most famous landmark, the late-Gothic **Frauenkirche** (Church of Our Lady; 1468–88). In contrast to the heavy red-brick exterior, the interior is a soaring passage of light thanks to a coat of startling whitewash. It has a fabulous altar by Asam and Ernst but is otherwise fairly spartan.

Local legend has it that Jörg von Halspach, builder of the Frauenkirche, struck a deal with Satan. The devil agreed to lend Halspach money only if he built the church without a single window. When the structure was finished, Halspach led him to a spot in the foyer where not a single window could be seen. Furious, Satan stamped his foot and stormed off, leaving a hoofed footprint in the pavement. The trick no longer works due to restoration work, but the outline (which looks more like that of a modern loafer) remains.

TOP FIVE VIEWS OF MUNICH

- **Frauenkirche** – put the Alps and Altstadt at your feet (below)
- **Bavaria statue** – see Oktoberfest meadow through her eyes (p81)
- **Olympiaturm** – ogle panoramic views of up to 100km (p76)
- **Monopteros** – survey the charms of the Englischer Garten (p74)
- **Friedensengel** – lord over the gurgling Isar River (p78)

Note the tomb of Ludwig the Bavarian, guarded by knights and noblemen, in the choir. There are good views of the city from the 98m-tall south **tower** (adult/child €2.50/free; ☻ 10am-5pm Mon-Sat Apr-Oct).

DEUTSCHES JAGD- UND FISCHEREIMUSEUM

On the main shopping drag you'll find the **Deutsches Jagd- und Fischereimuseum** (German Hunting & Fishing Museum; Map pp56-7; ☎ 220 522; Neuhauser Strasse 2; adult/child €3/2; ☻ 9am-5pm Tue, Wed & Fri-Sun, 9.30am-9pm Mon & Thu). Although it contains room after room of stuffed animals and antlers, this place is not just for rod-and-rifle freaks. Among the more intriguing exhibits are rococo hunting sledges, Stone Age fishing tackle and Chinese scroll paintings. The museum is in the former Augustinerkirche (1290) and boasts lavish interior decoration.

MICHAELSKIRCHE & AROUND

The **Michaelskirche** (Church of St Michael; Map pp56-7; Kaufingerstrasse 52) reflects a transition from Renaissance to baroque, its most distinctive feature being the 20m-wide barrel-vaulted ceiling – without supporting pillars. It's a solid building, reconstructed with extra care after the first version collapsed in the 16th century.

The main façade reflects the triumph of Catholicism over Protestantism: up above is Christ holding up a golden globe – the earth – while the bronze statue between the two entrance portals shows the archangel Michael in combat with the devil. The church crypt contains the tombs of some Wittelsbachs, including the humble final resting place of 'Mad King' Ludwig II. Outside the church is the **Richard Strauss Brunnen**, a modern fountain with streams of water that recall the *Dance of the Seven Veils* in Strauss' opera *Salomé*.

A little further on, at Neuhauser Strasse 48, is the **Bürgersaalkirche**, its inconspicuous façade belying the fact that it's a church. Built in the early 18th century, the church is a place of pilgrimage and contains the tomb of Rupert Mayer, a Jesuit priest and noted Nazi opponent who was beatified in 1987. Neuhauser Strasse culminates in **Karlsplatz**, punctuated by the medieval **Karlstor**.

Karlsplatz to Sendlinger Strasse

On Eisenmannstrasse, you'll see the ornate **Damenstiftskirche** to your left. Further south stands the **Sendlinger Tor**, the 14th-century southern gate.

ASAMKIRCHE

At Sendlinger Strasse 62 is the small St Johann Nepomuk church, better known as the **Asamkirche** (1733–46), designed and built by the talented Asam brothers. The brothers lived next door and this was originally their private chapel. Working jointly with his brother, Cosmas Damian, Asam had the luxury of designing the church exactly to his own specifications, unencumbered by the demands of a patron. One neat trick was that the main altar could be seen through a window from his house next door.

The jaw-dropping interior shows a harmonious unity of architecture, painting and sculpture. Scarcely a surface is unembellished, and it's almost too much for this pocket-sized interior (9m by 28m). As you enter note the golden skeleton of Death trying to cut the string of Life.

MÜNCHENER STADTMUSEUM

The **Münchener Stadtmuseum** (Munich City Museum; Map pp56-7; ☎ 2332 5586; St-Jakobs-Platz; adult/child €2.50/1.50; ☒ 10am-6pm Tue-Sun) has a permanent exhibit that traces the evolution of the city from royal residence to modern metropolis. Look out for the large-scale model of Munich in 1572 and the delightful *Moriskentänzer* (Morris Dancers; 1480) exhibition, which houses an ensemble of 10 half-metre–tall wooden figurines.

Don't miss the new ground-floor exhibit entitled **Nationalsozialismus in München** (Na-

tional Socialism in Munich), which examines the city's role in the Nazis' disastrous rise to power after 1918. Few labels are in English but the visuals are excellent, with a vast collection including photographs, propaganda posters, uniforms and flags, underground resistance papers and letters from concentration camp victims. Partitions of riveted steel provide a sobering backdrop for the displays.

The upper floors house the speciality collections. The **Musikinstrumenten Museum** (Musical Instruments Museum) holds a curious assembly of 2000 instruments from around the world, including entire sets of Indonesian ceremonial gongs, 19th-century skull-neck violins and more recent oddities such as a contrabass flute. The main chamber serves as a regular concert venue. The **Mode Museum** (Fashion Museum) has changing exhibits of clothing from the 18th century to today. The **Puppentheater-Museum** (Puppet Theatre Museum) has an astonishing collection of dolls and marionettes, with frequent *Punch and Judy* shows for the kiddies, along with mechanical funfair figures and slot machines. The newly revamped **Foto Museum** (Photography Museum) is a collection focusing on the early years of the medium, beginning around 1840.

Also part of the premises is the **Filmmuseum**, an institution in its own right that owns a huge archive of German silent movies. Its cinema presents two or three movies nightly (€4 each).

VIKTUALIENMARKT

The bustling **Viktualienmarkt** (Map pp56-7) is one of Europe's great food markets. In summer the entire place is transformed into one of the finest beer gardens, while in winter people huddle for warmth and schnapps in the small pubs around the square. The merchandise and food are top quality and arranged in semipermanent stands. A contingent of Bavarian butchers occupies the wooden huts along the back of St Peterskirche, selling tasty smoked ham and sausage packed in blue and white packaging like the Bavarian flag.

Shooting up from the centre of the square is the **Maypole**, bearing craftsmen's symbols and the traditional blue-and-white Bavarian stripes. On the south side of the square you'll see a statue of famous comedian **Karl**

Valentin, often holding fresh flowers left by a thoughtful local.

Immediately southwest of the market stalls is the **Schrannenhalle** (Map pp56-7), a reconstructed 19th-century grain market hall. Unveiled in May 2005, the 400m-long glass-and-iron structure harbours restaurants and craft shops and is a bright, airy venue for cultural events. Some of the decorative trim is from the original hall that burnt down in 1932.

Maxvorstadt

Northeast of the Altstadt, **Maxvorstadt** was the first stab at suburban planning by King Maximilian I. The district expanded apace under Ludwig I, who sponsored a new home for his private art collection at the Neue Pinakothek. He also conceived Ludwigstrasse, a broad and flashy boulevard lined with neoclassical edifices, which runs from Odeonsplatz to the Siegestor.

With its nine museums, all within walking distance of one another, Maxvorstadt is nirvana for culture vultures. There are two clusters: one around Königsplatz and the other – the trio of Pinakothek art museums – just north of here.

Northern Maxvorstadt, at the point where it spills into Schwabing is also Munich's 'Latin quarter', home to the city's three largest universities, the Technische Universität, the Ludwig-Maximilians-Universität (LMU) and the Fachhochschule München (Munich Polytechnic). Since many students also live in the neighbourhood, the streets are filled with time-killing pubs, cafés and boutiques.

KÖNIGSPLATZ
Northwest of the Altstadt is **Königsplatz** (Map p60; take U2 or tram No 27), a Greek-revivalist square created in a fit of monument-building by Ludwig I. It is anchored by the Doric-columned **Propyläen** gateway and orbited by three museums of ancient classics. The area between the buildings was once a vast expanse of pavement that, with three monuments serving as classical props, became an ideal spot for Nazi parades. After liberation the Allies grassed it over for the sake of denazification.

Only the foundations remain of two Nazi-purposed buildings at the east end of the square, as they were too close to utility lines to be demolished. They too have been denazified by planting foliage on top.

Peaceful and green today, the terrain is sometimes transformed for summer concerts, and the monuments are flooded with light and shadows with great effect.

GLYPTOTHEK
Munich's oldest museum, and one of its most fascinating, is the **Glyptothek** (Map p60; ☎ 286 100; Königsplatz 3; adult/child €3/2, free Sun, combined with Antikensammlungen €5/3; ☻ 10am-5pm Tue-Wed & Fri-Sun, 10am-8pm Thu). Like all the buildings on Königsplatz, the Glyptothek is a piece of Greek fantasy with its shock of alabaster columns, raised nobly above lawn level by a broad set of stairs. Greek and Roman sculpture, classical marbles and portraits of ancient kings are but a few delights of this comprehensive collection, 'acquired' under dubious circumstances by Ludwig I during a visit to Italy.

Among the most precious exhibits are sculptures from the Greek Aphaia Temple in Aegina, excavated by archaeologists in the early 19th century. Not to be missed either is the Barberini Faun, a marble statue of a sexy sleeping satyr with meticulous anatomical detail. Rooms X to XII contain superb busts, including one of a youthful Alexander the Great and several of Emperor Augustus. Also of note are the tomb reliefs of Mnesarete.

The inner courtyard has a calm and pleasant café where, in summer, classical theatre takes place under the stars.

ANTIKENSAMMLUNGEN
One of Germany's best antiquities collections is housed in the **Antikensammlungen** (Antiquities Collection; Map p60; ☎ 598 359; Königsplatz 1; adult/child €3/2, free Sun; ☻ 10am-5pm Tue & Thu-Sun, 10am-8pm Wed). It features vases, gold and silver jewellery and ornaments, bronze work, and Greek and Roman sculptures and statues. The collection, though dimly lit in parts, ranks right up there with that of the British Museum and the Louvre.

HOCHSCHULE FÜR MUSIK
The most sinister building in Munich stands just northeast of Königsplatz. The **Hochschule für Musik** (College of Music; Map p60; ☎ 289 03; Arcisstrasse 12) used to be the local Nazi headquarters, the place where Neville

Chamberlain made the agreement to cede the Czech Sudetenland to Hitler to ensure 'peace in our time'.

LENBACHHAUS

Franz von Lenbach, a leading portraitist of the late 19th century, used his considerable fortune to knock together this fabulous villa. Lenbach's widow sold it to the city in 1924 and threw in a bunch of his works as part of the deal. Today it is open as the **Städtische Galerie im Lenbachhaus** (☎ 2333 2000; Luisenstrasse 33; adult/child incl Kunstbau €4/2, during special exhibits €6/3; ☉ 10am-6pm Tue-Sun). The museum space is bright and pleasant, that is, apart from the dark upstairs rooms as Lenbach knew them, restored for the display of his own works.

The biggest draw are the paintings by members of Der Blaue Reiter (The Blue Rider), a movement begun in 1911 by Franz Marc and Wassily Kandinsky. The group, which also included Paul Klee, Alexej Jawlenski, August Macke and Gabriele Münter, is regarded as the high point of German expressionism. The irony here is that Lenbach himself opposed the Secessionist painters who paved the way for the innovations of the Blue Rider group. Also look for paintings by Lenbach, including some of his 80-plus portraits of Bismarck.

Another focal point is on contemporary art, especially by avant-gardists such as Joseph Beuys, Anselm Kiefer and Dan Flavin. Works by these and other practitioners are shown on a rotating basis in the nearby **Kunstbau**, a 120m-long underground room above the U-Bahn station Königsplatz.

PALÄONTOLOGISCHES MUSEUM

Bone up on prehistoric creatures at the **Paläontologisches Museum** (Palaeontological Museum; Map p60; ☎ 2180 6630; Richard-Wagner-Strasse 10; admission free; ☉ 8am-4pm Mon-Thu, to 2pm Fri, closed Sat & Sun). The displays include a giant elk from Ireland with 3m-tall antlers, an ancient Bavarian elephant and a sabre-toothed tiger from California. The museum also has a rare specimen of archaeopteryx, thought to be either the first bird or a birdlike dinosaur. This one's a must-see for kids.

ALTE PINAKOTHEK

A treasure-trove of the works of Old European Masters awaits visitors in the **Alte Pinakothek** (Map p60; ☎ 2380 5216; Barer Strasse 27, enter from Theresienstrasse; adult/child €5/3.50, free Sun; ☉ 10am-5pm, to 8pm Tue, closed Mon). Housed in a neoclassical temple commissioned by King Ludwig I, it is one of the most important collections in the world and a delicacy not just for art connoisseurs.

Nearly all the paintings were collected or commissioned by various Wittelsbach rulers, and mirror their eclectic tastes over the centuries. The collection ranges from the 14th to the 18th centuries. Its strong point is the selection of old German masters. The oldest works are altar paintings, of which the *Kirchenväteraltar* (Altar of the Early Church Fathers) by Michael Pacher stands out. Lucas Cranach the Elder's *Crucifixion* (1503) is an emotional rendition of the suffering Jesus.

Perhaps the most important room is the so-called **Dürersaal** upstairs. Here hangs Albrecht Dürer's famous Christlike *Self-Portrait* (about 1500), showing the gaze of an artist brimming with self-confidence. Also here is his final major work, *The Four Apostles,* which depicts John, Peter, Paul and Mark as rather humble men in a more sober interpretation of Christianity as per the Reformation. Compare this to Matthias Grünewald's *Sts Erasmus and Maurice,* which shows the saints dressed in rich robes like kings.

For a secular theme, inspect Albrecht Altdorfer's *Battle of Alexander the Great* (1529), which captures in dizzying detail a scene from a 6th-century war pitting Greeks against Persians.

The museum also owns a world-class collection of old Dutch masters, including an altarpiece by Rogier van der Weyden called *The Adoration of the Magi, The Seven Joys of Mary* by Hans Memling, *Danae* by Jan Gossaert and *The Land of Cockayne* by Pieter Bruegel the Elder.

Rubens fans will rejoice at the depth of the collection here. One of his most memorable portraits is that of *Hélène Fourment* (1631), a youthful beauty who was the aging Rubens' second wife. Other 17th-century Flemish artists represented include Anthony Van Dyck and Rembrandt with his intensely emotional *Passion Cycle.*

There are also scattered but outstanding examples of art from southern Europe, including such Italian masters as Botticelli, Rafael, da Vinci and Titian. The Spanish section boasts works by El Greco, Murillo and Velázquez, while the French have Nicolas Poussin, Claude Lorrain and François Boucher.

Free audio guides (in four languages, including English) are available in the lobby. These include commentary on about 90 works.

NEUE PINAKOTHEK

The **Neue Pinakothek** (Map p60; ☎ 2380 5195; Barer Strasse 29, enter from Theresienstrasse; adult/child €5/3.50, free Sun; ☉ 10am-5pm, to 8pm Wed, closed Tue) picks up where the Alte Pinakothek leaves off. It contains an extensive collection of 18th- to early-20th-century paintings and sculpture, from rococo to *Jugendstil* (Art Nouveau).

The core of the exhibit, though, is 19th-century German art from the private stock of King Ludwig I, who had nearly 400 paintings when he died in 1868. An entire room is dedicated to Hans Marées (1837–87), who specialised in realistic country scenes injected with a touch of sentimentality, as well as portraits. His *Youth Leading a Horse and Nymph* (1883) was one of his most harmonious. Marées was scarcely appreciated during his lifetime, however, and his pictures were carted off to Schleissheim after their first showing at the museum.

Munich society painters such as Wilhelm von Kaulbach and Karl von Piloty are here too, and their art reflected a renewed interest in German history during the latter part of the 19th century. The king had a special affinity for the 'Roman Germans', a group of neoclassicists centred around Johann Koch who stuck mainly to Italian landscapes.

Among the most memorable canvases are those by the Romantic painter Caspar David Friedrich, such as his *Riesengebirge Landscape with Rising Mist*. His landscapes and the work of portraitist Thomas Gainsborough are filled with emotionalism and an ominous mood.

French impressionists such as Degas always draw sizable crowds, as do the post-impressionists such as Van Gogh – one of his famous *Sunflowers* (1888) is on display. There are also several works by Gauguin, including *Breton Peasant Women* (1894); and by Manet including *Breakfast in the Studio* (1869).

Two particularly off-beat works featured are Walter Crane's *The Seeds of Neptune*, which shows watery steeds galloping on incoming waves, and Goya's chilling kitchen still life, *Plucked Turkey*.

PINAKOTHEK DER MODERNE

Germany's biggest museum of modern art is the **Pinakothek der Moderne** (Map p60; ☎ 2380 5360; Barer Strasse 40, enter from Theresienstrasse; adult/child €9/5, free Sun; ☉ 10am-5pm Tue-Wed & Sat & Sun, to 8pm Thu & Fri, closed Mon). Opened in 2002, the museum took six years to build and is the largest to emerge in Germany since WWII. The spectacular interior is dominated by a huge eyelike dome, spreading soft natural light throughout the blanched white galleries of the four-storey interior. Many of the building's walls are curved, leading the viewer softly from one discovery to the next, and right angles are disrupted by diagonals.

The museum brings together quite a few significant collections of 20th-century art, design, sculpture, photography and video under a single roof. To achieve this the museum tapped a variety of sources including the State Graphics Collection of 400,000 drawings, prints and engravings, as well as university archives and the Bavarian royal family. Duke Franz von Wittelsbach (see the boxed text on p83) contributed his private collection of more than 800 works of contemporary art.

There are oils and prints by household names such as Picasso, Dali, Klee, Kandinsky and Warhol, and many lesser-known works that will be fresh to many visitors. A piece likely to become a signature work is Joseph Beuys' *End of the 20th Century*, comprising 21 mostly prone columns of basalt strewn about an otherwise blank chamber.

The basement floor covers the evolution of design from the industrial revolution to today, and is billed as the world's largest collection. Themed areas are dedicated to car production, computer culture, the '60s and '70s, jewellery, and the use of bentwood and plywood. You'll find classics such as Eames chairs and early Apple Macs but also obscure items such as a display of electric kettles designed for AEG in 1909.

From 2007 the gallery will be expanded to include the **Museum Brandhorst**, to be located directly behind the Pinakothek der Moderne. It will be devoted to postmodern artists stretching into the 21st century.

MUSEUM REICH DER KRISTALLE

Ensconced in the **Museum Reich der Kristalle** (Museum of the Crystal Realm; Map p60; ☎ 2180 4312; Theresienstrasse 41, enter from Barer Strasse; adult/child €1.50/1; ☉ 1-5pm Tue-Sun) is a truly dazzling collection of crystals. Exhibits demystify the formation of crystals and their underlying molecular structures. A large Russian emerald and numerous diamonds are among the most prized possessions.

SIEMENSFORUM

About 350m southeast of the Pinakothek der Moderne is the **SiemensForum** (Map p60; ☎ 6363 2660; Oskar-von-Miller-Ring 20; admission free; ☉ 9am-5pm, closed Sat). It's a fun, hands-on kind of place with five floors of promotional exhibits on electronics and microelectronics, ranging from the first Morse telegraph to the multimedia PC, and chews over 140 years of company history in the process.

Schwabing

Until 1890 Schwabing was its own little peaceful village north of Munich, where the moneyed built marvellous villas within walking distance of the Englischer Garten to the east. The Academy of Arts was founded in Schwabing and the district hummed with creative thinkers, a period that lasted till 1914.

Today Schwabing still boasts some of the finest examples of *Jugendstil* design in Munich. Thanks to the university, the district bristles with pubs and bars, but many now have a *schicki-micki* (yuppie) rather than a bohemian bent. The more intriguing places cluster in the area west of Leopoldstrasse and its southern continuation, Ludwigstrasse, where they rub shoulders with second-hand bookshops, edgy boutiques and restaurants. The liveliest streets are Amalienstrasse, Türkenstrasse and Schellingstrasse.

OLD SCHWABING

The church with the bold clock face on the north side of Münchner Freiheit station is the **Erlöserkirche** (Map p59; Germaniastrasse 4), built at the turn of the 20th century. It was a time of transition after Art Nouveau hit the scene, and architects were experimenting with the new style. Its exterior is neo-Romanesque but behind the heavy doors there's a wealth of Art Nouveau details – floral ornamentation such as the impressive piece on the pillars was commonplace. The coffered ceiling has great acoustics and classical concerts are often held here.

Towards the Englischer Garten to the east, **Wedekindplatz** is the heart of Old Schwabing. It still has a touch of the Bohemian thanks to the gritty bars and alternative theatre houses nearby. Thomas Mann lived here from 1899 to 1901 while he penned his famous novel *Buddenbrooks*. In the 1960s this part of Schwabing was swimming in beatniks and hippies, and the German take on the 1968 revolution got underway here as much as in Berlin, Cologne or Frankfurt.

The streets just south of Wedekindplatz are lined with beautiful villas and town houses, and exude a much more peaceful atmosphere. South of the square you'll pass the baroque garden of **Schloss Suresne** (Map p59; Werneck-Schlösschen; Werneckstrasse 1, enter from Mandlstrasse), a petite palace built in 1718 for one of Elector Max' government officials. His impoverished widow sold off the estate in 1756 and it changed hands 27 more times until purchased by the Catholic Church in 1937. Paul Klee had a studio here from 1919 to 1922. It now houses the Katholische Akademie in Bayern (Catholic Academy in Bavaria).

The **Seidlvilla** (Map p59; ☎ 342 687; Nikolaiplatz 1B) is another gorgeous residence that has served as a community centre and art gallery since 1991. The gate's often shut but check the opening times; you may be able to ring the buzzer and just stroll in.

LEOPOLDSTRASSE & AROUND

Like all grand boulevards, **Leopoldstrasse** – the Champs Élysées of Munich – is a catwalk for the masses. It's a busy thoroughfare, sure, but this wide and shady promenade in full view of passing traffic is perfect for showing off the goods, especially during the sports-car rush on warm summer evenings. The task is made easier by the rows of streetside café tables packed with aspirants. Other times of day draw a broader range of humanity; try Sunday for

---

DETOUR

From the Münchner Freiheit U-Bahn stop in Schwabing, walk three blocks south on busy Leopold-strasse. Then turn right into Ainmillerstrasse, one of Munich's Art Nouveau showcases. The crowning glory is No 22, a vintage façade with startling blue-and-gold arches topped with Roman helmed heads, and a stucco of Adam and Eve reclining under the Tree of Knowledge. Take the following right into Friedrichstrasse and admire the gilded artwork at No 3. Continue two blocks north to the church, turn right and walk two blocks to rejoin Leopoldstrasse. The U-Bahn station is one block north.

---

more dog-walking locals and a community of art vendors.

Just west of here, in an unremarkable (and unmarked) flat at Kaiserstrasse 46, lived Lenin from 1900 to 1901. Under the alias of Meyer – his real name was Vladimir Ulyanov – the Soviet leader-to-be published two periodicals: the influential underground *Der Funke* (Spark) as well as *Die Morgenröte* (Dawn). He also wrote some essays and articles under the name Lenin for the first time, including *What is to be done?*, which laid down principles for the October Revolution of 1917.

The **Akademie der Bildenden Künste** (Academy of Fine Arts; Map p59; Georgenstrasse) is housed in a three-storey neo-Renaissance building. Founded in 1808 by Maximilian I, it advanced to become one of Europe's leading arts schools in the second half of the 19th century and still has a fine reputation today. Famous students included Max Slevogt, Franz von Lenbach and Wilhelm Leibl and, in the early 20th century, Lovis Corinth, Paul Klee, Wassily Kandinsky, Franz Marc and others who went on to become modern-art pioneers.

Near the Giselastrasse U-Bahn station looms Jonathan Borofsky's sculpture **Walking Man** (Map p59), a white, three-storey alien captured in midstride.

SIEGESTOR

One of Munich's classic landmarks is the monumental **Siegestor** (Victory Gate; 1852). Modelled on Constantine's arch in Rome, and crowned by a triumphant Bavaria riding in a lion-drawn chariot, this triumphal arch was built to honour the Bavarian army for ejecting Napoleon from his German colony.

After heavy damage in WWII the arch was turned into a peace memorial. The inscription on the upper section reads: *Dem Sieg*

geweiht, vom Kriege zerstört, zum Frieden mahnend (Dedicated to victory, destroyed by war, calling for peace).

LUDWIGSTRASSE

South of the Siegestor begins Ludwigstrasse, an impressive, very European boulevard that reflected the ambitions of the Bavarian kingdom. King Ludwig I commissioned it in 1816 while he was crown prince in a bid to turn Munich into an 'Athens of the North'. He didn't quite succeed, but the remarkably uniform and well-proportioned row of neoclassical piles is a credit to court architects von Klenze and von Gärtner. The boulevard culminates at the Feldherrnhalle on Odeonsplatz.

LUDWIG-MAXIMILIANS-UNIVERSITÄT

A political football of its rulers, this prestigious university was shunted around Bavaria like a substitute teacher in the first part of its existence. Founded in Ingolstadt in 1472, and thus one of the world's oldest, the university moved to Landshut in the 19th century and finally to Munich in the early years of the Bavarian monarchy. The final move was ordered by King Maximilian II, and students 'thanked' the king by forcing his abdication in 1848. Over the years the university has fostered some great minds including Wilhelm Röntgen, the discoverer of the X-ray.

Geschwister-Scholl-Platz, a square anchored by two huge, bowl-shaped fountains and dominated by the main building, is the beating heart of the university . Inside the main building, the most striking features are the large, vaulted assembly hall and the bright, airy atrium.

The square itself, which links the university with the priests' seminary opposite, was named for Hans and Sophie Scholl, students and founding members of Die Weisse Rose

(The White Rose) resistance group (see the boxed text below). A memorial exhibit called **Denk Stätte** (Map p59; ☎ 2180 3053; Geschwister-Scholl-Platz 1; admission free; ⏰ 10am-4pm Mon-Fri, to 9pm Thu) is in the lower mezzanine behind the foyer. It includes a library dedicated to the WWII resistance, along with photos and documents about the various groups' activities.

LUDWIGSKIRCHE

Just south of the university stands the alabaster-towered **Ludwigskirche** (Church of St Ludwig; Map p59; ☎ 288 334; Ludwigstrasse 20; ⏰ 8am-8pm), built between 1829 and 1844 in Florentine style. There's only one showpiece inside, the *Last Judgment* fresco by Peter Cornelius. It is one of the world's largest frescoes and was intended by the artist to rival Michelangelo's own *Last Judgement*.

BAYERISCHE STAATSBIBLIOTHEK

The next major building south of the church is the **Bayerische Staatsbibliothek** (Bavarian State Library; Map p59; Ludwigstrasse 16), also built by von Gärtner (1832–43). The four sculptures atop the stairway are Aristotle, Hippocrates, Homer and Thucydides. With around 7.2 million volumes, this library holds the most extensive scientific collection in Germany, not to mention 250,000 maps, 800 atlases and over 42,000 periodicals. Also on view are 16th-century globes of the earth and cosmos made for Duke Albrecht V.

Englischer Garten

The **Englischer Garten** is nestled between the Altstadt, Schwabing and the Isar River. One of the largest city parks in Europe, it's a great place for strolling, drinking, sunbathing, paddleboating and even surfing (p84). In hot weather hundreds of naked sunbathers can loll in the park on a normal working day, with their jackets, ties and dresses stacked neatly beside them.

A favourite playground for Müncheners and visitors alike, the Englischer Garten is a great oasis for relaxing and outdoor fun, with or without clothing. It's actually one of the world's largest metropolitan parks – bigger than London's Hyde Park or New York's Central Park. Starting just north of Prinzregentenstrasse, it stretches north for about 5km between the district of Schwabing and the Isar River.

DIE WEISSE ROSE

During the Third Reich public demonstrations against the Nazis were rare; after 1933, intimidation and the instant 'justice' of the Gestapo and SS served as powerful disincentives. One of the few rebellious groups was the ill-fated Die Weisse Rose (The White Rose), led by Munich university students Hans and Sophie Scholl.

The young Hans joined the Hitler Jugend (Hitler Youth), and his older sister, Inge, became a group leader in its female counterpart, the Bund Deutscher Mädel (League of German Girls). But soon Hans became disillusioned with the Nazis' methods and attempted to forge a resistance group within the Hitler Youth. This triggered a Gestapo raid on the Scholl home in Ulm in 1937, and the family were marked as enemies of the state.

In 1942, out of a group of fellow medical students, Hans and Sophie formed Die Weisse Rose, which aimed to encourage Germans to resist Hitler. Its members acted cautiously at first, creeping through the streets of Munich and smearing slogans such as 'Freedom!' or 'Down With Hitler!' on walls. Growing bolder, they printed and distributed anti-Nazi leaflets, planting them in telephone boxes and sending them to contacts in other German cities. The leaflets, which would be dropped by Allied planes in the later stages of the war, reported on the mass extermination of the Jews and other Nazi atrocities. One read: 'We shall not be silent – we are your guilty conscience. The White Rose will not leave you in peace.'

In February 1943 Hans and Sophie took a suitcase of leaflets to university and placed stacks outside each lecture hall. Then, from a top landing, Sophie dumped the remaining brochures into an inner courtyard. A janitor saw her, and both were arrested and charged with treason along with their best friend, Christoph Probst. After a sham trial the three were condemned to death and beheaded the same afternoon. Sophie hoped that thousands would be stirred to action by their self-sacrifice, but there would be no more resistance at Munich university – in fact, some fellow students applauded the executions.

'DEGENERATE' ART

Expressionism, surrealism, Dadaism and other modern artistic styles were definitely not Hitler's favourite movements. The Nazis created a popular offensive against such so-called 'Jewish subversion' and 'artistic Bolshevism'. This peaked around 1937, when the German term *Entartung* (degeneracy) was borrowed from biology to describe virtually all modern movements. That year, paintings by Klee, Beckmann, Dix and others were exhibited at Munich's Deutsches Haus der Kunst, defaced with signatures in protest.

About 20,000 people visited the exhibition daily, most to frown upon the works. If that wasn't enough, a year later a law allowed for the forced removal of degenerate works from private collections. Many art collectors, however, managed to keep their prized works out of Nazi hands. In Murnau, Gabriele Münter hid her entire collection of her own work, as well as that by other Blue Rider artists like Kandinsky, from the Nazis. But the fate of many other artists' works was less fortunate: although a lot of works were sold abroad to rake in foreign currency, in 1939 about 4000 paintings were burnt publicly in Berlin and lost forever.

After WWII the monolithic building was renamed **Haus der Kunst** (Map p59; ☎ 2112 7113; Prinzregentenstrasse 1; ⌚ 10am-8pm Mon-Sun, till 10pm Thu), and today its enormous spaces are used for high-calibre shows of paintings, photography or modern art installations, often all at once.

The Englischer Garten was conceived in 1789 – in what happened to be the year of the French Revolution – as a 'garden for the people' by Elector Karl Theodor. He assigned the design job to the most unlikely Minister of War, an American named Benjamin Thompson, who in turn looked to Friedrich von Sckell for assistance. Karl Theodor considered naming the park after himself but chose 'Englischer Garten', not a bad idea given the basic landscape design was indeed English.

Müncheners quickly embraced the park. It is an artist's study in contrasts, with paths that piddle around in dark stands of mature oaks and maples before emerging into sunlit meadows of lush grass. Locals are mindful of its popularity and tolerate the close quarters of bicyclists, walkers and joggers. Street musicians dodge balls from frolicking children, and students sprawl on the grass to chat about missed lectures.

Sooner or later you'll find your way to the **Kleinhesseloher See**, a lovely lake at the centre of the park. You can rent a paddle boat for a swing around the three little islands before taking a foamy one at the Seehaus beer garden (p98).

South of the lake, the most famous beer garden is at the **Chinesischer Turm**. Tables sprawl in the shadow of the Chinese pagoda, which was built during an oriental craze in the 18th century. Further south, at the top of a gentle hill, is the **Monopteros** (Map p59; 1838), a Greek folly with pearly white columns. The ledges are often crowded by the dangling legs of visitors enjoying balmy summer nights.

Another hint of Asia awaits further south, at the **Japanisches Teehaus** (Japanese Teahouse; Map p59; ☎ 224 319). Built during the 1972 Olympics as a gesture of friendship, it is set in the middle of an incredibly cute duck pond. Authentic tea ceremonies take place here every second and fourth weekend between April and October at 3pm, 4pm and 5pm.

Don't even think about spending the night. Police patrol frequently and muggers, drug fiends and proselytisers keep the park awake till dawn.

Olympiapark & Around

Memories of the Olympic Games held in 1972 may be fading but its host complex is still very much alive and kicking. The 290m tall Olympiaturm (Olympic Tower) is the focal point and overlooks the massive, undulating 'tented' roof of the Olympic Stadium, Hall and swimming centre.

Now the complex is open as a collection of public facilities, for special and public events. Most weekends there's a grandstand featuring local bands of varying quality, but the schedule can hold some pleasant surprises. Both the swimming centre and ice-skating rink are open to the public. There's an **Info Pavilion** (Map p60; ☎ 3067 2414) at the Olympia-Eissportzentrum (ice-skating rink).

Wandering around the grounds is free but you'll have to pay to see inside the

Olympic Stadium (Map p60; adult/child €1.50/0.80; 8.30am-6pm mid-Apr–Sep, 9am-4.30pm Oct–mid-Apr, closed on events days). From April to October you can take a **Soccer Tour** (adult/child €5/3.50; 1hr), which visits the Olympic Stadium, VIP area and locker rooms, or an **Adventure Tour** (adult/child €7/5; 90 min) that covers the entire Olympiapark both on foot and in a little train. When the weather's good you can enjoy stunning views of the city from the top of the **Olympiaturm** (Map p60; adult/child €3/2; 9am-midnight, last trip 11.30pm).

The tower is also the unlikely venue of the new **Rock Museum** (☎ 834 9860; free admission; 9am-midnight), exhibiting signed guitars, gold records and memorabilia from three decades of collecting by an aficionado. The displays up here are also strewn inside the revolving restaurant.

BMW MUSEUM

Next to the Olympic Tower in Olympic Park is the temporary **BMW Museum** (Map p60; ☎ 3822 3307; Petuelring 130; adult/child €2/1.50; 10am-10pm Apr-Oct, 10am-8pm Nov-Mar). It projects a big presence from a small space, with highlights from its splendid car and motorcycle collection parked in a translucent globe that can carry projections from within. The museum is normally housed in the company headquarters – look northeast across the autobahn to see the striking silver cylinders – but it's undergoing a revamp through to 2007.

The **BMW factory** (Map p60; ☎ 3822 3306; Petuelring 130), next to the head office, still offers free tours of the factory line weekdays at 6pm (in English Tuesday and Thursday only). Tours are laden with PR but it's fascinating to see the gleaming roadsters in their embryonic state.

Ludwigsvorstadt & Westend

The area of **Ludwigsvorstadt** is sight-poor apart from the bouncy architecture around Karlsplatz. The district acts, in essence, as a bridge between the Hauptbahnhof and the more alluring sights of the Altstadt to the east.

Southwest of the train station, the **Westend** area is the stomping ground of several breweries including Hacker-Pschorr and Augustiner, who set up shop here in the 19th century. The most venerable section is around Holzapfelstrasse, Westendstrasse and Schwanthalerstrasse. Gentrification is underway and art galleries are springing up where labourers once bedded.

Near the western edge of the Westend is **Golliersplatz** (Map pp56-7), a leafy oasis where neighbourhood children play. It's the site of a lively flea market in summer.

KARLSPLATZ

The western gateway to the Altstadt, busy Karlsplatz is anchored by the medieval **Karlstor** and an enormous modern **fountain**, a favoured meeting spot. It marks the western end of the pedestrian-only shopping street Neuhauser Strasse, and is also a major junction for the U- and S-Bahn.

In 1791 unpopular city ruler Karl Theodor ordered the city wall to be torn down, sparing only the Karlstor and ordering the square to be named after himself. The locals, however, had had enough of Karl and continued to refer to the square as **Stachus**, most likely derived from a beer garden called Wirtshaus zum Stachus, which operated near the gate after 1755.

JUSTIZPALAST

The dignified edifice rising up just west of Karlsplatz is the **Justizpalast** (Palace of Justice; Elisenstrasse 1a), built from 1891 to 1898 in a cocktail of neo-Renaissance and neo-baroque styles. It was here that Hans and Sophie Scholl were tried for 'civil disobedience' and condemned to death in 1943 (see the boxed text on p74). Behind it, the **Neuer Justizpalast** (New Palace of Justice), with its red-brick façade and stepped gables, is more of a neo-Gothic confection.

ALTER BOTANISCHER GARTEN

Behind the courthouses, the **Alter Botanischer Garten** (Old Botanical Garden; Map pp56-7) is a nice place to cool your heels after an Altstadt shopping spree. Created under King Maximilian in 1814, the tender specimens were moved after WWII to a clean-air spot behind Schloss Nymphenburg. All remaining 'foreign' plants were removed under the Nazis in 1935, who turned it into a pleasant, if rather generic, park. The ferocious **Neptunbrunnen** (Neptune fountain; Map pp56-7), on the south side, dates back to the same year. The neoclassical entrance gate is called the Kleine Propyläen and is a leftover from the original gardens.

LENBACHPLATZ

A short walk northeast of Karlsplatz, Lenbachplatz is fringed by a number of ornate neoclassical buildings. The edifice at No 2 is home to both the Deutsche Bank and the Börse (Bavarian Stock Exchange).

Next door at No 6 is the impressive **Palais am Lenbachplatz** (Map pp56-7), designed in the late 19th century as one of the first dual-purpose buildings, combining home and office. Its main tenant is the trendy restaurant and bar **Lenbach** which has a back entrance (in Ottostrasse) illuminated by two Olympic-style torches. British design maven Terence Conran created the interior.

On the opposite (eastern) side of Lenbachplatz stands the neo-Renaissance **Künstlerhaus am Lenbachplatz** (Lenbachplatz 8), built in 1900. The front has been invaded by the Mövenpick restaurant chain, but the interiors are stunning, especially the Venetian Room, a sweeping ballroom styled like an Italian palazzo and decorated by Munich artist Franz von Lenbach. The exterior is brilliantly lit at night.

In the middle of the square is the splendid **Wittelsbacher Brunnen**, a weighty fountain whose two groups of figures illustrate the beneficial and destructive power of water.

Gärtnerplatzviertel & Glockenbachviertel

Southeast of the Altstadt, the **Gärtnerplatz district** is fast catching up with Schwabing and Haidhausen as the place to be after dark. It's also the hub of Munich's gay and lesbian scene that trips over into the **Glockenbachviertel** to the southwest.

Everyone gravitates towards the circular Gärtnerplatz, lorded over by the splendid **Staatstheater am Gärtnerplatz** (Map pp56-7). Founded by citizens in 1865, the theatre was taken over by Ludwig I after the owners went bankrupt. It opened with Jacques Offenbach's *Salon Pitzelberger* and light opera has been the main fare here ever since.

The Glockenbachviertel derived its name, which means 'bell brook quarter', from a foundry once located on a stream nearby. Many of the city's carvers and woodworkers lived here, giving rise to street names such as Baumstrasse (Tree St) and Holzstrasse (Wood St).

Müllerstrasse links the two neighbourhoods and is chock-full of cafés and bars

flying the rainbow flag. The area also has plenty of cool boutiques and second-hand shops catering for a mixed crowd. Other good streets to explore are Fraunhoferstrasse and Hans-Sachs-Strasse.

The loveliest spot is undoubtedly the path along the babbling brook, the **Glockenbach**, which runs south along Pestalozzistrasse. It's the sole survivor of a network of creeks that once crisscrossed Munich; the rest have been rerouted or paved over. It parallels the **Alter Südlicher Friedhof** (Map pp56-7), a cemetery that's a popular, if final destination for many Munich celebrities (there's a plaque with names and grave locations near the entrance).

JÜDISCHES MUSEUM MÜNCHEN

The Gärtnerplatzviertel sprung up from the former Jewish quarter, a reminder of which is the small **Jüdisches Museum München** (Jewish Museum; Map pp56-7; ☎ 2000 9693; Reichenbachstrasse 27; admission free, donations encouraged; ☑ 9am-noon Wed & 2-6pm Tue-Thu). It presents temporary exhibits chronicling the fate of the Jews in Munich and Bavaria. A synagogue and community house are in the same building.

In 2007 the museum will move to a new **Jüdisches Gemeindzentrum** (Jewish Community Centre; Map pp56-7) on St-Jakobs-Platz, right behind the Stadtmuseum. The modern complex will encompass a synagogue, school and cultural centre and is a major step towards a renewal of the Jewish presence in the city. The site on St-Jakobs-Platz is located near that of a monumental Romanesque synagogue that was burnt and razed by the Nazis in 1938.

Bogenhausen

A short walk from the centre, and even shorter with the aid of a chauffeur, Bogenhausen has no problems with flaunting its wealth. Elegant villas sprang up here from the 1870s onwards and the area is peppered with gilded Art Nouveau façades.

Good streets on which to soak up the refinement include Möhlstrasse, branching northeast from the Europa-Platz near the Friedensengel. Mansions for the superrich line this chic street; many are the reserve of foreign consulates and law offices. East of here (via Siebertstrasse and Ismaninger Strasse) is Holbeinstrasse, a treasure chest of Art Nouveau houses; all of them, in fact, are listed monuments. The one at No 7 is a particularly fine example.

Prinzregentenstrasse, the main artery, divides Bogenhausen from the lively quarter of Haidhausen (p80) to the south.

FRIEDENSENGEL

Just east of the Isar River, the **Friedensengel** (Angel of Peace; Map p58) statue stands guard from its perch atop a 20m-high column. The graceful, gilded female is a replica of the Nike figure found on the Greek mountain of Olympia. It commemorates the 1871 Treaty of Versailles, which ended the Franco-Prussian War, and the base contains some shimmering golden frescoes. On New Year's Eve the steps around the monument are party central.

MUSEUM VILLA STUCK

Franz von Stuck was a leading *Jugendstil* painter with a rebellious streak. His former *fin-de-siècle* home has been reincarnated as the **Museum Villa Stuck** (Map p58; ☎ 455 5510; Prinzregentenstrasse 60; admission €1; ☯ 10am-6pm Tue-Sun). Stuck's villa, built in 1897, is a stronghold of swank, with dark-wood wainscoting, tapestries and handmade furniture. The overall impression is a weighty one and forms the perfect backdrop for the exhibits, including some of Stuck's own dark, heavily Romantic works. The historic rooms, artist's old studio and garden with Art Nouveau pergola have just been reopened to the public after a 13-year renovation.

Of note here is the painting *Die Sünde* (Sin; 1912), which has an unabashed eroticism that caused quite a stir back in the old days. Changing exhibits focus on art by Stuck's contemporaries as well as later 20th-century avant-gardists and contemporary artists.

PRINZREGENTENTHEATER

One of Bogenhausen's main landmarks is the **Prinzregententheater** (Map p58; ☎ 2185 2899; Prinzregentenplatz 12). This dramatic mix of Art Nouveau and neoclassical styles was built for Prince-Regent Luitpold as a festival house for Richard Wagner operas. After WWII it housed the Bavarian State Opera, then took three decades to renovate before reopening in 1996 to the strains of Wagner's *Tristan und Isolde*. The Bavarian

Theatre Academy also has its home here; students often perform in the small Akademietheater.

HYPOVEREINSBANK TOWER

Northern Bogenhausen has some rather daring postmodern architecture. The building that definitely takes the cake is the headquarters of the **HypoVereinsbank** (Arabellastrasse 12), built in 1981. One of Munich's few skyscrapers, the eye-popping design consists of a quartet of cylindrical towers whose silvery aluminium shell gives it a distinctly space-age feel. Take the U-Bahn U4 to Richard-Strauss Platz.

Lehel

Just east of the Altstadt proper, **Lehel** (pronounced lay-hl) was in the Middle Ages, a layover for the poor, craftspeople and artisans who were kept outside the city walls. Today, the district's quiet streets are lined with lovely residential buildings dating from the *Gründerzeit* period in the late 19th century, built for the well-to-do.

ST-ANNA-PLATZ

Flanked by two pretty churches, St-Anna-Platz is the spiritual centre of Lehel. The **Klosterkirche St Anna** (Map p58; ☎ 211 260; St-Anna-Platz 21; ☯ 6am-7pm), built between 1723 and 1733, drew on some of the biggest names in church construction including Cosmas Damian Asam, who painted the stunning ceiling fresco.

On the square's eastern side looms **St Annakirche** (Map p58; ☎ 212 1820; St-Anna-Platz 5; ☯ 8am-6pm), which came into the picture in the late 19th century after the Klosterkirche became too small for its growing congregation. A neo-Romanesque pile by Gabriel von Seidl, it is considered a supreme example of revival architecture and worth a look for its huge altar and impressive nave paintings.

Author Lion Feuchtwanger grew up in the house at No 2 on the square and, in the 1920s, wrote the novels *Erfolg* (Success), a critique of early-20th-century Munich, as well as the classic *Jud Süss*.

BAYERISCHES NATIONALMUSEUM

Off the southeastern corner of the Englischer Garten is a highlight of Munich's thriving museum scene, the **Bayerisches Na-**

tionalmuseum (Bavarian National Museum; Map p59; ☎ 211 2401; Prinzregentenstrasse 3; adult/child €3/2, free Sun; ☺ 10am-5pm Tue-Sun, to 8pm Thu). It's chock-full of exhibits illustrating the art, folklore and cultural history of southern Germany and Bavaria in particular.

The ground floor has treasures from the early Middle Ages to the rococo period, including evocative carved sculptures by Erasmus Grasser and Tilman Riemenschneider, two of the greatest of the genre, although the works by Johann Baptist Straub and Ignaz Günther are nothing to sneeze at either. Upstairs, the eastern wing concentrates on the 19th century. Highlights include Nymphenburg porcelain, precious glass and an exquisite collection of *Jugendstil* items.

The west wing has specialised collections of musical instruments, games and silverware, including a ridiculously ostentatious silver table setting once owned by the Hildesheim prince-bishop. By contrast, the basement shows the ways of life of the simple peasant folk through a series of period rooms. Also here is a celebrated collection of cots from the 17th to the 19th centuries.

ARCHÄOLOGISCHE STAATSSAMMLUNG

Behind the Bayerishce Nationalmuseum, you can trace the settlement of Bavaria from the Stone Age to the early Middle Ages at the **Archäologische Staatssammlung** (Archaeological Collection; Map p59; ☎ 211 2402; Lerchenfeldstrasse 2; adult/child €2.50/1.50, free Sun; ☺ 9am-4.30pm, closed Mon). The exhibit features objects from Celtic, Roman and Germanic civilisations, including a well-preserved body of a ritually sacrificed young girl.

SCHACK-GALERIE

Count Adolf Friedrich von Schack (1815–94) was a great fan of 19th-century Romantic painters such as Böcklin, Feuerbach and Moritz von Schwind. His collection is now housed in the former Prussian embassy, the **Schack-Galerie** (Map p58; ☎ 2380 5224; Prinzregentenstrasse 9; adult/child €2.50/2; ☺ 10am-5pm Wed-Mon). A tour of this intimate space is like an escape into the idealised fantasy worlds created by these artists.

MAXIMILIANSTRASSE

The section of Maximilianstrasse that links the Altstadt with Haidhausen is one of Munich's grandest royal boulevards. Starting at the Residenz, it travels east for just over 1km to the Maximilianeum, the seat of the Bayerischer Landtag (Bavarian State Government). It makes for an interesting stroll that takes you past posh hotels and elegant fashion boutiques, as well as a mishmash of architectural styles ranging from Bavarian rustic to Italian and English Gothic.

Built between 1852 and 1875, the avenue was essentially an ego trip of King Max II. He harnessed the skills of architect Friedrich von Bürklein to create this unique hotchpotch that, perhaps not surprisingly, became known as the 'Maximilianic Style'.

Maximilianstrasse is also home to several of Munich's finest theatrical venues, including the Residenztheater, the Nationaltheater, the Kammerspiele and the Kleine Komödie am Max II (p102).

DEUTSCHES MUSEUM

You could spend days wandering the **Deutsches Museum** (German Museum; Map p58; ☎ 217 91; Museumsinsel 1; adult/child/family €7.50/5/15, child under 6 free; ☺ 9am-5pm), said to be the world's largest science and technology museum. It's on an island southeast of Isartor station and features just about anything ever invented.

There are loads of interactive displays (including glass blowing and papermaking), model coal and salt mines, and wonderful sections on musical instruments, caves, geodesy, microelectronics and astronomy. To see the entire thing you'd have to wander over a distance of about 100km, so target a few sections.

Demonstrations take place throughout the day; a popular one is in the power hall where a staff member is raised in the insulated Faraday Cage, which is then zapped with a 220,000V bolt of lightning. There's often a live performance in the musical-instrument section too.

STAATLICHES MUSEUM FÜR VÖLKERKUNDE

Offering an eye-popping journey through exotic cultures and civilisations is the **Staatliches Museum für Völkerkunde** (State Museum of Ethnology; Map p58; ☎ 210 1360; Maximilianstrasse 42; adult/child under 18 €3/free; ☺ 9.30am-5.15pm Tue-Sun). The museum's collection, a bonanza of non-European art and objects, is one of the most complete anywhere and is strongest in sculpture from West and Central Africa, Peruvian

MUNICH

ceramics, jewellery and even mummy parts, and artefacts from Micronesia and the South Pacific.

MAX II DENKMAL

Next up, in the middle of a traffic circle, is a bronze statue of a balding King Max II gazing down upon 'his' boulevard. Clinging to the base are four rather stern-looking 'children' holding the coats of arms of the Bavarian tribes of Bavaria, Franconia, Swabia as well as the Palatinate.

MAXIMILIANBRÜCKE & PRATERINSEL

Carrying on, you'll soon cross the Isar on Maximiliansbrücke (1905), designed by Friedrich von Thiersch and adorned with photogenic sculptures. Below you'll see the gravelly shores of the river island known as Praterinsel, a popular casual bathing spot in summer.

Also on the island, in a former schnapps distillery, is the **Aktionsforum Praterinsel** (Map p58; ☎ 2123 830; Praterinsel 3-4), an art and cultural centre with studios for around 20 artists and an active events schedule including exhibits, open-air performances and parties.

On the island's southern tip, in a beautiful white building, is the **Alpines Museum** (Map p58; ☎ 211 2240; Praterinsel 5; adult/child under 14 €3/1; ☯ 1-6pm Tue-Fri, 11am-6pm Sat & Sun). Maintained by the Deutscher Alpenverein (German Alpine Association), it has loads of mountain paintings, graphics, scientific instruments and a detailed history of the organisation.

MAXIMILIANEUM

Just past the bridge, and technically already in Haidhausen, is the crowning glory of Maximilianstrasse: the **Maximilianeum** (Map p58), completed in 1874, a decade after the king's sudden death. It's an imposing structure, drawn like a theatre curtain across a hilltop, bedecked with mosaics, paintings and other artistic objects. There's a free exhibit about the Bavarian parliament, which moved here in 1949.

Since 1876, the building has also been the seat of a study foundation for Bavarian scholars and home to an art gallery. Until 1918, the Royal Servant School was here as well. North and south of the structure is an undulating park called the **Maximiliananlagen**, which is a haven for cyclists in summer and tobogganists in winter.

DETOUR

The beautiful rushing Isar River is a pleasure to see from its islands. From Steindorfstrasse (Map p58) cross the bridge leading to the Praterinsel and stroll 500m south along the path, a leafy park on your left (with the Alpines Museum, p80) and the clear chilly waters on your right. The land falls away and you cross a footbridge over to the Museuminsel, which has an alluring patch of greenery where people feed ducks, strum guitars and walk their dogs. At Ludwigsbrücke you're right across from the Deutsches Museum.

Haidhausen

In the 19th century, Haidhausen bulged at the seams to provide homes for the factory workers, artisans, masons and tradespeople who powered the Industrial Revolution. It got all trendy after students and artists moved in during the 1960s, and again when the Gasteig Cultural Centre opened in 1985. These days Haidhausen still has an artsy attitude and if you're talking food and drink, many think it outranks Schwabing.

KULTURZENTRUM GASTEIG & AROUND

Haidhausen is home to one of Munich's finest cultural venues, the **Kulturzentrum Gasteig** (Gasteig Culture Centre; p102), a postmodern, boxy, glass-and-brick complex with a design that caused quite a controversy during construction back in the '70s and '80s. Things have settled down since and today more than two million people use the centre every year. The name 'Gasteig' is derived from the Bavarian term 'gaacher Steig', meaning 'steep trail'.

There are four concert halls, including the 2500-seat Philharmonie, the permanent home of the Münchener Philharmoniker, which also hosts renowned international orchestras. More-intimate venues at the centre are the Carl-Orff-Saal (590 seats) and the Kleiner Konzertsaal (Small Concert Hall; 190 seats). The Black Box (250 seats) presents mostly experimental theatre and dance. Also here is the Richard Strauss Conservatory, a huge municipal library branch and an adult education school.

Right on the Isar, west of the Gasteig, is the lovely **Müllersches Volksbad** (p84), Munich's first public swimming pool and an awesome Art Nouveau structure dating from 1901. Nearby is the giant **Muffathalle** (p101) culture centre, which was converted from an old power plant.

The prim church ensemble north of here is the **St Nikolai & Lorettokapelle** (Map p58). St Nikolai was first built in 1315 in Gothic style only to go for baroque three centuries later. The design of the little Loreto Chapel emulates the Gnadenkapelle in Altötting (p154). Outside, the covered walkway protects the remarkable Stations of the Cross reliefs made of Nymphenburg porcelain.

WIENER PLATZ

Walking north from the Gasteig on Innere Wienerstrasse will take you to Wiener Platz, which has a daily produce market.

East of the square stands the slender red pinnacle of the huge **St-Johann-Baptist-Kirche** (Map p58). Dubbed 'Haidhausen's Cathedral', the church boasts 21 neo-Gothic windows decorated with a wonderful cycle of religious paintings. The surrounding square is pleasant, with its leafy park and town houses, and is well shielded from the traffic noise of busy Max-Weber-Platz just to the north.

One architectural gem located nearby is the incongruous, timber-framed **Kriechbaumhof** (Map p58) at Preysingstrasse 71. Restored to its original 17th-century form, it's home today to an Alpining group.

Theresienwiese

The **Theresienwiese** (Theresa Meadow), better known as 'Wiesn', just southwest of the Altstadt is the site of the annual Oktoberfest (pp88–9). At the western end of the meadow is the **Ruhmeshalle** (Hall of Fame) guarding solemn statues of Bavarian leaders, as well as the **Bavaria statue** (Map pp56-7; adult/child €3/2; ⏰ 9am-noon & 2-4pm Tue-Sun). This iron lady has a cunning design that makes her seem solid, but actually you can climb via the knee joint up to the head for a great view of the Oktoberfest.

VERKEHRSZENTRUM

Sheltered in an historical trade fair hall, the new **Verkehrszentrum** (Transport & Mobility Centre; Map pp56-7; ☎ 217 9529; Theresienhöhe 14a; adult/child €2.50/1.50; ⏰ 9am-5pm, to 8pm Thu) shows fascinating exhibits on famous and pioneering research and inventions, cars, boats and trains and the history of car racing, with hands-on experiments and demonstrations. Kids can construct their own Lego-like racing vehicles and then negotiate their way on a mini-racetrack.

In 2006 the museum will open a new section showing the Deutsches Museum's entire vehicle collection, ranging from the first carlike vehicle to the first German high-speed train, the ICE.

Neuhausen

Northwest of the Hauptbahnhof, **Neuhausen**, one of Munich's oldest districts, has a long and cosy association with the royal family. It has an air of relaxed confidence and a pretty good dining scene, although there aren't many sights here to explore.

Neuhausen's development took a giant leap forward in the 17th century, when it became the servants' quarter of the newly built Schloss Nymphenburg (below). During the early 19th century Neuhausen was revamped as a residential pad for the well-heeled, with the villas along the Nymphenburg Canal resembling second-string royal residences.

Nymphenburger Strasse was actually one of the first commuter roads into Munich, laid down to ease transport of the royals into town. The city's first tram – a horse-drawn vehicle – served the boulevard from 1876.

Modern, bustling **Rotkreuzplatz** is the aesthetically challenged centre of Neuhausen. Its only redeeming value is the large number of good restaurants, cafés and bars around here.

In southern Neuhausen, at the corner of Marsstrasse and Wredestrasse, is the hugely popular **Circus Krone** (Map p60; ☎ 545 8000; Zirkus-Krone-Strasse 1-6; ⏰ Dec-Apr), a Munich fixture for decades. Performances run from December to April, and then, when it's all over, the circus leaves in a grand procession with elephants and camels driven along Arnulfstrasse towards the Hauptbahnhof. The hall is left to host rock concerts and other events during the rest of the year.

Schloss Nymphenburg

If the Residenz hasn't satisfied your passion for palaces, visit the amazing **Schloss Nymphenburg** (Nymphenburg Palace; Map p60; ☎ 179

080; combined ticket to everything except Marstallmuseum adult/child €10/8), about 5km northwest of the Altstadt. Begun in 1664 as a villa for Electress Adelaide of Savoy, the palace and gardens were continually expanded and built upon over the next century to create the royal family's summer residence. To get there take tram No 17 or 41.

SCHLOSS

The main **building** (adult/child €5/4; ⏰ 9am-6pm, 9am-8pm Thu) consists of a main villa and two wings. The circuit begins upstairs in the **Steinerner Saal** (Stone Hall), which is a two-storey dining hall with fantastic stucco and frescoes by Johann Baptist Zimmermann. The **Gobelinzimmer**, with stunning detailed tapestries, is almost as good. The tour also takes in the **Wappenzimmer** (Heraldic Room) and the **Chinesisches Lackkabinett** (Chinese Lacquer Room), but take time out to see the cute chapel in the western wing.

The rooms are all sumptuous, but one of the most majestic is the **Schönheitengalerie** (Gallery of Beauties), in the southern wing, formerly the apartments of Queen Caroline. It's now the home to 38 portraits of women whom Ludwig I considered beautiful; most famous of these is *Schöne Münchnerin*, the portrait of Hélène Sedlmayr, daughter of a shoemaker. There's also a smouldering one of court dancer Lola Montez, who cost Ludwig his crown, for more information see the boxed text on p22).

Also on display are the coaches and riding gear of the royal family in the **Marstallmuseum** (adult/child €4/3; ⏰ 9am-6pm, 9am-8pm Thu). This includes the wedding coach of Ludwig II that was never used after his engagement to Princess Sophie fell apart.

On the 1st floor is a collection of porcelain made by the famous Nymphenburger Manufaktur. Also known as the Sammlung Bäuml, it presents the entire product palette from the company's founding in 1747 to 1930.

The north wing is occupied by the **Museum Mensch & Natur** (Museum of Humankind & Nature; adult/student over 15 €2.50/1.50, children under 15 free with parent; ⏰ 9am-5pm Tue-Sun). This natural history museum delves into the mysteries of life and earth such as crystal formation, the industry of bees and basic genetics. This is a fun place to bring children for the interactive displays (in German).

GARDENS & OUTBUILDINGS

The royal gardens are a magnificently sculpted English park. In front of the palace entrance is a long and wide canal, a popular spot to feed the swans. In winter it freezes over for ice-skating and the slow but graceful sport of curling. At the eastern end of the canal is the **Hubertus Fountain**, a huge braying stag that spouts water. Behind the castle, the royal gardens ramble on around the extension of the Nymphenburg Canal.

The gardens are enchanting and give forth a number of intriguing buildings and follies. The place was laid out by the same man who designed the Englischer Garten, the architect Friedrich von Sckell, and here too the design has an English landscape flavour.

The chief folly, and quite frilly to boot, the **Amalienburg** (Map p60) is a small hunting lodge with a large domed central room. The place drips with crystal and gilt decoration; don't miss the amazing Spiegelsaal (Mirror Hall). The two-storey **Pagodenburg** (Map p60) was built in the early 18th century as a Chinese teahouse. It echoes the Chinesischer Turm in the Englischer Garten. More than 2000 ceramic tiles painted with landscapes, figures and ornamentation cover its walls. The **Badenburg** (Map p60) is a sauna and bathing house that still has its original heating system. Elsewhere in the park, the **Magdalenenklause** (Map p60) was built as an artificial hermitage in a deliberately 'ruined' style.

Entrance details for all the **outbuildings** (adult/child €2/1; ⏰ 9am-6pm, 9am-8pm Thursday) are the same.

NEUER BOTANISCHER GARTEN

If you get excited about window-box geraniums, you'll be positively ecstatic about the **Neuer Botanischer Garten** (New Botanical Garden; Map p60; ☎ 1786 1350; Menzinger Strasse 65; adult/youth €3/1, child under 12 free; ⏰ 9am-7pm May-Aug, 9am-6pm Apr & Sep, 9am-4.30pm Nov-Jan, 9am-5pm Feb-Mar & Oct). Built in the early 20th century on a tract just north of Schloss Nymphenburg, the grounds sprawl with over 22 hectares of weird and wonderful species. The Victorian-style greenhouses include a famous collection of tropical and subtropical plants in the **Palmenhaus**. Throughout the gardens, you'll come across some whimsical statues from the palace's porcelain factory.

THE BAVARIAN WHO WOULD BE KING – OF ENGLAND

Depending on whose story you believe, Bavaria's Duke Franz may actually be Britain's legal monarch. That's what the Jacobites maintain – that King James II was deposed illegally, and that the Wittelsbachs are the rightful heirs to the British throne. Queen Elizabeth II and her ancestors are thus 'usurpers'.

The dispute dates back to Britain's Glorious Revolution in 1688, when King James II, member of the Catholic House of Stuart, was removed from the throne. Three centuries later, the Windsors haven't forgotten. Travelling to Munich in 1987, Prince Charles quipped: 'I hope Prince Franz of Bavaria does not insist too strongly on his right.'

As it happens he does not. The duke – whose full name is Franz Bonaventura Adalbert Maria von Wittelsbach – lays no claims to the keys of Buckingham Palace. But he does, on occasion, use the title Senior Representative of the House of Stuart.

The Jacobites, who enjoy a clannish following, may have had a point up until 1807 when Henry Benedict Stuart, the last remaining Stuart in the male line, died. But after that the claim becomes tenuous. The bloodline twists and turns from Charles I's daughter through the royal houses of France, Sardinia, Modena, and – where it rests today – Bavaria.

Whatever their aspirations, the Wittelsbachs continue to play an active role in the land they once ruled. The Bavarian state provides a residence and office at Schloss Nymphenburg (p81) for the head of the royal house.

Unlike the Windsors, the duke has no interest in hunting or horses, nor does he make tabloid headlines. His highness loves modern art and acts as patron to avant-garde artists, often when they are drawing the most controversy. A member of the international committee of New York's Museum of Modern Art, Duke Franz began collecting the works of Georg Baselitz shortly after his painting 'The Great Piss-Up' was condemned as immoral when first exhibited in West Berlin.

The duke's focus on cutting-edge art is somewhat unusual, since the collections of European royalty tend to focus on the old masters. Franz was in fact a driving force behind the establishment of Munich's new Pinakothek der Moderne (p71).

As Duke Franz (born 1933) has no children, the next in line to the British throne would be his niece's son, Joseph, the sovereign heir of Liechtenstein – that is, if the Jacobites had their way.

Outer Districts

SCHLOSS BLUTENBURG

Idyllically encircled by the little Würm River, **Schloss Blutenburg** (Map pp54-5; ☎ 891 2110; cnr Pippinger Strasse & Verdistrasse) creates the illusion of a moated castle. First mentioned in 1425, there's evidence that it's older still. Duke Albrecht III enlarged the complex and his son added the beautiful chapel, considered a sterling example of the late Gothic. Inside, the altar paintings by Jan Polack and the stained-glass windows are definitely worth a closer look.

In 1676, a certain Freiherr von Berchem acquired the palace, which was already in bad shape. He tried to fix it up as much as possible, but eventually money ran out and his heirs sold it back to Elector Max Emanuel in the early 18th century. Now state-owned, it underwent a sweeping restoration in the 1980s and today houses **Internationale Jugendbibliothek** (International Youth Library; ☎ 891 2110; ⏰ 10am-4pm Mon-Fri), a unique research and lending library with about half a million children's books in 130 languages. Schloss Blutenburg is about 11km northwest of the Altstadt.

MÜNCHENER TIERPARK HELLABRUNN

Around 6km south of the centre, about 5000 animals are housed at Munich's 'geo-zoo' (with sections dividing animals by continents). The **Münchener Tierpark Hellabrunn** (Hellabrunn Zoo; Map pp54-5; ☎ 625 080; Tierparkstrasse 30; adult/child €9/6; ⏰ 8am-6pm Apr-Sep, 9am-5pm Oct-Mar) was one of the first of its kind and has some 460 species, including rhinos, elephants, and gazelles. It's absolutely worth the admission if only to gain access to the petting zoo, which crawls with friendly animals that you can feed. To get here take the U-Bahn to Thalkirchen or bus No 52.

BAVARIA FILMSTADT

An often-missed treasure is the **Bavaria Filmstadt** (Map pp54-5; ☎ 6499 2304; Bavariafilmplatz 7;

adult/child €10/7, with stunt show & cinema €17/14; tours 9am-4pm) in the southern suburb of Geiselgasteig. You'll see sets from such hits as *Enemy Mine, Das Boot, Cabaret* and *The Never-Ending Story*, all of which were filmed here. A more recent set is provided by *Asterix and Obelix*, the comic-based film that was a hit in Europe, set in the age of the Romans and Gauls. Numerous German TV series and films are still shot here as well.

On top of that there's a 3-D cinema with seats that lurch to the thrills on the screen (ie a space race or descent into a silver mine). There are also stunt shows at noon, 1.30pm and 3pm. To get here take the U-Bahn to Silberhornstrasse, then tram No 25 to Bavariafilmplatz. The Filmstadt is about 14km southwest of the Altstadt.

ACTIVITIES

Munich makes a perfect base for outdoor activities. For information about hiking and climbing, contact the Munich chapter of the **Deutscher Alpenverein** (German Alpine Club; Map pp56-7; ☎ 551 7000; Bayerstrasse 21), near the Hauptbahnhof.

For gear and equipment, **Sport Schuster** (Map pp56-7; Rosenstrasse 1-5), and the better **Sport Scheck** (Map pp56-7; ☎ 216 60; Sendlinger Strasse 6), nearby, both have multiple floors of everything imaginable for the adventurer, from simple camping equipment to expedition wear, plus excellent bookshops.

Boating

One spot in town to take a leisurely boat trip is the Englischer Garten's Kleinhesseloher See. Rowing or pedal boats cost around €7 per half-hour for up to four people. Hire boats are also available at Olympiapark.

Cycling

Munich is an excellent place for cycling, particularly along the Isar River.

Radius Tours & Bikes (Map pp56-7; ☎ 5502 9374; www.radiusmunich.com; at the end of tracks 31-33 in the Hauptbahnhof; 10am-6pm May–mid-Oct) hires out bikes from €3 per hour and €14 per day, with a €50 deposit. Staff speak English and are happy to provide tips and advice on touring around Munich.

Skating

Monday nights are **Blade Night**, an organised roll through town (May to August) that starts and ends with a big street party. The refreshment stands open at 7pm and thousands of bladers hit the streets at 9pm for a leisurely 10km to 20km tour of different neighbourhoods. Starting point is near the Hackerbrücke at Wredestrasse (Map p60), northwest of the Hauptbahnhof. Detailed route maps are posted at www.muenchner -blade-night.de.

Surfing

At the southern tip of the Englischer Garten is an artificially created wave located in a deep-chilled creek known as the Eisbach where surfers practise their moves. The sport was introduced after WWII by an American GI who knew how to cruise on a primitive waxed plank.

Swimming

Bathing in the Isar River isn't advisable because of pollution, though many locals do. The two best public swimming pool options are the **Olympia-Schwimmhalle** (Map p60; ☎ 3067 2290; Olympiapark; adult/child €3.50/2.50; 7am-11pm), and the spectacular Art Nouveau **Müllersches Volksbad** (Map p58; ☎ 2361 3434; Rosenheimer Strasse 1; adult/child €3.20/2.50; 7.30am-11pm) in Haidhausen. Four-hour sauna sessions cost €11 (women only Tuesday and Friday).

ALTSTADT WALKING TOUR

This circuit covers the highlights within Munich's historic centre over a pleasant stretch of about 4km, or 1½ to two hours.

Start at Marienplatz (p63), the heart and soul of Munich. The glockenspiel spins into action at the **Neues Rathaus (1**; p64), the impressive Gothic town hall with six courtyards and multiple towers. Head southeast across the square, past the Fischbrunnen to the **Altes Rathaus (2**; p64), an older Gothic masterpiece with a statue of Romeo's heartthrob Juliet on the south side.

Pass east underneath the arches of the Altes Rathaus, turn left on Maderbräustrasse and continue to Orlandostrasse to the celebrated, if infamous, **Hofbräuhaus (3**; p97). Feel free to stroll in, check the vaulted ceiling, oompah band and Nazi-era hall upstairs.

Distance: 4km
Duration: 1½ to 2 hours

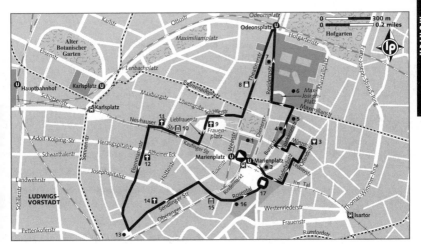

Do a zigzag special by turning west into Münzstrasse, left into Sparkassenstrasse and right again into Ledererstrasse, with Burgstrasse at its end. Turn north here to reach the **Alter Hof** (4; p64), the royals' residence until 1474. Note the ornate 'Monkey Tower' on the southern side of the courtyard. Exit to the north, pass the **Münzhof** (5; mint; p65) and turn left on Maximilianstrasse, Munich's ultranice shopping street. At Max-Joseph-Platz, the square with the imposing black statue of Maximilian I, consider spending a few hours at the **Residenz** (6; p65), one-time royal palace and a great Munich museum.

From the west exit of the Residenz, turn right, pet one of the bronze lions for luck and stroll to the **Feldherrnhalle** (7; p66), the hall honouring field marshals. It's better known as the spot where Hitler clashed with police in 1923 and was arrested. Cross the square in front of the hall, veer left on Theatinerstrasse and you'll pass the minimalist shopping complex **Fünf Höfe** (8; p67). Just past it turn right on Schäfflerstrasse to encounter another Munich symbol, the onion-towered **Frauenkirche** (9; p67), which shelters the tombs of Wittelsbach rulers.

Walk south on Liebfrauenstrasse to Kaufinger Strasse, the main shopping drag, turn right and you'll reach the **Deutsches Jagd-und Fischereimuseum** (10; p67). The shiny boar here is like the Residenz lions: rub and get lucky. Stroll west to the vaulted **Michaelskirche** (11; p67) and Richard Strauss Fountain, an homage to both Strauss and Wilde.

Backtrack a few steps on Neuhauser Strasse and turn right on Eisenmannstrasse. Pass the **Damenstiftkirche (12)** and continue south to **Sendlinger Tor (13)**, the city's southern gate from the 14th century. Bear northeast on Sendlinger Strasse to reach the **Asamkirche** (14; p68), the most ornate baroque church in Munich and one of its smallest. Carry on along Sendlinger Strasse, then turn right into Dultstrasse to reach the **Münchener Stadtmuseum** (15; p68), the city museum, with a huge vacant site for the future Jewish Community Centre next door. Pass behind the Stadtmuseum into Sebastiansplatz and raise you eyes towards the spanking new **Schrannenhalle** (16; p69), the old grain hall that's risen from the ashes. Just north of here is the **Viktualienmarkt** (17; p68), a tantalising array of colours and aromas from around the globe, with a beer garden at its centre – that's a prime spot to finish this tour.

MUNICH FOR CHILDREN

Munich is a great city for children. Many of the museums have hands-on exhibits to play with, the zoo is stunning and there are lots of parks and children's theatre events. The Munich tourist office has an excellent publication called *Familienspass in München* (Family Fun in Munich), which lists the sights, activities, sports, playgrounds and events suitable for families, all in English.

You can safely leave the little ones at **Münchner Kindl** (Map pp56–7; ☎ 2423 1600; www .muenchnerkindlgruppe.de in German; Burgstrasse 6; per hr

BIZARRE MUNICH MUSEUMS

Munich's most bizarre sight is just a short walk east of Viktualienmarkt.

Zentrum für Aussergewöhnliche Museen (Centre for Unusual Museums; Map pp56-7; ☎ 290 4121; Westenriederstrasse 41; adult/child €4/3; ☼ 10am-6pm) This motley crew of misfits includes a collection of chamber pots, perfume bottles, Easter bunnies and locks. There's also a collection of items associated with 'Sisi' (that's Empress Elisabeth of Austria to you). We could make lots of jokes about this place, but to paraphrase Groucho Marx, it doesn't need our help.

Kartoffelmuseum (Potato Museum; Map p58; ☎ 404 050; Grafingerstrasse 2; admission free; ☼ 9am-6pm Fri, 11am-5pm Sat) This claims to be the only museum in the world devoted to the tuber in art history, and they may well be right. From oils and watercolours to engravings, posters and naive glass painting, the displays give the lowdown on one of the world's great staples.

€4.50, 1st hr free; ☼ 9am-6pm Mon-Fri, 10am-4pm Sat). Kids 18 months to 10 years old are welcome in this toy-filled refuge near Marienplatz.

A sure-fire hit is **Münchener Tierpark Hellabrunn** (p83), which has a huge petting section and an aviary, as well as a magnificent park. The **Deutsches Museum** (p79) has plenty of hands-on science exhibits and a reconstructed coal mine done up as a cave. The darling puppet collection in the **Stadtmuseum** (p68) includes a stage with regular performances. Older children will be more interested in the fiery stunt show at **Bavaria Filmstadt** (p83). The **Paläontologisches Museum** (p70) has dinosaur skeletons that'll amaze humans of any age.

Children's theatres and circus include:
Circus Krone (Map p60; ☎ 545 8000; Zirkus-Krone-Strasse 1-6; ☼ Dec-Apr) An enduring favourite and venerable Munich tradition.
Münchner Marionettentheater (Map pp56-7; ☎ 265 712; Blumenstrasse 32) Munich's main puppet theatre often shows Mozart's musical plays.
Münchner Theater für Kinder (Map p60; ☎ 593 858; Dachauer Strasse 46) Children's performances year-round.

TOURS

Mike's Bike Tours (Map pp56-7; ☎ 2554 3988; www .mikesbiketours.com; standard/extended tour €22/33; ☼ Apr–mid-Nov) Offers guided bike tours of the city. The standard tour covers about 6.4km in four hours (with a 45-minute beer garden break); the extended tour goes for seven hours and covers 16km. Tours leave from the archway of the Altes Rathaus on Marienplatz (in front of the Toy Museum).
Original Munich Walks (☎ 5502 9374; www.radius munich.com) Offers a variety of different walks, all starting under the glockenspiel on Marienplatz; the two-hour City Walk (adult/child under 14/youth under 26 €10/free/9; ☼ 10am May-Oct) covers the heart of the city and gives good historical background and architectural information;

the 2½-hour Third Reich Tour (prices as above; ☼ 3pm Apr-Oct) visits all major sites associated with the growth of the Nazi movement.

Panorama Tours (☎ 5502 8995; Arnulfstrasse 8; adult/ child €11/6; ☼ 10 times daily) Runs one-hour bus tours around Munich leaving from the Hertie department store, opposite the Hauptbahnhof. Longer themed tours are offered on a regular schedule as well (around €23). The commentary is given in two languages, which can get tedious.
Taxi Sightseeing Tours (☎ 0175-481 2848; www .taxi-guide-muenchen.de; for up to 8 people €73) One-hour taxi tours are available in a variety of languages and you get to decide the route with your driver.

FESTIVALS & EVENTS

Munich always seems to have something to celebrate. The list below gives just a few of the highlights; for more information check www.muenchen-tourist.de.

January/February
Fasching Six-week carnival beginning 7 January with all kinds of merriment including music, costume parades and hundreds of fancy-dress balls. Check the Munich visitors' website at www.muenchen-tourist.de for events.

February/March
Starkbierzeit The traditional serving of potent spring beers accompanied by dancing and quaint competitions such as stone-lifting. The biggest and best-known venue is the Löwenbräukeller (www.loewenbraeukeller.com).

April
Frühlingsfest Theresienwiese fills with beer tents and amusements for the Spring Festival, a mini Oktoberfest, which runs for the last two weeks of April.

May
Maidult Traditional fair held for nine days in early May on Mariahilfplatz with crafts, antiques and some quirky junk.

June/July

Christopher Street Day Gay festival and parade culminating in a big party on Marienplatz. Second weekend in July.

Jakobidult Summer fair on Mariahilfplatz much like the Maidult (left).

Munich Film Festival (www.filmfest-muenchen.de) World premieres of international and independent films in the last week of June.

Opera Festival (☎ 2185 1021; www.bayerische.staats oper.de) Month-long festival of opera concluding on 31 July with Wagner's *Meistersinger von Nürnberg*.

Tollwood Festival (☎ 383 8500; www.tollwood.de in German) World culture festival with nightly concerts from around the world at the Olympiapark from mid-June to mid-July.

August

Tanzwerkstatt Europa (☎ 724 2515; www.jointadven tures.net) Performances and workshops for modern dance, drama and readings held over 10 days in early August.

September/October

Bundesgartenschau (www.buga2005.de in German) The German Horticultural Show BUGA hits the new fairgrounds in Riem with a blaze of flowers and cultural events, and a special landscaped park. Runs through early October, in 2005 only.

Oktoberfest (www.oktoberfest.de) Legendary beer-swilling party running from mid-September to the first Sunday in October.

November/December

Christkindlmarkt (www.christkindlmarkt.de in German) Traditional Christmas market on Marienplatz.

SLEEPING

Room rates in Munich can be high and may rise a bit during the summer, but they skyrocket during Oktoberfest. At any time you'd be well advised to book ahead.

The hostels are the cheapest options – the most popular ones are located northwest of the centre in cosmopolitan Neuhausen. There are also lots of budget pensions and hotels, of varying standards, clustered around the Hauptbahnhof. This area is swamped with places to stay and has an increasing number of upmarket options. The Altstadt has the largest choice of top-end hotels.

Altstadt

BUDGET

Hotel Blauer Bock (Map pp56-7; ☎ 231 780; hotel blauerbock@aol.com; Sebastiansplatz 9; s/d from €41/66, s/d with bathroom from €60/93) This hotel once provided beds for Benedictine monks and coachmen for the grain market nearby. It's comfy, familiar and spacious, although the interiors could do with an update. The corner room No 4 overlooks the Schrannenhalle (p69).

MIDRANGE

Hotel Schlicker (Map pp56-7; ☎ 242 8870; www .hotel-schlicker.de; Im Tal 8; s €85-115, d €115-200; P 🖳) The charming 400-year-old Schlicker is ideally located near Viktualienmarkt and is a pretty good deal for its spacious, modern rooms. Prices don't go up in the summer or at Oktoberfest, but the place is very popular and reservations are advisable.

Hotel Alcron (Map pp56-7; ☎ 228 3511; Ledererstrasse 13; www.hotel-alcron.de in German; s €60-70, d €80-95; ✗ 🖳) This quaint hotel is perfectly situated just stumbling distance from the Hofbräuhaus. A wonderful spiral wooden staircase leads up to the small, simple rooms that have traditional furnishings and offer comfortable beds to sleep off any excesses.

TOP END

Bayerischer Hof (Map pp56-7; ☎ 212 00; www.bay erischerhof.de; Promenadeplatz 2-6; s €170-228, d €276-406; P ✗ 🖳 🖳 🖳; wheelchair access) One of the *grande dames* of the Munich hotel trade is the lovely Bayerischer Hof. The historic hotel boasts a super-central location, a pool and a jazz club. Marble, antiques and oil paintings line the walls and you can dine until you drop at any one of the three fabulous restaurants. Children are welcome.

Kempinski Vier Jahreszeiten München (Map pp56-7; ☎ 212 50; www.kempinski-vierjahreszeiten.de; Maximilianstrasse 17; s €275-475, d €395-545; P ✗ 🖳 🖳 🖳) This illustrious hotel has a grand façade featuring the four seasons, the four continents and statues of the managers. Each room has a tasteful individuality, although not as many amenities as you may expect. Still the suites are palatial and the elegant rooftop pool is in a class of its own.

Hotel Mandarin Oriental Munich (Map pp56-7; ☎ 200 980; www.mandarinoriental.com; Neuturmstrasse 1; s from €295, d from €329; ste €540-2200; P ✗ 🖳 🖳 🖳; wheelchair access) The first thing this gorgeously restored neo-Renaissance villa hits you with is its ceremonial staircase; the next is its high-powered clientele. Paul McCartney, Bill Clinton and Prince Charles

OKTOBERFEST

Rio has its Carnaval, Cannes its film festival, Indianapolis its 500. But they all take a back seat to the world's biggest party: Munich's Oktoberfest – an unapologetic assault on the senses and sensibility. Incomparable Bavarian brew, the smell of oxen roasting on a spit, and the roar of more than six million people combine to put an entire city on sensory overload. For 16 wild days in late September, Munich is ruled by lovers of beer and pretzels, food and foolishness, rides, parties, music and almost every other indulgence under the sun.

Oktoberfest is a small temporary city with its own infrastructure. It employs about 12,000 people and has its own police force, lost and found office, childcare centre, fire brigade, consumer protection unit, baggage checkroom, post office and first-aid station. It installs its own sewage system, power stations and U-Bahn terminal. And to channel beer in the appropriate manner, there are a thousand-plus Portacabins, although even these cannot stop large numbers of visitors from heading off into the darkness when nature calls to indulge in what the Bavarians call 'wildes Bieseln' (wild peeing).

Other revellers contain their rollicking excursions to the bright lights of the carnival with its roller coaster, Ferris wheel and all sorts of low-key and high-tech rides. Wide-eyed five-year-olds clutch giant gingerbread hearts like prized possessions. The sweet aroma of roasted almonds wafts through the air. Nights become a mesmerising mosaic of smoke, boisterous song, and ruddy faces illuminated by strobes and enough dazzling lights to put Las Vegas to shame.

In the giant beer tents, an endless stream of foaming amber-coloured beer cascades into the famous gargantuan steins in a futile effort to parch the thirst of the crowds. Oompah music, provided by some of the best brass bands in Bavaria, has crowds roaring and swaying. Locals in dirndls and lederhosen hoist, guzzle and toast with a UN of visitors. It's a sight to behold, at least once in a lifetime.

HISTORY

The world's biggest party had its origins in a simple horse race. In 1810 Bavarian Crown Prince Ludwig – later King Ludwig I – married Princess Therese of Saxe-Hildburghausen, and following the wedding a horse race was held at the city gates. The six-day celebration was such a rip-roaring success that it became an annual event, was extended and moved forward to start in September so that visitors would enjoy warmer weather. Faced with all those fine suds, the horse race became little more than a sideshow and was finally dropped in 1938.

FACTS & FIGURES

Gluttony is big business at the Oktoberfest, which draws some six million visitors every year and pumps nearly €1 billion into the local economy. Nearly half that amount is spent on the festival grounds for the following:

Beer 6.3 million litres	**Pork knuckles** 56,036 servings
Chicken 487,487 birds	**Pork sausage** 190,635 pairs
Coffee, tea 189,000 cups	**Sparkling wine** 22,000 bottles
Fish 48,600kg	**Water, lemonade** 722,000 bottles
Oxen 91 animals	**Wine** 36,000L

HIGHLIGHTS

Brewer's Parade

The parade through the city centre, travelling from Sonnenstrasse to the fairgrounds via Schwanthalerstrasse, begins at 11am on the first day of the festival. At noon, the lord mayor stands before the thirsty crowds at Theresienwiese. With due pomp and ceremony, he slams home a wooden tap with a mallet. The beer flows forth, the crowds cheer and the mayor exclaims: 'Ozapft ist's!' (It's tapped!).

Costume Procession
On the second day of the festival, starting at 10am, a young girl on horseback dressed as the Münchener Kindl, the child monk from the city's coat of arms, leads 8000 performers from all over Europe (wearing pretzel bras and other traditional drunkenwear) through the streets of the city centre.

Folklore International
About 500 performers from the costume procession stage musical, dance and folklore performances in the Circus Krone building on Arnulfstrasse at 8pm on the first evening of Oktoberfest.

Gay Meeting
There's a big gay meeting on the first Sunday of Oktoberfest at the Bräurosl tent, with legions of butch-looking guys in leather pants. It is timed to coincide with a gay leather convention; it's huge fun and open to all.

Schicht'l Tent
On the midway, amid the high-tech roar, a few nostalgic favourites have survived. Among these are the magic shows at Schicht'l Tent where beheadings are a speciality. Generations have gasped at this bloody sleight of hand, which is no mean feat. Even master illusionist David Copperfield has paid his respects by losing his head.

Flea Circus
Oktoberfest also boasts Germany's last remaining flea circus – a fixture since the 19th century – where trained pests provide the oomph for miniature chariots that outweigh them a thousandfold.

THE LOWDOWN
Oktoberfest runs from mid-September to early October at the Theresienwiese, a 15-minute walk southwest of the Hauptbahnhof (or one stop on the U4 or U5 to Theresienwiese). If you're asking directions, say 'd'Wiesn' (dee-veezen), the nickname for the grounds. Trams and buses heading that way have signs reading 'Zur Festwiese' (literally 'to the Festival Meadow').

There are 16 tents, which open between 10am and 10.30am (as early as 9am on Sunday) and close at 11.30pm. Only Käfers Wiesnschenke and the Wein-und Sektzelt are licensed until 1am. Regardless, it's a good idea to leave by 10pm as crowds can get a bit unruly when the beer supplies are turned off.

Predictably the beer tents are most crowded all day on Saturday and Sunday, but for lighter traffic try a weekday afternoon. Until Friday of the first week the evenings aren't swamped either. Tuesday is Family Day with reduced prices for sideshows and rides.

Admission to the tents is free but there's no central reservation system for tables. With a lot of advance planning, you can apply for a table with the tent owners directly. For addresses, see the website of the Munich tourist office (www.muenchen-tourist.de).

An Oktoberfest brew is big but not cheap: a 1L *Mass* (tankard) costs around €7, payable with special tokens sold by the tents. As for the food, consider eating before you arrive as the reluctance to part with €6 for a chicken leg tends to fade after a litre or two of amber liquid. The streets around, especially off the eastern edge, are filled with shops making inexpensive doner kebabs, pizzas and filled pastries.

Make sure to reserve a room as early as you can (like a year in advance). Hotels book out very quickly and the prices skyrocket during the fair. If you show up during Oktoberfest, expect to find only extremely pricey rooms – if any at all – in Munich. Latecomers may have to resort to nearby cities such as Augsburg, Garmisch-Partenkirchen or Bad Tölz, all under an hour's train ride away.

THE AUTHOR'S CHOICE

Looking for a night at someplace extra-special? This fabulous Altstadt hotel just cries out to be visited.

Cortiina (☎ 242 2490; www.cortiina.com; Ledererstrasse 8; s/d €146/186; ⓟ ⌧ ⌧ ▣) This stunning modern hotel is a great place for anyone looking for stylish elegance without the antiques. The design is chic and minimalist without losing any comfort. Dark wood and low lighting run throughout the hotel, while the bedrooms are lined with oak panelling and have parquet floors and individual furnishings, as well as glass-encased bathrooms lined with Jura stone.

are among recent guests. Service is polite almost to a fault, with liveried servants wherever you look. Garage parking and breakfast add €18 and €19, respectively, to your final tally.

Hotel Olympic (Map pp56-7; ☎ 231 890; www .hotel-olympic.de; Hans-Sachs-Strasse 4, Glockenbachviertel; s €90-150, d €140-180; ⓟ ⌧ ⌧) Just south of the Altstadt, in one of Munich's prettiest streets. Classy Art Deco furnishings and the fine artworks on display lend these spacious rooms the air of an art gallery. The hotel sits on a picturesque little courtyard and most rooms get a peek.

Maxvorstadt
MIDRANGE
Hotel Königswache (Map p60; ☎ 542 7570; www .koenigswache.de; Steinheilstrasse 7; s €87-94, d €108-118; ⓟ ▣) After a day of high art this hotel's Monty Python approach can be quite refreshing. Court trappings such as guardhouses, a suit of armour and royal portraits are a wonderful foil to the rooms, which are surprisingly modern and well equipped. It's within walking distance of the Pinakothek museums.

Schwabing & Englischer Garten
BUDGET
Pension Frank (Map p59; ☎ 281 451; www.pension -frank.de; Schellingstrasse 24; s/d €45/57) Large rooms and a convivial atmosphere make this small pension a popular choice with young backpackers and with school groups. Rooms (all with shared bathroom) have lovely wrought-iron beds and there is a small col-

lection of English novels and a communal kitchen.

MIDRANGE
Cosmopolitan Hotel (Map p59; ☎ 383 810; www .cosmopolitan-hotel.de in German; Hohenzollern Strasse 5; s/d €100/110; ⓟ ⌧) The Cosmopolitan is a good-value modern hotel with comfortable, tastefully furnished rooms that feature plenty of dark wood and subtle lighting. Ideally located for access to Schwabing's nightlife, it's the place for party animals to get their beauty sleep.

Gästehaus Englischer Garten (Map p59; ☎ 383 9410; www.hotelenglischergarten.de; Liebergesellstrasse 8; s/d €68/73, s/d with bathroom €99/107; ⓟ) Steps away from the Englischer Garten, this cosy pension occupies a graceful old mill, which has a private garden for breakfast on warm summer mornings. Most of the antique-filled rooms have private bathrooms and TV. Reserve well ahead.

TOP END
München Park Hilton (Map p59; ☎ 384 50; www .hilton.de; Am Tucherpark 7; s/d €233-365; ⓟ ⌧ ⌧ ▣) This is a modern 15-storey tower in which every room has picture windows overlooking the Englischer Garten. Facilities include a sauna and a lovely view of the Isar from its terrace restaurant.

Ludwigsvorstadt & Westend
BUDGET
Wombat's (Map pp56-7; ☎ 5998 9180; www.wombats -hostels.com; Senefelderstrasse 1; dm/d €15/58; ⓟ ▣) Of all the hostel-hotels popping up in Munich this pert little number does the best job in combining style with location. Past the glassed-in courtyard you'll find a friendly expat staff, pleasant if modular furnishings and private showers and toilets in every room (dorms and doubles only). A welcome drink is thrown in at the in-house bar with pool table.

Hotel Jedermann (Map pp56-7; ☎ 543 240; www .hotel-jedermann.de; Bayerstrasse 95; s €34-99, d €49-149; ⓟ ⌧ ⌧ ▣) This nicely renovated hotel is excellent value with small but comfortable rooms and data ports. Some have air-con, a rarity in this category. The Anglophile staff speak English and family rooms have connecting doors.

Hotel Monaco (Map pp56-7; ☎ 545 9940; www .hotel-monaco.de; Schillerstrasse 9; s €55-155, d €66-165;

✕ ▣) On the 5th floor of this inauspicious building you'll find an exercise in floral elegance. Artful paper roses adorn the halls, layers of swag and net curtains line the windows and there's a good variety of rooms. It's a cosy effect, if that's what you like.

Easy Palace (Map pp56-7; ☎ 558 7970; www .easypalace.de; Mozartstrasse 4; dm/s/d €16.90/29/50; **P** ▣) This new hostel has a good range of facilities from pool tables to bike hire and luggage storage. The rooms are fairly simple but comfortable and the management is friendly.

MIDRANGE

Hotel Atlas (Map pp56-7; ☎ 889 8000; www.hotel -atlas.com; Landwehrstrasse 65; s/d €80/105; **P** ✕ ; wheelchair access) The fine hardwood furniture, Mediterranean granite and excellent bathrooms (with floor heating) put this place head and shoulders above the competition at this price. The fancy wellness studio offers pick-me-ups such as herbal baths, algae wraps and rose-oil massages. Ask for a room overlooking the quiet inner courtyard.

Alpen Hotel (Map pp56-7; ☎ 559 330; www.alpen hotel-muenchen.de in German; Adolf-Kolping-Strasse 14; s €75-135, d €95-195; ✕ ▣) This place manages to combine an old-fashioned Alpine inn with a boutique hotel. The newer rooms are as sleek as a catwalk but many have a countrified look (No 23 has a big four-poster bed). The sitting room features a big portrait of 'Sisi' over the fireplace.

Belle Blue Hotel Garni (Map pp56-7; ☎ 550 6260; www.hotel-belleblue.com; Schillerstrasse 21; s/d from €75/85; ✕ ✕ ▣) This chic little hotel employs a tried-and-true design formula to great effect. Flawless colour schemes, snazzy bath fixtures and tailor-made furniture let you overlook the fact that the rooms are a little snug. Still good value though, and your hosts are kind.

Hotel-Pension Mariandl (Map pp56-7; ☎ 534 108; www.hotelmariandl.com; Goethestrasse 51; s/d from €60/80) There's old-world charm and huge rooms with high ceilings and giant windows at this neo-Gothic mansion overlooking Beethovenplatz. The downstairs restaurant has live jazz or classical music nightly at 8pm (see p96 and p102). Children are welcome.

Hotel Petri (Map pp56-7; ☎ 581 099; www .hotel-petri.de; Aindorferstrasse 82; s €55-95, d €80-120;

P ✕ ▣ ✿) This is one of the best deals in the Westend. Rooms have distinctive antique wooden furniture and a TV, and there's also a garden and a small indoor swimming pool.

Hotel Uhland (Map pp56-7; ☎ 543 350; www .hotel-uhland.de; Uhlandstrasse 1; s €66-125, d €77-170; **P** ▣) Just east of the Theresienwiese you'll find this lovely Art Nouveau villa with its relaxed atmosphere and English-speaking staff. The large, comfy rooms (some with a tiny balcony), quaint garden and good service make it an enduring favourite with visitors. There's also an Internet terminal for guests.

Hotel St Paul (Map pp56-7; ☎ 5440 7800; www .hotel-stpaul.de; St Pauls Strasse 7; s €77-107, d €92-168; **P** ✕) This is a popular Oktoberfest option, being right next to the Theresienwiese U-Bahn stop. Front rooms have a splendid view of St Paul's Church while ones in the rear overlook a leafy courtyard, a good spot for breakfast.

Creatif Hotel Elephant (Map pp56-7; ☎ 555 785; www.munich-service.de; Lämmerstrasse 6; s €49-149, d €59-189; **P** ✕) This sparkling new hotel offers a range of simple rooms with modern décor and good facilities. It's family run and the service is extremely friendly with a big welcome for children.

Hotel Seibel (Map pp56-7; ☎ 540 1420; www .seibel-hotels-munich.de; Theresienhöhe 9; s €59-149, d €79-189; ✕) This hotel has a pleasant atmosphere, very pleasant staff, Bavarian-style rooms with lovely wrought-iron beds and hardwood furniture. Rooms at the back are quieter, away from the busy thoroughfare at the front.

Hotel Schweitz (Map pp56-7; ☎ 543 6960; www .hotel-schweiz.de; Goethestrasse 26; s €63-90, d €90-165; **P** ✕ ▣) Recently renovated and upgraded, this modern hotel has bright but cosy rooms with maple-wood furniture. The 6th floor features a modest wellness area with infrared sauna and an open-air terrace.

Meininger's (Map pp56-7; ☎ 030-6663 6100; www .meininger-hostels.de; Landsbergerstrasse 20; dm/s/d €19/49/78; **P** ✕ ▣) A few minutes' drive west of the Hauptbahnhof, and on the doorstep of the Augustiner brewery, this sprawling, modern hostel-hotel has amenities similar to Wombat's (opposite) but with underground parking and a rooftop terrace.

Other recommendations:

Hotel Bristol (Map pp56-7; ☎ 5951 5154; www
.bristol-muc.com; Pettenkofer Strasse 2; s €62-125, d
€83-150; Ⓟ ⊠ 🖵) Looks humble from the street but
is modern and well furnished.

Hotel Brunnenhof (Map pp56-7; ☎ 545 100; www
.brunnenhof.de; Schillerstrasse 36; s/d €80/95; Ⓟ 🖵 ;
wheelchair access) Bright, airy rooms, in a central yet quiet
location.

Gärtnerplatzviertel & Glockenbachviertel

MIDRANGE

Pension am Gärtnerplatztheater (Map pp56-7;
☎ 202 5170; www.pension-gaertnerplatztheater.de;
Klenzestrasse 45; s/d €50/80) Escape the tourist
rabble, or reality altogether, in this slightly
warped establishment in the cool Gärtnerplatz quarter. The décor includes antique-
filled rooms labelled Sisi and Ludwig, but
you can't argue with the reasonable prices
and quality ambience.

Lehel

MIDRANGE

Hotel Adria (Map p58; ☎ 293 081; www.adria
-muenchen.de; Liebigstrasse 8a; s €95-123, d €105-144;
⊠ 🖵) This pleasant hotel is run with efficiency and has a welcoming setting. Rooms
are decked out in Mediterranean hues, out-
fitted with all the major accoutrements and
have thoughtful touches such as foreign
newspapers. Take up where you left off the
night before with a champagne breakfast.

Parkhotel im Lehel (Map p58; ☎ 211 050; www
.golden-leaf-hotel.de; Unsöldstrasse 10; s/d from €78/89;
Ⓟ ⊠ 🖵) This hospitable place offers a
quiet, convenient alternative to the Altstadt –
smallish rooms are equipped with little perks
such as fruit bowls and big perks such as
fantastically comfortable beds. Special deals
are available all the time.

TOP END

Opera-Garni (Map p58; ☎ 5210 4940; www.hotel
-opera.de; Annastrasse 10; r €165-245, ste €245-325;
⊠ 🖵) Step inside the Opera-Garni and
you'll step back in time. This charming
hotel is pure old-world elegance and refinement. Breakfast is served in the garden
between graceful statues and the sumptuous rooms are stunningly decorated with
individual combinations of rich colours,
lush fabrics and an abundance of antiques,
chandeliers and Persian carpets.

Neuhausen

BUDGET

Jugendherberge München (Map p60; ☎ 131 156;
www.jhmuenchen.de in German; Wendl-Dietrich-Strasse
20; dm €23; ⏱ closed Dec; ⊠) This is the most
central DJH hostel and is northwest of the
Altstadt. Although it's relatively loud and
very busy, it's also popular and friendly.
There's no curfew or daytime closing, and
there's a restaurant, garden and bikes for
hire.

MIDRANGE

Hotel Laimer Hof (Map p60; ☎ 1780 380; www.laimer
hof.de; Laimer Strasse 40; s/d from €69/89; Ⓟ) Run by
possibly the nicest couple on the planet, this
cute little villa – incidentally a listed monument – has a relaxed country feel despite
being just five minutes' walk from Schloss
Nymphenburg. Of the 23 rooms, those on
the upper floors have the most character
and best views.

Outer Districts

BUDGET

Campingplatz Thalkirchen (Map pp54-5; ☎ 7243
0808; fax 724 3177; Zentralländstrasse 49; per tent/car/per-
son from €3/4.30/4.50; ⏱ mid-Mar–Oct) This is the
closest camp site to the city centre but can
get very crowded. It's scenically located on
the Isar River, 5km southwest of the city
centre. Take the U-Bahn 3 to Thalkirchen,
then bus No 57 to Thalkirchen or it's a 15-
minute walk.

Campingplatz Nord-West (Map pp54-5; ☎ 150
6936; www.campingplatz-nord-west.de in German; Auf den
Schrederwiesen 3; per tent/car/person from €3.10/2.60/3.90)
A pleasant camp site about 2km from both
the Olympic Park and Schloss Nymphenburg. It's also within walking distance of
three swimming lakes.

Long-Term Rentals

If you're planning to stay in Munich for
a month or longer, you may consider
renting through a *Mitwohnzentrale* (flat-
sharing agency). Accommodation can be
anything from rooms in shared student
flats to furnished apartments.

Generally speaking, a room in a flat costs
about €330 to €450 per month, while a one-
bedroom apartment ranges from €430 to
€700. Commission (up to one month's
rent) and VAT (16%) must be added to the
rental rate.

Agencies to try include:

City Mitwohnzentrale (Map pp56-7; ☎ 194 30; www
.mwz-muenchen.de; Lämmerstrasse 4)

Mitwohnzentrale an der Uni (Map p59; ☎ 286
6060; www.mwz-munich.de; Adalbertstrasse 6)

Mitwohnzentrale – Mr. Lodge (Map p60; ☎ 340
8230; www.mrlodge.de; Barerstrasse 32)

EATING

As the culinary hub of southern Germany,
Munich does not suffer from inferiority
complexes. One in four residents is a for-
eigner, which translates into a fanfare of
national cuisines – Bavarian is a given, but
the southern Mediterranean is well represented alongside some good Asian and Tex-
Mex. There's something for every palate,
and generally, for every wallet.

The Altstadt is a safe bet for traditional
Bavarian dishes. Cosmopolitan Neuhausen
has the greatest selection of cuisines, some
of them quite innovative and good value.
More upmarket fare can be found in the
Glockenbachviertel and Bogenhausen.

Bavarian/German

Hundskugel (Map pp56-7; ☎ 264 272; Hotterstrasse 18,
Altstadt; mains €9-20) Munich's oldest restaurant,
founded in 1440, feels a bit like an old-fashioned doll's house it's so tiny. It's famous for
its honest Bavarian home cooking but you'll
have to squeeze in as best you can.

Fraunhofer (Map pp56-7; ☎ 266 460; Fraunhoferstrasse 9, Gärtnerplatzviertel; mains €5.50-12) This
bustling restaurant is a homely place where

the olde-worlde atmosphere (mounted animal heads and a portrait of Ludwig II)
contrasts with the menu, which offers fresh
takes on classical fare, and the hip, inter-
generational crowd.

  Unionsbräu Haidhausen (Map p58; ☎ 477 677;
Einsteinstrasse 42, Haidhausen; mains €6-13) Dried
hops dangle from the ceiling of this sophisticated brew-pub that caters to business
types at lunchtime and a more rollicking
crew after dark. There's a jazz club in the
basement (p101).

  Bratwurstherzl (Map pp56-7; ☎ 295 113; Dreifaltigkeitsplatz 1, Altstadt; mains €6-10; ⌚ lunch Mon-Sat, dinner Mon-Fri) Cosy panelling and a vaulted brick
ceiling set the tone of this traditional chow
house, where dishes have a Franconian
twist. A plate of six Nuremberg sausages
with sauerkraut is €8.

  Ratskeller (Map pp56-7; ☎ 219 9890; Marienplatz
8, Altstadt; mains €10-18) No animal is safe from
the menu of this vast, cavernous restaurant,
underneath the historic Rathaus. The quality is dependably high, service is efficient,
and the surroundings couldn't get much
more atmospheric.

Other recommendations:

Andechser am Dom (Map pp56-7; ☎ 298 481; Wein-
strasse 7a, Altstadt; mains €5-14.50) Traditional restaurant
frequented by a bourgeois crowd. Great views from the
rooftop terrace.

Wirtshaus in der Au (Map p58; ☎ 448 1400; Lilienstrasse 51, Haidhausen; mains €7-16) Creative Bavarian
cuisine in an unpretentious setting.

Weisses Bräuhaus (Map pp56-7; ☎ 299 875; Im Tal
10, Altstadt; mains €7-15) The *Weisswurst* (veal sausage)
served here sets the city's standard.

Italian

Ruffini (Map p60; ☎ 161 160; Orffstrasse 22l, Neuhausen;
meals €7-10) In fine weather you'll be lucky to
snag a seat on the great rooftop terrace of
this sprawling restaurant-café. It attracts a
casual crowd for its generous breakfasts, delicious Italian salads and pastas, and creamy
cakes at the attached bakery. There's no table
service on the terrace, so you'll have to balance your own tray up a steep staircase.

  La Fiorentina (Map pp56-7; ☎ 534 185; Goethestrasse 41, Ludwigsvorstadt; mains €7.50-12) This small
local hang-out has a cosy atmosphere that
attracts a young, unpretentious crowd. It
serves up good-value Tuscan country cooking, mouth-watering pizzas and lovingly
prepared daily specials.

Il Mulino (Map p60; ☎ 523 3335; Görresstrasse 1, Maxvorstadt; mains €5-10) In business for more than two decades, this classy little restaurant continually woos back a loyal clientele with delicious pizzas and pasta sauces that hit the spot. In summer, the cool leafy beer garden fills up quickly. Service is snappy.

Hippocampus (Map p58; ☎ 475 855; Mühlbaurstrasse 5, Bogenhausen; mains €15-28) One of Munich's top restaurants, this trendy, upmarket place, right near the Prinzregententheater, serves a great range of Italian specials. It has a stylish interior, romantic ambience and celebrity clientele.

Riva (Map pp56-7; ☎ 220 240; Im Tal 44, Altstadt; mains €7-15) The thin-crust pizza is to die for, as they say, and generously laden with tried-and-true toppings such as mushrooms and pepperoni or creative variations such as the shrimp-leek-ginger combo. Make reservations, or come before dinner time to get your fill.

Asian

Sho-ya (Map pp56-7; ☎ 523 6249; Gabelsbergerstrasse 85, Maxvorstadt; sushi €10-15) It may look innocuous on the outside but this place is proudly hailed as one of the best sushi joints in town. It's ideally located and serves giant *ebi* (shrimp) and superb *maguro* (tuna). The basement boasts a lively karaoke bar.

Shida (Map pp56-7; ☎ 269 336; Klenzestrasse 32, Gärtnerplatzviertel; mains €11-16) Shida's excellent Thai food and intimate atmosphere are justly famous and perennially popular. It's only the size of a shoe box but packs a mean punch in the food stakes. Reservations are essential.

Punjabi (Map pp56-7; ☎ 2554 2424; Zweibrückenstrasse 15, Isar-Vorstadt; mains €5.50-7.50) Excellent, tasty Indian specialities, from vegetarian samosas to fiery curries and tandooris cooked in a traditional clay oven. Top it off with a baked banana served with honey and grated coconut, and waddle home.

Der Kleine Chinese (Map pp56-7; ☎ 202 1132; Fraunhoferstrasse 35, Gärtnerplatzviertel; mains €5-8) This place is a good-value option with cheap sit-down meals served in snug quarters lit by surreal egg-shaped lanterns.

French

Rue des Halles (Map p58; ☎ 485 675; Steinstrasse 18, Haidhausen; mains €19-28; ☽ dinner) Excellent French cuisine attracts a 'Rolls-Royce crowd' to this bright, modern restaurant near the Gasteig. Count on about €80 for a three-course meal, including a glass of wine.

La Bretagne (Map p58; ☎ 487 220; Rablstrasse 37, Haidhausen; mains €17-20; ☽ dinner) This intimate Breton restaurant has a loyal following for its seafood specialities and traditional French fare. Self-control is needed if you want to leave room for the divine desserts. Bookings recommended.

Kleinschmidtz (Map pp56-7; ☎ 608 518; Fraunhoferstrasse 13, Gärtnerplatzviertel; mains €18-23, 3-course meal €30-50; ☽ dinner) Serious foodies flock to this snug eatery where the chef whips up interesting concoctions using choice seasonal ingredients.

Greek

Taverna Paros (Map p58; ☎ 470 2995; Kirchenstrasse 21, Haidhausen; mains €8-18; ☽ dinner) The simple wooden tables and photos of earthy Greek islanders belie the sophistication of this splendid little eatery. The lamb roast stuffed with feta cheese (€13) will melt in your mouth.

Spanish

Casa de Tapas (Map p60; ☎ 2731 2288; Bauerstrasse 2, Schwabing; tapas €3-6, mains €9.50-14; ☽ lunch Mon-Sat, dinner nightly) The painted ceiling and rustic décor of this convivial tapas bar will transport you to the Iberian Peninsula. Cocktails are a great deal during happy hour from 4pm to 8pm. It's pretty small, so reserve ahead, come early or forget about a table.

Bar Tapas (Map p59; ☎ 390 919; Amalienstrasse 97, Schwabing; tapas €3.30, mains €5-8; ☽ dinner) Beautiful people flock to Bar Tapas to nibble on manchego cheese and *jamón serrano* (cured ham), or just to chat over candlelight and red wine. This is a good place to suss out intentions before the night gets going.

El Cortijo (Map p59; ☎ 331 116; Feilitzschstrasse 32, Schwabing; mains €9-18; ☽ dinner, closed Sun) At this classic Spanish restaurant, the cooking has an accent on seafood and heavy meat dishes. A glass of port is thrown in as a thank you. The paella for two costs €22.

Jewish

Cohen's (Map p59; ☎ 280 9545; Theresienstrasse 31, Schwabing; mains €9-14) Tucked away in a courtyard, this well-lit, modern place serves up big portions of German and Eastern European dishes that change with the seasons. Specials include *Königsberger Klopse* (veal dumplings in caper sauce) and gefilte fish.

Latin American

Joe Peña's (Map pp56-7; ☎ 226 463; Buttermelcherstrasse 17, Gärtnerplatzviertel; mains €11-17) This festive cantina-style restaurant is regarded as Munich's best Tex-Mex place and can get very crowded, especially during happy hour (5pm to 8pm). The food is tasty but slightly calibrated to Germanic tastes.

Zapata (Map 3; ☎ 166 5822; Schulstrasse 44, Neuhausen; mains €9-15; ☾ dinner) Munich's revolutionary diner is packed full of sombreros, saddles, cactuses, good food and some refined piña colada drinkers. The menu includes all the usual suspects served up in decent portions and at reasonable prices.

Sausalitos (Map p59; ☎ 281 594; Türkenstrasse 50, Schwabing; mains €9-12) Close to the university, this is the 'in' Mexican place for students. After 8pm it fills up with fashion victims and usually has standing room only. The menu is stocked with all the standards from burritos to fajitas and nachos, and you can watch it all being prepared in the open kitchen. The margaritas are killer.

Turkish

There's more to Turkish food than the ubiquitous doner kebab and these restaurants are here to prove it.

Diyar (Map p58; ☎ 4895 0497; Wörthstrasse 10, Haidhausen; appetisers €4.50-8, mains €7-16) When the belly dancers arrive, this place turns into party central. But even on less-eventful evenings, this unassuming restaurant offers good value and a fun ambience. Try the grilled meats or make a meal of the hot and cold appetisers; there're also a few meatless mains.

Dersim (Map p60; ☎ 123 5454; Jutastrasse 5, Neuhausen; mains €7-14; ☾ dinner) This place is light years away from the doner stands near the Hauptbahnhof but still affordable. The chef's forte is lamb and the aromas are wonderful as almost everything is bought fresh from the markets.

Pardi (Map p60; ☎ 131 850; Volkartstrasse 24, Neuhausen; mains €10-19) If you've never tasted authentic Turkish food this is a fine place to get an introduction. Complexion-friendly candlelight, a stylish bar and friendly service immediately put you at ease. Lamb is

the star of the show here, although the extensive menu has plenty of other options in store.

Vegetarian

There are more vegetarian eateries in Munich than elsewhere in Bavaria but the choice is somewhat limited.

Buxs (Map pp56-7; ☎ 291 9550; Frauenstrasse 9, Altstadt; dishes per 100g €2; ☾ closed Sat evening & Sun) Freedom of choice reigns at this bright, modern self-service place that serves around 50 varieties of soups, salads and antipastos, not to mention the glorious smoothies and desserts. Weigh your appetite carefully as all items are sold per 100g.

Prinz Myschkin (Map pp56-7; ☎ 265 596; Hackenstrasse 2, Altstadt; mains €8-16.50; ☾ Mon-Sat) Considered by many to be Munich's best vegetarian restaurant, this spacious, trendy haunt has an impressive Italian-and Asian-influenced menu including some macrobiotic choices. If you just want a light snack half portions are available.

Ignaz (Map p60; ☎ 271 6093; Georgenstrasse 67, Schwabing; mains €7-9; ☾ 8am-10pm Mon-Sat, 9am-10pm Sun) This is a nonsmoking eatery with vegetable quiches, pastas, soups and salads, plus a few meaty selections that come in handy when dining with carnivores. The good-value lunch buffet is served Monday to Friday only.

Café Gollier (Map pp56-7; ☎ 501 673; Gollierstrasse 83, Westend; mains €7.50-12) This wonderful place is worth a detour to the western Westend for its generous portions of tasty fare direct from a brick oven. All menu items are made with organic ingredients including the beers and sugar-free soft drinks.

Cafés & Bistros

Munich cafés are enticing places to linger, to chat, write postcards, read the paper or simply watch the world go by. Most are casual eateries attracting people of all ages and lifestyles. The menu may be limited to simple snacks, although many cafés serve substantial meals. The afternoon *Kaffee und Kuchen* (coffee and cake) is a classic German café tradition.

ALTSTADT & AROUND

Dukatz im Literaturhaus (Map pp56-7; ☎ 291 9600; Salvatorplatz 1, Altstadt; mains €5-21) A stomping ground for the chic and the intellectual, the Dukatz serves up designer sandwiches and latte macchiato in its café section and impressive mains in its restaurant.

Cáfé am Beethovenplatz (Map pp56–7; ☎ 5440 4348; Goethestrasse 51, Ludwigsvorstadt; mains €4.50–10) This relaxed café with a musical theme has high ceilings, chandeliers and a winning atmosphere. The breakfast selections are named after famous composers and the divine evening meals are accompanied by live jazz or classical music.

Woerners (Map pp56–7; ☎ 265 231; Marienplatz 1, Altstadt; mains €6–15) Two cafés merge into one here: the outdoor Cáfe am Dom on the ground floor, giving some of the best seating on the square, and upstairs, Cáfe Reber, a Munich institution with parquet floors, crystal chandeliers and a long, long history.

Interview (Map pp56–7; ☎ 202 1649; Gärtnerplatz 1, Gärtnerplatzviertel; mains €6–15; ☺ closed Sun evening) This is a pleasant street-side café with popular front-row views of the Theater am Gärtnerplatz. Specialities include grilled fish and creative pasta using seasonal ingredients. Breakfast is served till 5pm.

Other recommendations:

Stadtcafé (Map pp56–7; ☎ 266 949; Stadtmuseum, St-Jakobs-Platz 1, Altstadt; meals €5–12) Culture haunt at the city museum with panorama windows and lovely courtyard.

Forum (Map pp56–7; ☎ 268 818; Corneliusstrasse 2, Altstadt; mains €8–14) A great place any time of day with good breakfasts, extra good desserts and a lively bar.

SCHWABING

Friesische Teestube (Map p59; ☎ 348 519; Pündter Platz 2, Schwabing; mains €4–8; ☺ 10am–10pm) This aromatic little café with 155 types of tea is set up as a living room, with wooden cabinets, antique clocks and comfy padded divans. It serves breakfast and bistro fare such as pizzas, homemade cakes and cured-ham platters.

Tresznjewski (Map p60; ☎ 282 349; Theresienstrasse 72, Maxvorstadt; mains €8–15) This classy brasserie has daring artworks and waiters in full-length aprons. It appeals to the trendy set, and serves up a varied menu from intriguing pastas and sandwiches to simple burgers and *Bratwurst*.

Other recommendations:

Bobolovsky's (Map p59; ☎ 297 363; Ursulastrasse 10, Schwabing; mains €7–11; ☺ 9am–1am) Bustling bistro that takes the happy hour concept to new lengths.

News Bar (Map p59; ☎ 281 787; Amalienstrasse 55, Schwabing; mains €5–10) Trendy café with newspapers – great for whiling away the hours.

HAIDHAUSEN

Café Voilá (Map p58; ☎ 489 1654; Wörthstrasse 5, Haidhausen; mains €5–10) High stucco ceilings, giant mirrors and large windows make this café a great place for watching the world go by. It's buzzing for breakfast and later in the day for fairly priced baguettes, burgers and creative vegetarian dishes.

Creperie Bernard Bernard (Map p58; ☎ 480 1173; Innere-Wiener-Strasse 32, Haidhausen; mains €5–8; ☺ dinner Mon–Sat) The best crepes in town can be found at this small place, which serves up delicious savouries oozing goats cheese or shrimp and lavish desserts dripping with the finest French *chocolat*.

Quick Eats

In Munich alone 100,000 *Weisswurst* are eaten every day. Tradition has it they're best eaten before noon, but that was in the days before refrigeration.

Throughout the city, branches of **Vinzenzmurr** (Altstadt; Map pp56–7; ☎ 260 4765; Rosenstrasse 7; Ludwigvorstadt; Map pp56–7; ☎ 264 189; Sendlinger Strasse 38; Karlsplatz; Map pp56–7; ☎ 598 180; Sonnenstrasse 4) have hot buffets and prepared meals; a very good lunch – such as *Schweinebraten mit Knödel* (roast pork with dumplings) and gravy – can be as low as €4, and hamburgers cost about €2.50. Some branches even have salad bars.

For quick snacks, any **Müller bakery** (Map pp56–7; ☎ 594 713; Sonnenstrasse 2, Altstadt) offers coffee and pretzels or bread rolls covered with melted cheese and bacon or ham. On Neuhausen's Rotkreuzplatz, **Schneider's Feinbäckerei** (Map p60; ☎ 264 744; Volkartstrasse 48, Neuhausen) is one of Munich's best bakeries, making scrumptious rolls, loaves and cakes.

Doner kebabs and pizza rule the fastfood scene in Munich. South of the Hauptbahnhof on Bayerstrasse are plenty of tourist traps, but one gem is **Ristorante Ca' doro** (Map pp56–7; cnr Senefelder Strasse, Ludwigvorstadt), serving generous slices of piping-hot pizza from a mere €1.60. **Kebab Antep** (Map pp56–7; ☎ 532 236; Schwanthalerstrasse 45, entry from Goethestrasse, Ludwigvorstadt; kebabs €2.75) makes great kebabs, spinach pie and other vegetarian offerings.

Another good spot, just north of the Frauenkirchen, is **Münchner Suppenküche** (Map pp56-7; Schäfflerstrasse 7, Altstadt; dishes €3-6; 🕑 Mon-Sat), an old-fashioned soup kitchen known for its chicken casseroles, chilli con carne and other filling snacks.

There are plenty of chances to grab a bite in Schwabing. **Reiter Imbiss** (Map p59; Hohenzollernstrasse 24, Schwabing; meals around €3) is a butcher-snack bar combo with heaps of budget-priced sandwiches and meaty stuff; there's also a salad bar. On Schwabing's main drag, **Wok Man** (Map p59; Leopoldstrasse 68, Schwabing; mains €4.50-6) dishes up a good selection of decent Chinese food.

Near the Neue Pinakothek, **Indisches Fast Food** (Map p60; Barer Strasse 46, Maxvorstadt; mains €5-8) serves up heaped spoonfuls of fragrant basmati rice with tasty Indian standards.

Self-Catering

Supermarkets large and small can be found throughout the city. **Norma** (Map pp56-7; Landwehrstrasse 26) and **Aldi** (Map pp56-7; Rundfunkplatz 4, Ludwigvorstadt) are the cheapest places to buy staples, but for a last-minute stock-up before your train leaves, hit **Tengelmann** (Map pp56-7; Bayerstrasse 5, Ludwigvorstadt), just opposite the Hauptbahnhof. The supermarket in the basement of the **Kaufhof** (Map pp56-7; ☎ 512 50; Karlsplatz 21-24, Altstadt) department store, opposite Karlsplatz, has a far more upmarket selection, plus goodies including fresh mozzarella, superb sliced meats and cheeses, and a good bakery.

At **Viktualienmarkt** (Map pp56-7; 🕑 10am-6pm Mon-Fri, 10am-3pm Sat), south of Marienplatz, deep-pocketed travellers can put together a gourmet picnic of breads, cheeses and salad to take off to a beer garden or the Englischer Garten. **Nordsee** (Map pp56-7; ☎ 221 186) has good, well-priced seafood; **Caseus** (Map pp56-7; ☎ 266 155) is a wonderful cheese-and-wine shop. Behind it you'll find the juice bar **Müller** (Map pp56-7; ☎ 267 79), which offers great fruity concoctions. Right next to the maypole, look for **Oliven & Essiggurken** (Map pp56-7; ☎ 260 4223), with its olives and pickles plus marinated garlic and loads more.

More prosperous picnickers may prefer the legendary delicatessens, **Alois Dallmayr** (Map pp56-7; ☎ 213 50; Dienerstrasse 14) or **Käfer** (Map p58; ☎ 416 8310; Prinzregentenstrasse 73). Both carry an amazing range of exotic foods imported from every corner of the earth.

DRINKING

Beer drinking is an integral part of Munich's nightlife, and indeed daily life. Bavarians down around 160L of the amber liquid every year, or almost one-third more than the national average.

The Altstadt is the traditional home of the beer hall, with larger ones scattered in the other districts. Trendy *schicki-mickis* flock to the designer bars of the Gärtnerplatzviertel or studenty Schwabing, typically cruising the main drag along Leopoldstrasse; Schellingstrasse and Amalienstrasse draw a more relaxed share of the action. Haidhausen is the truer 'Latin quarter' nowadays, with the preclub set favouring Innere Wiener Strasse and the streets around Weissenburger Platz.

Beer Halls & Gardens

Bavaria's brews are best sampled in the venerable old beer halls and gardens. People come here primarily to imbibe so the food served tends to be an afterthought. (For the fare available at beer halls, see the boxed text on p99.) A few places allow you to bring along a picnic lunch, but in most cases outside food is forbidden.

Most places listed here are either gardens or gardens-cum-restaurants: almost all open from 10am to at least 10pm. Even in the touristy places, be careful not to sit at the *Stammtisch,* a table reserved for regulars (there will be a brass plaque).

You sometimes have to pay a *Pfand* (deposit) for the glasses (usually €2.50). Beer costs €4.50 to €6.50 per litre.

ALTSTADT & AROUND

Hofbräuhaus (Map pp56-7; ☎ 221 676; Am Platzl 9, Altstadt) This is certainly the best-known and most celebrated beer hall in Bavaria but it is generally so packed with tipsy tourists that it loses all sense of authenticity. A live band plays Bavarian folk music most of the day.

Augustiner-Grossgaststätte (Map pp56-7; ☎ 5519 9257; Neuhauser Strasse 27, Altstadt) This sprawling place has a less-raucous atmosphere and better food. Altogether it's a much more authentic example of an old-style Munich beer hall, complete with hidden courtyards and hunting trophies on the walls.

Braunauer Hof (Map pp56-7; ☎ 223 613; Frauenstrasse 42, Gärtnerplatzviertel) Near the Isartor, this

A ROYAL 'BREW-HA-HA'

By Bavarian law, as stubborn as it seems, the only breweries allowed to serve beer at the Oktoberfest are the six biggies that produce right within the city boundaries: Spaten, Augustiner, Hofbräu, Hacker-Pschorr, Löwenbräu and Paulaner. Smaller breweries and hopefuls from nearby towns, quality aside, are not permitted.

Not surprisingly this rule has raised a hue and cry among non-Munich brewers, most notably one Prinz Luitpold von Bayern. A direct descendant of Ludwig I, he has, for more than two decades, made a sport of tweaking the brewery barons. Every year the prince – who happens to own the Kaltenberg brewery outside Munich – submits his Wiesen application to the city fathers. And every year he is shot down.

One time, though, His Royal Highness was sure he'd bagged his precious tent. He gambled with a big Munich brewer that he'd succeed; if not, the prince would trudge the 48km from Kaltenberg to the Oktoberfest carrying a stein brimming with the cold stuff. The brewery gods threw the dice and yes, the prince gathered himself together and set out for Oktoberfest with 1500 followers and the national media in hot pursuit.

Accompanied by brass bands, several coaches, the local shooting club as well as sausage and beer wagons, he arrived at the Wiesen entrance at noon on the last day of Oktoberfest. City officials tried to bar them from entering, but the prince and his loyal following – cheered on by the crowds – finally triumphed and crashed the gates. The prince was charged with duress, slander and resisting a public official (later dropped). Sales of Kaltenberg skyrocketed.

pleasingly twisted beer garden is centred on a snug courtyard. There's a hedge maze, a fresco with a bizarre bunch of historical figures and a golden bull that's illuminated at night.

Also recommended:

Viktualienmarkt (Map pp56-7; ☎ 297 545; Viktualienmarkt 6, Altstadt) A Munich institution since 1807, with tables shaded by enormous chestnut trees.

Augustiner Bräustuben (Map pp56-7; ☎ 507 047; Landsberger Strasse 19, Altstadt) Hang-out of the Augustiner brewery staff, drenched in the heartiest of atmospheres.

ENGLISCHER GARTEN

No visit to Munich is complete without a brew in the Englischer Garten.

Chinesischer Turm (Map p59; ☎ 383 8730; Englischer Garten 3, Schwabing) This is Munich's oldest beer garden, opened in 1791. A very mixed crowd of businessfolk, tourists and junkies clump around this classic Chinese pagoda, entertained by what has to be the world's drunkest oompah band (in the tower above the crowd, fenced in like the Blues Brothers).

Hirschau (Map p59; ☎ 369 942; Gysslingstrasse 15, Schwabing) This beer garden is much less crowded but attracts a more smug crowd for the open-air pop and disco. Spaten and Franziskaner are on tap. Take U Bahn 6 to Dietlindenstrasse, then it's a 15-minute walk.

Seehaus (Map p59; ☎ 381 6130; Kleinhesselohe 3, Schwabing) Be prepared for a competitive jostle with the *schicki-micki* crowd and tourists for space in this hugely popular beer garden. It's right on the Kleinhesseloher See with dreamy views of the lake and the park. Paulaner is the featured libation.

NEUHAUSEN

Löwenbräukeller (Map p60; ☎ 526 021; Nymphenburger Strasse 2, Neuhausen) You can't get much more authentic than this earthiest of Bavarian beer halls. The 'cellar' is upstairs, with a grand ballroom seating a couple of thousand enthusiastic drinkers with nary a tourist in sight. On stage you'll be treated to traditional heel-slapping dances such as the *Schuhplattler*. The huge beer garden serves a great variety of Löwenbräu beers, which curiously enjoy more prestige abroad than in Germany.

Augustiner Keller (Map pp56-7; ☎ 594 393; Arnulfstrasse 52, Neuhausen) This enormous place, about 500m west of the Hauptbahnhof, is a giant leafy beer garden buzzing with life and good cheer. It's one of the oldest and biggest beer gardens in Munich with space for 5000 and a playground for children. The spot is beautiful and the atmosphere laidback – ideal for leisurely drinking.

Hirschgarten (Map p60; ☎ 172 591; Hirschgartenallee 1, Nymphenburg) Locals and some savvy tourists flock to the Hirschgarten, just south of Schloss Nymphenburg. The shady garden is enormous, the largest in town, with bench space for up to 8000 revellers. But the real attraction is the deer wandering just the other side of the fence. To get there take the S Bahn to Laim.

Taxisgarten (Map p60; ☎ 156 827; Taxisstrasse 12, Neuhausen) North of Rotkreuzplatz, this is another peaceful place mainly frequented by local families. Freshly baked pretzels, homemade *Obatzda* (a cheese spread, see the boxed text below) and its famous ribs go down especially well with mugs of Franziskaner and Spaten. Take bus No 177 from Rotkreuzplatz to Klugstrasse.

Pubs & Bars
ALTSTADT & AROUND
Schumann's (Map pp56-7; ☎ 229 060; Odeonsplatz 6-7, Altstadt) Urbane and sophisticated, Schumann's has a hard-won reputation as Munich's best cocktail maker, with more than 220 varieties on offer. It even publishes its own bar books and some tales of celebrity drinking.

Jodlerwirt (Map pp56-7; ☎ 467 3524; Althofstrasse 4, Altstadt) In an alley north of Marienplatz, this totally untouristed place vibrates with yodelling sessions in the cramped bar upstairs. Come late evening, everyone locks arms and newcomers are soon rocking and singing with complete strangers.

Master's Home (Map pp56-7; ☎ 229 909; Frauenstrasse 11, Altstadt) This is a wonderfully quirky cellar just east of the Viktualienmarkt. The off-centre décor time warps you back to the colonial era – antique furnishings, plenty of knick-knacks and oddities such as a room built around a bathtub.

Nage & Sauge (Map p58; ☎ 298 803; Mariannenstrasse 2, Lehel; 5.15am-1am) Stylish yet earthy, this split-level candlelit bar has cosy nooks perfect for a romantic tête-à-tête over a crispy focaccia. It's popular but nicely off the beaten track in a quiet backstreet of Lehel.

Other recommendations:
Baader Café (Map pp56-7; ☎ 201 0638; Baaderstrasse 47, Isarvorstadt) A literary think-and-drink place with a high celebrity quotient and possibly the best Sunday brunch in town.
Pacific Times (Map pp56-7; ☎ 2023 9470; Baaderstrasse 28, Isarvorstadt) Trendy joint decked out in dark wood and wicker chairs to attract the beautiful people.

SCHWABING
If you want a variety of hip bars within spitting distance of each other, then Leopoldstrasse is for you.

Alter Simpl (Map p59; ☎ 272 3083; Türkenstrasse 57, Schwabing) This watering hole has good jazz, a reasonable menu (€5 to €13) and an art-house vibe. Thomas Mann and Hermann Hesse were among the writers and artists that used to meet here in the early 20th century. Charming vintage covers of

---

AND THERE'S FOOD, TOO

Bavarian beer gardens have their own peculiar rules, but you can master them as quickly as saying *Prost* (cheers).

Tables laid with a cloth and utensils are reserved for people ordering food, not for the drinking hordes. But if you get hungry, you'll know what to expect – the menus are pretty similar. Typical dishes include roast chicken (about €9 for a half), *Steckerlfisch* (grilled mackerel on a stick, also around €9), huge pretzels (€3) and meaty fixtures such as *Schweinebraten* (pork roast) and schnitzel (€9 to €12). Spare ribs (about €11.50) are probably not worth it except at Taxisgarten.

Radi is a huge, mild radish that's eaten with beer; you can buy prepared radish for about €4.50. For do-it-yourselfers this is a cinch: buy a radish at the market and a *Radimesser* (radish knife) at any department store, stick it down in the centre and twist the handle round and round, creating a radish spiral. Then, just like the pros, smother the cut end of the radish with salt until it 'cries' to reduce bitterness (and increase your thirst!).

Obatzda (*oh*-bats-dah) is Bavarian for 'mixed up' – this cream cheese-like speciality (about €4 to €6) is made of butter, ripe Camembert, onion and caraway. Spread it on a *Brez'n* (pretzel) or bread.

Another speciality is *Leberkäs* (liver cheese), which is nothing to do with liver or cheese but instead a type of meatloaf that gets its name from its shape. It's usually eaten with sweet mustard and soft pretzels.

the satirical magazine *Simplicissimus* (p28) adorn the walls.

Atzinger (Map p59; ☎ 282 880; Schellingstrasse 9, Schwabing) Generations of students have downed beer and chowed on simple but satisfying fare at this classic haunt with wood panelling and framed poster art.

Roxy (Map p59; ☎ 349 292; Leopoldstrasse 48, Schwabing) The place to talent spot and people watch, this slick bar attracts a designer crowd keen to hang out, look good and sip cocktails. By day it offers surprisingly good food at decent prices.

Millennium (Map p59; ☎ 3839 8430; Leopoldstrasse 42, Schwabing) Another spot to see and be seen is this funky, orange place with a strangely sloping ceiling and quirky seating. Mingle with the cocktail crew by night and then come back in the morning for the great breakfast.

News Café (Map p59; ☎ 3838 0600; Leopoldstrasse 74, Schwabing) Plush leather seating, rows of glowing red lamps and African-inspired art make this hip joint a great place to hang out. It serves light food and a multitude of cocktails.

Brik (Map p59; ☎ 2899 6630; Schellingstrasse 24, Schwabing; sushi €5-10) This slick Japanese-style café, bar and lounge is a temple of minimalism and draws a hip crowd as much for the delicious sushi snacks as for the drinks.

HAIDHAUSEN

Dreigroschenkeller (Map p58; ☎ 489 0290; Lilienstrasse 2, Haidhausen) Cosy and labyrinthine, this cellar pub has rooms based upon Bertolt Brecht's *Die Dreigroschenoper* (The Three-Penny Opera), ranging from a prison cell to a red-satin salon. There's great beer and wine, and an extensive menu (mostly hearty German stuff).

Julep's (Map p58; ☎ 448 0044; Breisacherstrasse 18, Haidhausen) This place is decked out like a Prohibition-era bar and comes with a cocktail menu as long and confusing as a Dostoevsky novel. Happy hour is from 5pm to 8pm and all night Sunday.

Kilombo (Map p58; ☎ 485 298; Senftlstrasse 9, Haidhausen) Looks like an old locals' bar from the street but is a surprise inside, with a scuffed chic that just seemed to happen: simple, old wooden chairs, plastic table tops and a scratched-up piano, but definitely cool.

Lisboa Bar (Map p58; ☎ 448 2274; Breisacher Strasse 2, Haidhausen) The only Munich bar with a branch in the Portuguese capital. Dim and romantic, with Portuguese knick-knacks and Fado music spreading an atmosphere of melancholy and passion. It's said to serve the best caipirinhas in town.

NEUHAUSEN

Kreitmayr's (Map p60; ☎ 448 9140; Kreitmayrstrasse 15, Neuhausen) Situated just east of Erzgiessereistrasse, Kreitmayr's is a real bar-crawler's bar, with bar food, good drinks, a pool table, darts and pinball, and live music on Thursday (from Irish folk to jazz). It also has a beer garden in summer.

Irish Pubs

Munich has a huge Irish expat population; if you're out looking for friendly, English-speaking people, you're in luck. Most of the pubs have live music at least once a week and seem to cluster in Schwabing.

Günther Murphy's Irish Tavern (Map p59; ☎ 398 911; Nikolaistrasse 9a, Schwabing) One of the most popular Irish pubs in Munich, and within crawling distance of the Englischer Garten, this cellar bar is often packed to the gills with a mix of locals, expats and tourists.

Shamrock (Map p59; ☎ 331 081; Trautenwolfstrasse 6, Schwabing) Shamrock is fun, loud, boisterous and crowded every night. Arrive early if you want a table and be prepared to squeeze your way to the bar if you stay on late. Live sports are shown on a big screen.

Molly Malone's (Map p58; ☎ 688 7510; Kellerstrasse 21, Haidhausen) This award-winning Irish pub is a better bet if you'd actually like a quiet drink or a decent conversation. It's famous for its authentic fish and chips and has over 100 types of whiskey on hand.

ENTERTAINMENT

Munich's entertainment scene covers the gamut in supreme style. Apart from discos, pubs and beer halls, try not to miss the city's excellent classical, jazz and opera venues.

Listings Publications

Go München (www.gomuenchen.com in German; €3) The 'what's on' guide to the city for exhibitions, concerts and so on.

In München (www.in-muenchen.de in German; free) The best source of information; available free at bars, restaurants and ticket outlets.

München im… (free) Good tourist office listing of almost everything the city has to offer every month.

Münchner Stadtmagazin (€2.50) Complete guide to the city's bars, discos, clubs, concerts and nightlife in general.

Munich Found (www.munichfound.de; €3) English-language magazine with somewhat useful listings.

Tickets

Tickets to entertainment and sports events are available at official Kartenvorverkauf (ticket outlets).

Kartenvorverkauf Karlsplatz (Map pp56-7; ☎ 5450 6060); Marienplatz (Map pp56-7; ☎ 264 640) Branches all over the city and kiosks in these U-Bahn stations.

München Ticket (Map pp56-7; ☎ 5481 8181; www .muenchenticket.de in German; Neues Rathaus)

Clubs

Munich has a thriving club scene with something to suit most tastes. Bouncers are notoriously rude and discerning though, so dress to kill and keep your cool. The cover prices for discos vary but average between €4 and €10.

Kultfabrik & Optimolwerke (Map p58; www .kultfabrik.info in German; Grafingerstrasse 6, Haidhausen) Munich's veritable village of pubs, bars and clubs is a party animal's mecca where you can roam from '80s disco to hip-hop, trance and heavy metal. If you're an aficionado of Russian pop try Kalinka, a trendy place decked out with lots of red velvet, dancing girls and a giant bust of Lenin. Other options include Black Raven, a loud, head-banging metal hang-out where a black uniform and body piercings are *de rigueur*; Living4, which plays a good mix of hip-hop, Latin and house; and Milch & Bar, a more mainstream choice catering to disco divas. Much of the action will migrate to a vast new clubland, Kultpark Nord, north of town near the Allianz Arena (Map pp54-5) sometime in 2006.

P1 (Map p59; ☎ 211 1140; Prinzregentenstrasse 1, Schwabing) P1 is a bit of a Munich institution and remains the see-and-be-seen place for celebrities and wannabes. Dress to kill, say you're a 'regular' and pray the bouncer buys it. Mick Jagger stops by from time to time but a more frequent guest is FC Bayern goalie Oliver Kahn.

Atomic Cafe (Map pp56-7; ☎ 3077 7870; Neuturm-strasse 5, Altstadt) Lava lamps and sofas recall the 1960s, but the legions of twisting and gyrating twenty-somethings are definitely new millennium.

Titanic City (Map p59; Nordendstrasse 64, entrance on Kürfürstenplatz, Schwabing; ☑ Wed-Sun) This Schwabing institution feeds the dark side with bands such as Rammstein and Fits of Rage, but shifts gear into roots and classic rock at the drop of a drumstick. This is a reliable choice and free of teenyboppers.

Muffathalle (Map p58; ☎ 4587 5075; Zellstrasse 4, Haidhausen) This multihall complex holds large concerts and, in summer, an open-air disco on Friday with drum 'n bass, acid jazz and hip-hop (it's always crowded, so expect long queues).

Backstage (Map p60; ☎ 183 330; Helmholzstrasse 18, Neuhausen) Less pretentious, this concert venue and disco offers crossover, psychedelic, hip-hop, trash and various other alternative sounds.

Live Music

ROCK

Schlachthof (Map pp56-7; ☎ 765 448; Zenettistrasse 9) Concerts and disco mega-parties are held regularly at this vast venue, right in front of a huge abattoir complex. It attracts a thirtysomething crowd.

Large rock concerts are staged at Olympiapark. Most other rock venues are also listed under Clubs (left). For something a little different try **Brunnenhof der Residenz** (Map pp56-7; ☎ 936 093; Residenzstrasse 1, Altstadt), which hosts open-air performances from rock, jazz and swing to classical and opera, in stunning surroundings.

JAZZ

Munich has a hot jazz scene with plenty of possibilities.

Jazzclub Unterfahrt im Einstein (Map p58; ☎ 448 2794; Einsteinstrasse 42, Haidhausen) This is perhaps the best-known place in town with live gigs from 9pm, and sometimes it pulls international stars such as Al Porcino and his big band. There's a small art gallery in one corner and open jam sessions on Sunday nights.

Jazzbar Vogler (Map pp56-7; ☎ 294 662; Rumfod-strasse 17, Gärtnerplatzviertel; ☑ Tue-Sun) Conceived as a 'cultural living room' by ex-journalist Vogler, this intimate watering hole has grown into one of the town's top jazz venues. The musicians are some of Munich's baddest cats, especially the talents who come to tickle the grand piano.

Jazzy's (Map p58; ☎ 2166 8447; Steinsdorfstrasse 21, Lehel) This classy jazz club, on the banks of

MUNICH

the Isar, dishes up a combination of killer cocktails and live jazz every night from 8pm. It's also popular with the trendy set for its enormous Sunday brunch.

Café am Beethovenplatz (Map pp56-7; ☎ 5440 4348; Goethestrasse 51, Ludwigsvorstadt) Dine on fine foods while you sit back and enjoy the nightly concerts in this atmospheric café. Weekdays generally feature live jazz or classical music and the jazz accompaniment to Sunday lunch is absolute heaven.

Waldwirtschaft Grosshesselohe (Map pp54-5; ☎ 795 088; Georg-Kalb-Strasse 3) In a southern suburb, this is a popular beer garden known for some mean Dixieland and other jazz played daily to the consternation of local residents.

CLASSICAL MUSIC & OPERA

Philharmonie im Gasteig (Map p58; ☎ 480 980; www .gasteig.de in German; Rosenheimer Strasse 5, Haidhausen) Munich's premier high-brow cultural venue has a packed schedule as home to the city's philharmonic orchestra. The Symphonieorchestra des Bayerischen Rundfunks (Bavarian Radio Symphony Orchestra) is also based here, and performs on Sunday throughout the year.

Nationaltheater (Map pp56-7; box office ☎ 2185 1920; www.staatstheater.bayern.de; Max-Joseph-Platz 2, Altstadt; ☺ box office 10am-6pm Mon-Fri, 10am-1pm Sat) The Bayerische Staatsoper (Bavarian State Opera) performs here. It is also the site of many cultural events, particularly during the opera festival in July. You can buy tickets at regular outlets or at the box office.

Staatstheater am Gärtnerplatz (Map pp56-7; box office ☎ 2185 1960; www.staatstheater-am-gaertner platz.de; Gärtnerplatz 3, Gärtnerplatzviertel) This venue has occasional classical concerts, but opera, operetta, jazz, ballet and musicals also feature on the entertainment menu.

Cinemas

For show information check any of the listings publications. Admission usually ranges from €6.50 to €8.50 though one day a week, usually Monday or Tuesday, is *Kinotag* (cinema day) with reduced prices. Non-German films in mainstream cinemas are almost always dubbed. Films showing in the original language with subtitles are denoted *OmU* (Original mit Untertiteln); those without subtitles are denoted *OV* (Originalversion) or *OF* (Originalfassung).

Amerika Haus (Map p60; ☎ 552 5370; Karolinenplatz 3, Ludwigsvorstadt) shows undubbed films, as do the following movie theatres:

Filmmuseum (Map pp56-7; ☎ 2332 4150; Münchener Stadtmuseum, St-Jakobs-Platz 1, Altstadt)

Atelier (Map pp56-7; ☎ 591 918; Sonnenstrasse 12, Ludwigsvorstadt)

Atlantis (Map pp56-7; ☎ 555 152; Schwanthalerstrasse 2, Ludwigsvorstadt)

Museum-Lichtspiele (Map p58; ☎ 482 403; Lilienstrasse 2, Haidhausen)

Cinema (Map p60; ☎ 555 255; Nymphenburger Strasse 31, Neuhausen)

Theatre

Munich has a lively theatre scene. The two biggest companies are the Bayerisches Staatsschauspiel (Bavarian State Theatre) and the Münchener Kammerspiele (Munich Studio Theatre). The **Bayerisches Staatsschauspiel** (tickets ☎ 2185 1940) performs at the **Residenztheater** (Map pp56-7; Max-Joseph-Platz 1, Altstadt), the intimate rococo **Altes Residenztheater** (also known as Cuvilliés Theatre, also within the Residenz) and at the **Theater im Marstall** (Map pp56-7; Marstallplatz, Altstadt), behind the Nationaltheater (see left).

Münchener Kammerspiele (Map pp56-7; ☎ 2333 7000; Maximilianstrasse 26-28, Altstadt) This theatre stages large productions of serious drama from German playwrights or works translated into German.

Deutsches Theater (Map pp56-7; ☎ 5523 4444; Schwanthalerstrasse 13, Ludwigsvorstadt) Munich's answer to the West End: touring road shows (usually popular musicals such as *Beauty and the Beast*) perform here.

Kulturzentrum Gasteig (Map p58; ☎ 480 980; Rosenheimer Strasse 5, Haidhausen) A major cultural centre with theatre, classical music and other special events in its several halls.

Other venues include the **Prinzregententheater** (Map p58; ☎ 2185 2959; Prinzregentenplatz 12, Haidhausen) and the **Kleine Komödie am Max II** (Map p58; ☎ 221 859; Maximilianstrasse 47, Lehel), which shows lightweight comedy.

Gay & Lesbian Venues

Munich has a thriving gay and lesbian scene that's far and away the best in Bavaria. The best listings can be found in the Rosa Seiten (Pink Pages; €3.50) or Our Munich (free), a monthly guide to gay and lesbian life in the city. You can pick up both at the **Weissblauer Gay Shop** (Map p60; ☎ 522 352; Theresienstrasse 130,

Neuhausen) or **Black Jump** (Map p58; ☎ 4800 4332; Orleansstrasse 51, Haidhausen). Another good bet for information is the website www.munich-cruising.de.

Information and support for gay men and lesbians is available through **Schwules Kommunikations und Kulturzentrum** (Map pp56-7; information ☎ 2602 2819; Müllerstrasse 43, Ludwigsvorstadt; ⚐ 7-11pm), dubbed 'the Sub' and **LeTra/Lesbentelefon** (Map pp56-7; ☎ 725 4272; Angertorstrasse 3, Gärtnerplatzviertel; ⚐ 2.30-5pm Mon & Wed, 10.30am-1pm Tue, 7-9pm Thu).

BARS & CAFÉS

Nightlife is centred in the so-called 'Bermuda Triangle' formed by Sendlinger Tor, Gärtnerplatz and the Isartor.

Morizz (Map pp56-7; ☎ 201 6776; Klenzestrasse 43, Gärtnerplatzviertel) The spot to hang out in town, Morizz resembles an Art Deco Paris bar with red leather armchairs and plenty of mirrors. The service is impeccable, the food's good and the wine and whiskey list will keep anyone happy. It's quiet early in the evening but livens up as the night wears on.

Deutsche Eiche (Map pp56-7; ☎ 231 1660; Reichenbachstrasse 13, Gärtnerplatzviertel) A Munich institution, this was once filmmaker Rainer Werner Fassbinder's favourite hang-out. It's still a popular spot and packs in a mixed crowd for its comfort food and fast service. See also the boxed text on p92.

Iwan (Map pp56-7; ☎ 554 933; Josephspitalstrasse 15, Altstadt) Iwan was once an ultrachic and extremely exclusive place that's broadened its clientele. The two floors host a very mixed crowd that spills out into the leafy courtyard in summer.

Nil (Map pp56-7; ☎ 265 545; Hans-Sachs-Strasse 2, Glockenbachviertel) This place attracts a young, fun-loving crowd and a handful of faded German stars to its octagon bar. The atmosphere is pretty chilled though and it's a good place to see and be seen.

Bei Carla (Map pp56-7; ☎ 227 901; Baaderstrasse 16, Gärtnerplatzviertel) Behind the drab façade is this fine, energised and exclusively lesbian bar. It's a popular spot with a good mixed-age crowd, lots of regulars and snack foods if you're feeling peckish.

Stud (Map pp56-7; ☎ 260 8403; Thalkirchner Strasse 2, Glockenbachviertel; ⚐ Thu-Sun) This is a Levi's-and-leather place with a dark, coal-mine–like interior and lots of butch guys with no

hair. The clientele is gay and lesbian but they're always looking for more lesbians. It's men only on Sunday.

Other recommendations:
Fortuna Musikbar (Map pp56-7; ☎ 554 070; Maximiliansplatz 5, Altstadt) Popular lesbian bar and disco.
New York (Map pp56-7; ☎ 591 056; Sonnenstrasse 25, Altstadt) Posing, preening and cruising club with nonstop high-energy dance music.
Cabaret Mrs Henderson (Map pp56-7; ☎ 263 469; Müllerstrasse 1, Gärtnerplatzviertel) The best transvestite show in town.

SHOPPING

Fashionistas with a flexible credit card should head for Maximilianstrasse, Theatinerstrasse, Residenzstrasse and Brienner Strasse in the Altstadt. For high-street shops and department stores try the pedestrian area around Marienplatz, Neuhausser Strasse and Kaufingerstrasse. For trendier street clothes Gärtnerplatzviertel, Glockenbachviertel, Schwabing and Haidhausen all have smaller alternative boutiques. Beer steins and *Masses* are available at all the department stores, as well as from the beer halls.

Ludwig Beck (Map pp56-7; ☎ 2423 1575; Marienplatz 11, Altstadt) Munich's most venerable department store has some chic, reasonably priced clothes, a large CD shop, a coffee bar and restaurant. It also has a branch of Heinemann's, which makes some of Germany's finest filled chocolates.

Foto-Video Sauter (Map pp56-7; ☎ 551 5040; Sonnenstrasse 26, Altstadt) A good stock of all the top names fills the shelves at this photography emporium. Good deals can be had on Leica cameras and binoculars.

Manufactum (Map pp56-7; ☎ 2424 3669; Kardinal-Faulhaber-Strasse 5, Altstadt) In the exclusive Fünf Höfe mall, Manufactum specialises in hits of traditional German design and manufacturing. Look for chunky Kaweco pens designed in 1883, Porsche pepper mills and that bathroom classic, 4711 Kölnisch Wasser.

Porzellan Manufaktur Nymphenburg (Schloss Nymphenburg Map p60; ☎ 1791 9710; Schloss Nymphenburg, Nymphenburg; ⚐ 10am-5pm Mon-Fri; Altstadt Map pp56-7; ☎ 242 428; Odeonsplatz 1, Altstadt) Has been in the business of making fine porcelain for Bavarian royals since 1747. Go for a classic botanical work or figurine, or instead for radically minimalist pieces by contemporary designers.

Heels Angels (Map pp56-7; ☎ 201 0136; Klenze-strasse 45, Gärtnerplatzviertel; ✆ by appointment) Tucked behind a courtyard near Gärtner-platz, this studio workshop custom-makes leather boots and shoes with an alternative feel, from mock mukluks to studded wooden sandals.

Bavarian dress is the most distinctive of traditional German clothing and can be bought in specialist shops and most larger department stores. **Loden-Frey** (Map pp56-7; ☎ 210 390; Maffeistrasse 5-7, Altstadt) stocks a wide range of Bavarian wear. Expect to pay at least €200 for a good leather jacket, pair of lederhosen or dirndl dress.

Holareidulijö (Map p60; ☎ 271 7745; Schelling-strasse 81, Ludwigvorstadt) gets its quirky name from a phonetic yodel, appropriate for a store that carries preloved lederhosen and other folkwear in good condition.

The **Christkindlmarkt** (Christmas market; Map pp56-7; ✆ Dec) on Marienplatz is large and well stocked but predictably expensive. The **Auer Dult** (Map p58; ✆ 9am-8pm), a huge flea market on Mariahilfplatz in Au, has great buys and takes place during the last weeks of April, July and October.

GETTING THERE & AWAY
Air
Munich's sparkling **Flughafen München** (Munich International Airport; ☎ 975 00, flight inquiries ☎ 9752 1313; www.munich-airport.de) is easy to navigate and second in importance only to Frankfurt for international and domestic flights. The main carrier is **Lufthansa** (Map pp56-7; ☎ 01805-838 4267; Lenbachplatz 1). Other international airlines serving Munich include Air France, British Airways, Delta, easyJet, El Al, Scandinavian Airlines (SAS) and United. For contact and flight information see p284 .

Bus
Munich is a stop for **Busabout** (in the UK ☎ 020 7950 1661; www.busabout.com), with links to Austria, Croatia, Italy, Paris, Amsterdam and other cities.

Europabus (see the boxed text on p227) links Munich to the Romantic Road. For details of fares and timetables inquire at **EurAide** (Map pp56-7; ☎ 593 889; www.euraide.de; Room 3, track 11, Hauptbahnhof; ✆ 8am-12.30pm & 2-6pm May-Sep; 8am-noon & 2-5pm Oct-Apr) or **Deut-sche Touring** (Map pp56-7; ☎ 8898 9513; www .deutsche-touring.com), near platform No 26, off Arnulfstrasse on the north side of the Hauptbahnhof.

BEX BerlinLinienBus (Map pp56-7; ☎ 030-861 9331; www.bex.de in German; Hauptbahnhof, Altstadt) runs daily buses between Berlin and Munich (one-way/return €43/€79, 8½ hours), via Ingolstadt, Nuremberg, Bayreuth and Leipzig.

Car & Motorcycle
Munich has autobahns radiating on all sides. Take the A9 to Nuremberg, the A92-A3 to Passau, the A8 to Salzburg, the A95 to Garmisch-Partenkirchen and the A8 to Ulm or Stuttgart.

All major car-hire companies have offices at the airport. Sixt (Budget), Hertz, Avis and Europcar have counters on the 2nd level of the Hauptbahnhof. An independent car hire company with good rates is **Allround** (Map pp56-7; ☎ 723 8383; www.allround rent.de; Boschetsriederstrasse 12) whose smallest car goes for €35 per day, including 300km, 16% VAT and insurance.

For info about shared rides, contact **ADM-Mitfahrzentrale** (Map pp56-7; ☎ 194 40; www .mitfahrzentralen.de in German; Lämmerstrasse 4; ✆ 8am-8pm Mon-Sat), near the Hauptbahnhof. Sample fares (including commission) are: Vienna (€25), Berlin (€32), Amsterdam (€43), Paris (€46), Prague (€26) and Florence (€35).

Train
Train services from Munich are excellent. There are rapid connections at least every two hours to all major cities in Germany, as well as frequent but usually nondirect services to European cities such as Vienna (€63, five hours), Prague (€73, 6½ hours) and Zürich (€58, 4¼ hours).

There are direct connections to Berlin (€89 to €111, 6½ hours) and Hamburg (€111, six hours). Going to Frankfurt (€69, 3½ hours) usually requires a change in Fulda, Würzburg or Mannheim.

Prague extensions are sold at the rail-pass counters in the Reisezentrum at the Hauptbahnhof, or through EurAide (left).

GETTING AROUND
Central Munich is compact enough for exploring on foot. To get to the outlying suburbs make use of the public transport network, which is extensive and efficient.

Café crowd on Marienplatz (p63), Munich

Viktualienmarkt (p68), Munich

Marienplatz (p63) and Frauenkirche (p67), Munich

View of Salzburg (p114)

CHRIS

Altstadt (old town; p114), Salzburg

CHRIS MELLOR

Schloss Mirabell (p116), Salzburg

MARK

Wolfgang Amadeus Mozart (p116)

MARK HONAN

To/From the Airport

Munich's Flughafen München is connected by the S1 and S8 to the Hauptbahnhof – €9.50 with a single ticket or €7.60 if using eight strips of a *Streifenkarte* (see below). The trip takes about 40 minutes and runs every 20 minutes from 3.30am until around 12.30am.

The **Lufthansa Airport Bus** (☎ 323 040) travels at 20-minute intervals from Arnulfstrasse near the Hauptbahnhof (one-way/return €9.50/15, 45 minutes) between 5.10am and 9.40pm. A taxi from the airport to the Altstadt costs about €45 to €60.

Car & Motorcycle

It's not worth driving in the city centre; many streets are pedestrian-only, ticket enforcement is Orwellian and parking is a nightmare. The tourist office map shows city car parks, which generally charge about €1.50 to €2 per hour.

Public Transport

Getting around is easy on Munich's excellent public-transport network (MVV). The system is zone-based, and most places of interest to visitors (except Dachau and the airport) are within the 'blue' *Innenraum* (inner-zone).

Tickets are valid for the S-Bahn, U-Bahn, trams and buses but must be time-stamped in the machines at station entrances and aboard buses and trams before use. Failure to validate a ticket puts you at the mercy of ticket inspectors (usually in plain clothes) who speak perfect English, have seen and heard all possible excuses and possess admirable efficiency when it comes to handing out fines (around €40) for unauthorised travel.

Short rides (four bus or tram stops; two U-Bahn or S-Bahn stops) cost €1, longer trips cost €2.10. It's cheaper to buy a strip-card of 10 tickets called a *Streifenkarte* for €9.50, and stamp one strip (€0.95) per adult on rides of two or less tram or U-Bahn stops, two strips (€1.90) for longer journeys.

Some of the other deals on offer include:

Bayern-Ticket (€24) See p291 for more information.

Day passes One-/three-day per person €4.50/€11 for the inner zone; one-/three-day Partner-Tageskarte (€8/€18) for unlimited travel in all four zones for up to five people.

Isarcard (€14) Weekly pass covering all four zones but valid Monday to Sunday only – if you buy on Wednesday, it's still only good until Sunday.

Rail passes are also valid on S-Bahn trains. Bicycle transport costs €2.10 per trip or €2.50 for a day pass, but is forbidden between 6am and 9am and 4pm and 6pm Monday to Friday.

The U-Bahn ceases operation at around 12.30am Monday to Friday and 1.30am on weekends, but a network of *Nachtbusse* (night buses) operates. Pick up the latest route and time schedule from any tourist office.

Taxi

Taxis cost €3.70 at flag fall, plus €1.20 to €1.45 per kilometre and are not much more convenient than public transport. For a radio-dispatched taxi, ring ☎ 216 10 or ☎ 194 10. Taxi ranks are indicated on the city's tourist map.

AROUND MUNICH

STARNBERGER FÜNF-SEEN-LAND

pop 85,000 / elev 584m

Once a royal retreat and still popular with politicians, celebrities and the merely moneyed, Starnberger See (Lake Starnberg) is a fast and easy escape from the urban bustle of Munich for a weekend on the water.

The town of Starnberg, at the northern end of the lake, is the heart of the Fünf-Seen-Land (Five Lakes District). Starnberger See and the Ammersee are the two largest lakes, set in a glacial plain but within easy reach of Munich. The smaller Pilsensee, Wörthsee and Wesslinger See offer a more secluded charm.

This area has long been a favourite with the Bavarian nobility. The 19th-century 'fairy-tale' king Ludwig II – 'Kini' to his adoring fans – had a soft spot for the Starnberger See. That is until he mysteriously drowned in the lake on the eastern shore. Ludwig's bosom buddy, Empress Sisi of Austria (1837–98), spent many a summer staying in Possenhofen on the western shore; her descendent Otto von Habsburg – head of the Austrian royal family – still lives in nearby Pöcking.

The present head of the Wittelsbach family, the art-loving Duke Franz (see the boxed text on p83), still uses Ludwig's former palace in Berg.

Information

District tourist office (☎ 08151-906 00; www.sta5.de in German; Wittelsbacherstrasse 2c, Starnberg; ☼ 8am-6pm Mon-Fri Nov-May, also 9am-1pm Sat May-mid-Oct) A short walk north of Bahnhofsplatz, with a free room-finding service and help for onward transport to other lake towns.

Sights

STARNBERG

At the north end of the lake, the town of Starnberg is the gateway to the lake district but lacks any lasting allure, so most people head straight on to the other communities. The main train station in Starnberg is just steps away from the cruise-boat landing docks, pedal-boat hire and the district tourist office.

Just west of the Bahnhof is the **Heimatmuseum** (☎ 08151-772 132; Possenhofener Strasse 5, entry Bahnhofsplatz; adult/child €1.50/0.75; ☼ 10am-noon & 2-5pm Tue-Sun, closed Feb). In a nicely restored wooden farmhouse, this extensive local history museum includes a prized sculpture by Ignaz Günther and a model of the 17th-century state yacht **Bucentaur**, which

ploughed the lake under the brute power of Roman-style rowers.

Starnberg is just 30 minutes by S6 from Munich (two zones or four strips of a *Streifenkarte*). Note that all bus connections to other lake towns depart from the new high-tech S-Bahn station at Starnberg Nord, still confused by weary commuters with the lakeside Starnberg stop.

BERG

On the eastern shore of the Starnberger See is **Schloss Berg**, the summer residence of King Ludwig II and the place where he spent his final days. The palace and its lovely gardens are still inhabited by the Wittelsbach family and closed to prying eyes.

You are free, however, to walk through its wooded park to the **Votivkapelle** (Votive Chapel; ☎ 08151-5276; admission free; ☼ 9am-5pm Apr-Oct). Built in honour of Ludwig and shrouded by mature trees, this pompous little Romanesque chapel overlooks the spot in the lake – marked by a simple cross, erected years later by his mother – where Ludwig's dead body was supposedly found. Visitors are allowed glimpses into the spartan interior from the entrance chamber.

Bus No 961 travels from Starnberg to Berg (correct stop: Berg am See) throughout the day, less often at weekends.

POSSENHOFEN & FELDAFING

Austrian empress Sisi, cousin of Ludwig II, spent her childhood summers at **Schloss Possenhofen**, a chunky cream-coloured palace on the western lakeshore. The complex today houses fancy apartments and is closed to the public, but its lush park dappled with mature leafy trees is perfect for picnics and sunbathing. Access is free but it gets crowded on sunny summer weekends.

Sisi was so taken with the area that she returned here as an adult to spend summers in what is now the **Kaiserin Elisabeth Hotel** (☎ 08157-930 90; Tutzinger Strasse 2-6, Feldafing), a couple of kilometres south. A larger-than-life sculpture in the garden shows her with a book in a relaxed repose, gazing back at the hotel. You can eat in the rustic **Ludwigstüberl** (p109) or the stuffy restaurant where aproned waiters serve the 'Sisi Menu', featuring dishes Sisi allegedly had the day Ludwig died.

Sisi and Ludwig frequently rendezvoused on the romantic offshore **Roseninsel** (Rose Island), where Ludwig also received other illustrious guests, Richard Wagner among them. Neglected for a century after the king's passing, the island, rose garden and summerhouse have been recently restored and reopened to the public. Ferryman Norbert Pohlus will take you to the island on his historical rowboat **Plette** (☎ 08171-722 22 66; adult/child under 15 €4/2; Easter-Oct in good weather). There's a two-passenger minimum.

Fans of Art Nouveau villas should take a spin around Feldafing, which also has a popular swimming beach, the **Strandbad Feldafing** (☎ 08157-82 00; adult/child Mon-Fri €1.50/1.30, Sat & Sun €2.50/1.50; 10am-10pm Jun-Sep, 10am-10pm Thu-Sun Oct-May).

Possenhofen and Feldafing are both stops on the S6 from Munich (40 minutes).

BUCHHEIM MUSEUM

About 1km north of Bernried, right on the Starnberger See, is the amazing **Buchheim Museum** (☎ 08158-997 060; Bernried; adult/child €8.50/3.50; combined boat & museum ticket €16; 10am-6pm Tue-Sun Apr-Oct, 10am-5pm Tue-Sun Nov-Mar) This is the private collection of Lothar-Günther Buchheim, best known as author of *Das Boot*, the novel that inspired the famous film. The museum stirred a great deal of controversy before it was finished in 2001, thanks to its postmodern design and its wilful mix of artworks, including the owner's own efforts. The foregarden of the museum greets visitors with a bronzed statue of a BMW sprouting octopuslike tentacles.

Expressionist paintings by the early 20th-century group Die Brücke (The Bridge) form the heart and soul of the museum. Shapes and figures teeter on the abstract without ever quite getting there, with bright, emotional colours and unusual perspectives by leading lights such as Kirchner, Nolde and Pechstein. The Nazis, predictably, called this work subversive and had much of it destroyed.

Then prepare for a zany contrast – of arts and crafts from around the world, the 'make love not war' silk-screen prints from Buchheim's own workshops and glass cases containing several thousand paperweights. Connecting halls are watched over by bizarre circus figures, creating an atmosphere of childlike wonder. Crusty in his public appearances, Buchheim's eyes suddenly light up when he talks about the collective imagination – hence the subtitle 'Museum of Fantasy'.

The building itself is a handsome, streamlined vessel of wood and white stucco by Günter Behnisch, architect of Munich's Olympiastadion. The shiplike effect is emphasized by a 12m-long footbridge on stilts jutting out over the lake. Initially Buchheim aimed to build the museum near Feldafing before public opposition forced him to relocate to this site.

RegionalBahn (RB) trains make the trip from Munich to Bernried in 40 minutes, with a change in Tutzing (€6.60). From the station, it's a 15-minute walk north to the museum. From May to October you can reach the museum via an hour-long boat trip from Starnberg; departures are three times every afternoon.

ANDECHS

One of the district's main attractions is the Benedictine **Kloster Andechs** (Andechs Monastery; ☎ 08152-3760; Bergstrasse 2, Andechs; church admission free). Founded in the 10th century, the monastery remains an important place of pilgrimage, although more visitors are probably drawn by the monks' formidable brews, some of Bavaria's finest.

The offertory candles in the Holy Chapel are among Germany's oldest; standout specimens in the special candle vault are over 1m tall. Famous relics include branches from Christ's crown of thorns and a victory cross of Charlemagne, who annexed Bavaria while conquering most of Western Europe in the 9th century.

The church was originally Gothic but was made over into rococo later on. It boasts a riot of frescoes, sculptures and a sophisticated altar designed by Munich court architect Cuvilliés. During the year, the altar picture can be lowered to change the scenes from Christ's Passion and Salvation. In summer concerts are held featuring works by Carl Orff, the composer of *Carmina Burana* (see the boxed text on p137) who is buried inside the church.

Most visitors to the 'Holy Mountain', as Andechs is known, really come to worship at the **Braustüberl**, the monastery's beer hall and garden. The resident monks have been brewing beer for over 500 years. Six varieties are on offer, from the rich and velvety Doppelbock Dunkel to the fresh, unfiltered Weissbier. The place is often so overrun it's easy to forget that you're in a religious institution, pious as your love for the brew may be. Summer weekends can be insanely busy.

From June to October, you can take tours (adult/child €3/1.50; ☻ 3pm Mon-Fri) of the monastery, or a brewery tour (adult/student/child €3/1.50/free; ☻ 1.30pm Mon & Tue).

Andechs is served three times daily (twice on Sunday) by bus No 951 from the S-Bahn station in Starnberg Nord (S6; 35 minutes) and the one in Herrsching (S5; 10 minutes). The last bus from Andechs to Herrsching leaves at 6.40pm, to Starnberg at 4.43pm.

DIESSEN

About 11km west of Andechs, in the southwestern corner of the Ammersee, the small town of Diessen is home to the **Marienmünster** (☎ 08807-948 940; ☻ 8am-noon & 2-6pm), one of the area's most magnificent baroque churches. Part of a monastery complex, this festive symphony in white stucco, red marble and gold leaf involved some of the most accomplished artists of the 18th century. The painting above the altar showing Mary ascending into heaven had to be sent from Italy because its artist, the master Giovanni Battista Tiepolo, preferred to work in Venice.

Activities

If cruises are too tame, consider taking a spin around the lake under your own steam. Boat hire is available on the Starnberger See, the Ammersee and the Wörthsee. In Starnberg, **Paul Dechant** (☎ 08151-121 06; Bootshaus 2, Starnberg), near the train station, has rowing, pedal and electric-powered boats for €11 per hour. In Herrsching, near Andechs on the Ammersee, **Alfred Schlamp** (☎ 08152-969 533; Summerstrasse 30, Herrsching) charges €6 per hour for his pedal and rowing boats.

A bicycle is an excellent way to explore the area. The tour around Starnberger See, for instance, is 50km and partly travels along dedicated bike paths with no car traffic. For guided bike tours contact **Bike It** (☎ 08151-746 430; Maximilianstrasse 4, Starnberg; tours from €25, bike hire per day from €15-20). There's a famous in-line skating stretch on the eastern shore between Berg and Ambach.

There are **10 marked hiking** trails in the district. A delightful half-day trip starts in Tutzing and goes via a moderate ascent to the Ilkahöhe, which is a 730m hill with panoramic views of the lake and the surrounding countryside.

BOAT CRUISES

From Easter to mid-October, **Bayerische-Seen-Schifffahrt** (☎ 120 23) runs scheduled boat services on the Starnberger See and the Ammersee, a leisurely way to explore the region. In Starnberg, boats leave from the landing docks just south of the main station. The company also offers narrated tours of both lakes, varying from one to four hours and costing from €7 to €14. Tours on the Starnberger See pass by five palaces as well as the Ludwig II cross.

Sleeping

DJH Hostel Possenhofen (☎ 08157-996 611; www.jugendherberge.de/jh/possenhofen in German; Kurt-Stieler-Strasse 18, Pöcking-Possenhofen; dm €20.45, s/d incl breakfast €26.50/53; P 🖳) This cavernous new hostel, just 250m from Starnberger See, caters to school groups and families but has a number of singles and doubles with full facilities.

Hotel Garni Kefer (☎ 08157-931 70; www.hotel-kefer.de In German; Hindenburgstrasse 12, Pöcking-Possenhofen; s €39-62, d €62-76; P) This is an old-fashioned hotel in a pretty villa with white carved balconies, some with lake views over the treetops. Rooms are spacious and the beds comfy with thick fluffy duvets. Spa-type niceties such as sauna and steam bath are included.

Landgasthof zur Linde (☎ 08157-933 180; www.linde-wieling.de in German; Wieling 5, Feldafing; s €45-85, d €70-115; P) Flower boxes spilling over with geraniums offer a cheerful welcome to this 34-room Alpine-style inn, about 2km south of the Feldafing train station. Rooms are furnished in modern country style and there's a good restaurant with a beer garden as well.

Hotel Schlossgut (☎ 08177-93 23; www.schlossgut.de; Oberambach 1, Oberambach; s/d from €97/130, ste from €235; breakfast €15; P ✗ 🐱 🖳 🍴) This palatial hotel doubles as a health farm with extras such as cosmetic, allergy and mud treatments. After a loll in the private swimming pond or deluxe sauna you can take dinner with certified organic ingredients in the first-class restaurant.

The Five Lakes District has six camp sites, one on the Ammersee, **Campingplatz St Alban** (☎ 08807-7305; Diessen), one on the Wörthsee, **Campingplatz Woerl** (☎ 08152-764 45), one on the Pilsensee, **Campingplatz Strandbad Pilsensee** (☎ 08152-7232) and three on Starnberger See, including **Campingplatz Hirsch** (☎ 08177-546) in Münsing-Ambach on the eastern shore. For details, call or check with the tourist office (p106).

Eating

Braustüberl (☎ 08152-376 261; Bergstrasse 2, Andechs; ⏰ 10am-8.45pm) Crispy grilled pork knuckles and steaming pretzels are the things to get at this beer hall right on the 'Holy Mountain'. A self-service deli sells most items by weight (eg 100g pork knuckle for €1.70). To avoid standing in line for half an hour, bring your own picnic for the designated tables in the beer garden.

Ludwigstüberl (☎ 08157-930 90; Tutzinger Strasse 2-6, Feldafing; Brotzeit €6.50-8.50, mains €11-19; ⏰ dinner Wed-Mon, lunch on Sun, closed Tue) On cold nights it's a treat to sit near the fireplace in this cosy tavern, digging into a soulful menu ranging from salads to roast beef. Bookings are recommended. It's part of the Kaiserin Elisabeth Hotel; don't confuse this place with the stuffy hotel restaurant.

Forsthaus Ilkahöhe (☎ 08158-8242; Auf der Il-kahöhe, Tutzing; mains €16-23; ⏰ Wed-Sun) It's hard to tell what's more appealing: the gourmet regional cuisine or the idyllic hilltop setting, with spectacular views of the Starnberger See and the Alps. Come for a full meal or just a foamy *Mass* in the beer garden, open daily in fine weather.

Gasthaus Zum Fischmeister (☎ 08177-533; Seeuferstrasse 31, Ambach; mains €13-28; ⏰ Wed-Sun) Munich's glamour pack often hangs out in this high-octane pub right by the ferry docks. The ambience is of easy prosperity but not snobby. Fish is its prized speciality: try a tender whitefish or char taken straight from the Starnberger See.

Getting There & Away

Starnberg lies 25km southwest of central Munich – a half-hour's journey by car or S-Bahn on the S6 line. The S6 links Munich with Starnberg and the towns along the eastern shore of the Starnberger See (Possenhofen, Feldafing and Tutzing); the S5 goes from Munich to Herrsching am Am-

mersee. Bus services throughout the region are good.

DACHAU
☎ 08131 / pop 39,000 / elev 508

Mention Dachau and the instant association is with the Nazi concentration camp, visited by more than 800,000 people each year. Few of them realise that there was a Dachau some 1100 years before the camp was built. Fewer still ever make it to the town's little Altstadt with its historic buildings, a pretty Renaissance palace and garden.

In the 19th century, Dachau had a thriving artists colony, which included Lovis Corinth and Max Liebermann. Their work can be seen in the **Dachauer Gemäldegalerie** (☎ 567 50; Konrad-Adenauer-Str 3; ⏰ 11am-5pm Wed-Fri, 1-5pm Sat-Sun), next to the tourist office. Even today, about 100 artists live in Dachau.

Orientation & Information

Dachau's Bahnhof is about 3.5km southwest of the concentration camp memorial and about 1km southeast of the Altstadt, where you'll find the **tourist office** (☎ 752 86; www.dachau.info; Konrad-Adenauer-Strasse 1, Dachau; ⏰ 9am-1pm Mon-Wed & Fri, 2-6pm Thu).

Sights
SCHLOSS DACHAU

First built as a medieval castle for local nobles, **Schloss Dachau** (☎ 879 23; Schlossstrasse 7, Dachau; adult/child €2/1; ⏰ 9am-6pm Tue-Sun Apr-Sep, 10am-4pm Tue-Sun Oct-Mar) was transformed into a monolithic complex in the 16th century for the Wittelsbach dukes, who in turn made it their summer palace. The palace then fell into disrepair and just one of its four wings survived, namely the baroque number you see today. Behind its creamy façade is a festival hall with a magnificent Renaissance ceiling that glorifies the Wittelsbach rulers. This is also the delightful setting of the Dachauer Schlosskonzerte, which is a classical concert series (tickets about €17 to €28).

Behind the Schloss, the **Hofgarten** (admission free; ⏰ 7am-dusk, latest 8pm) harbours an orchard, a rose garden and lovers' paths sheltered by a leafy canopy. The terrace of the Schlosscafé overlooks this oasis of calm.

DACHAU CONCENTRATION CAMP MEMORIAL

The Dachau concentration camp was the Nazi's first, built by Heinrich Himmler in March 1933 to house political prisoners. All in all it 'processed' more than 200,000 inmates, killing at least 32,000, and is now a haunting memorial. Note that children under 12 may find the experience too disturbing. Expect to spend two to three hours here to fully absorb the exhibits.

> The way to freedom is to follow one's orders; exhibit honesty, orderliness, cleanliness, sobriety, truthfulness, the ability to sacrifice and love of the Fatherland.
>
> *Inscription from the roof of the concentration camp at Dachau*

Information

The **memorial** (☎ 669 970; www.kz-gedenkstaette-dachau.de; Alte Römerstrasse 75, Dachau; admission free; 🕓 9am-5pm Tue-Sun) is in the northeastern corner of Dachau. Free map-pamphlets in about a dozen languages are available at the main entrance. For more in-depth descriptions, pick up the brochure *Concentration Camp Dachau* (€2) or the detailed catalogue (€7). Proceeds go directly to the Survivors Association of Dachau.

A 22-minute English-language documentary runs at 11.30am, 2pm and 3.30pm. If you think you've seen it all, this film may cause you to think again.

The Memorial

You approach the memorial through the **Jourhaus**, originally the only entrance to the compound. Set in wrought iron, the chilling slogan '*Arbeit Macht Frei*' (Work Sets You Free) hits you at the gate.

The first stop is the **Documentary Exhibit** housed in the former utility building, where the kitchen, baths and storage rooms were located. A wall-sized map shows camp locations throughout Germany and Central Europe, with special symbols for the extermination camps.

The exhibit consists of photographs and models of the camp, its officers and prisoners, and of horrifying 'scientific experiments' carried out by Nazi doctors. Other exhibits include a whipping block, a chart showing the system for prisoner identification by category (Jews, homosexuals, Jehovah's Witnesses, Poles, Roma and other 'asocial' types) and documents relating to the camp and the persecution of 'degenerate' authors banned by the party. There are also exhibits on the rise of the Nazi party and the establishment of the camp system.

Outside this building, in the former roll-call square, is the **International Memorial** (1968), inscribed in English, French, Yiddish, German and Russian, which reads 'Never Again'. Behind the exhibit building, the **bunker** was the notorious camp prison where inmates were tortured; some of the cells are too tiny for prisoners to sit, let alone lie down. Executions took place in the prison yard.

You can visit a single re-created barrack block and try to imagine the horrifying conditions in which the prisoners lived. The bulk of inmates were housed in rows of large barracks, now demolished, which used to line the main road north of the roll-call square. The **crematorium** is in the camp's far northwestern corner. Also here is a gas chamber, disguised as a shower room, which was never used. Instead, prisoners marked for gassing were sent to other camps. Outside the crematorium is a statue to 'honour the dead and warn the living' and a Russian Orthodox chapel. Nearby are Jewish and Catholic memorials as well as a Protestant church.

Tours

A guided tour is highly recommended, but be absolutely sure to join only ones authorized by the memorial staff, such as those listed below. Some unauthorized tours provide tourists with no more than a recorded audio guide or, more gallingly, have even been known to provide inaccurate details about the site.

Dachauer Forum (☎ 996 880; ticket €3; 🕓 1.30pm Tue-Fri, noon Sat & Sun Jun-Sep; noon Sat & Sun Oct-May; 2-3 hr) Informative tours by dedicated volunteers in English, departing from the main hall. The same guides also give half-hour introductions (€1.50; 🕓 noon Tue-Sat May-Oct, Thu & Sat & Sun Nov-Apr).

Radius Tours & Bikes (☎ 5502 9374; www.radiusmunich.com; ticket €19; 🕓 9.20am & 12.40pm Tue-Sun Apr-Oct, 12.40pm Nov-Mar; 5 hr) These excellent English-language tours leave from opposite track 31 in the Hauptbahnhof. Tickets include public transportation from Munich, and bookings are advised.

Self-guided Audio Tour (adult/child €3/2; up to 2 hr)
For putting together your own tour covering history, key buildings and the exhibits. Available from the ticket desk.

Getting There & Away

The S2 (direction: Laim) leaves Munich Hauptbahnhof every 20 minutes and makes the journey to Dachau Hauptbahnhof in 22 minutes. You'll need a two-zone ticket (four strips of a *Streifenkarte*), including the bus connection. From here change to local bus No 724 or 726 and show your stamped ticket to the driver. By car, follow Dachauer Strasse straight out to Dachau and follow the KZ-Gedenkstätte signs. Parking is €1.75.

SCHLEISSHEIM
☎ 089 / pop 5700 / elev 486m
The northern Munich suburb of Schleissheim has not one but three palaces and an aviation museum to boot.

Sights
NEUES SCHLOSS SCHLEISSHEIM
The crown jewel of the palatial trio is the **Neues Schloss Schleissheim** (☎ 315 8720; Max-Emanuel-Platz 1, Schleissheim; adult/youth €4/3, with Schloss Lustheim €5/4, child under 15 years free; ☾ 9am-6pm Apr-Sep, 10am-4pm Oct-Mar, closed Mon). Modelled after Versailles, this pompous pile was dreamed up in 1701 by Prince-Elector Max Emanuel, in expectation that he'd be crowned emperor. But Max, who fled into exile during the War of Spanish Succession, had to wait nearly 20 years to see it realised.

The overblown dimensions, starting with the 330m-long façade, give credence to the view that Max was a bit deluded. Inside you're treated to room after enormous room of stylish period furniture, a heavily stuccoed dining hall and a vaulted ceiling smothered in frescoes by Cosmas Damian Asam, among the most expensive artists of the period. The palace is the pearl in an impressive baroque park with canal and cascading waterfall.

The palace is home to the **Gemäldegalerie** (Dachau Paintings Gallery), a selection of European baroque art drawn from the Bavarian State Collection. The ground floor displays works by Italian, German and Spanish artists, while the upstairs focuses on Flemish greats including Brueghel and van Dyck.

ALTES SCHLOSS SCHLEISSHEIM
Nearby, the Renaissance **Altes Schloss Schleissheim** (☎ 315 5272; Maximilianshof 1; adult/youth €3/2; ☾ 9am-6pm Apr-Sep, 10am-4pm Oct-Mar, closed Mon) is a shadow of its former self, having been badly damaged in WWII. It houses exhibits on religious festivals, with a prominent section on Easter eggs, and another on Prussia.

SCHLOSS LUSTHEIM
On a little island at the eastern end of the Schlosspark stands the fanciful hunting palace **Schloss Lustheim** (☎ 315 8720; adult/youth €3/2; ☾ 9am-6pm Apr-Sep, 10am-4pm Oct-Mar, closed Mon). Frescoes inside pay tribute to the hunting goddess Diana, but your eyes may be drawn more to the display of opulent Meissner porcelain, billed as the second-best after the collection in Dresden.

FLUGWERFT SCHLEISSHEIM
Near the palaces, on what is Germany's oldest airfield (1912), is **Flugwerft Schleissheim** (☎ 315 7140; Effnerstrasse 18; adult/child €3.50/2.50; ☾ 9am-5pm), the aviation branch of the Deutsches Museum. Displays are housed in a cohesive mix of historical and modern halls that show off 60-odd planes, helicopters, hang-gliders and engines. This *tour de force* includes a MiG-21 – the Soviets' notorious fighter jet – and an F-4E Phantom, a familiar sight on TV screens during the Vietnam War. Also on view is a reconstruction of Otto Lilienthal's 1894 glider, with a revolutionary wing shaped like Batman's cape.

Getting There & Away
Take the S1 (direction: Freising) to Ober-schleissheim. It's about a 15-minute walk from the station along Mittenheimer Strasse towards the palaces. By car, take Leopoldstrasse north until it becomes Ingolstädter Strasse. Then take the A99 to the Neuherberg exit, at the south end of the airfield.

FREISING
☎ 08161 / pop 42,000 / elev 448m
A few stops north on the S-Bahn, Freising is a bedroom community for Munich but retains the feel of a traditional market town. For a thousand years, Freising was the spiritual and cultural centre of southern

Bavaria. In 1821 the bishop bowed to the inevitable and moved his seat to Munich. Freising sank in the ecclesiastical ranking but hung onto its religious gems, the main reasons to visit today.

Orientation & Information

The bulk of Freising's sights are in the Altstadt on or around the Lehrberg (Teaching Hill), site of the cathedral complex and more popularly known as the Domberg. For information, visit the **tourist office** (☎ 541 22; www.freising.de in German; Marienplatz 7, Freising; 🕑 9am-4.30pm Mon-Fri Oct-Mar, 9am-4.30pm Mon-Fri, 9am-noon Sat Apr-Sep).

Sights

Freising's charming **Altstadt** is crisscrossed by a tangle of lanes lined by baroque and Renaissance townhouses, immaculately restored and clean almost to a fault.

Looming over the old town is the Domberg, a whitewashed hub of religious power with the twin-towered **Dom St Maria and St Korbinian** (☎ 18 10; 🕑 8am-noon & 2-5pm, to 6pm May-Oct) as its focal point. Originally a 12th-century Romanesque basilica, much of the interior bears witness to later periods. But the best treasures lie in the crypt, site of Korbinian's mortal remains. In this forest of wilful pillars – and no two are carved alike – you'll find the famous Bestiensäule (Beast Pillar), with an epic allegory of Christianity fighting the crocodilelike monsters of evil.

The church is a head-turning masterpiece of the Asam brothers, the megastars whose baroque frescoes grace the most pious ceilings of Bavaria. Remnants from the Gothic era include the choir stalls and the painting, *Lamentation of Christ*, in the left aisle. The altar painting by Rubens is a copy of the original in the Alte Pinakothek museum in Munich.

East of the Dom are the cloisters, whose halls drip with fancy stucco and a thousand years' homage in marble plaques to the bishops of Freising. The baroque hall of the **cathedral library** (🕑 2-3pm Mon-Fri mid-May–mid-Oct), shines with the gold-and-white fantasies of François Cuvilliés, designer of the magnificent Cuvilliés Theatre in Munich.

At the western end of the hill is the **Domberg Museum** (☎ 487 90; Domberg 21, Freising; adult/child €2/1; 🕑 10am-5pm Tue-Sun). This is in fact the largest ecclesiastical museum in Germany, with displays precious enough to deserve an armed guard. You can feast your eyes on bejewelled gold vessels, reliquaries and ceremonial regalia, but also some of the world's finest nativity scenes. The highlight is the *Lukasbild*, a 12th-century Byzantine icon set in its own diminutive silver altar. Upstairs you'll discover works by Rubens and other masters.

Southwest of the Domberg, there's a former Benedictine monastery that hosts, among other university faculties, a respected college of beer brewing. Also here is the **Staatsbrauerei Weihenstephan**, a brewery with the plausible claim of being the world's oldest, founded in 1040. **Guided tours** (☎ 53 60; ticket €2; 🕑 2pm Mon-Thu) round the modern tanks leave you hankering at the end for a foamy golden *Weissbier* (wheat beer), available in the beer garden or vaulted cellar of the Bräustüberl. Bookings are advised.

Getting There & Away

Freising is about 35km northwest of Munich at the northern terminus of the S1 (€4.20, 25 minutes). The Domberg and Altstadt are a 10-minute walk from the train station. By car, take Leopoldstrasse north and turn right on Schenkendorfstrasse. Then take the A9 north and the A92 to the Freising-Mitte exit.

Salzburg & Upper Bavaria

CONTENTS

HIGHLIGHTS

- **Going for Baroque**
  Exploring the graceful squares and spires of Mozart's birthplace, Salzburg (pp114–25)

- **Sinister Views**
  Bearing witness to a tortured past at the Eagle's Nest near Berchtesgaden (p148

- **Warped Fantasy**
  Marvelling at the ludicrous riches of Ludwig's Schloss Linderhof (p132)

- **Getting High**
  Taking a pulse-quickening cable car to the top of the Zugspitze (2964m; p127)

- **I Can See Clearly Now**
  Splashing in the pristine emerald-green lakes of the Tölzer Land (pp134–7)

- POP: 12 MILLION
- AREA: 70,625 SQ KM

Quaint, invigorating and absolutely gorgeous, this Alpine region embraces with a gusto that leaves city-dwellers gasping. The air seems more bracing, the skies blow a cobalt blue and the lakes are ridiculously clean and sparkling. It's enough to convert the most dedicated lummox to the great outdoors.

You'll also find clichés in spades: the thigh-slapping lederhosen lads, the foaming mugs of beer and platters groaning beneath portions of pork roast with sauerkraut. An admirable job is done in exploiting these popular images, but the story is presented with such sincerity that you can't resist playing along.

Much of the region is rural, endowed with the kind of scenery that is the stuff of postcards. Nature and architecture blend harmoniously just about everywhere you look. Overall, people here are patriotic, politically conservative, overwhelmingly Roman Catholic and proud of their traditions.

Though it's an Austrian city, elegant Salzburg is included in this guide for its historical ties and closeness to Bavaria. Mozart's birthplace enjoys the attractions of the nearby Salzkammergut and a prestigious festival that draws masses of classical music-lovers every year. The old town, impossibly charming and picturesque, is deservedly a Unesco World Heritage site.

The region is a paradise for outdoor activities, offering everything from leisurely dips and Alpine hikes to thrilling swooshes through some of Europe's most alluring ski areas.

SALZBURG

☎ 0043-662 (in Germany), 0662 (in Austria, but outside of Salzburg) / pop 147,000

A stone's throw across the German border, Salzburg is blessed with one of Europe's most evocative settings. Bathed in a soft glow, and lorded over by a majestic fortress, its landmark spires, domes and plazas bring the city's heyday to mind, when it settled matters with a wave of the sceptre – not only in the church but also in the fine arts.

Much of the excitement can be explained by a hard-up, hard-partying composer who died desperately young. During his lifetime, Wolfgang Amadeus Mozart wooed many women but actually received precious little support from his home town. But in his eternal shadow there has emerged a Mozartplatz, a Mozarteum music academy, two Mozart museums and even *Mozartkugeln*, a chocolate treat filled with marzipan.

Many English-speakers, however, come to relive an Oscar-winning film: since 1964, the city and nearby hills have been alive to the *Sound of Music*.

HISTORY

Salzburg was the chief town in the region as far back as Roman times. In the 13th century, the bishops were promoted to prince-archbishops, meaning they gained control over an area that stretched into Bavaria and as far as Italy. Their economic power was from mining – of gold, certainly, but even more so of salt, the so-called 'white gold'.

Wolf Dietrich von Raitenau, an influential prince-archbishop, gave Salzburg its baroque look. But that didn't prevent him from being arrested in a dispute with powerful Bavaria over salt. Dietrich conveniently died in prison.

Salzburg pursued a course of neutrality, keeping out of the Thirty Years' War in the 17th century and the War of the Austrian Succession a century later. But by then its power and prosperity were dwindling. France and Bavaria briefly controlled Salzburg before it became part of Austria in 1816.

ORIENTATION

The Salzach River bisects Salzburg's centre. The old town, mostly a pedestrian precinct on the southern bank, is watched over by a hilltop fortress – the Festung Hohensalzburg – and is home to most of the attractions.

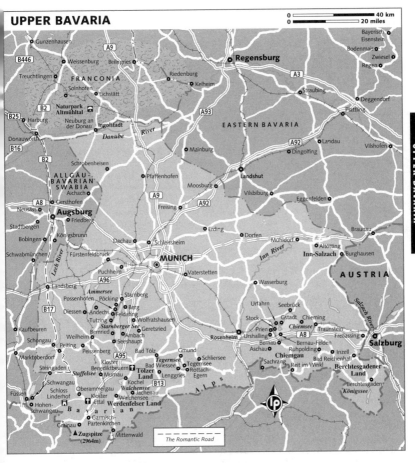

UPPER BAVARIA

The Romantic Road

Mirabellplatz, on the northern bank, is a hub for public and tour buses. The Hauptbahnhof is about 1km north of Mirabellplatz.

INFORMATION
Bookshops
News & Books (☎ 846 390; platform 2a, Hauptbahnhof) Has a good pick of international newspapers and magazines.

Emergency
Ambulance (☎ 144)
Police Headquarters (☎ 133; Rudolfskai 2)

Internet Access
Cybar (☎ 844 822; Mozartplatz 5; per min €0.15; ☺ 10am-11pm) There's a 10-minute minimum at this Internet café, next to the tourist office.

Laundry
Bubble Point Waschsalon (☎ 876 381; Karl-Wumb-Strasse 3; ☺ 7am-11pm) Across from the train station, this modern place charges €4.50 per wash and €2 for the dryer, and has Internet access.

Medical Services
Landeskrankenhaus St-Johanns-Spital (☎ 448 20; Müllner Hauptstrasse 48) District hospital, just north of the Mönchsberg.

Money
Banks in the city centre usually open from 9am to 6.30pm Monday to Friday and until noon on Saturday.
American Express (☎ 808 00; Mozartplatz 5; ☺ 9am-5.30pm Mon-Fri, 9am-noon Sat) Also exchanges money.

AMADEUS, AMADEUS

Wolfgang Amadeus Mozart was only 35 years old when he died in 1791, yet he composed 626 works including operas, symphonies, concertos, string quartets and quintets as well as sonatas for piano and violin. Haydn proclaimed him the 'greatest composer' of all time, and Schubert effused that the 'magic of Mozart's music lights the darkness of our lives'.

Born in Salzburg, Mozart learned how to play the harpsichord at age three. Two years later his father, Leopold, gave a small violin to the child prodigy who, without the benefit of lessons, played well enough a few days later to join a professional quartet. Leopold was quick to exploit his son's astounding talent, taking Wolfgang and his sister Nannerl (four years older and also gifted) on a European concert tour.

At 14, Mozart was appointed director of the archbishop of Salzburg's orchestra. He later settled in Vienna, where he enjoyed his most productive years. Something of a ladies' man, at age 24 Wolfgang boasted, 'If I had married everyone I jested with, I would have well over 200 wives'. A year later Mozart married Constanze Weber, though he fancied her sister too.

In Vienna, Mozart suffered his worst bouts of compulsive gambling – losing large sums in billiards, ninepins and cards. He lived too hard and fast for his own good, ate poorly and attended all-night parties probably like those depicted in the Oscar-winning film *Amadeus* (1985). He lies buried in Vienna's St Marx cemetery; the exact location is not known.

Österreichische Verkehrsbank (☽ 8.30am-7pm Mon-Fri, 8.30am-2.30pm Sat) Fine for changing cash, but save your travellers cheques for American Express.

Post

Post office Altstadt (Residenzplatz 9; ☽ 7am-7pm Mon-Fri, 8am-10pm Sat); Hauptbahnhof (☽ 6am-8.30pm Mon-Fri, 8am-2pm Sat, 1-6pm Sun)

Tourist Information

Salzburg has six tourist office branches, including one at the airport and three on the outskirts near autobahn exits and major highways (open April to October only).

All tourist offices sell a city map for €0.70, although you could just as easily make do with the free *Hotelplan* (hotel map). Offices and hotels also sell the Salzburg Card, which provides museum admission, public transport and a bevy of reductions for everything from car hire to concerts. The card costs €19/€26/€32 for 24/48/72 hours. For telephone and online hotel reservations, general inquiries and requests for printed brochures and information contact **Salzburg Information** (☎ 889 870; www.salzburginfo.at; Auerspergstrasse 7, 5020 Salzburg, Austria).

The most useful offices:

Altstadt tourist office (☎ 8898 7330; Mozartplatz 7; ☽ 9am-7pm Sun Jul & Aug, 9am-6pm Mon-Sat Oct-Apr) A large bustling office that runs like clockwork.

Hauptbahnhof tourist office (☎ 8898 7340; platform 2a; ☽ 8.45am-7.45pm) Tiny and usually packed with bleary-eyed travellers.

Travel Agencies

American Express (☎ 808 00; Mozartplatz 5; ☽ 9am-5.30pm Mon-Fri, 9am-noon Sat) Next to the Altstadt tourist office.

STA Travel (☎ 458 733; Fanny-von-Lehner-Strasse 1; ☽ 9am-6pm Mon-Fri) Student travel agency near the train station.

SIGHTS & ACTIVITIES
Mozart Wohnhaus

Salzburg has not one but two museums dedicated to its famous son: the *Wohnhaus* (residence) and *Geburtshaus* (birthplace; p120). Both museums are popular and feature largely overlapping displays, including musical instruments, sheet music and Mozart memorabilia.

If you've only got time for one, the **Wohnhaus** (☎ 8742 2740; www.mozarteum.at in German; Makartplatz 8; adult/child under 14/youth 15-18/student €6/1.50/2/5; ☽ 9am-6pm Sep-Jun, 9am-7pm Jul & Aug) is the place to see. Once known as the Tanzmeistersaal, this townhouse is where Mozart lived from 1773 to 1780. The music room has been transformed into an exhibit where commentary about his family, travels and achievements is activated by infrared signals and accompanied by musical excerpts. There's also a free film museum with an archive of celluloid images of the maestro.

Schloss Mirabell

This palace was built by the worldly Prince-Archbishop Wolf Dietrich for his mistress in 1606. Its charming gardens have manicured hedges, flowers in fleur-de-lys patterns and groups of statues adorning the pools. The building houses the city administration, but you can peek inside at the marble staircase draped with baroque sculptures. Upstairs, the gilt-and-stucco Marmorsaal (Hall of Marble) is used for weddings and **classical concerts** (tickets ☎ 848 586; www.salzburger-schlosskonzerte.at).

Friedhof St Sebastian

Behind the 16th-century church of St Sebastian in Linzer Gasse is a small **cemetery** dominated by the templelike mausoleum of Prince-Archbishop Wolf Dietrich. In a wonderful piece of arrogance, the cleric commands the faithful to 'piously commemorate the founder of this chapel' (ie himself). The **Mozart family grave** is the third on your left as you walk towards the mausoleum.

Historically the biggest celebrity to be buried here is Paracelsus, the resourceful scientist who's considered the founder of modern medicine. Look for his grave on the steps leading up to the church at the end of the walkway.

Kapuzinerberg

A path winds up from Linzer Gasse to a splendid lookout over the river at the **Kapuzinerkloster**, a weighty-looking monastery dating from 1594. Archbishop Dietrich von Raitenau had it expanded, basically to make himself and Salzburg look good. You hike up past six little 18th-century baroque chapels, and half-way up you encounter the Felixpforte, which announces the first stupendous view over Salzburg. Look for the sign to the lookout 'Hettwer Bastei'.

Festung Hohensalzburg

One of the largest fortresses in Europe, the **Festung Hohensalzburg** (☎ 8424 3011; www.salzburg-burgen.at; Mönchsberg 34; grounds & interior audio tour adult/child €3.60/2; ⏰ 9am-6pm mid-Mar–mid-Jun, 9am-7pm mid-Jun–mid-Sep, 9am-5pm mid-Sep–mid-Mar) is literally Salzburg's high point. Begun in 1077, it was enlarged and modified by various archbishops. The most influential was papal ally Leonhard von Keutschach (r 1495–1519), whose personal motif, the turnip, is strewn about the castle. Wandering through the bishops' lavish staterooms (adorned with a ridiculous amount of gold

studs, Gothic woodcarvings and elaborate ironwork) is like seeing a giant treasure chest from the inside.

The **Burgmuseum** features rambling exhibits on fortress history, the medieval judicial system, military practices and – incongruously – marionettes. Many people get a kick out of the torture chamber that displays 'masks of ridicule' and imaginative tools of the trade. A hands-on display plays period tunes on rare old instruments such as a Turkish snake. Plan about 90 minutes to see it all.

If you don't roam around inside, you can still enjoy the sweeping views over the city and south to the Alps, explore the courtyards and visit the terrace café. The **grounds** (⏰ 9am-7.30pm Jun-Aug, 9am-7pm May & Oct-Mar, 9am-5.30pm Apr) are open slightly longer hours.

Getting to the fortress means either a 15-minute wheeze uphill or a ride aboard the **Festungsbahn** (☎ 8884 9750; Festungsgasse 4; return with admission to grounds adult/child €8.50/4.50). This is Austria's oldest funicular railway (1892) with rides leaving every 10 minutes.

Museum der Moderne

Salzburg's new **Museum der Moderne** (Museum of Modern Art; ☎ 842 220; www.museumdermoderne.at; Mönchsberg 32; adult/child under 15 €8/6, incl Rupertinum €12/8; ⏰ 10am-6pm Tue & Thu-Sun, 10am-9pm Mon & Wed) thrusts the city into the big league of contemporary art spaces. The museum adorns the Mönchsberg 'like a piece of picture frame', enthused the local newspaper *Kurier* at the opening in October 2004. Some locals mumble it looks more like a 'bunker'. Everyone seems to agree, though, that the spacious interiors are attractive and well designed.

Visitors are whisked 60m up the **Mönchsberg lift** (one way/return €1.60/2.60) direct to the museum ticket desk, and proceed via a

---

TOP SALZBURG VIEWS

- **Mönchsberg** (above) – terrace of the Museum der Moderne
- **Festung Hohensalzburg** (left) – former stronghold of archbishops
- **Kapuzinerberg** (left) – a monk's privileged look at Salzburg

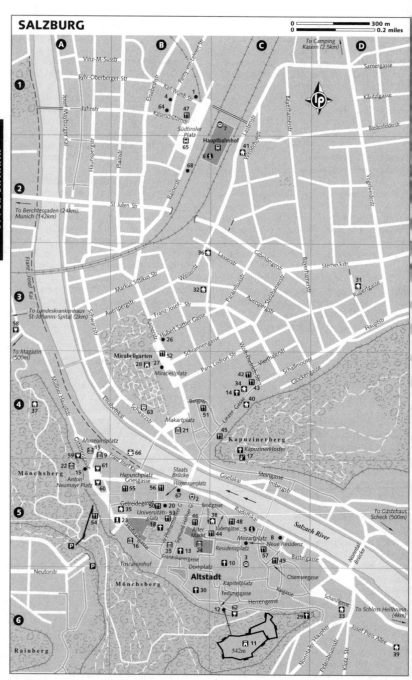

SALZBURG

monumental stairway (or second lift) to four levels of halls in an S-shaped floor plan, with picture windows at regular intervals. The collection spans from modern (eg Cézanne and Monet) to leading lights of the present, such as Sylvie Fleury, Rosemarie Trockel or Heimo Zobernig. This is a challenging exhibit that doesn't rely on household names.

Guided tours are given on Wednesday at 6.30pm (free), plus on Saturday at 2pm and Sunday at 11am (both €2). The terrace of the museum's designer restaurant **M32** (☎ 841 000; mains €5-14; ⏰ 10am-1am) affords stupendous views of Salzburg.

Stift Nonnberg

Founded in around 700 AD the **Stift Nonnberg** (Nonnberg Convent) is the oldest in the German-speaking world. The convent church, in late-Gothic style, is enclosed by a courtyard and dates from the late 15th century. Note the main doorway, with figures of the Virgin Mary flanked by John the Baptist and St Erentrud, the first abbess, on one side and an angel and kneeling nun on the other. There's an ornate high altar and a vast crypt containing the tomb of St Erentrud.

To get here from the fortress, go down via Festungsgasse to the lower station of the funicular, and then into the churchyard on your left.

Dom

The vast **Dom** (cathedral; Domplatz) was one of the earliest baroque churches north of the Alps. There's been a church in this spot since the 8th century, but the current one emerged after 1614 when a fire razed the earlier building. The blueprint foresaw a colossal structure 139m long, but Archbishop Wolf Dietrich opted for a more modest layout in the shape of a cross, with entrances converging on the altar aisle from three sides.

The main façade to the west, made of Salzburg marble, is framed by two symmetrical towers. Below them are four large statues of apostles: Peter (with keys) and Paul (with sword), as well as the patron saints Virgil and Rupert (with salt barrel and church model). The modern bronze doors are decorated with allegories of faith, hope and charity.

Inside the cathedral, it's hard not to be impressed by the rich stucco, paintings and the beautiful dome. Light floods into the dome interior through a ring of windows above striking orange-coloured frescoes.

A descent into the crypt reveals tombs of the prince-archbishops and a Romanesque crucifix. The Romanesque font, meanwhile, is where the infant Mozart was baptized in 1756.

The **Dommuseum** (Cathedral Museum; ☎ 844 189; Domoratorien; adult/child under 18 & student €5/1.50;

10am-5pm Mon-Sat, 11am-6pm Sun, closed Nov-Apr), inside the Dom, contains ecclesiastical treasures and art from as far back as the Middle Ages.

Residenz

The town palace, the **Residenz** (☎ 8042 2690; Residenzplatz 1; adult/child 6-16 incl Residenz Galerie €7.30/2.50; 10am-5pm) is where the archbishops entertained guests. It was also here that Austrian Emperor Franz-Josef received Napoleon III in 1867 and Germany's Kaiser Wilhelm a few years later in 1871.

The self-guided audio tour affords a good look at the extravagant lifestyle of these men of the cloth. The lavish baroque interiors have period furniture and dark, imposing frescoes framed in swirls of stucco.

The tour also gives access to the 15 state rooms of the **Residenz Galerie** (☎ 840 451; gallery only adult/child/student €5/2/4; 10am-5pm Tue-Sun) on the 2nd floor. Gems on display include Dutch and Flemish masters such as Rembrandt, Rubens and Brueghel, as well as by 19th-century Austrian artists such as Waldmüller, Amerling, Makart and Ender.

Franziskanerkirche

Dark and unappealing at first, the **Franziskanerkirche** (Franciscan church), on Franziskanergasse, has a surprise in store: an amazing sunlit hall choir. The roof is upheld by a circle of pillars spilling up into a vaulted canopy, making the whole affair resemble a stone forest. The freestanding high altar is a baroque riot in gold-and-pink marble, integrating an exquisitely carved Madonna.

Stiftskirche St Peter

The church's origin is actually Romanesque (1143), although this is hard to believe given the 18th-century baroque cloak it wears today. The interior is stuffed with rich stucco, flamboyant frescoes and emotive paintings. To the right, in one of the 15 side altars, is a memorial tombstone to composer Johann Michael Haydn, the younger brother of Joseph.

To the rear of the graveyard are the **Katakomben** (catacombs; ☎ 844 5760; adult/child & student €1/0.60; 10.30am-5pm Tue-Sun May-Sep, 10.30am-3.30pm Wed-Thu, 10.30am-4pm Fri-Sun Oct-Apr), hewn out of the rocks of the Mönchsberg and dating from the early days of Christianity.

Rupertinum

Occupying a 17th-century palace, the **Rupertinum** (☎ 842 220; Wiener-Philharmoniker-Gasse 9; adult/child under 15 €6/4, incl Museum der Moderne €12/8; 10am-6pm Tue-Sun, to 9pm Wed Sep-Jun, 10am-6pm Mon-Sun, to 9pm Wed Jul & Aug) is an extension of the Museum der Moderne (p117). Apart from contemporary art exhibits, the Rupertinum prides itself on its collection of paintings by Austrian expressionist Oskar Kokoschka (1886–1980). Also here is the **Austrian Photography Gallery** focusing on 1950s' and '60s' works including those of Inge Morath, master of the celebrity portrait.

Kollegienkirche

Located on Universitätsplatz, the **Kollegienkirche** (Collegiate Church) is considered the crowning achievement of Johann Bernhard Fischer von Erlach, a star architect of the 18th century. For a baroque church its interior is surprisingly austere except for the altar, where puffy clouds billow into the heavens – a special effect of the era. There are chapels dedicated to the patron saints of the four major university faculties: Thomas Aquinas (theology), Ivo (jurisprudence), Luke (medicine) and Catherine (philosophy).

Mozart Geburtshaus

The smaller of the two Mozart museums is the **Geburtshaus** (☎ 844 313; www.mozarteum .at in German; Getreidegasse 9; adult/child under 14/youth 15-18/student €6/1.50/2/5, incl Wohnhaus €9/2.50/3/7; 9am-6pm Sep-Jun, 9am-7pm Jul & Aug), the place of Wolfgang's birth. The musical genius composed nearly all the works of his youth here, during the first 17 years of his life. There's an assortment of instruments, including the little violin he played as a child, as well as manuscripts, letters and family portraits.

Pferdeschwemme

The horse trough known as the **Pferdeschwemme** (Herbert-von-Karajan-Platz) was a fancy drinking spot for the archbishops' mounts. Its centrepiece, a sculpture called *Rossebändiger* (Horse tamer), by Michael Bernhard Mandl, reminds us who was in charge. The backdrop consists of seven frescoes of rearing equine 'pin-ups' including Pegasus, the mythological steed who bucked Bellerophon on his bid to visit the gods on Mt Olympus.

WOLFGANG TURNS 250

When Mozart celebrates a big birthday, Salzburg pulls out all the stops. Busy enough during regular years, in 2006 the Salzburg Festival agenda will bulge to include gala banquets, recitals devoted to the maestro's travel impressions, highlights of his favoured genres (Masses to marionettes), and 'Mozartiades' that combine music, pictures and explanatory chats.

Several key buildings are receiving a make-over in the festival district. The Kleines Schauspielhaus, a famous small theatre and main concert venue of the festival, has been all but razed for a roomier high-tech auditorium **Haus für Mozart** (House for Mozart), due to be unveiled in July 2006.

If you want to reserve tickets for the 2006 festival, by all means don't tarry. Salzburg usually draws about seven million visitors a year, but festival organisers are expecting more than twice that number during the course of 2006.

For online ticket orders check out www.mozart2006.net and for phone orders contact the **Salzburger Festspiele** (Salzburg Festival; ☎ 8045 588).

Haus der Natur

Visitors who make it past the mechanical dinosaur in the **Haus der Natur** (☎ 842 653; Museumplatz 5; adult/child €4.50/2.50; 9am-5pm) will enjoy coral-filled fish tanks, an excellent reptile house and a space hall featuring full-scale rockets. Few labels are in English but the bulk of displays (such as the graphic close-up of open-heart surgery on the 4th floor) require little explanation.

Carolino Augusteum Museum

Pretty much Salzburg's local history museum, the **Carolino Augusteum Museum** (☎ 620 808; Museumsplatz 1; adult/child under 19 & student €3.50/1.10; 9am-5pm Fri-Wed, 9am-8pm Thu) contains a well-presented collection of Roman mosaics, Gothic statues and paintings by local artists. The museum will be closed from October to December 2005 as it relocates to the Neue Residenz palace in the Altstadt (old town). Here it will reopen with a special exhibit called **Viva Mozart** (☎ 620 808; Mozartplatz 1; adult/child under 14 €8/6; audio guide free; 9am-6pm, till 8pm Thu 27 Jan 2006–7 Jan 2007), an interactive birthday party' that takes guests through changing scenes of the great musician's extraordinary life.

TOURS

One-hour **walking tours** (€8; 12.15pm Apr-Oct, closed Sun Nov-Mar) of the Altstadt leave from the tourist office at Mozartplatz. **Top Bike** (☎ 06272-4656; 10am-5pm Apr-Sep, 9am-7pm Jul & Aug) Altstadt (Franz-Josef-Kai 1); Hauptbahnhof (Hauptbahnhof) rents out self-guided audio tours of Mozart sights (€5 for two hours).

The *Sound of Music* tour is enduringly popular with English-speaking visitors,

despite its many detractors. Tour operators include **Salzburg Sightseeing Tours** (☎ 881 616; Mirabellplatz 2) and **Salzburg Panorama Tours** (☎ 874 029; cnr Mirabellplatz & St-Andra-Kirche). Tours depart twice daily, last about four hours and cost €33. **Bob's Special Tours** (☎ 849 511; www.bobstours.com; Rudolfskai 38) takes groups of four to 18 people on minivan tours including the *Sound of Music* (adult/child €35/€29); reserve ahead.

The tour buses stop at film locations including the church at Mondsee (site of Maria and the Baron's wedding), the gazebo in Schloss Hellbrunn (scene of Liesl and Rolf's duet *I Am 16 Going On 17*) and Schloss Leopoldskron (the family home). If you take it lightly, it can be brilliant fun: it's hard to forget manic Julie Andrews impersonators flouncing in the fields, screeching 'the hills are alive' in voices to wake the dead.

Glassed-in tour boats run by **Salzburg Stadt-Schiff-Fahrt** (☎ 825 858; adult/child €10/6; 10am-5pm May & Sep, 9.30am-6pm Jun, 9.30am-7pm Jul & Aug) leave throughout the day from Salzach Insel river dock. The 45-minute tours take in views of Salzburg, and there's a longer tour to Schloss Hellbrunn outside of town.

FESTIVALS & EVENTS

The **Salzburger Festspiele** (Salzburg Festival; ☎ 8045 500; www.salzburgfestival.at; late Jul-end Aug) is the heavyweight on the cultural calendar. It includes concerts ranging from Mozart (of course!) to contemporary music, opera and theatre. Several events take place daily in different locations; ticket prices range from €4 to €360. Demand for tickets usually far exceeds supply, so make reservations early. Other important festivals are the **Oster-festspiele** at Easter, comprising choir and orchestra concerts with the Berliner Philharmoniker and guest ensembles, as well as the **Pfingstkonzerte**, a series of classical concerts on the weekend of Whit Sunday and Pentecost. **Mozartwoche** (Mozart Week) draws conductors, soloists and orchestras of international renown in late January. Tickets and information for all these events are available from **Salzburg Ticket Service** (☎ 840 310; www.salzburgticket.com).

SLEEPING

The *Hotelplan* from the tourist office gives current prices for hotels, pensions, hostels and camp sites. All prices here are quoted for the high season, which usually means during the annual Salzburg Festival from late July to the end of August. Rooms include private bathroom and breakfast unless otherwise mentioned.

For hotel reservations, contact Salzburg Information (p115). The Altstadt tourist office (p115) makes in-person room reservations for only €2.20. The tourist offices also have a list of private rooms (per person from €30), but for those you'll have to make your own reservations.

Budget

Gasthaus Hinterbrühl (☎ 846 798; www.downtown hotel.at; Schanzlgasse 12; s/d/t €37/44/50; breakfast €5) One of the few Altstadt budget options, this place is a bit of a rough diamond but still a gem, built right into the remnants of the old city wall. Up the narrow winding staircase you'll find no-nonsense rooms with shared bathrooms. The downstairs restaurant is as rustic as they come, and if you're lucky you'll see the grizzled angler who delivers the day's catch wrapped in newspaper.

Jugend & Familiengästehaus Salzburg (☎ 8426 700; www.jgh.at; Josef-Preis-Allee 18; d/q/8-bed per person with breakfast €24/18/14; 🖳) This large, modern and busy facility, is definitely the city's most comfortable and central hostel. Salzburg has no shortage of hostels so check with the tourist office if this one is full.

Camping Kasern (☎ 450 576; www.camping-kasern -salzburg.com; Carl-Zuckmayer-Strasse 26; per person/car/tent €4.50/3/3; 🕙 Apr–Oct; 🖳) Chock-full of modern amenities, including guest laundry, cooking facilities and a TV and video room, this camp site is just north of the A1 Nord exit. From

the Hauptbahnhof, take any bus labelled 'Zentrum' to Mirabellplatz. Then cross the road to the corner of Paris-Lodron-Strasse, take bus No 15 towards Kasern-Bergheim and alight at Jägerwirt.

Other recommendations:

Pension Sandwirt (☎ 874 351; fax 874 351; Lastenstrasse 6a; s/d €24/48) Run by possibly the nicest couple on earth, near the train station.

Pension Junger Fuchs (☎ 875 496; Linzer Gasse 54; s/d from €26/38) Good location with few frills, although the rooms are nicer than the cramped hallways suggest.

Midrange

Hotel zur Goldenen Ente (☎ 845 622; www.ente .at; Goldgasse 10; s/d €82/125; 🖳) This charming place, hidden in a back lane of the Altstadt, occupies a 700-year-old house that retains original features such as bare wooden beams and vaulted ceilings in the good on-site restaurant. Its two single and 15 double rooms are tastefully renovated in country-house style with antique furnishings. Touches such as guest bathrobes and big fluffy towels complete the open-arms welcome.

Gästehaus Scheck (☎ 6232 680; www.hotel-scheck .com; Rennbahnstrasse 11; s/d €79/98; 🅿) In a quiet lane, 10 minutes' walk from the old town, this family-run guesthouse has a pretty garden with patio surrounded by mature trees. Furnishings are of a high standard: the private bathrooms shine with classy tile work and some rooms have four-poster beds.

Hotel Amadeus (☎ 871 401; www.hotelamadeus .at in German; Linzer Gasse 43-45; s/d/t €82/150/175) The best of several small hotels along atmospheric Linzer Gasse, Amadeus offers country-style rooms bathed in cheery Mozart-friendly hues right next to the St Sebastian graveyard (p117). All rooms have cable TV, including the few cheaper ones with shared facilities. The breakfast room sparkles in dazzling white and blue.

Centro Hotel (☎ 882 221; www.centro-hotel.at Auerspergstrasse 24; s/d €68/108; 🗶 🖳) Just minutes from Schloss Mirabell, this modern family-friendly hotel pulls in the crowds who appreciate the spacious rooms, shady courtyard and private terraces. Secure child beds and highchairs are available on request. The owner's pooch is cute too.

Other recommendations:

Bergland Hotel (☎ 872 318; www.berglandhotel.at in German; Rupertgasse 15; s/d €56/86) Fine modern rooms, with an Alpine style perkier than most.

Hotel Lasserhof (☎ 873 388; www.lasserhof.com; Lasserstrasse 47; s/d/t from €59/93/108) A cordial, multilingual staff and a mix of modern and rustic furnishings.

Top End
Hotel Goldener Hirsch (☎ 808 40; www.goldener hirsch.com; Getreidegasse 37; d from €145, ste from €292; P X X 🖵) This venerable family-owned inn, close to Mozart's birthplace, dates from 1407. Rooms exude the character of an elegant hunting lodge, with massive oak wardrobes and telephones installed on antique trunks. Little pamperings include a turndown service, and staff happily caters to individual wishes such as infant beds and nonsmoking rooms.

Hotel Schloss Mönchstein (☎ 8485 550; www .monchstein.at in German; Mönchsberg Park 26; r from €251, ste from €375; P X X 🖵) This 17th-century abode of ecclesiastical bigwigs is nestled in a remote corner atop the Mönchsberg. The interiors boast a tasteful mix of modern and period furnishings with bird's-eye views of Salzburg. Intimate meals can be taken in the tiny watchtower that houses one of several fine restaurants. Rich and famous guests have included Russia's Catherine the Great, who gave her hosts one of her royal waistbands as a parting gift.

EATING
From traditional Austrian to pizza and nouvelle cuisine, Salzburg's culinary scene has something to please most palates.

Budget
Stadtalm (☎ 841 729; Mönchsberg 19c; mains €4-11; ⦾ 11am-midnight May-Sep, 11am-7pm Oct-Apr) The place to cool your heels after a bracing hike. From its lofty perch atop the Mönchsberg, the Stadtalm offers some of the best views of Salzburg plus a convivial ambience, good brews and Austrian food. Take the footpath up from near Max-Reinhardt-Platz, or the Mönchsberg lift.

Bio Bistro Spicy Spices (☎ 870 712; Wolf-Dietrich-Strasse 1; mains €4-11; ⦾ 10am-6.30pm Mon-Fri, 10am-1pm Sat) This Indian-vegan joint has chilled music, an abundance of organic options and seasonings that hit all the buttons from gentle to incendiary. Dishes are carefully labelled to ensure vegan integrity.

Café Tomaselli (☎ 844 488; Alter Markt 9; light meals €3-7, coffee & cake €4) Austrians have a refined coffeehouse culture. This most famous café draws a young but intellectual crowd through its doors to the two floors of wood-panelling, chandeliers, and oil paintings in gilded wood frames. Mozart's wife Constanze lived here with her second husband.

Other recommendations:
Café Pepita (☎ 881 576; Linzer Gasse 12; dishes €7-9; ⦾ closed Sun) A symphony of stuffed baguettes and salads.
Café Konditorei Fürst (☎ 843 759; Brodgasse 13; snacks €3-6, coffee & cake €4) Old-time café where *Mozartkugeln* was invented.

Midrange
Marc's (☎ 840 935; Chiemseegasse 5; mains €7-15; ⦾ closed Sun) Legions of trendy young things are drawn by the wine tastings, warm ambience and sophisticated dishes that have an Italo-Austrian accent. Start the evening with a wine aperitif from the bar (400 to choose from) before taking dinner in the tunnel-shaped, vaulted hall.

Zum Eulenspiegel (☎ 843 180; Hagenauerplatz 2; mains €7-21) A shade touristy for sure, but with food this good, who's to complain? The trademark dish is a superb fish soup Provençale (€7.50), and many ingredients come fresher-than-fresh from its own farms. Endless knick-knacks, dark wood-panelling and quaint sayings sell the image of old Austria to great effect.

Zwettler's (☎ 840 044; Kaigasse 3; mains €6-14) Dumplings served in umpteen ways figure

---

AUTHOR'S CHOICE

Sleek and stylish, **Magazin** (☎ 8415 8430; Augustinergasse 13; mains €14-35; ⦾ noon-2pm, 6.30-10pm Tue-Sat) is the first Salzburg restaurant to combine the best of nouvelle cuisine with civil defence. The building is something of an architectural feat that includes an ultrachic, two-storey wine bar and cellar hewn out of the north face of the Mönchsberg. The main dining area offers the biggest surprise, however, a single table with 26 seats in a former air-raid shelter, a tunnel chamber made absolutely romantic by soft backlighting. The menu is brief, innovative and French-inspired, served on beautiful white china like precious works of art. The in-house shop sells a fine assortment of wines, deli goods, cut flowers and cooking utensils. Reservations are advised.

big on the menu of this cosy inn, although its delicious desserts are the real diet disasters. Try *Salzburger Nockerl'n* (a sweet soufflé), *Mohr im Hemd* ('shirted moor'; chocolate cake with whipped cream), *Palatschinken* (pancake with jam) or *Kaiserschmarrn* (shredded pancake).

Sternbräu (☎ 842 140; Griesgasse 23/Getreidegasse 34; mains €8-15) In this labyrinth of themed dining halls you can pick from a supercasual to formal ambience, although in summer you may want to opt for the garden with self-service buffet and pizzeria. Otherwise, the food's mostly Austrian. This is the place that presents the *Sound of Music* dinner show (see right).

Other recommendations:

Ährlich (☎ 871 275; Wolf-Dietrich-Strasse 7; mains €11-17) Creative organic restaurant, not just for veggies.

K&K am Waagplatz (☎ 842 156; Waagplatz 2; mains €11-21) Traditional restaurant with a warren of cosy dining rooms and excellent set meals.

Top End

Pergeo (☎ 870 899; Priesterhausgasse 20; mains €25-41; closed Sat & Sun) This little culinary temple resembles a bistro for a simple bite, but is far from it. From this tiny kitchen unfolds the most carefully thought-out, masterfully prepared dishes such as fresh trout fillets with swirls of horseradish cream and caviar, served with the perfect wine.

Quick Eats & Self-Catering

Eurospar (8am-7pm Mon-Fri, 8am-5pm Sat) is a large supermarket by the Hauptbahnhof with a self-service restaurant. The produce markets on **Mirabellplatz** (Thu morning) and **Universitätsplatz** (7am-7pm Mon-Fri, 6am-3pm Sat) are the best places in town to snack and run – or just to linger at the colourful stands. **Nordsee Imbiss** (Getreidegasse 11; sandwiches €2-5, meals €6-10) is a takeaway heaven with an ice-filled seafood bar.

DRINKING

Beer halls are popular in Salzburg. The area along Rudolfskai near the Stadtsbrücke is a hub of nightlife, including several music clubs and Irish pubs.

Stieglkeller (☎ 842 681; Festungsgasse 10; mains €12-15; 10am-11pm May-Sep) Situated on a steep path at the foot of the fortress, this venerable beer hall and garden (established in 1492) has excellent views of the Altstadt.

The locals head upstairs for self-service beer and the open-air terrace where the beer tastes twice as good.

Republic (☎ 841 613; Anton Neumayr Platz 2; from 8am) This is one of Salzburg's most diverse and energetic bars, in American '50s style with a disco, restaurant, café and a desperately hip clientele. If that isn't enough it also serves breakfast.

Augustiner Bräustübl (☎ 431 246; Augustinergasse 4; 3-11pm Mon-Sat, 2.30-11pm Sun) Monks supply the lubrication at this rambling old pub that's a picture of Austrian *Gesellikeit* (cosiness). You can also buy meat, bread and salads in the deli shops in the foyer, then eat inside or in the large, shady beer garden. The brew is tapped direct from oak barrels.

Other recommendations:

Bar Flip (☎ 843 643; Gsättengasse 17) Dark, cavernous cocktail bar with yellow oil drums for tables.

Humboldt (☎ 843 171; Gsättengasse 4-5) Does a good trade in tapas, cocktails and flirting.

ENTERTAINMENT

You'd have to be either extremely drunk or a serious fanatic to truly appreciate the **Sound of Music show**, which is nonetheless popular. Besides the famous melodies you'll be treated to Austrian folklore tunes once sung by the von Trapps, plus a bit of Mozart and Strauss thrown in for the highbrow crowd. There's even a video interview with Maria von Trapp. All this can be absorbed over a dinner featuring 'schnitzel with noodles and crisp apple strudels' and other menu items inspired by the musical. Performances are at the **Sternbräu Dinner Theatre** (☎ 826 617; Griesgasse 23; dinner & show €43, drink & show €31; 8.30pm May-Oct). Tickets are available at hotels, the tourist offices and the box office.

Not just for kiddies, the **Salzburger Marionettentheater** (☎ 872 406; Schwarzstrasse 24; adult €18-35, child €14; box office 9am-1pm & 2h preperformance) enjoys international renown for the grand operas that are performed with the most extraordinary marionettes. On the programme are not only Mozart standards such as *Don Giovanni, The Marriage of Figaro* or the *Magic Flute,* but also masterworks by Rossini, Tchaikovsky and Prokofiev. The performances are accompanied by world-famous orchestras in majestic rococo surrounds.

GETTING THERE & AWAY
Bus
Regional buses depart from outside the main (west) exit of the Hauptbahnhof and from Mirabellplatz. Bavarian communities served throughout the day include Berchtesgaden (bus No 9450, 45 minutes), and Bad Reichenhall, served about hourly by bus No 9527 (one hour).

Car & Motorcycle
The A8 autobahn connects Munich and Salzburg. If you travel beyond Salzburg on autobahns you'll need to purchase a Vignette, a pass available at petrol stations, rest stops and auto-club offices. A 10-day pass costs €4.30 for motorcycles and €7.60 for cars; if you're caught without it, you'll have to buy a 24-hour pass costing €65/€120 or face an even stiffer fine.

Car-hire agencies in Salzburg include **Avis** (☎ 877 278; Ferdinand-Porsche-Strasse 7), near the Hauptbahnhof, and **Hertz** (☎ 852 086), in the same building around the corner.

Train
Connections are good from Bavarian cities to Salzburg. Regional trains depart from Munich every 30 to 60 minutes (€21, two hours) with stops in the Chiemsee towns of Prien and Bernau, among others. EuroCity (EC) trains make the trip nonstop in 90 minutes (€25). RegionalBahn (RB) trains travel from Bad Reichenhall in 30 minutes (€4.20) and from Berchtesgaden in 45 minutes (€6.90).

GETTING AROUND
Bus
Salzburg is crisscrossed by 19 bus routes. Single-trip tickets are €1.80, day passes (transferable) €3.40, weekly passes €11. Bus drivers only sell single tickets; all others must be bought from vending machines, *Tabak* (tobacco shops) or the tourist offices.

Car & Motorcycle
Driving in the city centre is hard work. Much of the Altstadt is pedestrian-only and parking is limited and expensive. The largest car park near the centre is the Altstadt Garage below the Mönchsberg.

Other Transport
Taxis (☎ 8111) cost €3 at flagfall (€3.70 between 9pm and 6am), plus about €1.50 per kilometre in the centre or €1.80 outside the city.

Top Bike Salzburg (☎ 06272-4656; ☺ 10am-5pm Apr-Sep, 9am-7pm Jul & Aug) Altstadt (Franz-Josef-Kai 1); Hauptbahnhof (Hauptbahnhof) hires out bicycles for two/four hours for €6/€10 and €15 for all day, with discounts for longer periods.

Rates for *Fiaker* (pony-and-trap) for up to four passengers cost about €33 for 25 minutes and €66 for 50 minutes, but you can bargain some drivers down.

UPPER BAVARIA

Upper Bavaria is quite large and diverse, stretching from Ingolstadt in the north to Garmisch-Partenkirchen in the south and Berchtesgaden in the southeast. This is the Bavarian heartland, and many locals are quick to point out that only they are the 'original' Bavarians, unlike the 'newcomer' Franconians and Swabians, who only became Bavarian in the early 19th century. In the west, the Lech River heralds the start of the Allgäu-Bavarian Swabia region.

Although in many villages time seems to stand still, the tourism industry throughout the region is state of the art. Every place has a helpful tourist office, there's good public transport and finding accommodation to suit every budget is almost never a problem.

WERDENFELSER LAND
In the southern Alps of Upper Bavaria, the Werdenfelser Land stretches from the foothills into the shadow of the Karwendel and Wetterstein mountain ranges. Here towers the mighty Zugspitze (2964m), the tallest mountain in Germany. The most well-known towns are the skiing resort of Garmisch-Partenkirchen, and Oberammergau with its famous Passion Play. North of here, Murnau is a nice lakeside resort that was once the home of a famous artists' colony.

Garmisch-Partenkirchen
☎ 08821 / pop 27,500 / elev 708m
The year-round resort of Garmisch-Partenkirchen is a favourite haunt for outdoor enthusiasts. The gateway to the best skiing in Germany, it offers access to three ski fields, including those on Germany's highest

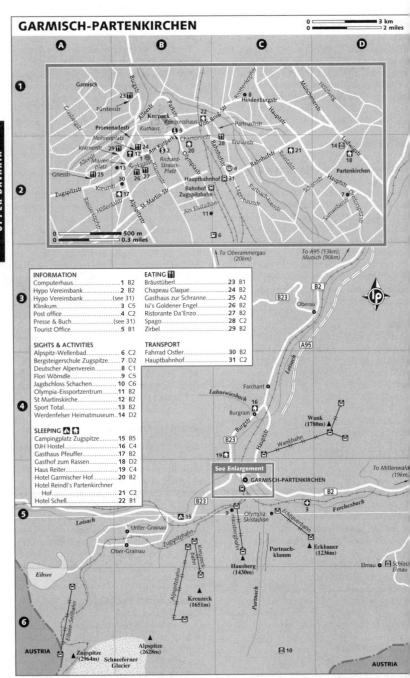

GARMISCH-PARTENKIRCHEN

INFORMATION	
Computerhaus	**1** B2
Hypo Vereinsbank	**2** B2
Hypo Vereinsbank	(see 31)
Klinikum	**3** C5
Post office	**4** C2
Presse & Buch	(see 31)
Tourist Office	**5** B1

SIGHTS & ACTIVITIES	
Alpspitz-Wellenbad	**6** C2
Bergsteigerschule Zugspitze	**7** D2
Deutscher Alpenverein	**8** C1
Flori Wörndle	**9** C5
Jagdschloss Schachen	**10** C6
Olympia-Eissportzentrum	**11** B2
St Martinskirche	**12** B2
Sport Total	**13** B2
Werdenfelser Heimatmuseum	**14** D2

SLEEPING	
Campingplatz Zugspitze	**15** B5
DJH Hostel	**16** C4
Gasthaus Pfeuffer	**17** B2
Gasthof zum Rassen	**18** D2
Haus Reiter	**19** C4
Hotel Garmischer Hof	**20** B2
Hotel Reindl's Partenkirchner Hof	**21** C2
Hotel Schell	**22** B1

EATING	
Bräustüberl	**23** B1
Chapeau Claque	**24** B2
Gasthaus zur Schranne	**25** A2
Isi's Goldener Engel	**26** B2
Ristorante Da'Enzo	**27** B2
Spago	**28** C2
Zirbel	**29** B2

TRANSPORT	
Fahrrad Ostler	**30** B2
Hauptbahnhof	**31** C2

mountain, the Zugspitze (2964m). The towns of Garmisch and Partenkirchen were merged on the occasion of the 1936 Winter Olympics and continue to host key international skiing events. Today, each town retains its own distinct flair: Garmisch has the more cosmopolitan and urban flair, while Partenkirchen preserves more of an old-world Alpine village feel.

Garmisch-Partenkirchen also makes a handy base for excursions to Ludwig II's palaces, including nearby Schloss Linderhof and the lesser known Jagdschloss Schachen.

ORIENTATION

The train tracks that divide the two towns culminate at the Hauptbahnhof. From here, turn west on St-Martin-Strasse to get to Garmisch and east on Bahnhofstrasse to get to Partenkirchen.

INFORMATION

Computerhaus (☎ 0171-602 4876; Klammstrasse; per hr €4; ⏰ 10am-6pm Mon-Fri, 10am-noon Sat) Internet access.

HypoVereinsbank (Am Kurpark 13) There is another branch located in the Hauptbahnhof.

Klinikum (☎ 770; Auenstrasse 6) Hospital in the southeastern corner of town near the Eckbauerbahn valley station.

Post office (Bahnhofplatz)

Presse & Buch (☎ 4400; Hauptbahnhof) Sells around 300 international magazines and newspapers as well as books.

Tourist office (☎ 180 700; www.garmisch-parten kirchen.de; Richard-Strauss-Platz 1, Garmisch; ⏰ 8am-6pm Mon-Sat, 10am-noon Sun) There's an electronic room-reservation board outside, or call the 24-hour automated hotline for room availability.

SIGHTS

Town Centre

In Garmisch, a short walk north of Marienplatz, the 18th-century **St Martinskirche** (St Martin's Church; Kramerstrasse) is decorated with stucco-framed frescoes telling the story of the life of St Martin. Note the pulpit, which shows sculptures of the four evangelists, three virtues and Moses. Enamel name tags on many pews indicate the seats of regular churchgoers.

The heart of Partenkirchen is **Ludwigstrasse**, lined with houses painted in traditional *Lüftlmalerei* style (see the boxed text above). Ludwigstrasse was on a trading route and

---

LÜFTLMALEREI

Throughout Alpine Bavaria you'll find centuries-old houses with façades decorated in a style called *Lüftlmalerei*, a type of trompe l'oeil painting that became popular in the 18th century. The term literally means 'air painting', but is actually derived from the name of the house *'Zum Lüftl'*, which was owned by Oberammergau's Franz Seraph Zwink (1748–92), who pioneered the practice. Images usually have a religious flavour, but some also show hilarious beer hall scenes or other secular themes. The best examples are in Oberammergau.

---

remains the commercial drag in this part of town.

Fires in the 19th century destroyed most of the medieval buildings here. One notable exception is the **Werdenfelser Heimatmuseum** (Werdenfelser Local History Museum; ☎ 2134; Ludwigstrasse 47, Partenkirchen; adult/child €1.50/0.50; ⏰ 10am-1pm Tue-Sun & 3-6pm Tue-Fri). It illustrates the history of the region through exhibits ranging from prehistory to the 20th century. Look for a Madonna sculpture by Ignaz Günther (1725–75), costumes and masks for carnival, Oberammergau woodcarvings and a replica violinmaking workshop.

Zugspitze

Views from Germany's rooftop are quite literally breathtaking, especially during *Föhn* (an intense autumn wind) weather when they extend into four countries. Skiing and hiking are the main activities here and to get to the top, you can walk (see p127), take a cogwheel train or a cable car.

The **Zugspitzbahn** (the cogwheel train) has its own station right behind the Hauptbahnhof. From here it chugs along the mountain base to the Eibsee, a forest lake, then winds its way through a mountain tunnel up to the Schneeferner Glacier (2600m). From here a cable car makes the final ascent to the summit.

Alternatively, the **Eibsee-Seilbahn**, a steep cable car, sways and swings its way straight up to the summit from the Eibsee lake in about 10 minutes (not for the faint-hearted!). Most people come up on the train and take the cable car back down, but it works just as well the other way around. The entire trip

SALZBURG & UPPER BAVARIA

for an adult/child costs €35/€21 in winter and €43/€29.50 in summer. Winter rates include a day ski pass.

Expect serious crowds at peak times in winter and through much of the summer. Skiers may find it easier, but a bit slower, to schlep their gear up on the train, which offers exterior ski-holders.

Jagdschloss Schachen

High in the mountains above Garmisch-Partenkirchen, at a lofty 1866m, the **Jagdschloss Schachen** (Schachen Hunting Lodge; ☎ 2996; adult/child under 14 €2.50/free; ☺ tours 11am & 2pm Jun–Oct) was Ludwig II's little-known hunting lodge. It can be reached via the Partnachklamm (below) in a gruelling four-hour hike, or in three hours from Schloss Elmau. This plain wooden hut has some surprisingly magnificent rooms.

Inside is a Ludwig extravaganza of the first order, especially in the so-called Maurischer Saal (Moorish Room; also known as the Turkish Room) on the 1st floor. It's straight out of *The Thousand and One Nights*, complete with fine carpets, peacock feathers, a fountain and brightly pigmented glass windows. Here, the king escaped to his fantasy world, ordering his servants to don turbans and smoke water pipes. The downstairs is more functional, with a dining room, study, bedroom and chapel.

Partnachklamm

One of the area's main tourist attractions is the magnificent **Partnachklamm** (☎ 3167; adult/child €2/1), a narrow 700m-long gorge with walls rising up to 80m. A circular walk hewn from the rock takes you through the gorge, which is spectacular in winter when you can walk beneath curtains of icicles and frozen waterfalls. You can get there by horse-drawn carriage, bus or on your own two feet.

ACTIVITIES
Skiing

Garmisch-Partenkirchen has the longest ski season in Bavaria, running from November to May in the higher elevations. There are three ski fields: the Zugspitze plateau (2964m), the three-part Classic Ski Area (Alpspitze, 2050m; Hausberg, 1340m; Kreuzeck, 1651m; day pass per adult/child €29/€18.50) and the Eckbauer (1236m; day pass per adult/child €17/€11.50). A Happy

Ski Card (three-day minimum, per adult/child €83/€50) covers all three ski areas plus three other ski areas around the Zugspitze, including Mittenwald (p130). Local buses serve all the valley stations.

Cross-country ski trails run along the main valleys, including a long section from Garmisch to Mittenwald. Call ☎ 797 979 for a weather or snow report.

For ski hire and courses:
Flori Wörndle (☎ 583 00; www.skischule-woerndle.de; Am Hausberg 4, Hausberg)
Sport Total (☎ 1425; www.agentursporttotal.de; Marienplatz 18) It also organises paragliding, mountain biking, rafting and ballooning.

Hiking

Garmisch-Partenkirchen is prime hiking territory and mountain guides are at the tourist office on Monday and Thursday between 4pm and 6pm to give help and information to hikers. At other times brochures and maps with route suggestions for all levels are available.

Hiking to the Zugspitze summit is only possible in the summer months and not recommended for those without mountaineering experience.

For guided hikes and courses:
Bergsteigerschule Zugspitze (☎ 589 99; Dreitorspitzstrasse 13, Partenkirchen)
Deutscher Alpenverein (☎ 2701; Hindenburgstrasse 38, Partenkirchen)

Other Activities

Built for the 1936 Olympics, the **Olympia Eissportzentrum** (☎ 753 291; Am Eisstadion; adult/child €3.80/2.20) is one of the largest ice-skating complexes in Germany with one large and two smaller rinks. Besides skating you can play hockey and curling. It's open daily, but check for skating times.

The **Alpspitz-Wellenbad** (☎ 753 313; Klammstrasse 47; adult/child per 3hr €4.50/2.50, all day €6/3.40; ☺ 9am–9pm Mon-Sat, 9am-7pm Sun) is a fun pool with waves and a large sauna landscape.

FESTIVALS & EVENTS

Garmisch-Partenkirchen hosts many big skiing and jumping competitions, but on 6 January the focus is on the quirky **Hornschlittenrennen**. About 100 teams of four daredevils each race down a 1200m-long narrow ice track aboard historic wooden sledges, competing for the title of Bavarian

Champion. It's a fun event that each year attracts as many as 10,000 spectators.

The highlight of the cultural calendar is the **Richard-Strauss-Tage** in June, a music festival honouring the composer, who had a villa here from 1908 until his death in 1949. **Concerts** (tickets ☎ 752 545) featuring top international talent take place throughout town.

SLEEPING

There is an electronic outdoor room-reservation board at the tourist office and a 24-hour **reservation hotline** (☎ 194 12).

Hotel Reindl's Partenkirchner Hof (☎ 9438 520; www.reindls.de; Bahnhofstrasse 15, Partenkirchen; s €72-135, d €120-220; P ⊠ 🖳 🖳) It doesn't get much better than this – an elegant, three-winged luxury hotel stacked with perks, a wine bar and a top-notch restaurant. Its country-style rooms have touches of royalty and splendid mountain views.

Hotel Schell (☎ 9575; www.hotel-schell.de; Partnachauenstrasse 3, Partenkirchen; s/d from €25/45; P) This traditional Alpine home is a real winner for its friendly service and spotless, good-value rooms. It's close to the Hauptbahnhof but very quiet and children and adults alike will enjoy the garden.

Gasthof zum Rassen (☎ 2089; www.gasthof-rassen.de in German; Ludwigstrasse 45, Partenkirchen; s €32-53, d €52-90; P ⊠) Bright, modern rooms contrast with the traditional lobby of this beautifully frescoed 14th-century building. A former brewery, the massive event hall houses the oldest *Bauerntheater* (peasants' theatre) in Bavaria.

Hotel Garmischer Hof (☎ 9110; www.garmischer-hof.de; Chamonixstrasse 10, Garmisch; s €55-75, d €84-124; P 🖳) This top-notch establishment has contemporary rooms, some with Zugspitze views, and lots of amenities. Children are welcome and the downstairs restaurant, although a bit stuffy, comes recommended.

Campingplatz Zugspitze (☎ 3180; www.zugspitzcamping.de in German; Griesener Strasse 4, Grainau; per tent/person/vehicle €3/5/3) The camp site nearest to Garmisch has good sanitary and cooking facilities and the Alps on its doorstep. It's along the B23 towards Grainau. Take the blue-and-white bus outside the Hauptbahnhof in the direction of the Eibsee.

Other recommendations:

Haus Reiter (☎ 2223; www.reiter-gap.com; Burgstrasse 55; s €20-30, d €40-60; P ⊠) Chalet-style guesthouse with modern rooms and garden.

Gasthaus Pfeuffer (☎ 2238; fax 4617; Kreuzstrasse 9, Garmisch; d €40-60; P) Central and simple guesthouse with cable TV.

DJH hostel (☎ 2980; www.jugendherberge.de/jh/garmisch in German; Jochstrasse 10; B&B with linen €15.85-16.45) A modern 200-bed facility in a gorgeous spot, set to reopen in September 2005.

EATING & DRINKING

Isi's Goldener Engel (☎ 948 757; Bankgasse 5, Garmisch; mains €8-18) This local favourite has wacky décor that blends frescoes, stags' heads and a gilded stucco ceiling. The huge menu selection ranges from simple schnitzel to game dishes, though the best deal is the generous lunch special.

Spago (☎ 966 555; Partnachstrasse 50, Partenkirchen; mains €6-8) This trendy café and restaurant, just off the main drag, makes a nice change from all the tradition. The slick design, outdoor seating area and international menu serve a local clientele rather than the tourist rabble.

Ristorante Da'enzo (☎ 722 26; Bankgasse 16, Garmisch; mains €5.50-17) Tables inside and out throng with fresh-faced punters at this popular local winner for fine Italian cooking. The menu includes excellent pasta and pizza as well as delicious fish and meat dishes.

Bräustüberl (☎ 2312; Fürstenstrasse 23, Garmisch; mains €5-17) This place, a bit outside the centre, is quintessential Bavarian, complete with enormous enamel coal-burning stove and dirndl-clad waitresses. The dining room is to the right, the beer hall to the left.

Chapeau Claque (☎ 713 00; Mohrenplatz 10, Garmisch; meals €5-9) Do stop at this cosy and very French wine bar-bistro with soft lighting and friendly service. Meals include various potato dishes, soups and baguette sandwiches.

Other recommendations:

Zirbel (☎ 7671; Promenadestrasse 2, Garmisch; meals €4-14) Relaxed, tunnel-shaped pub serving snacks and small meals.

Gasthaus zur Schranne (☎ 1699; Griesstrasse 4, Garmisch; mains €8-14; 🕑 closed Thu) Atmosphere-laden tavern featuring regional snacks and daily specials.

Berggaststätte Schachenhaus (☎ 2996) Serves food and drink, and has simple sleeping quarters.

GETTING THERE & AROUND

Garmisch is serviced by hourly trains from Munich (€14.70, 1½ hours) and special packages combine the return trip with a

Zugspitze day ski pass. RVO bus No 1084 travels to Oberstdorf with stops at the Wieskirche, Neuschwanstein and Hohenschwanstein and then Füssen. The A95 from Munich is the direct road route.

Bus tickets cost €1 for journeys in town. For bike hire try **Fahrrad Ostler** (☎ 33 62; Kreuzstrasse 1, Garmisch; per day €10-14).

Mittenwald

☎ 08823 / pop 8300 / elev 913m

Stunningly picturesque Mittenwald, 20km southeast of Garmisch-Partenkirchen, was a famous violinmaking centre long before the first tourists ever arrived. Nowadays the sleepy village is a favourite Alpine getaway for weary urban types, with its clear air and snow-capped peaks. The narrow, winding streets reveal Alpine views at every corner and the ornate gables and beautifully frescoed walls give it a charming, but authentic, feel.

INFORMATION

HypoVereinsbank (Obermarkt 30)
Post office (Bahnhofsplatz 1) Opposite the train station.
Tourist office (☎ 339 81; www.mittenwald.de in German; Dammkarstrasse 3; ⏰ 8am-5pm Mon-Fri, 9am-noon Sat, 10am-noon Sun May-Sep only)

SIGHTS

Action in the centre revolves around the **Pfarrkirche St Peter und Paul** (Church of St Peter and Paul), standing at the eastern end of Obermarkt like the dot in an exclamation mark. It has a rather jolly steeple with a helmet-shaped copper top and a painted façade. Inside, take a sec to view the colourful frescoes starring the church's patron saints, Peter and Paul.

The **Geigenbaumuseum** (Violinmaking Museum; ☎ 2511; Ballenhausgasse 3; adult/concession €2.50/1.50; ⏰ 10am-1pm daily & 3-6pm Tue-Fri) displays 200 instruments from the violin family, from kiddie models to the contrabass. Matthias Klotz (1653–1743) is the man credited with turning Mittenwald into a centre of violinmaking. His grandson fashioned an instrument Mozart played and a violinmaking school still exists today.

West of here, **Obermarkt** is lined by stately houses decorated with *Lüftlmalerei* (see the boxed text on p127). Note especially **Gasthaus Alpenrose** (Obermarkt 1), which uses secular themes to convey a religious message: at the bottom are the four virtues, in the middle the five senses and on top the Virgin Mary ringed by angels and saints. The **Neunerhaus** (Obermarkt 24) is another eyecatcher.

Special events in Mittenwald include Fasnacht (carnival) held in late February or early March, when locals in traditional masks, handed down through families over centuries, mix old rituals with modern celebrations and attempt to drive out winter.

ACTIVITIES
Hiking
Mittenwald is an excellent place for hiking. Popular local hikes with cable-car access go to the Alpspitze (2628m), the Wank (1780m), Mt Karwendel (2384m) and the Wettersteinspitze (2297m). Return tickets to the Karwendel, which boasts Germany's second-highest cable-car route cost €19/€11 per adult/child.

A easy walk runs through the **Leutaschklamm** (Leutasch Gorge; admission free; ⏰ 9am-6pm mid-May–late Oct). In June and July, the light creates a pretty rainbow reflected in a waterfall, which you can see if you start out early. It's 11km return and takes two to three hours. The path goes to Leutasch in Austria, so bring a passport.

The gondola of the **Karwendelbahn cable car** (☎ 5396, 8480; adult/child one-way €12.50/9, return €20/11.50; ⏰ 8.30am-5pm) takes you to Germany's second-highest mountain station at 2244m. Running times depend on the season and weather. From there, it's a six- to eight-hour hike across eight peaks over 2000m, offering wonderful panoramic views.

Skiing
The Karwendel ski field has one of Germany's longest runs (7km). A major adrenalin rush for advanced skiers is the 7km **Dammkar run** (☎ 8480; day passes adult/child €27/18; ⏰ 9am-4.30pm), the country's first free-riding ski area (unprepared pistes), reached via a 400m tunnel from the Karwendelbahn mountain station.

Beginner and intermediate skiers will probably find the Kranzberg (1400m) more to their liking. The **Kranzbergbahn chairlift** (☎ 1553; day passes adult/child €19/13; ⏰ 9am-4.30pm) ferries skiers to the St Anton station, where you can return to the valley or take T-bar lifts to other runs. There are also combined day ski passes covering the Karwendel and Kranzberg fields.

For equipment hire and ski or snowboard instruction, contact the **Erste Skischule Mittenwald** (☎ 3582; Bahnhofsplatz). A three-hour ski lesson costs €30, with rates lower from the second day.

SLEEPING & EATING

There are only a few hotels and restaurants in town.

Hotel-Gasthof Alpenrose (☎ 927 00; www.alpenrose-mittenwald.de; Obermarkt 1; s €25-35, d €50-70; mains €7.50-15; P) This is the town gem, an ornate 18th-century inn with cosy rooms and old-style eating. Live Bavarian music is played almost nightly.

Gästehaus Sonnenbichl (☎ 922 30; www.sonnenbichl-tourismus.de; Klausnerweg 32; s/d €44/88; P) This four-storey, English-speaking guesthouse is on a gentle slope five minutes' walk from the centre. It has stupendous views of the Karwendel, a wonderful terrace and a pretty garden falling away into the valley. Rooms are in extraspacious country style.

Gröblalm (☎ 9110; www.groeblalm.de in German; Gröblalm 1-2; s €33-52, d €62-87) For peace and quiet head to Gröblalm, a sprawling mountain lodge that combines rustic Alpine décor with health club perks including a sauna and solarium. The restaurant has heaps of local colour and the views across the valley are superb.

Restaurant Arnspitze (☎ 2425; Innsbrucker Strasse 68; mains €15.50-23; closed Tue) For local gourmet fare head to this star-laden restaurant, about 1km south of town. The menu features gems such as locally caught whitefish but also fusion-style fare. It has a nice two-bed apartment (€34 per night) for short stays.

The **DJH hostel** (☎ 1701; www.jugendherberge.de/jh/mittenwald in German; Buckelwiesen 7; dm €15.85-16.45; closed mid-Nov–late Dec) is rather inconveniently located 4km north of town.

GETTING THERE & AWAY

Mittenwald is served by hourly trains from Munich (€17.10, two hours), Garmisch-Partenkirchen (€3.30, 22 minutes) and Innsbruck (€8.90, one hour).

RVO bus No 9608 connects Mittenwald with Garmisch-Partenkirchen (30 minutes) several times a day though the timetable changes frequently.

Oberammergau

☎ 08822 / pop 5400 / elev 850m

Some 20km north of Garmisch-Partenkirchen lies Oberammergau, a study in genuine piety as well as religious kitsch and commercialism. It's also a crafts centre, noted for its woodcarvings and glass paintings. Set in a wide valley surrounded by forest and mountains, this undeniably beautiful village is packed with souvenir shops and tourists.

For information visit the **tourist office** (☎ 923 10; www.oberammergau.de; Eugen-Papst-Strasse 9a; 8.30am-6pm Mon-Fri, 9am-5pm Sat, 1-5pm Sun mid-Jun–mid-Oct, 8.30am-6pm Mon-Fri, to noon Sat mid-Oct–mid-Jun). Staff can help find accommodation.

SIGHTS & ACTIVITIES

Oberammergau is famous for its epic **Passion Play**, performed by the townspeople every decade (the next one is in 2010) since 1634 to give thanks for being spared from the plague. Tours of the **Passionstheater** (☎ 923 10; Passionswiese 1; tour adult/child €2.50/1; tours 9.30am-5pm May-Oct, 10am-4pm Nov-Apr) include a history of the play and a peek at the costumes and sets. In the years between the Passion Plays spectacular opera events are held once a month between July and September. Ask at the tourist office for details.

The town's other claim to fame are the eye-popping house façades painted in *Lüftlmalerei* (see the boxed text on p127). Images usually have a religious flavour, but some also show hilarious beer hall scenes or fairy-tale motifs, such as *Hansel & Gretl* at Ettaler Strasse No 41, and *Little Red Riding Hood* at Ettaler Strasse 48. The *pièce de résistance*, however, is the **Pilatushaus** (☎ 923 10; Ludwig-Thoma-Strasse 10; admission free; 1-6pm Mon-Fri May-Oct), which also contains a gallery and several workshops.

Oberammergau is also famous for its intricate woodcarvings, a tradition that harkens back to the Middle Ages. American pop artist Jeff Koons used to order carvings from Oberammergau craftsmen to use as the basis of his own creations. About 120 active artisans chisel away in workshops around town, churning out everything from saints and angels to animals and corkscrews. Opening its doors to visitors is Oberammergau's prestigious **Schnitzschule** (Carving School; ☎ 35 42; Ludwig-Lang-Strasse 3; admission free; 9-11am Tue &

Thu). It's closed during school holidays and exam periods.

Some of the most accomplished work can be seen in the newly revamped **Oberammergau Museum** (☎ 941 36; Dorfstrasse 8; adult/child €3/1; ◷ 10am-5pm Tue-Sun) and at **Pfarrkirche St Peter und Paul** (Herkulan-Schwaiger-Gasse 5), which has a graveyard chock-full of elaborate headstones and crosses.

About 1.5km east of the town centre is the valley station of the **Laber-Bergbahn** (☎ 47 70; Ludwig-Lang-Strasse 59; adult/child one-way/return €8/12.50; ◷ 9am-4.30pm Sep-Jun, 9am-5.30pm Jul & Aug). This gondola ferries hikers, skiers and sightseers to the peak of Mt Laber (1684m), which also has a restaurant and gorgeous views of the valley and Alps. Day ski passes for adult/child cost €34/€21, and half-day passes are available.

Oberammergau is also favoured for **hiking** and **cycling**. Popular nearby destinations include Linderhof (12km) and Ettal (5km). The tourist office can make suggestions and sells maps.

SLEEPING & EATING

Gasthof zur Rose (☎ 4706; www.hotel-oberammergau.de; Dedlerstrasse 9; s/d €35/58; mains €8-16; ◷ restaurant closed Mon) This is a beautifully kept traditional inn, rustic but with modern amenities in a quieter side street. The restaurant specialises in fish and venison.

Hotel Alte Post (☎ 9100; www.ogau.de; Dorfstrasse 19; s €45-68, d €65-85; mains €8-16; P ☒ ☲) In the centre of town, this cute place with frescoed façade has been an inn since 1612. It has a popular restaurant, and some rooms overlook the bustling main street and terrace café.

DJH hostel (☎ 4114; www.jugendherberge.de/jh/oberammergau in German; Malensteinweg 10; B&B with linen €15.35; ◷ closed mid-Nov–late Dec) The hostel is about a 15-minute walk south of the Bahnhof, on the western bank of the Ammer. This well-run, 132-bed facility is as clean as a whistle and perfectly located for enthusiasts of Alpine hiking and skiing.

Gasthaus zum Stern (☎ 867; Dorfstrasse 33; Brotzeit €4-8.50, mains €7-13) The fare here is stick-to-the-ribs Bavarian but includes less-common game such as rabbit goulash. The house also serves *Hasenbräu* (rabbit brew) in the comfy dining room and beer garden.

La Montanara (☎ 6258; Schnitzlergasse 10; pizzas €2.50-7.50, mains €5-15) This trattoria has a

cheerful wine-themed décor, serves pizzas and offers a full menu of meat dishes.

GETTING THERE & AROUND

Hourly trains connect Munich with Oberammergau with a change at Murnau (€14.60, 1¾ hours). RVO bus No 9606 operates between Oberammergau and both Garmisch-Partenkirchen and Füssen almost hourly. You can hire mountain bikes at **Ammergauer Radlladen** (☎ 14 28; Schnitzlergasse 12) for €13 per day.

Ettal

☎ 08822 / pop 850 / elev 877m

About 5km south of Oberammergau lies tiny Ettal, which would be another turn in the road but for its famous monastery **Kloster Ettal** (☎ 740; admission free; ◷ 8am-6pm). Ludwig der Bayer founded the place in 1330 out of gratitude for surviving a trip to Rome. He brought along a marble Madonna, now the monastery's prize possession and part of the high altar. A fire devastated most of the old Gothic structure but all was rebuilt in the sugary rococo style you see today.

This imposing complex has a vast courtyard, weighty dome and a façade wearing larger-than-life-sized statues of the apostles. As you enter through the Gothic portal, note the tympanum above the entrance showing the Crucifixion, with Ludwig der Bayer and his wife looking on.

In the nave all eyes are drawn to the ceiling, caused by a visual trick of the era. The dome fresco shows a hearty celebration of the Trinity by St Benedict and his followers, with (count them) 431 individual figures. The painting then blends cleverly into the stucco. You'll see more such tricks by master artist Zimmermann at the Wieskirche (p259) .

The monastery still has about 50 to 60 Benedictine monks in residence. They're an enterprising bunch who manage not only a prestigious boarding school, but also a publishing business, a hotel-restaurant, brewery and distillery. The famous Ettaler Klosterlikör comes from here.

If you need information or help with finding a place to stay, drop by the **Verkehrsamt** (☎ 3534; Ammergauer Strasse 8; ◷ 8am-noon Mon-Fri).

Schloss Linderhof

The pocket-sized palace of **Schloss Linderhof** (☎ 08822-920 30; adult/child Apr–mid-Oct €6/5, mid-

Oct–Mar €4/3; parking €2; 9am-6pm Apr–mid-Oct, 10am-4pm mid-Oct–Mar), about 13km west of Oberammergau, is probably also Ludwig II's most magnificent. Finished in 1878, the Linderhof hugs the hillside in a fantasy landscape of French gardens, fountains and follies. The reclusive Ludwig used the palace as a retreat and hardly ever received visitors here. Like Herrenchiemsee (p139), Linderhof was inspired by Versailles and dedicated to Louis XIV, Ludwig's idol.

Linderhof is full of unbelievable treasures and myth-laden frescoes, evidence of the king's creativity as well as his ostentatious taste. The largest room is his **private bedroom**, heavily ornamented and centred on an enormous 108-candle crystal chandelier weighing 500kg. An artificial waterfall, built to cool the room in summer, cascades just outside the window. The **dining room** reflects the king's fetish for privacy and new invention; its central fixture is a 'magic table' that sinks through the floor to the kitchen, allowing Ludwig to dine without seeing his servants.

The gardens and outbuildings, which are open April to October, are as fascinating as the castle itself. The highlight is the oriental-style **Moorish Kiosk** where Ludwig, often dressed in oriental costume, presided over late-night entertainment from an elaborate peacock throne. Also worth a visit is the **Venus Grotto**, an artificial stalactite cave inspired by a stage set for Wagner's *Tannhäuser*. Underwater lighting illuminates the room and Ludwig's conch-shaped boat with cherub prow.

Bus No 9622 makes the trip out to Linderhof from Oberammergau twice daily on weekdays and four times at weekends, while RVO bus No 9606 comes from Garmisch-Partenkirchen (€6.50, 1½ hours).

Murnau
☎ 08841 / pop 11,000 / elev 700m

Murnau, about 25km north of either Garmisch or Oberammergau, lost its medieval look to a raging fire in the mid-19th century, but made its mark decades later as a cradle of the modern art movement. It all began in 1909 when the painter Gabriele Münter (1877–1962), a friend of Wassily Kandinsky, bought a simple country house in this town on the Staffelsee, a large lake. Until the outbreak of WWI in 1914, the

two spent their summers here together, often joined by fellow artists including Alex Jawlensky, August Macke, Franz Marc and other avant-gardists. Their gatherings ultimately led to the founding, in 1911, of the artists' group Der Blaue Reiter (The Blue Rider) by Kandinsky and Marc. Marc later moved to the nearby Kochelsee (p136).

Münter, herself no slouch in the artistic sphere, stayed in Murnau until her death. During the Nazi era, she fiercely safeguarded an amazing treasure trove of paintings, especially Kandinsky's, which were considered 'degenerate' by the regime. In 1957, she donated her entire collection to the Städtische Galerie im Lenbachhaus (p70) in Munich.

ORIENTATION & INFORMATION
Murnau's Bahnhof and main bus station is about 700m northwest of the town centre. Take Bahnhofweg to Bahnhofstrasse south, which gets you to Gabriele-Münter-Platz and the tourist office. One block east is Obermarkt, the main artery, with the Schlossmuseum up on a low hill. The Staffelsee is about 1km west of Obermarkt. For information, stop by the **tourist office** (☎ 614 10; www.murnau.de; Kohlgruber Strasse 1; 8.30am-noon & 2-6pm Mon-Fri, 8.30am-noon Sat May-Oct, 8.30am-5pm Mon-Fri, 9am-noon Sat Nov-Apr).

SIGHTS & ACTIVITIES
The **Gabriele-Münter-Haus** (☎ 628 880; Kottmüllerallee 6; adult/child under 18 €2.50/free; 2-5pm Tue-Sun), south of the tourist office via Burggraben, was recently restored to the time when Münter lived there with Kandinsky. Highlights include the furniture that the two of them painted, as well as an amazing staircase decorated by Kandinsky. Two rooms focus on the book *The Blue Rider Almanac,* a collection of essays and illustrations that was a ground-breaking manifesto on avant-garde art.

One of Murnau's geographical features that attracted many artists was the pleasant **Staffelsee** and its seven islands. The lake's clear water is among the warmest in the region, making it ideal for swimming. You can also cycle or walk around its 18km circumference or hire row or pedal boats (from €4 per hour for row boats and €6 per hour for pedal boats). From May to October, boats shuttle between the three lake communities (Murnau, Seehausen and Uffing) four times daily. The entire round trip costs €7/€3.50.

Back in town, attractions include the **Schlossmuseum** (☎ 476 207; Schlosshof 4-5; adult/child €3.50/1.50; 🕑 10am-5pm Tue-Sun Oct-Jun, 10am-6pm Tue-Sun Jul-Sep), with permanent exhibits about Der Blaue Reiter, Münter's later works, the writer Ödon von Horváth, the history of the palace, Murnau landscapes and painted glass. Also worth a look is the **Münter-Brunnen**, a modern fountain on Gabriele-Münter-Platz by the local sculptor Hansi Angerer. It recreates the floor plan of the Münter Haus, with the Kandinsky staircase as its focal point.

SLEEPING & EATING

Gasthof Alter Wirt (☎ 1434; www.alter-wirt-murnau .de in German; Untermarkt 12; s/d €29/56; wheelchair access) This old inn in the pedestrian centre has traditional Bavarian rooms with classy old hardwood furnishings. There's a good in-house restaurant downstairs.

Griesbräu (☎ 1422; www.griesbraeu.de; Obermarkt 37; s/d €40/70; meals €6-12; 🕑 restaurant closed Mon & Tue; wheelchair access) This popular brewpub serves its wonderful, amber-coloured Weissbier alongside the brewing vats in the back courtyard. It also serves meaty stuff such as roast piglet and chicken, and there's a country restaurant.

GETTING THERE & AWAY

Direct RB trains go hourly to Munich (€11.50, one hour), Garmisch-Partenkirchen (€4.30, 26 minutes) and Oberammergau (€4.30, 40 minutes). To get to Kochel, take RVO bus No 9611 (40 minutes), which has departures almost hourly. Murnau is on the B2.

TÖLZER LAND

The Tölzer Land, some 50km south of Munich, is a fabulous outdoor playground anchored by two beautiful Alpine lakes – the Walchensee and the Kochelsee – and centred on the spa town of Bad Tölz (below). Its gorgeous landscape has attracted many artists including Blue Rider member Franz Marc, he of *The Blue Horses* fame.

Bad Tölz

☎ 08041 / pop 17,700 / elev 659m

Bad Tölz is a beautiful town in a beautiful location. Its sloping main street winds its

way through frescoed houses and a host of quaint shops, bars and cafés. The town, known mainly for its spas, is a favourite day trip for Munich residents who come for its giant swimming complex, Alpine slide and rafting trips down the Isar River. It's also the gateway to the Tölzer Land region.

Every year on 6 November, the town celebrates the patron saint of horses, Leonhard, with the famous **Leonhardifahrt**, a pilgrimage up to the Leonhardi chapel on Kalvarienberg. It features townsfolk dressed in traditional lederhosen and fancy dirndls, brass bands and up to 80 flower-festooned horse-drawn carts.

ORIENTATION

The Isar separates the town's spa quarter in the west from the Altstadt in the east. The train station is near the eastern edge of town, about a 20-minute walk from the river.

INFORMATION

City tourist offices (☎ 786 70; www.bad-toelz.de in German; 🕑 9am-noon Mon-Sat & 2-5.30pm Mon-Fri) Heimatmuseum (Markstrasse 48; 🕑 closed noon-2pm Mon-Fri); Max-Höfler-Platz (**Max-Höfler-Platz 1**) Book accommodation and organise tours.

Tölzer Land tourist office (☎ 505 206; www .toelzer-land.de in German; Professor-Max-Lange-Platz 1) For regional information.

SIGHTS & ACTIVITIES

Cobblestoned and car-free, the **Marktstrasse** gently slopes through the Altstadt flanked by statuesque townhouses with painted façades and overhanging eaves. It is also home to the **Heimatmuseum** (☎ 504 688; Marktstrasse 48; adult/child €2/1; 🕑 10am-noon & 2-4pm, closed Mon). The sprawling exhibit touches on practically all aspects of local culture and history. Look out for the displays of painted armoires – the so-called Tölzer Kisten – as well as beer steins, folkloric garments and some pretty odd religious items.

In a side alley a few steps south of Marktstrasse, through Kirchgasse, is the **Pfarrkirche Maria Himmelfahrt** (Church of the Assumption; ☎ 761 260; Frauenfreithof), a late-Gothic, three-nave hall church with some brilliantly painted glass windows and an expressive floating Madonna. Wandering down Marktstrasse, you'll soon spot the baroque **Franziskanerkirche** (Franciscan Church; ☎ 769 60; Franziskanergasse

) across the Isar. Flanked by lovely gardens, its stark whitewashed interior is enlivened by several beautiful altars.

Above the town, on Kalvarienberg, looms Bad Tölz' landmark, the twin-towered **Kalvarienbergkirche** (Cavalry Church). This enormous baroque church, with its large central staircase, is also the site of the tiny **Leonhardikapelle** (Leonhardi Chapel; 1718), the destination of the Leonhardi pilgrimage.

In the spa section of town, west of the Isar River, you'll find the fantastic complex **Alpamare** (☎ 509 991; www.alpamare.de; Ludwigstrasse 14; 4hr pass adult/child €23/17, day pass €30/20; ☺ 9am-9pm Mon-Thu, 9am-10pm Fri-Sun). The huge centre has heated indoor and outdoor mineral pools, a wave and surfing pool, and a series of wicked waterslides (including Germany's longest, the 330m-long Alpabob-Wildwasser). Though you could, of course, opt to just relax in the saunas and solariums before retiring to the hotel (rooms from €112). There's a bus stop on Wilhelmstrasse nearby, served almost hourly from the Hauptbahnhof 3km away. Parking is free.

About 3km southwest of the old town, the 'Blomberg' (1248m) is a family-friendly mountain with a natural toboggan track in winter and fairly easy hiking and a fun Alpine slide in summer.

The **Alpine slide** is a fibreglass track that snakes over a kilometre down the mountain from the middle station. You ride down through the 17 hairpin bends on little wheeled bobsleds that have a joystick to control braking (push forward to go, pull back to brake). You can reach speeds of up to 50km/h, but chances are if you do, you're going to either ram a rider ahead of you or fly off the track. If you do try for speed, wear a long-sleeved shirt and jeans.

Unless you're walking, getting up the hill involves a chairlift ride aboard the **Blombergbahn** (☎ 3726; top station adult/child return €7/3, midday one-way €2; ☺ 9am-6pm May-Oct, to 4pm Nov-Apr weather permitting). Riding up to the midway station and sliding down costs €4/€3 per adult/child, with discounts for multiple trips. In winter, day passes that are good for skiing or toboggan track are €15/€13 per adult/child; sledges are hired out for €3 per day.

GETTING THERE & AWAY

Bad Tölz has hourly train connections with Munich on the private Bayerische Oberlandbahn (BOB; €10.20, one hour). Alternatively, take the S-Bahn line S2 from central Munich to Holzkirchen, then change to the BOB.

Walchensee

☎ 08858 / pop 500

Both the Kochelsee and the Walchensee are crystal-clear Alpine lakes, encircled by a spectacular mountainous landscape. Of the two, the latter is considerably larger, more accessible and offers a greater spectrum of water-sports activities. Its pebbled beaches are crowded with swimmers and sun worshippers in the summer months, when water temperatures max out at a tolerable 23°C.

Rumours of Nazi treasure buried in the depth of the lake continue to draw divers, but the lake's real fame is as a hot spot of the windsurfing scene. This is due to a peculiar microclimate, which generates strong breezes during fine-weather days. These start building at about 11am and usually don't die off until around 4pm or 5pm. It's a phenomenon that occasionally brings in the sport's elite, such as Robbie Naish of Hawaii. Things can get crowded on weekends.

Operators hiring out gear and offering lessons include **Windsurf-Center Walchensee** (Seestrasse 10; per hr/day €16/40), and **Surfschule Reinhard Post** (Einsiedl; per hr/day €16/40).

Numerous hiking trails crisscross the Tölzer Land, from easy spins around the lake to lung-searing mountain climbs. A particularly rewarding day hike with superb views takes you to the peak of the Herzogstand at 1731m, one of King Ludwig's favourite mountains. You can start either near Urfeld on the northern shore of the Walchensee or in Schlehdorf/Raut on the Kochelsee. If you don't feel like climbing to the top but still want to enjoy the views, catch a gondola ride on the **Herzogstandbahn** (☎ 236; adult/child one-way €7/4, return €12/6.50; ☺ 9am-5.15pm Apr-Oct, 9am-4.15pm Nov-Mar).

A spectacular way to extend this tour is by taking the craggy ridge walk from Mt Herzogstand to Mt Heimgarten (1790m). The route requires you to clutch the cables and is not for the vertigo-prone. From here, you could either double back or work your way downhill to the town of Walchensee. All local tourist offices sell hiking maps.

Walchensee is about 35km southwest of Bad Tölz. It is connected with Kochel via the spectacularly windy Kesselbergstrasse. Bus No 9610 makes the trip out here from Bad Tölz up to six times daily (one hour).

Kochel am See

☎ 08851 / pop 4100

The evocative landscape of Kochel, with its rich and varied palette of colours and lake motifs, greatly inspired one of the most influential early-20th-century German painters, Franz Marc (1880–1916). Along with Wasilly Kandinsky, a sometime resident of nearby Murnau (p133), Marc was a founding member of the artists' group, Der Blaue Reiter (The Blue Rider; 1911). He is best remembered for his paintings featuring animals, horses in particular.

Marc began visiting the area while still a student at the Munich Academy of Arts, where his father was a professor. He lived here on and off starting in 1908, finally buying a house in 1914. Mon ths later, he volunteered for WWI and was killed in action in 1916. He's buried in Kochel cemetery.

A lovely villa here is home to the **Franz Marc Museum** (☎ 7114; Herzogstandweg 43; adult/child €4/3; 2-6pm Mar–mid-Jan). Aside from about 20 paintings it presents watercolours, sketches and drawings, as well as personal effects such as his pipe and his school report card. Works by Kandinsky, Münter, Jawlensky and other friends complement his work.

The **tourist office** (☎ 338; www.kochel.de; Kalmbachstrasse 11) will help you to find accommodation.

There are a few hotels and pensions on the two lakes, but they are mainly found in Kochel. Sitting grandly on the shores of the Kochelsee, **Gasthaus Edeltraut** (☎ 8858-262; gasthofedeltraut@aol.com; Seestrasse 90; s/d €28/52; mains €6-14) has a beer garden big enough to warrant its own maypole. It also has comfy farm-style rooms, its own boat hire and a traditional restaurant.

The better of two camp sites, **Campingplatz Renken** (☎ 5776; fax 5776; Mittenwalder Strasse 106; per adult/car & tent €5.70/6; Apr-Sep) is located right on the lake. Renken counts a restaurant, cooking facilities and children's playground among its amenities. Bavaria's smallest **DJH hostel** (☎ 5296; www.jugendherberge .de/jh/kochel in German; Badstrasse 2; dm €15.35), a

traditional Alpine-style house with just 3 beds, is in Kochel.

Kochel is about 22km southwest of Ba■ Tölz and is served several times daily b bus Nos 9610 and 9612 from Bad Tölz vi Benediktbeuern (40 minutes). Trains fron Munich connect with Kochel hourly, with change in Tutzing (€11.50, one hour).

Kloster Benediktbeuern

About 14km southwest of Bad Tölz, th **Kloster Benediktbeuern** (☎ 08857-880; Don-Bosco Strasse 1; adult/child €3/2) is one of the oldes monasteries in Bavaria, founded in AI 739. Destroyed by Hungarian marauder in 955, it was quickly rebuilt and remaine■ a powerful and prestigious institution unt the early 1800s, when an optical laborator was opened on the grounds.

It was here that famed physicist Josep■ von Fraunhofer (1787–1826) developed nev types of glass, worked to perfect his optica instruments for manufacture and discov ered the 'Fraunhofer lines', the dark lines i the sun's spectrum. In 1930 an Italian orde took over the monastery, and today operate two small universities on the grounds.

The heavily stuccoed **Basilika St Benedik** (8am-5pm, services 9am Easter-early Nov) is classi Italian baroque. The ceiling frescoes, diml lit by candlelight, are by Georg Asam, fathe of the famous Asam brothers.

Of greater importance is the small **Anas tasiakapelle** (Anastasia Chapel; 8am-5pm), th product of some of the most talented bar oque artists who worked in Bavaria. As yo enter, on your right is the charming tale i German of how the monks faced imminen attack in the 18th century from maraud ers about to cross the frozen Kochelsee. Fo help the clerics prayed to Anastasia, a marty who died in 1053. A warm *Föhn* wind cam up, melting the ice and drowning the attack ers. The monks were spared and Anastasia' place in history was secured.

There's also a small **exhibit** (admission fre 9am-6pm Mar-Oct) in the original worksho rooms giving some technical details c optical glassmaking and a few about Fraun hofer himself.

In summer, a series of classical concert■ the **Benediktbeurer Konzerte**, takes place i the basilica or in a baroque festival ha (tickets cost €15 to €20, student discount available).

DAVID PEEVERS

Lederhosen detail (p26)

MARTIN MOOS

Oktoberfest (p88), Munich

MARTIN MOOS

Oktoberfest (p88), Munich

Christkindlmarkt (p87), Munich

PAUL BERNHARDT

Marktplatz (p230), Rothenburg ob der Tauber

Veste Oberhaus (p170), Passau

Haidplatz, Regensburg (p158)

Fresco on exterior of the Altes Rathaus
(p200), Bamberg

The monastery also runs a **Gästehaus** (☎ 881 95; www.kloster-benediktbeuern.de in German; s/d €22/44, s/d with shower €31/53). Rooms are newly furnished and not the least institutional, with TVs and access to an earthy pub.

From Munich, regional trains travel hourly to Benediktbeuern (€9.70, one hour, change in Tutzing). From Bad Tölz, take bus Nos 9610 or 9612; the trip takes 30 minutes.

Lenggries
☎ 08045 / pop 9300 / elev 700m

About 10km south of Bad Tölz, via the B13, Lenggries is the gateway to the **Brauneck ski field**, which offers runs suitable for beginners to advanced skiers. Day passes for adults/children aged to 15 are €23/€13, and a free bus operates from December to mid-March.

Lenggries is also a popular departure point for white-water canoeing, kayaking and rafting trips on the Isar River. **Kajakschule Oberland** (☎ 916 916; www.viactiva.de in German; Ganghoferstrasse 4) is one of the most experienced outfitters around. Courses start at €109, equipment can be hired for €23 per day. Four-hour rafting tours start at €49, including equipment.

The **tourist office** (☎ 500 820; www.lenggries.de; Marktstrasse 1) can help you find accommodation. There are a few guesthouses with singles for about €35 and doubles for €70.

Der Altwirt (☎ 8085; www.altwirt-lenggries.de; Marktstrasse 13; s €40-45, d €64-74; mains €7-15; P ☐) is the oldest hotel in town, housed in a massive inn built in 1469, with traditionally decorated rooms, a sauna and solarium, and a good restaurant. It's popular among skiers in winter and has its own storage room for ski equipment.

Lenggries is the final stop on the BOB private railway from Munich (for details see p135). Bus Nos 9564 and 9553 from Bad Tölz also travel here up to eight times daily (less often on weekends).

TEGERNSEE
☎ 08022 / pop 25,000 / elev 726m

With an Alpine stage in the background and surrounded by forests, Tegernsee lake is in an ideal setting. This fact has not gone unnoticed by Germany's money elite – from Munich bankers to Berlin politicos – many of whom have their weekend villas here. You'll find few places with a higher concentration of people parading around with their necks and fingers dripping with jewels, and their shiny S-class Mercedes parked nearby.

The lake has four resort towns: Gmund on the northern shore is the most low-key; Tegernsee on the eastern shore is the most historical; Rottach-Egern in the south the ritziest; and Bad Wiessee in the west, with its curative iodine springs, the healthiest. Summer activities include swimming, cycling, hiking, boating and windsurfing. In winter, skiing and snowboarding are options as is, sometimes, ice-skating on the frozen lake.

Information
Bad Wiessee tourist office (☎ 860 30; www.bad -wiessee.de; Adrian-Stoop-Strasse 20, Bad Wiessee)
Gmund tourist office (☎ 750 527; www.gmund.de; Kirchenweg 6, Gmund)
Rottach-Egern tourist office (☎ 671 341; www .rottach-egern.de; Nördliche Hauptstrasse 9, Rottach-Egern) With Internet access.

SALZBURG & UPPER BAVARIA

CARMINA BURANA

Medieval love poems in a dead language don't usually make it into film soundtracks. But through composer Carl Orff (1895–1982), the rants of a hedonistic band of Germans have survived to titillate, amuse and become soundtracks for a host of films including *The Omen*, *Excalibur* and *The Doors*.

Carmina Burana (literally, 'Songs of Beuern') is a collection of about 250 raging, erotic and humorous poems composed by goliards (defrocked monks, minstrels and wastrels). The 13th-century manuscript was found, by accident, in the monastery of Benediktbeuern in 1803.

Early in his career, Orff was mainly a music educator whose life was forever changed after he wrote his famous secular cantata, which disregards the notation of the Latin originals. The epic premiered in Frankfurt in 1937 to immediate acclaim. In treating these celebrations of eroticism, gluttony, drinking and gambling, his choral and instrumental arrangements were light-hearted, inspirational and downright frightening. Through the driving strains of the *Carmina Burana*, one fact about the 13th century is made abundantly clear: they sure knew how to party.

DETOUR

This leisurely drive, 18km in total, takes you past velvety meadows dotted with traditional Alpine barns. From Lenggries, take Wegscheider Strasse 2km south and turn right on the road marked Jachenau. Well off the busy highways, the soundtrack is of burbling brooks and tinkling cowbells. You'll pass through a clutch of hamlets until you reach pretty **Jachenau** village, with bucolic *Lüftlmalerei* paintings along Dorfstrasse. Continuing west, pay the road toll (€2) at the little wooden hut and carry on till you reach **Walchensee**. The road follows the south shore of this emerald-green lake, and there are numerous picnic spots along the way. Carry on another 8km to the B11, turn right and soon you're in Walchensee village.

Tegernsee tourist office (☎ 180 140; www.tegernsee.de; Hauptstrasse 2, Tegernsee)

Sights

TEGERNSEE

The name of a town as well as the lake, Tegernsee once had considerable pull on the monastic scene. Founded in 746 by Benedictine monks, Tegernsee had a library that was the envy of the religious elite – even at the Vatican.

Eventually the Wittelsbach royal family bought the place and turned it into one of their summer residences. Today the complex contains a brewery owned by Duke Max von Wittelsbach. You can sample the family suds in the famous **Bräustüberl** (opposite). The **Pfarrkirche St Quirinus** (Church of St Quirin), with frescoes by Georg Asam, completes the 'Bavarian Trinity' of palace, brewery and church. The complex also houses a high school.

Fans of biting caricature should check out the **Olaf-Gulbransson-Museum** (☎ 3338; Im Kurgarten, Tegernsee; adult/child €4/1; ☺ 11am-5pm Tue-Sun). The Norwegian-born Gulbransson (1873–1958) worked for the Munich-based satirical magazine *Simplicissimus* but spent much of his adult life in Tegernsee. The museum shows the entire range of his work, from cartoons to oils and drawings. His caricatures of Kaiser Wilhelm are world famous.

ROTTACH-EGERN

The two-part town of Rottach-Egern is the most glamorous of the lakeside communities. Its streets are lined by beautiful old houses with painted shutters and façades, many more, with overhanging eaves and wooden balconies, cling to the slopes of nearby hills. For superb views, take the **Wallbergbahn** (☎ 70 53 70; Am Höhenrain 5-7, Rottach-Egern; adult/child one-way €8.50/4.50, return €14/7; ☺ 8.45am-5pm Apr-Oct, 8.45am-4.30pm Nov-Mar) a cable car to the top of Mt Wallberg at 1772m where there's a restaurant and trailheads. Thanks to good thermal wind conditions, this is also prime terrain for hang-gliding and paragliding.

If you have your own vehicle, a drive up the mountain on the Wallbergstrasse, a panoramic toll route to the Moosalm restaurant, is another fun thing to do.

Sleeping & Eating

Hotel Garni Reiffenstuel (☎ 927 350; www.reiffenstuel.de; Seestrasse 67, Rottach-Egern; s €60, d €69-94; ℗) This friendly lakeside hotel has its own swimming beach, boat hire and a vast rear garden for taking the rays. Its countrified rooms are spacious and comfy, most with views of the lake and Alps beyond.

Hotel Bachmair am See (☎ 2720; www.bachmair.de; Seestrasse 47, Rottach-Egern; s €120-145, d €175-270; ℗ ✗ ✗ 🖳 🖳) The ritziest old resort on the lake is like a little village unto itself. Facilities include a shopping arcade, a panoramic terrace, restaurants and a fancy fitness centre, with its own cave pool. Rooms are decorated in ultraelegant country style.

Bräustüberl (☎ 4141; Schlossplatz 1, Tegernsee; meals €3.50-9) If you're willing to brave the thick smoke, you can join beer-guzzling tour groups and grizzled locals for sausages, *Leberkäs* (pork and beer meatloaf) and local cheeses at this historic beer hall. It's in the palace right on the lakeside.

Getting There & Around

The Tegernsee is about 50km south of Munich. The town of Tegernsee is served by the BOB, a private railway from Munich, with a change in Schaftlach (€8.80, one hour).

The BOB also goes to Bad Tölz, again changing in Schaftlach (€3.20, about one hour, depending on connection), or you can take bus No 9557 via Gmund and Bad Wiessee (1¼ hours).

Bus No 9559 connects the lake communities every 30 to 60 minutes.

CHIEMSEE
☎ 08051 / elev 518m

The Bavarian Sea, as Chiemsee is affectionately known, is a haven for water rats, stressed-out city dwellers and anyone on the grand palace tour. Most visitors come to see King Ludwig II's homage to Versailles – Schloss Herrenchiemsee – built on one of the islands. But the lake's natural beauty and its huge reputation for water sports draw a huge following.

The towns of Prien am Chiemsee and, about 5km south, Bernau am Chiemsee, both on the Munich–Salzburg rail line, are perfect bases for exploring the lake. Of the two, Prien is the larger and more commercial.

Information
You can surf the Web for free in the lobbies at all three locations.

Bernau tourist office (☎ 986 80; www.bernau -am-chiemsee.de; Aschauer Strasse 10, Bernau; 🕑 8am-5pm Mon-Fri, 8-4pm Sat May-Sep, 8am-3.30pm Fri Oct-Apr)

Chiemsee Info-Center (☎ 965 550; www.chiemsee .de; 🕑 9am-7pm Mon-Fri, 10am-4pm Sat & Sun) On the southern lakeshore, just off the autobahn exit Bernau-Felden, the centre covers information for the whole area.

Prien tourist office (☎ 690 50; www.tourismus.prien .de in German; Alte Rathausstrasse 11, Prien)

Sights

SCHLOSS HERRENCHIEMSEE
Herreninsel in the Chiemsee is home to a fantastic palace born of Ludwig II's warped imagination: **Schloss Herrenchiemsee** (☎ 688 70; www.herren-chiemsee.de; adult/child under 18 €7/ free; 🕑 tours continuously 9am-5.15pm Apr-Sep, 10am-4.40pm Oct-Mar). Begun in 1878, it was never intended as a residence but as a homage to absolutist monarchy, as epitomised by Ludwig's hero the French 'Sun King', Louis XIV. Ludwig spent only 10 days here and even then was rarely seen, preferring to read at night and sleep all day.

The palace is both a knock-off and an attempt to one-up Versailles, with larger and more lavishly decorated rooms. Ludwig managed to spend more money on this palace than on Neuschwanstein and Linderhof combined. When cash ran out in 1885, one year before his death, 50 rooms remained unfinished.

The rooms that were actually completed each outdo each other in opulence. The vast **Gesandtentreppe** (Ambassador Staircase), a double staircase leading to a frescoed gallery and topped by a glass roof, is the first visual knockout on the guided tour but fades in comparison to the stunning **Grosse Spiegelgalerie** (Great Hall of Mirrors). This tunnel of light runs the length of the garden (98m; 10m longer than that in Versailles!) and sports 52 candelabra and 33 great glass chandeliers with 7000 candles, which took 70 servants half an hour to light. In late July it becomes a superb venue for classical concerts.

Resembling a chapel the **Paradeschlafzim-mer** (State Bedroom) features a canopied bed perching altarlike on a pedestal behind a golden balustrade. This was the heart of the palace, where morning and evening audiences were held. It is the king's bedroom, however, the **Kleines Blaues Schlafzimmer** (Little Blue Bedroom), which tops the bill. The decoration is sickly sweet, encrusted with gilded stucco and wildly extravagant carvings. The room is bathed in a soft blue light emanating from a glass globe at the foot of the bed. It supposedly took 18 months for a technician to perfect the lamp to the king's satisfaction.

Admission to the palace also entitles you to a spin around the **König-Ludwig II-Museum**, where you can see the king's christening and coronation robes, blueprints for more manic architectural projects and his death mask.

To get to the palace take the ferry from Prien-Stock (€5.70 return, 15 to 20 minutes) or from Bernau-Felden (€7.30, 25 minutes), operates May to October. From the boat landing on Herreninsel, it's about a 20-minute walk through lovely gardens to the palace. The palace tour, offered in German or English, takes 30 minutes.

FRAUENINSEL
This island is home to the **Frauenwörth Abbey**, founded in the late 8th century and one of the oldest nunneries in Bavaria. The abbey church (10th century), whose freestanding campanile sports a distinctive onion dome (11th century), is worth a visit. Opposite the church is the AD 860 Carolingian **Torhalle** (Gatehouse; ☎ 08054-7256; admission €1.50; 🕑 11am-6pm May-Oct). It houses

medieval *objets d'art*, sculpture and changing exhibits of Chiemsee painters from the 18th to the 20th centuries.

Return ferry fare, including a stop at Herreninsel, is €6.80 from Prien-Stock and €7.30 from Bernau-Felden.

Activities

SWIMMING & BOATING

The swimming beaches most easily accessed are at Chieming and Gstadt (both free) on the lake's east and north shores, respectively. The small beach at Urfahrn, about 5km west of Gstadt, is particularly nice. Hire boats, available at many beaches, range from €5 to €20 per hour, depending on the type. In Prien, **Bootsverleih Stöffl** (☎ 2000; Seestrasse 64) has two-seater paddle boats for €4.50 per hour and electric boats for €9 to €19.

The futuristic-looking glass roof by the harbour in Prien-Stock shelters **Prienavera** (☎ 609 570; Seestrasse 120; adult/child 3hr pass €8/3.50, day pass €10/5; ☺ hr seasonal, usually 10am-9pm). It's an enormous pool complex with sauna, steam baths, slides, Jacuzzi and fitness area. The name is a weak pun on the Italian 'primavera', meaning 'spring'.

Sleeping

The tourist offices can set up private rooms in town and in farmhouses from €18 per person.

Hotel Bonnschlössl (☎ 890 11; www.alter-wirt-bernau.de; Kirchplatz 9, Bernau; s €46-72, d €72-104; P ✿) For something special yet affordable, head over to this charming hotel set in a fully restored 1477 palace with faux turrets. Rooms are stylish and packed with amenities. You can take breakfast on the terrace overlooking a wonderful rambling garden.

Hotel Neuer am See (☎ 609 960; www.neuer-am-see.de in German; Seestrasse 104, Prien; s €44-64, d €80-94, ste €94-118; P) This friendly hotel, about 150m from Prien harbour, has pretty country-style rooms, almost all with a balcony and many with views of the Chiemsee and beyond to the Alps. The on-site café-restaurant is especially proud of its homemade cakes and its fish dishes made with varieties plucked fresh from the lake.

Hotel Garni Möwe (☎ 5004; www.hotel-garni-moewe.de in German; Seepromenade 111, Prien; s €60-65, d €70-86; P) This traditional Bavarian hotel sits right on the lakefront and offers excellent value. It has its own bike and boat hire as well as a sauna and fitness centre and the large garden is a bonus for anyone travelling with children.

DJH hostel (☎ 687 70; www.jugendherberge.de/jh/prien in German; Carl-Braun-Strasse 66; dm €17.45; ☺ closed Dec–mid-Jan) Prien's hostel is a 15-minute walk from the Hauptbahnhof and can sleep 130 people in 23 rooms. The hostel has lots of games and activities and a green conscience. There's also an environmental study centre for young people here.

Panorama Camping Harras (☎ 904 60; www.camping-harras.de; Harrasser Strasse 135, Prien; per person/tent/car €5.40/3/1.60) This camp site is scenically located on a peninsula with its own private beach. It offers catamaran and surfboard hire and has a restaurant with lakeview terrace. Prices are 15% higher for stays under four days.

Eating

Badehaus (☎ 970 300; Rasthausstrasse 11, Bernau; mains €6-15) Near the Chiemsee Info-Center and the lakeshore, this contemporary beer hall is done up in the nostalgic style of a bathhouse. It has quirky décor and gourmet fare enjoyed by a mix of locals and visitors. A special attraction is the so-called 'beer bath', a glass tub filled (sometimes) with a mix of beer and water.

Der Alte Wirt (☎ 890 11; Kirchplatz 9, Bernau; Brotzeit €4-9, mains €7-16; ☺ Tue-Sun) For great Bavarian cuisine with swift service, drop by this listed monument, a massive half-timbered inn with five centuries of history. The *Leberkäse* is clearly the star of the menu, but the meat dishes are uniformly excellent; having an in-house butcher doesn't hurt. The waitresses dart around the dining halls as if on roller blades.

Westernacher am See (☎ 4722; Seestrasse 115, Prien; mains €8-16) This lakeside dining haven has a multiple personality, with a cosy restaurant, cocktail bar, café, beer garden and glassed-in winter terrace. Its speciality is modern twists on old Bavarian favourites. It also has spacious double rooms (€88) with a splendid view of the Chiemsee.

Hacienda (☎ 4448; Seestrasse 94, Prien; tapas €2-13, mains €7-14; ☺ dinner Mon-Sat) For something a little more hip, slick Hacienda serves up some delicious tapas and traditional Spanish food including *jamón serrano* (cured ham) and a mean paella. The crowd is

---

DETOUR: URSCHALLING

While at the Chiemsee, take a few minutes to visit the exquisite Romanesque **St Jakobuskirche** (Church of St Jakobus), tucked away in the hamlet of **Urschalling**, west of the lake. The outside looks conventionally Bavarian, with onion dome and whitewashed walls, but the interior reveals a series of primitive frescoes in a charming, very Italian style. Little is known about the 15th-century artist who let fly in the face of convention by depicting God as a woman – and in fact, this unusual take on the Holy Trinity (located on the altar ceiling) continues to stir debate today. The Church frowned on the representation and in 1550, the frescoes were painted over. These striking artworks might still be forgotten if a cleaning woman hadn't rediscovered them in 1923.

To get to the church from Prien am Chiemsee, take Bernauer Strasse south for 2km, turn right into Urschallinger Strasse and drive half a kilometre. If you find the doors locked, get a key from the **sexton** (☎ 5886).

---

young and lively and heads straight for the cocktails.

Getting There & Around

Prien and Bernau are served by hourly trains from Munich (€13.30, one hour). Hourly bus No 9505 connects the two lake towns. Local buses run from Prien Bahnhof to the harbour in Stock. You can also take the historic Chiemseebahn (1887), the world's oldest narrow-gauge steam train (one way/return €2/€3; May to September).

Ferries operated by **Chiemsee Schifffahrt** (☎ 6090; Seestrasse 108, Prien) ply the lake every hour with stops at Herreninsel, Fraueninsel, Seebruck and Chieming on a schedule that changes seasonally. You can circumnavigate the entire lake and make all these stops (getting off and catching the next ferry that comes your way) for €9.50. Children aged six to 15 get a 50% discount.

Radsport Reischenböck (☎ 4631; Bahnhofsplatz 6, Prien) hires out city bikes for €8 per day and mountain bikes for €15.

WASSERBURG AM INN

☎ 08071 / pop 12,000 / elev 419m

The old and picturesque salt-trading town of Wasserburg, about 28km north of the Chiemsee and 60km east of Munich, hangs like a teardrop in a crook of the Inn, where it is overlooked by majestic tree-covered cliffs. The town eventually lost its salt licence and the ships of white gold have given way to tractor-trailers. But the medieval Altstadt remains a place where the clocks seem to tick more slowly, even in the high season.

The **main tourist office** (☎ 105 22; www.wasser burg.de in German; Marienplatz 2; 9am-5pm Mon-Fri,

10am-2pm Sat May-Sep, 9am-3pm Mon-Fri, 10am-1pm Sat Oct-Apr) is entered via Salzsenderzeile, on the right side of the Rathaus (town hall). The old town is easily explored on foot.

Sights

On the south side of the Altstadt, the old **bridge gate** bears witness to Wasserburg's medieval past. While standing on the Rote Brücke (Red Bridge), check out the mural painted in 1568 depicting knights in armour, waving the banners of Bavaria and Wasserburg, and above them, Jupiter on an eagle with a lily branch, lightning and a sceptre.

On the main square at Marienplatz, the pretty Gothic **Rathaus** (☎ 1050; tours adult/child €2.50/1; tours hourly 10am-4pm Tue-Fri, half-hourly Sat & Sun) was quite versatile, having been a bakery and corn store as well as a Bavarian administration centre. The highlight here is its dark-wood panelled council chamber, retained more or less in its 15th-century state. The much newer banqueting hall (also on the tour) is used for concerts.

Wasserburg's museums are innovative to be sure, targeting niches others don't (bother to) reach. The **Wegmacher Museum** (Road Construction Museum; ☎ 918 50; admission free; 8-11am Mon-Fri, 1-3pm Mon-Thu) has over 1500 exhibits of tools and equipment used since Roman times to lay out our roads and bridges. The ferocious old steam rollers have heaps of personality and come from as far afield as Russia.

Activities

Boat trips on the Inn are popular in summer. The 45-minute tours (€6; 2.15pm & 3.15pm Thu-Tue May-Sep) depart from the south end of the Rote Brücke. A sculpture path runs along the Inn's shore, which has a pebbly beach for picnicking and sunning.

Tours

You can join **group tours** of the Altstadt and of the beer catacombs, the 200-year-old storage vaults tunnelled deep into the hill opposite. Ask at the tourist office for details.

Sleeping & Eating

Hotel Paulaner Stuben (☎ 3903; www.paulaner stuben-wasserburg.de; Marienplatz 9; s €21-23, d €35, s/d with shower €35/50; meals €6-16) It occupies a fabulous patrician's house, dripping with stucco and one of the region's finest rococo façades. Many rooms have a front-row view of the Gothic town hall opposite, and there's a feel-good restaurant serving local game.

Hotel Fletzinger (☎ 908 90; www.hotel-fletzinger .de; Fletzingergasse 1; s €51-77, d €77-87; **P**) This traditional Bavarian inn offers rooms with carved antique bedsteads and it doesn't skimp on the perks, including fresh fruit and newspapers every morning. Guests drift in and out of its prime location near the Rathaus. It has a beer garden out back.

Weisses Rössl (☎ 502 91; Herrengasse 1; mains €8-17, 3-course meals €23-34; ⏰ lunch & dinner, closed Mon-Tue & Sun afternoon) This intimate dining spot is one of the town's best, often featuring a gourmet take on game and regional favourites. The chef pours his soul into every meal, and even basic items such as *Spätzle* (noodles) get a new lease on life.

Stechl-Keller (☎ 925 159; Marienplatz 6; mains €5-8; ⏰ 8am-1am) This traditional-looking *Gasthof* (inn) serves bistro-type pizzas and salads to a youthful crowd. The big streetside terrace is buzzing any time of day.

Getting There & Away

Wasserburg's train station is in Reitmehring, 5km to the northwest of the Altstadt and reachable via RVO bus 9414 (€1); the other direction goes to Prien am Chiemsee. Trains to Munich run every one to two hours and involve a change at Grafing (€8.70, 1¼ hours). There are also a half-dozen trains daily to Altötting (€8.70, one hour), with a change at Mühldorf.

CHIEMGAU

Cradled by the Chiemgauer Alps but a stone's throw from crystalline lakes, the Chiemgau is a perfect year-round outdoor

playground. Hiking, mountain biking and bicycle touring are popular activities, and winter brings downhill and cross-country skiing. Like most areas in the Bavarian Alps, the Chiemgau is dotted with *Almen*, rustic mountain restaurants serving local specialities in the summer months.

Aschau

☎ 08052 / pop 5400 / elev 615m

About 5km south of the Chiemsee (p139), tiny Aschau sits pretty at the foot of the craggy Mt Kampenwand (1669m), in the forested Prien Valley. It offers an excellent base to the Chiemsee lake in the summer rush, being a bit off the beaten track. It also has one of Germany's star-quality restaurants. About 10km deeper into the valley is the mountain village Sachrang, on the Austrian border.

Aschau's **tourist office** (☎ 904 937; www.aschau .de in German; Kampenwandstrasse 38; ⏰ 8am-6pm Mon-Fri, 9am-noon Sat, 10am-noon Sun May–mid-Oct, closed lunch, Sat & Sun mid-Oct–Apr) is on the town's main drag.

SIGHTS & ACTIVITIES

The Gothic parish church is worth a look, but the main sight is the hilltop **Schloss Hohenaschau** (guided tours adult/child incl museum €2.50/1.50; ⏰ 9.30am, 10.30am, 11.30am Tue-Fri May-Sep, Thu only Apr & Oct). It has 12th-century origins but has lost much of its medieval look. Although now a government-owned holiday retreat, large sections, including the chapel, prison, festival halls and interior courtyard, may be visited on the guided tours. Also inside is the **Prientalmuseum** (Prien Valley Museum; ⏰ during castle tours & 1.30-5pm Sun Apr-Oct), which chronicles local history. From here, it's about a 15-minute walk up to the castle.

South of the castle is the **Kampenwandbahn** (cable car; ☎ 4411, 906 4420; An der Bergbahn 8; adult/child 5-15 one-way 5-15 €9.50/5, return €13.50/7.50; ⏰ 8.30am-5pm May-Oct, 8.30am-5.30pm Jul & Aug, 9am-4.30pm Dec-Apr). It's a 15-minute gondola ride to the top, where there's a restaurant and trailheads, including a 1.5km groomed trail in winter. Skiers have 12km of pistes to play with, including the 5km valley run (all-day ski passes cost €20/€12.50 per adult/child, less if you start later in the day).

SLEEPING & EATING

Aschau can accommodate up to 3200 overnight guests. Prices are very competitive and there some very classy options.

Prillerhof (☎ 906 370; www.prillerhof.de; Höhenbergstrasse 1; s €28-33, d €54-72) Run by an award-winning young hotelier, this is one of the most feel-good and good-value places in the region. Generously sized, the modern rooms have such luxury touches as pantry kitchen, balcony and fluffy bathrobes. A sauna, Jacuzzi and steam room invite you to relax after a day in the mountains or on the lake. There's even a guest laundry.

Gasthof zum Baumbach (☎ 957 90; www.bayern gast.de/zum-baumbach in German; Kampenwandstrasse 75; s/d from €48/76; mains €7.50-14; closed Mon) Its smartly renovated rooms are modern and cheerful, some with balcony views of Schloss Hohenaschau. The restaurant serves fresh regional cuisine, including low-fat and meat-free selections and is, along with the beer garden, a popular gathering place.

Residenz Heinz Winkler (☎ 179 90; www.residenz -heinz-winkler.de; Kirchplatz 1; r €150-275, ste €250-350; mains €32-45, 3-course meals from €70) Heinz Winkler is one of Germany's top chefs, with three Michelin stars and numerous other awards to his credit. You can sample his supreme creations at the classically elegant Venezianisches Restaurant, part of the historic hotel that Winkler modernised in 1989. There are two-storey suites here, as well as cooking courses (from €350) throughout the year.

GETTING THERE & AWAY

Regional trains link Prien with Aschau hourly (€1.60, 15 minutes). From Bernau, there is a shuttle to Aschau and Sachrang (Monday to Saturday only; free to overnight visitors).

Ruhpolding, Inzell & Reit im Winkl

In the eastern Chiemgau lie the three classic resorts of Ruhpolding, Inzell (about 13km east), and Reit im Winkl (about 24km southwest). Tourism is the main source of income here and things can be a bit of a squeeze in July and August and during ski season.

INFORMATION

Inzell tourist office (☎ 08665-988 50; www.inzell.de in German; Rathausplatz 5, Inzell) With Internet access.

Reit im Winkl tourist office (☎ 08640-800 20; www .reit-im-winkl.de; Rathausplatz 1, Reit im Winkel)

Ruhpolding tourist office (☎ 08663-880 60; www .ruhpolding.de; Hauptstrasse 60, Ruhpolding)

SIGHTS & ACTIVITIES

Ruhpolding's four small **museums** celebrate local heritage with exhibits on everything from bellmaking to rural religious art and farming implements. The onion-domed parish church of **St Georg** shelters a precious Romanesque Madonna (altar on the right), a frilly rococo pulpit and a modern jewelled cross.

From Ruhpolding, cable cars go to the top of the **Rauschberg** (1672m) and the **Unternberg** (1450m), or you can hike up in two to three hours.

Vita Alpina (☎ 08663-9388; Brander Strasse 1; 3hr without/with sauna €9/11.70; 9am-9pm) is the local wellness complex in Ruhpolding, with wave pool, steam bath, saunas, outdoor pool with massage jets and a 76m waterslide.

Fans of two-wheelers can look forward to **cycling** through beautiful scenery on easy to challenging routes. Classic mountain bike routes are the moderate **Chiemgau MTB Marathon**, with a 65km and a 130km version starting in Ruhpolding; and the 45km **Reit im Winkl-Unken** tour for moderate to advanced riders. Less-athletic types may prefer the **Chiemgau Radweg**, which connects the three communities via a 34km route along the valley floor past several small mountain lakes. Bicycles may be hired in all communities.

Cross-country skiing is big in the Chiemgau with more than 60km of groomed trails in Ruhpolding, 30km in Inzell and 90km in Reit im Winkl. Ruhpolding, in fact, is home to the national biathlon training centre and regularly hosts the World Cup. A nice and easy cross-country terrain is the 'Drei Seen' area between Ruhpolding and Reit im Winkl. The 30km 'Chiemgau-Marathon-Loipe' from Reit im Winkl to Inzell is a good challenge.

There's **downhill skiing** at the Unternberg, but snow levels are not always reliable at these altitudes, although if nature fails, snowmaking machines kick into gear. The Chiemgau's top ski area is the **Winklmoos-Alm/Steinplatte** (1870m) near Reit im Winkl. It's the stomping ground of Rosi Mittermaier, who won two gold medals and one silver medal at the 1976 Winter Olympic Games. Lifts usually operate from late November to mid-April with day passes costing €33.50, including the bus from Seegatterl.

All three resort towns have ski schools and these also hire out skiing equipment, including boots, skis and poles, as well as snowboards (about €10 per day).

SLEEPING & EATING
There's no shortage of quality private rooms and hotels, with farmhouses being a popular alternative. The Chiemgau, in fact, is the only holiday region in Bavaria that also puts farmhouses into various 'star' categories, as is often done with hotels. The tourist offices can help you sift through the bewildering choices.

Gasthof Hirschbichler (☎ 08665-555; www.gasthof -hirschbichler.de in German; Traunsteiner Strasse 25, Inzell; s/d €25/50; Brotzeit €4-10, mains €7-11) Large rooms, a central location and a good-value restaurant with its own butcher are the main assets of this friendly place.

Hotel Pension Edelweiss (☎ 08640-988 90; www .edelweiss-hotel.de in German; Am Grünbühel 1, Reit im Winkl; s/d from €34/52) In a quiet yet central location, this is a family-friendly charmer in a towering half-timbered house, featuring Bavarian country-style rooms and a sunny terrace.

Hotel Alpen Sonne (☎ 08663-880 40; www.alpen -sonne.de in German; Obergschwendter Strasse 17, Ruhpolding; s €41-61, d €66-97; meals €7-13; 🐕) Here you'll find newly renovated, modern rooms with all amenities, some with balcony overlooking a pretty slope with chairlift. It also has an indoor pool with sauna, and a decent in-house restaurant serving Bavarian fare.

GETTING THERE & AROUND
If you're travelling by train from Munich, change in Traunstein (€16.50, 1½ hours). Ruhpolding, Inzell and Reit im Winkl are all connected by regional bus No 9506 with several departures throughout the day. Bus No 9505 travels from Prien am Chiemsee to Reit im Winkl via Bernau. Bus No 9526 goes to Bad Reichenhall from Inzell.

BAD REICHENHALL
☎ 08651 / pop 16,400 / elev 471m
Bad Reichenhall, on the River Saalach, sits serenely at the foot of the Berchtesgadener and Chiemgauer Alps. Its history and prosperity has quite literally been built on salt, which has been hauled from the underground mines since Roman days. To this day, Bad Reichenhall – meaning a spa 'rich in salt' – remains the largest supplier of table salt in Germany.

It's also a famous spa town thanks to its richly concentrated briny springs. Prominent guests such as King Maximilian II took the waters here. Spas aren't quite the rage they used to be, however, and a charming air of faded elegance persists.

Bad Reichenhall is equidistant (about 20km) to Berchtesgaden and Salzburg, and makes a good alternative base for outdoor and cultural explorations.

Orientation
The Altstadt of Bad Reichenhall is compact, designed as it was for a strolling public, but the rest of the town is rather sprawling. The Hauptbahnhof is a short walk east of the historic centre, with the pedestrianised Ludwigstrasse as the main drag.

Information
Cafe Amadeo (☎ 64041; Poststrasse 29; per hr €2; 🕑 8am-1am) Internet access.
Post office (☎ 778 150; Hauptbahnhof; 🕑 8am-6pm Mon-Fri, 8am-12.30pm Sat)
Sparkasse (Bahnhofstrasse 17)
Tourist office (☎ 6060; www.bad-reichenhall.de; Wittelsbacher Strasse 15; 🕑 8am-5.30pm Mon-Fri, 9am-noon Sat Apr-Oct, 8am-5pm Mon-Fri, 9am-noon Sat Nov-Mar, 9am-noon Sun May-Sep)
Volksbank (Ludwigstrasse 3)

Sights
The bulk of sights are in the Altstadt. About 150m east of the tourist office, and signposted just about everywhere in town, lies the **Kurpark** (admission free; 🕑 7am-10pm Apr-Oct, 7am-6pm Nov-Mar), the town's historic spa gardens. An entrance fee is charged during concerts but most days you can stroll right on in.

Enter the gardens from the east (right) side at the neobaroque **Kurhaus.** There's often a little band inside playing schmalzy evergreens for fox-trotting guests. The bizarre elongated structure opposite the Kurhaus is the **Gradierwerk**, an open-air inhalatorium from 1912 that would be rather quaint if it weren't so darned big. The core of this 170m-long, 14m-high building is wrapped in 250,000 blackthorn twigs that are constantly drizzled with salty spring water, creating a fine, healthy mist for those wandering the ambulatory (as if the Alpine air weren't pristine enough already). The Gradierwerk is usually in operation from April to November.

Also in the park is the **Wandelhalle**, a performance rotunda for the 40-piece **Philharmonisches Orchester** (☎ 8661; adult/child €5/2.50; Kurkarte holders free; ⏰ concerts Tue-Sun). In fine weather, concerts are held in the Kurpark's summer pavilion.

Just east of the Kurpark you'll run into the long pedestrian Salzburger Strasse, which turns into Ludwigstrasse at its southern tip. Here you'll come upon a local institution, **Café Reber**, at No 10. The red awnings and fluttering flags scream 'tourist trap' but you'll soon realize it's tongue-in-cheek; some afternoons there's even a zoot-suited maestro playing the gold piano. Stop by for coffee and cake or sample their *Mozartkugeln*, a chocolate treat with a nougat and pistachio centre (good but considered to be slightly inferior to the Salzburg originals). In a square adjoining the café there's a cutesy sculpture of Mozart and his wife.

Nearby lies the biggest reminder of the town's hidden wealth, the **Alte Saline & Salzmuseum** (Old Salt Works & Salt Museum; ☎ 700 2146; Salinenstrasse; adult/child €5.20/3.20; ⏰ 10am-11.30pm & 2-4pm Apr-Oct, 2-6pm Tue & Thu Nov-Mar). A fire destroyed the original 16th-century salt works in 1834, giving King Ludwig I an excuse to rebuild with fancy Industrial Revolution machinery. Guided hour-long tours (in German) lead you through a network of tunnels and bring you face to face with mighty water wheels and pumps. Afterwards you're free to bone up on 'white gold' (ie salt) in the museum.

A few steps south of the Alte Saline, the main square of Rathausplatz is dominated by the **Alte Rathaus**. Built in 1849, the frescoes you see were only added in 1924, depicting Charlemagne, St Rupert, Friedrich Barbarossa and (of course) Ludwig I.

On the north side of town, about 500m west of the Kurpark, stands the massive **Basilika St Zeno** (Salzburger Strasse 33), one of Bavaria's grandest basilicas. This three-nave Gothic church is renowned for its artistic treasures, starting with the fantastic ribbed entrance portal with vivid Romanesque sculpture. Inside you'll find an ornate pulpit, baptismal font and choir stalls all from around 1520, as well as a covered walkway with severe Gothic arches.

Activities

Bad Reichenhall offers the full monty of outdoor activities. There are many easy hiking trails starting in town, but for a more challenging foray, head up Mt Hochstaufen (1771m) north of the town. The climb to the top takes about three hours from the **Padinger Alm** (☎ 44 39; ⏰ closed Mon), a mountain restaurant at 667m.

South of town, a **cable car** (☎ 2127; one-way/return €9.50/15; ⏰ 9am-5pm) gently rocks its way up the 1613m Predigtstuhl at least once hourly. It's a nostalgic experience, in cars still based on 1928 designs. The valley station is on Südtiroler Platz in the southern suburb of Kirchberg (bus No 1). There's a restaurant at the top as well as numerous trailheads.

The local chapter of the **Deutscher Alpenverein** (☎ 3731; Innsbrucker Strasse 16) is based at Sport-Rehrl. **Club Aktiv** (☎ 672 38; Frühlingstrasse 61) and **Sport Müller** (☎ 3776; Spitalgasse 3) are outfitters that can organise various outdoor activities, including mountain biking, canyoning, skiing and mountain climbing.

Give yourself a pampering at the sparkling new **Rupertustherme** (☎ 01805-606 706; Friedrich-Ebert-Allee 21; 4hr ticket €12, incl sauna €15; ⏰ 9am-10pm Mon-Sat, 9am-8pm Sun). The 360 degrees of picture windows let you feel like you're swimming through the Alps, and some of the heated salt pools are outside in the fresh mountain air.

Sleeping

Prices listed here are for rooms with private bathroom and include *Kurtaxe* (resort tax). Your euros go a long way here, and standards are remarkably high for the money.

Pension Schwarzenbach (☎ 4472; www.pension-schwarzenbach.com in German; Nonn 91; s/d from €21/42; **P**) Your charming hosts at this lovely pension, which has terrific views of the town and the mountains, work hard to make you feel at home. Several hikes start right outside the door.

Hotel Eisenrieth (☎ 9610; www.hotel-eisenrieth.de in German; Luitpoldstrasse 23; s/d from €33/50; **P**) You can be sure to get a good night's sleep at this quiet and peaceful hotel in the spa district. Many rooms are balconied. The owners speak both English and French.

Hotel Pension Erika (☎ 953 60; www.hotel-pension-erika.de in German; Adolf Schmid Strasse 3; s/d from €38/68; **P** 🐾) This delightful 50-room palazzo-style hotel has oodles of old-style elegance downstairs but snappy modern rooms. It has a fantastic garden for lolling about with the Alps in your lap.

Hotel Neu-Meran (☎ 4078; www.hotel-neu-meran
.de in German; Nonn 94; s €52-83, d €104-166; P ☻)
This is among Bad Reichenhall's most stylish places, with beautifully furnished sunny
rooms, a top-notch chef in the kitchen and
a fitness centre with sauna, steam room and
small gym.

Eating

There is a fair range of restaurants in town,
with their own particular take on Alpine
cuisine.

Bürgerbräu (☎ 6089; Waaggasse 2; mains €6-12)
Right next to the Rathaus, everything about
this traditional Bavarian beer hall is big,
including the menu and the portions and,
hopefully, your appetite. Each of the rooms
has a different ceiling (eg coffered, vaulted).

Café Reber (☎ 600 3174; Ludwigstrasse 10; mains
€6-10; ☺ 9am-6pm) This famous coffee-and-
cake café also serves a few hot dishes at
lunch time. Piano music is piped out to the
terrace tables.

Piccolino (☎ 984 343; Schachtstrasse 2; mains €9-25;
☺ closed Sat lunch & Sun) This pint-sized Tuscan-
style bistro is run by a delightful couple (he
cooks, she serves) and offers a small menu
of freshly prepared, seasonal cuisine. Standards are frighteningly high and as the sign
says, pizza is not served.

Aegidi Keller (☎ 653 33; Poststrasse 20; mains €6-
17) This medieval wine cellar from 1159 has
a diverse repertoire that varies daily, from
braised lamb and *Tellerfleisch* (boiled beef
with creamy horseradish) to paella and stone-
oven pizza. It has a pretty inner courtyard
open in summer, and even does takeaway.

Schwabenbräu (☎ 969 50; Salzburger Strasse 22;
Brotzeit €3-6, mains €8-13, dinner buffet €7) For a cold
snack or casual meal (from salads to roasts),
come to this convivial place with a young
clientele and a small beer garden. It's about
2km north of the spa district.

Getting There & Around

RB trains from Berchtesgaden depart hourly
(€3.30, 30 minutes). There are direct trains
to Salzburg (€4.30, 30 minutes), and regional
buses Nos 9527 and 9528 travel straight to
Salzburg's Mirabellplatz several times daily
(30 to 45 minutes). Bus No 9526 goes to
Inzell in the Chiemgau.

Bad Reichenhall is served by an extensive
bus network. Pick up a map at the tourist
office.

BERCHTESGADEN & BERCHTESGADENER LAND

☎ 08652 / pop 7700 / elev 550

Hiding in one of Bavaria's remotest corners, the Berchtesgadener Land is a self-
contained universe of wooded hilltops
and valleys, hemmed in by six different
mountain ranges along the Austrian border. Germany's second-highest mountain,
the Watzmann (2713m), towers above the
crystalline lakes, rushing streams and quiet
Alpine villages.

About half the area is protected as the
Nationalpark Berchtesgaden, home to the
pristine Königssee, Germany's highest
lake. The park also offers wonderful hiking
and other outdoor opportunities. In summer the mountaintop Eagle's Nest, a lodge
built by the Nazis, is a major draw, as is the
Dokumentation Obersalzberg, a museum
chronicling the region's dark history as the
Nazi party's southern headquarters.

Berchtesgadener Land is steeped in
fantastic tales of myth and legend. Some
say if you hike the trails, and bump into
a *Wildfrau* (mountain woman), it brings
luck. An encounter with a dwarf, however,
spells trouble.

History

Through word, paintings and song, the great
natural beauty of Berchtesgaden has been
celebrated for centuries. The area struck
terror into the hearts of its first settlers, a
band of Augustinian monks sent here to
establish a monastery in around 1100. They
found a land so wild, and so inhospitable,
that they suspected dragons might inhabit
it. Their worst fears seemed justified when,
one dark winter night, a thunderstorm
tore the roofs off their cottages and land-
slides shook the valley. The brothers fled
the godforsaken enclave to seek shelter in a
neighbouring monastery. Their archbishop,
though, would have none of this dragon
business and ordered the monks back to
Berchtesgaden.

In the 16th century, Berchtesgaden be-
came a sovereign state within the Holy
Roman Empire, ruled by a prince-abbot
until 1810 when it became part of the
Kingdom of Bavaria. To its chagrin today,
Berchtesgaden played a pivotal role in the
Third Reich. For more information, see the
boxed text on p149.

BERCHTESGADENER LAND

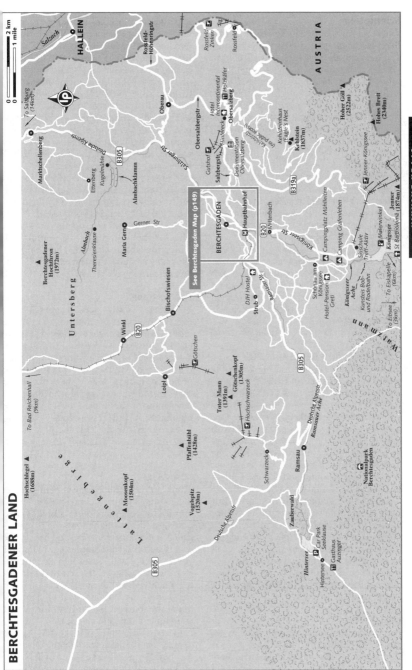

SALZBURG &
UPPER BAVARIA

Orientation

The main town in Berchtesgadener Land is Berchtesgaden, home to the Hauptbahnhof and the central bus station as well as most hotels, restaurants and the main tourist office branch. About 5km south of town is the Königssee community of Schönau, while the Obersalzberg is about 4km east, Marktschellenberg some 9km north, Ramsau about 9km west and Bischofswiesen 5km northwest.

Information

HypoVereinsbank (Weihnachtsschützenplatz 2½) Changes foreign currency.

Nationalpark-Haus Berchtesgaden (National Park information office; ☎ 643 43; www.nationalpark -berchtesgaden.de in German; Franziskanerplatz 7, Berchtesgaden; ☒ 9am-5pm Mon-Sat)

Post office (cnr Angergasse & Ludwig-Ganghofer-Strasse)

Tourist office (☎ 9670; www.berchtesgadener-land.de in German; Königsseer Strasse 2; ☒ 9am-6pm Mon-Sat, 10am-1pm & 2-6pm Sun May–mid-Oct, 9am-5pm Mon-Fri, 9am-noon Sat mid-Oct–Apr) Has a free room-booking service, public Internet terminal and an electronic room-reservation board outside.

Sights

DOKUMENTATION OBERSALZBERG

From 1933 to 1945, Obersalzberg was the southern headquarters of Hitler's Nazi government, a sinister period that's given the full historical treatment at the fascinating **Dokumentation Obersalzberg** (☎ 947 960; www .obersalzburg.de in German; Salzbergstrasse 41; adult/child under 16 €2.50/free; ☒ 9am-5pm Apr-Oct, 10am-3pm Tue-Sun Nov-Apr). The exhibit chronicles the forced takeover of the area, the construction of the compound and the daily life of the Nazi elite. All facets of Nazi terror are illuminated, including Hitler's near-mythical appeal, his racial politics, the resistance movement, foreign policy and the death camps. If you only have time for one big attraction in Berchtesgaden, this is it. A small section of the underground bunker network is also open for touring. To get there take bus No 9538 from the Hauptbahnhof in Berchtesgaden.

EAGLE'S NEST

Berchtesgaden's most sinister draw is on top of Mt Kehlstein, a sheer-sided peak at Obersalzberg. This was where Martin Bormann, one of Hitler's henchmen, engaged 3000 workers to build a diplomatic meeting house for the *Führer's* 50th birthday. Perched at 1834m, the innocent-looking lodge (called Kehlsteinhaus in German) occupies one of Germany's most breathtakingly scenic spots. Ironically, Hitler is said to have suffered from vertigo and rarely enjoyed the spectacular views himself.

The Kehlsteinhaus opens to visitors from mid-May to October. To get here from the centre of Berchtesgaden, first drive 4km east on the B319 (Salzbergstrasse) to the Kehlstein bus departure area on the Obersalzberg, or take bus 9549 (€3.90 return) there from the Hauptbahnhof. From here the road is closed to private traffic and you must take a special **bus** (adult/child €13.50/12.50; ☒ 7.40am-4pm, 35 minutes) up the mountain. The final 124m stretch to the summit is in a luxurious, brass-clad lift. The Kehlsteinhaus now contains a **restaurant** (☎ 2969) that donates profits to charity.

SALZBERGWERK

Berchtesgaden was once a major salt-mining centre and a 90-minute tour of the local **Salzbergwerk** (salt mines; ☎ 600 20; adult/child €12.50/11; ☒ 9am-5pm May–mid-Oct, 12.30-3.30pm Mon-Sat mid-Oct–Apr) is well worth considering. It's more fun that it sounds, with traditional protective miners' gear to be worn and a ride down a whooshing wooden slide into the depths of the mine. Down below, the highlights include mysteriously glowing salt grottoes and the crossing of a 100m-long subterranean salt lake on a wooden raft.

KÖNIGSSEE

The beautiful, emerald-green Königssee is the country's highest lake, elevation 603m. Framed by steep mountain walls, it lies like a misplaced fjord 5km south of Berchtesgaden and is enchanting beyond belief. The waters descend to a staggering 200m and you can see down, down into the crystal-clear depths, with water so clean it's drinking quality. But the surface can also be treacherous, and like the snowy slopes of the peaks above, is plagued by storms that whip up at a moment's notice.

Electric boat tours (€10.80, two hours) operate on the lake year-round. On their way out they glide past a statue of St Nepomuk; a rock that downed a boatload of

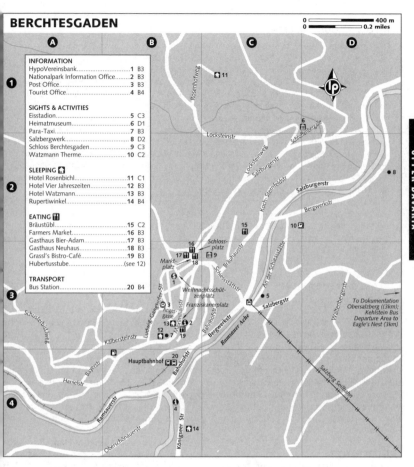

BERCHTESGADEN

INFORMATION
HypoVereinsbank	1 B3
Nationalpark Information Office	2 B3
Post Office	3 B3
Tourist Office	4 B4

SIGHTS & ACTIVITIES
Eisstadion	5 C3
Heimatmuseum	6 D1
Para-Taxi	7 B3
Salzbergwerk	8 D2
Schloss Berchtesgaden	9 C3
Watzmann Therme	10 C2

SLEEPING
Hotel Rosenbichl	11 C1
Hotel Vier Jahreszeiten	12 B3
Hotel Watzmann	13 B3
Rupertiwinkel	14 B4

EATING
Bräustübl	15 C2
Farmers Market	16 B3
Gasthaus Bier-Adam	17 B3
Gasthaus Neuhaus	18 B3
Grassl's Bistro-Café	19 B3
Hubertusstube	(see 12)

TRANSPORT
Bus Station	20 B4

pilgrims in 1688; and tumbling almost vertically above the boat, an Alpine waterfall.

The first stop is **St Bartholomä**, a quaint onion-domed chapel that is the lake's most enduring image. It dates back to the 12th century but looks much different today after the baroque flourishes were poured onto it centuries later. The boat will stop and the guide will hoist his flügelhorn and play a tune towards the amazing **Echo Wall**. It's usually a familiar old chestnut such as *Que Sera Sera* but the response is really quite breathtaking – bouncing back seven times, in total, between the cliffs of the Watzmann and the surrounding peaks. The effect only fails when there's a heavy fog. A few years back, some yokels hid in

the ridges and bleated out their own echo, a quite different one, back to the captain as a joke.

In the valley, about an hour's hike from the dock at St Bartholomä, is the **Eiskapelle**. As snow gathers in the corner of the rocks here, a dome emerges that reaches heights of over 200m. In summer as the ice melts, the water digs tunnels and creates a huge opening in the solid ice.

You can also explore the lakeshore yourself, passing the bustling tourist village filled with stands peddling souvenirs, for a nice and easy 3.5km return walk to the secluded **Malerwinkel** (Painter's Corner), a lookout point famed for its picturesque vantage point.

HITLER'S MOUNTAIN RETREAT

Of all the German towns tainted by the pall of the Third Reich, Berchtesgaden has been cursed with a larger share than most. Hitler fell in love with nearby Obersalzberg in the 1920s and bought a small country home here, later enlarged into the imposing Berghof.

After becoming chancellor in 1933, he established part-time headquarters here and brought the party brass with him. They bought or confiscated over 31 sq km of land, tore down ancient farmhouses, erected a 2m-high barbed-wire fence, built guardhouses along the three access roads, and eventually turned Obersalzberg into the fortified, southern headquarters of the NSDAP (National Socialist German Workers' Party). In 1938, Hitler hosted British Prime Minister Neville Chamberlain here for the first of a series of negotiations (later continued in Munich with other European leaders), which led to the infamous promise of 'peace in our time' at the expense of the invasion of Czechoslovakia. Little is left of Hitler's 'Alpine Fortress' today. In the final days of WWII, the Royal Air Force levelled much of the Obersalzberg, though the Eagle's Nest, Hitler's mountaintop eyrie, was left strangely unscathed.

To learn more, visit the excellent Dokumentation Obersalzberg, which opened in 2000 and has been a wild success, far exceeding visitor projections. The latest controversy is a new luxury hotel, the Hotel Intercontinental (p152) recently built on the nearby site of the Platterhof, once a Nazi 'people's hotel', despite protests that the project would erase a piece of the very history the centre aims to illuminate. It seems that for Berchtesgaden there's just no escaping from Hitler's shadow.

SCHLOSS BERCHTESGADEN

In Berchtesgaden's main square, the **Schloss Berchtesgaden** (royal palace; ☎ 947 980; Schlossplatz; adult/child €7/3; ☼ tours 10am-1pm & 2-4pm mid-May–mid-Oct, 11am & 2pm mid-Oct–mid-May) is a bit overlooked by the crowds who immediately rush to the mountains. Crown Prince Rupprecht decorated many rooms with objects from the royal Wittelsbachs' own art collection. Prepare for hunting weapons, sumptuous furniture, fine porcelain and paintings by Bavarian artists. This royal collection has a bit of a backwoods flavour.

HEIMATMUSEUM

A short walk from the centre of town, the **Heimatmuseum** (Local History Museum; ☎ 4410; Schroffenbergalle 6; adult/child €2/1; ☼ 10am-4pm Tue-Sun) is one of the Alps' most interesting folk museums. It's a diverse collection located in the 400-year-old Schloss Adelsheim, and sadly undervisited. One exhibit traces the tradition of Berchtesgaden's hand-fashioned wooden boxes, made from pine by the region's poor farmers, gilded or painted and then decorated with local flowers or other traditional designs. At the peak of the trade, 40,000 boxes a week were produced to hold everything from hats to letters. Other rooms display carved flutes, religious art, gingerbread moulds, toys and the marionettes used by a family of travelling performers from 1870 to 1936.

Activities

HIKING

The wilds of the 210-sq-km **Nationalpark Berchtesgaden** unquestionably offer some of the best hiking in Germany. A dense network of trails crisscrosses diverse landscapes, from placid lakeshores and craggy peaks to scenic valleys and lush mountain meadows. A good introduction is a 2km path up from St Bartholomä beside the Königssee to the Watzmann-Ostwand – scores of mountaineers have died attempting to climb this massive 2000m rock face. Another popular hike goes from the southern end of the Königssee to the Obersee.

We've outlined further hikes below, but for more suggestions see the brochure *Berg + Tal* (Hill + Dale), published by the Berchtesgaden tourist office. Maps are available there as well as at the Nationalpark information office, whose knowledgeable staff are the best source all around.

Zauberwald

This is an easy 1.5km hike along the shores of the idyllic **Hintersee**, just west of Ramsau, where rowing boats share the water with ducks. The trail continues through the 'Magic Forest' where huge boulders are haphazardly piled along the creek. It starts at the car park Seeklause and should take no more than one to 1½ hours of leisurely walking time. May to July are the best months.

Almbachklamm

A moderate 8.5km hike takes you through the dramatic Almbach gorge (adult/child €2/€1), which offers terrific views of the rushing stream, pools and waterfalls. It starts at the **Kugelmühle**, Germany's oldest functioning marble mill (1683). The gorge is 4km northeast of Berchtesgaden and 2km south of Marktschellenberg, and slowly climbs up to the dam at Theresienklause. From here, it spills out into a lovely valley, which leads to the village of Ettenberg with its pilgrimage church. This is a good spot for a picnic or a *Brotzeit* (snack) before heading down a steepish trail back to Marktschellenberg. This hike has an elevation gain of 320m and will take about three hours (walking time only). The best time of year is between May and October.

SKIING

Skiing conditions, especially for downhill, in the Berchtesgadener Land are not as reliable as in other Alpine resorts such as Garmisch-Partenkirchen, but snowmaking equipment does its part in stretching the season.

There are five ski areas (five-day passes for adults/children under 14 cost €105/€55 for all lifts) with about 50km of slopes, plenty of ski schools and outfitters. There are also about 60km of groomed cross-country tracks. Call ahead for snow conditions (☎ 967 297, recording in German).

The **Götschen** is the training centre of the German women's skiing team as well as popular snowboarding terrain. Evening skiing is a blast when the slopes are flooded with lights and music.

The **Jenner-Königssee area** (☎ 958 10; www .jennerbahn.de in German; daily/6-day passes €23.50/94) is the biggest of the ski fields, with pistes varying from 630m to 1800m, and is suitable for more-experienced skiers.

Good family playgrounds are **Gutshof**, in the Obersalzberg area, and **Rossfeld-Zinken**, on the border with Austria, which has a separate snowboarding piste with half-pipe. Day passes, which include the trip on the local bus and toll fees, cost around €20.

Finally, there's **Hochschwarzeck**, which has a tobogganing track and other attractions.

For equipment hire and courses:

Skischule Treff-Aktiv (☎ 667 10, 0171-726 4289; www .treffaktiv.de in German; Jennerbahnstrasse 14, Schönau) It also organises mountaineering, rafting and hikes.

OTHER WINTER SPORTS

Speed freaks will love the **Kunsteis Bob- und Rodelbahn** (☎ 9670, 1760; Schönau). It's a 1.3km-long ice canal with an 11% incline and 18 curves, including a full loop. You can go down in a regular guest bobsleigh but if that's too tame, whiz down at up to 120km/h with a professional racer in a four-person racing bob (per person €80).

There is ice skating at the **Eisstadion** (☎ 614 05; An der Schiessstätte; adult/child €3/1.50), or you could head out to the Hintersee, which is usually frozen in winter.

PARAGLIDING

If you haven't earned your wings yet, fly tandem with a qualified instructor on a flight with **Para-Taxi Berchtesgadener Land** (☎ 948 450; www.parataxi.de in German; Maximilianstrasse 16; 15min €115, 20-30min €150, 30-45min €180) that's as soft as silk and always too short, but long enough to get hooked.

WATZMANN THERME

Berchtesgaden's thermal wellness and fun activity pool complex, **Watzmann Therme**

CRUEL KING WATZMANN

The placid meadows surrounding St Bartholomä stand in stark contrast to the 1800m of grey massif soaring behind it – the mythical Mt Watzmann. Legend has it that the two big and seven smaller peaks represent a sadistic king, his queen and their children who, after terrorising the land for years, morphed into stone as punishment for their cruelty. 'King' Watzmann, the middle peak, rises to an elevation of almost 2700m and is the highest point in the national park. Its eastern face ranks as one of the most dangerous climbs in the Alpine region. More than 100 people have lost their lives attempting climbs since the peak was first scaled in 1881. Most accidents are caused by rocks, which dislodge from the unstable limestone, crashing down on the unsuspecting climbers below. This climb should only be attempted by the very experienced and in the company of a skilled mountain guide.

(☎ 946 40; Bergwerkstrase 54; tickets 2hr/4hr/day €8/10.50/15; ☯ 10am-10pm) has several indoor and outdoor pools with various hydrotherapeutic treatment stations, a sauna and fabulous Alpine views.

Tours

An excellent way to experience the creepy legacy of the Obersalzberg area, including the Kehlsteinhaus and the underground bunker system, is by taking a four-hour tour with **Eagle's Nest Tours** (☎ 649 71; www .eagles-nest-tours.com; adult/child under 12 €40/30; ☯ 1.30pm mid-May–Oct). Buses depart from the tourist office and reservations are advised, although a second service runs at 8.30am when there is sufficient demand.

Sleeping

Berchtesgaden has plenty of private rooms from €25 per person. Check with the tourist office about availability. Unless otherwise noted, lodging options listed below are in the town of Berchtesgaden.

Hotel Intercontinental (☎ 975 50; www.inter continental.com; Hintereck 1; s/d/ste from €150/250/290; P ☒ ☒ ☐ ☒) An upscale palace in the clouds (1000m), the Interconti has bulge-bracket luxuries such as all-season terraces, a library with fireplace, 24-hour fitness centre and state-of-the-art rooms – if you can accept its controversial location on the Obersalzberg (see the boxed text on p149).

Hotel Vier Jahreszeiten (☎ 9520; millers-hotel@t -online.de; Maximilianstrasse 20; s €67-72, d €87-138; P ☒) An Alpine lodge with more than a touch of the modern, including a pool, sauna and solarium, for starters. All categories get a piece of the comforts, not to mention panoramic views of the mountains. It has an excellent restaurant (right).

Hotel Rosenbichl (☎ 944 00; www.hotel-rosenbichl .de; Rosenhofweg 24; s €55, d €78-98; P ☒) This traditional hotel in the middle of the protected nature zone offers exceptional value. The rooms are spacious and modern and there's also a sauna, whirlpool, solarium and a fitness studio.

Rupertiwinkel (☎ 4187; info@gaestehaus-ruperti winkel.de; Königseer Strasse 29; s/d €25/45; P) This incredibly friendly, English-speaking pension is just past the tourist office and within walking distance of the station. The comfortable, modern rooms are great value and some have spacious balconies.

Hotel-Pension Greti (☎ 946 50; www.pension-greti .de; Waldhauserstrasse 20, Schönau; r €24-52; P) Warm and welcoming, and just a 15-minute walk from the Königssee, all of Greti's rooms are in a well-appointed country style and have balconies. The panelled cellar bar is perfect for winding down postpiste.

Hotel Watzmann (☎ 2055; fax 5174; Franziskaner-platz 2; s €25-39, d €44-68; ☯ closed Nov–mid-Dec; P ☒) There's a good range of rooms at this rambling time-warped place in the centre of town. The rooms are small but reasonable value and just ooze character with their quirky traditional décor and animal hides mounted on the walls.

DJH hostel (☎ 943 70; www.jugendherberge.de/jh /strub/index.html; Gebirgsjägerstrasse 52; dm under 27s only €14.85-15.55; ☯ closed Nov-late Dec) This 360-bed hostel is situated in the suburb of Strub and has great views of Mt Watzmann. It's a 25-minute walk from the Hauptbahnhof or a short journey on bus No 9539.

The nicest camp sites are near the Königssee in Schönau and include **Camping-platz Mühlleiten** (☎ 4584; www.camping-muehlleiten .de; Königseer Strasse 70; per camp site/person €5/4.70) and **Camping Grafenlehen** (☎ 4140; www.camping -grafenlehen.de; Königsseerfussweg 71; per camp site/person €6/5.20).

Eating & Drinking

Hubertusstube (☎ 9520; Maximilianstrasse 20; mains €10-22) Part of the Hotel Vier Jahreszeiten, this restaurant offers rich pickings such as venison and sirloin steak specialities as well as a good choice of vegetarian dishes. The dining areas all have fine views of the mountains.

Grassl's Bistro-Café (☎ 2524; Maximilianstrasse 11; mains €3-9; ☯ 9am-6pm Mon-Sat) This cosy café with the porcelain knick-knacks is an ideal lunch spot, not least for the breathtaking terrace. Besides its array of soups, sandwiches and daily specials, try its snow-capped Mt Watzmann chocolates.

Gasthaus Neuhaus (☎ 2182; Marktplatz 1; mains €5-14) This huge place serves *Brotzeiten* and more-substantial old-style Bavarian fare, including seasonal specials and vegetarian fare. The daily three-course menu is easy on the pocket at €9, and there's a beer garden with live music on summer evenings.

Bräustübl (☎ 1423; Bräuhausstrasse 13; Brotzeit €3.50-9, mains €5-16) This venerable pub-eatery now has organic schnitzel but remains comfy and familiar, located by a pretty courtyard

ST NICK'S SCARY HELPERS

Pagan rites and rituals were an important part of everyday life in Berchtesgadener Land as far back as the 8th century. Especially in the mountains, cut off from change and progress, these traditions were carried on despite the growing reach of the Catholic Church.

One of the most popular customs in Berchtesgaden revolves around the *Buttnmandl* – centuries-old folk characters who stomp and growl their way through towns and villages to chase away the demons of winter. These fearsome creatures (read: young men aged 16 to 30) are wrapped from head to toe in hand-threshed straw or hairy hides, and don furry masks with long slobbering tongues. Large cowbells hung from their backs clank with every step to awaken mother nature in time for spring. Several dark, hairy characters with hooves, known as *Kramperl* or *Gangerl,* help to direct the collective madness.

In the Middle Ages, as the tradition of St Nicholas spread throughout Europe, this 'heathen' practice was coupled with the Christmas holidays. This allowed people to retain the beliefs of their forebears (and the Church to keep them under control). Nowadays about a dozen *Buttnmandl* and a couple of *Kramperl* join St Nick every year to impress on children the need to be good – and woe betide anyone who steals a stalk of lucky straw. Long switches are still flicked at the legs of young girls as an ancient fertility rite. The *Kramperl* herd the *Buttnmandl* together and pass on orders from St Nick, who is dressed as a bishop and carries a staff.

In the town of Berchtesgaden the ritual is kicked off by an organised *Buttnmandl* 'run' on 5 December, as enthusiastic crowds greet St Nick on horseback complete with a parade, folk music and police escort. But dates vary in the countryside, where some *Buttnmandls* are still marauding at Christmas.

at the old brewery. It also has a beer hall that puts on a heel-whacking Bavarian stage show every Saturday night in summer.

Holzkäfer (☎ 621 07; Buchenhöhe 40; dishes €4-9; ☒ 2pm-1am Wed-Mon; wheelchair access) If you're driving, this funky log cabin restaurant in the Obersalzberg hills is a great spot. Crammed with antlers, carvings and backwoods oddities, it's great for an evening drink or a light meal.

Other possibilities:

Gasthaus Bier-Adam (☎ 2390; Markt 22; mains €6-14) Cheerful place with a good range of traditional fare and a nonsmokers' dining room.

Gasthaus Auzinger (☎ 08657-230; Hirschbichlstrasse 3, Ramsau; mains €6-11; ☒ Fri-Wed) Former artists' haunt serving farmers' favourites near the Hintersee.

Farmers market (Marktplatz; ☒ 8-11am Fri Apr-Oct) An incredible array of fresh produce and meats.

Getting There & Away

For the quickest train connections to Berchtesgaden, it's usually best to take a Munich to Salzburg train and change at Freilassing (€29, 2½ hours). There are direct trains from Salzburg (€7.20, 1¼ hours), although RVO bus No 9540 makes the trip in about 45 minutes and has more departures. Berchtesgaden is south of the Munich–Salzburg A8 autobahn.

Getting Around

The various communities of the Berchtesgadener Land are well connected by **RVO bus** (☎ 944 820). Pick up a detailed schedule at the tourist office. To get to the Königssee, take bus No 9541 or 9542. Bus No 9538 goes up the Obersalzberg. For a taxi call ☎ 4041.

INN-SALZACH
Altötting

☎ 08671 / pop 13,000 / elev 403m

What Lourdes is to France, Altötting is to Bavaria. Every year more than a million Roman Catholic pilgrims descend upon this innocuous little town to pay their respects to the Mary – a limewood sculpture, clad in festive robes and blackened from centuries of exposure to candle soot. Mary arrived in Altötting in about 1330, worked a few miracles and soon became one of the most popular women in Europe. Kings, dukes and popes including Pope John Paul II have stopped by.

Over the centuries, additional churches were built to deal with the burgeoning throng. Today there are six major ones in the town centre alone, all huddled around Kapellplatz. In the streets, nuns in habits, frocked priests and robed monks mingle with the mostly elderly pilgrims. Souvenir shops hawk items that register a perfect 10 on the 'kitsch-ometer' but that are happily snapped up by the faithful.

There's definitely something fascinating, almost exotic, about this place, even if religion doesn't do it for you. Note that the town all but shuts down from mid-November to early March.

ORIENTATION & INFORMATION

Altötting's compact centre is anchored by Kapellplatz, a short walk north of the Bahnhof. For information, stop by the **tourist and pilgrimage office** (☎ 8069; www.altoetting.de in German; Kapellplatz 2a; ☒ 8am-noon & 2-5pm Mon-Fri, 9am-noon Sat May-Oct, 8am-noon & 2-5pm Mon-Thu, 8am-noon Fri Nov-Apr).

SIGHTS

Church fans will be in heaven in Altötting. The one not to be missed is the **Gnadenkapelle**, a tiny 8th-century octagonal chapel in the middle of Kapellplatz. Here you can visit the miraculous Mary perched in her silver and gold altar. She's guarded by the sculptures of two kneeling men – a prince and a bishop – as well as the hearts of Wittelsbach rulers, including Ludwig II. These are enshrined in silver urns tucked away in niches on the opposite wall.

Inside the chapel and all over the covered outside walkway encircling it, more than 2000 *ex voto* tablets attest to the fact that Mary has been busy in the miracle department. You'll often see devout pilgrims shouldering heavy crosses and schlepping them around the ambulatory, sometimes crawling on their knees, and reciting the rosary in religious ecstasy.

The big twin-towered church south of the chapel is the Gothic **Stiftskirche**. It's the third on the site and the successor of a Romanesque basilica, of which only the western portal survives. Inside, the best sight is a large clock topped by a scythe-wielding silver skeleton, every second signalling someone's death with each swing. Known as the Tod von Eding, the macabre fellow was inspired by the black plague, which raged through local lands in 1634.

Proceed to the Gothic cloister, which has some frescoes, ancient tombstones and, incongruously, photographs of local *Wehrmacht* members killed during WWII. The

double chapel in the southeastern corner contains the grave of Thirty Years' War general, Count von Tilly.

Attached to the church's northern façade is the **Schatzkammer** (Treasury; ☎ 5166; adult/child €2/1; ☒ 10am-noon & 2-4pm Tue-Sun Apr-Oct). The *pièce de résistance* here is the exquisite Goldene Rössl (Golden Horse), a small silver-and-gold altar smothered with pearls and jewels that was wrought in Paris in 1404. It has just been painstakingly restored and gleams like new. Beneath the tableau is a horse held steady by a servant for his master, French King Charles VI; he's the one depicted on the altar praying to Mary.

East of the Gnadenkapelle, the late-baroque **Kirche St Magdalena** (1697) is clothed in heavy stucco. On the northern side of Kapellplatz is the **Wallfahrts- und Heimatmuseum** (Pilgrimage & Local History Museum; ☎ 5166; adult/child €1.50/0.50; ☒ 2-4pm Tue-Fri, 10am-3pm Sat & Sun Apr-Oct), where scale models, folk art and paintings help tell the town's history and the impact of pilgrimages.

A short walk east of the Kapellplatz, in Kreszentiaheimstrasse, is one of Altötting's most unusual sights, the **Panorama** (☎ 6934; adult/child €3/2; ☒ 9am-5pm Mar-Oct, 11am-2pm Sat & Sun Nov-Feb). It's a monumental 360-degree painting, created by Gebhard Fugel in 1902 to 1903, of the classical Jerusalem during Jesus' Crucifixion. A 30-minute surround-sound narration takes you back to the events leading up to this fateful day. If you speak German it's quite impressive. In winter the Panorama only opens for groups of 10 or more.

Across the street, the **Mechanische Krippe** (Mechanical Creche; ☎ 66 53; Kreszentiaheimstrasse 18; adult/child €1.50/1; ☒ 9am-5pm Mar-Dec) features about 130 wooden figurines carved by Oberammergau's masters in 1926 to 1928.

SLEEPING & EATING

Hotel Zwölf Apostel (☎ 969 60; info@hotel-zwoelf-apostel.de; Bruder-Konrad-Platz 3-4; s €40, d €60-65; ☒) This is one of the oldest inns in town, with spruced-up, modern rooms with TV (some even with direct-dial phones!) as well as a good restaurant. It's on the rear square behind the basilica, far enough from the crowds to ensure a sound sleep.

Hotel Zur Post (☎ 5040, 6214; www.zurpostaltoetting.de; Kapellplatz 2; s €50-97, d €108-135; lunch mains €5-12.50, dinner €6.50-20; ℗) Although this is Altötting's flagship hotel, the rooms are surprisingly small and nothing special. The integrated 'Roman' spa and sauna complex, however, with separate sections for men and women, is superb. At the restaurant the chef gives traditional favourites the creative treatment.

Brotzeitstüberl (☎ 6904; Kapellplatz 13; snacks €1.50-5; ☺ from 5pm or 6pm Mon-Sat) This is a simple but tasty snack place near the Stiftskirche, which serves things like ham and cheese baguettes, *Leberkäs* and schnitzel.

More cafés and cheaper eateries are on the southern side of Kapellplatz, including **La Piazzetta** (☎ 138 54; Kapellplatz 24; dishes €3.50-8), a bistro-type place that does pizza, pasta and salads. The terrace tables give a fine view of the Gnadenkapelle.

GETTING THERE & AWAY

Coming from Munich by train requires a change in Mühldorf (€14.60, 1¾ hours). From Landshut, regional trains take about 1¼ hours, also via Mühldorf (€9.70). Trains to Burghausen leave at least hourly (€3.30, 25 minutes). Altötting is just off the B12, about 93km due east of Munich.

Burghausen

☎ 08677 / pop 20,000 / elev 350m

About 15km southeast of Altötting, Burghausen was once a mover and shaker in Europe, a flourishing centre of the salt trade and a regional seat of government. Decline set in, as it tends to do, and by the 17th century Burghausen's star had dimmed. But there was a bright side: the town escaped the march of progress, preserving its medieval appearance for posterity.

The lovely Altstadt hugs a gentle bend of the Salzach River – which separates it from Austria – and is lorded over by the castle complex. It is billed as Europe's longest, seated grandly atop a mountain ridge. The modern part of town is north of here, spawned by the arrival of the chemical industry in the early 20th century, which still provides jobs for about 10,000 people today.

Burghausen's Bahnhof, in the modern town, is connected to the Stadtplatz, the main Altstadt square, by bus No 1. There's a **tourist office** (☎ 967 6932; www.burghausen.de; Stadtplatz 112; ☺ 8.30am-5pm Mon-Fri, 10am-1pm Sat, 10amnoon Sun Jul-Sep) in town and another branch (Burg 9) near the northern end of the castle, about 50m south of Curaplatz.

The best views of the castle and the Altstadt are from the Austrian side. Cross the bridge over the Salzach and either drive or walk uphill to the viewpoint.

SIGHTS
Burg zu Burghausen

Stretching out for 1034m, and visible from anywhere in the Altstadt, Burghausen's namesake **Burg** (castle) consists of several groups of buildings wrapped around six courtyards. The dukes lived in the lap of luxury, although there was a fair amount of discord as the nobles tended to keep their ex-wives cooped up in the same complex. The main castle at the southern end has an inner core dating back to 1255 and now houses several museums. Entrance to the castle grounds is free.

The **Historisches Stadtmuseum** (Museum of Municipal History; ☎ 651 98; adult/child under 18 €2/free; ☺ 9am-6.30pm May-Sep, 10am-4.30pm mid-Mar–Apr & Oct, closed Oct–mid-Mar) is the local history museum. It has predictable displays but the rooms, all 30 of them, ooze atmosphere, including the Gothic *Kemenate,* the wing once inhabited by the duchess and her entourage. The duke and his fellows used to congregate in the section of rooms of what is now the **Staatliche Sammlungen** (State Galleries; ☎ 4659; adult/child under 18 €3/free; ☺ 9am-5pm Apr-Oct, 9am-5pm Nov-Mar), which house a collection of late-Gothic paintings by Bavarian artists as well as furniture from the 15th and 16th centuries.

In the fourth courtyard is the **Folterturm** (Torture Tower; ☎ 641 90; adult/child €1.80/0.60; ☺ 9am-6pm mid-Mar–Oct, 9am-6pm Sat & Sun Nov–mid-Mar). The old tower houses a bone-chilling torture chamber, prison cells and dungeons connected via a subterranean walkway to **Hexenturm** (Witches' Tower). The last person was beheaded here in 1831.

In the sixth courtyard, the interesting **Haus der Fotografie** (House of Photography; ☎ 4734; adult/child under 18 €2/free; ☺ 10am-6pm Wed-Sun Apr-Oct) chronicles the history of photography, with a decent array of classic old cameras. It has numerous galleries in attractive quarters that were once the old pension-master's office.

There are several ways to the castle. If you're driving, you'll find a car park at its northern end near Curaplatz. Trails leading to the Altstadt are in the second and sixth courtyards while another, via the Georgstor, heads down the other side to the Wöhrsee, a large recreational lake.

From March to October, tours (in German) leave from the tourist office at Burg 9 on weekends and holidays at 11am and 2pm.

Altstadt

The action in the old town hinges on the **Stadtplatz**. It's an elongated square with Italian flair and framed by candy-coloured town houses topped by red tile roofs. Edifices worth inspection include the magnificent **Tauffkirchenpalais** (Stadtplatz 97), where Napoleon stayed briefly in 1809; the former **Regierungsgebäude** (Government Building; Stadtplatz 108), bearing some elaborate coats of arms and topped by a trio of copper-domed turrets; and the **Rathaus** (Stadtplatz 112), which now houses the main tourist office. The southern end of the square is punctuated by the **Pfarrkirche St Jakob** from where a painted arch leads to the pedestrianised In den Grüben, the former craftsmen's quarter.

Many of the Gothic buildings along here house charming boutiques, wine taverns, pubs and restaurants. At No 193 is the **Mautnerschloss**, the former toll collector's home, which now houses a **jazz cellar** (☎ 887 140) and a study centre for contemporary music.

FESTIVALS & EVENTS

Burghausen is famous for its jazz festivals, especially the **Internationale Jazzwoche** (International Jazz Week; www.b-jazz.com in German) in April and May, which has drawn the crème de la crème of musicians – Ella Fitzgerald to Count Basie – to this little town since 1970.

SLEEPING & EATING

The tourist offices can help you find private rooms from €18 per person.

Hotel Post (☎ 9650; Stadtplatz 39; s €69-72, d €89-95; meals €8-20; **P**) This is one of the nicest hotels in town with comfortable rooms, a beer garden sprawling onto Stadtplatz, and a good restaurant serving Bavarian food. The courteous staff wear traditional costume.

Altstadt Pension (☎ 878 686; In den Grüben 138/142; s/d from €38/51; **P**) This pension with bright flowers and solid pine furniture is tucked away in an alley south of the main square. You can have breakfast in the riverside beer garden at the rear, or just watch the rowers plying the Salzach.

DJH hostel (☎ 4187; www.jugendherberge.de/jh /burghausen in German; Kapuzinergasse 235; dm incl breakfast €15.45-17.95) Burghausen's hostel is inside a former monastery at the southern end of the Altstadt and will take guests over 27 years.

Zum Andechser (☎ 881 8231; Am Stadtplatz; mains €6.50-13) Come here for monkish brews and the usual range of Bavarian specialities, consumed either in the woodsy interior or on the big terrace facing Stadtplatz.

Trastavere (☎ 3999; Stadtplatz 111; mains €4-15) This is a youthful bistro with a good Italian restaurant in the vaulted cellar. The rear terrace has delightful views out over the icy Salzach.

GETTING THERE & AWAY

Trains from Altötting make the trip to Burghausen at least hourly (€3.30, 25 minutes). Burghausen is on the B20.

Eastern Bavaria

EASTERN BAVARIA

HIGHLIGHTS

■ **Green Getaway**
Returning to nature amid the thick forest of the Nationalpark Bayerischer Wald (p175)

■ **History Lesson**
Encountering a pantheon of Germany's greatest minds and achievers at Walhalla (p166)

■ **Chilling Out**
Cruising leisurely through the spectacular Danube Gorge (p166)

■ **Party Town**
Drinking tasty brews amid medieval splendour in amiable Regensburg (p158)

■ **Epic Drink-Up**
Letting your hair down at Straubing's boisterous Gäubodenfest (p167)

■ **Architectural Splendour**
Exploring three rivers, a lordly fortress and baroque buildings in pretty Passau (p169)

Walhalla
Regensburg ★ ★
★ Danube Gorge Straubing
★ Nationalpark
Bayerischer Wald
Passau ★

■ POP: 2.25 MILLION   ■ AREA: 20,000 SQ KM

Celts, Romans, missionaries, kings and Kaisers, merchants, farmers, students – for more than two millennia people have been drawn to Ostbayern (Eastern Bavaria), a charismatic pastiche of undulating farmland and thick sweeps of forests anchored by proud cities drenched in history and romance. Through it all wends the Danube, an epic river that has captured the imagination of poets and painters and delivered power and prosperity during times when Munich was still little more than a far-off dream.

Eastern Bavaria is a low-key destination, far removed from the theme park–like bustle of Schloss Neuschwanstein or the see-and-be-seen hub of Garmisch-Partenkirchen. The pace of life is unhurried, the locals are welcoming and genuinely glad to see you, and their traditions haven't been hijacked by Hollywood or kitsch promoters.

Start by visiting the cities, each of which will charm you in different ways. Regensburg's blend of medieval looks and 21st-century verve is nothing short of infectious. Landshut's proud castle, Straubing's treasure-packed churches and Passau's baroque Altstadt (old town) will all carve out distinct niches in your memory. East of the Danube, the Bavarian Forest is a glorious sprawl of spruce and fir sprinkled with easy-going villages. Germany's oldest national park is here, the remote and partly untamed Nationalpark Bayerischer Wald. Great hiking and skiing, a centuries-old tradition of glassmaking, the absence of mass tourism and amazingly low-priced lodging (of high standard) are just a few of the assets that make this region perfect for an unforgettable and thoroughly fun getaway.

REGENSBURG

☎ 0941 / pop 142,000 / elev 330m

At once ancient and vibrant, Regensburg is one of Bavaria's most beautiful cities and is among the best-preserved medieval towns in Europe. Its magic reveals itself in countless, often surprising, places. You'll find it in a leafy beer garden overlooking the Danube, in the romantic Altstadt with its honeycomb of teensy lanes spilling onto buzzing piazzas, and in the soaring spires of the Dom (cathedral). This is a city where you can eat pizza in a former Gothic chapel, lean against a wall erected by the Romans and see the house where Oskar Schindler lived. There are excellent restaurants, lively nightlife (thanks to a large student population) no fewer than three local breweries and enough engaging sights to keep you busy for at least a couple of days.

History

'Regensburg is so beautifully situated, someone had to settle here,' rhapsodised Johann Wolfgang von Goethe. And indeed, that's just what's happened for more than 2000 years. The Romans built a giant fortress here, St Boniface founded a bishopric and the Bavarian dukes made the town their capital. That is until they were ousted by Charlemagne under whom it became the hub of his ever-expanding Frankish empire. Regensburg's prominence rose steadily through the Middle Ages, and so did its fortunes, especially after the completion of the Steinerne Brücke (Stone Bridge) in 1146. As the only permanent bridge across the Danube, it put the city smack-bang in the middle of important trade routes, thus turning it into a medieval trading metropolis. The Altstadt's characteristic town houses, with their jutting tall towers, date back to this period.

Alas, competition from Augsburg and Nuremberg eventually brought on Regensburg's decline, although it regained some prestige as the seat of the Perpetual Diet (permanent parliament) of the Holy Roman Empire from 1663 to 1806.

Spared wartime destruction, today's city preserves its medieval character, at least in the Altstadt, but is also the thriving capital of the Oberpfalz (Upper Palatinate) region with a university, modern industries and a proud heritage.

Orientation

Regensburg's major sights cluster in the Altstadt, which is hemmed in by the Danube

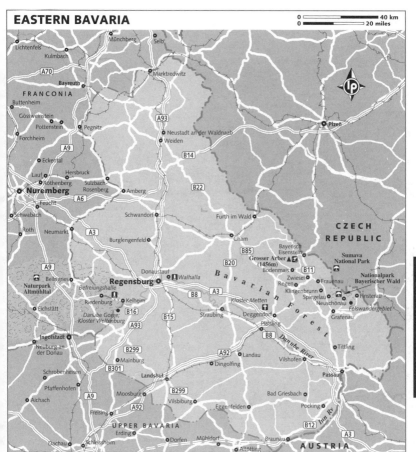

EASTERN BAVARIA

EASTERN BAVARIA

on the northern flank and is almost entirely closed to private vehicle traffic (driving to your hotel is OK). The Hauptbahnhof (central train station) is about a 10-minute walk south of the heart of the Altstadt, ie the area around the Dom.

Information

BOOKSHOPS
Bücher Pustet (☎ 569 70; Gesandtenstrasse 6-8) Good selection of maps and English-language travel guides and novels.
Presse + Buch (☎ 585 750; inside Hauptbahnhof) English books and magazines.

EMERGENCY
Ambulance (☎ 192 22)

Police (☎ 110, nonemergencies ☎ 5060; Minoritenweg 1)

INTERNET ACCESS
C@fe Netzblick (☎ 599 9700; Am Römling 9; per hr €2.50; ⏰ 6pm-1am)
City Point (☎ 584 3091; Wahlenstrasse 6; per min 5¢; ⏰ 9am-10.30pm)

LIBRARIES
Stadtbücherei (public library; ☎ 507 2470; Haidplatz 8; ⏰ 10am-6.30pm Mon-Fri, 10am-1pm Sat) English-language books and magazines in the American Library on the 2nd floor.

MEDICAL SERVICES
Evangelisches Krankenhaus (Protestant Hospital; ☎ 504 00; Emmeramsplatz 10)

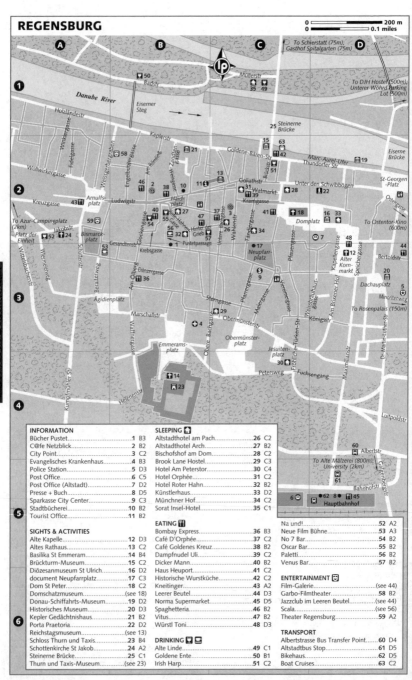

REGENSBURG

0 — 200 m
0 — 0.1 miles

MONEY
Sparkasse City Center (Neupfarrplatz 10; ⊗ 24hr)
Automated foreign-exchange machine.

POST
Post office Altstadt (Domplatz 3) Hauptbahnhof (Bahnhofstrasse 16) The Hauptbahnhof branch also changes money.

TOURIST INFORMATION
Tourist office (☎ 507 4410; www.regensburg.de; Altes
Rathaus; ⊗ 9.15am-6pm Mon-Fri, 9.15am-4pm Sat,
9.30am-4pm Sun & holidays)

Sights
DOM ST PETER & AROUND
Regensburg's soaring landmark, the **Dom St
Peter** (St Peter's Cathedral; ☎ 597 1002; Domplatz; admission free, tours in German adult/concession €2.50/1.50;
⊗ 6.30am-6pm Apr-Oct, to 5pm Nov-Mar, tours 10am,
11am, 2pm Mon-Sat, 1pm & 2pm Sun May-Oct, 11am Mon-
Sat, 1pm Sun Nov-Apr) ranks among Bavaria's
grandest Gothic cathedrals. Construction
began in the late 13th century, mostly as a
vanity project to show off the city's prosperity. Inside the dark, cavernous cathedral,
prized possessions include kaleidoscopic
stained-glass windows and a pair of charming sculptures attached to pillars just west
of the altar. One shows the Angel of the Annunciation, his smiling mug beaming at the
Virgin on the opposite pillar as he delivers
the news of her pregnancy.

Attached to the Dom, in the former bishop's residence, the **Domschatzmuseum** (Cathedral
Treasury; ☎ 576 45; adult/child under 14 €2/1; ⊗ 10am-
5pm Tue-Sat, noon-5pm Sun Apr-Oct, 10am-4pm Fri & Sat,
noon-4pm Sun Dec-Mar) brims with vestments,
monstrances, tapestries and other riches.
More religious treasure awaits nearby in
the **Diözesanmuseum St Ulrich** (☎ 516 88; Domplatz 2; adult/child/student €2/1/1; ⊗ 10am-5pm Tue-Sun
Apr-Oct), which is inside a medieval church.
Combination tickets for both museums
cost €3/€2 per adult/child.

Just north of the Dom, the arched gate
called **Porta Praetoria** (Unter den Schwibbögen) is
the most impressive reminder of Regens-
burg's Roman heritage. It was built in AD
179 by Emperor Marcus Aurelius as part of
the Castra Regina fortress. To see more remains of the Roman wall, stroll along Unter
den Schwibbögen.

South of the Dom, the graceful **Alte Kapelle**
(Old Chapel; Alter Kornmarkt 8) wows visitors with
rich and harmonious rococo decorations

but, at its core, is actually about 1000 years
old. The church is only open during services, but peering through the wrought-iron
gate will give you at least partial views.

HISTORISCHES MUSEUM
A medieval monastery provides a suitably
atmospheric backdrop for the city's **Historisches Museum** (Historical Museum; ☎ 507 2448;
Dachauplatz 2-4; adult/concession €2.20/1.10; ⊗ 10am-
4pm Tue-Sun, to 8pm Thu). The collections trace
through the region's history from the Stone
Age to the 19th century, with special emphasis on the Roman period and Regensburg's medieval glory days.

ALONG THE DANUBE
A veritable miracle of engineering in its
time, the arched **Steinerne Brücke** (Stone
Bridge) was cobbled together in only 11
years (1135–46) and for centuries remained
the only solid crossing along the entire Danube. According to legend, its crafty builder
promised the devil the first soul to cross
the bridge – if he let him beat the cathedral builder who had bet on completing his
church first. The bridge builder won and
hoodwinked Satan too, for the first to cross
the bridge were a dog, a cat and a chicken.

Ensconced in its southern tower is the
Brückturm-Museum (Bridge Tower Museum; ☎ 567
6015; Weisse-Lamm-Gasse 1; adult/concession €2/1.50;
⊗ 10am-5pm Apr-Oct), which houses a small
historical exhibit about this unique bridge,
although most people come for the bird's-
eye views from the top.

A short walk east along the Danube, the
Donau-Schiffahrts-Museum (Danube Navigation Museum; ☎ 507 5888; Marc-Aurel-Ufer; adult/concession
€2/1.50; ⊗ 10am-5pm Apr-Oct) is an historic pad-
dle-wheel steam tugboat with exhibits on
the history of navigation on the river.

Just west of the bridge is the **Kepler
Gedächtnishaus** (Kepler Memorial House; ☎ 507 3442;
Keplerstrasse 5; adult/concession €2.20/1.10; tours €2/1;
⊗ 10.30am-4pm Sat, Sun & holidays), the house
where the astronomer and mathematician
Johannes Kepler (1571–1630) lived and
died. Exhibits trace the man's life and scientific accomplishments, especially his laws
of planetary motion.

ALTES RATHAUS & REICHSTAGSMUSEUM
The seat of the *Reichstag* (parliament) from
1663 to 1803, the **Altes Rathaus** (old town

hall) is now home to Regensburg's three mayors, the tourist office and the **Reichstagsmuseum** (☎ 507 4411; adult/concession €3/2; ☿ tours 9.30-4pm Mon-Sat, 10am-4pm Sun Apr-Oct, 10am-4pm Nov-Mar, tours in English 3.30pm Mon-Sat). Tours take in not only the richly decorated **Reichssaal** (Imperial Hall), where the delegates convened, but also the stomach-turning torture chamber in the basement. Walk into the old holding cell and look down to the dungeon before entering the interrogation room, which bristles with scary tools of the trade. Ouch!

DOCUMENT NEUPFARRPLATZ

Regensburg had a thriving Jewish community centred on today's Neupfarrplatz, but in the early 16th century, with the city on the brink of bankruptcy, the townspeople expelled all Jews, razed their quarter and built a pilgrimage chapel on the site of the former synagogue (later replaced by today's Neupfarrkirche). Excavations on the square in the mid-1990s revealed remains of the old Jewish quarter, even older Roman buildings, a spectacular cache of gold coins and a Nazi bunker. The subterranean **document Neupfarrplatz** (☎ 507 3454; Neupfarrplatz; adult/concession €5/2.50; ☿ tours 2.30pm Thu-Sat Sep-Jun, Thu-Mon Jul & Aug) provides access to a small portion of the excavated area. Tours feature a multimedia presentation (in German) about the square's history, including the excavations and a nifty 3-D animation of the original synagogue. The space is also occasionally used for concerts and readings. Back up above, on the square itself, a work by renowned Israeli artist Dani Karavan graces the site of the former synagogue.

SCHLOSS THURN UND TAXIS & MUSEUMS

During the 15th century, Franz von Taxis (1459–1517) scratched out his place in history by establishing the first European postal system, which remained a family monopoly until the 19th century. To compensate for the loss, the family was given a new palace, the former Benedictine monastery of St Emmeram. Henceforth known as **Schloss Thurn und Taxis** (☎ 504 8133; www .thurnundtaxis.de; Emmeramsplatz 5; tours adult/concession €10.50/8; ☿ tours 11am, 2pm, 3pm & 4pm Mon-Fri, extra tour 10am Sat, Sun & holidays Apr-Sep, tours 10am, 11am, 2pm & 3pm Sat, Sun & holidays Nov-Mar), it soon

became one of the most modern palaces in Europe. Its residents enjoyed running water, central heating and a lavish interior of exquisite furniture, silver chandeliers, Gobelin tapestries, thick carpets and other items indispensable to the lifestyle of a noble family.

All this can only be seen on self-guided audio tours, which also include a look at the cloister of the **Basilika St Emmeram** (☎ 510 30; Emmeramsplatz 3; admission free; ☿ 10am-4.30pm, from 1pm Fri & noon Sun). The church itself is a masterpiece by the Asam brothers and sports a haunting crypt sheltering the remains of Sts Emmeram, Wolfgang and Ramwold, all three of them Regensburg bishops in the early days of Christianity.

The palace complex also contains the **Thurn und Taxis-Museum** (☎ 504 8133; www.thurn undtaxis.de; adult/concession €3.50/2.50, tours €6/4; ☿ tours 12.30pm & 3.30pm, self-touring 1-5pm Sat, Sun & holidays Apr-Oct, tours 1pm Sat, Sun & holidays Nov-Mar), which presents porcelain, glass, furniture and other items from the family's private collection.

SCHOTTENKIRCHE ST JAKOB

In the western Altstadt, the 12th-century main north portal of the **Schottenkirche St Jakob** (Scottish Church of St Jacob; Jakobstrasse 3) is considered one of the supreme examples of Romanesque architecture in Germany. Its numerous reliefs and sculptures (which were originally painted and covered in gold leaf) form an incredibly complicated iconography whose meaning continues to baffle even the experts.

Tours

English-language walking tours (☎ 507 4410; www.regensburg.de; Altes Rathaus; adult/concession/family €6/3/9; ☿ 1.30pm Wed & Sat May-Sep & Dec) Tours last 90 minutes and depart from the tourist office (p161). German tours are offered several times daily year-round.
Personenschifffahrt Klinger (☎ 521 04; adult/child/student €6.80/3/4.50; ☿ 10am-4pm mid-Mar–Oct) Operates 50-minute Danube cruises from the Steinerne Brücke landing docks. For boat cruises to Walhalla, see p166.

Festivals & Events

Bavarian Jazz Weekend (☎ 562 244; www.bayer isches-jazzweekend.de in German; throughout Altstadt; ☿ early or mid-Jul)
Christmas market (Neupfarrplatz & Schloss Thurn und Taxis; ☿ Dec)

Dult (Dultplatz; ⊙ Pentecost & late Aug) Oktoberfest-style party with beer tents, carousel rides, entertainment and vendors.

Schlossfestspiele (www.thurnundtaxis.de; Schloss Thurn und Taxis; ⊙ mid-Jul) Opera and classical music at the palace.

Sleeping
BUDGET
Hotel Am Peterstor (☎ 545 45; www.hotel-am-peterstor.de; Fröhliche-Türken-Strasse 12; s/d €40/55) The people running this neat little hotel know they're not offering you the Ritz, and that's just the point. Rooms are basic but more than adequate, the location is great and the rates won't make much of a dent in your wallet.

Backpackers will likely gravitate to the new independent and supercentral **Brook Lane Hostel** (☎ 690 0966; www.hostel-regensburg.de in German; Obere Bachgasse 21; dm €15, d with shared bath €30, linen €2). It's a snug place, with bunks for 10 in two dorms and one double room, plus a full kitchen and even a small supermarket downstairs. Otherwise, try the **DJH hostel** (☎ 574 02; jhregensburg@djh-bayern.de; Wöhrd-strasse 60; dm incl breakfast & linen €18.85), which is about a 10-minute walk east of the Altstadt. Campers should head to the riverside **Azur-Campingplatz** (☎ 270 025; www.azur-camping.de/regensburg in German; Weinweg 40; per person €4.50-6.80, camp sites €3.50-8), about 2km west of the Altstadt.

MIDRANGE
Künstlerhaus (☎ 571 34; www.himmelzimmer.de; Alter Kornmarkt 3; s €70-140, d €90-140) Regensburg's most eccentric hotel is a snug hideaway inside the Altstadt's narrowest house. Let your fantasies go wild in any of the four themed rooms, including the Space Room (calling all Trekkies), the Asian-style Wellness Suite or the romantic Himmel and Orient Suite.

Hotel Roter Hahn (☎ 595 090; www.roter-hahn.com; Rote-Hahnen-Gasse 10; s €75-105, d €87-130; P ⊠) The hotel lobby's timeworn beamed ceiling and historic stone well create a warm and welcoming ambience at this delightful hotel, which pairs ancient roots with up-to-date amenities. Breakfast is truly a gourmet spread – sparkling wine anyone? – and the restaurant top-rated.

Altstadthotel Arch (☎ 586 60; www.altstadthotel-arch.de in German; Haidplatz 4; s €71-97, d €96-130; ⊠) This landmark hotel in a medieval patrician

mansion puts you right onto charismatic Haidplatz, a beehive of activity on balmy summer nights. Rooms give off an air of understated elegance. For a touch of romance, book a beamed *Ratsherrenzimmer* (councilmen's room).

Altstadthotel am Pach (☎ 298 610; www.ampach.de in German; Untere Bachgasse 9; s €80-100, d €100-180; ⊠) People who have shaped Regensburg history – from Marcus Aurelius to Emperor Karl V – are commemorated in the 21 rooms of this sleek new hotel. Rooms vary in size but all are warmly furnished with thick carpets, comfy mattresses and a small refrigerator containing complimentary beer and water.

Münchner Hof (☎ 584 40; www.muenchner-hof.de; Tändlergasse 9; s €64-74, d €85-100; P ⊠) Another good option in this category, which offers good-sized rooms and modern conveniences within the Gothic walls.

TOP END
Bischofshof am Dom (☎ 584 60; www.hotel-bischofshof.de; Krauterermarkt 3; s €70-100, d €120-180; P ⊠) The rambling residence of generations of bishops is now a romantic hotel where stylish rooms wrap around a flower-filled courtyard (with a beer garden in summer). A special touch – some rooms feature original Roman walls. There's also a popular restaurant.

Sorat Insel-Hotel (☎ 810 40; www.sorat-hotels.com; Müllerstrasse 7; s €95-190, d €130-210; P ⊠ ⊠) The state-of-the-art Sorat has an awesome location on a Danube island with panoramic views of the town's skyline. The generously sized rooms and public areas all sport Art Deco touches, and service is impeccable.

Eating

RESTAURANTS

Kneitinger (☎ 524 55; Arnulfsplatz 3; meals €5-13; ⊗ 9am-11pm) Students to actors to town burghers all flock to this quintessential Bavarian brewery-pub for hearty home cooking and delicious house brews. It's been in business since 1530.

Leerer Beutel (☎ 589 97; Bertoldstrasse 9; mains €7-14) This chic restaurant in the cultural centre serves up creative regional fare with occasional excursions to France. The dining hall with its high, beamed ceiling, brick walls and original art makes for a fashionable backdrop.

Vitus (☎ 526 46; Hinter der Grieb 8; mains €5-15; ⊗ 10am-1am) Colourful canvasses mix with ancient beamed ceilings at this bustling place serving country-style French food, including delicious *Flammekuche* (Alsatian-style pizza). Sit in the rustic bar area, the restaurant with linen-draped tables or the child-friendly café section. Breakfast is served until 6pm.

Rosenpalais (☎ 599 7579; Minoritenweg 20; bistro mains €11-19, restaurant mains €25-30, multicourse gourmet dinners from €65; ⊗ closed Sun) Upstairs, in the elegant baroque dining rooms, Michelin-starred chef Christian Graf von Walderdorff pampers a Rolls Royce crowd of diners with fanciful creations inspired by the cuisines of Germany, the Mediterranean and Asia. Gourmets on a budget gather in the more convivial downstairs bistro.

Spaghetteria (☎ 563 695; Am Römling 12; dishes €5-8) A spirited crowd regularly invades this one-time Gothic chapel for the heavenly pastas, tangy sauces and an antipasto buffet as colourful as a Michelangelo painting.

Dicker Mann (☎ 573 70; Krebsgasse 6; dishes €9-12; ⊗ 10am-1am) Tucked into a narrow lane, this traditional restaurant oozes history but maintains a lively flair thanks in part to its young and upbeat staff. Pasta dishes and creative salads provide lighter counterpoints to the meat-laden menu. On a balmy night, grab a table in the lovely beer garden out the back.

Haus Heuport (☎ 599 8297; Domplatz 7; mains €15-25; ⊗ 9am-11pm Mar-Oct, 5-11pm Mon-Fri, 9am-11pm Sat & Sun Nov-Feb) Hump it up the grand old wooden staircase to this Gothic dining hall with front-row views of the Dom and dinners that are culinary celebrations. The weekend breakfast (served until 6pm,

reservations advised) is a megaevent, while in summer tables spill out onto the square where patrons can pick from a less-pricey bistro menu.

CAFÉS & BISTROS

Café D'Orphée (☎ 529 77; Untere Bachgasse 8; mains €12-15; ⊗ 9am-1am) This delightful brasserie with its red velvet banquettes, framed posters and gilded mirrors is so fabulously French, you half expect to glimpse the Eiffel Tower whilst gazing out the window. Paté, quiches and steak *au poivre* all make appearances on the menu that also features breakfast and vegetarian fare.

Café Goldenes Kreuz (☎ 572 32; Haidplatz 10; breakfast €3-7, cakes €1.50-3; ⊗ 7am-7pm Mon-Sat, 9am-7pm Sun) This classic Viennese-style coffeehouse is a great spot for breakfast or afternoon coffee and cake. It's inside the Kaiserherberge, an historic inn once popular with emperors, nobles and other famous folk.

QUICK EATS & SELF-CATERING

Historische Wurstküche (☎ 466 210; Thundorfer Strasse 3; meals €5.40-11; ⊗ 8am-7pm) Sausage has been the name of the game in this spot since 1135, purportedly making it the world's oldest sausage kitchen. Everyone loves the little links, grilled over beechwood and served with sauerkraut and sweet, grainy mustard.

If the Wurstküche is closed, your next best bet is **Würstl Toni** (Alter Kornmarkt; ⊗ till late), a simple stand with cult status among night owls.

There's a daily **farmer's market** (⊗ 9am-4pm) on Neupfarrplatz but for a decent-sized supermarket you'll have to head to **Norma Supermarket** (Hauptbahnhof).

Other quick tummy-filling stations:
Bombay Express (☎ 584 0954; Am Ölberg 3; mains €5-8; ⊗ Mon-Sat) Fragrant Indian curries made with choice ingredients for takeaway or eating at stand-up tables.
Dampfnudel Uli (☎ 532 97; Watmarkt 4; dishes under €5; ⊗ 10am-6pm Tue-Fri, 10am-3pm Sat) Serves steamed doughnuts with custard (€3.90), a Regensburg speciality.

Drinking

BEER GARDENS

All beer gardens are attached to year-round restaurants where no-nonsense dishes cost between €5 and €10.

Alte Linde (☎ 880 80; Müllerstrasse 1) Enjoy a mug of ale while taking in panoramic views of the Altstadt at this large and leafy beer garden on a Danube island, accessed via the romantic Steinerne Brücke – a lovely spot to while away a summer eve.

Goldene Ente (☎ 854 44; Badstrasse 32) This bustling place is a student favourite with a pretty riverside location, but service that sometimes moves slower than the Danube itself.

Gasthof Spitalgarten (☎ 847 74; St-Katharinen-Platz 1) Crossing the Danube on the Steinerne Brücke takes you to one of the oldest hospital breweries in Bavaria. The beer garden, filled with a convivial mix of young and old, locals and visitors, has grand views of the city, and friendly service.

PUBS & BARS

Paletti (☎ 515 93; Gesandtenstrasse 6, Pustetpassage; ◷ 8am-1am Mon-Sat, 3pm-1am Sun) Tucked into a covered passageway off Gesandtenstrasse, this buzzy Italian café-bar is a hip hang-out with see-and-be-seen windows and art-clad walls. Come to knock back thimble-sized espressos, dig into hearty pasta carbonara or sip a chilled pinot grigio. It's *dolce vita*, Regensburg-style.

Venus Bar (☎ 599 9923; Hinter der Grieb 5) Match your mood to the room in this smooth bar where you can sip wine in front of a flickering fireplace, plop onto leather couches for a quick bite or recline on pillows in a chilli-red backroom so saucily exotic Scheherazade would likely approve.

Neue Film Bühne (☎ 570 37; Bismarckplatz 9) Theatrical décor with clever Asiatic touches forms the backdrop of this trendy café-bar.

'OUT' & ABOUT IN REGENSBURG

Regensburg has a small but lively gay and lesbian scene. Popular hang-outs include the low-key pub **Na und!** (Jakobstrasse 7; ◷ from 8pm) and the café-bar **Schierstatt** (☎ 870 0762; An der Schierstatt 1; ◷ 10am-1am), which also draws some heels. On Thursday night, the latter is a popular warm-up stop for the legendary lesbigay party at **Scala** (☎ 522 93; Gesandtenstrasse 6, Pustetpassage; ◷ 11pm-3am). Good sources for plugging into the scene include the magazine *Just Different* and the website www.gay-regens burg.de (in German).

In summer, the terrace offers primo people-watching.

Also recommended:

No 7 Bar (Glockengasse 3) Mirrors and red mood-lighting make everyone look good.

Oscar Bar (☎ 630 8455; Rote-Hahnen-Gasse 2) Chic and sleek with a crowd to match.

Irish Harp (☎ 572 68; Brückstrasse 1) High-spirited Irish pub with occasional live music.

Entertainment

Look for *Logo*, the local what's-on guide, in cafés, bars and shops around town.

CINEMAS

Cinemas with occasional screenings of movies in their original language, including English:

Film-Galerie (☎ 560 901; Bertoldstrasse 9) Upstairs at the Leerer Beutel cultural centre.

Garbo-Filmtheater (☎ 575 86; Weissgerbergraben 11)

Ostentor-Kino (☎ 791 974; Adolf-Schmetzer-Strasse 5) Has a nice café.

LIVE MUSIC

Jazzclub im Leeren Beutel (☎ 563 375; Bertoldstrasse 9) Jazz is big in Regensburg and this fine venue is great for catching some smooth or swinging tunes from local and visiting talent. It shares premises with an art gallery, the Film-Galerie (above) and a stylish restaurant (opposite).

Alte Mälzerei (☎ 788 8150; Galgenbergstrasse 20) Local and international bands, cabaret, spoken word, dance parties – the programme at this cultural centre is unpredictable, eclectic and classy.

Theater Regensburg (☎ 507 2424; Bismarck-platz) The city's municipal theatre keeps the high-brow crowd entertained with a varied menu of opera, ballet, classical concerts and drama.

The cathedral's famous boys' choir, the Regensburger Domspatzen, sings at the 10am Sunday service in the Dom.

Getting There & Away

Regensburg has direct train connections to Munich (€19.20, 1½ hours), Nuremberg (€15.20, one hour), Passau (€21, 1½ hours) and Landshut (€9.70, 45 minutes).

Regensburg is approximately an hour's drive southeast of Nuremberg and northwest of Passau via the A3 autobahn. The A93 runs south to Munich.

Getting Around

BICYCLE

Bikehaus (☎ 599 8808; Bahnhofstrasse 17/18; bikes per day adult/child €9/6; ☺ 10am-7pm Mon-Sat) is a full-service outfit near the Hauptbahnhof with bike sales, hire, repair, storage and in-the-know staff happy to help you plan trips around the region.

BUS

The Altstadtbus loops frequently between the Hauptbahnhof and the Altstadt (per ride €0.50) daily except Sunday. Regular buses converge at the Albertstrasse stop, also just north of the train station. Single tickets cost €1.60 and day passes €3.30 on weekdays and €3 on weekends. Weekend passes are good for up to five people travelling together.

CAR & MOTORCYCLE

The Steinerne Brücke is closed to private vehicles. The main river crossings are via the Nibelungenbrücke and the Eiserne Brücke. Car parks in the Altstadt charge from €1.20 per hour and are well signposted. Parking is free at the Unterer Wöhrd lot on the northern bank near the Nibelungenbrücke from where it's about a 10-minute walk to the Altstadt.

TAXI

For a taxi call ☎ 194 10 or ☎ 520 52.

AROUND REGENSBURG

Walhalla

Modelled on the Parthenon in Athens, **Walhalla** (☎ 09403-961 680; adult/concession €3/2; ☺ 9am-5.45pm Apr-Sep, to 4.45pm Oct, 10am-11.45am & 1-3.45pm Nov-Mar) is a wonderfully opulent marble temple dedicated to the giants of Germanic thought and deed. It was the brainchild of King Ludwig I and designed by Leo von Klenze in 1842.

The gallery of 127 marble busts and 64 commemorative tablets (of statesmen, scientists and artists) dominates the interior, which is draped entirely in multicoloured marble. Every few years, the Bavarian government selects a new worthy German to be admitted to this illustrious circle. The latest (in 2003) was Sophie Scholl, a member of *Die Weisse Rose* Nazi resistance group (see the boxed text on p74). The sheer weight of the august personages may be a bit over-whelming, but if passing under the gaze of Beethoven, Luther and Einstein doesn't leave you at least a little in awe, you're probably holidaying in the wrong country.

Walhalla is about 10km east of Regensburg. Drivers should follow the road to Donaustauf along the northern bank of the Danube. In fine weather, the most pleasant way to get here is by boat cruise operated by **Regensburger Personenschifffahrt Klinger** (☎ 0941-5957 3818; adult/child under 14/student/family return €9.50/4.50/6.50/22; ☺ 10.30am & 2pm Apr-Oct) from Regensburg's Steinerne Brücke landing docks. Trips also include a 1¼-hour stop at Walhalla. Bus No 5 also makes the trip out here regularly from Regensburg's Hauptbahnhof.

Befreiungshalle

About 30km upstream from Regensburg awaits another monumental piece of architecture dreamed up by King Ludwig I, the grandiose **Befreiungshalle** (Hall of Liberation; ☎ 0941-682 070; Befreiungshallestrasse 3; adult/concession €3/2.50; ☺ 9am-6pm Fri-Wed, 9am-8pm Thu mid-Mar–Oct, 9am-4pm daily Nov–mid-Mar). This pale yellow cylinder, perched above the Danube near Kelheim, serves to commemorate Napoleon's defeat in 1815. Inside, the ring of supersized winged white marble sculptures of the Roman goddess Victoria is a real trip.

Danube Gorge & Kloster Weltenburg

In fine weather, it's well worth combining a visit of the Befreiungshalle with a trip through the glorious **Danube Gorge** (Donaudurchbruch). This is one of the most dramatic stretches of the river as it carves through craggy cliffs and past weathered rock formations.

The only way to enjoy this natural spectacle is from the water. You can either hire your own kayak or canoe or board one of the cruise boats leaving from the Danube landing docks in Kelheim from mid-March to October (one-way/return €3.80/€6.60, bicycles one-way/return €1.80/€3.60).

At the end of the 40-minute ride, boats dock at the **Kloster Weltenburg**, an ancient Benedictine abbey, which also operates the world's oldest monastic brewery (since 1050). Now state-of-the-art, it makes several varieties, including a *Dunkles* and a delicious *Bockbier*. The **Klosterschenke** (☎ 09441-

3682; Asamstrasse 32; ☻ 8am-7pm mid-Mar–Oct) is fronted by an idyllic chestnut-canopied beer garden that gets swarmed by revellers on warm weekends and around holidays.

For spiritual sustenance, pop into the **Klosterkirche Weltenburg**, a magnificent rococo church designed by the Asam brothers. Its most arresting feature is the high altar, which shows St George triumphant on horseback, with the slain dragon and rescued princess at his feet. See if you can spot the stucco sculpture of Cosmas Damian Asam leaning over the railing from the oval ceiling fresco.

The return boat trip from Kloster Weltenburg takes only 20 minutes.

STRAUBING
☎ 09421 / pop 44,000 / elev 331m

Straubing, some 45km southeast of Regensburg, has a storybook historic centre sprinkled with stately patrician houses and half a dozen churches. It is the heart of the Gäuboden, one of Bavaria's most fertile regions, a fact that wasn't lost on the Celts and Romans who first settled here a couple of millennia ago. Duke Ludwig the Kelheimer founded the 'modern' town in 1218, but most of its fine old buildings date back to its late-14th-century heyday as the seat of the duchy of Straubing-Holland. These days Straubing famously hosts the Gäubodenfest, one of Bavaria's largest beer parties (see right).

Orientation & Information
The historic centre, compact and easily walkable, is sandwiched between the Danube to the north and the Hauptbahnhof to the south. A short walk north on Bahnhofstrasse takes you straight to a pedestrianised thoroughfare referred to as Stadtplatz but actually divided into Theresienplatz and Ludwigsplatz by the *Stadtturm* (city tower). The **tourist office** (☎ 944 307; www .straubing.de in German; Theresienplatz 20; ☻ 9am-5pm Mon-Fri, to noon Sat) is in the Rathaus right by the *Stadtturm*.

Sights
Flanked by pastel-coloured town houses, the Stadtplatz is lorded over by Straubing's symbol, the Gothic **Stadtturm** (1316), a one-time watchtower decorated with a giant clock face and slender copper turrets. It sits right next to the richly gabled **Rathaus**

(Theresienplatz 20), which was once a merchant trading hall, and the gleaming golden **Dreifaltigkeitssäule** (Holy Trinity Column). The town burghers erected the latter in 1709 in hopes of being spared destruction by the occupying Austrians during the Spanish War of Succession. (PS: it worked.)

A few steps north of the *Stadtturm*, the **Basilika St Jakob** (Pfarrplatz) is an imposing late-Gothic hall church designed by master architect Hans von Burghausen. Standouts among its many treasures include the brilliant stained-glass windows and an altar remodelled in dazzling rococo by the Asam brothers.

East of here, is the small but exquisite **Gäubodenmuseum** (☎ 974 10; Frauenhoferstrasse 9; adult/concession €2.50/1.50; ☻ 10am-4pm Tue-Sun), which houses the Römerschatz, one of the most important collections of Roman treasures in Germany. Displays include ceremonial armour and ornate masks worn by both soldiers and horses.

The final collaboration by the Asam brothers, the exuberant **Ursulinenkirche** (Burggasse), is two blocks east of the museum. The ceiling fresco depicts the martyrdom of St Ursula surrounded by representations of the four then-known continents. Also nearby is the former ducal residence, the 14th-century **Herzogschloss** (Schlossplatz), which now houses government offices and a small collection of **religious art** (☎ 211 14; adult/concession €2.50/1.50; ☻ 10am-4pm Thu-Sun Apr-Jan). Also have a look at the palace's historic **Rittersaal** (Knights' Hall).

Straubing's oldest church, **Basilika St Peter** (Petersgasse) is worth the 15-minute stroll east along the Danube or via Donaugasse and Petersgasse. Built in 1180 on the site of a Roman fortress, it still boasts two portals, a Christ figure and a pietà from the Romanesque founding period. Surrounding the church is an eerie churchyard chock-full of moss-draped tombstones, some dating back as far as the 14th century. Also here are several small chapels, including the **Seelenkapelle** with a Dance of Death fresco cycle and the **Agnes-Bernauer-Kapelle** (see the boxed text on p168).

Festivals & Events
Every August, Straubing erupts into a beery roar for 10 days during the **Gäubodenfest**, an Oktoberfest-style party that began in 1812

THE WOEFUL TALE OF AGNES BERNAUER

Star-crossed love always makes for a good story. The year is 1432. Our tragic heroes are Albrecht, heir to the duchy of Bavaria, and Agnes Bernauer, the daughter of an Augsburg barber. The two meet at a tournament in Augsburg, fall madly in love and quickly – and secretly – marry. Naturally, Albrecht's family is seriously chagrined. A simple commoner for the future duke? Pleeeze!

Undaunted by such family squabbles, the couple lives happily for a few years, mostly in Straubing, and even has a daughter. Albrecht's dad, Duke Ernst I, meanwhile, is busily concocting a most twisted plot to get rid of poor Agnes. After sending his son on some fake out-of-town errand, he has the girl dragged before a sham tribunal, found guilty of witchcraft and sentenced to drowning in the Danube. Miraculously, she manages to get rid of her shackles and swim ashore – only to be finished off by the executioner. ('Medieval justice' is surely one of the greatest oxymorons of all time.)

Agnes' hubbie, though heartbroken at first, quickly finds solace in another marriage. His father, however, is haunted by the demons of remorse, which he seeks to appease by building a chapel in his ex-daughter-in-law's memory. It's still there today, right in the churchyard of the Basilika St Peter. These days, Straubing commemorates the tragic heroine with a torte named in her honour and the quadrennial Agnes-Bernauer-Festival (next one in 2007).

as a social gathering for grain farmers and now lubricates more than a million visitors. For details contact the tourist office (p167). The town also celebrates the quadrennial **Agnes-Bernauer-Festival** with the next one in 2007, see above.

Sleeping

Hotel-Restaurant Wittelsbach (☎ 9430; www.wittelsbach.org in German; Stadtgraben 25/26; s/d €46/67; meals €7-14; P ✗ ☷) Rooms at this family-run place exude homy, comfortable charm and are big enough to accommodate a small desk. Townspeople often crowd the restaurant, especially during theme nights (all-you-can-eat ribs, Mexican night etc).

Hotel-Restaurant Seethaler (☎ 939 50; www.hotel-seethaler.de in German; Theresienplatz 25; s/d/tr/q €65/95/110/127; meals €9-16; P ✗ ☲) Over 500 years old, this hotel oozes history and has an amazing lobby canopied by a painted and beamed Gothic ceiling. The lobby leads on to good-sized rooms packed with 21st-century amenities, including a minibar, cable TV and snazzy bathrooms, some with double sinks. There's also wireless LAN throughout. The restaurant serves up solid regional cuisine.

Hotel Theresientor (☎ 8490; www.hotel-theresientor.de in German; Theresienplatz 41; s €63-110, d €90-140; P ✗ ☷) This swanky new hotel flaunts an edgy, modern feel with rooms decked out in designer furniture and granite desks; the marble baths are nice as well. For the ultimate hideaway book the loft-style tower

suite with private terrace and splendid views. Rates include access to an off-site fitness centre.

Straubing has a small and basic **DJH hostel** (☎ 804 36; juhe-sr@web.de; Friedhofstrasse 12; dm incl breakfast €14.30; ☪ Apr-Oct) and a pleasant riverside **campingplatz** (☎ 897 94; www.msc-straubing.de in German; Wundermühlweg 9; camp sites €8-21; ☪ mid-Apr–mid-Oct).

Eating

Zum Geiss (☎ 963 922; Theresienplatz 40; mains €8-16; ☪ 9am-midnight) Despite a modern makeover, Straubing's oldest restaurant still serves traditional Bavarian food with the occasional nod to Austrian cuisine. In summer, tables around the stone fountain in the quiet back garden are the most coveted.

Gäubodenhof (☎ 122 75; Theresienplatz 8a; mains €6-13; ☪ 7.30am-11pm) Filled with knick-knacks and old-fashioned ambience, this is another good spot for a traditional meal. Vitamin junkies can load up at the fresh salad buffet. The owners also rent rooms (singles/doubles €43/€68).

Gaststätte Unterm Rain (☎ 227 72; Unterm Rain 15; mains €5-12; ☪ dinner, lunch Sun) This congenial restaurant-cum-beer garden, snuggled against the old town wall, serves sizable portions of hearty Bavarian cuisine (the schnitzels are reportedly big enough for two). Definitely try a mug of *Röhrl*, the local brew.

Every morning (except Sunday), a produce market enlivens Ludwigsplatz.

Other recommendations:

Cafe Krönner (☎ 109 94; Theresienplatz 22) This café's owners invented the Agnes-Bernauer-Torte.

Molise (☎ 105 08; Theresienplatz 38; dishes €6-20) Great pizza and pasta.

Getting There & Away

Straubing has direct train connections with Regensburg (€7, 30 minutes) but coming from Passau (€11, one hour) requires a change in Plattling. Drivers should take the Kirchhof exit off the A3 (Nuremberg–Passau) autobahn. There's free parking at Grossparkplatz Unter den Hagen, a five-minute walk south of Stadtplatz.

PASSAU

☎ 0851 / pop 51,000 / elev 302m

Passau may be right on the border with Austria, but there's an undeniable hint of Italy in its look and outlook, which is why romantic souls have nicknamed it 'Bavaria's Venice'. Water has quite literally shaped the town, which is spectacularly located at the confluence of the Danube, Inn and Ilz Rivers. It was the rivers that brought wealth to Passau, which for centuries was an important trading hub, especially for salt, the so-called 'white gold'. Christianity, meanwhile, brought prestige as Passau evolved into the largest bishopric in the Roman Empire. The powerful prince-bishops built much of the historic centre, a pleasing jumble of winding lanes, archways and fabulous architecture, mostly of the baroque persuasion.

Passau is a major river-cruise stop and is often deluged with day visitors. It is also the hub of long-distance cycling routes, eight of which converge here, and a good jumping-off point for explorations into Upper Austria.

Orientation

Passau's Altstadt is a narrow peninsula with the confluence of the Danube, Ilz and Inn at its eastern tip. The Hauptbahnhof is about a 10-minute walk west of the heart of the Altstadt (eg the Dom), where most sights, hotels and restaurants are located. The Veste Oberhaus and the DJH hostel are atop a steep hillside on the north side of the Danube.

Information

BOOKSHOP

Buchhandlung Rupprecht (☎ 931 270; Ludwigstrasse 18) Maps, travel books, English-language novels.

INTERNET ACCESS

CompPass (☎ 490 7164; Neuburger Strasse 19; per hr €3; ☽ 1-10pm) A laundromat is also here.

MONEY

Commerzbank (Ludwigstrasse 13)
Sparkasse (Ludwigstrasse 8)

POST

Post office (Bahnhofstrasse 27)

TOURIST INFORMATION

Tourist office (☎ 955 980; www.passau.de) Altstadt (Rathausplatz 3; ☽ 8.30am-6pm Mon-Fri, 9am-4pm Sat & Sun Easter–mid-Oct, 8.30am-5pm Mon-Thu, to 4pm Fri mid-Oct–Easter); Hauptbahnhof (Bahnhofstrasse 36; ☽ 9am-5pm Mon-Fri year-round, to 4pm Fri mid-Oct–Easter)

DETOUR: FURTH IM WALD

It's hard to imagine that sleepy, pretty **Furth im Wald**, on the far northwestern edge of the Bavarian Forest, is home to a fierce, fangy monster – a dragon of Godzilla proportions. Every August this epic creature is dragged out to reprise its starring role in the **Further Drachenstich** (Dragon Slaying; www.drachenstich.de), one of Bavaria's oldest and most popular festivals. There's lots of general merriment but the main event is an outdoor play that pits the valiant knight Udo against the 18m-long and 5m-tall high-tech monster, culminating in the beast's death by lance, complete with spewing blood and other melodramatic flourishes. The poor dragon, naturally, never wins as he symbolises war, death and starvation suffered by the local folks some 500 years back.

If you can't make it to the festival, you can still admire the giant critter – plus lots of other quirky exhibits – at the **Deutsches Drachenmuseum** (National Dragon Museum; ☎ 09973-802 585; Schlossplatz 4, Furth im Wald; adult/child/family €2.50/2/6.50; ☽ 10.15am-5pm Tue-Sun Easter-Oct, 2.15-5pm Tue & Thu, 11am-3pm Sat & Sun Nov-Apr). The exhibits are found inside the Stadtturm, which can be climbed for panoramic views. Furth im Wald is on the B20, about 50km north of the Straubing exit off the A3 autobahn.

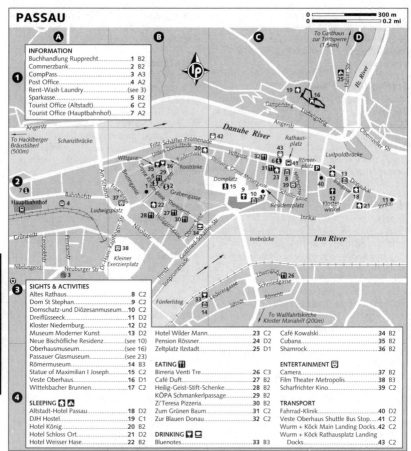

Sights

VESTE OBERHAUS

A 13th-century fortress, built by the prince-
bishops for defence purposes, **Veste Oberhaus**
towers over Passau with patriarchal pomp.
Not surprisingly, views of the city and into
Austria are superb from up here.

Inside the bastion is the **Oberhausmuseum**
(☎ 493 3512; Veste Oberhaus 125; permanent collections
adult/concession/family €5/4/10; ☺ 9am-5pm Mon-Fri,
10am-6pm Sat, Sun & holidays mid-Mar–Oct & 25 Dec-10
Jan), a regional history museum that goes
far beyond displaying dusty artefacts. The
biggest crowds turn out for the travelling
exhibits but the permanent collection also
yields some gems. You can uncover the
mysteries of medieval cathedral building or

learn what it took to become a knight. Passau's period as a centre of the salt trade is
explored as much as the life of tradespeople
and the role their guilds played in society.
Displays are labelled in English.

DOM ST STEPHAN

The characteristic green onion domes of
Passau's **Dom St Stephan** (St Stephen's Cathedral;
Domplatz; admission free; ☺ 6.30am-at least 6pm) float
serenely above the town's silhouette. There's
been a church in this spot since the late 5th
century, but what you see today is much
younger thanks to the Great Fire of 1662,
which ravaged much of the medieval town,
including the ancient cathedral. The rebuild-
ing job went to a team of Italians, notably

the architect Carlo Lurago and the stucco master Giovanni Battista Carlone. The result is an imposing and harmonious baroque house of worship filled with artwork, including frescoes inspired by a tapestry series by Peter Paul Rubens. The modern high altar is a 1953 work by Munich artist and professor Josef Henselmann. Carved in wood and dipped in silver, it shows the stoning of St Stephen in wrenchingly emotional detail.

The true pièce de résistance, though, is the cathedral organ, which has 17,974 pipes and ranks among the world's largest. Half-hour recitals take place at noon daily Monday to Saturday (adult/child €3/€1) and at 7.30pm on Thursday (adult/child €5/€3) from May to October and in December. Show up at least 30 minutes early to ensure a seat. The acoustics are so heavenly, you'd swear God himself was at the keyboards.

Outside on Domplatz stands a **statue of Maximilian I Joseph**, the first Bavarian king. In December a colourful Christmas market enlivens the square.

RESIDENZPLATZ

East of the Dom, Residenzplatz is framed mostly by show-off homes built by rich Passau patricians in centuries past, although pride of place clearly belongs to the 18th-century **Neue Bischöfliche Residenz** (New Bishop's Residence; Residenzplatz 8). Melchior Hefele, a student of Balthasar Neumann (the genius behind the Würzburg Residence, see p218), drafted the stucco-draped façade, as well as the glorious rococo staircase, which winds towards a wonderfully over-the-top ceiling fresco entitled *The Gods of Olympus Protecting Immortal Passau*.

The bishops resided in these splendid digs until 1871. Today, the diocese administration occupies most of the rooms, but several have been set aside for the **Domschatz-und Diözesanmuseum** (Cathedral Treasury & Museum; Residenzplatz 8; adult/child €1.50/0.50; 10am-4pm Mon-Sat May-Oct). The amazing range of ecclesiastical finery – including monstrances, vestments, sculptures and paintings – nicely exemplifies the wealth and power of the Church rulers. Be sure not to miss the baroque library, where frescoes by Giovanni Carlone provide the requisite flourish. The museum is accessed from inside the Dom except during the organ concerts when entry is via Residenzplatz.

At the square's centre is the **Wittelsbacher Brunnen** (1903), a sprightly fountain built 100 years after Napoleon decided that Passau would make a fitting addition to Bavaria. It shows Mary, Bavaria's patron saint, surrounded by allegories of the three local rivers.

ALTES RATHAUS

A short walk north of Residenzplatz, via Schrottgasse, is Passau's **Rathaus** (Rathausplatz 2), an attractive Gothic building embellished by its 19th-century landmark painted tower. A carillon chimes its merry tune several times daily (hours are listed on the wall, alongside historical flood-level markers).

The entrance on Schrottgasse takes you to the **Grosser Rathaussaal** (Great Assembly Room; adult/concession €1.50/1; 10am-4pm Apr-Oct & Dec) where large-scale paintings by 19th-century local artist Ferdinand Wagner show scenes from Passau's history with melodramatic flourish. If it's not being used for a wedding or a meeting, also sneak into the adjacent **Small Assembly Room** for a peek at the ceiling fresco featuring buxom beauties and a fierce-looking fellow, again as allegories of the three rivers.

PASSAUER GLASMUSEUM

Next to the Rathaus, inside the Hotel Wilder Mann (p173), the **Passauer Glasmuseum** (Passau Glass Museum; 350 71; Am Rathausplatz; adult/concession €5/3; 1-5pm) offers a survey of 250 years of Bohemian glasswork and crystal. Even if you charge through the place, you'll need at least an hour to see this warren of rooms filled with some 30,000 fragile pieces from the baroque, classical, Art Nouveau and Art Deco periods.

KLOSTER NIEDERNBURG

One of the most impressive structures in the eastern Altstadt, the **Kloster Niedernburg** (Niedernburg Abbey; 2012; Klosterwinkel; admission free; 8am-6pm) has origins in the 750s but didn't gain prominence until Benedictine nuns took it over in 1000. Inside the abbey church, the flower-bedecked tomb of one of its first abbesses, the much revered Queen Gisela, is the main point of interest. The sister of Heinrich II, Gisela said goodbye to the real world after the untimely death of her husband, Stephen of Hungary. The former convent complex, mostly built in

EASTERN BAVARIA

the 15th century, is now a Catholic girls' school.

MUSEUM MODERNER KUNST

Occupying a marvellously adapted Gothic building, the **Museum Moderner Kunst** (Museum of Modern Art; ☎ 383 8790; Bräugasse 17; adult/concession/family €5/3/10; ☒ 10am-7pm Tue-Sun Jul-Sep, 10am-6pm Oct-Jun) usually presents up to 10 high-calibre exhibits annually, which feature an international roster of 20th- and 21st-century artists. Some spotlight a single practitioner, including crowd-pleasers such as Salvador Dalí or Gustav Klimt, while others focus on themes as varied as football (soccer) or women.

DREIFLÜSSEECK

The tip of the Altstadt peninsula is known as the **Dreiflüsseeck** (Three Rivers Point) and is the only place from which you can actually see the Danube, Ilz and Inn all at once (except from above, of course). Views of the Veste Oberhaus are also memorable.

RÖMERMUSEUM

To study up on Passau's Roman origins, cross the Inn River and skip over to the **Römermuseum** (Roman Museum; ☎ 347 69; Lederergasse 43; adult/concession €2/1; ☒ 10am-noon & 2-4pm Tue-Sun Mar-May & Sep-Nov, 10am-noon & 1-4pm Jun-Aug). Ruins from the Roman fort, the Kastell Boitro, which stood here from AD 250 to 400 are still *in situ*. The museum itself displays archaeological items that were dug up during excavations here and elsewhere in eastern Bavaria and document both civilian and military life in those days.

WALLFAHRTSKIRCHE KLOSTER MARIAHILF

For a sweeping panorama of Passau's Altstadt and the Veste Oberhaus, it's well worth making the trip up to the hilltop **Wallfahrtskirche Kloster Mariahilf** (☎ 2356; Mariahilfberg 3; admission free), a baroque pilgrimage church. To get there, cross the Innbrücke, then turn left on Schmiedgasse, which takes you to Kapuzinerplatz, past the remnants of the old town wall. From here, visitors and praying pilgrims climb the 321 stairs of a covered flight whose walls are festooned with votive tablets. Inside the church, the object of devotion is a painting of Mary (actually a copy of the original by Lucas Cranach the Elder), which has been venerated since

1622. The church became famous after Emperor Leopold I prayed here in 1683 for divine help in defeating the Turks (with success, at least from his perspective).

Tours

From March to November, **Wurm + Köck** (☎ 929 292; www.donauschiffahrt.com in German; Höllgasse 26; tickets €6.50) runs 45-minute cruises around the Altstadt at least once hourly from the landing docks near Rathausplatz.

Starting in May, the same company also operates six-hour boat trips to Linz in Austria (one-way/return €21/€24, return by bus €25; 9am and 1pm Tuesday to Sunday May to September). Children aged four to 14 travel for half price; bicycles are free. Boats leave from the company's main landing docks near Untere Donaulände.

Festivals & Events

The annual **Festspiele Europäische Wochen** (Festival 'European Weeks'; www.ew-passau.de in German; tickets ☎ 752 020; ☒ mid-Jun–late Jul) brings together top international talent for opera, concerts, readings, theatre, film and art under a different theme each year. Events take place in and around Passau, Upper Austria and the Czech Republic.

Sleeping

BUDGET

Pension Rössner (☎ 931 350; www.pension-roessner .de; Bräugasse 19; s €35, d €45-60) This immaculate pension, in a restored mansion near the Dreiflüsseeck, offers great value for money and a friendly, cosy ambience. Each room is uniquely decorated and many have fortress views.

The beautifully renovated **DJH hostel** (☎ 493 780; jhpassau@djh-bayern.de; Veste Oberhaus 125; dm incl breakfast & linen €18.55) is right in the fortress. To get there, see p174. Campers should head to **Zeltplatz Ilzstadt** (☎ 414 57; Halser Strasse 34; camp sites per adult/child €5/4), idyllically located on the Ilz River, about a 15-minute walk from the Altstadt or catch bus Nos 1, 2, 3 or 4 to Kleiner Exerzierplatz-Ilzbrücke.

MIDRANGE & TOP END

Altstadt-Hotel Passau (☎ 3370; www.altstadt-hotel .de; Bräugasse 23-29; s €76-89, d €105-125; meals €13-22; ☒ ☒) Those fancying an arty vibe will be well sheltered in this pretty hotel, which offers a welcoming cocktail of class and comfort. The restaurant is tops and the bar a good place to reflect upon the day's exploits.

Hotel Schloss Ort (☎ 340 72; www.schlosshotel -passau.de in German; Im Ort 11; s €54-78, d €88-128; meals €15-25; P) Behind the walls of a snug medieval palace awaits this stylish little hotel, located a hop, skip and a jump from the Dreiflüsseeck. Romantics should book a room with a heavenly canopied bed. The restaurant serves ambitious German and international food in quiet, refined surrounds. In fine weather, the rush is on for the tables on the river-facing terrace.

Hotel Weisser Hase (☎ 921 10; www.weisser-hase .de; Heiliggeistgasse 1; s €75-95, d €120-145; P) A pedigree going back to 1512, good-sized rooms, wireless LAN and a central locale near good eating and shopping are among this hotel's winning attributes. The sauna is great for letting off some steam after a day of pounding the streets.

Hotel König (☎ 3850; www.hotel-koenig.de; Untere Donaulände 1; s €57-85, d €85-130; meals €8-11; P) This riverside property puts you smackbang in the middle of the Altstadt. Rooms spread out over two buildings but most come with pretty views of the Danube and the Veste Oberhaus. The restaurant has a partly covered terrace.

Hotel Wilder Mann (☎ 350 71; www.wilder-mann .com in German; Am Rathausplatz; s €49, d €78-138;) During its 19th-century heyday this hotel, in a rambling Danube-facing patrician residence, used to host royalty and celebrities, including Empress Elisabeth (Sisi) of Austria. These days, an air of faded grandeur hangs over the rooms, which are quite comfortable but equipped with amenities dating back to the first moon landing. The Passauer Glasmuseum (p171) and a gourmet restaurant are on the premises.

Eating
RESTAURANTS
Heilig-Geist-Stift-Schenke (☎ 2607; Heiliggeistgasse 4; mains €7-16; 10am-1am Thu-Tue) It's hard not to be charmed by the cosy tangle of rooms upstairs or the romantic garden, but wait until you see the vaulted and candlelit stone cellar (open from 6pm)! No matter where you sit, the food's universally good. Specialities include *Spiessbraten* (marinated meat licked by a beechwood fire) and the *Schlosserbuam,* a plum-based dessert.

Hacklberger Braüstüberl (☎ 583 82; Bräuhausplatz 7; mains €5-11; 9am-1am) A glass of *Zwickl bier*, this microbrewery's speciality, is just what the doctor ordered after a long day of traipsing around Passau. In summer there's no better place to enjoy it than in the parklike beer garden. The menu is an inspired mix of traditional and updated fare. It's on the northern Danube bank.

Birreria Venti Tre (☎ 490 5283; Schmiedgasse 23; mains €8-16; dinner) At this new trattoria, the décor, candlelit ambience and tasty food blend as perfectly as a traditional Tuscan stew. The spaghetti Renate (with shrimp and tomatoes) is recommended, as is the tiramisu. Nice garden, too.

Zur Blauen Donau (☎ 490 8660; Höllgasse 14; mains €17-23, 4-course menu around €40; dinner) It didn't take master chef Richard Kerscher long to capture the hearts and tummies of Passau foodies at his intimate new restaurant. Local hunters, farmers and fisherfolk supply many of the ingredients that are whipped into sophisticated concoctions in the open kitchen. The mousse au chocolat is killer, as are the great wines.

Zum Grünen Baum (☎ 356 35; Höllgasse 7; mains €6-10; 10am-1am) This darling eatery has some eccentric design touches (look for the 'cutlery chandelier') and a toy-filled, smoke-free backroom that's a winner with families. Organic beer and wine and lots of vegetarian dishes give this place a healthy bent. Clued-in locals know to leave room for dessert (ask for the unlisted 'variety platter').

Gasthaus zur Triftsperre (☎ 511 62; Triftsperrstrasse 15; mains €5-13; 10am-midnight Tue-Sun, Feb-Dec) It's a pleasant, easy 3km walk along the Ilz River to this earthy beer garden and restaurant. Regulars are drawn by the homemade cakes and fresh trout. If you don't feel like walking back, you could rent one of the rooms (singles/doubles €26/€38).

Other recommendations:
Café Duft (☎ 346 66; Theresienstrasse 22; breakfast €5-10, tapas €2.70; 9am-1am Mon-Sat, 10am-1am Sun) Casual and bustling any time of day.
Zi'Teresa Pizzeria (☎ 2138; Theresienstrasse 26; pizza €5-8.50, mains €10-18; 11.30am-11.30pm) Outstanding thin-crust pizzas.

QUICK EATS
For cheap eats, **KÖPA Schmankerlpassage** (Ludwigstrasse 6; 8am-6.30pm Mon-Sat) lets you stock up

on fresh fruit, vegetables and baked goods or scoff a hot meal (around €5) at the counter in the back. There's also a small salad bar.

A farmers market is held outside the Dom every Tuesday and Friday morning.

Drinking

Café Kowalski (☎ 2487; Oberer Sand 1; dishes €5-9; ◷ 10am-1am Sun-Wed, to 3am Fri & Sat) Conversation flows as freely as the wine or beer at this gregarious spot. If hunger strikes, there're burgers, schnitzels, pasta and sandwiches to keep your tummy happy. Views of the Inn River are gratis.

Cubana (☎ 490 9570; Rosstränke 9; ◷ Wed-Sun) Fans of fiery rhythms and cool drinks let their hair down at this popular bar and lounge. During happy hour (7pm to 9pm Wednesday to Saturday, all night Sunday) many cocktails are just €3.50.

Other good watering holes:

Bluenotes (☎ 343 77; Lederergasse 50) Across the Inn River; great cocktails and sometimes live music.

Shamrock (☎ 934 6093; Rosstränke 5-7) Passau's predictably boisterous Irish pub.

Entertainment

Camera (☎ 342 30; Am Ludwigsplatz; ◷ Thu-Mon) At this happening dance club a pretence-free crowd sweats it out on the dance floor, either to a DJ or the occasional live band (usually on Thursday). If you're facing McDonald's, the entrance is on the right.

Scharfrichter Kino (☎ 2655; Milchgasse 2) The former home of Passau's executioner is now a lively cultural centre that often rubs the city's establishment the wrong way (see the boxed text below). There's a stage for theatre and cabaret, a café and an alternative cinema that sometimes screens films in English.

Film Theater Metropolis (☎ 752 815; Dr-Hans-Kapfinger-Strasse 11) This multiplex shows mostly recent-release Hollywood movies, including some screenings in the original language (usually English).

Getting There & Away

Passau is served by direct trains from Munich (€26, 2¼ hours), Regensburg (€21, 1½ hours), Landshut (€15.90, 1¼ hours) and Nuremberg (€35, two hours). Change in Plattling for Zwiesel (€16, 1½ hours) and other Bavarian Forest towns.

Passau is just off the A3 autobahn from Nuremberg and Regensburg, which connects with the A92 to Munich near Deggendorf.

Getting Around

Central Passau is compact, so most sights are reachable on foot. The CityBus regularly connects the Bahnhof with the Altstadt (€0.50). Longer trips on Stadtwerke buses cost €1.50; day passes are €3.

The walk up the hill to Veste Oberhaus or the youth hostel, via Luitpoldbrücke and Ludwigsteig path, takes about 30 minutes. From mid-March to October, a **shuttle bus** (one-way/return €2/2.50; ◷ 10am-5pm Mon-Fri, 10am-6pm Sat, Sun & holidays) operates half-hourly from Rathausplatz.

LIFE IS A CABARET, OLD CHUM

It may be tiny, but Passau's Scharfrichterhaus – the former executioner's home turned cultural centre – has been a giant on Germany's political cabaret scene for over a quarter century.

Back in the '70s, Passau was a sleepy, provincial nest ruled entirely by the 'holy trinity' of the Catholic Church, the conservative Christlich-Soziale Union (CSU; Christian Social Union) party and the monopolist local newspaper. Someone needed to shake up this cocktail of conservatism, someone gutsy and gifted, someone such as satirists Bruno Jonas and Siegfried Zimmerschied. In their first show they poked fun at everyone from God to gardeners, much to the delight of their audience, but not so the establishment. The chief vicar sued for blasphemy, the newspaper refused to report about the show, and the city politicians ordered it closed it down.

But even after the power elite had dropped the axe, the counter-culture movement not only refused to die but quickly blossomed. Besides its regular programming, the Scharfrichterhaus has for the past 25 years staged the hugely popular **Passauer Kabarett-Tage** (Passau Cabaret Days), a festival that draws top-notch performers from throughout Germany. Each year, organisers also honour budding talent with the Oscar of the political cabaret scene, the *Scharfrichterbeil* (statuette shaped like an axe). These days, the Scharfrichterhaus is nothing short of a Passau institution, and the performers' sharp tongues are a source of pride, not ire, to most locals.

There are several public car parks near the Hauptbahnhof but only one in the Altstadt, at Römerplatz (per hour/day €1.10/€10).

Fahrrad-Klinik (☎ 334 11; Bräugasse 10) hires out bikes from €11 per day.

BAVARIAN FOREST

If you want to venture off the beaten track, look no further than the Bayerischer Wald (Bavarian Forest), a lovely landscape of meadows, moorland, mountains, raised bogs, streams and lakes embraced by woodlands as dense and thick as in the fairy tales. Much of the area is protected as the **Naturpark Bayerischer Wald**, which at 3077 sq km is Germany's largest. The nature park also embraces the Nationalpark Bayerischer Wald, a heavily protected expanse where nature is being allowed to slowly reclaim the forest (see the boxed text on p176).

Trees have always been the region's biggest natural asset and their abundance led to the birth of the local glass industry in the late 17th century. Glass is still produced here today, and all along the **Glasstrasse**, a 250km-long holiday route connecting Neustadt an der Waldnaab with Passau, you can visit glass-blowing studios, factories and stores.

Tourism is generally well organised and lodging options are not only plentiful and comfortable but also have the lowest price tags anywhere in Germany. Zwiesel and Bodenmais offer good infrastructure and are excellent gateways any time of year, including winter when skiing is a major draw. Note that many hotels, restaurants and museums are closed from November until mid-December.

For travel around the Bavarian Forest, the best value is the Bayerwald-Ticket (adult/family €5/€10), a day pass good for unlimited travel on bus and train.

The region also makes a good base for excursions to the Czech Republic; Prague is only three hours away by car or four hours by train from Bayerisch Eisenstein (one-way €18.80). Check passport and visa requirements with a Czech consulate before heading out.

Nationalpark Bayerischer Wald

A paradise for outdoor enthusiasts, the Nationalpark Bayerischer Wald was carved out in 1970 as Germany's first national park and expanded in 1997 to its current size of 243 sq km. It stretches from Bayerisch Eisenstein to Finsterau along the Czech border and seamlessly blends into the much larger Sumava National Park on the Czech side. Together the two parks form the largest contiguous woodland area in Central Europe. The thick forest, mostly a cocktail of mountain spruce with a dash of fir, is crisscrossed by hundreds of kilometres of hiking, biking and cross-country skiing trails. On the German side, three main mountains – Rachel, Lusen and Grosser Falkenstein – soar to between 1300m and 1450m. Deer, wild boar, lynx, fox, otter and countless bird species roam around this protected area.

INFORMATION

Hans-Eisenmann-Haus (☎ 08558-961 50; www.nationalpark-bayerischer-wald.de in German; Böhmstrasse 35, Neuschönau; ☼ 9am-5pm mid-May–Oct, 9am-4pm Christmas–mid-May) Main park information centre with exhibits, activity schedule, children's discovery room and library.

SIGHTS & ACTIVITIES

An easy and fun way to sample the park's ample charms is by taking a spin along the **Tierfreigelände** (animal preserve; admission free; ☼ 24hr), right by the parking lot at the Hans-Eisenmann-Haus. A 7km loop takes you past large outdoor habitats where you can observe wolves, lynxes, brown bears, red deer, owls and many other species. The trail is suitable for wheelchairs and child strollers. The best times to spot the critters are in the early morning and late afternoon.

Another popular trail goes from the DJH hostel (p172) to the **Lusen peak** (1373m), which has been eaten bare of its tree cover by the bark beetle but offers great views, sometimes as far as the Alps. The **Felswandergebiet**, near the park's southern edge, takes you past muscular rock formations. For longer hikes, the rangers at the Hans-Eisenmann-Haus are a fount of information and can provide maps.

For some insight into the region's cultural history, drop by the **Freilichtmuseum Finsterau** (☎ 08557-960 60; Museumstrasse 51, Finsterau; adult/child/family €3.50/1.50/7.50; ☼ 9am-6pm May-Sep, 9am-4pm Oct, 11am-4pm Christmas-Apr), an outdoor

---

NATURE KNOWS BEST

You're hiking along a gorgeous path beneath towering canopies of thick spruce when suddenly you burst into a clearing. A nearly apocalyptic scene assaults your eyes. Vast fields of dead, fallen trees; skeletal, grey, leafless, some still standing, others rotting on the forest floor. Your mind reels in horror at this battlefield of nature. What's going on here?

Welcome to the domain of the bark beetle, a voracious little scarab that has laid waste to enormous swaths of the Nationalpark Bayerischer Wald. They feed solely on spruce, which is found in abundance here since people – over centuries – have cleared the original mixed forest to fuel local ovens and glass smelters. Spruce were introduced because of their quick-yield growth, and the bark beetle couldn't have been more pleased. Since 'discovering' their new fecund habitat a decade or so ago, these nasty critters have devoured about 40 sq km, or nearly a sixth, of the park's trees, mostly in the higher elevations.

So why isn't anything being done to fight back? Well, you see, this is a national park and the motto is to let nature take its course without human interference. It's a controversial approach, to be sure, and one that initially did not sit too well with locals who feared the beetles would kill not only the trees but also the tourism industry. 'Patience, my dears,' said the environmentalists. And indeed, nature proved it has a way of tending to itself.

From beneath the corpses of fallen spruce, new life is asserting itself sprig by sprig. And most importantly, a greater variety of trees – mountain ash, beech and other deciduous species – is slowly taking root as well. Though they take more time to grow to maturity, these hardier trees will restore the park's original 'mixed-forest' blend where the spread of arboreal predators is held in check by the trees themselves. A forest that 'polices' itself. It'll take time, but eventually it'll be as thriving and self-sustaining as it once was.

---

museum featuring historic farmhouses, a smithy and an old inn brought here from places throughout the Bavarian Forest.

SLEEPING & EATING

The **DJH Neuschönau-Waldhäuser** (☎ 08553-6000; jhwaldhaeuser@djh-bayern.de; Herbergsweg 2; dm incl breakfast & linen €15.90) is the only lodging option right in the heart of the national park and an ideal base for outdoor explorations. It is closed at various times during the year, so call ahead. **Campingplatz Finsterau** (☎ 08557-768) in Finsterau and **Camping am Nationalpark** (☎ 08553-727) in Klingenbrunn just near Spiegelau are both on the park's perimeter.

In the northern park, near Zwiesel, an easy half-hour walk along a brook leads to the **Schwellhäusl** (☎ 09925-460; mains €5-8; ⌚ 10am-7.30pm), an historic forest lodge next to a little lake where you can fortify yourself with a cool beer or a hearty meal. Sit in the beer garden or inside amid mounted boar heads and a painting of King Ludwig II.

GETTING THERE & AROUND

From mid-May through to October, several roads within the national park are closed to private vehicles and served instead by the **Igel-Bus** (☎ 09920-5968; 1-/3-/7-day tickets €3.30/8.20/11). The natural-gas powered buses operate on four routes, including one connecting the Grafenau train station with the Hans-Eisenmann-Haus, the DJH hostel and the Lusen hiking area (Lusen-Bus). The Rachel-Bus provides access to the park from Spiegelau, a stop on the Waldbahn from Zwiesel to Grafenau (see p178). The Bayerwald-Ticket (see p175) is valid on all Igel-Bus lines.

Frauenau

☎ 09926 / pop 3000 / elev 624m

Frauenau bills itself as the 'glass heart of the Bavarian Forest' and is home to the outstanding **Glasmuseum** (www.glasmuseum-frauenau .de in German; Am Museumspark 1; adult/child/senior/student/family €5/2.50/4.50/4.50/11; ⌚ 9am-5pm Mon-Fri, 10am-4pm Sat, Sun & holidays), which has been completely overhauled and is scheduled to be up and running by mid-2005. Exhibits are housed in an extravagant building that also contains the local **tourist office** (☎ 941 00; www.frauenau.de in German; ⌚ 9am-noon & 1.30-4pm Mon-Fri year-round, 9.30-11.30am Sat mid-May–mid-Oct). Inside you're sent on an 'edutaining' tour through 4000 years of glass history, starting with the ancient Egyptians and ending with modern glass art from around the world. Other sections look at the glass industry's history in the region and the daily life and working conditions through the centuries.

Frauenau is also home to two of the most prestigious glass-blowing studios along the Glasstrasse, both of which offer tours for visitors. **Glasmanufaktur Freiherr von Poschinger** (☎ 940 10; Moosauhütte 14; adult/child €1/0.50; ☿ tours 10am, 11am, noon, 1pm & 2pm Mon-Fri & 10am, 11am, noon Sat Jun-Oct, 11am, noon, 1pm Mon-Fri Christmas-May), still helmed by the jovial baron himself, is the world's oldest family-run glass factory (since 1568). **Glashütte Eisch** (☎ 1890; Am Steg 7; adult/child €1/0.50; ☿ tours 9-11.30am & 1-2.45pm Mon-Thu, 9-11.45am Fri & Sat) is co-owned by Erwin Eisch, a world-famous artist who helped pioneer the glass-as-art movement in the 1960s. Both studios specialise in elegant, high-quality hand-blown items that are, of course, also for sale in their respective stores.

Zwiesel

☎ 09922 / pop 10,500 / elev 585m

Zwiesel is one of the area's bigger towns, and a good exploration base thanks to its train connections and bountiful and good-value lodging options.

INFORMATION

Naturpark Informationshaus (☎ 802 480; www.naturpark-bayer-wald.de; Infozentrum 3, along the B11; ☿ 9.30am-4.30pm Tue-Sun) Information and exhibits about the Naturpark Bayerischer Wald inside an experimental building that's completely energy self-sufficient.

Zwiesel tourist office (www.zwiesel-tourismus.de in German) Town centre (☎ 840 523;; Rathaus, Stadtplatz 27; ☿ 9am-5pm Mon-Fri, 10am-noon Sat Jul & Aug); Zwiesel-Süd (☎ 840 529; along the B11, near exit Zwiesel-Süd; ☿ 10am-1pm & 2-5pm Mon-Fri, 1-3pm Sat, 10am-noon Sun) Exact hours vary by season.

SIGHTS

The forest, local customs and glassmaking are some of the main themes of the **Waldmuseum** (Forest Museum; ☎ 608 88; www.waldmuseum-zwiesel.de in German; Stadtplatz 28; adult/concession €2/1; ☿ 9am-5pm Mon-Fri, 10am-noon & 2-6pm Sat & Sun mid-May–mid-Oct, 10am-noon & 2-5pm Mon-Fri, 10am-2pm Sat & Sun mid-Oct–mid-May). The exhibits explain the forest's special and unique flora and fauna and shows how they've changed over time. Other displays here include a collection of ornate snuff boxes and arty

creations from students of a local glass-making school.

Large glass factories include the well-known **Schott-Zwiesel Glaswerke** (☎ 982 49; Dr-Schott-Strasse 35; ☿ tours 11am Mon-Fri) and, in the Glaspark north of town, **Glashütte Theresienthal** (☎ 1030; Theresienthaler Strasse; ☿ tours 9.30am-1.30pm), which also runs a small museum. Both have shops, but you'll also find lots of smaller, less-commercial studios throughout town.

SLEEPING & EATING

Landhaus Karin (☎ 2187; www.schall-fewo.de in German; Buschweg 24; d €42, apt €24-50; **P**) Run by a delightful young couple, this child- and pet-friendly property sits right on the edge of the forest and has modern rooms and apartments. Rates include admission to a local fitness centre. The free city bus stops right outside.

Hotel-Gasthof Kapfhammer (☎ 843 10; www.hotel-kapfhammer.de; Holzweberstrasse 6-10; s/d €35/70; meals €8-15) British royalty has overnighted at this charming place, which nonetheless has a down-to-earth atmosphere and a good Bavarian restaurant.

Hotel Zur Waldbahn (☎ 3001; www.zurwaldbahn.de in German; Bahnhofplatz 2; s €46-59, d €70-90; meals €8-15; **P** ✗ ☺) Tradition and modern comforts combine at this charismatic inn, just steps from the Bahnhof. The breakfast buffet is an especially generous spread and even includes homemade jams. If you've treated yourself to dinner at the excellent restaurant, you can work it off in the good-size, modern pool, complete with soothing massage jets.

Angerresidenz (☎ 842 00; www.angerresidenz.de in German; Gebäudestrasse 16; 2-bedroom apt €50-70, 3-bedroom apt €80-110; **P** ✗ ☐) Next to a little park and river, this stylish retreat leaves few demands unfulfilled. Mornings start with fresh breakfast rolls brought right to the door of your spacious apartment with its distinctive designer furniture, terrace and fully equipped kitchen. Unwinding spots include a sauna, game and fitness rooms and even a nifty massage bed.

Azur-Ferienpark Bayerischer Wald (☎ 802 595; www.azur-camping.de/zwiesel/zwiesel.html in German; Waldesruhweg 34; per person €4.50-6.80, per camp site €5.50-8.50) A convenient camp site about 500m north of the train station, near public pools and sports facilities.

Weinanger (☎ 869 690; Angerstrasse 37; dishes €5-10; ☻ 7pm-1am Tue-Sat) If your stomach's not up for a full Bavarian meal, this cheerful wine bistro with its brick walls and polished wooden tables is a cosy alternative. French onion soup, cheeses and sandwiches all feature on the menu.

Another good dining option is the upscale **Marktstube** (☎ 6285; Angerstrasse 31; mains €10-14; ☻ Wed-Mon), which infuses some international touches into traditional Bavarian meals.

GETTING THERE & AWAY

Zwiesel is reached by rail from Munich via Plattling (€26.40, 2½ hours), Regensburg (€17.80, two hours) Landshut (€17.40, two hours), and Passau (€16, 1½ hours); most trains continue to Bayerisch Eisenstein, with connections to Prague.

The Waldbahn regional train makes hourly trips between Zwiesel and Bodenmais (€2.70, 20 minutes) and less frequently between Zwiesel and Grafenau (€5.90, 50 minutes). From Grafenau you can catch the Igel-Bus into the Nationalpark Bayerischer Wald (see p176).

Drivers coming from the A3 autobahn should get off at Deggendorf and follow the B11 to Zwiesel.

Bodenmais

☎ 09924 / pop 3500 / elev 689m

Beautifully located Bodenmais, about 15km northwest of Zwiesel, is the most popular resort town in the Bavarian Forest with more than 800,000 overnight visitors a year. Its main street is Bahnhofstrasse where glass and souvenir shops rub shoulders with hotels and restaurants.

INFORMATION

Internetecke Altes Rathaus (☎ 905 294; Bergknappenstrasse 10; ☻ 10am-noon & 1-5pm Mon-Thu, 10am-1pm Fri) Free Internet access.

Sparkasse (Marktplatz 4) Bank.

Tourist office (☎ 778 135; www.bodenmais.de in German; Bahnhofstrasse 56; ☻ 8am-5pm Mon-Fri, 9am-1pm Sat, 9am-noon Sun) Adjacent to the train station.

SIGHTS & ACTIVITIES

Bodenmais has excellent hiking and biking in summer but it really comes into its own during the ski season. There are 21km of groomed cross-country trails in the town

itself but most people head about 5km east to the **Bretterschachten** area (served by ski bus), which offers the most reliable conditions on 65km of tracks.

Downhill skiers head about 14km north of town to the **Grosser Arber** (1456m), the highest mountain in the Bavarian Forest. With mostly easy to moderate runs, this ski area is especially popular with families, although it has also hosted European and World Cup ski races. There's also a 'fun park' for snowboarders with various kickers, humps and steeps, plus a rail park. Ski passes cost €22 per day; other tickets are also available.

In summer, the mountain summit is a popular destination with hikers who can follow a thrilling trail leading along a creek, across a gorge and past waterfalls. The easy alternative to get to the top is a gondola ride aboard the **Arber-Bergbahn** (☎ 09925-941 40; one-way/return €5.50/8), which, incidentally, is owned by the royal Hohenzollern family. The valley station can be reached by bus No 8645 from Bodenmais. Buses also stop at the **Grosser Arbersee**, a pleasant lake.

SLEEPING & EATING

Sport-und Ferienpension Adam (☎ 902 270; www .sportpensionadam.de in German; Hirtenweg 1; d €40, apt €36-41; P) Run by a young family, this place has lovely rooms, a guest kitchen and a sauna. With its free mountain bike and cross-country ski hire, it's tailor-made for sporting types.

Gästehaus Graf (☎ 321; www.gaestehaus-graf.de in German; Jahnstrasse 30; d €43) Cross-country ski right out the door of this small inn, which is run by an energetic mother-and-daughter team. Rooms range in look from dowdy to bright and contemporary, and there's a guest kitchenette as well.

Riederin (☎ 7760; www.riederin.de in German; Riederin 1; d €114, with half-board €134; P ✗ ▯ ▣) This full-service resort has so much going on, you may never make it out the door. The wellness area alone – with indoor and outdoor pools, saunas and Jacuzzi – is an enticing pampering station. Then there's the tennis courts, six-hole golf course, massages, nonsmoking restaurants…yup, you'll be busy.

Feriengut-Hotel Böhmhof (☎ 943 00; www .feriengut-boehmhof.de; Böhmhof 1; d incl meals €123-138; P ✗ ▣) This deluxe country retreat with its mostly bright, airy and spacious rooms is another great spot for taking a break from the rat race. Rates include breakfast, afternoon cakes, snacks and a four-course dinner.

Zum Kimbacher (☎ 770 0140; Hadergasse 1; mains €7.50-12; ☺ 6pm-midnight Mon-Sat) Locals love this place for its imaginative décor, good wines and delicious Bavarian and Austrian food, including creative salads and crispy *Flamme-kuche* (a pizzalike dish). In summer, you dine outside with a view of the Bodenmais rooftops. Frequent live music, too.

Die Waidlerstub'n (☎ 822; Marktplatz; mains €4.50-13) Bodenmais' oldest restaurant has outdoor seating on the market square and an inspired menu of hearty specials, plus salads and some vegetarian choices.

SHOPPING

Waldglashütte Joska (☎ 7790; Am Moosbach 1) Observe all phases of the glassmaking process before stocking up on souvenirs. There's also a small museum.

Herrgottschnitzer von Bodenmais (☎ 393; Dreifaltigkeitsplatz 11) If you're in the market for hand-carved religious figurines, this famous workshop makes some of the finest and most accomplished in the entire region.

GETTING THERE & AWAY

The Waldbahn regional train connects Zwiesel with Bodenmais (€2.70, 20 minutes) hourly. Bus No 8645 goes from Bodenmais via the Grosser Arber to Bayerisch Eisenstein. Drivers should take the B11 to Zwiesel and then follow the signs to Bodenmais.

LANDSHUT

☎ 0871 / pop 60,000 / elev 385m

Landshut, about 70km northeast of Munich, is not shy about its looks and deservedly so. Its historic centre, filled with beautifully gabled, candy-coloured town mansions, is immaculately preserved and overlooked by a quintessential medieval castle. Both are reminders of the city's golden age in the 14th and 15th centuries when it was the seat of the Bavaria-Landshut duchy under the so-called 'Rich Dukes'. Every four years, the town forms the backdrop of the Landshuter Hochzeit, an historical festival that commemorates a royal wedding in 1475 (see the boxed text on p180).

Orientation

Landshut is bisected by the Isar River, which splits into two arms – the Kleine Isar and the Grosse Isar – near the town centre. Nearly all major sights are concentrated on the main thoroughfare, the partly pedestrianised Altstadt, which in this case refers only to a street, not the entire historic district. Altstadt is paralleled by another major street called Neustadt. The Hauptbahnhof is about 2km northwest of here. Bus Nos 1, 2, 3 or 6 connect the train station with the historic centre, or else it's a walk south on Luitpoldstrasse and across the Isar.

Information

Bücher Pustet (☎ 2001; Altstadt 28) Well-stocked bookshop.
Police (☎ 110, nonemergency ☎ 925 20)
Post office City Centre (Postplatz 395); Hauptbahnhof (Bahnhofsplatz 1a) The city centre branch is next to the Heiliggeistkirche.

DETOUR: KLOSTER METTEN

While driving on the A3 autobahn between Regensburg and Passau, **Kloster Metten** (☎ 0991-910 80; Abteistrasse 3; adult/concession €2/1; ☺ tours 10am & 3pm), an imposing Benedictine abbey in Metten about 6km from the Deggendorf exit, makes for a lovely break from the road. Founded in 766, it is one of Bavaria's oldest monasteries and got its dazzling baroque looks during the 18th century. Tours take in the **Klosterkirche** (church), where Cosmas Damian Asam painted the wall frescoes and the painting above the high altar. Even sweeter eye-candy awaits in the famous **Bibliothek** (library), a walk-in jewel box of gold leaf, stucco and frescoes held aloft by statues of Atlas. Tours usually also take in the **Festsaal** (festival hall), where classical concerts are held in summer. Look up to see especially endearing representations of the four continents, including the fellow with the feather headdress representing America.

The monastery is still active with monks running a prestigious boarding and grammar school as well as a book-binding business, nursery and small publishing house.

LANDSHUTER HOCHZEIT

Every four years, the people of Landshut really cut loose during the Landshuter Hochzeit when 2300 of them dress up in medieval costume to re-enact the 1475 marriage of Georg, son of Duke Ludwig the Rich, to Hedwig, daughter of the king of Poland. Held over four weekends in July, the megaparty features jousting tournaments, dances, medieval music, fun and games, markets and merriment all around. Up to 80,000 visitors invade the town on any given day.

By all accounts, the original event was a grandiose spectacle indeed. The wedding ceremony at Basilika St Martin, attended by the *crème de la crème* of European royalty, was followed by a bridal procession along Altstadt with the townspeople cheering on the happy newlyweds and their entourage. This kicked off a week-long free-for-all courtesy of the duke. The final gustatorial tally included around 320 oxen, 200,000 eggs, 2300 sheep and 11,500 geese, not to mention entire rivers of beer and wine.

Today's festival isn't quite as lavish, but it's a good party nonetheless. The next two are scheduled for 2005 and 2009, see the website www.landshuter-hochzeit.de for more information.

Sparkasse (Bischof-Sailer-Platz 431)
Tourist office (☎ 922 050; www.landshut.de in German; Rathaus, Altstadt 315; ☯ 9am-5pm Mon-Fri, 9am-noon Sat)

Sights
ALTSTADT

If it wasn't for the modern businesses ensconced on the ground floor of the historic gabled mansions, Landshut's Altstadt would easily time warp you back into the Middle Ages. Gothic town houses, painted in a rainbow of colours and with Renaissance and baroque embellishments, fringe both sides of this beautiful street, which is book ended by two churches. The main procession of the Landshuter Hochzeit (see the boxed text above) comes through here, which is especially fitting since some of the buildings have historical connections to the actual event.

Hedwig, the bride, stayed at the **Grasberger Haus** (Altstadt 300) with its lovely vaulted foyer, while the most illustrious guest, Emperor Friedrich III, shacked up in the **Pappenberger Haus** (Altstadt 81), right opposite the **Rathaus** (Altstadt 315), Landshut's triple-gabled town hall. Here, in the **Prunksaal** (state hall; admission free; ☯ 2-3pm Mon-Fri), the royal couple took their first spin on the dance floor. Murals, added in the 19th century, capture scenes from the wedding. Today, the hall offers a baronial setting for concerts and official functions.

A few steps south is the magnificent **Stadtresidenz** (City Residence; ☎ 924 110; Altstadt 79; adult/child under 18/senior €3/free/2; tours ☯ 9am-6pm Apr-Sep, 10am-4pm Nov-Mar, closed Mon), considered to be the first Renaissance palace north of the Alps. The arcaded courtyard leads to lavish rooms, including the **Italienischer Saal** (Italian Great Hall), with festive stucco and mythological frescoes.

Towards the southern end of Altstadt, one more mansion stands out: the **Alte Post** (Altstadt 28), which served as an assembly hall in the 16th century and later became a post office. The elaborately frescoed façade presents a who's who of Wittelsbach rulers.

BASILIKA ST MARTIN

Landshut's main church, the Gothic **Basilika St Martin** (Kirchgasse; ☯ 8am-6pm Apr-Sep, 8am-5pm Oct-Mar) is a superb architectural specimen of exquisite proportions brimming with art treasures. Considered the crowning achievement of architect Hans von Burghausen, its size and dignified appearance are an expression of the citizenry's enormous pride and wealth during the town's late-medieval heyday. Legend has it that the plan was to build the church so high as to be able to peer right into the dinner pot of the duke residing in the hilltop Burg Trausnitz. To this end, presumably, the steeple soars 130m above the town, making it the world's tallest brick tower.

Inside, a Triumphal Cross (1495), hewn from a single tree trunk and with a Jesus figure four times life-size, dangles above the choir. Other treasures include the Madonna (1518) in the right aisle, the oak choir stalls (1500) and the sculpture-festooned stone altar (1424).

The most bizarre sight, though, is the second stained-glass window in the left aisle, a 20th-century work. The sequence ostensibly depicts the life and martyrdom of St Castulus, but if you look closely you'll see that some of the saint's tormentors look like some bad guys from your history books: Hitler, Goebbels and Göring. The window, not surprisingly, has been nicknamed 'Nazifenster'.

BURG TRAUSNITZ

Founded in 1204, **Burg Trausnitz** (☎ 924 110; www.burgtrausnitz.de; adult/senior €4/3, combination ticket with Cabinet €6/4, child under 18 free; ⏱ 9am-6pm) imperiously overlooks Landshut from its hilltop perch. The castle is considered the seat of the Wittelsbach dynasty and served as residence of the local dukes until 1503. Each fiddled with its appearance and size to bring it into line with the style of the day. From the late-Romanesque period stems the **Georgskapelle**, a two-storey chapel later decorated with exquisite Gothic sculpture. The Renaissance brought the **Narrentreppe** (Fools' Stairs) decked out with cheeky murals depicting commedia dell'arte scenes.

Since 2004 the castle is home to its own museum, the **Kunst-und Wunderkammer** (Cabinet of Art & Curiosities; adult/senior €4/3, combination ticket with castle €6/4, child under 18 free; ⏱ 9am-6pm Apr-Sep, 10am-4pm Oct-Mar). It re-creates the wondrous collections of rarities, oddities and art amassed by inquisitive rulers during the Renaissance, including Landshut's own Prince Wilhelm. A fan made of peacock feathers, a stuffed Nile crocodile, a parrot-shaped clock and a cherry pit engraved with erotic scenes are all part of this eclectic and highly entertaining display.

The castle is reached via a set of stairs nicknamed 'Ochsenklavier' (oxen piano), which veers off Alte Bergstrasse. Views of the town are excellent from up here. Behind the castle, the **Hofgarten** makes for a nice stroll.

OTHER SIGHTS

The northern end of Altstadt is punctuated by the 15th-century **Heiliggeistkirche**, another von Burghausen work, which today functions both as a house of worship and as a museum of sacred art. The modern altar is by internationally renowned Landshut sculptor Fritz Koenig, who also founded the **Skulpturenmuseum** (☎ 890 21; Am Prantlgarten 1; adult/child/family €3.50/2/6.50; ⏱ 10.30am-1pm & 2-

5pm Tue-Sun). Exhibits are set up in former malt storage rooms hewn into the Hofberg mountain and so far have featured Koenig's own work and examples from his private collection.

Festivals & Events

Aside from the famous **Landshuter Hochzeit** (☎ 229 18; www.landshuter-hochzeit.de; ⏱ Jul), the town also hosts the biannual **Landshuter Hofmusiktage** (☎ 922 050; www.landshuter-hofmusiktage.com in German; ⏱ Jul), a European festival of medieval, Renaissance and baroque music held over two weeks in July (next one in 2006).

Sleeping

Hotel-Gasthof Ochsenwirt (☎ 234 39; www.ochsenwirt.net in German; Kalcherstrasse 30; s €50-85, d €75-90, child under 10 free; meals €8-15; ⏱ restaurant closed Tue; P ✗) Gear up for a day of sightseeing in the newly spruced-up rooms (parquet floors, large desks, comfy beds) of this cosy inn near the Burg Trausnitz. The restaurant serves no-nonsense Bavarian food, and there is also an inviting beer garden in summer. From Altstadt, take bus No 7 to Kalcherstrasse.

Stadthotel Herzog Ludwig (☎ 974 050; www.stadthotel-herzog-ludwig.de in German; Neustadt 519; s €70-90, d €90-110, children under 12 free; ✉ ✗) Spacious rooms with elegant furniture, wireless LAN and an on-site beauty clinic for those sudden rejuvenation needs are among the assets of this doesn't-get-more-central new kid on the block. The 'wedding suite' with its mirror-canopied bed looks like fun, but smoking in the rooms is a no-no.

Hotel Goldene Sonne (☎ 925 30; www.goldenesonne.de; Neustadt 250; s €70-120, d €100-110; meals €8-14; P ✗) Next to the Stadthotel, this lovely property successfully marries a long hospitality tradition with the latest amenities, including wireless LAN. Cheerful colours – blue, red and yellow – give the rooms a pleasing contemporary look. The restaurant is excellent (suckling pig is a speciality) and the beer garden is a great place for a drink or repast.

Landshut's **DJH hostel** (☎ 23449; jugendherberge@landshut.de; Richard-Schirrmann-Weg 6; dm incl breakfast & linen €19.45; ⏱ closed Christmas-early Jan; P) is in a cleverly modernised medieval building, about halfway between Altstadt and Burg Trausnitz. Campers can pitch their tents at the riverside **Campingplatz Landshut** (☎ 533 66; fax 533 66; Breslauer Strasse 122; per camp site/tent/person €5.50/3/4.50; ⏲ Apr-Sep).

Eating

Zum Ainmiller (☎ 211 63; Altstadt 195; mains €10-15; ⏲ closed Mon; ☒) This woodsy spot packs them in with honest-to-goodness Bavarian food that feeds both the belly and the soul. Even vegetarians have a better-than-usual selection. If possible, sit downstairs in the historic cellar with murals and tiled stove or in the courtyard with castle views.

Michelangelo (☎ 262 61; Altstadt 297; pizza & pasta €5-9, mains €10-18; ⏲ 8.30am-1am) Grab an outside table for a spot of people-watching or head inside where a statue of David serenely watches over diners munching on pizza, pasta and other favourites. On Thursday pasta costs just €4.

Restaurant Bernlochner (☎ 899 90; Ländtorplatz 5; mains €13-19) At this elegant restaurant, chef Helmut Krausler digs deep into his culinary repertoire to give pork, rabbit, quail or salmon the gourmet treatment. The result is refined German cuisine with clever international touches. In summer, it's best enjoyed outside with a view of the Isar River.

Ferrale (☎ 261 91; Neustadt 436; mains €5-13; ⏲ 9am-6pm Mon, 9am-midnight Tue-Sat) This neighbourhood Italian eatery fits like a well-worn glove and is much liked for its friendly service, pretty pastas and crunchy thin-crust pizzas. It's attached to a café-bar and gourmet deli.

Fürstenhof (☎ 925 50; Stethaimerstrasse 3; mains €16-25, set menus €33-66; ⏲ closed Sun) This is Landshut's silver-service restaurant whose chef Andre Greul managed to wrest a star from those notoriously finicky Michelin testers for his avant-garde interpretations of classic Franco-German cuisine. It's inside a romantic Art Nouveau villa that's also a hotel (singles/doubles from €85/€110).

Back on Altstadt, **Cafe Ganymed** (☎ 236 85; Altstadt 216; mains €8-12; ⏲ 9.30am-1am) is another popular noshing nook with a legendary all-you-can-eat Sunday brunch buffet (€10).

Getting There & Around

Landshut is directly connected by regional trains to Munich (€11.50, 45 minutes), Passau (€16.70, 1¼ hours) and Regensburg (€9.70, 45 minutes). The A92 runs right past the town, which is also at the crossroads of the B15 and B299.

The centre is eminently walkable, but there's also a good bus system (single trips €1.60, day passes €1.90). Parking is free for the first hour in the CCL shopping mall at Am Alten Viehmarkt, near the northern end of Neustadt.

Franconia

HIGHLIGHTS

▪ **Wining**
Wine tasting amid the vineyards in Sommerhausen (p223)

▪ **Dining**
Devouring Nuremberg's famous finger-sized sausages (p192)

▪ **City Stroll**
Ambling along the cobblestone streets of magnificent, World Heritage–listed Bamberg (p198)

▪ **Road Tripping**
Biking, bussing or driving the alluring Romantic Road (p226)

▪ **Green Haven**
Gliding the willow-fringed Altmühl River in a canoe (p239)

▪ **Architectural Wonder**
Admiring Balthasar Neumann's crowning achievement, the Residenz (p218) in Würzburg

▪ **Chill-Out Spot**
Gazing at valley vistas from the Burggarten (p232) outside Rothenburg ob der Tauber's medieval twin-turreted town gate

▪ **History Lesson**
Visiting the moving Deutsch-Deutsches Museum (see the boxed text on p212) in the once-divided village of Mödlareuth

Map labels: Mödlareuth ★ · Würzburg ★ · ★ Bamberg · ★ Sommerhausen · Nuremberg ★ · ★ Rothenburg ob der Tauber · ★ Romantic Road · ★ Altmühl River

▪ POP: 4.1 MILLION   ▪ AREA: 20,900 SQ KM

FRANCONIA

Occupying the northern part of Bavaria, Franconia is the largest of the state's holiday regions. It's also the most diverse, steeped in culture, art and architecture, with gently undulating hillsides, dense forests and sophisticated cities. Other treasures include lush vineyards strung along the Main River, medieval castles and palaces, nine nature parks and countless romantic villages.

Franconia consists of three administrative regions: Oberfranken (Upper Franconia), Mittelfranken (Central Franconia) and Unterfranken (Lower Franconia). The region only became part of Bavaria in the early 19th century under Napoleon and even now many of its people consider themselves 'Franconian' rather than 'Bavarian'. To that end, you'll find that their dialect, dress, food and traditions are distinctly different. This is not lederhosen and dirndl country, and the staunch conservatism, so prevalent further south, is often tempered with more liberal tendencies. Franconia also has a large proportion of Protestants, whereas the rest of Bavaria is predominantly Catholic.

Franconia abounds with historic cities, especially the famous trio of Nuremberg, (home of Albrecht Dürer and Hitler's Nazi party rallies); Bamberg, a Unesco World Heritage city; and Würzburg, with its architecture and spirited university atmosphere. The northern half of the Romantic Road runs through Franconia, where you'll find the enchanting medieval towns of Rothenburg ob der Tauber and Dinkelsbühl.

Franconia's superb wines (mostly whites) are bottled in the distinctive *Bocksbeutel*, a flattened teardrop-shaped flagon used exclusively for wines from this region and those from the Württemberg region west of here. Equally celebrated are Franconia's hundreds (yes, hundreds) of breweries and their unique brews.

NUREMBERG

☎ 0911 / pop 500,000 / elev 289m

Nuremberg (Nürnberg) is Bavaria's second-largest city and a major tourist magnet. It woos visitors with a wonderfully restored medieval Altstadt (old town), a grand castle, major museums and the world-famous Christkindlesmarkt (Christmas market). Other tantalising assets are the finger-sized Nürnberger Bratwürste (sausages), and *Lebkuchen* – large, soft gingerbread cookies, traditionally eaten at Christmas time but available here year-round.

History

During its medieval heyday, Nuremberg was, for centuries, the unofficial capital of the Holy Roman Empire and the preferred residence of German kings. Thanks to the 'Golden Bull', a law passed in 1356 by Emperor Karl IV, every newly elected king or emperor was required to hold his first gathering of parliament in Nuremberg. From 1424 to 1800, the city was also the empire's 'treasure chest', acting as guardian to the crown jewels and many of today's priceless artworks.

Especially in the 15th century, numerous artistic masters, local boy Albrecht Dürer foremost among them, lived and worked here, leaving their legacy throughout the city.

Starting with the Thirty Years' War, Nuremberg reached its nadir in 1806 under Napoleon, when the former Free Imperial City – weakened and bankrupt – was absorbed into the Kingdom of Bavaria. The city's comeback occurred as a result of industrialisation and a major milestone came in 1835 when Germany's first railway began operating between Nuremberg and Fürth.

In the 20th century, Nuremberg became linked with, and heavily burdened by, the legacy of the National Socialists. After seizing power in 1933, Hitler selected Nuremberg as the site for his mass party rallies. His main architect, Albert Speer, designed the grandiose grounds. In 1935, the infamous Nürnberger Gesetze (Nuremberg Laws), which stripped Jews of their German citizenship in addition

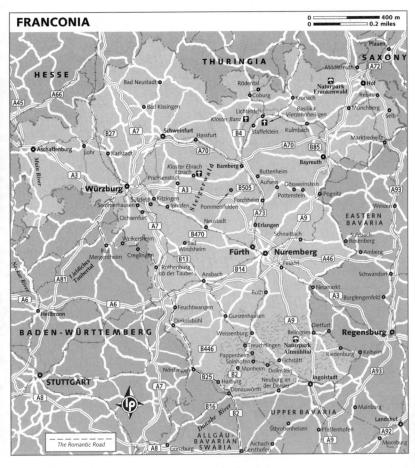

FRANCONIA

0 ————— 400 m
0 ————— 0.2 miles

The Romantic Road

to other repressive measures, were also enacted in the city.

Allied bombing raids killed about 6000 people and destroyed about 90% of the Altstadt. After WWII, numerous top Nazis were tried by an international military tribunal at the so-called Nuremberg Trials. Painstaking reconstruction – using the original stone – saw the restoration of almost all main buildings, including the castle and the three medieval Altstadt churches.

Postwar, Nuremberg has transformed itself into the 'City of Human Rights', hosting among other events the Human Rights Conference and the Nuremberg International Human Rights Award. Earlier this decade it received the Unesco Prize for Human Rights Education. Together with Fürth, it forms an important industrial region focused on engineering, printing and plastics, toys and food.

Orientation

Nuremberg's landmark Kaiserburg (Imperial Castle) lords over the Altstadt, home to most of the major sights and neatly enclosed by a reconstructed town wall. The placid Pegnitz River separates the quiet and statelier Sebalder Altstadt in the north from the southern Lorenzer Altstadt, which is a partly pedestrianised shopping precinct.

The Hauptbahnhof (central train station) is just outside the walls, southwest of the Altstadt. From here, Königstrasse, the main

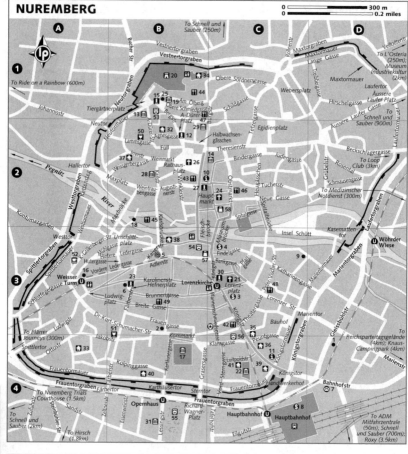

artery, runs north to Hauptmarkt, the main square.

The Reichsparteitagsgelände (Nazi Party Rally Grounds) is about 4km southeast of the Altstadt in Luitpoldhain, while the Nuremberg Trials courthouse is just west of the Altstadt. Fürth (p194) is 9km to the north.

Information
BOOKSHOPS
Buchhandlung Edelmann (☎ 992 060; Kornmarkt 8) English-language novels downstairs and Nuremberg's largest travel section upstairs.
Jakob Emie Buchandlung (☎ 224 783; Hefnersplatz 8) Multilanguage bookshop.

CULTURAL CENTRES
Amerika Haus (☎ 230 690; Gleissbühlstrasse 13) An impressive range of cultural and artistic programmes, an English-language discussion group, resource library and a cinema regularly screening first-run and classic US and UK films.

EMERGENCY
Bayerisches Rotes Kreuz (Bavarian Red Cross; ☎ 192 22) Ambulance service.
Medizinischer Notdienst (Clinic; ☎ 192 92; Kesslerplatz 5) Emergency medical care.
Police (☎ 110)

INTERNET ACCESS
Internet-Versteck (☎ 234 2557; Kaiserstrasse 17; per 15/60min €0.50/1; ☺ 11am-11pm Mon-Sat, 1-11pm Sun) Follow the signs up the stairs.

LAUNDRY
Schnell und Sauber (☎ 180 9400; ☺ 6am-midnight) This company has four coin laundries, all outside the Altstadt. Sulzbacher Strasse 86 in the east (tram No 8 to Deichslerstrasse), Allersberger Strasse 89 in the south (tram Nos 4, 7 and 9 to Schweiggerstrasse), Schwabacher Strasse 86 in the west (U2 to St Leonhard) and Schweppermannstrasse 27 in the north (tram No 9 to Krelingstrasse). A load costs €3.50; drying per 12 minutes is €1.

LIBRARIES
Stadtbibliothek (Central city library; ☎ 231 2672; Gewerbemuseumsplatz 4)

MONEY
Commerzbank (Königstrasse 21)
HypoVereinsbank (Königstrasse 3)
Reisebank (Hauptbahnhof)

POST
Post office (Bahnhofplatz 1)

TOURIST INFORMATION
Tourist office (www.tourismus.nuernberg.de) Hauptmarkt (☎ 233 6135; Hauptmarkt 18; ☺ 9am-6pm Mon-Sat, 10am-4pm Sun May-Sep, 10am-7pm daily during Christkindlesmarkt); Künstlerhaus (☎ 233 6131; Königstrasse 93; ☺ 9am-7pm Mon-Sat) Staff sell the Nürnberg + Fürth Card (€18), available to overnight visitors and good for two days of unlimited public transport and admission to most museums and attractions in both cities.

TRAVEL AGENCIES
Plärrer Journeys (☎ 929 760; Gostenhofer Hauptstrasse 27) A good general travel agency that also has a last-minute ticket desk at the airport.

Sights
HAUPTMARKT
This bustling square in the heart of the Altstadt is the site of markets and the famous Christkindlesmarkt (p191). At the eastern end is the ornate Gothic **Pfarrkirche Unsere Liebe Frau** (1350–58), also known as simply the Frauenkirche. The work of Prague cathedral builder Peter Parler, it is the oldest Gothic hall church in Bavaria and stands on the ground of Nuremberg's first synagogue. The western façade is beautifully ornamented and is where, every day at noon, crowds crane their necks to witness a spectacle called *Männleinlaufen*. It features seven figures, representing electoral princes, parading clockwise three times around Emperor Karl IV to chimed accompaniment. The scene commemorates the passage of the Golden Bull in 1356.

Near the tourist office the gargoyle-adorned 19m-tall **Schöner Brunnen** (Beautiful Fountain), a replica of the 14th-century original, rises from the square like a Gothic spire. Look for the seamless golden ring in the ornate wrought-iron gate. Local superstition has it that if you turn it three times, your wish will come true.

ALTES RATHAUS & ST SEBALDUSKIRCHE
Beneath the **Altes Rathaus** (old town hall; 1616–22), a hulk of a building with lovely Renaissance interiors, are the **Lochgefängnisse** (Medieval Dungeons; ☎ 231 2690; Rathausplatz; adult/concession €3/1.50; ☺ 20min tours half-hourly 10am-4.30pm Tue-Sun Apr-Oct, 10am-4.30pm Tue-Fri Nov-Mar, daily tours during the Christkindlesmarkt), consisting of 12 small cells and a torture chamber. Leaflets in languages other than German (€0.50) are free.

Opposite the Altes Rathaus is the 13th-century **St Sebalduskirche**, Nuremberg's oldest church, whose exterior is replete with religious sculptures and symbols. Check out the ornate carvings over the Bridal Doorway to the north, showing the Wise and Foolish Virgins. Inside, the bronze shrine of **St Sebald** is a Gothic and Renaissance masterpiece that took its maker, Peter Vischer the Elder, and his two sons more than 11 years to complete. (Vischer is in it too, sporting a skullcap.)

STADTMUSEUM FEMBOHAUS

North of here, Rathausplatz gives way to Burgstrasse whose main attraction is the municipal museum, the **Stadtmuseum Fembohaus** (City Museum; ☎ 231 2595; Burgstrasse 15; adult/concession €4/2 Noricama or general exhibit, combination ticket €6/3; ☻ 10am-5pm Tue, Wed & Fri-Sun, 10am-8pm Thu). Highlights of this entertaining overview of the city's history include the restored historic rooms of this 16th-century merchant house and a flashy Hollywood-esque multimedia show, Noricama, which journeys through Nuremberg history.

FELSENGÄNGE

Beneath the **Albrecht Dürer Monument** on Albrecht-Dürer-Platz are the chilly **Felsengänge** (Underground Cellars; ☎ 227 066; tours adult/concession €4/3; ☻ tours 11am, 1pm, 3pm & 5pm). Departing from Burgstrasse 19, tours descend to this four-storey subterranean warren dating from the 14th century, which once housed a brewery and a beer cellar. During WWII, it served as an air-raid shelter. Tours take a minimum of three people. Take a jacket against the chill (and note there are no toilets).

ALBRECHT-DÜRER-HAUS

Dürer, Germany's most famous Renaissance draughtsman, lived and worked at the **Albrecht-Dürer-Haus** (Albrecht Dürer House; ☎ 231 2568; Albrecht-Dürer-Strasse 39; adult/concession with audio-guide €5/2.50, with palm-held computer €12/8; ☻ 10am-5pm Fri-Wed, 10am-8pm Thu) from 1509 until his death in 1528. After a multimedia show, visitors embark on a self-guided tour (available in English) of the four-storey house, which is narrated by 'Agnes', Dürer's wife. Highlights are the hands-on demonstrations in the re-created studio and print shop on the 3rd floor and, in the attic, a

gallery featuring copies and originals of Dürer's work.

Special tours led by an actress dressed as Agnes take place at 6pm Thursday, 3pm Saturday and 11am Sunday; there's an English-language tour at 2pm Saturday.

TIERGÄRTNERPLATZ

Framed by charming half-timbered houses, on the **Tiergärtnerplatz** square's eastern edge stands the beautiful **Pilatushaus** fronted by Jürgen Goertz's 1984 bronze sculpture **Der Hase – Hommage á Dürer** (The Hare – A Tribute to Dürer). This nod to Dürer's watercolour original called *Junger Feldhase* (1502) shows the dire results of tampering with nature.

During WWII, prescient officials moved key artworks to the **Historischer Kunstbunker** (Historical Art Shelter; ☎ 227 066; Obere Schmiedgasse 52; tours €4/3; ☻ tours 3pm, minimum 3 people), a network of caves underneath the Kaiserburg (see below), as early as 1940. This was technically a form of resistance, since Hitler forbade such 'defeatist' thinking. There's also a film of the bombing of Nuremberg.

KAISERBURG

A must-see is the humongous **Kaiserburg** (Imperial Castle; ☎ 225 726; Burg; adult/concession with museum €6/5, well & tower only €3/2; ☻ 9am-6pm Apr-Sep, 10am-4pm Oct-Mar). Construction began during the reign of Hohenstaufen King Konrad III in the 12th century and dragged on for about 400 years. The complex, for centuries the receptacle of the Holy Roman Empire's treasures, consists of three parts: the Kaiserburg and Stadtburg (the Emperor's Palace and City Fortress), as well as the Burggrafenburg (Count's Residence), which was largely destroyed in 1420. Wedged between its surviving towers are the Kaiserstallung (Royal Stables), which today house the DJH hostel (p191).

Tardis-like sections open to visitors include the royal living quarters, the Imperial and Knights' Halls and the **Romanesque Doppelkapelle** (Twin Chapel). The latter poignantly illustrates medieval hierarchy: common folk sat in the dimly lit lower section, with the royals having entered up above directly from the palace.

Enjoy panoramic city views from atop the **Sinwellturm** (Sinwell Tower; 113 steps) or peer into the amazing 48m-deep **Tiefer**

Brunnen (Deep Well) – guides lower a platter of candles so you can see its depth, which still yields drinking water.

The **Kaiserburg Museum** (☎ 200 9540; Burg; adult/concession €6/5; ☺ 9am-6pm Apr-Sep, 10am-4pm Oct-Mar) chronicles the history of the castle and provides a survey of medieval defence techniques.

The grassy knoll at the southeast corner of the castle gardens, which are open seasonally, is **Am Ölberg**, a favourite spot to sit and gaze out over the city's rooftops.

SPIELZEUGMUSEUM

Nuremberg has long been a centre of toy manufacturing, and the **Spielzeugmuseum** (Toy Museum; ☎ 231 3164; Karlstrasse 13-15; adult/concession €4/2; ☺ 10am-5pm Tue & Thu-Sun, to 9pm Wed, extended hr during Jul & Aug, the Christkindlesmarkt & Toy Fair) presents them in their infinite variety – from historical wooden and paper toys to toy trains, books and computer games. Kids and kids at heart will delight in the play area.

South of here across Karlsbrücke brings you to a tiny island surrounded by a scenic stretch of the Pegnitz River. On the north bank is the covered wooden **Henkersteg** (Hangman's Bridge).

LUDWIGSPLATZ TO LORENZPLATZ

At the foot of the fortified **Weisser Turm** (White Tower; now the gateway to the U-Bahn station of the same name) stands the dramatic **Ehekarussell Brunnen** (Marriage Merry-Go-Round), a remarkable metallic fountain with six timeless interpretations of marriage based on a verse by medieval cobbler-poet Hans Sachs. Further east, another modern fountain, the **Peter-Henlein-Brunnen** on Hefnerplatz, is dedicated to the 16th-century tinkerer credited with making the first pocket watch.

The site of the Altstadt's other U-Bahn station, Lorenzplatz is dominated by the **Lorenzkirche** (Gothic Church of St Lawrence), which is chock-full with artistic highlights. Check out the 15th-century tabernacle in the left aisle whose delicate carved strands wind up to the vaulted ceiling. Remarkable also are the stained glass (including a rose window 9m in diameter) and Veit Stoss' *Engelsgruss* (Annunciation), a wooden carving with life-size figures, suspended above the high altar.

North of the church, the **Tugendbrunnen** (1589) is a fountain featuring the seven Virtues with a figure of Justice looking on.

GERMANISCHES NATIONALMUSEUM

Spanning from prehistory to the early 20th century the **Germanisches National Museum** (German National Museum; ☎ 133 10; Kartäusergasse 1; adult/concession €5/4, free 6-9pm Wed, English audio-guide €1.50; ☺ 10am-6pm Tue & Thu-Sun, 10am-9pm Wed) is the country's most important museum of German culture. It features works by German painters and sculptors, an archaeological collection, arms and armour, musical and scientific instruments and toys. Among its many highlights is Dürer's anatomically detailed *Hercules Slaying the Stymphalian Birds*. The research library has over 500,000 volumes and 1500 periodicals.

In Kartäusergasse at the museum's entrance is the **Way of Human Rights**, a symbolic row of 29 white concrete pillars (and one oak tree) bearing the 30 articles of the Universal Declaration of Human Rights. Each pillar is inscribed in German and, in succession, the language of peoples whose rights have been violated, with the verdant oak representing languages not explicitly mentioned.

VERKEHRSMUSEUM

Nuremberg's **Verkehrsmuseum** (Transportation Museum; Lessingstrasse 6; adult/concession €3/2; ☺ 9am-5pm Tue-Sun) combines two major exhibits under one roof: the **Deutsche Bahn Museum** (German Railway Museum; ☎ 442 233) and the **Museum für Kommunikation** (Museum of Telecommunications; ☎ 230 880). The former explores the origins and history of Germany's legendary railway system; the latter showcases development in telecommunications, including historic telephones dating back over 100 years.

NEUES MUSEUM

The interesting **Neues Museum** (New Museum; ☎ 240 200; Luitpoldstrasse 5, entry via Klarissenplatz; adult/concession €3.50/2.50, free Sun; ☺ 10am-8pm Tue-Fri, 10am-6pm Sat & Sun) presents a unique juxtaposition of international contemporary art and design.

Paralleling developments in both genres, the collection includes paintings, sculpture, photography, video art and installations. Equally stunning is the building itself, with a dramatic 100m curved glass façade that, literally and figuratively, reflects the stone town wall opposite.

MUSEUM INDUSTRIEKULTUR

This former screw-manufacturing plant now houses the **Museum Industruriekultur** (Museum of Industrial Culture; ☎ 231 3875; Sulzbacker Strasse 62; adult/concession €4/2; ☾ 9am-5pm Tue-Fri, 10am-6pm Sat & Sun), with quirky exhibits such as talking washing machines, a fully functional 1920s' cinema, and a kids' fun learning lab with various vehicles to 'test drive'.

REICHSPARTEITAGSGELÄNDE

Nuremberg's role during the Third Reich is emblazoned in minds around the world through the black-and-white images of rapturous Nazi supporters thronging the city's flag-lined streets as bayonet-bearing troops salute their Führer.

The rallies at the **Reichsparteitagsgelände** (Nazi Party Rally Grounds) were part of an orchestrated propaganda campaign that began as early as 1927 to garner support for the NSDAP. In 1933, the party planned a ridiculously large purpose-built complex in the southeastern Luitpoldhain suburb. Nazi leaders hoped to establish a metaphorical link between Nuremberg's illustrious past as *Reichstagstadt* (where parliament met during the Holy Roman Empire) and the Third Reich's new rally centre (the *Reichsparteitag*).

A **Documentationszentrum** (Documentation Centre; ☎ 231 5666; Bayernstrasse 110; adult/concession with audio-guide €5/2.50; ☾ 9am-6pm Mon-Fri, 10am-5pm Sat & Sun) puts the Nazi Party Rally Grounds into historical context and is also intended as a place of learning and dialogue. An outstanding exhibition called 'Fascination and Terror' examines the causes, relationships and consequences of the Nazi terror regime. Besides chronicling the rise of the NSDAP, it examines the cult around Hitler, the propaganda and reality of the party rallies, the Nuremberg Trials and more. It's in the north wing of the Kongresshalle.

Much of the actual Reichsparteitagsgelände was destroyed during 1945 bombing raids, but enough is left to sense the dimension and scale of this gargantuan complex. At the area's northwestern edge once stood the **Luitpoldarena**; designed for mass SS and SA parades, it's now a park.

The half-built **Kongresshalle** (Congress Hall), meant to outdo Rome's Colosseum in both scale and style, is the largest remaining Nazi building.

Most of the parades, rallies and events took place at the **Zeppelinfeld**, fronted by a 350m-long grandstand, the **Zeppelintribüne**. The grounds are bisected by the 60m-wide **Grosse Strasse** (Great Rd), which culminates, 2km south, at the **Märzfeld** (March Field), planned as a military exercise ground. West of the Grosse Strasse was to have been the **Deutsches Stadion**, with a seating capacity of 400,000. Its construction never progressed beyond the initial excavation; the hole later filled with groundwater to become today's Silbersee.

Nowadays the Zeppelintribüne grandstand hosts sporting events (including the Norisring car races in June) and rock concerts. During June 2006, the **Franken Stadion**, also here, will see five World Cup soccer matches (opposite) played out.

Take tram No 4 to Dutzendteich, or No 9 to Luitpoldhain.

NUREMBERG TRIALS COURTHOUSE

Schwurgerichtssaal 600 (Court Room 600), of what is today the Landgericht Nürnberg-Fürth, was where the captured Nazis were tried in 1945 to 1946 for crimes against peace and humanity. The Allies held the trials in Nuremberg for obvious symbolic reasons. They chose this still-operational **courthouse** (☎ 231 5421; Fürther Strasse 110, entry from Bärenschanzstrasse; adult/concession €2/1; ☾ tours hourly 1-4pm Sat & Sun) because it was easily accessible and one of the few such large structures to survive the war intact.

The trials resulted in the conviction and sentencing of 22 Nazi leaders and 150 underlings, and the execution of dozens until 1949. Among those condemned to death early on were Joachim von Ribbentrop, Alfred Rosenberg, Wilhelm Frick and Julius Streicher. Hermann Göring, the Reich's field marshal, cheated the hangman by taking a cyanide capsule in his cell hours before his scheduled execution.

Take U-Bahn U1 to Bärenschanze.

Tours

The tourist office runs 2½-hour English-language **walking tours** (adult/child under 14 incl admission to Kaiserburg €7.50/free; ☾ 1pm May-Oct

& during the Christkindlesmarkt) from the Haupt-markt branch (p187). They also operate 2½-hour **coach tours** (adult/child under 12 €11/5.50; ☺ 9.30am Apr-Oct & during the Christkindlesmarkt) in English and German, taking in the city's major sights including the Reichsparteit-agsgelände.

Nürnberger Altstadtrundfahrten (☎ 421 919; adult/concession €4/3.50; ☺ every 45min 10.30am-4pm Sun-Fri Apr-Oct) is a tourist choo-choo mod-elled on the world's first train, the Adler. Starting from the Hauptmarkt, it loops through the Altstadt for half-hour guided tours in German (also in English with a minimum of five people).

Festivals & Events

Every year, millions of visitors flock to Nuremberg's world-famous **Christkindles-markt** (☺ 9.30am-8pm Mon-Wed, 9.30am-9pm Thu-Sat, 10.30am-9pm Sun late Nov-24 Dec) to browse the stalls selling toys, trinkets, gingerbread and sweets while clutching steaming mugs of *Glühwein* (sweet mulled wine) and gorg-ing on *Bratwürste* (roast sausages). After dark, the brightly coloured lights create a fairy-tale spectacle. Adjoining the main market is the adorable children's **Kinder-weihnacht**, with such delights as carousels, miniature train rides and child-size food portions.

Nuremburg's Altstadt also comes to life during several summer festivals. The **Bardentreffen** in early August is an open-air medieval music festival. But the summer festival highlight is the 12-day **Altstadtfest** in September when the entire old town is taken over by music and theatre, stalls sell-ing speciality foods, craft stands and lots more. Auto-racing fans should check out the **Norisring Races**, a Formula Three race around the Zeppelintribüne in late June or early July.

June 2006 sees Nuremberg host five of Germany's **World Cup** soccer matches, on the 11th, 15th, 18th, 22nd and 25th, at Franken Stadion. Even if you don't have a ticket, expect a party atmosphere…and plenty of crowds.

Sleeping

Accommodation is tight during special events (above). That said, cheap rooms can be found at other times, especially if you book ahead.

BUDGET

Lette 'm Sleep (☎ 992 8128; www.backpackers.de; Frauentormauer 42; dm €15-19, d €44-52, linen €3; ☒ ▣) A backpacker favourite, this in-dependent, all-ages hostel is in a terrific location within the town wall just five min-utes' walk from the Hauptbahnhof. The retro-styled kitchen and common room with velour lounges and groovy lighting are great areas to chill, there's a free online computer and WiFi Internet access, tea and brewed coffee, and staff are wired into what's happening around town. Checkout is at noon.

DJH Jugendgästehaus (☎ 230 9360; www.djh.de in German; Burg 2; B&B with linen €20.45-23.45; ☒) In the former castle stables, about 20 to 30 minutes' walk north of the Hauptbahnhof, this spotless hostel has 317 beds in bright, airy dorms as well as a piano and table ten-nis.

Probst-Garni Hotel (☎ 203 433; fax 205 9336; Luit-poldstrasse 9; s/d €21/43, s/d with bathroom €41/55) Nu-remberg's most reasonably priced pension is a friendly place squeezed on the 3rd floor of a creaky but well-located building. Some singles are tiny, but other rooms are ad-equate. Rooms with bathrooms have TVs.

Campers can head to **Knaus-Camping-park 'Am Dutzendteich'** (☎ 981 2717; knaus.camp .nbg@freenet.de; Hans-Kalb-Strasse 56; per camp site/per-son €9.50/5) near the lakes in the Volkspark, southeast of the city. Take U-Bahn U1 to Messezentrum.

MIDRANGE

Hotel Deutscher Kaiser (☎ 242 660; www.deutscher -kaiser-hotel.de; Königstrasse 55; s €79-140, d €96-170; ℙ ☒ ▣) A grand sandstone staircase leads to ornately decorated rooms in this 1880s-built hotel in the Altstadt. Bathrooms are equipped with bidets and there's a fitness room, but the real gem is the elegant read-ing room with newspapers and magazines in German and English. Staff are profes-sional and genuine.

Hotel Elch (☎ 249 2980; www.hotel-elch.com; Irr-erstrasse 9; s €70, d €95; ℙ ☒) A 15th-century, half-timbered house has morphed into this snug narrow staircased hotel with a nice am-bience and warm, attentive service. Rooms pair rustic timber floorboards and furniture with modern telephones and TVs.

Hotel Victoria (☎ 240 50; www.hotelvictoria.de in German; Königstrasse 80; s/d €74/99; ℙ ☒ ▣)

Through the black-and-white photograph–lined corridors, rooms here are compact but stylish, with contemporary blonde wood furniture, crisp white sheets and minibars.

Hotel Lucas (☎ 227 845; www.hotel-lucas.de; Kaiserstrasse 22; s from €65, d from €90; ✕ ⌨) This trendy, modern hotel in the heart of the city offers excellent value. The rooms are an oasis of restrained international design and comfort and all have fax and ISDN connections. Good deals on weekend stays are available and there's public parking close by.

Am Jakobsmarkt (☎ 200 70; www.hotel-am-jakobs markt.de in German; Schottengasse 5; s €81-105, d €103-127; ⓟ ✕ ⌨) Choose from contemporary or traditional spacious rooms at this well-run place, reached via a tiny courtyard near the Spittlertor. Extras include a sauna, solarium and fitness room.

TOP END

Hotel Drei Raben (☎ 274 380; www.hotel-drei-raben .de; Königstrasse 63; r €100-185; ✕ ⌨) The design of this original hotel builds upon the legend of the three ravens perched on the building's chimney stack, who tell each other stories from Nuremberg lore. Each of the 'mythology' rooms uses décor and art including sandstone-sculpted bedheads and etched-glass bathroom doors to reflect a particular tale – from the life of Albrecht Dürer to the history of the local soccer club. Junior suites have claw-foot tubs. There's often dancing, cake and coffee in the downstairs bar on Sunday, as well as live jazz.

Agneshof (☎ 214 440; www.agneshof-nuernberg.de in German; Agnesgasse 10; s €90-175, d €105-225; ⓟ ✕ ⌨) Located in the preserved 'antiques quarter' near the St Sebalduskirche, the Agneshof's public areas have a sophisticated, artsy touch, as do the rooms, many featuring balconies with castle views. Polite staff and first-rate wellness facilities make it worth the money. In summer there's a pretty deck-chaired courtyard garden.

Eating

RESTAURANTS

Traditional Bavarian cooking is big in Nuremberg.

Barfüsser Kleines Brauhaus (☎ 204 242; Hallplatz 2; mains €6.60-12.80) Munch on hearty Franconian food or seasonal specials in this atmospheric brewery-pub. A staircase descends to a cavernous vaulted cellar where you'll

be surrounded by copper pipes direct from the brewery, framed old advertisements, and tabletop *Eichenholzfässchen* (individual five-litre oak-wood kegs). A lift provides wheelchair access.

Hütt'n (☎ 201 9881; Burgstrasse 19; mains €8-12; ☽ from 4pm Mon-Wed) A perpetually overflowing local haunt (be prepared to queue for a table), the special here is the *ofenfrische Krustenbraten*: roast port with crackling, dumplings and sauerkraut salad. There's also a near-endless variety of schnapps.

Burgwächter (☎ 222 126; Am Ölberg 10; mains €7-16) In the shadow of the castle, this is a great place with a terraced beer garden and terrific city views. The prime steaks and grilled cuts will please carnivores but vegetarians aren't forgotten, with homemade Swabian filled pastas and other meatless Bavarian specialities (which, contrary to appearances, isn't an oxymoron).

Bratwursthäusle (☎ 227 695; Rathaus-Platz 1; mains €8-14; ☽ closed Sun) Cooked on an open-flame grill in an island kitchen with its copper saucepans hanging overhead right in the centre of the restaurant, this place has some of the best *Rostbratwürste* (roast sausages) around. You can dine in the timbered restaurant or on the terrace with views of the Sebalduskirche, Rathaus and Hauptmarkt, but if you're in a hurry, loose change will get you three sausages in a bun.

International options:

L'Osteria (☎ 558 283; Pirckheimer Strasse 116; mains €6-12) The best pizza in town, with oodles of atmosphere and large bottles of wine to which you just help yourself.

Enchilada (☎ 244 8498; Obstmarkt 5; mains €8.40-15.90) Generous taco platters, burritos and nachos in a candlelit setting.

CAFÉS & QUICK EATS

Café am Trödelmarkt (☎ 208 877; Trödelmarkt 42; dishes €3.60-10.40) A gorgeous place on a sunny day, this café overlooks the covered Henker-steg. It's especially popular for its continental breakfasts, and has good blackboard specials.

Souptopia (☎ 240 6697; Lorenzer Strasse 27; soups €2.50-4; ☽ closed Sun) Homemade soups made fresh are the go here, with vegetarian and nonvegetarian choices, along with sandwiches and salads.

Wok Man (☎ 204 311; Breite Gasse 48; dishes €2-7; ☽ to 8pm Mon-Sat, closed Sun) This is a decent, self-service, Chinese fast-food place in the pedestrian zone with spring rolls and large platters of chow mein.

Drinking

Many of the best bars are in the pedestrian zone south of the Pegnitz.

Treibhaus (☎ 223 041; Karl-Grillenberger-Strasse 28; dishes €2.50-4.50) This bustling, smoky café is a Nuremberg institution, popular with students, shoppers and anyone else in search of an unpretentious and convivial ambience. Breakfast is served until the evening, but the hot and cold snacks are also worth a try.

Sausalitos (☎ 200 4889; Färber Strasse 10; meals €6-24) With its slick Santa Fe décor, this is the place where young hipsters congregate for copious cocktails. It's at its most rocking during Margarita Happy Hour between 11pm and 2am Monday to Thursday.

Café Lucas (☎ 227 845; Kaiserstrasse 22; meals €7.50-13.50) This two-storey café draws the designer set for convincing cocktails, snacks and a few choice larger meals; there's a nifty outside section with wooden tables on a platform overlooking the river.

Saigon Bar (☎ 244 8657; Lammsgasse 8; ☺ from 10pm Thu-Sun) Do as the Nurembergers do and make this your last stop after a night on the town. With a background beat of drum 'n bass, this essential late-night bar does a top-rate *caipirinha*, the Brazilian drink that's at least as popular in Bavaria as it is in Rio, made from smashed limes, brown sugar, crushed ice and white pitú rum.

Entertainment

Doppelpunkt, Nuremberg's popular free listings magazine for nightlife and cultural fixtures, is in German only, but it's easy to navigate, as is its website, www.doppelpunkt.de (in German). There's comprehensive information (in English) about gay and lesbian parties, clubs and events at www.nuernberg.gay-web.de.

LIVE MUSIC & NIGHTCLUBS

Stereo Deluxe (☎ 530 060; Klaragasse 8; admission from €5; ☺ Thu-Sat) First a home-grown, world-renowned record label for modern urban sound, this is now also a hip café with an in-the-groove club in the red strobe-lit basement. Very cool.

Hirsch (☎ 429 414; Vogelweiherstrasse 66; admission €6-10; ☺ 7pm-2am Sun-Thu, 9pm-5am Fri & Sat) A converted factory, the Hirsch has live alternative

music in two separate areas, as well as theme nights and a summer beer garden. On Friday and Saturday nights, DJs spin everything from drum 'n bass to acid jazz and '70s disco, with monthly Pink Hirsch gay parties.

Loop Club (☎ 686 767; Klingenhofstrasse 52; ☺ 10pm-4am Thu-Sat) With three dance areas and a languid chill-out zone with lounge music, this place attracts a slightly older crowd. Every Thursday is the 50 Cent party, with mixed drinks costing just that all night. Take the U-Bahn U2 to Herrnhütte, turn right and it's a five-minute walk. There's a Nightliner bus service back to town after the trains stop running.

Other recommendations:

Mach 1 (☎ 203 030; Kaiserstrasse 1-9; admission €4-6; ☺ Thu-Sat) Legendary dance temple with top international DJs and an infamously strict door policy. Dress to impress.

Hausbrauerei Altstadthof (☎ 221 570; Bergstrasse 19; ☺ Mon-Sat) Brewery-pub whose basement cellar resonates with live folk, blues and rock.

CINEMAS

Roxy (☎ 488 40; Julius-Lossmann-Strasse 116) Specialises in English- and French-language first-run films – take the Worzeldorferstrasse-bound tram No 8 and exit at the Südfriedhof stop.

THEATRE & CLASSICAL MUSIC

Altstadthof (☎ 244 9859; Bergstrasse 19; tickets €8-12) Tucked away in a complex that also includes a brewery-pub (above) and boutiques, this small independent theatre presents entertaining comedies and other light fare.

Städtische Bühnen (Municipal Theatres; box office ☎ 231 3575; Richard-Wagner-Platz 2-10; tickets €8-50) Nuremberg's magnificent theatre complex consists of the *Opernhaus* (opera house), the *Schauspielhaus* (drama theatre) and the *Kammerspiele* (chamber plays). The renovated Art Nouveau opera house presents opera, ballet and readings, while the latter two offer a varied programme of both classical and contemporary plays. The Nürnberger Philharmoniker also performs here.

Shopping

Lebkuchen Schmidt (☎ 896 60; Plobenhofstrasse 6, Hauptmarkt) Lebkuchen are a Nuremberg speciality and some of the best are made by Schmidt, whose shop windows are filled with decorative metal tins.

Käthe Wohlfahrt (☎ 240 5675; Königstrasse 8) This is the Nuremberg branch of the dazzling Rothenburg-based Christmas ornament emporium.

Getting There & Away

Nuremberg airport (☎ 937 00) is 7km north of the centre and served by regional and international carriers, including discount carrier Air Berlin, and Air France and Lufthansa.

InterCity Express or InterCity trains run hourly to/from Frankfurt (€50, 2¼ hours) and Munich (€38, 1¾ hours). Regional trains travel hourly to Bamberg (€9.40, one hour) and Würzburg (€14.40, 1¼ hours) and every other hour to Regensburg (€15.20, one hour).

Several autobahns including the Berlin–Munich A9, converge on Nuremberg, but only the north–south A73 joins B4, the ring road. There's an **ADM Mitfahrzentrale** (☎ 194 40; Hummelsteiner Weg 12) right behind the south exit of the Hauptbahnhof.

Getting Around

TO/FROM THE AIRPORT

Every second U-Bahn No 2 (every few minutes between 5am and 12.30am) runs from the Hauptbahnhof to the airport in 12 minutes (look for the plane symbol on the front of the train). A taxi between the airport and central Nuremberg costs about €15.

BICYCLE

Ride on a Rainbow (☎ 397 337; Adam-Kraft-Strasse 55; per day €10-18, week €44-99) hires out bikes of all sorts.

The tourist office (p187) sells the ADFC's *Fahrrad Stadtplan* (€4.50), a detailed map of the city and surrounding area. It also has a list of 'bicycle friendly' hotels in town that can store bicycles for travellers.

PUBLIC TRANSPORT

Walking's the ticket in the Altstadt. Tickets on the bus, tram and U-Bahn/S-Bahn network costs €1.40/€1.80 per short/long ride. A day pass for one/two adults costs €3.60/€6.20; Saturday passes are valid all weekend.

TAXI

The flagfall for a **taxi** (☎ 272 770) is €2.60.

AROUND NUREMBERG

Fürth

☎ 0911 / pop 110,000 / elev 297m

More than an appendage to Nuremburg, its big city neighbour to the south, Fürth is a spirited town with its own identity and

---

KASPAR HAUSER: THE CHILD FROM THE VOID

Sixteen-year-old Kaspar Hauser first surfaced in dire physical condition – barely able to stand or see in direct sunlight – in the Nuremberg square, Unschlittplatz, on Whit Monday in 1828.

Repeatedly uttering the phrase 'I want to be a rider like my father', he was thought to be retarded and held in a jail cell for two months, becoming a freak show. A local professor came to his rescue and within months the boy could speak, read and write and revealed that his past 12 years had been spent chained within a completely dark coffinlike cave. His 'keeper' had supplied food and water but beaten him if he made any noise.

In October 1829, an unknown assassin attempted to murder Kaspar Hauser. For his safety, he was removed from the local professor's care and eventually ended up in Ansbach in November 1831. In Ansbach he became close with the town's head judge, Anselm von Feuerbach. It was Feuerbach who first publicly advanced the controversial theory that Kaspar was in fact the prince of Baden – who reportedly died at birth – and thus was the rightful heir to the contested Baden throne. Feuerbach may well have been onto something, for he suddenly dropped dead of suspected poisoning.

On 14 December 1833, Kaspar was lured into an Ansbach park with the promise that he would be told who his true parents were. There he was stabbed in the chest; three days later he died from his wounds.

The mystery of Kaspar Hauser continues to live on in more than 3000 books and over 14,000 articles as well as two feature films by Werner Herzog and Peter Sehr. In 1996, the German news weekly *Der Spiegel* published the results of a DNA test proving that Kaspar had no relation to the House of Baden, but still the debate continues.

history. In 2007, it is celebrating its 1000-year anniversary.

Fürth once had the largest Jewish community in southern Germany, who began to settle here in 1528. The Third Reich regime forced about 1500 of them into emigration; those who stayed – about 900 – perished in the camps. Among the emigrants was the former US Secretary of State, Henry Kissinger, who was born here in 1923.

As a result of its shared role with Nuremberg as the site of Germany's first railway, Fürth lays claim as the world's smallest city to have its own subway system (three stops), though its compact size means walking across town is often speedier than waiting for a train.

For information, drop by the **tourist office** (☎ 406 615; www.fuerth.de; Bahnhofplatz 2; ☧ 9am-6pm Mon-Fri, to 1pm Sat).

SIGHTS

For an engaging and informative overview of the region's Jewish history from the Middle Ages to today, visit the **Jewish Museum of Franconia** (☎ 770 577; Königstrasse 89; adult/concession €3/1.50; ☧ 10am-5pm Sun-Fri, to 8pm Tue). A room for celebrating the Feast of Tabernacles and a ritual mikvah bath in the basement are tangible reminders of this 17th-century former Jewish home's heritage.

Admission here is also good for the branch museum in the village of **Schnaittach** (☎ 09153-7434; Museumsgasse 12-16, Schnaittach; ☧ 11am-5pm Sat & Sun), where you can tour the former synagogue, a mikvah and the cantor's and rabbi's quarters. Schnaittach is about 50km northeast of Nuremberg, off the A9. From Nuremberg Hauptbahnhof, trains make the 40-minute trip here hourly (every two hours on weekends; €3.90 each way).

A journey through 80 years of German radio and TV history awaits visitors of the **Rundfunkmuseum** (Radio Broadcasting Museum; ☎ 756 8110; Kurgartenstrasse 37; adult/concession €3/2; ☧ noon-5pm Tue-Fri, 10am-5pm Sat & Sun). Housed in the former headquarters of the Grundig electronics corporation, the 12 exhibit rooms chronicle events and milestones, from the first radio broadcast in Berlin in 1923 to the use of propaganda radio in WWII to the latest digital technology. Take U-Bahn U1 to Stadtgrenze, then it's a 200m walk.

FESTIVALS & EVENTS

Yiddish culture is celebrated during the **International Klezmer Festival** in March. Another major event is the 11-day **Michaelis-Kirchweih**, a huge street carnival with rides, food and merriment, in late September.

EATING

Die Kartoffel (☎ 770 554; Gustavstrasse 34; dishes €6-18.50) The chef at this rustic eatery has infinite imagination when it comes to turning the lowly potato into an interesting meal.

Gustavstrasse is home to several more restaurants and cafés, particularly near the quaint square, Waagplatz.

ENTERTAINMENT

Kultur Forum (☎ 973 840; www.kulturforum.fuerth.de in German; Würzburger Strasse 2; tickets €5-25) In 2004 this former slaughterhouse was refitted to incorporate a stunning glass foyer and a diverse programme of traditional theatre, poetry readings and children's performances in two separate halls.

Jazz has a strong following in Fürth; for information on venues and gigs, check the local listings magazines (see p193), or at record shops such as **Da capo** (☎ 785 666; Hornschuchpromenade 16a), which has a good jazz section.

GETTING THERE & AWAY

The U1 makes the trip from Nuremberg's Hauptbahnhof to Fürth several times hourly (€1.80, 15 minutes).

From Nuremberg, take Fürtherstrasse west, which leads directly here.

Erlangen

☎ 09131 / pop 101,000 / elev 279m

About 24km north of Nuremberg, Erlangen is a buzzing university and Siemens company town. Expelled from France by the 1683 Edict of Nantes, the Huguenots settled here and established the town as a preindustrial and trading centre. Cobblestone streets criss-crossed by students on bicycles, tree-lined shopping boulevards, ivy-covered buildings and a lovely Schloss (palace) make Erlangen worth a stop. Around Pentecost the **Erlanger Bergkirchweih**, a 12-day folk and beer festival on the Burgberg, takes place with the city as backdrop.

FRANCONIA

FEATURE: PROST!

When JRR Tolkien opened his *Fellowship of the Ring* with a rousing hobbit birthday party in the mythical Shire, he quite possibly drew his inspiration from Franconia's **St Annafest** (St Anna Festival; ☎ 09191-714 338; www.forchheim.de in German), held in the Kellerwald – 24 wooded beer gardens and medieval stone cellars deep in the forests of Forchheim (about half an hour from both Nuremberg and Bamberg), many of which are open year-round.

Of ancient origins, the St Annafest takes place over 10 days in late July and early August and draws around half a million local revellers who feast on platters of *Bratwürste* (sausages) while carnival acts and bands perform into the night… and, of course, swig the regionally produced brews.

Franconians love their beer, as evidenced by the region's 300-odd breweries, which make up almost half of Bavaria's total and one-third of Germany's; which means one brewery for every 4500 inhabitants. (By comparison, there are only 100 breweries in the entire US and just 30 in Japan.) Industrialisation arrived late to Franconia, and it's still largely untouched by globalisation, allowing these small, often family-run enterprises to endure.

Even Franconia's impressive figures are dwarfed by the village of **Aufsess** in Franconian Switzerland. With a population of 1500, it holds the world record for the greatest number of breweries per capita (four, one for about every 375 residents), as well as the record for the world's smallest brewery, **Kathi Bräu** (☎ 09198-277; Hechenhof 1). Right up until her death in 1993 at the age of 85, Kathi herself would regularly stand at the upper windows, arms folded and nodding with satisfaction as she surveyed her beer garden packed with loyal patrons and decree free beer for all. These days locals still have their own mugs behind the bar.

Aufsess' four breweries are linked by a round trip, 14km beer hiking trail through picturesque countryside. Set off from **Brauerei Reichold** (☎ 09204-271; www.reichold.de in German; Hochstahl 24; s/d from €26/42; mains €5.50-9.50; ☺ restaurant closed Mon & Tue), whose restaurant uses generations-old

---

ORIENTATION & INFORMATION

Hugenottenplatz is a short walk east of Bahnhofplatz from where the pedestrianised Hauptstrasse leads north to Schlossplatz and the Altstadt with lots of student-oriented bars and restaurants. The **tourist office** (☎ 895 10; www.erlangen.de in German; Nürnberger Strasse 24-26; ☺ 9.30am-6pm Mon-Fri) is on the 1st floor of the Grand Galerie shopping centre.

SIGHTS

The eye-catching **Schloss** houses the university administration. Right behind it is the picnic-friendly **Schlossgarten**, with its striking fountain, the Hugenottenbrunnen. Concerts occasionally take place in the park or in the adjacent **botanical garden** (☎ 852 2669; admission free; ☺ 8am-5.30pm Mon-Fri Apr-Oct, 8am-3pm Mon-Fri Nov-Mar). The greenhouses have shorter opening hours; call ahead or check with the tourist office.

Local history starting with the Huguenot settlement is chronicled at the **Stadtmuseum Erlangen** (☎ 862 400; Martin-Luther-Platz 9; adult/concession €2.50/1.50; ☺ 9am-1pm Tue-Fri, 2-5pm Tue & Wed, 11am-5pm Sat & Sun). It's in the beautiful, baroque Altstädter Rathaus, about 400m north of Schlossplatz.

EATING

Alter Simpl (☎ 256 26; Bohlenplatz 2; mains €6-12; ☺ Mon-Sat) On a square just off Friedrichstrasse awaits this warren of a restaurant with hearty (read: meaty) hot and cold dishes. Meat grilled over beech wood is a speciality.

Tio (☎ 817 191; Südliche Stradmauerstrasse 1a; meals €5-15) Over two striking levels of polished concrete, glass and steel, this trendy neon blue–lit place has smart, contemporary cuisine and good-value pizzas and pastas.

The bustling **farmers market** (Marktplatz; ☺ 10am-4pm Mon-Sat) overflows with produce. Look for the fast-food options as you exit the train station. Nordsee has an outlet at Hauptstrasse 30.

GETTING THERE & AROUND

Regional trains to Nuremberg leave several times hourly (€3.60, 15 minutes). Single local bus tickets are €1.40, day passes are €3.

Erlangen is on the A73 autobahn, just north of the A3.

Ansbach

☎ 0981 / pop 40,000 / elev 409m

About 50km southwest of Nuremberg, Ansbach still preserves the graceful charm

recipes. The owners will give you a trail map, a survival certificate if you make it all the way around, and, if you're keen, a list of another six breweries that can be added in as part of a wider trail.

At traditional Franconian guesthouses and breweries like these, if your drinking companions are still finishing their beers, as your final – and only your final – drink, ask for an equalising *Schnitt* – a half-serve of beer for half-price (you'll almost always end up being given more). These are limited to tap beer, which, in these parts, is by no means a raw deal.

If you prefer wheels over hiking boots, spin along the **Aischgründer Bierstrasse** (Aisch Valley Beer Route; www.bierstrasse.de) taking in seven breweries between Uhelfeld (near Bamberg) and Bad Windsheim (p235), near Rothenburg.

But if you'd rather imbibe than drive, contact the **Fränkische Bierstrasse** (Franconian Beer Route; www.bierfranken.de in German), which has details of about 30 breweries and options for tours. **TooT Tours** (☎ 07958-311; www.toot-tours.com) also run a special Beer Tour to hot spots throughout this beer lover's paradise.

There are endless ways to tap Franconia's unique beer culture. Just some include touring the world's most comprehensive beer museum, **Maisel's Brauerei-und-Büttnerei-Museum** (☎ 0921-401 234; Kulmbacher Strasse 40; tours €4; ☺ tour 2pm Mon-Sat) in Bayreuth and Bamberg's **Fränkisches Brauereimuseum** (Franconian Brewery Museum; ☎ 0951-530 16; Michaelsberg 10f; adult/concession €2/1.50; ☺ 1-5pm Wed-Sun Apr-Oct), where monks have been brewing since 1122. Or maybe take Bamberg's beer-tasting trip (p202), sampling the city's *Rauchbier* (smoked beer). As well check out the **Bayerisches Brauereimuseum** (brewery museum; ☎ 09221-805 14; Hofer Strasse 20; ☺ 10am-5pm Tue-Fri, 9am-5pm Sat & Sun Apr-Oct, 10am-5pm Tue-Sun Nov-Mar) in Kulmbach, sip the town's own unique brew, *Eisbock* (iced beer), and – if the hobbitlike St Annafest whets your palate – join in Kulmbach's rollicking beer festival which spills into the streets around late July or early August.

of the margravial residence it was for nearly 500 years. Founded as a Benedictine monastery by St Gumbertus in 748, the settlement came under the rule of the Hohenzollern clan in 1331, who made it their residence in 1456. Ansbach reached its cultural heyday in the early 18th century. The magnificent baroque palace and many of the statuesque town mansions lining the Altstadt's largely car-free lanes date back to this era. Ansbach is also associated with one of the most enduring crime stories revolving around the life and death of Kaspar Hauser (see the boxed text on p194). Today, it is the capital of the administrative district of Central Franconia, and exudes a cosmopolitan flair.

ORIENTATION

The train and bus stations are about a 10-minute walk south of the Altstadt, near the southwestern edge of the Hofgarten (Palace Garden). Walking north on Bischof-Meiser-Strasse will take you straight to the Residenz Ansbach; the Altstadt is just west of here.

INFORMATION

Tourist office (☎ 512 43; www.ansbach.de in German; Johann-Sebastian-Bach-Platz 1; ☺ 9am-5pm Mon-Fri,

10am-1pm Sat May-Oct, 9am-12.30pm & 2-5pm Mon-Fri Nov-Apr) Next to the Gumbertuskirche.

SIGHTS
Residenz Ansbach

Starting out in the 14th century as a moated castle, the margraves' opulent palace, the **Residenz Ansbach** (☎ 953 8390; Promenade 27; admission €4; ☺ tours hourly 9am-5pm Tue-Sun Apr-Sep, 10am-3pm Oct-Mar) went through a Renaissance make-over before getting its baroque looks in the first half of the 18th century, with Italian architect Gabriel de Gabrieli at the helm.

Compulsory tours are in German only (but ask for an English-language pamphlet). Buy your tickets in the net-vaulted **Gothic Hall**, where you can peruse glass-encased porcelain and faïences. Over the next 50 minutes, you'll see 27 magnificently furnished rooms, including the **Festsaal** (Banquet Hall) with a ceiling fresco by Carlo Carlone; the **Kachelsaal** (Tile Hall) smothered in 2800 hand-painted tiles; and the dizzying **Spiegelkabinett** (Mirror Cabinet) decked out with precious Meissen porcelain.

East of the palace, across the Promenade, is the sprawling **Hofgarten** whose architectural focus is the **Orangerie**.

FRANCONIA

Kaspar Hauser Sites

For background on the mystery and theories about Kaspar Hauser, visit the excellent exhibit at the **Markgrafenmuseum** (Margravial Museum; ☎ 977 5056; Kaspar-Hauser-Platz; adult/concession €2.50/1; ⊙ 10am-5pm May-Sep, 10am-5pm Tue-Sun Oct-Apr). Displays include the bloodstained undergarments Hauser wore on the day he was stabbed, the letter he carried when first found in Nuremberg and personal effects, including a pocket watch. Some German skills will be of help in understanding the exhibits.

In Platenstrasse, right in the Altstadt, the **Kaspar-Hauser-Denkmal** (1981) shows him both as the scruffy kid he was at his discovery and as the dapper man about town at the end of his life. A **Memorial Stone** marks the spot of the attack in the Hofgarten, just east of the Orangerie. Hauser is buried in the **Stadtfriedhof**, about 600m south of the Altstadt via Maximilianstrasse, where his tombstone reads: 'Here lies Kaspar Hauser, an enigma of his time, his birth unknown, his death a mystery'.

Gumbertuskirche

Behind the altar of the three-towered **Gumbertuskirche** (Church of St Gumbertus; Johann-Sebastian-Bach-Platz), a door leads through to the **Schwanenritterkapelle**, which is a late-Gothic chapel filled with elaborate epitaphs of members of the Order of the Swan. Below here, the **Fürstengruft** holds the sarcophagi of 25 Ansbach margraves. The adjacent Romanesque **crypt** (⊙ 10am-noon Sun year-round, 3-5pm Fri-Sun Apr-Oct) is the oldest section of the church.

FESTIVALS & EVENTS

Ansbach's rococo heritage is celebrated each year in late June during the **Ansbacher Rococo Festival**. Other highlights on the cultural calendar include the biannual **International Bach Week**, held in late July of odd-numbered years, and the **Kaspar Hauser Festival** in September of even-numbered years. Bookings for either should be made well ahead.

SLEEPING & EATING

Hotel Zum Lamm (☎ 969 9900; www.hotel-zum-lamm .de; Endresstrasse 23; s/d €55/78; meals €7-15; ⊙ restaurant closed Sun; P 🍽) Ask for one of the rustically furnished rooms at this friendly inn, which offers free parking and a traditional

Bavarian restaurant, which are surprisingly thin on the ground in Ansbach.

Hotel Schwarzer Bock (☎ 421 240; www.schwarzer bock.com; Pfarrstrasse 31; s €44-59, d €77-99; meals €7-14.50; ⊙ restaurant closed Sun evening; P 🍽) This rococo mansion in a central location in the Altstadt has nicely furnished, if old-fashioned, timber-floored rooms and an excellent restaurant serving creative Franconian fare. There's a small fitness room and a sunny beer garden.

Stadtcafé (☎ 7449; Martin-Luther-Platz 15; mains from €6.60) A popular meeting point for locals, you could easily graze here all day. Á la carte breakfast is served until 7pm, with the breakfast buffet – a veritable feast – from 7.30am to 11am. There are even special dishes for ovo-lacto vegetarians.

Tham (☎ 950 8988; Endresstrasse 12; mains €5.30-10.40) This Asian restaurant's menu spans numerous pages, but especially popular is the all-you-can-eat buffet lunch including soup, spring rolls and dessert served from 11.30am to 2pm Monday to Friday.

GETTING THERE & AWAY

Frequent trains depart from Nuremberg's Hauptbahnhof (€10.40, 45 minutes). Getting to Rothenburg ob der Tauber requires a change in Steinach (€10.20, 40 minutes). Ansbach lies at the juncture of the B13 and the B14, just north of the A6 autobahn.

BAMBERG

☎ 0951 / pop 70,000 / elev 240m

A high point of any trip to Franconia, Bamberg is truly magnificent. The city's abundance of fine historic buildings, their richness of styles and the almost complete absence of modern eyesores has made it a Unesco World Heritage site.

A bishopric studded with churches, Bamberg was built on seven hills and is therefore also known as the 'Franconian Rome'. Its 'Tiber' is the Regnitz whose canals give the city a laissez-faire feel. About 8000 students inject liveliness into streets, cafés and pubs. The world-renowned Bamberg Symphony Orchestra and the Calderón Theatre Festival draw thousands every year.

Bamberg is justly famous for its beer. There are 10 breweries in town and another 81 in the region, which collectively produce over 200 kinds of beer, including *Rauchbier*, a dark-red ale infused with the smoke of smouldering beech wood, giving it a smooth bacony flavour (it tastes much better than it sounds; vegies can rest assured there's no meat involved). The surrounding hills are dotted with wonderful beer gardens.

History
Bamberg's name derives from the Babenberg dynasty, who built a castle in the 9th century in the spot now occupied by the cathedral. In 1002, Emperor Heinrich II (973–1024) took over the castle, founded a bishopric five years later and thus laid the groundwork for the next 800 years of Bamberg's history as seat of the ruling prince-bishops.

The city reached another heyday in the 18th century under Prince-Bishop Lothar

Franz von Schönborn (1655–1729), who hired some of Europe's finest architects, including Balthasar Neumann and brothers Georg and Johann Dientzenhofer, to rid the town of its medieval look in favour of the more elegant and 'contemporary' baroque. Tax relief and other incentives were given to citizens willing to rebuild their homes; poorer folk simply plastered over the half-timbered façades. Many of these historic buildings stand intact because Bamberg emerged from the WWII bombing raids, miraculously, with hardly a scratch.

Orientation
Two waterways traverse Bamberg: the Rhine-Main-Danube-Canal, and, paralleling

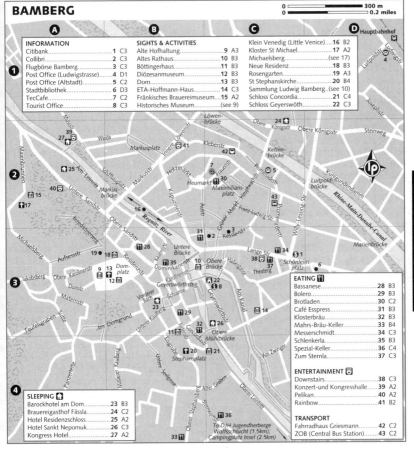

BAMBERG

0 ——— 300 m
0 ——— 0.2 miles

INFORMATION	
Citibank	1 C3
Collibri	2 C3
Flugbörse Bamberg	3 C3
Post Office (Ludwigstrasse)	4 D1
Post Office (Altstadt)	5 C2
Stadtbibliothek	6 D3
TecCafe	7 C2
Tourist Office	8 C3

SIGHTS & ACTIVITIES	
Alte Hofhaltung	9 A3
Altes Rathaus	10 B3
Böttingerhaus	11 B3
Diözesanmuseum	12 B3
Dom	13 B3
ETA-Hoffmann-Haus	14 C3
Fränkisches Brauereimuseum	15 A2
Historisches Museum	(see 9)

Klein Venedig (Little Venice)	16 B2
Kloster St Michael	17 A2
Michaelsberg	(see 17)
Neue Residenz	18 B3
Rosengarten	19 A3
St Stephanskirche	20 B4
Sammlung Ludwig Bamberg	(see 10)
Schloss Concordia	21 C4
Schloss Geyerswörth	22 C3

EATING	
Bassanese	28 B3
Bolero	29 B3
Brotladen	30 C2
Café Esspress	31 B3
Klosterbräu	32 B3
Mahrs-Bräu-Keller	33 B4
Messerschmidt	34 C3
Schlenkerla	35 B3
Spezial-Keller	36 C4
Zum Sternla	37 C3

ENTERTAINMENT	
Downstairs	38 C3
Konzert-und Kongresshalle	39 A2
Pelikan	40 A2
Rainbow	41 B2

TRANSPORT	
Fahrradhaus Griesmann	42 C2
ZOB (Central Bus Station)	43 C2

SLEEPING	
Barockhotel am Dom	23 B3
Brauereigasthof Fässla	24 C2
Hotel Residenzschloss	25 A2
Hotel Sankt Nepomuk	26 C3
Kongress Hotel	27 A2

To DJH Jugendherberge
Wolfsschlucht (1.5km);
Campingplatz Insel (2.5km)

FRANCONIA

it further south, the Regnitz River, which once separated the secular from the Episcopal part of town. The Hauptbahnhof is about 2km from the central Altstadt. The ZOB (city bus hub) is on Promenadestrasse, just north of Schönleinsplatz.

Information

BOOKSHOPS
Collibri (☎ 208 580; Austrasse 14) The city's best bookstore.

INTERNET ACCESS
TecCafe (☎ 201 494; Frauenstrasse 5; per 14min €1, half-price btwn noon & 2pm; ✆ to 10pm Sun-Thu, to 12am Fri & Sat)

LIBRARIES
Stadtbibliothek (☎ 981 90; Obere Königstrasse 4a)

MONEY
Citibank (Schönleinsplatz)

POST
Post office Altstadt (Promenadestrasse); Ludwigstrasse (Ludwigstrasse 25)

TOURIST INFORMATION
Tourist office (☎ 297 6200; www.bamberg.info in German; Geyersworthstrasse 3; ✆ 9.30am-6pm Mon-Fri, to 2.30pm Sat year-round, to 2.30pm Sun Apr-Dec) Staff here sell the Bamberg Card (one/two people €7.50/€14.50), good for 48 hours of admission to most city attractions, use of local buses and an English audio-guided tour.

TRAVEL AGENCIES
Flugbörse Bamberg (☎ 9253 0085; Kesslerstrasse 5)

Sights

SCHLOSS GEYERSWÖRTH
Originally the ancestral home of the patrician Geyer family, Prince-Bishop Ernst von Mengersdorf (r 1583–91) took such a liking to its picturesque river setting that he acquired the grounds and mansion and replaced it with **Schloss Geyerswörth** (Geyersworthplatz; ☎ 871 960). It's his coat of arms that graces the portal to the inner courtyard. The tower can be climbed for free from 9am to 5pm Monday to Thursday and to 1pm on Friday. Ask for the keys at the adjacent tourist office.

ALTES RATHAUS
The Geyersworthsteg, a small footbridge, crosses the Regnitz just outside the Schloss.

From here, you'll have the best views of the statuesque **Altes Rathaus** (Old Town Hall; 1461; Obere Brücke 1). It's actually right on the river, perched on a tiny artificial island between two bridges like a ship in dry dock. Gothic at its core, it got the baroque treatment in 1754. (Note the cherub's leg sticking out from the fresco on the east side, true to the 18th-century fad for trompe l'oeil painting.)

For closer views, turning at the end of the Geyersworthsteg, then right again onto Obere Brücke brings you face to façade with the imposing tower, a baroque addition by Balthasar Neumann. It provides access to the precious porcelain and faïences – mostly from Strassbourg and Meissen – housed in the **Sammlung Ludwig Bamberg** (Ludwig Gallery, Bamberg; ☎ 871 871; Obere Brücke 1; adult/concession €3.10/2.10; ✆ 9.30am-4.30pm Tue-Sun).

KLEIN VENEDIG
The 'Franconian Rome' also has its own **Klein Venedig** (Little Venice). A row of diminutive, half-timbered cottages – a former fisher folk colony – clasps the Regnitz' east bank between Markusbrücke and Untere Brücke. The little homes balance on poles set right into the water and are fronted by tiny gardens and terraces. In August, this forms the backdrop for the Sandkerwa festival (p202).

Klein Venedig is well worth a stroll but looks at least as pretty from a distance, especially in summer when red geraniums spill from flower boxes. Good vantage points are from the opposite bank along Am Leinritt and from the Untere Brücke near the Altes Rathaus.

BÖTTINGERHAUS & SCHLOSS CONCORDIA
Two of Bamberg's most beautiful baroque mansions are on the left bank in the southern Altstadt. Both are the former homes of wealthy privy councillor Ignaz Böttinger. The former, **Böttingerhaus** (1713; Judenstrasse 14; ☎ 230 27), is a heavily ornamented grand Italian palazzo shoehorned into narrow Judenstrasse. After the space outgrew his family of 14 three years later, Böttinger hired Johann Dietzenhofer to build the even grander **Schloss Concordia** (Concordiastrasse 28), a moated palace a short walk south of Böttingerhaus. It's now the home of the Künstlerhaus Villa Concordia, a statesponsored artists' residence, which hosts events and exhibits.

ST STEPHANSKIRCHE

Bamberg's main Protestant church, **St Stephanskirche** (Church of St Stephan; St Stephansplatz 4; ⊙9am-5pm) was consecrated in 1020 by Pope Benedikt VIII and turned baroque in the 17th century at the hands of Giovanni Bonalino and Antonio Petrini.

ETA-HOFFMANN-HAUS

Ernst Theodor Amadeus Hoffmann (1776–1822) was an 18th-century writer and composer, primarily known for using the fantastical and supernatural to probe the complexity of human experience. Hoffmann came to Bamberg in 1808 as the local theatre's music director, but lost his job after a disastrous first performance. He nevertheless stayed in town until 1813, working as a tutor and writer. His former home, **ETA-Hoffmann-Haus** (Schillerplatz 26; adult/concession €2/1; ⊙4-6pm Tue-Fri, 10am-noon Sat & Sun May-Oct), is now a small museum.

CATHEDRAL QUARTER

West of the Regnitz sprawls the former quarter of the prince-bishops, moored by the humungous hilltop Dom (cathedral) and dotted with various other religious buildings.

Dom

The quartet of spires of Bamberg's **Dom** (cathedral; Domplatz; ⊙9.30am-6pm Mon-Fri, 9.30-11.30am & 12.45-6pm Sat, 12.30-1.45pm & 2.45-6pm Sun May-Oct, 9.30am-5pm Mon-Sat, 12.30-1.45pm & 2.45-5pm Sun Nov-Mar) soars above the cityscape. Founded by Heinrich II in 1004, its current appearance dates to the early 13th century and is the outcome of a Romanesque-Gothic duel between church architects after the original and its immediate successor burnt down in the 12th century. Politics, rather than passing styles, dictated the final floor plan.

The uniformity is remarkable, considering that the plans changed each winter during 20 years of building. The pillars have the original light hues of Franconian sandstone thanks to Ludwig I, who ordered the cathedral cleansed of all postmedieval decoration in the early 19th century. From May to October free 30-minute organ concerts take place at noon on Saturday.

The interior contains superb and often intriguing works of art. In the north aisle, soon after entering, look for the famous **Lächelnde Engel** (Smiling Angel), who smirkingly hands the martyr's crown to the headless St Denis.

Nearby is the Dom's star attraction, the statue of the chivalric knight-king, the **Bamberger Reiter**. An enduring mystery, nobody has a clue as to either the name of the artist or the young king on the steed. The canopy above the statue represents the heavenly Jerusalem, an indication that this person may have been revered as a saint. The Nazis seized on the image of the heroic medieval ideal, which became a symbol of Aryan perfection.

In the west choir is the marble tomb of **Pope Clemens II**, the only papal burial place north of the Alps. Of the several altars, the **Bamberger Altar**, carved by Veit Stoss in 1523, is worth closer inspection. Because its central theme is the birth of Christ, it's also called the 'Christmas altar'.

Outside is the **Prince's Portal** (1225), which shows Christ in an ornate sculpture of the Last Judgement.

Diözesanmuseum

A door in the Dom's south aisle leads to the cloister and the former chapter house built by Balthasar Neumann in 1730, which is now home to the **Diözesanmuseum** (Cathedral Treasury; ☎502 316; Domplatz 5; adult/concession €3/2; ⊙10am-5pm Tue-Sun). There's Gothic sculpture and objects from the Dom's former baroque decoration on the ground floor, but the real treasures await upstairs. Besides a bevy of sculpture and liturgical objects, there's a superb collection of 11th-century textiles, including Heinrich II's famous 'star-spangled' cloak with heavy gold embroidery.

Alte Hofhaltung

Northwest of the Dom, the Renaissance-style **Alte Hofhaltung** (1570; Domplatz) is a former prince-bishops' palace, built on the site of an 11th-century fortress. Its prettiest section is the inner courtyard surrounded by half-timbered, balconied buildings, reached via the **Schöne Pforte** (Beautiful Gate; 1573). In summer, the Calderón Festival (p202) takes place in the courtyard.

The gabled Ratsstube (Council Chamber) is home of the **Historisches Museum** (Historical Museum; ☎871 142; In der Alten Hofhaltung; adult/concession €2.10/1.50; ⊙9am-5pm Tue-Sun May-Oct), with an eclectic mix of art and historical

FRANCONIA

exhibits. Highlights include a model of the pilgrimage church Basilika Vierzehnheiligen (p215) and the 'Bamberger Götzen', ancient stone sculptures found in the region.

Neue Residenz

Across Domplatz, the stately **Neue Residenz** (New Residence; ☎ 519 390; Domplatz 8; adult/concession €4/3; ☼ 9am-6pm Apr-Sep, 10am-4pm Oct-Mar) served as the home of Bamberg's prince-bishops from 1703 until secularisation in 1802.

You can shuffle through about 40 stuccoed rooms stuffed with furniture and tapestries from the 17th and 18th centuries. Showpieces are the dizzying **Kaisersaal** (Imperial Hall) upstairs, whose ceiling is smothered with a complex allegorical fresco by Melchior Seidl.

The edifice also shelters the **Bayerische Staatsgalerie** (Bavarian State Gallery), whose strengths are in medieval, Renaissance and baroque paintings, with works by Anthony Van Dyck, Hans Baldung Grien and Cranach the Elder. Grien's haunting *Die Sintflut* (The Deluge; 1516) is especially worth a closer look.

After your culture fix, unwind in the residence's small but exquisite baroque **Rosengarten** (Rose Garden), with calming views of the Altstadt's sea of red rooftops below.

Michaelsberg

From Domplatz, Aufsesstrasse leads to **Michaelsberg** for a rather steep climb up to the top of Michaelsberg and the former Benedictine **Kloster St Michael** (1610), now a home for the elderly. The monastery church is a must-see for its baroque art and the meticulous depictions of nearly 600 medicinal plants and flowers on the vaulted ceiling. The manicured garden terrace boasts a splendid city panorama.

The vaulted cellars of the ex-monastery are an atmospheric backdrop for the **Fränkisches Brauereimuseum** (Franconian Brewery Museum; ☎ 530 16; Michaelsberg 10f; adult/concession €2/1.50; ☼ 1-5pm Wed-Sun Apr-Oct). Exhibits show plaster(ed) dummies of monks, who began making beer here as early as 1122. There's plenty of historical equipment and documentation of the beermaking process.

Tours

In addition to English audio-guided city tours (p200), two-hour guided **walking tours**

(adult/concession €5/3.50; ☼ tours 10.30am & 2pm Mon-Sat Apr-Oct, 2pm Mon-Sat, 11am Sun Nov-Mar) in German depart from the tourist office.

A terrific deal is the Bamberg **beer-tasting trip** (ticket €20), which allows you to brewery-hop at your own pace. The tourist office can kit you out with a 36-page brochure with a map of the breweries, their history and detailed, wine connoisseur–like descriptions of their brews, along with a decent-quality day pack, vouchers for five half litres of beer, and a beer mug.

Festivals & Events

Kids will love the **street magician festival**, held in and around Grüner Markt for three days in mid-July.

Locals and visitors alike let their hair down during the **Sandkerwa**, held throughout the Altstadt around the fourth weekend in August. Highlights include the *Fischerstechen*, a kind of boat jousting, and a big fireworks finale.

On the third weekend in October every year, the entire Altstadt turns into a **flea and antique market**, with plenty of bargains.

Besides the **Christmas market** on Maximilianplatz, another favourite December tradition, especially with children, is following the **Bamberger Krippenweg**, an enchanting route of 34 nativity scenes set up in churches and museums throughout the city.

German speakers may also like to check out the popular **Calderón Festspiele**, an open-air theatre festival in the courtyard of the Alte Hofhaltung in late June.

Sleeping

Barockhotel am Dom (☎ 540 31; fax 540 21; Vorderer Bach 4; s €62-65, d €83-88; ℗ ✗) In the Cathedral Quarter, this gracious place embodies Bamberg's baroque heritage. Peaceful rooms include TV and direct-dial phones, and there's a lift. Enjoy breakfast in the grand 14th-century cross-vaulted Gothic room.

Brauereigasthof Fässla (☎ 265 16; www.faessla .de; Obere Königstrasse 19-21; s/d €37/55; meals €7-10; ☼ restaurant closed Sun; ℗) Those interested in serious research of the local beer offerings should consider staying in this guesthouse, north of the Rhine-Main-Danube-Canal, whose snug rooms are a mere staircase up from the pub and muraled *Schwemm* (covered courtyard). Chairs at the popular on-site restaurant are embossed with Fässla's cute coat of arms – a gnome rolling a giant beer barrel.

Hotel Sankt Nepomuk (☎ 984 20; www.hotel-nepo muk.de; Obere Mühlbrücke 9; s/d €80/112; meals €15-25; **P**) This is a classy but family-friendly establishment in an A-frame-shaped former mill right on the Regnitz. It has a superb gourmet restaurant, rustic rooms are fully equipped and you can hire bicycles here.

Hotel Residenzschloss (☎ 609 10; www.residenz schloss.com; Untere Sandstrasse 32; s €128-148, d €159-179; **P** ✗ ▣) Opposite the concert hall, Bamberg's top hotel in an historic former hospital caters for deep-pocketed travellers but its rooms are truly palatial. Facilities include a Roman-style steam bath and whirlpool. (It's owned by Warsteiner, Germany's largest brewery, hence the piano bar's beverage of choice.)

Kongress Hotel (☎ 609 1888; www.welcome-to -bamberg.com; Mussstrasse 7; s/d €99/119; **P** ✗ 😄) What this modern riverfront hotel lacks in quaintness it makes up for with efficient service, extras including hairdryers and cable TV, and an excellent breakfast buffet. More than a dozen rooms are wheelchair-friendly or have full wheelchair access.

DJH Jugendherberge Wolfsschlucht (☎ 560 02; www.djh.de in German; Oberer Leinritt 70; dm incl linen & breakfast €14.85, d €35.70; closed mid-Dec–Jan) About 2km from the Altstadt, on the west bank of the Regnitz. Take bus No 18 from the ZOB to Rodelbahn. From here walk northeast to the riverbank and turn left; it's just past the minigolf range.

Campingplatz Insel (☎ 563 20; www.campinginsel .de; Am Campingplatz 1; per camp site/adult €6.70/3.90) The camping options are limited to this well-equipped place, which has high-grade bathroom amenities and is located in a riverside spot convenient to public transport. Take bus No 18 from ZOB to Campingplatz.

At the time of writing, plans were well ahead for a new, central independent all-ages hostel – check www.hostel-bamberg.de or with the tourist office.

Eating

Local specialities include the *Fränkischer Sauerbraten* (beef, first marinated, then braised) and the *Bamberger Zwiebel* (stuffed onions cooked in beer sauce). The *Bamberger Hörnla*, usually just referred to as a *Bamberger*, is an ultrabuttery version of a croissant.

RESTAURANTS

Bolero (☎ 509 0290; Judenstrasse 7-9; tapas €2.80, mains €5-15; ✦ from 5pm) About 30 different tapas are the mainstay of this sprawling bodega. Rustic wooden tables and candlelight transport you straight to southern Spain, as does the beer garden's brio.

Messerschmidt (☎ 297 800; Lange Strasse 41; mains €10-21) In the birth house of plane engineer Willy Messerschmidt, who also founded his first company here in 1923, is this stylish gourmet regional restaurant. It oozes old-world tradition with its dark wood, white-linen table settings and formal service. Above the ornately moulded exterior is a charming alfresco terrace overlooking a pretty park. The attached wine tavern has a looser atmosphere but the same prices.

Zum Sternla (☎ 28750; Lange Strasse 46; mains €6.90-11.50) Bamberg's oldest *Wirtshaus* (inn), Zum Sternla was established in 1380 and it would seem the camaraderie amongst its patrons has changed little in the intervening years. Staples include pork dishes, steaks, dumplings and sauerkraut, as well as specials, but it's a great, nontouristy place for traditional *Brotzeit* (snack), or just a pretzel and a beer.

BREWERIES

Bamberg's ten breweries make over 60 different types of beer. All have integrated restaurants, which is a great opportunity to try local dishes and, of course, what's on tap.

Spezial-Keller (☎ 548 87; Sternwartstrasse; dishes €4-10; ✦ Tue-Sun) Spezial-Keller's smoky *Rauchbier* (smoky ale) is superb. Coupled with great views of the Dom and the Altstadt from the beer garden, this place is well worth at least one visit. Every year in November, crowds gather here to ring in *Bockbier* (malty beer) season.

Schlenkerla (☎ 560 60; Dominikanerstrasse 6; dishes €2.50-9.50; ✦ Wed-Mon) This 16th-century restaurant at the foot of the Dom is famous for its tasty Franconian specialities and its *Rauchbier*, served directly from the oak barrel (€2.05 per half-litre mug).

Mahrs-Bräu-Keller (☎ 534 86; Oberer Stephansberg 36; dishes €3-10; ✦ Tue-Sun) Wash down the house speciality – pizza cooked over beech wood in an outdoor stone oven – with Pilsner at this Art Deco cellar.

FRANCONIA

Klosterbräu (☎ 522 65; Obere Mühlbrücke 3; mains €5-10; ⏱ Thu-Tue) This beautiful half-timbered brewery is Bamberg's oldest. It's usually bristling with a youthful clientele, and its excellent beers are perfect for washing down the solid fare.

CAFÉS

Bassanese (☎ 509 568; Karolinenstrasse 2; snacks €4-8; ⏱ to 7pm) Right in front of the Rathaus on the bridge, enjoy authentic Italian *gelato*, strudels and handmade chocolates in wicker chairs on the cobblestones while taking in the views.

Café Esspress (☎ 204 666; Austrasse 33; dishes €2-12.80) This student-oriented place changes stripes throughout the day, from breakfast café to lunch spot to coffeehouse to restaurant and cocktail bar at night.

QUICK EATS & SELF-CATERING

You'll find fast-food options around the intersection of Obere Königstrasse and Luitpoldstrasse, especially Chinese and Turkish food, for around €2 to €6.

The daily local **produce market** (Grüner Markt) is a good place to stock up. On Saturday, head to the organic **Bauernmarkt** (farmers market; Maximilianplatz).

The owner of **Brotladen** (☎ 474 47; Fleischstrasse 3) drives to village bakeries all over the region early each morning to amass over 50 different types of bread.

Drinking & Entertainment

Consult the free listings magazines *Franky*, *Treff* or *Fränkische Nacht*, usually found in pubs, for the latest 'in' spots and events. Bamberg's beer devotees have over 300 pubs in which to worship.

Pelikan (☎ 603 410; Untere Sandstrasse 45) Up there with the best, Pelikan is a candlelit place with occasional live music and a Thai-oriented menu (€2.20 to €12.50). In summer, head for the convivial beer garden in the inner courtyard.

Downstairs (☎ 208 3786; Generalsgasse 3; ⏱ from 10pm Tue, from 11pm Thu-Sat) An underground vibe reigns at this cool basement bar and dance club where DJs spin techno and alternative tunes (no chart music).

Rainbow (☎ 863 2173; Innere Löwenstrasse 6; ⏱ Tue-Sun) The most popular gay club in town.

Fans of classical music should try to catch a concert by the famous Bamberger Symphoniker orchestra, which usually plays in the modern **Konzert-und Kongresshalle** (☎ 964 7100; Mussstrasse 1; tickets €19-35.50), on the Regnitz north of the Altstadt.

Shopping

Bamberg's main shopping drags are the pedestrianised Grüner Markt, which runs south from Maximilianplatz (referred to locally as Maxplatz), and the parallel Austrasse, with lots of owner-run shops and one-off boutiques preluded by tempting pavement sale racks. Also dotted throughout the Altstadt are around 30 antique stores.

Getting There & Away

There are at least hourly Regional Express and RegionalBahn trains from Nuremberg (€9.40, RE/RB 45/60 minutes) and from Würzburg (€14.20, one hour), as well as ICE trains every two hours from Munich (€44, three hours) and Berlin (€63, 4¼ hours). Bamberg is just south of A70 (Schweinfurt–Kulmbach–Bayreuth) and at the start of the A73 to Nuremberg.

Getting Around

Walking is the best option in town, but you can also hire bicycles at **Fahrradhaus Griesmann** (☎ 229 67; Kleberstrasse 25; per day €5-8). The tourist office (p200) has a good selection of bicycle-path maps of the vicinity.

Cars are a pain in town, so park on the outskirts and walk or take a bus (per trip €1, or €7.50 for a Bamberg Card good for 48 hours of unlimited travel). Several buses, including Nos 1, 2 and 14 connect the train station with the **ZOB** (Promenade Strasse). Bus No 10 goes from the ZOB to the Domplatz. Contact taxis on ☎ 150 15 and the flagfall is €2.60.

AROUND BAMBERG

The rural area to the west and south of Bamberg is known as the **Steigerwald**. Much of it is a nature park, blanketed by beech and oak forest, and prime hiking and cycling territory. Local rulers took quite a liking to the land as well, giving culture vultures a fine palace and monastery towards which to steer.

The Steigerwald is not well served by public transport. If you're not motorised, bicycles are the best option for getting around.

Pommersfelden

When deciding on a location for a summer residence, Prince-Bishop Lothar Franz von Schönborn picked Pommersfelden, a little village about 20km south of Bamberg just off the B505. Called **Schloss Weissenstein** (☎ 09548-981 80; Schlossplatz 1; admission & 30min/60min tour €3/5; ☑ 10am-5pm Apr-Oct), his palace is a good example of the baroque exuberance so beloved by the bishop.

Johann Dientzenhofer was the lead architect of the horseshoe-shaped palace. Inside, the dominant feature is a three-storey double staircase, canopied by a ceiling fresco of Apollo by Johann Rudolf Byss. Upstairs, the highlight is the **Marmorsaal** (Marble Hall), an ostentatious banquet hall used for festivities and concerts. Both staircase and hall are seen on the 30-minute tour. The 60-minute tour also takes in the bishop's private quarters, the mirror room and a gallery of Italian, Dutch and German 17th- and 18th-century paintings. Don't miss a stroll through the fabulous **park** (admission €0.50; ☑ year-round). The palace, by the way, is still owned by the current count of Schönborn.

Kloster Ebrach

About 35km west of Bamberg on the B22, **Kloster Ebrach** (☎ 09553-266) probably wins the award for most unusual use of a former monastery: it's now a prison for juvenile offenders.

An outgrowth of Bavaria's first Cistercian abbey, founded in 1127, the current complex dates to the 18th century and is primarily the work of Johann Dientzenhofer. Balthasar Neumann contributed the magnificent **Kaisersaal** (Imperial Hall) and staircase. You can see both on **guided tours** (adult/concession €2.50/1.25; ☑ 10.30am & 2.30pm Apr-Oct), usually led by prison guards.

Of greater interest is the attached **monastery church** (☑ 10am-noon & 2-6pm mid-Apr–Oct), whose oldest section is the **Romanesque Chapel of St Michael**, consecrated in 1134. Construction of the main basilica, which ranks as a fine example of early-Gothic architecture, began in 1200, concluding in 1285. It's built in the classic shape of a cross, consisting of a three-nave basilica and a transept. The kaleidoscopic rose window in the western façade adds a touch of mysticism. The interior received the usual baroque face-lift in the 18th century.

FRÄNKISCHE SCHWEIZ

The Fränkische Schweiz (Franconian Switzerland) is a triangular rural region between Bayreuth, Nuremberg and Bamberg, so named for its enchanting landscape rather than any geopolitical relationship with its namesake. You'll find narrow valleys carved by sprightly streams, majestic medieval castles perched on craggy hilltops, and otherworldly rock formations with more than a thousand mysterious caves. Sprinkled throughout the storybook-pretty villages of half-timbered 'gingerbread' houses (iced with shimmering snow in winter) are about 70 breweries. Artists, especially the late-18th-century Romantic poets, have long been inspired by this setting.

The slow pace of hiking, mountain biking, canoeing and kayaking best facilitates appreciation of this area, which is also extremely popular with rock climbers who have more than 5000 routes to grapple with.

To try these and other pursuits, look out for a new, independent, all-ages outdoor activities hostel, **Factory 41** (☎ 95515-918 905; Hauptstrasse 41, Plankenfels), due to have opened in the village of Plankenfels by the time you're reading this – check www.factory41.de for details.

The region has a central **information office** (☎ 09194-797 779; www.fraenkische-schweiz.com in German; Oberes Tor 1, Ebermannstadt; ☑ 8am-4.30pm Mon-Thu, 8am-noon Fri). If the office is closed, look for information leaflets inside the police station in the same building.

The B470 is the main route through the Fränkische Schweiz, which is best explored under your own steam.

Pottenstein

☎ 09243 / pop 5500

Pottenstein is a picture-perfect village that is home to Germany's largest stalagmite and stalactite caverns, the **Teufelshöhle** (Devil's Cavern; ☎ 208; adult/concession €3.50/2.50; ☑ 9am-5pm Apr-Oct, 10am-3pm Tue, Sat & Sun Nov-Mar, 10am-3pm 26 Dec-6 Jan). Tours through this glittering underground world cover a distance of 1.5km and last 45 minutes; a highlight is the reconstructed skeleton of a prehistoric bear. In summer, concerts are held in the entrance foyer. The cavern is about 2km outside of Pottenstein, right on the B470. Bus 232 stops here or it's a nice walk from town. Overlooking Pottenstein is the well-preserved 11th-century

FRANCONIA

Burg Pottenstein (☎ 7221; adult/concession €3.50/2; ◷ 10am-5pm Tue-Sun May-Oct), which is now a private museum. On tours, you'll see furnished historical rooms, arms and armour, glass, porcelain and ceramics and an art exhibit.

Pottenstein has a **tourist office** (☎ 708 41; www.pottenstein.de in German; Forchheimer Strasse 1; ◷ 8am-5pm Mon-Fri, 10am-noon Sat May-Sep, 9am-noon & 2-4pm Mon-Fri Oct-Apr).

The nearest train station is in Pegnitz, 14km east of Pottenstein. From here, buses travel west along the B470.

Gössweinstein

☎ 09242 / pop 1500 / elev 500m

A colossal **Basilika** (☎ 264; ◷ 8am-6pm May-Oct) dominates this pint-size village. Balthasar Neumann created this honey-coloured vision in stone between 1730 and 1739, with Prince-Bishop Carl von Schönborn footing the bill. Some of the many altars have unusual features, such as the golden globe of the main altar and the tooth extractor wielded by Apollonia, the patron saint of dentists. Behind the basilica is the 'Grotto of Lourdes', a replica of the famous pilgrimage church in France.

Above town looms the tower and stepgabled roofline of **Burg Gössweinstein** (☎ 456; adult/concession €1.80/1; ◷ 10am-6pm Easter-Oct), whose history goes back to the 11th century. It got its current neo-Gothic look little more than a hundred years ago under Freiherr von Sohlern, whose descendants still own the place. You'll have panoramic views from up here.

There's a small **tourist office** (☎ 456; www .goessweinstein.de in German; Burgstrasse 6; ◷ 8am-noon & 2-5pm Mon-Fri, 9am-noon Sat Easter-Oct, 8am-noon & 2-4pm Mon-Thu, 8am-noon Fri Nov-Easter).

Coming from Bayreuth or Nuremberg, take the RE train to Pegnitz, then change to bus No 232, which travels west along the B470, stopping in Pottenstein and Gössweinstein.

Buttenheim

☎ 09545 / pop 3417 / elev 273m

The house in which Löb (aka Levi) Strauss was born is now the faded-blue shuttered **Levi-Strauss-Museum** (☎ 442 602; Marktstrasse 33; adult/concession €2.60/1.30; ◷ 2-6pm Tue & Thu, 11am-5pm Sat & Sun Nov-Feb; 2-5pm Tue & Thu, 11am-5pm Sat & Sun Mar-Oct). Löb lived here until his teenage years when his cloth-dealer father died. He and his mother then followed his older brothers to America, where he staked out his claim by supplying gold rush miners with their supplies, and later, the 'waist overalls' that would inspire global fashion.

At this refreshingly uncommercial museum, you can trace the life of the jeans inventor, from his humble roots to his stratospheric success. Upstairs focuses on the production of jeans, from the fabric to the rivets. Also here is a collection of vintage Levi's jeans and a short film. A few doors up an outlet retails cutting-edge Levi's garb.

Buttenheim has a train station and is served directly from Nuremberg (€6.90, 50 minutes) and Bamberg (€2.60, 12 minutes); coming from Bayreuth requires a change in Nuremberg (€19.80, 2½ hours).

BAYREUTH

☎ 0921 / pop 73,000 / elev 345m

Since the inaugural Richard Wagner Festival in 1876, 'Wagner' and 'Bayreuth' have been as intimately linked as Tristan and Isolde. Every year in August, this quiet bourgeois town in Upper Franconia plays host to an international galaxy of musicians, singers and opera pilgrims at the opera festival started by the cantankerous composer himself.

Bayreuth was first mentioned in 1194 as Baierrute, a name that roughly translates as 'Bavarians' forest clearing'. Owned by the Nuremberg burgraves since 1248, it became the margravial seat of the Brandenburg-Kulmbach-Ansbach in 1603. The glory days arrived in 1735 when Wilhelmine, sister of King Frederick the Great of Prussia, married Margrave Friedrich. Wilhelmine invited the finest artists, poets, composers and architects in Europe to court. As a result, the city became home to some superb rococo and baroque architecture, the Eremitage and the Margravial Opera House among them.

Wagner arrived on the scene more than 100 years later, in 1872 (see the boxed text on p209). Once settled in Bayreuth, his presence attracted the philosopher Friedrich Nietzsche as well as composers Franz Liszt and Anton Bruckner.

Like Ludwig II before him, Hitler worshipped Wagner and maintained close relations with his daughter-in-law Winifred, at one time even proposing marriage to her. After the war, Bayreuth at first suffered under the weight of this association, but in recent years, the family feuds about the successor of current festival director Wolfgang Wagner, a grandson of the composer, have dominated the headlines along with the fate of the plastic statues of Wagner's dog, Russ (see the boxed text on p210).

Orientation

The Hauptbahnhof is about five to 10 minutes' walk north of the historic, cobblestoned centre. Head south on Bahnhofstrasse to Luitpoldplatz and on to the pedestrianised Maximilianstrasse, the main drag, also known as Markt. The central bus station (ZOB) is also on Markt. The Eremitage is about 6km east and the Festspielhaus 1.5km north of the town centre.

Information

BOOKSHOPS

Gondrom (☎ 757 260; Maximilianstrase 18) One of the biggest bookshops in town.

EMERGENCY

Fire & Medical Services (☎ 112)
Police (☎ 110)

INTERNET ACCESS

Café Ponte (☎ 871 0503; Opernstrasse 24; ☼ 8am-1am Sun-Wed, 9am-2am Thu-Sat)

MONEY

Commerzbank (Luitpoldplatz 8) Opposite the tourist office.

POST

Post office Hauptbahnhof (Hauptbahnhof); Sternplatz (Kanzleistrasse 3)

TOURIST INFORMATION

Tourist office (☎ 885 88; www.bayreuth.de; Luitpoldplatz 9; ☼ 9am-6pm Mon-Fri, 9.30am-1pm Sat) Staff sell the three-day Bayreuth Card (€9), which entitles you to unlimited trips on city buses, entrance to nine museums and a guided city walk (in German). You can also get a Combination Ticket (adult/concession €7/6), valid for the Neues Schloss and the Margravial Opera House; and the Bayreuth of Margravine Wilhelmine ticket (adult/concession €13/11), which includes entry to the Neues Schloss, the Margravial Opera House, the Eremitage, Sanspareil and Schloss Fantaisie.

TRAVEL AGENCIES

Reisebüro Bayreuth (☎ 8850) This full-service travel agency shares space with the tourist office.

Sights

TOWN CENTRE

Except during the Wagner Festival in July and August, Bayreuth streets can be very quiet, though the town's strong musical traditions ensure that there are good dramatic and orchestral performances year-round.

A favourite musical venue is the **Markgräfliches Opernhaus** (Margravial Opera House; ☎ 759 6922; Opernstrasse 14; adult/child under 18/concession €5/free/4; ☼ 9am-6pm Apr-Sep, 10am-4pm Oct-Mar, closed during rehearsal & performance days). Designed between 1744 and 1748 by Giuseppe Galli Bibiena from Bologna, this stunning baroque masterpiece was Germany's largest opera house until 1871. Yet Richard Wagner deemed the place too quaint for his serious work, and conducted here just once. German speakers will especially enjoy the 45-minute multimedia show, with projected images of the royals and lurid lighting. In May or June the house hosts a festival of opera and ballet, the **Fränkische Festwoche**.

South of here is Wilhelmine's **Neues Schloss** (New Palace; ☎ 759 690; Ludwigstrasse 21; adult/child under 18/concession €4/free/3; ☼ 9am-6pm Apr-Sep, 10am-4pm Oct-Mar), the margravial residence after 1753. On the ground floor is a collection of porcelain made in Bayreuth in the 18th century. The Cedar Room is the site of the annual VIP opening celebrations of the Wagner Festival. Behind the palace sprawls the vast, leafy **Hofgarten** (admission free; ☼ 24hr).

To learn more about the man behind the myth, visit Haus Wahnfried, the composer's former home on the northern edge of Hofgarten, which now contains the **Richard-Wagner-Museum** (☎ 757 2816; Richard-Wagner-Strasse 48; adult/concession Sep-Jun €4/2, admission Jul & Aug €4.50; ☼ 9am-5pm Fri-Mon & Wed, 9am-8pm Tue & Thu Apr-Oct, 10am-5pm Nov-Mar). Wagner had this lovely mansion built with cash sent by King Ludwig II. Inside is an undynamic, if comprehensive, chronological exhibit about Wagner's life, with glass cases crammed with documents, photographs, clothing, coins, porcelain and personal effects. Unless you're a Wagner fan or at least a German speaker, it's hard to fully appreciate this museum. The composer is buried in the garden, as is his wife, Cosima. At the base of their graves, look for the small tombstone where Wagner's dog, Russ (see the boxed text on p210) lies buried.

Along with Wagner, the composer and virtuoso Franz Liszt (1811–86) was one of

FRANCONIA

the seminal figures of classical music in 19th-century Europe. Within earshot of Haus Wahnfried is the house where he died, now the **Franz-Liszt-Museum** (☎ 516 6488; Wahnfriedstrasse 9; adult/concession €1.50/0.50; ⏰ 10am-noon & 2-5pm Sep-Jun, 10am-5pm Jul & Aug). Liszt was the father of Cosima, Wagner's wife. On view are a sparkling grand piano, his death mask, correspondence and portraits.

A few doors north, in the former home of Wagner's daughter, Eva, is the **Jean-Paul-Museum** (☎ 507 1444; Wahnfriedstrasse 1; adult/concession €1.50/0.50; ⏰ 10am-noon & 2-5pm Sep-Jun, 10am-5pm Jul & Aug). The imaginative and large-living 19th-century Romantic poet Jean Paul (Johann Friedrich Richter) lived in Bayreuth from 1804 until his death in 1825.

OUTSIDE THE TOWN CENTRE

North of the Hauptbahnhof, the **Festspielhaus** (☎ 787 80; Festspielhügel 1-2; adult/concession €2.50/2; ⏰ tours 10am, 10.45am, 2.15pm & 3pm Tue-Sun, closed Nov, during rehearsals & the Wagner Festival), built in 1872, was also constructed with Ludwig II's backing. The acoustics of the place are truly amazing as its builders took the body density of a packed house into account. Take bus No 5 to Am Festspielhaus.

About 6km east of the centre is the **Eremitage**, a lush park surrounding the **Altes Schloss** (☎ 759 6937; Eremitage; adult/child under 18/concession €2.50/free/2; ⏰ 9am-6pm Fri-Wed, 9am-8pm Thu Apr–mid-Oct), Friedrich and Wilhelmine's summer residence. Take bus No 2 or 3 from Markt.

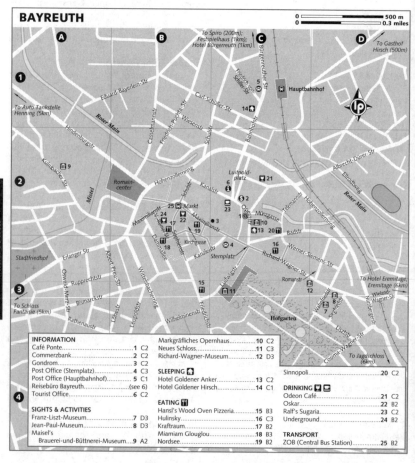

BAYREUTH

ALL WORK WHILE PLAYING

Born in Leipzig, Richard Wagner (1813–83) spent the last years of his life in Bayreuth, arriving from Switzerland with his second wife, Cosima, on 24 April 1872. With the financial backing of Ludwig II, his biggest patron, protector (and groupie), Wagner built his spectacular house, Haus Wahnfried.

Wagner's commanding operas, including *Götterdämmerung* (The Twilight of the Gods), *Parsifal*, *Tannhäuser* and *Tristan und Isolde*, supported his grandiose belief that listening to opera should be work (his *The Ring of the Nibelungen* is literally four days long), not a frivolous form of entertainment.

This theory extends to the acoustic architecture in the festival hall Wagner himself designed: the orchestra performs beneath the stage (and hence are able to wear shorts and T-shirts), and reflecting boards and surfaces send the sound up and onto the stage, where it bounces from the wall behind the singers and, intertwined with the singers' voices, finally makes its way to the house. This inverted design means the orchestra actually performs in a mirror reversal of their usual positions, no mean feat for a musician, or a conductor.

Wagner is also well known for his reprehensible personal qualities as a notorious womaniser, an infamous anti-Semite and a hardliner towards 'non-Europeans'. Because of his extreme views, even fun-loving Friedrich Nietzsche called Wagner's works 'inherently reactionary, and inhumane'. Conversely, the Nazis embraced them as a symbol of Aryan might, and even today the 'correctness' of supporting Wagnerian music and the Wagner Festival in Bayreuth is strenuously debated by music aficionados.

Also here is the Eremitage's **Neues Schloss** (not to be confused with the Schloss of the same name in town), which is anchored by a mosaic Sun Temple topped by a gilded Apollo sculpture. Gracing the Neues Schloss are the grottoes, whose fountains start gushing on the hour between 10am and 5pm from May to mid-October (10 minutes later in the Lower Grotto). The bus trip out here takes about 20 minutes and costs €1.70. The winter-garden café in the Orangerie is a nice place to stop for a break.

For a fascinating insight to the brewing process, head to the enormous **Maisel's Brauerei-und-Büttnerei-Museum** (☎ 401 234; Kulmbacher Strasse 40; tours €4; ♡ tours 2pm Mon-Sat), northwest of the town centre. A one-hour guided tour (in German) plumbs the sweet-smelling depths of this 2400-sq-metre, 19th-century plant, covering all aspects of the business (including barrelmaking). Beer was brewed here until the 1970s (the plant's now housed in modern premises next door), and the *Guinness Book of World Records* lists it as the world's most comprehensive beer museum. Over 4500 beer mugs occupy several rooms, and there's a huge collection of old advertising posters in the former cooling room, some extremely valuable. Arguably, the best part is the foaming glass of *Weissbier* (wheat beer) served at the end in the

bottling room, now a private saloon with old-fashioned slot machines.

About 5km west of Bayreuth is **Schloss Fantaisie** (☎ 7314 0011; Bamberger Strasse 3; adult/concession €3/2; ♡ 9am-6pm Tue-Sun Apr-Sep, 10am-4pm 1-15 Oct), a divine rococo palace where Duchess Elisabeth Friederike Sophie (1732–80), the daughter of Margravine Wilhelmine, sought solace after a failed marriage to Carl Eugen von Württemberg. It's surrounded by lush gardens incorporating an exhibit about the art of landscaping.

Festivals & Events

The **Richard Wagner Festival** (www.festspiele.de in German) runs for 30 days from late July to August, with each performance attended by an audience of 1900. Tickets cost from €5 to €170, and demand is insane – the current waiting time is nine years! To apply, send a letter (no phone, fax or email) requesting a ticket order form to the Bayreuther Festspiele, Kartenbüro, Postfach 100 262, 95402 Bayreuth, before September of the year before you want to attend and return it to the booking office by 15 October. You'll need to write in every year until you secure tickets. If you've ordered tickets before, you should automatically receive an order form.

During the festival, returned tickets are sold at the *Festivalhalle* (festival hall) between 10am and noon on performance days and 90 minutes before curtain. People have been known to bring sleeping bags to camp overnight – along with their finery in their backpacks, just in case. Plenty of (illegal) scalpers cruise the queues, charging up to five times the ticket price.

The lucky concertgoers face another endurance test. The opening notes of some operas ring out in the afternoon so people can get home by midnight. Adding to that, the seats are hard wood, ventilation is poor and there's no air conditioning. But hang in there: on blisteringly hot days, water is sprayed on the roof during the interval!

Sleeping

Be warned that sleeping options – like the tickets themselves – are rare as hen's teeth during the Richard Wagner Festival, with most accommodation booked out months in advance. Accordingly, prices at this time are unpredictable and can escalate dramatically.

Jagdschloss Thiergarten (☎ 09209-9840; www.schlosshotel-thiergarten.de; Oberthiergärtner Strasse 36; r €80-170; meals €11-25; P ✗ ⬚) A former hunting castle (whose idle huntsmen would shoot from the upper windows), this gorgeous place has its own white deer loping in the gardens and luxurious rooms with canopied beds. The gourmet, traditional restaurant has a domed 13m ceiling, and there's a library and bar with open fireplace. The hotel is 6km from Bayreuth, to get there take Nürnbergerstrasse south of the city, past (not on) the autobahn exits, turn right on Wolfsbacherstrasse and follow it until just after it crosses the autobahn. The hotel is inaccessable by public transport, but if you don't have your own car, staff can organise transport from town.

Hotel Goldener Anker (☎ 650 51; www.anker-bayreuth.de; Opernstrasse 6; s €65-105, d €95-175; P ✗) The refined elegance of this hotel, owned by the same family since the 16th century, is hard to beat. Its 35 rooms are quiet and have TVs and telephones. It's just a few steps from the opera house in the pedestrian area, but there's vehicle access to the hotel's onsite parking.

Gasthof Hirsch (☎ 267 14; fax 853 142; St Georgen Strasse 6; dm/d €20/40; P) This charming guesthouse is the best budget option in Bayreuth, with delightfully furnished rooms in doubles or a three-bed dorm with its own piano. Bathrooms are shared, but there are hot and cold water basins in all rooms, and there's parking out front. The ultimate sweetener is the homemade apple-and-mint, cinnamon or Calvados jam served at breakfast.

Hotel Goldener Hirsch (☎ 230 46; goldener.hirsch@bayreuth-online.de; Bahnhofstrasse 13; s €55-75, d €69-89; P ✗ ⬚) This landmark site has had the same name since 1753 and has been a hotel since 1900. Behind its forest-green exterior public areas have a '70s flair, but rooms are spacious, and some have bathtubs. It's well positioned close to the train station.

Hotel Bürgerreuth (☎ 784 00; www.minuzzi.de in German; An der Bürgerreuth 20; s €45-60, d €70-80; P ✗ ⬚) On Green Hill, just north of the Festspielhaus, with views over the town, this is a classy abode popular with music-lovers (Louis Armstrong once stayed here). An Italian flair prevails throughout; most evident in the restaurant, considered one of Bayreuth's finest. Rooms are furnished with all modern amenities.

Hotel Eremitage (☎ 799 9730; www.eremitage-gastro.de in German; Eremitage 6; s €50-70, d €90-140;

GONE TO THE DOGS

Controversy of a different sort recently struck the Richard Wagner Festival. German sculptor Ottmar Hoerl created and installed hundreds of 70cm plastic replicas of Wagner's beloved mutt, Russ, all over the city, as a way to humanise the oft-reviled composer.

But though locals and visitors adored the dogs, to Hoerl's outrage, Bayreuth's authorities enforced a 'mile ban' around the Festspielhaus, purportedly to prevent other artists from using the festival as a canvas for their own art. In light of the dogs' popularity, festival organisers distanced themselves from the decision. The 800 or so other statues were not affected by the ban – though they too continue to diminish in numbers. Numerous Russ likenesses have been stolen, with authorities warning of severe punishment for perpetrators (ironic, given the authorities' 'dog catchers' rounding up of statues). When we visited, more than one souvenired pup was spotted in the possession of dog-loving Bavarians in far-flung corners of the state.

meals €10-20; ⊗ restaurant closed Nov-Mar; Ⓟ) Right by the Eremitage, this hotel is small (just 11 beds) but choice. Rooms have views of the park and a good range of comforts such as a minibar and cable TV, as well as lovely drapes and furnishings. Its gourmet restaurant and stone-walled beer garden enjoy a loyal following.

Eating

Bayreuth's dining options, in addition to those attached to the hotels recommended under Sleeping, span the globe.

Miamiam Glouglou (☎ 656 66; Von-Römer-Strasse 28; mains €10-16) Pretend you're in Paris at this delightful candlelit restaurant serving classic French bistro cuisine such as omelettes and crepes at good-value prices.

Sinnopoli (☎ 620 17; Badstrasse 13; mains €5.50-9.50) Eccentric lamps and art form a suitable backdrop for this contemporary place, with creative handmade pastas (half-price between 5pm and 7pm), baguettes, casseroles and specials.

Kraftraum (☎ 800 2515; Sophienstrasse 16; mains €4.40-8) This vegetarian restaurant has plenty to tempt the most committed carnivores. Pastas and jacket potatoes form the basis of the menu, alongside *gnoosh* (small appetite) offerings. Best of all is the smorgasbord Sunday brunch of muesli, stewed apple, pancakes, antipasto platters, salmon, cheese and loads more.

Spiro (☎ 260 29; Bürgerreuther-Strasse 25; mains €5-10; ⊗ Thu-Tue) Even the small portions at this home-style blue-and-white Greek restaurant are enormous. The gyros with french fries, salad and tzatziki is especially good, as is the fried eggplant.

Hansl's Wood Oven Pizzeria (☎ 543 44; Friedrichstrasse 15; pizzas €5-9) Bayreuth's best pizza is at this little hole in the wall. A check-list menu lets you choose your own gourmet toppings, after which you get to name your creation. Help yourself to the free spiced chilli olive oil. In summer, long outdoor tables ease the squeezed-to-capacity crowd inside.

Fast-food options include **Hulinsky** (Richard-Wagner-Strasse 25), a bakery-deli with sandwiches and baked goods, and the central **Nordsee** (Maximilianstrasse 39).

Drinking

Oskar (☎ 516 0553; Maximilianstrasse 33; dishes €4.80-11.90) In the old town hall (later a police station), this flowing Bavarian beer hall–style place bustles from morning to night. Sit in the busy bar, a cosy, hops-decorated room, or the winter garden. It's especially busy between 5pm and 7pm when cocktails are half-price. Dumplings, the house speciality, dominate the menu.

Ralf's Sugaria (☎ 6080 0900; Luitpoldplatz 3; snacks €3.50-5) A café by day and cocktail bar by night, the tutti-frutti décor at this trendy new place reflects the yummy ice cream produced on the premises (a glass window lets you see it being made). Live bands perform twice a month, and there's a large outdoor seating area.

Odeon Café (☎ 150 1010; Alexanderstrasse 7; mains around €7) An L-shaped seating area wraps around the dark-timbered bar, where the cocktail list is a hardcover book some 60 pages long, with a nourishing menu available to help soak them up.

Underground (☎ 633 47; Von-Römer-Strasse 15) Designed like a London tube, this bar-café has a mixed gay and straight clientele.

Getting There & Away

Bayreuth is a stop on the ICE train line from Dresden to Nuremberg. Regional trains to Nuremberg also depart hourly (€14.20, one hour). Getting to Bamberg requires a change in Lichtenfels (€18.20, 1½ hours). There are two exits to Bayreuth off the A9, which bring you to the eastern side of town.

Getting Around

Bus tickets per trip are €1.70. Bus Nos 3, 5 and 9 travel from the Hauptbahnhof right to the Markt in the town centre. For bike hire, try **Auto Tankstelle Henning** (☎ 575 4122; Bayreutherstrasse 32; per day/week €6/30), which has multiple drop-off points around town. **Taxis** (☎ 660 60) are available and the flagfall is €2.50.

AROUND BAYREUTH
Kulmbach

☎ 09221 / pop 30,000 / elev 306m

About 30km northwest of Bayreuth, Kulmbach is a mecca for beer-lovers, as it is home to four large and several smaller breweries as well as the town's famous *Eisbock* (iced beer). Frost transforms the alcohol into a kind of molasses, making it one of the strongest beers in the world. If you're in town in late

DETOUR: LITTLE BERLIN

Imagine a quiet village of around 55 residents torn in two by a heavily guarded, eerily lit 700m wall smack bang in the middle of its tiny lanes. For the villagers of Mödlareuth, aka Little Berlin, this was their fate for 24 years beginning in 1966. Direct contact between neighbours was suddenly and forcibly forbidden. Brothers still living only 20m from each other were now prohibited from even waving in greeting.

Mödlareuth's first division came after WWI, but it was relatively benign. One half of the village now belonged to the state of Thuringia, the other to the state of Bavaria, but both were part of a united Germany and village life continued harmoniously as it had for centuries. But this demarcation was to have calamitous consequences.

Following Hitler's downfall in 1945, the Allies carved Germany into four occupational zones with the Soviet zone evolving into East Germany and the British, French and American zones forming West Germany. Germany was now a country divided, first by ideology and, starting in 1961, also physically with the construction of the Berlin Wall and, what Churchill called the 'Iron Curtain' of the Cold War.

Mödlareuth again found itself quite literally caught in the middle. Just as had happened in Berlin, the little village was divided into two separate halves, first by a 2m-high fence, then by an ominous concrete wall. On the East German side, a land mine–ridden 'death strip' shadowed this ribbon of terror, with splinter mines installed along another metal lattice fence that was erected after a successful escape over the wall in 1973. All this was guarded around the clock by an alarmed fence connected to a command centre.

It took an average of six weeks for people living in the West German half of the village to obtain permission to cross. Residents in the East, of course, were not allowed to visit the western side of the village at all. Neighbours and families may as well have been on opposite sides of the world.

On the morning of 10 November 1989, a Trabi (East German two-stroke engine Trabant cars) spotted on the western side of Mödlareuth was the villagers' first-hand confirmation of the wall's historic fall in Berlin the day before – though the impenetrable barriers through the village meant people had to use the checkpoint border crossing 60km away just to get to the other side. It would be another month before the first pedestrian access opened, and it wasn't until the wall was razed on 17 June 1990 that residents were once more able to drive freely through their streets.

Today, the **Deutsch-Deutsches Museum** (German-German Museum; ☎ 09295-1334; Mödlareuth 13; adult/concession €2/1; ⊙ 9am-6pm Mar-Oct, 9am-5pm Mon-Fri, 10am-5pm Sat & Sun Nov-Feb) has preserved sections of the wall and also presents rotating exhibits, such as escape craft and items salvaged from ill-fated attempts to cross the border. A poignant film (in English, German and French) shows the history of this village, whose teensy population before, during and after the years of division has remained static.

Despite the village's bleak history, the museum is an uplifting demonstration of the triumph of human spirit, in large part due to the skill and emotional sensitivity of its local founder and curator, the filmmaker and photographer Arndt Schaffner.

Mödlareuth lies 66km northwest of Bayreuth. Driving from Bayreuth, follow the A9 north for 46km, then the A72 east for 9.5km. Take the Hof/Töpen exit and follow the signs to Töpen (3km). In the centre of town, turn right onto Mödlareutherstrasse for another 3km. When you see the tank and the helicopter, you're there.

July or early August, the **Kulmbacher Bierfest**, a large beer festival, is a treat.

For an overview of the local brewing history, stop by the **Bayerisches Brauereimuseum** (Bavarian Brewery Museum; ☎ 805 14; Hofer Strasse 20; ⊙ 10am-5pm Tue-Fri, 9am-5pm Sat & Sun Apr-Oct, 10am-5pm Tue-Sun Nov-Mar).

Kulmbach's other claim to fame is an exquisite medieval fortress, the **Plassenburg** (☎ 947 505; adult/concession €4/3; ⊙ 9am-6pm Apr-Oct, 10am-4pm Tue-Sun Nov-Mar). Behind the foreboding bastions of this castle awaits a royal residence of considerable charm. Especially worth a visit is the arcaded Renaissance

Schöner Hof (Beautiful Courtyard), which is the setting for summer concerts.

A jail in the 19th century, the fortress now contains several museums as well as the re-created staterooms. Entire armies of tin figurines can be admired at the Plassenburg's **Deutsche Zinnfigurenmuseum** (German Tin Figurine Museum). With 300,000 of the objects it's the world's largest of its kind, including about 170 dioramas re-creating historical or mythological scenes. Also on the fortress grounds are a museum of historical weapons and armour and a gallery of paintings featuring battle and hunting scenes. A shuttle bus makes the trip up here every half-hour.

Kulmbach's **tourist office** (☎ 958 80; www .kulmbach.de in German; Sutte 2; ⏰ 9am-5.30pm Mon, Tue & Thu, 9am-4pm Wed) has walking-tour maps in English.

From Bayreuth, a few regional trains make direct trips (€5.70, 40 minutes). Drivers should take the B85.

Kronach & the Frankenwald
☎ 09261 / pop 20,000 / elev 307m

Another 22km further north is the lovely medieval town of Kronach, sheltered by a fortified wall, embraced by two little rivers and crowned by a fortress. It celebrated its 1000th birthday in 2003 and is perhaps best known as the birthplace, in 1472, of the eponymous painter Lucas Cranach the Elder.

Kronach is also the gateway to the **Naturpark Frankenwald**, a dense forest area with deep valleys carved by rivers and creeks. Popular with hikers and other outdoor enthusiasts, it also supplies as many as a million Christmas trees for German homes each year.

Start your explorations in the old town centre, here called the *Obere Stadt* (upper town). Navigate the narrow alleys lined with half-timbered houses, eventually coming to the Gothic **Pfarrkirche St Johannes** for a look at its north portal topped with an emotive stone sculpture of St John the Baptist (1498). Then head up to the never-conquered **Festung Rosenberg** (☎ 604 10; adult/ concession incl entrance to Fränkische Galerie €3.50/2; ⏰ 9am-5.30pm Tue-Sun Apr-Oct, 10am-4pm Tue-Sun Nov-Mar), one of the largest fortresses in Germany. It's accessed by an early-baroque gate built in 1662 by Antonio Petrini. Entry incorporates a tour (in German), the high-light of which is descending to the maze of dungeons.

Entry prices to the complex increase slightly when there's a feature exhibition at the on-site **Fränkische Galerie** (☎ 604 10; adult/concession €2.50/1, combination ticket with Festung Rosenberg €3.50/2; ⏰ 9.30am-5pm Apr-Oct, 10am-4pm Nov-Mar), where you can admire sculpture and altar paintings by Franconian artists working between the 13th and the 16th centuries. Highlights include works by Tilmann Riemenschneider and the Dürer disciple Hans von Kulmbach.

Kronach has a **tourist office** (☎ 972 36; www .kronach.de; Marktplatz 5; ⏰ 10am-5pm Mon-Fri, 10am-2pm Sat May-Sep, 10am-4pm Mon-Fri Oct-Apr). Also in town is the **Frankenwald Tourismus Service Center** (☎ 6015; www.frankenwald.de in German; Adolf-Kolping-Strasse 1; ⏰ 9am-6pm Mon-Fri).

Kronach is about 45km northwest of Bayreuth and 33km east of Coburg. Regional trains to and from Bayreuth require a change in Hochstadt (€11.10, 1¾ hours); to and from Coburg, you must change in Lichtenfels (€6.90, one hour). Take the B85 if you're driving.

COBURG
☎ 09561 / pop 42,000 / elev 297m

If marriage is diplomacy by another means, Coburg's rulers were surely masters of the art. Over four centuries, the princes and princesses of the House of Saxe-Coburg intrigued, romanced and ultimately wed into the dynasties of Belgium, Bulgaria, Denmark, Portugal, Russia, Sweden and, most prominently, Great Britain. The crowning achievement came in 1857, when Albert of Saxe-Coburg-Gotha took vows with his first cousin Queen Victoria, founding the present British royal family (which quietly adopted the name of Windsor during WWI).

Coburg actually remained an independent duchy until the end of WWI but then voted to join Bavaria in 1920. Today visitors come to Coburg to visit its proud Veste Coburg, one of Germany's finest medieval fortresses.

Orientation

Coburg's Bahnhof (train station) and central bus station are northwest of the Altstadt. To get to the Markt, head south on Lossaustrasse, then east on Judengasse.

FRANCONIA

Information

Post office (Hindenburgstrasse 6) You can change money at the Postbank here.

Tourist office (☎ 741 80; www.coburg-tourist.de; Herrngasse 4; ☒ 9am-6.30pm Mon-Fri, 9am-1pm Sat Apr-Oct, 9am-5pm Mon-Fri Nov-Mar) Just off the Markt; staff have information about a single ticket to most of Coburg's sites for €7.

Sights

VESTE COBURG

Enthroned above town in a triple ring of fortified walls, the **Veste Coburg** is a storybook medieval fortress that harbours the amazing **Kunst Sammlungen** (Gallery; ☎ 8790; adult/concession €3/2.50; ☒ 10am-5pm Tue-Sun Apr-Oct, 1-4pm Tue-Sun Nov-Mar). As you enter the main building, look out for the original Napoleonic copper cannon, inscribed with the signature 'N'. Besides works by such star painters as Rembrandt, Dürer and Cranach the Elder, the vast collection here also encompasses 350,000 copper etchings and lots of fancifully decorated sledges and carriages.

In 1530, Protestant reformer Martin Luther, under imperial ban, sought refuge at the fortress for about half a year. His former quarters are an historical highlight. Audio guides in English cost €1.50, as do entertaining kids' audio guides (German only).

The **Veste-Express** (one-way/return €2/3; ☒ Apr-Oct), a tourist train, makes the trip to the fortress every 30 minutes. Bus No 8 goes uphill year-round from Herrngasse near the Markt (€1.25 each way). The fitness-inclined can also walk up a steepish path for about 30 minutes.

SCHLOSS EHRENBURG

In 1547, Coburg's dukes moved into a new residence, right in town, the **Schloss Ehrenburg** (☎ 767 57; Schlossplatz; tours adult/concession/child under 18 €4/3/free, combination ticket with Schloss Rosenau €6/5/free; ☒ 9am-3pm Tue-Sun). This tapestry-lined palace is of 16th-century origin and only got its neo-Gothic mantle in the 19th century. Albert spent his childhood here and Queen Victoria stayed in a room with Germany's first flushing toilet (1860). The most splendid room is the **Riesensaal** (Hall of Giants), whose baroque ceiling is supported by 28 statues of Atlas. Tours are in German only.

MARKT

A statue of Prince Albert anchors Coburg's central square. Flanking its north side is the ornate **Stadthaus** (Town House), a Renaissance edifice with a trio of stepped gables, red trim and a pretty oriel. Its counterpart is the baroque **Rathaus**, which sports blue-and-gold trim; one of its corners is graced by a two-storey oriel.

Festivals & Events

In mid-July, Coburg explodes during the annual **Samba Festival**, which draws around 50 bands, 2000 dancers and up to 200,000 revellers.

Sleeping

Coburger Tor (☎ 250 74; fax 288 74; Ketschendorfer Strasse 22; s €59-80, d €80-130; ☒ restaurant from 6pm Mon-Sat) A refined ambience, impeccable service, olde-worlde rooms with thoughtful décor and the attached gourmet restaurant make this place a winner. It's about a 15-minute walk south of the Altstadt.

Gasthof Fink (☎ 249 40; www.gasthof-fink.de; Lützelbucher Strasse 24; s €25-45, d €48-64; ☒ restaurant closed Mon; P ☒) With welcoming English-speaking staff, this family-friendly inn, about 4km outside town, encompasses two buildings just across from each other. The original *Gasthof* (inn) has quaint attic-style rooms with shared or private bathrooms, while the more expensive but excellent rooms in the contemporary Landhaus Fink all have private bathrooms, telephones and large balconies or courtyards. There's a wheelchair-equipped room on the ground floor. Take bus No 4.

DJH hostel (☎ 153 30; www.djh.de in German; Parkstrasse 2; B&B with linen €14.20; P ☒) Coburg's 128-bed hostel is in a mock castle surrounded by gardens 2km from town. Take bus No 1 from Theatergasse or the Bahnhof (€1.25).

Eating

The Coburg sausage is a local speciality; pick one up from the rolling kitchens on the Markt (€1.59).

München Hofbräu (☎ 234 923; Kleine Johannisgasse 8; mains €5-17) The charming staff at this cosy timber-lined traditional restaurant will guide you through a menu specialising in curry-spiced sausages and infinite pork dishes. There's a play area for kids with books, pencils, toys and games.

Ratskeller (☎ 924 00; Markt 1; mains €5-15)
Housed within Coburg's spectacular town
hall, this polished place serves good regional dishes from Thuringia and Franconia in an elegant setting with padded
red-leather seating.

Café Prinz Albert (☎ 945 20; Ketschengasse 27;
dishes €2.90-5; ⊙ to 6.30pm) Reflecting Coburg's
links with the British royals in both its décor
and menu, this is a fine place for a snack or
coffee and cake, or the Prince Albert breakfast – a cross-cultural marriage of sausages,
eggs and Bamberger croissants.

Getting There & Away
Direct trains travel from Bamberg (€8.40,
45 minutes) and Nuremberg (€16.20, 1¾
hours) every other hour. They also travel
between Coburg and Bayreuth (€12.90, two
hours), Kronach (€6.90, 1 hour), and Kulmbach (€8.40, 45 minutes), which requires a
change in Lichtenfels.

AROUND COBURG
Rödental
☎ 09563 / pop 14,422 / elev 306m
The village of Rödental, about 6km northeast of Coburg, is known for its palace, and
as the home of the Goebel factory, makers of the world-famous Hummel ceramic
figurines.

Schloss Rosenau (☎ 308 413; Rosenau 1; adult/
concession/child under 18 €4/3/free, with Schloss Ehrenhof
€6/5/free; ⊙ 9am-5pm Apr-Sep, 10am-3pm Oct-Mar) is
the birthplace of Prince Albert (1819) and a
favourite palace of his later wife Queen Victoria. Medieval at its core, Albert's father,
Ernst I, had it revamped in neo-Gothic style.
A highlight is the ornate Marmorsaal (Marble Hall) on the ground floor. The Orangerie
in the romantic English garden contains the
renowned **Museum für Moderne Glas** (Museum of
Modern Glass; ☎ 1606; admission €1; ⊙ 10am-1pm &
1.30-5pm Tue-Sun Apr-Oct, 1-4pm Tue-Sun Nov-Mar).

The Goebel family has been manufacturing porcelain figurines since 1871, but they're
most famous for the so-called **Hummelfiguren**,
cutesy statuettes with names such as 'Apple
Tree Boy' or 'Goose Girl' that grace the cabinets of millions of collectors worldwide. Each
design was created by a nun named Maria
Innocentia, who trained at the Munich Academy of Fine Arts. At the company-run **Information Centre** (☎ 09503-923 03; Coburger Strasse 7;
admission free; ⊙ 9am-5pm Mon-Fri, 9am-noon Sat) you'll

get an overview of the art of porcelainmak-
ing, observe artists at work and peruse precious collector's items in the museum.

Buses No 715 and No 8312 make several trips a day from Coburg's Bahnhof
to Rödental. It stops at the Goebel factory
from where it's a 20-minute walk or short
taxi ride (about €5) to the Schloss. Drivers
should head for Neustädter Strasse and follow the signs.

Basilika Vierzehnheiligen
About 25km south of Coburg is an ornate,
gilded 18th-century pilgrimage church,
the **Basilika Vierzehnheiligen** (☎ 09571-950 80;
Vierzehnheiligen 2; admission free; ⊙ 6.30am-7pm Apr-
Oct, 7.30am-dusk Nov-Mar). It stands in the spot
where, in 1445, a young shepherd reported
having recurring visions of the infant Jesus
flanked by the 14 Nothelfer (Holy Helpers),
a group of saints invoked in times of adversity since the 14th-century black plague
epidemic. The shepherd reported the 'little
ones' asking for a chapel to be built right
here so that they might have a place from
which to work their miracles. Lo and behold, miracles did happen and the chapel,
consecrated in 1448, quickly became a
popular place of pilgrimage for royals and
paupers alike.

When in 1741 the original church was
close to collapse, the local abbot commissioned Balthasar Neumann to build a
new one. Along with the Würzburg Residenz, Basilika Vierzehnheiligen is widely
regarded as one of Neumann's crowning
achievements. Inside, attention focuses on
the amazing freestanding altar, supposedly
placed right on the spot of the initial ap-
parition. The work of stucco artists Johann
Michael and Franz Xaver Feichtmayr of
Wessobrunn, it is studded with statues of
the 14 saints with one of the infant Jesus
balancing up on top.

The church is maintained by the attached
Franciscan monastery, whose six brothers
provide spiritual counselling to pilgrims.

The wonderful **Alte Klosterbrauerei**
(☎ 09571-3488; snacks €3-5; ⊙ 10am-8pm) is round
the back of Vierzehnheiligen, up the hill
past the wooden stands peddling kitsch.
Grab a table in the sprawling beer garden
with stunning views and quaff a half litre of
the bracing '*Nothelfertrunk*' beer for €1.85.
Snacks include hearty bread-and-sausage

platters, but you can also bring in your own food. Stay long enough and you may glimpse the nun in habit who lugs in cases for refilling.

Kloster Banz

Across the valley, **Kloster Banz** (☎ 09573-5592) is a former 11th-century Benedictine monastery turned conference centre for a conservative political think tank. Today's Italian baroque complex (1698–1719) is the work of Leonard and Johann Dietzenhofer. The **church** (🕑 9am-noon & 2-5pm May-Oct, 9am-noon & 2-4pm Nov-Apr) features bright ceiling frescoes, altars to the Three Wise Men and the 14 Holy Helpers, and intricately carved choir stalls. There's a lovely view from the Franz Josef Strauss memorial, which is dedicated to the former party leader of the Christliche-Soziale Union (Christian Social Union; CSU). Also here is a neat fossil collection at the **Naturhistorische Sammlung** (Petrefaktensammlung, Natural History Collection; ☎ 09573-337 44; adult/concession €1.50/1, 🕑 9am-noon & 2-5pm May-Oct, 9am-noon & 2-4pm Mar-Apr).

GETTING THERE & AWAY

Regional trains connect Coburg with Lichtenfels (€4.20, 22 minutes) from where there are infrequent buses to Basilika Vierzehnheiligen. A taxi from Lichtenfels to either Vierzehnheiligen or Kloster Banz is about €5. Vierzehnheiligen and Kloster Banz are near Staffelstein and Lichtenfels, just off the B173, about a 30-minute drive from Coburg.

FRANCONIA

WÜRZBURG

☎ 0931 / pop 130,000 / elev 182m

Vibrant Würzburg straddles the Main River and is the northern gateway to the Romantic Road and the capital of Fränkisches Weinland (Franconian Wine Country). Decimated in WWII when fire bombs destroyed almost 90% of the centre, the city put enormous efforts into restoring its major attractions, and the overall recovery has been remarkable. Today it's a vibrant university town (more than one-fifth of the population are students), humming with café-bars, hip clubs and a fantastic festival programme. In 2004, the city celebrated its 1300-year anniversary.

As you explore Würzburg, you'll repeatedly come across the work of two men who have shaped its artistic and architectural legacy: Tilman Riemenschneider and Balthasar Neumann. The latter was the main brain behind the Residenz, a magnificent palace ranked as a Unesco World Heritage site.

History

Würzburg was a Franconian duchy when, in 686, three roving Irish missionaries – Kilian, Totnan and Kolonat – passed through and proposed that Duke Gosbert convert to Christianity...and ditch his wife. Gosbert was purportedly mulling it over when his wife had the three bumped off in 689. When the murders were discovered decades later, the three martyrs became saints, Würzburg a pilgrimage city and, in 742, a bishopric.

For the next 1060 years, the bishops wielded enormous power as both secular and religious rulers, to the chagrin of the citizens. The prince-bishops, from their hilltop fortress of Marienberg, quashed two bloody uprisings – in 1400 and again in 1525 during the Peasants' War. Julius Echter von Mespelbrunn (1545–1617) brought the Reformation's resulting instability under control by turning the city into a centre of the Counter-Reformation.

Würzburg's 'golden age' arrived with the election of three artistically inclined prince-bishops from the House of Schönborn; the Residenz was built on their shift. Napoleon finally put an end to ecclesiastic rule in 1802; 14 years later, Würzburg became part of Bavaria.

Orientation

Würzburg's Altstadt is, perhaps not coincidently, shaped something like a bishop's hat. Duplicating this bishop's hat shape in an outer layer is the leafy Ringpark, which borders the city (its designer, Jöhns Person Lindahl, shot himself 22 years after its completion in 1878 because citizens didn't like the nongeometric English-style gardens – though it's now beloved by those seeking shade and serenity). Kaiserstrasse, running south from the station into the Altstadt, is the main shopping strip. The Main River forms the western boundary of the Altstadt and the fortress is found on the west bank. Alte Mainbrücke, a 15th-century stone footbridge, is the most

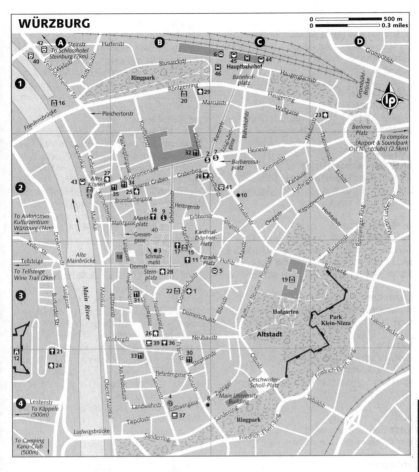

WÜRZBURG

0 ——————— 500 m
0 ——————— 0.3 miles

scenic route across the river. The Residenz is located on the Altstadt's eastern edge. At the northern end of the Altstadt is the Hauptbahnhof and the central bus station is just west of here.

Information

BOOKSHOPS
Hugendubel (☎ 354 040; Schmalzmarkt 12) Good stock of English-language novels and travel guides.

EMERGENCY
After-hours emergencies (☎ 192 22)
Ärztliche Notfallpraxis (☎ 322 833; Domerschul-strasse 1; ⏱ 1-10pm Wed, 8am-10pm Fri-Sun) This medical clinic has a doctor on duty.

INTERNET ACCESS
N@tcity (☎ 3041 9494; Sanderstrasse 27; per 12min €0.70, happy hour rates 9-10am Sun-Thu & 9.30pm-12am per 12min €0.50; ⏱ 9am-12am Mon-Thu, 9am-1am Fri & Sat, Sun 1pm-12am) A huge state-of-the-art Internet café.

LIBRARIES
Stadtbücherei (city library; ☎ 373 294; Falkenhaus am Markt) In the same building as the tourist office.

MONEY
Deutsche Bank (Juliuspromenade 66)
Postbank (Bahnhofplatz 2)
Sparkasse (Barbarossaplatz) Has an ATM that changes foreign notes.

POST
Post offices Altstadt (Paradeplatz); Bahnhof (Bahnhofs-platz 2) Telephone and fax services available.

TOURIST INFORMATION
Tourist office (☎ 372 398; www.wuerzburg.de; Markt-platz; ⏱ 10am-6pm year-round, closed Sun Nov-Mar) In the baroque masterpiece Falkenhaus.

TRAVEL AGENCIES
STA Travel (☎ 521 76; Zwinger 6) The local market leader for student travel.

UNIVERSITIES
Julius-Maximilian Universität (☎ 310; www.uni -wuerzburg.de; Sanderring 2) Established in 1582 by Julius Echter von Mespelbrunn (Alois Alzheimer took his medical degree here in 1887), Würzburg's largest university is scattered across town, with its main administrative building at Sanderring 2 in the southern Altstadt. It's especially renowned in the fields of economics, biochemistry and technology.

Sights

RESIDENZ
The impressive **Residenz** (☎ 355 170; Balthasar-Neumann-Promenade; adult/concession €5/4; ⏱ 9am-6pm Apr-Oct, 10am-4pm Oct-Mar, guided tours 11am & 3pm) is one of the most important and beautiful baroque palaces in southern Germany. Some sections can only be seen on guided tours.

In 1719, Johann Philipp Franz von Schönborn, unhappy with his old-fashioned digs up in Marienberg Fortress, hired a young architect by the name of Balthasar Neumann to build a new palace in town. Neumann's enormous horseshoe-shaped creation took 24 years to construct and another 30 or so to finish the eye-popping interior. In WWII, only the central section escaped unharmed; the rest required extensive restoration.

Almost immediately upon entering, you'll see Neumann's brilliant **Grand Staircase**, a single central set of steps that splits and zigzags up to the 1st floor. In 1750, Italian Giovanni Battista Tiepolo – then at the pinnacle of his career – smothered the vast vaulted ceiling with what still is the world's largest fresco. It allegorically depicts the four then-known continents (Europe, Africa, America and Asia) and is essentially a celebration of the arts and a glorification of the prince-bishop as patron *extraordinaire*.

The white stucco of the **Weisser Saal** (White Hall) is a soothing interlude before the next sensory onslaught: the opulent **Kaisersaal** (Imperial Hall). It's canopied by yet another impressive Tiepolo fresco, this one depicting Emperor Barbarossa.

Of the meticulously restored staterooms, the **Spiegelkabinett** (Mirror Hall) is the most memorable. Gilded stucco drips from its ceiling and walls, which are covered with a unique mirrorlike glass painted with figural, floral and animal motifs.

Hofkirche & Hofgarten
In the residence's south wing, the **Hofkirche** (Court Church; admission free; ⏱ hr vary, check with information desk or tourist office) is another Neumann and Tiepolo co-production. It matches the residence in its splendour and brilliant proportions and features side altars by the Italian artist.

Behind the Residenz, the **Hofgarten** (admission free; ⏱ dawn-dusk) has whimsical sculptures of children, mostly by court sculptor Peter Wagner. Concerts, festivals and special events take place here during the warmer months. Enter through intricate wrought-iron gates into the lovely French- and English-style gardens, partly built on the old baroque bastions.

Martin-von-Wagner Museum
Martin von Wagner (1777–1858) was a painter, sculptor and art procurer for King Ludwig I. His extensive private collection forms the basis of the **Martin-von-Wagner Museum** (☎ 312 288; Residenzplatz 2, enter next to the Hofkirche; admission free).

There are three departments in the museum. The **Antikensammlung** (Antiquities Collection; 2-5pm Tue-Sat) focuses on Greek, Roman and Egyptian ceramics, vases, figurines and marble sculptures from 1500 BC to AD 300. The **Gemäldegalerie** (Art Gallery; 9.30am-12.30pm Tue-Sat) has primarily German, Dutch and Italian paintings from the 15th to the 19th centuries, including works by Tiepolo. Finally, the **Graphische Sammlung** (Graphics Collection; 4-6pm Tue & Thu) consists of drawings, copperplate etchings and woodcuts, including some by Albrecht Dürer.

RATHAUS & GRAFENECKART
Adjoining Würzburg's **Rathaus**, the 1659 red building **Grafeneckart** (Domstrasse; admission free; 8am-11pm) houses a scale model of the WWII bombing, which starkly depicts the extent of the damage to the city following the night of 16 March 1945, when 5000 citizens lost their lives.

DOM ST KILIAN
Würzburg's **Dom St Kilian** (St Kilia's Cathedral; 10am-5pm Mon-Sat, 1-6pm Sun Easter-Oct, 10am-noon & 2-5pm Mon-Sat, 1-6pm Sun Nov-Easter), built between 1040 and 1237, is one of the largest Romanesque cathedrals in Germany, although numerous alterations have added Gothic, Renaissance and baroque elements. Most famous is the row of elaborate tombstones affixed to the pillars, especially those of Bishops Rudolf von Scherenberg (died in 1495) and Lorenz von Bibra (died in 1519) on the left, hewn from red marble by Tilman Riemenschneider. Attached to the north transept is the festive **Schönbornkapelle**, the final resting place of the Schönborn bishops, designed by Balthasar Neumann.

WÜRZBURGER DOMSCHATZ
A Neumann-designed town house harbours the **Würzburger Domschatz** (Cathedral Treasury; ☎ 3866 5600; Plattnerstrasse; adult/concession €2.50/1.75; 2-5pm Tue-Sun). Displays of ministerial garments, golden and bejewelled liturgical items and bishops' insignia are accompanied by spiritual music and intimate spotlighting.

NEUMÜNSTER
Abutting the Dom, the **Neumünster** (☎ 321 1830; 7am-6pm) is a Romanesque church built in the 11th century on the site of the martyrdom of Sts Kilian, Kolonat and Totnan, who lie buried in its crypt. The Gothic tower and choir stem from the 13th century, while the baroque period brought the addition of the dome and ornamented façade. The north exit leads to the lovely **Lusamgärtlein** (a cloister) with the grave of the celebrated medieval minstrel Walther von der Vogelweide.

MARIENKAPELLE
Next to the tourist office on Markt, the late-Gothic **Marienkapelle** (☎ 321 1830; Marktplatz; 8am-6.30pm), built between 1377 and 1481, is a testimony to the wealth and self-confidence of Würzburg's medieval townspeople. Balthasar Neumann was laid to rest in this dignified hall church, next to numerous Franconian knights and burghers. Among them is Konrad von Schaumberg (died in 1499) for whom Riemenschneider designed the tombstone. The prolific sculptor produced the sandstone figures of Adam and Eve above the entrance portal.

RÖNTGEN MUSEUM GEDÄCHTNISSTÄTTE
Würzburg's most famous modern scion is Wilhelm Conrad Röntgen, the discoverer of the X-ray in 1895, for which he received the Nobel prize for physics in 1901. His laboratory, including the instruments he used, are the heart of the **Röntgen Museum Gedächtnisstätte** (☎ 351 1103; Röntgenring 8; admission free; 8am-4pm Mon-Thu, 8am-3pm Fri).

MUSEUM IM KULTURSPEICHER
Housed in an historic riverside granary that's been cleverly converted into a cultural centre, the **Museum im Kulturspeicher** (Museum in the Cultural Memory; ☎ 322 250; Veitshöchheimer Strasse 5; adult/concession €3/1.50; 11am-7pm Wed, 11am-9pm Thu, 11am-6pm Fri-Sun) houses the **Municipal**

Gallery with art from the 19th to the 21st centuries including works by regional artists Otto Modersohn and Erich Heckel. Under the same roof is the **Sammlung Ruppert**, a collection of post-1945 European concrete art with sculpture, paintings and photographs by such artists as Victor Vasarely and Auguste Herbin.

Besides the two museums, the Kulturspeicher also incorporates a café, shop and a small stage, which is now the performance space of the **Kabarettbühne Bockshorn**, recently relocated from Sommerhausen, which has satirical sketches and stand-up comedy (in German) on its program.

FESTUNG MARIENBERG

On the Main's left bank, **Festung Marienberg** (Marienberg Fortress) has presided over Würzburg since the city's prince-bishops commenced its construction in 1201 atop castle ruins from the 8th century; they governed from here until 1719. Only Swedish troops in the Thirty Years' War managed to scale the fortress walls in 1631. Today, the sweeping views over the city's red rooftops and vine-covered hills are doubly impressive given the devastation of WWII. In summer, the sprawling, gently sloping lawns are strewn with picnickers taking in the panorama.

Besides the fortress' museums, the circular **Marienkirche** (706) is a major point of interest. For many centuries, the bishops had their intestines buried here, while their bodies rested in the Dom St Kilian and their hearts at the monastery in Ebrach. The **Maschikuliturm** (1724), a defensive tower, is another Balthasar Neumann creation.

The fortress is a 30-minute walk up the hill from the Alte Mainbrücke via the **Tellsteige trail**, which is part of the 4km-long **Weinwanderweg** (wine hiking trail) through the vineyards around Marienberg. From Easter to October, bus No 9 makes the trip to the castle from the central bus station.

Fürstenbaumuseum

The fortress' residential wing now holds the **Fürstenbaumuseum** (☎ 355 1753; adult/concession €4/3; ☺ 9am-6pm Tue-Sun Apr-Oct, 10am-4pm Tue-Sun Oct-Mar). On the 1st floor, the reconstructed apartments of the prince-bishops give you a good idea of the pompous lifestyle in which these rulers wallowed. A highlight is the

Echtersche Familienteppich, a huge tapestry showing the entire family of Julius Echter von Mespelbrunn including, oddly, their ages.

On display upstairs is a comprehensive overview of the city's history.

Mainfränkisches Museum

The fortress' baroque Zeughaus (Armoury; 1712) houses the **Mainfränkisches Museum** (☎ 205 940; Festung Marienberg; adult/concession €3/1.50; ☺ 10am-5pm Tue-Sun Apr-Oct, 10am-4pm Tue-Sun Nov-Mar). The historic rooms provide a suitable backdrop for the high-quality displays, including a world-famous collection of Tilman Riemenschneider sculptures. In another section, porcelain, glass, furniture and other such objects illustrate life during the baroque and rococo eras; from the same period are the sketches and drawings by Neumann and Tiepolo. In the Kelterhalle, where wine was once produced, is an exhibit about winemaking.

ST BURKHARD & KÄPPELE

On your way up to the fortress, you'll pass **St Burkhard** (☎ 424 12; ☺ 8am-6pm Apr-Oct, 8am-4.30pm Nov-Mar), a Romanesque basilica with a Gothic extension. Treasures include a Madonna by Riemenschneider and a 14th-century relief depicting the Crucifixion.

Further south, in a prime location atop the Nikolausberg, the **Käppele** (☎ 726 70; ☺ 8am-7pm), built in 1752, is a triple onion-domed pilgrimage church designed by Neumann. The Stations of the Cross featuring life-size figures by Peter Wagner lead up to the church. Inside, the votive tablets in the so-called 'Mirakelgang' (Miracle Aisle) are worth a look. The outside terrace is a great spot for photographs of the Marienberg and the city beyond.

Tours

The tourist office runs one-hour English-language **city walks** (€5; ☺ 6pm May-Oct). If you'd prefer to explore at your own pace, you can hire an **audio-guide tour** (also in English; €5) to tour the city's sights.

WINERY TOURS

The fortified **Alter Kranen** (Old Crane; 1773) was designed by Balthasar Neumann's son Franz Ignaz Michael to service a dock on the river south of Friedensbrücke. It is now the **Haus des Frankenweins** (☎ 390 1111; Kranenkai 1), where you can sample some of Franconia's finest wines (from €1.50 per glass) in historic rooms.

The historic **Weingut Juliusspital** (☎ 393 1406; Juliuspromenade 19; tour €5; ☷ tours 2pm Fri & 5pm Sat mid-Apr–Oct) offers tours (in German) that take in the splendid old wine cellars, rooms and courtyards, finishing with a glass of wine. Equally atmospheric, the **Bürgerspital Weingut** (☎ 350 3403; Theaterstrasse 19; tour €5; ☷ tours 2pm Sat Mar-Oct) also conducts tours, with a small bottle of the local vintage included in the bargain.

Festivals & Events

The largest European festival of its kind, the **Africa-Festival** (☎ 150 60; www.africafestival .org) is held in a Woodstock-like venue, on the meadows northwest of the river at Mainwiesen, around late May or early June, complete with markets, food stalls and, if it rains, lots of mud. It's a 15-minute walk from the Hauptbahnhof, or take tram Nos 2 or 4 to Talavera and follow the drums.

Also held here for 10 days during June is the **Umsonst & Draussen** (☎ 883 521; www.umsonst -und-draussen.de in German), a huge free live-music festival held over two stages with high-profile local and international bands.

Every May, the weekend-long **Weindorf** (Wine Village; ☎ 728 57; www.weindorfwuerzburg.de in German) takes place on the Marktplatz.

Thousands flock to the **Würzburger Mozart-fest** (☎ 372 336) held in the Residenz courtyard and garden in late May or early June, with the golden façade of the palace providing a perfect backdrop.

Sleeping

BUDGET

DJH Jugendgästehaus (☎ 425 90; www.djh.de in German; Burkarder Strasse 44; dm incl breakfast & linen €18-26.80) On the hillside below the fortress, this hostel has room for 254 in three- to eight-bed dorms. Take tram No 3 or 5 to Ludwigsbrücke then walk for five minutes north along river.

Pension Spehnkuch (☎ 547 52; www.pension -spehnkuch.de in German; Röntgenring 7; s/d €29/52) Up a narrow flight of stairs, 100m from the train station, this somewhat cramped pension has zero frills, but rooms are clean and the English-speaking staff welcoming, making it popular with budget-minded travellers from

around the world. Breakfast is served in a sunny room with a balcony, and there's free 24-hour parking on the street below.

Camping Kanu-Club (☎ 725 36; Mergentheimer Strasse 13b; per person/tent €2.50) On the west bank of the Main. Take tram No 3 or 5 to Judenbühlweg. The tram stops right out front.

By the time you're reading this, a new, independent, all-ages hostel, **Babelfish** (☎ 304 0430; www.babelfish-hostel.de; Prymstrasse 3), operated by two fun-loving locals, was scheduled to have opened a hop, skip and a jump from the train station and Altstadt.

MIDRANGE & TOP END

Hotel Rebstock (☎ 309 30; www.rebstock.com; Neubaustrasse 7; s/d from €81/206; meals €14-22; P ☒ ☒ ▣) Würzburg's top hotel, in a meticulously restored rococo town house, has eminent class, outstanding service and superb comfort. Exquisitely furnished rooms evocative of the south of France lack no amenities. The white tableclothed restaurant gets top marks for its outstanding and inventive international cuisine.

Schlosshotel Steinburg (☎ 970 20; www.steinburg .com; Auf dem Steinberg; s €80-105, d €130-150; P ☒ ☒) A perfect first (or last) stop on the Romantic Road, this former palace is framed by vineyards with two terraces affording magical views over the city. Individually designed rooms are appropriately gorgeous, and there's a Romanesque indoor pool and sauna.

Hotel Zum Winzermännle (☎ 541 56; www.winzer maennle.de; Domstrasse 32; s without bathroom €30-35, d without bathroom €55-65, s with bathroom €52-60, d with bathroom €75-90, f €90-130; ▣) This former winery (its name means 'the little wine farmer') was rebuilt in its original style after the war as a guesthouse by the same charming family. Rooms are cavernous and all have telephones and TVs. It's right in the city's pedestrianised heart with public parking nearby; guest vehicles are permitted to stop outside to drop off luggage.

Hotel Residence (☎ 535 46; hotel-residence -wuerzburg@t-online.de; Juliuspromenade 1; s €58-85, d €80-114; P) With pretty dormer windows and tastefully decorated rooms, this charming hotel, replete with all the trimmings, is near the river and the congress centre, within strolling distance of the city's main sights.

Hotel Dortmunder Hof (☎ 561 63; www.dortmunder -hof.de; Innerer Graben 22; s €40-65, d €70-100) In a handy position two blocks from Markt, this cyclist-friendly place is in a pretty lemon-coloured building, with clean, comfy rooms including cable TV. Parking can be arranged nearby.

Eating

Würzburg has a vast array of places to eat and drink, with plenty of quality restaurants and student hangouts among them. See also right for café-bar recommendations.

Backöfele (☎ 590 59; Ursulinergasse 2; mains €6-18) Don't miss this rustic restaurant with cobblestone floors, candlelit tables and exposed timber beams complemented by innovative twists on traditional game, steak and fish dishes. For starters, try the *Fränkische Most-suppe* – a frothy Franconian wine soup with aromatic cinnamon croutons. Bookings are advisable.

Juliusspital (☎ 540 80; Juliuspromenade 19; mains €8.90-15.90) This attractive *Weinstube* (traditional wine bar) features fabulous Franconian delicacies. The Juliusspital itself was first founded as a hospital and poor people's home by Julius Echter von Mespelbrunn in 1576. In the basement is an Aladdin's cave–like bakery, which also has a clutch of tables.

Auflauf (☎ 571 343; Peterplatz 5; Brotzeit €2-9, mains from €6.50) At this always-busy, unpretentious place with blue-and-white décor and timber tables you can order homemade gnocchi, gratins and the signature *Aufläufe* (casseroles) à la carte – or create your own *Auflauf* from a choice of main ingredients and sauces, plus melba cheese. Between 10pm and 11pm every night, two people can also get a terrific deal on a baguette, two *Aufläufe* mains and two servings of ice cream or coffee for €15.50.

QUICK EATS

Simsim (☎ 161 53; Innerer Graben 11; dishes €3-7) Outstanding Arabic food including felafel to take away or eat in mosaic-tiled surrounds.

Natur-Feinkostladen (☎ 189 81; Sanderstrasse 2a; dishes from €2) Health-food snacks and grain burgers, with a specialist organic grocery next door.

Schlenamer Eck (☎ 547 04; Juliuspromenade 24; dishes from €2) Perch on high stools to tuck into doner kebabs, chicken wings and vegetarian bruschettas.

Drinking

Würzburg is chock-a-block with student café-bars that stay open late and also serve good cheap food, especially along Neubaustrasse and Sanderstrasse.

MUCK (☎ 465 1144; Sanderstrasse 29; dishes €2.40-5.50) This fun place has loads of board games to while away the day. One of the earliest openers in town (officially 8am, though you'll often find them serving at 7am) it does a great house breakfast with bread rolls, croissants, salami (which can be swapped for vegie options) and cheeses plus orange juice and a mammoth, individual, refillable pot of coffee. At night, it has the laid-back feel of a party at a friend's house.

Schönborn (☎ 404 4818; Marktplatz 30; meals €4.80-7.90) Overlooking the market square across from the tourist office, this big, airy place with a curved central staircase backed by a mural has terrific pizzas and pastas as well as a great variety of dips and gourmet salads. There's an extensive cocktail list; happy hour is 6.30pm to 8.30pm and all night Wednesday.

Standard (☎ 511 40; Oberthuerstrasse 11a; dishes €3-6.80) Beneath a corrugated-iron ceiling and stainless-steel fans are newspaper racks, textile art and soulful jazz, with focaccias and pasta on the menu. Downstairs there's a second dimly lit bar where bands and DJs play a couple of times or more a week.

Also recommended:

Le Clochard Bistro (☎ 129 07; Neubaustrasse 20; food €4-7; ⏰ from 5pm Mon & Tue) Cosy creperie and bar with open fireplace. Tuesday nights are nonsmoking.

Uni-Café (☎ 156 72; Neubaustrasse 2; snacks €3-6.50) Hugely popular café set over two levels, with a student-priced, daily changing set menu and buzzy bar.

Entertainment

Fritz (www.fritz-wuerzburg.de in German) is the town's monthly listing magazine, available free at pubs and cafés.

Autonomes Kulturzentrum Würzburg (AKW; ☎ 417 800; www.akw-info.de in German; Frankfurterstrasse 87; ⏰ Thu-Sat, pub only Sun) Within this 1880s brewery complex are artist studios, a small independent theatre, disco and split-level bar with squashy sofas to sink into. Bands, mostly indy and alternative, perform regularly, and in summer there's a bustling beer garden with an open-air cinema screening art-house films on Monday nights. AKW also holds regular gay parties and women-only party nights. Take the No 2 or 4 tram to the Siebold-Museum stop and follow the signs (or the crowds).

Omnibus (☎ 561 21; Theaterstrasse 10) This venue, established in 1970, is the best place for live funk, blues, soul and old-time rock 'n roll.

Serious party animals should head to the **complex** (Gattingerstrasse 17; ☾ Tue, Wed, Fri & Sat) in eastern Würzburg. Dance temples include **Airport** (☎ 237 71), which throbs with a mix of techno, house, blackbeat and disco; and **Soundpark Ost** (☎ 230 80), which has two rooms for dancing to a wild mix of musical styles and a third for resting eardrums. Take bus No 26 from the central bus station.

Also recommended:

Das Boot (☎ 593 53; Veitshöchheimer Strasse 14; ☾ Mon & Thu-Sat) Permanently moored party boat and a Würzburg institution, with a Thai restaurant, English bar and Machine Room dance area on board.

Zauberberg (☎ 329 2680; www.zauberberg.info; Veitshöchheimer Strasse 20; ☾ Thu-Sat) Nightclub beloved by locals for its summer beer garden, regular reggae nights and Moroccan tent chill-out area serving mint tea.

Getting There & Away

Trains frequently serve Bamberg (€14.20, one hour), Nuremberg (€14.40, 1¼ hours), Aschaffenburg (€12.90, 1¼ hours) and Rothenburg ob der Tauber (€9.70, 1¼ hours), which requires a change in Steinach.

The Romantic Road Europabus stops at the main bus station next to the Hauptbahnhof.

A central car-hire agency is **Europcar** (☎ 120 60; Bahnhofsplatz 5).

Getting Around

Würzburg is best seen on foot. Single bus or tram tickets in town are €1.40, with day passes costing €8.50. **Taxi** (☎ 194 10) flagfall is €2.50, with short distances (eg between the Hauptbahnhof and Altstadt) capped at this amount.

Bicycle hire shops include the **Fahrradstation** (☎ 574 45; fahrradstation-wuerzburg@freenet.de; Hauptbahnhof; per day €10; ☾ closed Sun & Mon). This company also allows you to cycle along the Romantic Road and send the bike back on the Europabus (the cost to do this from Füssen to Würzburg is €25).

FRANCONIAN WINE COUNTRY

Würzburg is at the centre of the Fränkisches Weinland (Franconian Wine Country), which is roughly hemmed in by three low mountain ranges: the Spessart to the west, the Rhön to the north and the Steigerwald to the east. The Main River snakes through here on its 524km trip from the Fichtelgebirge to the Rhine at Mainz. Along the way, it passes by dozens of delightful villages seemingly lifted straight from a Grimm's fairy tale.

For visitors, there are lots of things to do involving the grape, including strolls through the vineyards, wine festivals or sampling the local crop right at a wine estate, with plenty of art and architecture fixes along the way.

We probably shouldn't encourage you to visit the region by car, but the fact is, if you intend to go to several villages, it is the easiest and most convenient way to travel. Public transportation is an option as long as you start in Würzburg, as connections between most villages are limited or nonexistent.

Sommerhausen

☎ 09333 / pop 1700

An almost Gallic charm prevails in this tiny, romantic wine village, whose cobbled streets lead right into the vineyards. Artists continue to fall in love with this place; you can see their work exhibited in several galleries around town. It's the birthplace, in 1651, of the first German immigrant to enter the US, Franz Daniel Pastorius.

There's a **tourist office** (☎ /fax 8256; Hauptstrasse 15; ☾ 9am-noon Mon & Wed-Fri). Otherwise, the **Landhaus Kunstgewerbe** (☎ 1061; Jahnstrasse 11; ☾ 10am-1pm & 2-7pm Mon-Sat) also has some information.

Other worthwhile sights include a 15th-century castle, a step-gabled town hall and a church, as well as Germany's smallest theatre, the **Torturmtheater** (☎ 268; Torturm), which is inside a tiny tower above the town wall and has just 50 seats. It was founded in 1946 by Luigi Malipiero, an Italian painter and set designer, and still enjoys a cult following for its cleverly staged productions.

Sommerhausen's stock in trade is, of course, its excellent wines. Twelve estates offer tastings, although by prior arrangement only. These include **Weingut Artur**

FRANCONIA

Steinmann (☎ 904 60; Am Plan 4), which charges €9 for five tastings and €17 for eight accompanied by a hearty *Brotzeit*. **Weinbau Wagner** (☎ 431; Sonnenhof) charges €11 for five tastings and €14 for eight with *Brotzeit*.

The olde-worlde **Weinhaus Düll** (☎ 220; www.weinhaus-duell.de in German; Maingasse 5; r €56-60; meals €7-14; ☺ restaurant from 5pm Mon-Fri, 11.30am Sat & Sun) inn is a charming overnight option with lovingly decorated rooms including private bathrooms and TVs. The restaurant has lots of fresh and seasonal fare, including game, as well as quite a few vegetarian selections. A speciality is sauerkraut soup.

Sommerhausen is served by bus No 8066 from Würzburg's central bus station (30 minutes). It's on the B13, about 15km south of Würzburg.

Sulzfeld
☎ 09321 / pop 1250
Sulzfeld, with its quiet, cobbled lanes, feels far removed from the hubbub of modern life. Hugging a bank of the Main, it hasn't grown much beyond the perimeter of its completely preserved medieval wall, which runs for 900m and is fortified by 18 towers. Access is through three picturesque gates.

A good place to soak up the atmosphere is on Marktplatz, dominated by the three-storey gabled **Rathaus** (1609). Built at the instigation of Prince-Bishop Julius Echter, its impressive size was a demonstration of the superior wealth of the Würzburg bishopric over its Protestant rivals, the margraves of Ansbach. The ornate **St Mary's Column** has anchored the square since 1724.

Many of the Altstadt's houses are decorated with ornate sculptures. Various saints and the Madonna with child are popular motifs; there's an especially neat Trinity where Klostergasse meets Friesengasse.

The town is famous for its *Meterbratwurst*, which is 100cm of sausage curled up like a pretzel. The Gasthaus zum Goldenen Löwen at the Markt claims to have invented it, but other places in town do just as good a job. With salad, the whole thing usually costs around €11; half metres are €6 to €7.

An enjoyable place to stop for the night is the 15th-century, half-timbered inn, **Gasthaus zum Stern** (☎ 133 50; www.stern-sulzfeld.de in German; Pointgasse 5; s €24-36, d €50-60), where the owners make their own wine served in the pretty beer garden or hearty Franconian restaurant.

To get to Sulzfeld by public transport catch one of the three weekday buses (No 8112) in Kitzingen, which is served by trains from Würzburg and Iphofen. Sulzfeld is about 24km southeast of Würzburg and 3km south of Kitzingen, the wine country's administrative centre, which is on the B8; from here follow the signs to Sulzfeld.

Iphofen
☎ 09323 / pop 4500
East of the Main, Iphofen has preserved a medieval flair largely because of its nearly intact towered and gated town wall. Some of the best Franconian wines grow nearby, including the famous Julius-Echter-Berg.

Iphofen's train station is south of the Altstadt. The **tourist office** (☎ 870 306; www.iphofen.de in German; Kirchplatz 7; ☺ 10am-6pm Mon-Fri, 10am-2pm Sat) is just north of the central Marktplatz.

SIGHTS
The tourist office adjoins the stainless-steel and glass **Vinothek Iphofen** (☎ 870 317; Kirchplatz 7; ☺ 11am-6pm Tue-Fri, 11am-5pm Sat & Sat), where you can sample and buy superior wines produced by 21 local vintners. Tastings start at €1.50 per 100mL.

The interior of Iphofen's parish church, the **St-Veits-Kirche**, is bathed in yellow and white hues, enhanced by the luminous stained-glass windows. Art treasures include a Madonna and sculptures of John the Baptist and the apostle John, which are (inconclusively) ascribed to Riemenschneider.

Take a stroll around the church to the landmark **Rödelseer Tor** (1456), a begging-to-be-photographed half-timbered town gate topped by a steep red-tile roof.

On the north side of Markt is the **Rathaus**, a baroque confection from 1716 with a double staircase typical of this region. South of the square, a 17th-century palace houses the **Knauf-Museum** (☎ 315 28; Am Marktplatz; admission €2; ☺ 10am-noon & 2-5pm Tue-Sat, 2-6pm Sun mid-Mar–Oct). Sponsored by the main local employer, the gypsum factory Knauf, it has 20 rooms filled with replica plaster casts of famous reliefs from such ancient cultures as Egypt, Mesopotamia, Rome and Persia.

SLEEPING & EATING
Hotel & Restaurant Zehntkeller (☎ 8440; www.zehntkeller.de in German; Bahnhofstrasse 12; s €65-85,

d €98-126; meals €15-30; P ⊡) Iphofen's most historic abode was once an administrative building for Würzburg's prince-bishops. Today it's a favourite weekend escape for Würzburgers, offering traditional but classy rooms and superior modern international cuisine.

Huhn – Das Kleine Hotel (☎ 1246; hotel-huhn@t -online.de; Mainbernheimer Strasse 10; s €52, d €72; P) About 300m west of the Altstadt, this hospitable place offers romantically furnished rooms with all amenities including TVs and telephones.

Right on Markt, **Café Dill** (☎ 870 413; Marktplatz; dishes €2-5.20) serves homemade soups, salads, and pastas in a snazzy contemporary setting.

GETTING THERE & AWAY

Regional trains from Würzburg (€5.70, 25 minutes) run hourly. Iphofen is on the B8, about 30km southeast of Würzburg. Bikes can be hired at **Zweirad-Hermann** (☎ 3331; Bahnhofstrasse 36; per day €6).

Prichsenstadt

☎ 09383 / pop 3200

On the western edge of the Steigerwald forest, Prichsenstadt is one of the jewels of Old Franconia, as yet undiscovered by mass tourism and imbued with a dreamy, unspoilt quality. Half-timbered and baroque houses line its little lanes, with ancient inns beckoning you to enjoy a glass of crisp white wine. The nicest way to enter is via the twin-turreted western gate.

The **tourist office** (☎ 975 00; Karlsplatz 5; 8am-noon Mon, Tue, Thu & Fri, 4-6pm Wed) is in the Rathaus.

A town oddity is Hans Klein's private **Mineral & Fossil Museum** (☎ 7008; Schulinstrasse 28; admission free; 9am-6pm). Displayed in his courtyard is an amazingly quirky array of stuff ranging from geodes to dinosaur teeth. Klein is not always around, but you're welcome to browse and leave money on the honour system if you decide to buy something.

If you want to spend the night, try **Alte Schmiede** (☎ 972 20; fax 972 249; Karlsplatz 7; s/d €30/50; meals €4.50-10), a 12th-century former blacksmith's forgery that lays claim as Prichsenstadt's oldest building. Its cosy restaurant dishes up honest-to-goodness mains such as roast duck with dumplings

and stuffed cabbage rolls. A wooden fish dangling by the door means that fresh carp or trout is on the menu, and it also has scrummy *Kuchen* (cake).

Nondrivers coming from Würzburg should take the regional train to Kitzingen, then change to bus No 8150. Prichsenstadt is about 40km east of Würzburg and about 50km west of Bamberg, on the B286 just north of the A3.

ASCHAFFENBURG

☎ 06021 / pop 69,000

This charming city of cobbled lanes and half-timbered houses makes a good day trip from Würzburg or Frankfurt. Its proximity to the latter means, in both appearance and mentality, it's more Hessian than Bavarian. Ludwig I, who took a liking to the place, nicknamed it his 'Bavarian Nice', an allusion to the Mediterranean microclimate here that allows the growth of figs and lemons.

The **tourist office** (☎ 395 800; www.info-aschaffen burg.de in German; Schlossplatz 1; 9am-5pm Mon-Fri, 10am-1pm Sat) runs 90-minute guided walks in German (€3.50) on Sunday at 2pm through the Altstadt from April to October, and through the castle from November to March.

Aschaffenburg's most spectacular draw is the magnificent Renaissance **Schloss Johannisburg**, the summer residence of the Mainz archbishops. Today it is home to the **Schlossmuseum** (☎ 386 570; Schlossplatz 4; adult/concession €4/3, combination ticket with Pompejanum €6/5; 9am-6pm Apr-Sep, 10am-4pm Oct-Mar, closed Mon). The modest interior has plenty of oil paintings and period furniture, but the true highlight is the stunning collection of architectural cork models depicting landmarks from ancient Rome.

Behind the beautiful palace garden is the **Pompejanum** (☎ 218 012; adult/child under 15 €4/free; 9am-6pm Tue-Sun Apr–mid-Oct). Built for King Ludwig I, this replica of a Pompeii villa is complete with frescoes, mosaics and Roman antiquities.

On Stiftsplatz you'll come upon the **Stiftskirche**, with origins in the 10th century but now an oddly skewed but impressive mix of Romanesque, Gothic and baroque styles. The attached **Stiftsmuseum** (☎ 444 7950; adult/concession €2.50/1.50; 11am-5pm Tue-Sun) is home to some intriguing relics and paintings.

FRANCONIA

Three kilometres west of town lies **Park Schönbusch**, a shady 18th-century expanse dotted with ornamental ponds and follies, and the **Schlösschen** (☎ 873 08; Kleine Schönbusch-allee 1; tour adult/concession €3/2; ⏰ tours in German hourly 9am-6pm Tue-Sun Apr-Sep), a country retreat of the archbishops.

Wholehearted Franconian fare can be found at the tiny **Schlossgass' 16** (☎ 123 13; Schlossgasse 16; mains €8-13) wine tavern, and **Wirtshaus Zum Fegerer** (☎ 156 46; Schlossgasse 14; mains €8-15), an inviting traditional inn.

Trains from Würzburg (€12.90, 1¼ hours) and Frankfurt (€13.60, 40 minutes) operate at least hourly. The A3 autobahn runs right past town.

NORTHERN ROMANTIC ROAD

The Northern Romantic Road starts in Würzburg (p216) and travels south through the Liebliches Taubertal (Tauber Valley), weaving in and out of the neighbouring state of Baden-Württemberg, while remaining within the historical boundaries of Franconia. It continues south via Rothenburg ob der Tauber and Dinkelsbühl. See p256 for the southern section starting in Nördlingen.

South of Würzburg, the Romantic Road plunges into the Liebliches Taubertal, a heavenly valley carved by the placid Tauber River.

Bad Mergentheim

☎ 07931 / pop 22,000 / elev 210m

Bad Mergentheim's history is inextricably tied to two things: its underground springs and the order of the Teutonic Knights. Evidence suggests that Stone Age and Celtic tribes enjoyed the local salt springs, which then somehow dropped from the radar screen for nearly two millennia. In 1826, a shepherd rediscovered them quite by accident, and their healing qualities have since turned Bad Mergentheim into a thriving spa town.

It's a departure from its earlier incarnation as the seat of the order of the Teutonic Knights, a Europe-wide military and religious order founded during the Third Crusade in 1191. The first knights settled in Mergentheim at the invitation of the local rulers the count of Hohenlohe, in 1219. After wrangling the town rights from Ludwig the Bavarian in 1340, the knights governed the town unchallenged and signif-

icantly advanced its infrastructure. In 1525, the order lost its Prussian territories after the leader, Albrecht von Hohenzollern, converted to Protestantism. The remaining Catholics, led by Walther von Cronberg, consolidated in Mergentheim where the order remained until dispossessed by Napoleon in 1809. It continues to exist today in Austria, ostensibly as a charity.

ORIENTATION & INFORMATION

The Tauber River divides Bad Mergentheim's peaceful spa centre on the northern bank from the bustling medieval Altstadt, where you'll find the **tourist office** (☎ 571 31; www.bad-mergentheim.de in German; Marktplatz 3; ⏰ 9am-5pm Mon-Fri, 10am-4pm Sat Apr-Oct, 9am-noon & 2.30-5pm Mon-Fri, 10am-2pm Sun Nov-Mar).

SIGHTS

The town's heart beats on Marktplatz, where many stately half-timbered and gabled town houses still reflect its medieval heyday. The knight balancing atop the octagonal fountain is Teutonic Grand Master Wolfgang Schutzbar, on whose watch the freestanding **Renaissance Rathaus** (1564), on the square's southern end, was built. Behind the Rathaus, the Gothic **Marienkirche** has some nifty medieval frescoes and also the bronze epitaph to Grand Master Walther von Cronberg by Hans Vischer.

East of the Marktplatz, via Burgstrasse, is the **Deutschordenschloss**, the former residence of the grand masters. The corner towers have impressive Renaissance spiral staircases, especially the so-called Berwarttreppe in the lobby of the **Deutschordensmuseum** (☎ 522 12; Schloss 16; adult/concession €3.50/2.50; ⏰ 10.30am-5pm Tue-Sun Apr-Oct, 2-5pm Tue-Sat, 10.30am-5pm Sun Nov-Mar). Exhibits here are rather eclectic, ranging from an overview of the Teutonic order to local history and 19th-century dolls houses. A tour of the lavish state rooms includes the early neoclassical **Kapitelsaal** (Chapter Hall) with its coffered ceiling. Several grand masters are buried in the baroque **Schlosskirche**, with design contributions by Balthasar Neumann and François Cuvilliés.

SLEEPING & EATING

Gasthof Johanniter (☎ 7502; fax 7927; Deutschorden-platz 5; s/d €32/52; meals €7-14.50; ⏰ restaurant closed Mon) Directly opposite the Schloss, this quintessential German guesthouse is the

---

TRAVELLING THE ROMANTIC ROAD

Train and bus are viable means of transport if you want to see short segments of the Romantic Road, but you'll find them complicated, tedious and slow for covering the entire route.

For flexibility and convenience, the ideal way to explore the Romantic Road in depth is, of course, by car (just follow the brown-and-white 'Romantische Strasse' signs).

If you'd rather let someone else do the driving, from April to October the **Deutsche Touring Europabus** (☎ 069-790 30; www.deutsche-touring.com) runs one coach daily in each direction between Frankfurt and Füssen, with short stops in nearly all towns and villages along the way. Buses leave at 8am daily from the train stations in either town and take about 12 hours to complete the route nonstop.

You can break the journey as often as you like, but plan your stops carefully as you'll have to wait a full day for the next bus to come around (reserve a seat before disembarking). Tickets are available either for the entire distance or for shorter segments between any of the stops.

Tickets for the entire route one-way/return cost around €74/€103. Sample fares for segments include: Würzburg–Rothenburg €17/€24, Rothenburg–Füssen €41/€57, Rothenburg–Munich €34/€47, and Frankfurt–Munich €67/€94. Eurail and German Rail pass holders get a 60% discount; InterRail pass holders, seniors and children aged four to 12 pay half price; students and those under 27 qualify for 10% off. If you want to take your bicycle, you'll need to make a reservation at least three days before the date of travel by calling ☎ 069-790 350. The cost is €6 for journeys of up to 12 stops or €12 for longer trips.

Tickets are available online at www.touring-germany.com or the **Frankfurt Hauptbahnhof** (Mannheimer Strasse 15, use the south exit) as well as at many travel agencies, railway stations and **EurAide** (☎ 089-593 889; euraide@compuserve.com) at the Munich Hauptbahnhof. Deutsche Touring can also assist with route planning and book accommodation. Packages are available at www .touring-germany.com; follow the links to independent tours.

The Romantic Road is heady in summer, but the cooler months have their own allure: toasty open fires, misty valleys, snow-capped villages and peaks, and best of all, few, if any, crowds. Prices are often significantly cheaper at this time. Make sure your vehicle is fitted with winter or all-season tyres if you're driving. If you don't have your own wheels, Rothenburg-based **TooT Tours** (☎ 07958-311; www.toot-tours.com) can create customised itineraries for one to seven people year-round, with flexible start and end points. Expert English-speaking local guides provide in-depth commentary, and arrange accommodation to fit your budget for multiday trips.

With its gentle gradients and ever-changing scenery, the Romantic Road makes an ideal bike trip. Tourist offices keep lists of 'bicycle-friendly hotels' and have information about public storage facilities.

The English-language website www.romantischestrasse.de is also an excellent source of information for planning a romantic road trip.

---

best value in town. Equally good value is the restaurant where the house speciality is roast beef with homemade pasta and salad; vegetarians are also well catered for.

Hotel Deutschmeister (☎ 9620; www.hotel-deutsch meister.de in German; Ochsengasse 7; s/d €43/74; meals €6-15; ⓧ restaurant closed Mon; ⊠) Just off Marktplatz, this is a traditional favourite with a good restaurant that's known for its seafood dishes. Rooms are unadorned but well equipped.

Schurk Markelsheim (☎ 2132; Hauptstrasse 57; mains €8.50-16.50; ⓧ from 5pm Mon-Sat, from 11.30am Sun) Six kilometres southwest of Bad Mergentheim, in the suburb of Markelsheim along the Romantic Road, this enchanting restaurant is well worth the drive (or seven-minute train trip). Under a vine-covered winter-garden roof strung with fairy lights, elegantly prepared dishes include herb-crusted escalope of turkey with noodles in cream sauce and fresh regional vegetables, and a trilogy of fish with lobster sauce, accompanied by a superb selection of wines.

GETTING THERE & AWAY

Regional trains connect Bad Mergentheim with Würzburg (€8.70, 55 minutes) and with Weikersheim (€4.20, 15 minutes) every two hours. The Europabus stops at the car park Altstadt-Mitte.

Bad Mergentheim is 49km south of Würzburg on the B290 (Romantic Road).

Weikersheim

☎ 07934 / pop 7555 / elev 227m

Weikersheim is the ancestral home and former residence of the counts and princes of Hohenlohe, a Franconian dynasty from the 12th century. It's a tranquil little town with what action there is centred on the recently restored Marktplatz. Here you'll find the church, the Rathaus, the **tourist office** (☎ 102; www.weikersheim.de in German; Ⓨ 9am-5.30pm Mon-Fri) and several hotels and restaurants.

Announcing its presence with a crest-festooned gate and onion-domed church steeple is the stunning **Schloss Weikersheim** (☎ 992 950; adult/concession €4.50/2.50; Ⓨ 9am-6pm Apr-Oct, 10am-noon & 1.30-4.30pm Nov-Mar). Exquisitely furnished in 16th- and 18th-century furniture, it's backed by an even more impressive symmetrical baroque garden.

After the last of the local Hohenlohes died childless in the 18th century, the palace was pretty much frozen in time. The furniture, wall coverings and artworks are all original. Highlights of the one-hour tour include the **Chinesisches Spiegelkabinett** (Chinese Mirror Cabinet) teeming with hundreds of Oriental figurines, and the **Rittersaal** (Knights' Hall). This tall banqueting hall pays homage to the family's favourite pastime: the hunt. The coffered ceiling shows hunting scenes, while a menagerie of stucco animals – deer, boar and even a badly proportioned elephant (the artist had never seen one in real life) – inhabits the walls.

The palace's upper-storey windows gaze out over the gardens, whose expansiveness culminates in an arcaded **Orangerie**. About 50 sculptures enliven the park, but the highlight is the whimsical **Zwergengallerie** (Gnome Gallery).

The castle can only be seen by guided tour in German, but ask to be lent an English-language leaflet for an overview of the rooms. Tours commence on the hour. Admission also entitles you to peruse the **Alchemie-Ausstellung** (Alchemy Exhibition) in the former palace kitchen. Palace builder Count Wolfgang II dabbled in the wondrous pseudo-science of alchemy and his story, ideas and experiments are given centre stage here.

Within the grounds, the castle has its own **winery** (☎ 298; Ⓨ 8am-noon & 1-5pm Mon-Fri year-round, 10-3pm Sat Apr-Oct) overlooking the bottling cellar, with tastings from €5.

The refined **Hotel Laurentius** (☎ 910 80; www.hotel-laurentius.de in German; Marktplatz 5; s €54-62, d €90-98; meals €7-20; Ⓨ restaurant Wed-Sun) also gets a gong for its gourmet restaurant with vaulted ceiling. Smaller meals such as pastas are served in the brasserie. The family also operates a nearby guesthouse (single rooms cost €30 and doubles €55).

Regional trains from Bad Mergentheim (€4.20, 15 minutes) come through every two hours. Bus No 7883 runs to Creglingen more or less hourly (15 minutes). The Europabus stops at Marktplatz.

Weikersheim is about 13km due east of Bad Mergentheim on the Romantic Road.

Creglingen

☎ 07933 / pop 5000 / elev 270m

The main reason people stop in Creglingen is to view Tilman Riemenschneider's exquisite carved limewood Marienaltar in the **Hergottskirche** (☎ 338; Kirchplatz 2; adult/concession €1.50/1; Ⓨ 9.15am-5.30pm Apr-Oct, 10am-noon & 1-4pm Tue-Sun Nov-Mar), built in 1389. In 1384, a local ploughman found a 'sacred host' in his field, a 'miracle' that inspired the local rulers, the counts of Hohenlohe, to sponsor a church on the site. More than 100 years later, Riemenschneider created his filigreed, unpainted masterpiece, which is a glorification of the Virgin Mary. Stashed away during the Reformation, the altar was still in mint condition when rediscovered in the 19th century.

Some of the finest work is in the predella (bottom portion), where some believe Riemenschneider has immortalised himself in the right scene showing Jesus in the temple surrounded by the scribes (he's purportedly the central figure in the group on the right). The church also contains several other altars, which are lengthily described in the leaflet (also in English) you'll get with admission.

Across the street from the church is the quirky **Fingerhutmuseum** (Thimble Museum; ☎ 370; Kohlesmühle; adult/concession €1.50/.50; Ⓨ 10am-12.30pm & 2-5pm Apr-Oct, 1-4pm Nov-Mar). Master thimblemaker Thorvald Greif presides over a priceless collection of more than 3000 of these diminutive sewing aids.

A PUB WITHOUT BORDERS

Along the Romantic Road, about 7km after you leave Creglingen and 13km before arriving in Rothenburg ob der Tauber, is **Holdermüle** (☎ 07933-912317; Archshofen 108; mains around €6.50; ☿ closed Nov–week before Easter), a quaint-as-it-gets pub divided by the Bavaria/Baden-Württemberg state border, which literally runs right through the middle of the building.

Tables in Bavaria (on the eastern side) have the state's blue and white colours on the tablecloths; Baden-Württemberg's tablecloths, on the western side of the room, are its state's yellow and black.

The hearty menu, which includes superb homemade soups, uses both states' produce. As for the opening hours, according to the owners, 'if cyclists show up at 9am they'll get a drink; closing is when the last guest leaves'.

Some are true pieces of art and highly valuable, especially those made of gold, silver or hand-painted fine porcelain. One of the most precious is 2500 years old and made of bronze.

The church and Fingerhutmuseum are both about 600m south of the village centre where the **Jüdisches Museum** (Jewish Museum; ☎ 7010; Badgasse 3; admission by donation; ☿ 2-5pm Sun) opened in November 2004. Incorporating English labelling and multimedia displays, the museum's permanent exhibition, *Roots and Destinations*, interprets the Jews' life both within the district and after they left. The museum and its collections were largely donated by American Arthur Obermayer, whose ancestors first lived in this same house 11 generations ago.

Also in the village centre, the **Lindleinturm-Museum** (☎ 7237; Stadtgraben 12; admission free; ☿ 10am-noon Fri, 10am-noon & 2-5pm Sat & Sun Apr-Oct & year-round by appointment) takes the cake for the most bizarre museum. This tower, once part of the medieval town fortifications, was the tiny home of Margarete Böttiger, a crotchety woman who bought the place in 1927 and lived here until shortly before her death in 1995 at age 98.

A servant, Margarete remained unmarried, preferring the company of felines, which is why locals called the tower 'Katzenturm' (Cat Tower), a term she so detested that she sought legal prevention for a huge sum against its use by the local authorities, even from beyond her grave. Modern technology, even central heating and hot water, were anathema to her. A lasting legacy: she decreed that her tower be turned into a museum – sort of a shrine to herself – and bequeathed most of her life savings to the town for its upkeep.

Creglingen is also the home of Capelle, makers of the medieval-style clothes worn by Germany's craftsmen *auf der walz* (on the walk), who spend three years and one day travelling the country and the world to perfect their trade to a high standard, a tradition that endures today.

The **tourist office** (☎ 631; www.creglingen.de in German; Bad Mergentheimer Strasse 14), northwest of the town centre, can help with finding a place to stay, including an apartment larger and infinitely more modern than Margarete Böttiger's also located within the town wall towers (€40 for two to six people).

Bus No 7883 makes the trip out to Weikersheim about hourly (15 minutes), but getting to Rothenburg is a veritable odyssey with multiple changeovers. The Europabus makes a 15-minute stop right at the Hergottskirche. Creglingen is 13km west of Weikersheim and 20km northwest of Rothenburg ob der Tauber.

Rothenburg ob der Tauber

☎ 09861 / pop 12,000 / elev 425m

A well-polished gem from the Middle Ages, Rothenburg ob der Tauber (above the Tauber River) is the main tourist stop along the northern Romantic Road. With its web of cobbled lanes hugged by higgledy-piggledy houses and encircled by towered walls, it's almost impossibly charming. At times, though, it can feel a bit like a medieval theme park. In summer and during the Christmas season especially, Rothenburg gets uncomfortably crowded with day-trippers (an estimated 2 million per year) clogging the narrow streets.

Rothenburg is at its most romantic when the yellow lamplight casts its spell long after the last tour buses have left.

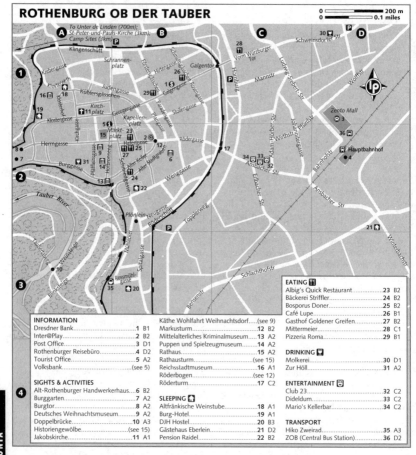

ROTHENBURG OB DER TAUBER

HISTORY

The recorded history of Rothenburg begins in 970 with the construction of a castle at the southern end of what is now the Spital quarter. In the 12th century, the town was brought under the control of the Hohenstaufen dynasty, which built another castle in 1142 and obtained town rights in 1172, which allowed them to build the fortifications. In 1274, Rothenburg became a Free Imperial City but suffered serious setbacks after an earthquake in 1356. During the Peasants' War, the town sided with Florian Geyer, the leader of the ultimately unsuccessful uprising. The town was besieged during the Thirty Years' War (1618–48), and in 1802 it became part of Bavaria. In

WWII, the Allies had slated Rothenburg for the same consummate bombing as neighbouring towns, but an American general in love with the town ultimately prevented its complete destruction.

ORIENTATION

Rothenburg is surrounded by an intact 3.5km-long town wall of which 2.5km are walkable. From the Bahnhof it's a five- to 10-minute walk west along Ansbacher Strasse to the Rödertor, one of the main entrance gates to the Altstadt (you'll find a large city map at the platform when you get off the train). From here, Rödergasse, then Hafengasse, lead straight to Marktplatz, the central square. The main shopping drag is Schmiedgasse, which runs south from Marktplatz to the Plönlein, a scenic fork in the road anchored by an ochre-yellows half-timbered cottage and fountain that's become Rothenburg's unofficial emblem.

INFORMATION

Dresdner Bank (Galgengasse 23)

Inter@Play (☎ 933 5599; Milchmarkt 3; per 20/60min €1/3; 8am-2am Sun-Thu, to 3am Fri & Sat)

KL Foto-Galerie (☎ 862 66; Rödergasse 11) Basic postal services.

Post office (Zentro Mall, Bahnhofstrasse 15) Opposite the Bahnhof.

Rothenburger Reisebüro (☎ 4611) This place in the train station books Europabus and train transport.

Tourist office (☎ 404 800, 24hr room referral hotline ☎ 194 12; www.rothenburg.de in German; Marktplatz 2; 9am-noon & 1-6pm Mon-Fri, 10am-3pm Sat & Sun May-Oct, 9am-noon & 1-5pm Mon-Fri, 10am-1pm Sat Nov-Apr) There are some leaflets and an electronic room-reservation board in the foyer, which is always open.

Volksbank (Marktplatz) Just to the right of the tourist office with an ATM.

SIGHTS

The **Rathaus** on the Marktplatz was built in Gothic style during the 14th century but was partly reconstructed during the Renaissance after half was ravaged by fire. The 220-step viewing platform of the **Rathausturm** (Town Hall Tower; ☎ 404 39; adult/concession €1/.50; 9.30am-12.30pm & 1.30-5.30pm Apr-Oct, noon-3pm Dec) provides majestic views over the town and the Tauber Valley. Below the Rathaus, the

subterranean prison and torture room at the **Historiengewölbe** (Historical Vaults; ☎ 867 51; adult/concession €2/1.50; 9.30am-5.30pm Apr-Oct, 1-4pm Dec) are creepy enough to get under your skin.

North of the Marktplatz is the **Jakobskirche** (Gothic Church of St Jacob; ☎ 700 620; Klostergasse 15; adult/concession €1.50/0.50; 9am-5.15pm Apr-Oct, 10am-5pm Dec, 10am-noon & 2-4pm Nov & Jan-Mar), with glorious 14th-century stained-glass windows. The church's *pièce de résistance* is the carved **Heilig Blut Altar** (Sacred Blood Altar), created by Tilman Riemenschneider, on a raised platform at the western end of the main nave. Rothenburg's town council commissioned the work in 1499 to find a suitably grand setting for its treasured reliquary: a capsule made of rock crystal said to contain three drops of Christ's blood. It is integrated within the gilded cross above the main scene, which depicts the Last Supper, unusually with Judas at the centre, receiving bread from Christ.

A short walk northwest of the Jakobskirche is this former Dominican convent turned **Reichsstadtmuseum** (Imperial City Museum; ☎ 939 043; Klosterhof 5; adult/concession €3/2; 10am-5pm Apr-Oct, 1-4pm Nov-Mar). The historical beamed rooms where the nuns used to eat, sleep and work now showcase local art, culture and history. Highlights include the superb *Rothenburger Passion* (1494), a cycle of 12 panels by Martinus Schwarz, and the oldest convent kitchen in Germany, as well as the recently acquired Baumann collection

---

DRINK & YE SHALL BE FREE

The year is 1631. The Thirty Years' War – pitching Catholics against Protestants – has been raging for 13 years, finally reaching the gates of Rothenburg ob der Tauber. Catholic General Tilly and 60,000 of his troops have besieged the Protestant market town, demanding its surrender. The town resists at first but eventually cannot stave off the onslaught of marauding soldiers. The mayor and other town dignitaries are captured and sentenced to death.

And that's pretty much where history ends and the legend of Meistertrunk begins.

As the tale goes, in an amazing display of chutzpah, Rothenburg's town council tries to sate Tilly's blood lust by proffering a 3.25L mug of wine. After a sip or two, Tilly challenges the men: 'If one of you has the courage to step forward and to down this mug of wine in one gulp, then I shall spare the town and the lives of the councilmen!' Mayor Georg Nusch accepts the challenge and – lo and behold – succeeds! And that's why you can still wander though Rothenburg's wonderful medieval lanes today. Or, so they say…

Of course, it's pretty much accepted that the wine legend is hooey, and that Tilly was placated with hard cash. Nevertheless, local poet Adam Hörber couldn't resist turning the tale into a play that since 1881, has been performed every Whitsuntide. It's also reenacted several times by the clock figures on the building housing the tourist office.

of superior quality weapons and armour. There's also a huge tankard holding 3.25L, once used to welcome official visitors; it inspired the legend of the Meistertrunk (see the boxed text on p231). The **Klostergarten** (Apr-Oct) behind the museum (enter from Klosterhof) is a quiet place to shake off the throngs.

The beautiful **Burggarten** (Castle Garden) occupies the site of the former Hohenstaufen castle of 1142, with panoramic views over the Tauber Valley. After an earthquake levelled the complex, only the **Blasiuskapelle** (Chapel of St Blaise) was rebuilt. Today it's a war memorial. To get to the park, you'll pass through the twin-turreted **Burgtor** (Castle Gate). Look up to see the ghoulish mask on the façade; wannabe attackers of the city were repelled by hot pitch poured through its mouth.

For more sweeping vistas, head east along Burggasse where you can also see the **Doppelbrücke**, a double-decker bridge ideal for watching the fireworks displays during the Reichsstadt-Festtage (right). Also visible is the head of a trail that leads down the valley and over to the pretty **St-Peter-und-Pauls-Kirche** in Detwang, which contains another stunning Riemenschneider altar.

Medieval justice was not for the squeamish, as you'll discover walking through the fascinating **Mittelalterliches Kriminalmuseum** (Medieval Crime Museum; ☎ 5359; Burggasse 3; adult/concession €3.50/2.30; 9.30am-6pm Apr-Oct, 2-4pm Nov & Jan-Mar, 1-4pm Dec). In addition to gruesome tools of torture and execution, this place documents legal history going back 1000 years, including famous criminal cases, legal proceedings in the Middle Ages, witch trials and so on. Display panels are in English.

Collector *extraordinaire*, Katharina Engels, has assembled an amazing range of dolls and toys at the **Puppen und Spielzeugmuseum** (Doll & Toy Museum; ☎ 7330; Hofbronnengasse 13; adult/concession €4/3.50; 9.30am-6pm Mar-Dec, 11am-5pm Jan & Feb). Teddy bears and wooden toys, carousels and marionette theatres, tin figurines and infinite dolls made of porcelain, paper, wood and wax, along with dolls houses, doll tea services, doll stores and more are traditionally displayed in glass cases and there's a 'dolled-up' shop in front.

German Christmas customs through the ages are on show at the **Deutsches Weihnachtmuseum** (German Christmas Museum;

☎ 409 365; Herrngasse 1; adult/concession €4/2.50; 10am-5.30pm Easter–mid-Jan, 10am-5.30pm Sat & Sun mid-Jan–Easter), operated by the Käthe Wohlfahrt emporium (p234). Many of the exhibits, including a great collection of nutcrackers, are donations or loans from private individuals.

Walking east of Marktplatz on Hafengasse leads you past the particularly scenic – and incessantly photographed – ensemble of the **Markusturm** (Marcus Tower) and the **Röderbogen** (Röder Arch).

Just south of here, down a little alley, is the **Alt-Rothenburger Handwerkerhaus** (Old Rothenburg's Artisans House; ☎ 942 80; Alter Stadtgraben 26; adult/concession €2.20/1.60; 11am-5pm Mon-Fri, 10am-5pm Sat & Sun Apr-Oct, 2-4pm Nov-7 Jan). Numerous artisans – including coopers, weavers, cobblers and potters – have had their workshops in this house during its 700-year existence. Because the last person to inhabit it had an apparent phobia of all things modern, preferring to live without running water or electricity, it offers a fairly authentic look at medieval living conditions.

Hafengasse turns into Rödergasse, which is punctuated by the **Röderturm**. It can be climbed for nice city views (admission is charged), though it's staffed by volunteers and not often open. At the top is a small photographic exhibit about the air raid on Rothenburg in 1945.

TOURS

The tourist office runs 90-minute English-language **walking tours** (ticket €4; 2pm Apr-Oct) from outside the Rathaus. **Private group tours** (☎ 07958-570) in English and German are also available. Also starting at the Rathaus, an atmospheric walking tour of the Altstadt is conducted every evening by the **Nachtwächter** (night watchman; tours English/German €4/3; tours English 7.55pm Apr-Dec; German 9.30pm Apr-Dec), dressed in traditional long black robes and toting a *Hellebarde* – a combined spear, hook and axe, from which dangles his candle-lantern.

FESTIVALS & EVENTS

The **Historisches Festspiel 'Der Meistertrunk'** (see the boxed text on p231) takes place around town each year on Whitsuntide. The festival features parades, dances and a medieval market. The highlight is the reenactment of the mythical Meistertrunk story in the

DAVID PEEVERS

Residenz (p218), Würzburg

Kaiserburg (p188), Nuremberg

ADINA TOVY AMSEL

MARK DAFFEY

Schloss Hohenschwangau (p262),
Füssen

Grounds of Schloss Linderhof (p132), near Ettal

ANDREW LUBRAN

Eibsee, Garmisch-Partenkirchen (p127)

Partnachklamm (p128), Garmisch-
Partenkirchen

Boating on the Königsee (p148),
Berchtesgaden

Kaisersaal (Emperor's Hall) of the Rathaus. Check with the tourist office on how to obtain tickets.

The play itself is also performed during the **Reichsstadt-Festtage** (Imperial City Festival) in early September, when the entire town's history is staged in the city streets; and twice more during the **Rothenburger Herbst**, a harvest celebration in October.

Featuring colourful dancing couples, the **Historischer Schäfertanz** (Historical Shepherds' Dance), takes places several times between April and October on Marktplatz.

Rothenburg is enchanting year-round, but perhaps never more so than during the **Christmas market**, held every December on the Marktplatz, when the brightly coloured stalls twinkle between the Rathaus and St Jakobskirche (see also p234).

Check with the tourist office for specific dates.

SLEEPING
Despite its popularity Rothenburg has surprisingly good-value accommodation.

Pension Raidel (☎ 3115; www.romanticroad.com/raidel; Wenggasse 3; s/d with bathroom €39/49, without bathroom €19/39; P) An utter delight, with 500-year-old exposed beams studded with wooden nails, quaint wallpapering and pastel sheets, and musical instruments for guests to play, this narrow half-timbered inn is right in the Altstadt. Rooms without their own bathroom have basins and the cosy breakfast room has an original copper boiler.

Burg-Hotel (☎ 948 90; www.burghotel.rothenburg.de; Klostergasse 1-3; s/d from €90/100; P ✗ 🖳) This intimate 15-room hotel is built right into the town fortifications. All rooms have private sitting areas and there's an elegant guest lounge with an antique baby grand piano, and a sun-drenched terrace overlooking the valley. If you're looking for a romantic getaway, this is it – the views are phenomenal.

Altfränkische Weinstube (☎ 6404; www.romanticroad.com/altfraenkische-weinstube; Klosterhof 7; s €48, d €55-65; meals €5.50-14.50; ✗) Tucked away in a quiet side street near the Reichsstadtmuseum, this enchanting inn has atmosphere-laden rooms all with bath tubs, and most with four-poster or canopied beds. At the restaurant guests are treated to romantic lighting and good-value regional food. The two-decades-old English Conversation Club – an ever-changing group of English-speaking visitors and locals headed by its charismatic founder 'Hermann the German' – meets here on Wednesday nights; everyone is welcome.

Gästehaus Eberlein (☎ 4672; www.eberlein.rothenburg.de; Winterbachstrasse 4; s €35-40, d €55-65; P ✗ 🖳) A familial atmosphere welcomes you at this modern-style inn, which is handily positioned behind the train station, and just off the A7 (from the Rothenburg exit, turn left at the first traffic lights, then left again). It's only a seven-minute walk into town. There's a pretty winter garden, and some rooms have telephones.

DJH hostel (☎ 941 60; www.djh.de in German; Mühlacker 1; dm €18.10-18.50, s €24.10-24.40, d €48.20-48.80; ✗ 🖳) Rothenburg's hostel is often heavily booked, frequently by rambunctious school groups. Occupying two enormous renovated old buildings – a former horse-powered mill and hospital – the rambling dining hall can also provide full board.

In the outlying town of Detwang, about 1.5km below the Altstadt, are two camp sites: the **Campingplatz Tauber-Idyll** (☎ 3177; Camping-Tauber-Idyll@t-online.de; Detwang 28; per tent/person €4.50/4; ✆ Easter-late Oct) and **Campingplatz Tauber-Romantik** (☎ 6191; info@camping-tauberromantik.de; Detwang 39; per tent/person €4.40/4; ✆ Easter-late Oct), which are both situated in an idyllic nature preserve on the Tauber River.

EATING
Restaurants
Café Lupe (☎ 875 117; Galgengasse 13; dishes €3.10-5.50; ✆ to 6pm Mon-Thu & Sun) With French-washed walls and glazed tiles, this unpretentious café is where locals come to escape the tourist crowds. It has a good variety of breakfast options and light meals such as filled baguettes, as well as excellent coffee.

Pizzeria Roma (☎ 4540; Galgengasse 19; dishes €5.50-9.50; ✆ Thu-Tue) In addition to piping-hot pizzas, this elongated eatery does some authentic Italian meat- and fish-based meals.

Gasthof Goldener Greifen (☎ 2281; Obere Schmiedgasse 5; dishes €6.30-13; ✆ closed Sun evening) Classic regional fare focussing on schnitzel, sausages and pork is dished up in this homey restaurant with heavy timber tables in the heart of the Altstadt, and the three-course special is fine value.

Unter den Linden (☎ 5909; Kurze Steige 1; meals €5-10; ✆ Easter-Oct) On the riverbank, this scenic beer garden has inexpensive meals and

FRANCONIA

FRANCONIA

THE AUTHOR'S CHOICE

Mittermeier (☎ 945 40; Vorm Würzburger Tor; mains €22-26) This classy establishment just outside the Würzburger gate serves high-quality, newly Michelin-starred cuisine in four settings: a buttercup-yellow à la carte restaurant, the ornately furnished German Room, the black-and-white tiled 'Temple', and a beautiful alfresco terrace. Artistic chefs use locally harvested produce, often grown specially, to create masterpieces such as a Tauber Forest saddle of venison with chanterelles, mango sauerkraut and handmade potato noodles. The 400-strong wine list is among the best in Franconia. If price is no object, consider spending the night in a sumptuous suite at the attached hotel (singles from €63, doubles from €70 and suites from €160).

---

local beer and is a favourite with cyclists. There's a kids' play area and a tepee bonfire when the autumn leaves start to fall. Be sure to try the homemade cheese.

Quick Eats

Bosporus Doner (Hafengasse 2; dishes €2.50-6) Delicious doner kebabs and other Middle Eastern goodies, including meat-free selections, can be eaten here or taken away.

Albig's Quick Restaurant (Hafengasse 3; dishes €1.50-6.50) This is a decent-priced trough, with half chickens, schnitzels, fries, burgers and other satisfying fare.

Bäckerei Striffler (☎ 6788; Untere Schmiedegasse 1) Rothenburg's enticing bakery windows are piled high with mountains of the town's pastry speciality, *Schneeballen* (snowballs) – dough ribbons loosely shaped into balls then deep-fried and dipped in cinnamon or powdered sugar. (Local tip: don't bite into one or you'll be wearing a small avalanche, instead smash it inside its paper bag and eat it in pieces.) Not only does this place make the best in town, but it also has a mouthwatering array of cakes.

DRINKING

Zur Höll (☎ 4229; Burggasse 8; dishes €3.10-14) If someone tells you to 'go to hell' in Rothenburg, consider it good advice. This wine tavern, in the town's oldest building (c 1100), plays on its name with all manner

of devil motifs, and there's a roaring open fire in winter. Franconian and international wines are served by the glass and bottle, and a selection of snacks and main dishes as well as a soup special are also available.

Molkerei (☎ 933 310; Schweinsdorfer Strasse 25b; ⊙ Wed-Sun) Updated industrial décor and cavernous open-plan spaces attract the young and hip at this reincarnated old dairy, with its cow-painted bathrooms and aluminium ceiling pipes. In summer there's a popular terrace, and the kitchen churns out great pizzas, pastas and steaks for the herds.

ENTERTAINMENT

Rothenburg is not exactly a party town but **Club 23** (☎ 3686; Ansbacherstrasse 1; ⊙ Thu-Sat), just outside the Rödertor near the Bahnhof, has been throwing dance parties since the disco era. In the same wedge of town, known by locals as the Bermuda Triangle, are several other late-night bars including the laid-back **Dideldum** (☎ 936 9369; Ansbacherstrasse 15e; ⊙ Wed-Mon), and **Mario's Kellerbar** (☎ 0173-167 0415; Ansbacherstrasse; ⊙ 7pm-5am), with amped up hip-hop.

SHOPPING

In keeping with the olde-worlde charm, a city ordinance requires all shop signs to be traditional wrought iron.

Käthe Wohlfahrt Weihnachtsdorf (☎ 4090; Herrngasse 1) Eternal Christmas reigns at this emporium, with its mind-boggling assortment of quality decorations, ornaments and souvenirs. Prices and visitor numbers are accordingly high, and during the Christmas market crush an entry fee of €1 is charged, which is refunded if you buy something (if you don't, it's donated to charity).

Though much frequented by tourists, the **Christmas market** is worth saving some luggage space for, with lots of traditional, often handcrafted items.

Kitchenware shops in the Altstadt also sell *Schneeballeneisen* (around €15) – long metal pincherlike contraptions for making your own snowballs at home.

GETTING THERE & AWAY

Rothenburg is on a branch line to Steinach, with hourly trains from 5am to 8pm. From Steinach there's frequent direct train service with Würzburg (€9.40, 1¼ hours). Travel from Munich (from €32, three hours) may require two or three changes in Steinach, Treuchtlingen, and in some cases Augsburg. The Europabus stops at the train station.

Rothenburg has its own exit off the A7 between Würzburg and Ulm.

Designated cycle tracks are signposted along the Romantic Road. Coming from Creglingen, cyclists can follow the 'Liebliches Taubertal' bicycle track through the Tauber Valley; or the 'Altmühl' track from the Altmühltal Naturpark. Less known, but also well signposted is the 'Aischtal' bicycle track, which starts in Bamberg and wends here via Bad Windsheim.

GETTING AROUND

Rothenburg's Altstadt is closed to nonresident vehicles from 11am to 4pm and 7pm to 9am Monday to Friday and all day on weekends; hotel guests are exempt. Galgentor is the only gate that's always open.

There are five car parks just outside the northern, northeastern and southeastern walls. Of these, P5 and the lower part of P4 (both in the northeast) are free, while the upper part of P4 costs €2 all day; the others are more expensive. For a taxi call ☎ 7227; flagfall is €2.45.

Some hotels have bicycle hire, or you can try **Hiko Zweirad** (☎ 3495; Am Mühlacker; per half/full day €2.50/5).

If you want to go the whole romantic hog, horse-drawn carriage rides of 25 to 30 minutes through the city cost about €6 per person, but you can haggle for a better price with some drivers. You'll find them in the Altstadt, usually on Schrannenplatz or Marktplatz.

Around Rothenburg

BAD WINDSHEIM

In the delightful little town of Bad Windsheim, about 27km northeast of Rothenburg, the **Fränkisches Freilandmuseum** (☎ 09841-668 00; Eisweiherweg 1; adult/concession €4.50/3.50; 9am-6pm Tue-Sun mid-Mar–mid-Oct, 10am-5pm Tue-Sun mid-Oct–end Oct, 10am-4pm Nov–mid-Dec) is the largest open-air museum in Bavaria. Reassembled in this 45-hectare park are some 70 homes and farmhouses, most of them original, from different Franconian regions. Each one is a little mini-museum, providing insight into the changing social, cultural and religious customs and traditions from the 15th century to today. Pride of place goes to a group of medieval buildings including a thatched farmhouse from 1367.

From Rothenburg, take the A7 to the B470 east.

> **THE GREAT DIVIDE**
>
> Just a few hundred metres south of the Schillingfürst exit on the B25 (Romantic Road) you'll cross the **European Water Divide**, marked with a green sign by the roadside. Every single drop of rain that falls south of here flows into the Danube to the Black Sea; every drop that falls north flows to the Rhine and ultimately the North Sea.

SCHILLINGFÜRST

Worth a visit as you continue south from Rothenburg along the Romantic Road is the **Bayerischer Jagdfalkenhof** (☎ 09868-222; Schloss Schillingfürst, Am Wall; adult/concession €7/4; shows 11am & 3pm May-Sep, additional show 5pm May-Aug), a falconry filled with birds of prey set against the dramatic backdrop of a magnificent castle. Between March and October, flight shows allow you to see these prehistoric-like eagles, falcons, hawks and vultures respond to a series of signals to land directly on their trainer's hands.

From Rothenburg, follow the B25 for 10km, then follow the signs to your left.

Feuchtwangen

☎ 09852 / pop 12,700 / elev 450m

En route to Rothenburg or Dinkelsbühl, travellers often bypass Feuchtwangen (literal translation 'wet cheeks'), which is a shame because its historic Altstadt rewards a stop. Its Marktplatz is ringed by a harmonious ensemble of half-timbered and step-gabled town houses and anchored by the **Röhrenbrunnen** (1727), a pretty fountain guarded by a statue of Minerva. The **tourist office** (☎ 904 55; Marktplatz 1; 9am-6.30pm Mon-Fri 1-5pm, Sat & Sun May-Sep, 9am-5pm Mon-Fri Oct-Apr) is in the former town hall.

SIGHTS & ACTIVITIES

From the northern end of the Marktplatz, steps lead to a Romanesque **cloister**, site of the **Kreuzgangspiele**, a prestigious summer open-air theatre festival. The cloister is actually part of the **Stiftskirche** (13th to 14th centuries), a former monastery church with an eye-catching altar by Michael Wolgemut, a teacher of Albrecht Dürer. Next door, the **Johanniskirche** (1257) is also worth a look for its choir frescoes and baroque altar.

East of the Markt is the excellent **Frankenmuseum** (☎ 2575; Museumstrasse 19; adult/child €2/0.50; ☼ 10am-5pm Wed-Sun May-Sep, 2-5pm Mar-Apr & Oct-Dec). Baroque to late-19th-century rooms provide glimpses of life, while others feature often endearingly naive folk art and a precious collection of faïences.

The multistorey, glass monolith **Spielbank** (casino) is just off the A7 autobahn (exit 111).

GETTING THERE & AWAY

The Europabus stops at the Busbahnhof, the main bus station. Feuchtwangen is on the B25. It's best reached using your own wheels, as regional buses are infrequent and timetables complicated.

Dinkelsbühl

☎ 09851 / pop 11,700 / elev 442m

It's a pleasant walk of about an hour around Dinkelsbühl's fortified wall, its 18 towers and four gates. Situated on the Wörnitz River, Dinkelsbühl traces its roots to a royal residence founded by Carolingian kings in the 8th century. Located at the intersection of two major trade routes, the town rose to prominence in the Middle Ages, primarily as a centre of textile manufacturing. Dinkelsbühl was spared destruction both during the Thirty Years' War and WWII, leaving its lovely medieval Altstadt virtually intact.

ORIENTATION & INFORMATION

The Altstadt is five minutes' walk west of the Busbahnhof, via Wörnitzer Tor. The post office and police station are next to the Busbahnhof. The **tourist office** (☎ 902 40; www.dinkelsbuehl.de in German; Marktplatz; ☼ 9am-6pm Mon-Fri, 10am-4pm Sat, 10am-1pm Sun Apr-Oct, 9am-5pm Mon-Fri, 10am-1pm Sat Nov-Mar) is located on Marktplatz, also known as Weinmarkt, opposite the Münster St Georg; enter via Segringer Strasse.

SIGHTS

Weinmarkt, the main square, is lined by a row of picture-perfect Renaissance mansions in mint condition. The corner building is the step-gabled and turreted **Ratsherrntrinkstube**,

which once hosted Emperor Karl V and King Gustav Adolf of Sweden and is now home to the tourist office. While here, duck into the **Hetzelhof**, the picturesque courtyard of a patrician town house, which is entered via a narrow passageway on the opposite side of the street.

North of the Ratsherrntrinkstube is the broad-shouldered **Schranne**, a former granary. Look for a little box on its north wall; after 11pm two €2 coins will illuminate the town's most important landmarks for one hour.

Standing sentry over Weinmarkt is **Münster St Georg**, one of southern Germany's purest late-Gothic hall churches. It's filled with treasures such as the **Sebastiansaltar** (1520), donated by the archers' guild, which graphically depicts the martyrdom of St Sebastian (he was shot full of arrows). A curiosity is the so-called **'Pretzl Window'** donated by the bakers' guild; it forms the upper section of the last window in the right aisle.

If you follow Martin-Luther-Strasse north past the Schranne, you'll soon get to the **Spitalanlage**, founded in 1280 as a hospital and now a seniors' residence and home of the **Historisches Museum** (☎ 3293; Dr-Martin-Luther-Strasse 6b; adult/concession €3/1; ☼ 10am-4pm Tue-Sun). The church was added in 1380, but only some frescoes on the north wall survive from that period. The **Spitalhof** behind the complex is a pretty spot for a break.

Just outside the western town gate, the mind-bending **Museum of the 3rd Dimension** (☎ 6336; Nördlinger Tor; adult/concession €7/6; ☼ 10am-6pm Apr-Oct, 11am-4pm Sat & Sun Nov-Mar) is probably the first dedicated entirely to simulating acid trips. Inside are three floors of holographic images, stereoscopes and attention-grabbing 3-D imagery (especially in the nude section on the 3rd floor) and much, much more.

TOURS

One-hour **walking tours** (ticket €2.50; ☼ 2.30pm & 8.30pm Apr-Oct, 2.30pm Sat & Sun Nov-Mar) in German depart from the Münster St Georg. A night watchman takes visitors on a free German tour at 9pm from April to October (Saturday only November to March).

FESTIVALS & EVENTS

In the third week of July, Dinkelsbühl celebrates the 10-day **Kinderzeche** (Children's Festival), commemorating how, in the Thirty Years' War, the town's children persuaded the invading Swedish troops to spare the town from devastation. The festivities include a pageant, reenactments in the Stadtfestsaal, lots of music and other entertainment.

SLEEPING & EATING

Note that single private rooms in town are rare.

Goldenes Lamm (☎ 2267; www.goldenes .de; Lange Gasse 26-28; s €35-48, d €59-70; meals €5-20; ☺ restaurant closed Wed Oct-May; P ☒) An ancient wooden staircase leads up to the pleasant rooms, which are topped by a rooftop garden deck strewn with comfy armchairs. The attached restaurant and beer garden are local favourites.

Flair Hotel Weisses Ross (☎ 579 890; www.flairhotel .com/weissesross in German; Staingasse 12; s €46-63, d €64-99; meals €9.50-15.30) A gathering place for artists for over a century, this enchanting hotel has comfortable rooms and a gourmet restaurant with *Gemütlichkeit* (cosiness) galore.

DCC-Campingplatz Romantische Strasse (☎ 7817; www.campingpark-dinkelsbuehl.de; Kobeltsmühle 2; per tent €8.50, if arriving by bike €6, per person €4.70, if arriving by bike €3.20) This year-round campsite lies on a swimming lake about 300m northeast of Wörnitzer Tor.

Weib's Brauhaus (☎ 579 490; Untere Schmiedgasse 13; meals €2.40-10.90) A woman brew master presides over the copper vats at this lively restaurant-pub. Many dishes are made with the house brew, including the popular *Weib's Töpfle* ('woman's pot') of pork medallions and deep-fried mashed potato.

Café Extrablatt (☎ 2297; Weinmarkt 10; meals €3-10.80) With menus designed like newspapers, this trendy bistro bustles morning to night and serves big breakfasts, reams of regional fare and invigorating salads.

Deutsches Haus (☎ 6058; Weinmarkt 3; mains €7.50-17.50) If you look at this historic building from the Rothenburg gate at the north of the street its central windows appear straight, but when standing directly in front you'll see this is an illusion created by its 13th-century architects, and the façade is actually off-kilter. Inside, superbly painted ceilings and mahogany panelling crown this formal restaurant. Traditionally prepared game and fish are house specialities, though the vegetarian meals, like panfried potato and carrot with mushroom cream sauce, are limited in number but not in quality.

GETTING THERE & AROUND

Dinkelsbühl is not served by trains. Regional buses to Rothenburg (€5.50, one hour) and Nördlingen (€4.50, 40 minutes) stop at the Busbahnhof. The Europabus stops right in the Altstadt at Schweinemarkt.

The tourist office hires out bicycles for €3.60 per day or €15.35 per week. From Easter to October, the Altstadt is closed to vehicles from noon to 6pm Sunday.

NATURPARK ALTMÜHLTAL

The Naturpark Altmühltal (Altmühl Valley Nature Park) covers some of Bavaria's most gorgeous land. Meandering through little valleys is the Altmühl River, a gentle stream that morphs into the mighty Rhein-Main-Donau-Kanal (Rhine-Main-Danube-Canal; see the boxed text on p241) near Beilngries before emptying into the Danube at Kelheim. It's a region largely undiscovered by international travellers, who make up only 5% of all tourists here. The earliest 'visitors' were the Romans, whose empire's northern boundary – the Limes – ran right through today's park.

The main town and gateway for park excursions is Eichstätt. Within a picturesque valley, Eichstätt is home to the only Catholic university in Germany (since 1980 with 4500 students). Razed by the Swedes during the Thirty Years' War (1618–48), it was rebuilt by Italian architects, notably Gabriel de Gabrieli and Maurizio Pedetti, who imbued it with a Mediterranean flair.

You can explore the park on your own by car or via extremely well-marked hiking and cycling trails. Canoeing, for an hour or several days, is also popular.

Orientation

The park sprawls over 2900 sq km west of Regensburg (p158), south of the A6 autobahn, east of Gunzenhausen and north of Ingolstadt (p242). The A9 runs right through it north–south.

Eichstätt is somewhat south of the park's centre and home to the central information centre. Other larger towns include Gunzenhausen, Treuchtlingen, Weissenburg and Pappenheim west of Eichstätt and Beilngries, Riedenburg and Kelheim east of Eichstätt.

Information

Staff at the excellent **Informationszentrum Naturpark Altmühltal** (Altmühltal Nature Park information centre; ☎ 08421-987 60; www.naturpark-altmuehltal .de in German; Notre Dame 1, 85072 Eichstätt; ☑ 9am-5pm Mon-Sat, 10am-5pm Sun Easter-Oct, 9am-noon & 2-4pm Mon-Thu, 10am-noon Fri Nov-Easter) can put together an entire itinerary for free and send you (for face value) maps and charts of the area and information on bike, boat and car hire. They can also help you find accommodation, although they don't reserve rooms. Upstairs are exhibits about the park's wildlife and habitats and there's a re-creation of its landscapes in the garden.

Information is also available from local tourist offices in towns throughout the park.

Sights

EICHSTÄTT

The town centre is dominated by the richly adorned **Dom**. Stand-out features include an enormous stained-glass window by Hans Holbein the Elder; the Pappenheimer Altar (1489–97) carved from sandstone and depicting a pilgrimage from Pappenheim to Jerusalem; and the seated statue of St Willibald, the town's first bishop.

Behind the Dom is the baroque **Residenz** (Residenzplatz; admission €1; ☑ tours 11am & 3pm Mon-Thu, 11am Fri, 10.15am, 11am, 11.45am, 2pm, 2.45pm & 3.30pm Sat & Sun Apr-Oct), built between 1725 and 1736. It's a Gabrieli building and former prince-bishops' palace with a stunning main staircase and a Spiegelsaal (Games Room), with its mirrors and fresco of Greek mythology. In the square is a golden statue of Mary atop a 19m-high column.

The **Markt**, a baroque square north of the Dom, is the heart of the partly pedestrianised Altstadt. About 300m northwest of here, on Westenstrasse, is the **Kloster St Walburga**, the burial site of Willibald's sister and a pilgrimage site: every year between mid-October and late February, water oozes from Walburga's relics and drips down into a catchment. The nuns bottle diluted versions of this *Walburgaöl* (Walburga oil) and give it away to the faithful. The walls in the upper chapel are covered with beautiful *ex voto* tablets as thank yous to the saint.

Overlooking the town centre is the hilltop castle of **Willibaldsburg** (1355–1725),

home of the **Jura-Museum** (Jurassic Museum; ☎ 08421-4730; Burgstrasse 19; adult/concession for both museum and castle €4/3; ☑ 9am-6pm Tue-Sun Apr-Sep, 10am-4pm Tue-Sun Nov-Mar), which is great even if fossils usually don't quicken your pulse. Highlights are a locally found archaeopteryx and aquariums with living specimens of the same animal species that were fossilised eons ago. Also up here is the **Museum of Pre-History & Early History** (☎ 08421-894 50), where a 6000-year-old mammoth skeleton is a must-see.

Near the car park, the **Bastiongarten** (admission free; ☑ 9am-6pm Apr-Sep), a garden built onto the castle ramparts, is probably better known as the 'Garden at Eichstätt' (there's a hefty coffee-table book of the same name, with copper plates of the original plantings). Re-created in 1997, the garden was first established by the scientifically minded and status-craving Prince-Bishop Johann Konrad von Gemmingen in the early 17th century and featured rare-for-the-times specimens such as tulips.

Looking across the valley, you can make out the **limestone quarry** (adult/concession €2/1, chisel & hammer hire per day €1.50; ☑ 9.30am-6pm;) where you can dig for fossils. Drive up or take a bus from Domplatz (€1, 10 minutes). Bus times are irregular – check with the tourist office. At the base of the quarry is the **Museum Bergér** (☎ 08421-4683; Harthof; adult/ child €2/0.50; ☑ 1.30-5pm Mon-Sat, 10am-noon Sun Apr-Oct or by request), which displays geological samples.

In 2008, Eichstätt celebrates the 1100th anniversary of the year its bishops got the rights to build fortifications, hold markets, and mint their own coins.

The local **tourist office** (☎ 08421-988 00; www .eichstaett.de in German; Domplatz 8; ☑ 9am-6pm Mon-Sat, 10am-1pm Sun Apr-Oct, 10am-noon & 2-4pm Mon-Thu, to noon Fri Nov-Mar), next to the Dom, runs 1½-hour **walking tours** in German (€3) from April to October at 1.30pm Saturday (also Wednesday at 1.30pm in July and August, and Monday at 1.30 in August).

Eichstätt has two train stations. Mainline trains stop at the Bahnhof, 5km from the centre, from where diesel trains shuttle to the Stadtbahnhof (main train station; south of the Altmühl River near the city centre). From the Stadtbahnhof, Willibaldsburg is about 1km southwest up Burgstrasse.

RIEDENBURG

Riedenburg is the main town along the canalised Altmühl. It's known as the 'Three-Castle-Town', but two of the three, Tachenstein and Rabenstein, are all but ruins. Only **Burg Rosenburg** (☎ 09442-2752; ☺ 9am-5pm Tue-Sun Mar-Oct, shows 11am & 3pm Tue-Sun) lords over the town. Originally it was the dream castle of a medieval minstrel who also happened to be a falconer. Today, a falconer picks up the tradition with a flock of not just falcons, but also eagles, vultures and other birds of prey.

BURG PRUNN

It has been ceaselessly photographed and inspired many poets and painters, and for good reason: **Burg Prunn** (☎ 09442-3323; adult/child under 18/concession €4/free/3/; ☺ tours 9am-5pm Apr-Oct, 10am-3.30pm Nov-Mar, closed Mon) is what everyone thinks of as the quintessential medieval castle. Framed by woods, its turrets and towers stand sentinel on a rocky bluff above the canal. It's truly a magnificent sight from below, perhaps even more impressive than from close-up. In 1569, Wiguläus Hundt, a local researcher, happened upon a hand-written copy of the medieval *Nibelungen* song, which became known as the 'Prunner Codex' and is now in the Bavarian State Library in Munich. The epic inspired Richard Wagner's *Nibelungen* opera cycle.

Activities

CANOEING & KAYAKING

Glide past craggy limestone rocks, duck beneath trembling willows or pull up to a pebbled beach for a picnic. Exploring the Altmühltal by canoe or kayak is the ultimate way to experience the park's picturesque charms at a gentle pace. The slow-moving river meanders for about 150km, with lots of little dams along the way, as well as a few fun pseudo-rapids about 10km northwest of Dollnstein. Just past Solnhofen, you'll be passing the '12 Apostles', a particularly memorable rock formation.

Canoeing and kayaking are hugely popular and it's a good idea to book boats and accommodation in advance. The main boat touring season is from May to September. During hot summers, the water level in the Altmühl can sometimes sink too low for navigation, so check in advance with the tourist office. Always pack sunblock and insect repellent.

Several companies offer canoe tours for half-/one-/two-/three-day trips costing about €21/€26/€111/€160, including the boat, transfer back to the embarkation point and, for overnight tours, luggage transfer and lodging. The two main outfitters are **San-Aktiv Tours** (☎ 09831-4936; www.san-aktiv-tours.com; Bühringer Strasse 8, Gunzenhausen) and **Natour** (☎ 09141-922 929; www.natour.de in German; Gänswirtshaus 34, Weissenburg).

If you prefer going it alone, you can also hire one- and two-person canoes from numerous companies all along the river. The canoes cost about €12.50 for a one-person and €25 for a two-person per day. For an additional fee, staff will haul you and the boats to or from your embarkation point (sample fee: Eichstätt–Solnhofen €25 for the first boat, then €3 for each additional boat). Besides San-Aktiv Tours and Natour, some other companies include **Franken-Boot** (☎ 09142-4645; Treuchtlingen), **Lemming Tours** (☎ 09145-235; Solnhofen) and **Bootsverleih Otto Rehm** (☎ 08422-987 654; Dollnstein). Or try **Fahrradgarage** (☎ 08421-2110; www.fahrradgarage.de in German; Herzoggasse 3, Eichstätt), run by friendly, English-speaking Frank Warmuth. You can get a full list of hire outlets from the Informationszentrum Naturpark Altmühltal (opposite).

CYCLING

With around 800km of trails – most of them away from traffic – the Altmühltal is ideal for leisurely bicycle touring. The weather is most dependable from June to August, but the downside is that trails can get quite crowded, especially on weekends. Advance room reservations are a good idea during this time.

The most popular route is the 160km Altmühltal Radweg from Gunzenhausen to Kelheim, much of it paralleling the Altmühl. To get away from the crowds, venture into the serene side valleys.

The Informationszentrum Naturpark Altmühltal (opposite) has a list of bike hire outlets. Rates start at about €7.50 per day.

Fahrradgarage (above) hires out bicycles for €7.50 per day. Staff will bring the bikes to you or transport you and the bikes to anywhere in the park for an extra fee.

Most hire companies will also store bicycles; Fahrradgarage charges €0.50 per hour or €1.75 per day.

FRANCONIA

HIKING

Spring and autumn are the best times for hiking along the park's 3000km of marked trails, including over a dozen long-distance routes. The most scenic is the **Altmühltalweg**, which winds for 140km along the river from Treuchtlingen to Kelheim, though sections of it must be shared with bicyclists. The new **Panorama** trail from Gunzenhausen to Kelheim traverses 160 elevated kilometres taking in spectacular views. Hiking-trail markers are yellow.

ROCK CLIMBING

The Jurassic limestone mountains in the Altmühltal have long exerted their challenge on rock hounds. You'll find rocks suitable for climbing in the areas of Dollnstein, Konstein and Aicha, and Prunn and Essing, with degrees of difficulty ranging from III to X (XI being the toughest).

Sport IN (☎ 0841-472 23; Jesuitenstrasse 17, Ingolstadt), offers a set programme of rock-climbing excursions, or contact German Alpine Association teacher **Michael Steinhoff** (☎ 08421-998 92) to create a customised tour.

Tours

There's no question that, despite its adverse impact on nature, the controversial Rhine-Main-Danube-Canal between Beilngries, in the mid-northeast of the Altmühl, and Kelheim, in the far east, passes through some glorious countryside. The **Altmühltal bicycle trail** rambles along here, but the nicest way to travel the canal is by boat. From May to early October, several companies run trips from Kelheim to Riedenburg (roughly halfway to Beilngries), with stops in Essing and Prunn; try **Personenschiffahrt** (☎ 09441-5858; www.schiffahrt-kelheim.de in German; one-way way/return to Riedenburg €6.50/11, 2hr). Some boats continue on to Beilngries and Berching, where you can catch a shuttle bus (operated by the boat companies) back to Kelheim. Note that boats leave from the Altmühl landing docks in Kelheim, not the Danube landing docks.

You can also start your journey in Berching or Beilngries, but there are far fewer departures. Check the schedule with the **Beilngries tourist office** (☎ 08641-8435; www.beilngries.de in German; Hauptstrasse 14; ☯ 9am-noon & 2-7pm Mon-Sat, 10am-noon Sun May–mid-Oct, 9am-noon & 2-4pm Mon-Fri mid-Oct–Apr).

For tours from Kelheim through the Danube Gorge and to Kloster Weltenburg, see p166.

Sleeping & Eating

EICHSTÄTT

Gasthof Sonne (☎ 08421-6791; www.sonne-eichstaett.de in German; Buchtal 17; s €36-42, d €56-68; meals €8-12; P ✗) Most of the generously sized rooms at this friendly place open onto balconies. The owners also operate a well-respected restaurant, due to have undergone a major face-lift by the time you're reading this.

Fuchs (☎ 08421-6789; Ostenstrasse 8; s/d €40/60; P) Supercentral, this spick-and-span hotel with underfloor heating in the bathrooms adjoins a confectionery and cake shop (cakes €2), with a sunny courtyard dining area.

Hotel Adler (☎ 08421-6767; www.ei-online.de/adler in German; Marktplatz 22; s €41-51, d €82-102; P) In a refitted 300-year-old building right on Markt, this ambient hotel offers all the trappings, including bike and boat hire and a generous breakfast buffet. There's also wheelchair access.

Camping Daum (☎ 08421-5455; fax 807 63; Westenstrasse 47; per camp site €6; ☯ closed during Volksfest) This all-seasons camp site is on the northern bank of the Altmühl River, about 1km east of the town centre. Note that it's closed during the 10-day oompah-pah-ing Volksfest (Eichstätt's version of Oktoberfest) around late August or early September, which takes place right next door. Also note that, though motorised campervans are permitted, towed caravans aren't.

Café im Paradeis (☎ 08421-3313; Markt 9; dishes €2.50-12.50) Recharge with a nourishing homemade soup, or a (primarily meat-based) bigger meal surrounded by antiques in the cosy back room or outside on the terrace, which offers primo people-watching.

On the Markt, **Metzgerei Schneider** (☎ 909 80; Marktplatz 14) has sausages of every conceivable sort, and markets are held here on Wednesday and Saturday mornings.

ELSEWHERE IN NATURPARK ALTMÜHLTAL

Camping is allowed only in designated areas along the river for €3 per tent. Individual travellers do not need reservations. You'll find hotels, pensions, guesthouses and hostels in all villages and towns throughout the park.

BAVARIA'S TOWER OF BABEL?

When the Rhine-Main-Danube-Canal opened on 25 September 1992, it created a 3500km-long continuous waterway from the North Sea to the Black Sea. It was an amazing feat that many had tried and failed to accomplish, starting with Charlemagne in 793. In the 19th century, King Ludwig I gave it a whack, but more than 100 locks made navigation on his 'Ludwig Kanal' impractical. Only in the 20th century, after 72 years of planning and 32 years of construction, did the willow-draped natural banks of the Altmühl finally yield to an asphalt canal 55m wide and 4m deep. It was a triumph of engineering and a tragedy for nature.

It is estimated that the canalisation of the 171km stretch between Bamberg and Kelheim has caused the loss of about 18 million sq metres of biotopes and pastures. This has destroyed the habitat of dozens of plant and animal species, including several on the endangered list. Experts fear that four out of five resident species will likely disappear, despite the creation of artificial biotopes. The towns along the canal, which once drew their tranquil identity from the gentle river, now seem oddly remote.

Economically, the canal is a flop as well. Built at a cost of more than €3 billion, it continues to operate far below its potential and manages to generate less than 10% of its maintenance costs through shipping fees. Meanwhile, tourist boats flood the villages with mass tourism.

Former federal transportation minister, Volker Hauff, has called the canal 'the most stupid construction project since the Tower of Babel'. Plans have been mooted, however, to extend the canalisation even further by straightening and deepening the Danube between Straubing and Vilshofen on the southern edge of the Bavarian Forest. Another environmental disaster in the making? Stay tuned.

Gasthaus Zur Krone (☎ 09091-508 776; Markplatz 7, Monheim; s/d €25/50; meals €8-16; **P**) In the mid-west of the park, this comfortable place offers a superior standard at budget rates and a cosy traditional restaurant.

Gasthof Xaver Bösl (☎ 08423-247; Marktstrasse 25, Titting; s €23-27, d €46-54; meals €4-8; **P**) It's not fancy, but this small tangerine-coloured inn in the park's midnorth has a sauna and lovely terrace. The charming owner makes sausages that he sells in his own *Metzgerei* (butchery) and serves at the guesthouse's restaurant.

Schloss Arnsberg (☎ 08465-3154; Kipfenberg-Arnsberg; s €37.50-40, d €75-80; meals €12-20; **P**) Six kilometres from the mideast village of Kipfenberg, this historic castle is perched atop a sheer rockface with sweeping views. Rooms are appropriately regally proportioned, and the restaurant has top-notch regional cuisine.

Hotel Die Gams (☎ 08461-6100; www.hotel-gams. de in German; Hauptstrasse 16, Beilngries; s/d €59/77; meals €10-20) This is a classy place to stay with flowing rooms, some of which have whirlpool spas in bathrooms that are bigger than most single rooms. There's also a lift. The downstairs restaurant has friendly staff and excellent German and international cuisine.

Getting There & Away
On the main Nuremburg–Munich line, there's a train service hourly or better between Ingolstadt and Eichstätt (€4.20, 20 minutes).

Bus No 9226 takes about 1½ hours from Beilngries to Ingolstadt.

Getting Around
BUS
The FreizeitBus Altmühltal-Donautal operates from mid-April to October; buses are equipped to transport bicycles. All-day tickets cost €7.50 for passengers with bicycles, €5 for passengers without, or €19.50 per family with bikes, €14 without.

Route FzB1 runs from Regensburg to Kelheim to Riedenburg on weekends and holidays only. Route FzB2 travels between Treuchtlingen, Eichstätt, Beilngries, Dietfurt and Riedenburg with all-day service on weekends and holidays and restricted service on weekdays. Bus No 9232 connects Beilngries with Eichstätt several times daily in 45 minutes.

TRAIN
Trains run between Eichstätt Bahnhof and Treuchtlingen hourly or better (€3.90, 25 minutes), and at least hourly between

Treuchtlingen and Gunzenhausen (€5.70, 15 minutes). RE trains from Munich that travel through Eichstätt Bahnhof also stop in Dollnstein, Solnhofen and Pappenheim. Some require a change in Ingolstadt.

INGOLSTADT

☎ 0841 / pop 120,000 / elev 374m

Even by high German standards Ingolstadt is unusually prosperous. Audi, the upmarket auto manufacturer, has its headquarters here, and alongside are the oil refineries that help run those sleek beasts.

But walking the streets of the medieval centre, where wagons rattled over cobblestone, it's easy to forget all about modern industry. It boasts a harmonious ensemble of comely buildings, a museum church with the largest flat fresco ever made and a fascinating military museum. And few people know that Frankenstein was born here, that is, in the author's imagination.

Although it's technically part of Upper Bavaria, in practical terms Ingolstadt makes for an excellent gateway to the Naturpark Altmühltal (p237), which is why it is covered in this chapter.

Orientation

The Hauptbahnhof is 2.5km southeast of the Altstadt; bus Nos 10, 11, 15 and 16 make the trip every few minutes (€1.60). The Danube flows south of the Altstadt and the Audi factory is about 2km north of the centre.

Information

INTERNET ACCESS

Stadtbücherei (city library; ☎ 305 1831; Hallstrasse 2-4; free)

MONEY

Dresdner Bank (Rathausplatz 3)

POST

Post office (☻ 8.30-6pm Mon-Fri, 9am-1pm Sat) Altstadt (Am Stein 8); Hauptbahnhof (**Hauptbahnhof**)

TOURIST INFORMATION

Tourist office (☎ 305 3030; www.ingolstadt.de/tour ismus; Rathausplatz 2; ☻ 8am-5.30pm Mon-Fri, 9am-2pm Sat, 10am-3pm Sun)

Sights

ASAMKIRCHE MARIA DE VICTORIA

The crown jewel among Ingolstadt's sights

is the **Asamkirche Maria de Victoria** (☎ 175 18; Neubaustrasse 11/2; adult/child €2/1.50; ☻ 9am-noon & 1-5pm Tue-Sun Mar-Oct, 10am-noon & 1-4pm Nov-Mar), a baroque masterpiece designed by brothers Cosmas Damian and Egid Quirin Asam, between 1732 and 1736.

Its shining glory is the trompe l'oeil ceiling (painted in just six weeks in 1735), which is the world's largest fresco on a flat surface. It is a mesmerising piece of work full of stunning visual illusions. Stand on the little circle in the diamond tile near the door and look over your left shoulder at the archer with the flaming red turban. Wherever you walk in the room the arrow points right at you. Focus on anything – the Horn of Plenty, Moses' staff, the treasure chest – and it will appear to dramatically alter when you move around the room. Asam took the secret methods he used in the painting to his grave.

Before leaving ask the caretaker, Herr Homm, to let you into the side chamber for a look at the **Lepanto Monstrance**, a gold and silver depiction of the Battle of Lepanto (1571).

DEUTSCHES MEDIZINHISTORISCHES MUSEUM

Located in Ingolstadt university's stately Old Anatomy building, the **Deutsches Medizinhistorisches Museum** (German Museum of Medical History; ☎ 305 1860; Anatomiestrasse 18/20; adult/child under 16 €3/free; ☻ 10am-noon & 2-5pm Tue-Sun) wends its way through the evolution of medical science. Pack a strong stomach for the visit.

The ground floor eases you in with birthing chairs, enema syringes and lancets for blood-letting. Upstairs things get closer to the bone with displays of human skeletons, preserved musculature and organs, fetuses of conjoined twins, a pregnant uterus and a cyclops. Once you've seen this you can grasp Shelley's inspiration (see the boxed text on p245).

Although presented in a completely scientific, almost clinical, fashion, there's an undeniable ghoulishness to the place. Afterwards you can recover in the bucolic medicinal plant garden, which includes a garden of smells and touch-signs for the blind.

NEUES SCHLOSS & BAYERISCHES ARMEE MUSEUM

The ostentatious **Neues Schloss** (New Palace) was built for Ludwig the Bearded in 1418.

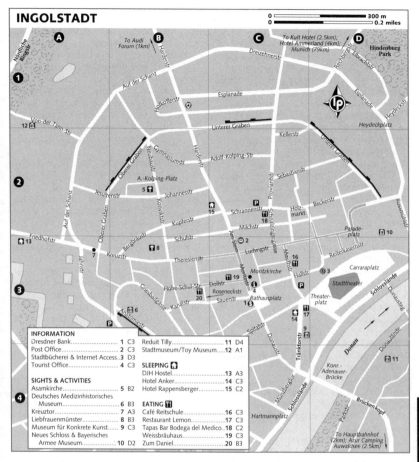

INGOLSTADT

0 — 300 m
0 — 0.2 miles

INFORMATION
Dresdner Bank...........................1 C3
Post Office.................................2 C3
Stadtbücherei & Internet Access..3 D3
Tourist Office............................4 C3

SIGHTS & ACTIVITIES
Asamkirche...............................5 B2
Deutsches Medizinhistorisches
Museum.................................6 B3
Kreuztor..................................7 A3
Liebfrauenmünster....................8 B3
Museum für Konkrete Kunst......9 C3
Neues Schloss & Bayerisches
Armee Museum.....................10 D2

Reduit Tilly..............................11 D4
Stadtmuseum/Toy Museum.....12 A1

SLEEPING
DJH Hostel..............................13 A3
Hotel Anker............................14 C3
Hotel Rappensberger...............15 C2

EATING
Café Reitschule........................16 C3
Restaurant Lemon....................17 C3
Tapas Bar Bodega del Medico..18 C2
Weissbräuhaus.........................19 C3
Zum Daniel.............................20 B3

Fresh from a trip to wealth-laden France, Ludwig borrowed heavily from Gallic design and created an ostentatious new home with 3m-thick walls, Gothic net-vaulting and individually carved doorways. Today the building houses the **Bayerisches Armee Museum** (Bavarian Military Museum ☎ 937 70; Paradeplatz 4; adult/child €3/2.50, all Sun €1, with Reduit Tilly €4/3; ☯ 8.45am-4.30pm Tue-Sun). The exhibits include armaments from the 14th century to WWII and a collection of 17,000 tin soldiers.

Part II of the museum is situated in the **Reduit Tilly** (same admission and hours as Neues Schloss), across the river, named for the Thirty Years' War general, it features exhibits covering the history of WWI and post-WWII Germany.

MUSEUM MOBILE

This high-tech museum is Ingolstadt's newest attraction and part of the **Audi Forum** (☎ 283 4444; Ettinger Strasse 40; adult/child under 18 €2/1, tour €4/2; ☯ 9am-8pm). The exhibits on three floors chronicle the automotive company's history, from its humble beginnings in 1899 to all of its latest successes. Some 50 cars and 20 motorbikes are on view to the public. 14 prototypes that perpetually glide past visitors on an open lift are also on display. One-hour tours (some in English) run twice hourly. Take bus No 11 to the terminus.

Car nuts can go on a two-hour tour of the **Audi factory** (toll-free ☎ 0800-282 4444; tour free; ☯ 9am-2pm production days only).

LIEBFRAUENMÜNSTER

The city's minster was founded by Duke Ludwig the Bearded in 1425 and built up over the next 100 years. Ostensibly a classic Gothic hall church, its most distinctive exterior feature is the pair of oblique square towers that flank the main entrance. Inside, subtle colours and a nave flooded with light intensify the magnificence of the soaring ceiling vaults where strands of delicate stonework sensuously intertwine into geometric filigree patterns. Somehow the whole thing seems completely organic.

Also worth a closer look are the brilliant stained-glass windows and the high altar by Hans Mielich (1560).

KREUZTOR

The Gothic **Kreuztor** (1385), red brick and with a fairy-tale outline, was one of the four main gates into the city until the 19th century and is now the emblem of Ingolstadt. This and the main gate within the Neues Schloss are all that remain of the city gates, but the former fortifications, now flats, still encircle the city.

OTHER ATTRACTIONS

Modern art buffs will love the **Museum für Konkrete Kunst** (Museum of Concrete Art; ☎ 305 1871; Tränktorstrasse 6-8; adult/child €3/1.50; ⏲ 11am-6pm Tue-Sun), which has a beautiful sculpture garden and fascinating displays, with international works, on the development of concrete art.

The **Stadtmuseum** (City Museum; ☎ 305 1885; Auf der Schanz 45; adult/child €3/1.50; ⏲ 9am-5pm Tue-Fri, 10am-5pm Sat & Sun) houses oodles of ancient artefacts as well as the **Toy Museum**, with playthings and mechanical toys from the 18th to 20th centuries.

Sleeping

DJH hostel (☎ 341 77; www.jugendherberge.de/jh/ingolstadt in German; Friedhofstrasse 4-1/2; dm €14.85-15.35; ⏲ closed mid-Dec–Jan; wheelchair access) This beautiful hostel is in a renovated city fortress (1828), about 150m west of the Kreuztor. It's a well-equipped place near the swimming pool and skating rink.

Hotel Ammerland (☎ 953450; www.hotel-ammerland .de; Ziegeleistrasse 64; s €55-95, d €70-120; P ☒ ▣) This charming hotel, about 4km north of the Altstadt, is an excellent choice. A recent makeover improved amenities and rooms are

nicely decorated in lively colours. Some of the pricier ones are themed 'Golfing', 'Africa' or 'Matisse'. The in-house bar is amazing.

Hotel Anker (☎ 300 05; www.hotel-restaurant -anker.de in German; Tränktorstrasse 1; s €52, d €80-84; meals €5-13) Bright, modern rooms, reasonable rates and friendly service make this family-run hotel a good central choice. Rooms in this five-storey orange house have direct-dial phone and cable TV, and the typical German restaurant attracts a loyal local following.

Hotel Rappensberger (☎ 31 40; www.rappens berger.de; Harderstrasse 3; s €80-135, d €90-165; P) This small stylish hotel has well-designed modern rooms in a very convenient location close to the centre of town. It's attached to a lively traditional pub that gets busy in the evenings.

Kult Hotel (☎ 951 00; www.kult-hotel.de in German; Theodor-Heussstrasse 25; s €120-150, d €130-165; P ☒ ▣) This stunning designer hotel is all clean lines and attention to detail with chrome features and natural fabrics in muted colours adorning the wonderful rooms. Look out for special offers that reduce the rack rates considerably.

Azur Campingplatz Auwaldsee (☎ 961 1616; www.azur-camping.de/ingolstadt; per tent/person/car €4.20/5.50/7) This huge forested camp site at Auwaldsee, a lake about 3km southeast of the city centre, has a shop and restaurant and you can hire rowing and sailing boats. An infrequent bus No 60 goes this way; a taxi from the centre will cost about €9.

Eating

Local drinkers are especially proud that the world's oldest health and safety regulation, Germany's Beer Purity Law of 1516, was issued in Ingolstadt. To find out why, try a mug of smooth Herrnbräu, Nordbräu or Ingobräu.

Dollstrasse and Theresienstrasse are packed with places to eat and drink and are a good bet on any night. The **markets** (Theaterplatz; ⏲ Wed & Sat) are great places to stock up on fresh produce, baked goods and other goodies.

Zum Daniel (☎ 352 72; Roseneckstrasse 1; mains €5.50-9; ⏲ closed Mon) This is the oldest pub in town and just drips with character and tradition. The Daniel has a Frankenstein exhibit upstairs and, according to some locals, the town's best pork roast.

FRANKENSTEIN'S BABY

Mary Shelley's *Frankenstein*, published in 1818, is one of the most enduring monster tales ever written. The story is well known: young scientist Viktor Frankenstein travels to Ingolstadt to study medicine. Here, he becomes obsessed with the idea of creating a human being and goes shopping for parts at the local cemetery. Unfortunately his creature is a problem child and promptly sets out to destroy its maker.

Why did Shelley pick Ingolstadt as her setting? For centuries, Ingolstadt, along with Prague and Vienna, was home to one of the most prominent universities in Central Europe. In the 18th century, a famous laboratory for scientists and medical doctors was housed in the Alte Anatomie (now the German Museum of Medical History). In the operating theatre, professors and students performed experiments on corpses and dead tissue. So Ingolstadt became Shelley's imaginary 'birthplace' of Frankenstein's monster.

Shelley originally became aware of Ingolstadt because it was the founding place of a secret society called the 'Illuminati'. Its list of illustrious members included Goethe and Herder as well as her husband, Percy Bysshe-Shelley.

Ingolstadt doesn't make a big deal out of Frankenstein, but German speakers may consider joining **Dr Frankenstein's Murder & Mystery Tour** (☎ 326 243; www.frankenstein.at in German; adult/concession €7/6; ☽ 10pm, 70min, check with the tourist office for dates), a spooky night-time walk led by a character dressed as the good old doctor. The evening concludes with a visit to 'Frankenstein's Kabinett', a re-created laboratory-cum-Frankenstein memorabilia room upstairs at Zum Daniel (opposite).

Restaurant Lemon (☎ 171 00; Tränktorstrasse 2; mains €9.50-17.50) This stylish modern restaurant specialises in gourmet food with Mediterranean flair. Both meat-lovers and vegetarians will be duly impressed with the colourful fresh ingredients and elegant presentation.

Café Reitschule (☎ 931 2870; Mauthstrasse 8; dishes €5-13) Dominated by a huge bar and some incongruous palm trees, this lively café is popular with a young crowd and serves up everything from soup, salads and schnitzel to hearty rump steaks.

Tapas Bar Bodega del Medico (☎ 379 5625; Schnalzingergasse 15; tapas €1.80-2.50; ☽ 6pm-2am, closed Sun) For tasty food and a wild night out try this spirited Spanish bar. The excellent tapas are cheap enough that you can try a whole selection and still leave room for cocktails.

Weissbräuhaus (☎ 328 90; Dollstrasse 3; Brotzeit €5-8, mains €9-15) This modern beer hall serves standard Bavarian dishes, including the delicious *Weissbräupfändl* (pork filet with homemade Spätzle noodles). There's a beer garden with a charming fountain out back.

Getting There & Around

Trains to Regensburg (€11.50, one hour) and Munich (€13.30, one hour) leave hourly. Single journeys on local buses cost €1.75.

AROUND INGOLSTADT
Neuburg an der Donau
☎ 08431 / pop 28,000 / elev 400m

Neuburg an der Donau scenically hugs the banks of the Danube, about 22km west of Ingolstadt, and makes for a good afternoon excursion. Neuburg had already been settled for around 1600 years when its heyday arrived in 1505. That year it became the capital of the principality of Pfalz-Neuburg, the so-called 'Junge Pfalz' (Young Palatinate). Starting with Count Ottheinrich, a succession of rulers built up the town with magnificent Renaissance and baroque edifices. Nearly all of these cluster in the *Obere Stadt* (upper town), atop the Stadtberg, a little hill rising above the Danube west of the Eisenbrücke, the main bridge into town. The bridge runs into Luitpoldstrasse, which divides the *Obere Stadt* from the newer commercial centre anchored by Spitalplatz. Beyond, along the Danube, is the sprawling Englischer Garten, a leafy oasis great for walking and cycling. The Bahnhof is about 1km south of the Danube. Bus No 3 loops between the station, the *Obere Stadt* and Spitalplatz at 30-minute intervals (€0.75 per ride).

Neuburg has a **tourist office** (☎ 552 40; www .neuburg-donau.de in German; Residenzstrasse A65, Obere Stadt; ☽ 9am-6pm Mon-Fri, 10am-noon & 2-5pm Sat & Sun).

FRANCONIA

SIGHTS

The *Obere Stadt* is as pretty as a film set, but time seems to move at the speed of drizzling honey. Visible from afar is the **Residenzschloss**, built between 1530 and 1545 by Count Ottheinrich. The palace courtyard is flanked by double arcades, which give it an Italianate look aided by sgraffito paintings on the façades. (Sgraffito is a decorative pattern, usually monochrome, which is scratched or inscribed on plaster or glaze.)

The **Schlosskapelle** is the oldest Protestant church in Bavaria (1543). Swathed in ceiling frescoes, the chapel is nicknamed 'Bavarian Sixtina', an allusion to the Vatican's Sistine Chapel. In 1665, Elector Philipp Wilhelm had the eastern wing added in baroque style and topped off by the towers that give the palace its distinctive silhouette.

The courtyard also gives access to the **Schlossmuseum** (Palace Museum; ☎ 8897; Residenzstrasse A2; adult/child €3/2; ☺ 9am-6pm Tue-Sun Apr-Sep, 10am-4pm Tue-Sun Oct-Mar), which has sections on prehistory as well as Neuburg's glory days as a royal residence. Also time for a spin around the garden with its fantastical grottoes, especially the **Blaue Grotte** (Blue Grotto) decorated with white Danube shells.

A short stroll west on Amalienstrasse takes you to the exquisite **Karlsplatz**, the heart of the *Obere Stadt*. Lined by ancient linden trees and meticulously restored historic houses, it is clearly dominated by the copper cupola of the late-Renaissance **Hofkirche** (1607–08). Planned as a Protestant church, it was actually finished by Jesuits. It is decorated in subdued baroque, with creamy white stucco and only hints of gold-leaf flourishes here and there.

The church dwarfs the comparatively modest **Rathaus** (1609) in the square's north-eastern corner, with its double staircase and a gallery on the ground floor. Of the various other ornate buildings around the square, the **Provinzialbibliothek** at the western end stands out for its yellow-and-pink exterior trim. Originally a church, it now houses an historical library and has a wonderful baroque festival hall upstairs, which can only be seen on guided tours (usually 2.30pm Wednesday, May to October).

Strolling west on Amalienstrasse takes you to the **Peterskirche**, where the altar sculptures by Johann Michael Fischer are noteworthy. Soon you'll pass through the terracotta **Oberes Tor**, a storybook 16th-century town gate flanked by stocky twin towers. East of here is the **Hutzeldörr**, a small park that parallels the town wall and eventually takes you back to the Schloss.

SLEEPING & EATING

Blaue Traube (☎ 8392; info@zur-blauen-traube.de; Amalienstrasse 49; s/d from €29/70; mains €4-11) With more traditional fare, this is the only place right on Karlsplatz. It also has about 20 rooms with furnishings that are torn in time: they have TVs but also heavy woodwork with an old ecclesiastical flavour.

Da Capo (☎ 427 00; Residenzstrasse A66; mains €9-15) Should hunger strike, you'll find a few options in the *Obere Stadt*, including this Italian bistro next to the tourist office. Pork scaloppine, red snapper and tagliatelle are served in the vaulted chambers.

Altstadtcafé (☎ 2786; Amalienstrasse A44; ☺ to 6.30pm) Try this place for hot dishes, your afternoon coffee-and-cake fix or maybe just a freshly squeezed OJ.

GETTING THERE & AWAY

Regional trains leave hourly from Ingolstadt (€3.30, 15 minutes). The B16 runs right past town and connects with the B13, which leads north to Ingolstadt.

Allgäu-Bavarian Swabia

HIGHLIGHTS

- **Fairytale Castle**
  Living the fantasy at King Ludwig II's iconic dream palace, Neuschwanstein (p261)

- **Adrenaline Rush**
  Airboarding the slopes of Oberstdorf (p271), the quintessential Alpine village

- **Chill-Out Spot**
  Soaking up the sunshine at Donauwörth's canal-woven linear park, the Promenade (p258)

- **Wind in Your Sails**
  Boating on chocolate-box pretty Lake Constance from the petite island of Lindau (p268)

- **To Market, To Market...**
  Wandering the brimming food stalls and eateries at Augsburg's bustling Stadtmarkt (town market; p255)

- POP: 1.8 MILLION
- AREA: 10,000 SQ KM

This double region of Allgäu-Bavarian Swabia (Allgäu-Bayerisch Schwaben), in the southwest of Bavaria, has a diverse landscape ranging from verdant rolling hills to rocky Alpine peaks.

In the north is the Ries Basin, created by a meteorite millions of years ago, with the medieval town of Nördlingen at its centre. Nördlingen is also the region's northernmost town on the Romantic Road, which winds southward to Füssen at the foot of the Allgäu Alps, whose dreamy setting inspired King Ludwig II to build his famous Neuschwanstein castle here. In the west the region is bounded by the Iller River as well as Lake Constance (Bodensee), where the lovely island of Lindau, with its Great Gatsby–style grandeur and cosmopolitan flair, holds forth as the only Bavarian town on this giant inland lake. In the east, the Lech River forms a natural boundary to Upper Bavaria.

The region's major metropolis is the chic city of Augsburg, just 70km west of Munich, founded by the Romans as a trading centre. It's the capital of Bavarian Swabia, which was once part of the medieval duchy of Swabia, the larger part of which now lies in the neighbouring state of Baden-Württemberg. The capital of the Allgäu, which more or less begins south of Augsburg, is the historic, cobblestoned town of Memmingen. Near here is the area known as 'Kneipp Country', in homage to the father of modern holistic therapy, local priest Sebastian Kneipp, whose 'cures' sprang from the area's climate and natural resources, and are now practised in spas across the country. Scattered with grazing cattle, some of the country's best cheeses are made in the Allgäu, which culminates at the Austrian border in Oberstdorf, a ski and snow sports resort that hosts international competitions.

AUGSBURG

☎ 0821 / pop 275,000 / elev 489m

A main stop on the Romantic Road, Augsburg is a city shaped by the Romans, by medieval artisans, bankers and traders and, in more recent times, by industry and technology. Traces of all these phases are evident throughout this delightful and stylish city, which is Bavaria's third largest and the administrative centre of Swabia.

History

Founded in 15 BC by the Romans as a an Imperial military camp called Augusta Vindelicum, Augsburg grew to be the capital of the then-province of Raetia.

A bishopric from the 8th century, Augsburg became a Free Imperial City in 1316, coming under the control of the Bavarian kingdom in 1805.

The city prospered in the Middle Ages as a major trading centre (mostly gold, silver and copper) and financial and banking hub. During the Renaissance, the self-made Jakob Fugger 'The Rich', in particular, amassed untold wealth, though his strong sense of social responsibility saw him establish the first social welfare estate in the world, the Fuggerei.

In 1518 Martin Luther was summoned to Augsburg to disavow his writings. Following his unequivocal refusal, in 1530 the reformers presented the *Confessio Augustana*, a summary of the Protestant doctrine, to Karl V, which led to the recognition of Lutheran faith as equal to the Catholic in 1555 in what went down in history as the Peace of Augsburg.

Augsburg's renewal from the scars of the Thirty Years' War came with industrialisation: in 1897 Rudolf Diesel invented the diesel engine here, and the ME163 built by the Messerschmidt factory was the most advanced fighter plane in WWII. This lead to Augsburg receiving a severe drubbing by Allied bombers. Its recovery has resulted in a reinvigorated city with a thriving cultural scene and Mediterranean flair.

Orientation

The Hauptbahnhof (central train station) is at the western end of Bahnhofstrasse, which intersects with Fuggerstrasse at the

ALLGÄU-BAVARIAN SWABIA

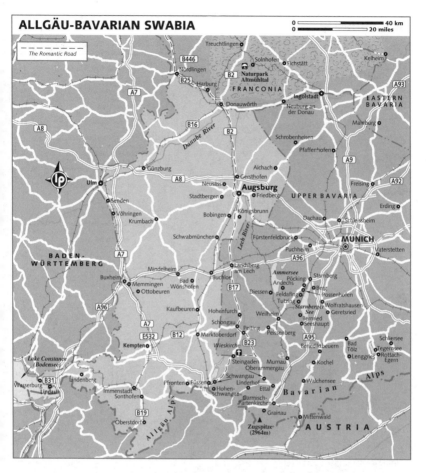

Königsplatz, the city's main bus transfer point. Parallel to Fuggerstrasse two blocks east is the city's main drag, Maximilianstrasse, which leads to Rathausplatz, the town square, the site of both the tourist office, and, during December, the Christmas market.

Information

BOOKSHOPS

Buchhandlung Rieger & Kranzfelder (☎ 517 880; Fugger Stadtpalast, Maximilianstrasse 36) Stocks English-language books.

EMERGENCY

Rotes Kreuz (Red Cross; ☎ 192 22) Call for a doctor or ambulance.

INTERNET ACCESS

Easy Internet Café (☎ 508 1878; Bahnhofstrasse 29; per hr €1; ⏰ 7am-midnight Mon-Fri, 8am-midnight Sat, 10am-midnight Sun) Cheapest coin-operated place in town.

MONEY

Citibank (Bahnhofstrasse 2) With an ATM.
HypoVereinsbank (Bahnhofstrasse 11) Also has an ATM.

POST

Post office Next to the Hauptbahnhof.

TOURIST INFORMATION

Tourist office (☎ 502 2070; www.augsburg-tourismus .de; Rathausplatz; ⏰ 9am-6pm Mon-Fri, to 5pm Nov-Mar, 10am-4pm Sat, 10am-2pm Sun) A €2 room-booking fee applies for bookings made in person.

www.lonelyplanet.com

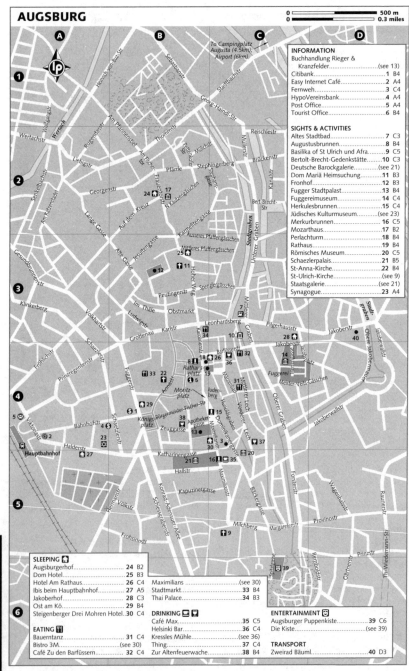

AUGSBURG

0 ————— 500 m
0 ————— 0.3 miles

To Campingplatz
Augusta (4.5km);
Airport (6km)

INFORMATION
Buchhandlung Rieger &
    Kranzfelder.........................(see 13)
Citibank...**1** B4
Easy Internet Café...........................**2** A4
Fernweh...**3** C4
HypoVereinsbank.............................**4** A4
Post Office.......................................**5** A4
Tourist Office...................................**6** B4

SIGHTS & ACTIVITIES
Altes Stadtbad................................**7** C3
Augustusbrunnen..............................**8** B4
Basilika of St Ulrich und Afra...........**9** C5
Bertolt-Brecht-Gedenkstätte...........**10** C3
Deutsche Barockgalerie.............(see 21)
Dom Mariä Heimsuchung...............**11** B3
Fronhof...**12** B3
Fugger Stadtpalast.........................**13** B4
Fuggereimuseum.............................**14** C4
Herkulesbrunnen.............................**15** C4
Jüdisches Kulturmuseum..........(see 23)
Merkurbrunnen...............................**16** C5
Mozarthaus....................................**17** B2
Perlachturm....................................**18** B4
Rathaus..**19** B4
Römisches Museum..........................**20** C5
Schaezlerpalais...............................**21** B5
St-Anna-Kirche................................**22** B4
St-Ulrich-Kirche........................(see 9)
Staatsgalerie..............................(see 21)
Synagogue......................................**23** A4

SLEEPING
Augsburgerhof..............................**24** B2
Dom Hotel.....................................**25** B3
Hotel Am Rathaus..........................**26** C4
Ibis beim Hauptbahnhof................**27** A5
Jakoberhof.....................................**28** C3
Ost am Kö......................................**29** B4
Steigenberger Drei Mohren Hotel..**30** C4

EATING
Bauerntanz.....................................**31** C4
Bistro 3M.................................(see 30)
Café Zu den Barfüssern...............**32** C4

Maximilians..............................(see 30)
Stadtmarkt.....................................**33** B4
Thai Palace....................................**34** B3

DRINKING
Café Max.......................................**35** C5
Helsinki Bar...................................**36** C4
Kressles Mühle..........................(see 36)
Thing...**37** C4
Zur Altenfeuerwache......................**38** B4

ENTERTAINMENT
Augsburger Puppenkiste................**39** C6
Die Kiste...................................(see 39)

TRANSPORT
Zweirad Bäuml...............................**40** D3

ALLGÄU-BAVARIAN SWABIA

TRAVEL AGENCIES
Fernweh (☎ 155 035; Dominikanergasse 10)

Sights
RATHAUSPLATZ
This large, pedestrianised square is the heart and soul of Augsburg's Altstadt (old town) and is anchored by the **Augustusbrunnen**, a fountain honouring the Roman emperor. The four figures represent the Lech River and the Wertach, Singold and Brunnenbach Brooks.

Looming over the square are the twin onion-domed spires of the Renaissance **Rathaus** (town hall), built by Elias Holl from 1615 to 1620 and crowned by a 4m-tall pine cone, the city's emblem (also an ancient fertility symbol). Upstairs is the **Goldener Saal** (Golden Hall; ☎ 324 9196; Rathausplatz; admission €1; ☺ 10am-6pm), a large banquet hall with an amazing gilded and coffered ceiling that is further interspersed with frescoes.

Next to the Rathaus is the **Perlachturm** (Perlach Tower; ☎ 502 070; Rathausplatz; adult/concession €1/0.50; ☺ 10am-6pm May-Oct, 2-7pm Sat & Sun Dec), a former guard tower, and also an Elias Holl creation. Climb to the top for panoramic city views.

DOM DISTRICT
North of the Rathausplatz, via Karolinenstrasse and Hoher Weg, is Augsburg's cathedral, the **Dom Mariä Heimsuchung**, with origins in the 10th century but 'Gothicised' and enlarged in the 14th and 15th centuries. The star treasures here are the so-called 'Prophets' Windows'. Depicting David, Daniel, Jonah, Hosea and Moses, they are among the oldest figurative stained-glass windows in Germany, dating from the 12th century.

The building west of the Dom is the **Fronhof**, the former bishop's palace. In the predecessor of the current 1743 building, the *Confessio Augustana* was proclaimed in 1530. It's a superb setting for an acclaimed concert series held here each July.

A short walk north of the Dom, the **Mozarthaus** (☎ 324 3894; Frauentorstrasse 30; adult/concession €1.50/1; ☺ 10am-5pm Tue-Sun) is where Leopold Mozart, Wolfgang Amadeus' father (who was also his music teacher and creator of the acclaimed 'violin technique'), was born in 1719. It's now a memorial museum.

ST-ANNA-KIRCHE
Founded as a Carmelite monastery in 1321, **St-Anna-Kirche** (Church of St Anna; ☎ 392 92; Im Annahof 2, off Annastrasse; ☺ 10am-noon Tue-Sat, 3-5pm Tue-Sun) hosted Martin Luther during his stay in 1518. His rooms have been turned into the **Lutherstiege**, a small museum about the Reformation. There's a portrait of Luther by Lucas Cranach the Elder in the eastern choir, while at the opposite end is the **Fuggerkapelle**, the chapel where Jakob Fugger and his brothers are buried. It is considered the first nonsecular Renaissance structure in Germany. Also pop into the lavishly frescoed **Goldschmiedekapelle** (Goldsmiths' Chapel; 1420).

MAXIMILIANSTRASSE
Rathausplatz marks the northern terminus of **Maximilianstrasse**, a grand boulevard lined by patrician mansions. Found along here are two impressive fountains that together with the Augustusbrunnen, were created for Augsburg's 1600th anniversary. The **Merkurbrunnen** (1599), at the intersection with Bürgermeister-Fischer-Strasse, is by Dutch artist Adriaen de Vries and features the god Mercury as a symbol of trade. Further south, near Hallstrasse, is the **Herkulesbrunnen** (1602), also by de Vries, which shows Hercules fighting the seven-headed Hydra. It's supposed to represent Augsburg's commercial importance.

In between the two fountains, at No 36–38, is the restored **Fugger Stadtpalast** (1515), the palatial town house and 'corporate' headquarters of Jakob Fugger. It embraces the **Damenhof** (Ladies' Court), a gorgeous inner courtyard arcaded in Italian Renaissance style. Outside marks the spot where Luther stood his ground in 1518.

In 1765 local banker Liebert von Liebenhofen commissioned an ebullient rococo palace, the **Schaezlerpalais** (☎ 324 4117; Maximilianstrasse 46; adult/concession €3/1.50; ☺ 10am-5pm Tue-Sun). Designed by Carl Albert von Lespilliez, a student of François Cuvilliés, the *pièce de résistance* is the 23m-long ballroom, a riot of carved decorations, stucco and mirrors topped off with a dashing ceiling fresco.

Today the palace houses two museums. The **Deutsche Barockgalerie** (German Baroque Gallery) offers an exhaustive survey of German 17th- and 18th-century artists, very

---

TAKING A CURE

Some call him the 'Water Doctor', some the 'Herb Priest'. Sebastian Kneipp's cures are widespread throughout Germany, with 60 health spas across the country, but it's the Allgäu's pristine mountain air, crystal-clear waters, high levels of sunshine and rich farming land that gave rise to modern holistic therapy.

The son of an impoverished Allgäu weaver, Kneipp was born in Stephansried, a little hamlet 3km from Ottobeuren (see the boxed text on p266) on 17 May 1821, coincidentally the same day Napoleon died in exile.

Kneipp had an early calling to the Catholic priesthood, but financial circumstances dictated it would be several years before he would be able to take up his studies in nearby Grönenbach. During his second year, he fell victim to tuberculosis and wouldn't have survived had he not come across a booklet by medical doctor Johann Siegmund Hahn about the curative properties of fresh water. He regularly immersed himself in the icy Danube, to the ridicule of his fellow students and teachers who told him in no uncertain terms he'd lose his scholarship if he continued with his radical ablutions. Despite this, he graduated and, his health improving, began his curate work first near Augsburg, then at Boos, near Memmingen, becoming not just a spiritual healer, but a physical one.

Arriving in Wörishofen in 1855 to oversee the convent's agricultural profitability, he observed the nuns actively toiling in the fields, and the fresh produce and especially the herbs they yielded, which would be integral to his later teachings. It was here in 1886 that he wrote *Meine Wasserkur* (My Cure by Water), the first of many books still used as reference works today. He recorded the findings of his ever-growing number of patients' treatments, thereby triggering Wörishofen's transformation from sleepy village to Bad Wörishofen, international spa resort, as well as Kneipp's own transformation from humble priest to miracle worker.

---

few of whom are household names. A deconsecrated church attached to the Schaezlerpalais now shelters the **Staatsgalerie** (Bavarian State Gallery), which has mostly Augsburg-related works by Old Masters, including a portrait of Jakob Fugger by Albrecht Dürer.

At the end of Maximilianstrasse looms the onion-domed tower of the late-Gothic **Basilika of St Ulrich and Afra**, formerly the abbey church of Augsburg's Benedictine monastery and the burial place of the town patrons.

Adjacent to the basilica and set at right angles, is the **St-Ulrich-Kirche**, which was a preaching hall of the monastery. A Lutheran church since 1524, its peaceful coexistence with its Catholic neighbour has long been a symbol of Augsburg's religious tolerance.

LECHVIERTEL

East of the Rathausplatz is the Lechviertel, sometimes also known as Jakobviertel, a largely pedestrianised district traversed by rushing little canals of the Lech River. Playwright and poet Bertolt Brecht (see the boxed text on p254) was born here in 1898 and his house has been turned into a memorial museum, the **Bertolt-Brecht-Gedenkstätte** (☎ 324 2779; Am Rain 7; adult/concession €1.50/1; ☼ 10am-4pm Wed-Sun).

Just north of the Brecht house, the **Altes Stadtbad** (☎ 324 9779; Leonhardsberg 15; day ticket adult/concession €4/2.40; ☼ 8am-7pm Mon-Tue, 8am-9pm Wed-Fri, 8am-8pm Sat, 8am-6pm Sun) is a fanciful Art Nouveau indoor swimming pool with richly ornamented tiles and stained-glass windows. It's worth a look even without taking a plunge.

RÖMISCHES MUSEUM

A couple of streets east of the Schaezlerpalais, the **Römisches Museum** (Roman Museum; ☎ 324 4134; Dominikanergasse 15; adult/concession €3/1.50; ☼ 10am-5pm Tue-Sun) presents Augsburg's Roman heritage inside a former monastery church (1515). Among the displays here are military items, weapons, sarcophagi, gold coins and tombstones.

FUGGEREI

Just east of the Lechviertel, across Oberer Graben, the ring road encircling the Altstadt, Jakob Fugger's legacy lives on. Between 200 and 300 people still live in this Catholic welfare settlement in now-modernised 60-

Kneipp's cures were founded on five pillars: hydrotherapy (a highly developed course of water treatment); exercise therapy; nutrition therapy using basic wholefoods; phytotherapy (the use of medicines on a herbal basis); and regulative therapy ('orderliness' in one's life, though Kneipp's fondness for the odd cigar – as parish priest he presided over plenty of weddings and christenings – backed up his belief in a balanced approach).

Authorities were suspicious of Kneipp's avant-garde philosophies, requiring him to appear in court in 1860 and 1866 under the Charlatan Act (both cases were dismissed). This didn't deter his devoted patients, the Rothschilds, Pope Leo XIII and Roosevelt among them. Kneipp became something of a celebrity and like all good celebrities, he went on tour, lecturing before roughly one million people, and curing Hungary's Archduke Joseph's ailments in the bargain. But it would be long after Kneipp's death, on 17 June 1897, before his theories were officially recognised.

Today, state ministries and state committees regulate establishments' right to carry the name 'Kneipp Health Resort' and (after 10 complaint-free years) 'Kneipp Spa'.

In the ski resort town of Oberstdorf alone, nine hotels offer Kneipp cures and over 30 guesthouses and restaurants feature 'Kneipp diet' dishes on their menus. Sprinkled along numerous footpaths are Kneipp tread baths and arm basins. Contact the **Oberstdorf tourist office** (www .oberstdorf.de; Bahnhof (☎ 700 217; ☺ 8.30am-8pm Mon-Fri, 9.30am-6pm Sat); Marktplatz ☎ 7000; Marktplatz 7; ☺ 8.30am-noon & 2-6pm Mon-Fri, 9.30am-noon Sat) for a comprehensive list and locations.

To embrace Kneipp's pillar of active physical movement, and take in some glorious countryside at the same time, you can take the **Kneipp Cycle Route** (☎ 08261-995 375; tourismus@lra.unterallgaeu .de), a 56km-long bicycle path linking the Kneipp hydrotherapy health resorts of Bad Wörishofen (whose buzzing shopping strip is called Kneipp Strasse), Ottobeuren and Bad Grönenbach. This area in the Unterallgäu (Lower Allgäu) is now known as 'Kneipp Country'. Details about the Allgäu's Kneipp cures and spas are also available at www.allgaeu.de, which has English sections.

sq-metre apartments, the rent having been frozen at 1 Rhenish guilder (now €1) per *year*, plus utilities and three daily prayers. During the day, bemused residents wave to tourists who are free to wander the car-free lanes of this gated community flanked by its 52 pin-neat houses and gardens.

To see how residents lived before running water and central heating, stop in at the **Fuggereimuseum** (☎ 450 3770; Mittlere Gasse 13; adult/concession €1/0.50; ☺ 9am-8pm May-Oct, 9am-6pm Nov-Apr). Franz Mozart, Wolfgang Amadeus' great-grandfather, once lived next door.

SYNAGOGUE
Augsburg's synagogue (1914–17), west of the Altstadt, is a beautiful Art Nouveau temple built by Heinrich Lömpel and Fritz Landauer. Devastated in 1938, it reopened in 1985 and, besides a prayer hall, contains the **Jüdisches Kulturmuseum** (Museum of Jewish Culture; ☎ 513 658; Halderstrasse 8; adult/concession €2/1; ☺ 9am-4pm Tue-Fri, 10am-5pm Sun). The permanent exhibit documents Jewish life in the region and explains traditions, rituals and customs using Judaica from the 17th to the 19th centuries. Tours run at 6pm on the first Wednesday of every month.

Tours
The tourist office runs two-hour guided **walking tours** (adult/concession €7/5; ☺ 2pm Apr-Oct, 2pm Sat Nov-Mar) in English and German from the Rathaus.

Festivals & Events
Mozart's legacy lives on in Augsburg in the form of the **Deutsches Mozartfest** (German Mozart Festival; www.deutsche-mozart-gesellschaft.de), which is every three years. The next is in May 2006, the 250th anniversary of the year of Wolfgang Amadeus' birth. The **Augsburger Mozartfest** (Augsburg Mozart Festival) takes place in the years between the German Mozart festivals.

Also in May 2006, from the 17th to the 28th, is the **Leopold Mozart International Violin Competition**, bringing together talented young violinists from around the world every four years. Contact the tourist office for dates and ticket information as well as details of other Mozart tours and celebrations.

Sleeping
BUDGET
Jakoberhof (☎ 510 030; www.jakoberhof.de; Jakoberstrasse 41; s with bathroom €39-49, d with bathroom

€54-64, s/d without bathroom €26/39; meals from €5; restaurant closed Nov-Mar; P X) One of the best budget options is this friendly pension, a collection of three buildings near the Fuggerei. It also has a decent Bavarian restaurant. Take tram No 1 or bus Nos 22 or 23.

Ibis beim Hauptbahnhof (☎ 501 60; www.ibishotel .com; Halderstrasse 25; r €49; P X) OK, it's a chain and lacking in character, but if you forgo the optional €9 breakfast per person, one or two people can stay at this place, a stone's throw from the train station, for €49 a night, making it one of the best deals in town.

Campingplatz Augusta (☎ 707 575; www.camping platz-augusta.de in German; Mühlhauser Strasse 54b; per tent/car/person €3.10/3.10/4.10, f €50) This year-round camp site with restaurant and kids' playground is on a swimming lake, some 7km from the city centre. Apart from camp sites, it has a few family rooms with bathrooms for three people. Take bus No 23 to the terminus, from where it's a 2km walk.

MIDRANGE & TOP END

Dom Hotel (☎ 343 930; www.domhotel-augsburg.de; Frauentorstrasse 8; s €64-105, d 74-125; P X) The former residence of Provost Johann, duke of Bavaria, Martin Luther hid in the garden here before his escape from the Catholic Cardinal Cajetan. Now a chic hotel with fabulous views of the cathedral

steeples, the contemporary rooms have cutting-edge, minimalist décor.

Ost am Kö (☎ 502 040; www.ostamkoe.de; Fuggerstrasse 4-6; s €65-95, d €74-120; P X) Behind the 1960s cube façade awaits this efficiently run, quality hotel with lots of personal touches and a rave-worthy buffet breakfast. It's on a busy street, but windows are soundproofed.

Hotel Am Rathaus (☎ 346 490; www.hotel-am -rathaus-augsburg.de in German; Am Hinteren Perlachberg 1; s/d from €80/110; P X) As central at it gets, moments to Rathausplatz and Maximilianstrasse, this boutique hotel has fresh neutral décor and a sunny little breakfast room. Ask about its weekend specials.

Augsburgerhof (☎ 343 050; www.augsburger-hof .de; Auf dem Kreuz 2; s €78-105, d €80-130; P X) The higher-priced rooms open onto the courtyard at this pretty, window-boxed hotel, but all are thoughtfully furnished and have cable TV and telephones. It's near the Mozarthaus, an easy stroll north of the Dom.

TOP END

Steigenberger Drei Mohren Hotel (☎ 503 60; www .augsburg.steigenberger.de in German; Maximilianstrasse 40; s/d from €106/175; P X) This stunning landmark hotel, flanked by the Schaezlerpalais and the Fugger Stadtpalast, is the oldest and best in Augsburg, with marble bathrooms and original art.

BRECHT: AUGSBURG'S BREAKAWAY SON

Bertolt Brecht was not fond of Augsburg, and Augsburg returned the sentiment.

The controversial playwright and poet was born in this city on 10 February 1898. Individualistic and rebellious, Brecht felt out of place in this tight, bourgeois community, abandoning it to study medicine in Munich, where he also began to write. His first play to reach the stage – *Trommeln in der Nacht* (Drums in the Night) – quickly turned Brecht into a household name in the theatre world.

Drawn to Berlin, a cultural hotbed throughout the 1920s, it was here where Brecht developed his theory of the 'epic theatre', which compels audiences to detach emotionally from the characters and to view the action critically and intellectually. His biggest success was *Die Dreigroschenoper* (The Threepenny Opera; 1928), featuring the enduring 'Mack the Knife'.

A staunch Marxist, Brecht went into exile during the Nazi years, surfaced in Hollywood as a scriptwriter, then left the USA under the scrutiny of the communist witch hunts of the McCarthy era. He returned to Germany in 1949, settling in East Berlin where he founded the Berliner Ensemble theatre company with his wife, Helene Weigel. Brecht died in Berlin on 14 August 1956, where he's buried.

Through all these years, Augsburg ignored Brecht as much as he had ignored it: the first time one of his plays was performed here was in 1982. It seems his birthplace has finally embraced one of its famous sons. Perhaps Brecht too would feel more at home in this now-progressive city.

Eating

RESTAURANTS

Café Zu den Barfüssern (☎ 450 4966; Barfüsserstrasse 10; dishes €1.90-2.40; ♥ to 6pm Mon-Sat) A few steps down from the street through a covered passageway brings you out to this pretty place on a little canal. It serves homemade cakes and pastries as well as a limited daily changing lunch menu.

Bauerntanz (☎ 153 644; Bauerntanzgässchen 1; mains €8.50-15) A local favourite, this good-value place has big portions of creative Swabian and Bavarian food using choice ingredients. There's outdoor seating in fine weather.

Thai Palace (☎ 368 33; Leonhardsberg 2; mains €8.50-17) The scents of Thailand grow stronger as you pass by the golden Buddha and climb the gold-trimmed staircase to this huge place with wraparound windows overlooking the bustling streets. The crowds that pack this place reflect the superior quality of the food. Entry is from Karolinenstrasse.

In the Steigenberger Drei Mohren Hotel (opposite) are two superb restaurants. **Bistro 3M** (mains €14.20-18.50), is a clubby place with red booths and French-influenced turkey, steak and guinea fowl as well as lots of vegetarian choices. **Maximilians** (mains €15-23; ♥ closed Sun dinner) offers a positively regal dining room with flowing white tablecloths. The Sunday jazz brunch is an elegant affair.

QUICK EATS

Along with dozens of stand-up eateries serving everything from Asian to Bavarian to Greek, brimming stalls at the **Stadtmarkt** (btwn Fuggerstrasse & Annastrasse; ♥ 7am-6pm Mon-Fri, 7am-2pm Sat) sell fresh produce, bread and meat in the Fleischhalle and the Viktualienhalle.

There are lots of fast-food joints in and around Bahnhofstrasse, and delightful cafés along Maximilianstrassse.

Drinking

Helsinki Bar (☎ 372 90; Barfüsserstrasse 4; dishes €4.10-5.50) The Nordic fare, blonde wood furnishings and suspended table lighting here attract a cool crowd.

Kressles Mühle (☎ 362 15; www.kresslesmuehle .de in German) Found behind Helsinki's intimate rooms, this is an alternative, a comedy club whose schedule includes poetry slams, stand-up and meditative gonging.

Café Max (☎ 154 700; Maximilianstrasse 67; dishes €3-10.50) Out the back of this café, where artsy types gather over authentic German, American, French and Italian breakfasts, is the select, sky-lit cocktail bar, Atrium.

Best beer garden bets:

Thing (☎ 395 05; Vorderer Lech 45) An Augsburg institution.

Zur Altenfeuerwache (☎ 511 685; Zeugplatz 4) This 17th-century armoury is now a trade school, cinema and a superb place for a brew.

Entertainment

In the southern Altstadt, next to the Heilig-Geist-Spital, modern and classic fairy tales – *Aladdin* to *Rumpelstiltsken* to *The Little Prince* – come to life at the celebrated marionette theatre **Augsburger Puppenkiste** (☎ 450 3450; Spitalgasse 15; afternoon ticket €7.80-9.80, evening ticket €14.50-19.80; ♥ shows 3pm & 7.30pm Wed & Sat, 2pm & 4pm Sun). The stars on strings are so endearing and the sets and costumes so elaborate that even non-German speakers will enjoy a show. It's often sold out, so if possible, make advance reservations or else check with the box office or the tourist office for remaining tickets.

The adjoining museum, **Die Kiste** (☎ 450 3450; admission €4.20; ♥ 10am-7pm Tue-Sun, last entry 6pm) takes visitors on a journey through the celebrated puppets' 50-year career on stage, TV and film.

Getting There & Away

AIR

Augsburg has a small regional airport that is the hub of Augsburg Air, a Lufthansa affiliate, with services to Hamburg, Berlin, Düsseldorf, Cologne and Frankfurt. It's about 6km north of the city centre; Munich's airport is about 90km due east.

CAR & MOTORCYCLE

Augsburg is just south off the A8, northwest of Munich. The northbound B2 and the southbound B17 are part of the Romantic Road.

TRAIN & BUS

Regional trains connect Augsburg and Munich at least hourly (€9.40, 50 minutes), with faster and pricier InterCity Express (ICE) and InterCity (IC) trains passing through as well. The Regional Express (RE) trains depart every other hour to Füssen (€14.40, two hours) and to Lindau (€23, three hours). The Europabus makes its stops at the Hauptbahnhof.

Getting Around

TO/FROM THE AIRPORT

The Augsburg **Flughafen Express** (☎ 08238-902 256; one-way/return €5/8; 20-35min) bus shuttle connects the airport with the Hauptbahnhof up to five times per day, but only from Monday to Friday.

The **Lufthansa Airport Bus** (☎ 0981 3152; one-way/return €15/24; 70min) runs between Augsburg's train station and the Munich airport six times daily.

PUBLIC TRANSPORT

Most rides within town on the bus and tram network cost €1; longer trips to the outlying suburbs are €2. A 24-hour ticket costs €5.20 and is good for up to three adults.

For bicycle hire, **Zweirad Bäuml** (☎ 336 21; Jakoberstrasse 70) has a good range of bikes from €10 per day or €50 per week.

SOUTHERN ROMANTIC ROAD

In this guide, we have divided the Romantic Road into two sections: the Northern Romantic Road from Würzburg to Dinkelsbühl through Franconia (p226), and the Southern Romantic Road from Nördlingen to Füssen, which goes through Bavarian Swabia and the Allgäu. For details about how to explore this route, see the boxed text on p227.

Nördlingen

☎ 09081 / pop 20,000 / elev 433m

About 70km northwest of Augsburg, Nördlingen lies within the flattened Ries Basin, a huge crater created more than 15 million years ago by a megameteorite. The basin is some 25km in diameter and was used by US astronauts training for the first moon landing.

The town's first recorded history dates back to 1100 and Nördlingen is still encircled by 14th-century town walls, punctuated by five gates, 16 towers and two bastions.

ORIENTATION

The train station is about a 15-minute walk southeast of the Altstadt. Nördlingen township is almost completely circular, with the St Georgskirche on Markt at its centre from where five main roads radiate towards the five town gates. The little Eger River traverses the northern Altstadt, separating the Gerberviertel (Tanner's Quarter), home to both the Stadtmuseum and the Ries Crater Museum, from the rest of the Altstadt.

INFORMATION

Tourist office (☎ 841 16; www.noerdlingen.de in German; Marktplatz 2; ⏰ 9am-6pm Mon-Thu, 9am-4.30pm Fri, 9.30am-1pm Sat Easter-Oct, 9am-5pm Mon-Thu, 9am-3.30pm Fri Nov-Easter)

SIGHTS

Circumnavigate the town by walking along the sentry walk of the covered town wall, and climb up at any of the five gates: **Baldinger Tor**, **Löpsinger Tor**, **Deininger Tor**, **Reimlinger Tor** or **Berger Tor**, located at the end of the streets bearing their names.

The football field–sized, late-Gothic **St Georgskirche** (Church of St George) got its baroque mantle in the 18th century. To truly appreciate Nördlingen's shape and the dished Ries Basin, scramble up the 350 steps of the church's 90m-tall **Daniel Tower** (adult/concession €1.75/1.20; ⏰ 9am-8pm Apr-Oct, 9am-5.30pm Nov-Mar). The guard, who actually lives up here, sounds out the watch every half-hour from 10pm to midnight.

The **Ries Crater Museum** (☎ 273 8220; Eugene-Shoemaker-Platz 1; adult/concession €3/1.80; ⏰ 10am-noon & 1.30-4.30pm Tue-Sun) is a modern museum in an ancient barn. It explores the formation of meteorites and the effects of such violent collisions on Earth. Rocks, including a genuine moon rock (on permanent loan from NASA), fossils and other geological displays shed light on the mystery of meteors.

The **Stadtmuseum** (☎ 273 8230; Vordere Gerbergasse 1; adult/concession €3/1.80; ⏰ 1.30-4.30pm Tue-Sun mid-Mar–early Nov) has costumes and displays on local history. More enlightening is an exhibition on the history of the town walls and fortification system at the **Stadtmauermuseum** (☎ 9180; Löpsinger Torturm; adult/concession €2.50/1.25; ⏰ 10am-4.30pm Apr-Oct).

TOURS

Guided walking tours (in German; €3, free if under 12) depart from the tourist office at 2pm from Easter to October, and also at 8.30pm from mid-May to mid-September.

FESTIVALS & EVENTS

The 10-day **Nördlinger Pfingstmesse**, held at Whitsuntide/Pentecost (dates vary), is the town's biggest party with beer tents, food stalls and entertainment taking over the Altstadt.

SLEEPING & EATING

Hotel Altreuter (☎ 4319; hotel-café-altreuter@nord schwaben.de; Marktplatz 11; s €33-45, d €48-64) Entry to this hotel is through a delectable sweet shop and café (snacks under €5). Its attractive, renovated rooms have TVs. There's also a public parking area in front of the hotel.

Kaiserhof Hotel Sonne (☎ 5067; www.kaiserhof -hotel-sonne.de in German; Marktplatz 3; s €55-65, d €75-120; meals €5.50-15; P ✕) Near the tourist office, Nördlingen's top digs have hosted an entire procession of emperors and their entourages since 1405. Rooms mix modern comforts with traditional charm, and there's an atmospheric regional restaurant.

Café Radlos (☎ 5040; www.cafe-radlos.de in German; Löpsinger Strasse 8; snacks €2.50-5, mains €4.20-11; ✕ closed Tue) Nördlingen is worth a visit for this hip café alone. Amid the art and photographic exhibits, magazine racks and lounge music, the global and regional cuisine includes plenty of vegetarian offerings. A raised stage with piano is the venue for regular live music, and once a month there's a themed Sunday breakfast buffet, which could be anything from Barbados to Brazil. Throw in an English menu, Internet access (€2 per 30 minutes), a kids' play area and a beer garden out back, and you may find yourself staying longer than planned.

La Fontana (☎ 211 021; Bei den Kornschrannen 2; mains €3.50-11.50; ✕ closed Mon) Housed in an enormous ochre-red barn (dating from 1602) with mezzanine seating, meals are upmarket Mediterranean, with good-value pizzas and pastas as well. Under the same raked roof is a market hall with farm-fresh meats, cheeses, breads and produce.

GETTING THERE & AROUND

Trains leave hourly to Donauwörth via Harburg (€4.20, 30 minutes) with connections to Augsburg and Munich. The Europabus stops at the Rathaus, as does regional bus No 501 to Dinkelsbühl and Feuchtwangen.

Nördlingen is on the B25, which connects with the B26 and B466. There are free car parks at all five city gates; some time restrictions apply.

For bicycle hire, try **Radsport Böckle** (☎ 801 040; Reimlinger Strasse 19; around €8).

Harburg

☎ 09080 / pop 5800

Perched above the Wörnitz River about 15km southeast of Nördlingen is the humungous **Schloss Harburg** (☎ 968 60; adult/concession €4.50/3; ✕ tours hourly 10am-5pm Tue-Sun Apr-Oct, closed Nov-Mar). With its medieval covered parapets, towers, turrets, keep and red-tiled roofs, it almost seems like a movie set. Construction commenced in 1150 under the Hohenstaufen emperors before passing into the possession of the counts and princes of Oettingen-Wallerstein in 1299, who still own it today. In July 2006 it will be the backdrop for a medieval extravaganza expected to attract more than 20,000 people, complete with jousting knights. Contact the Fürstliche Burgschenke (see the boxed text below) for more information.

The walk to Harburg's cute half-timbered **Altstadt** takes about 10 minutes from the castle, slightly more the other way

---

THE AUTHOR'S CHOICE

If you've ever entertained royal fantasies, there's no better place to live them out than within the soaring stone walls of historic Schloss Harburg at the luxuriant **Fürstliche Burgschenke** (☎ 1504; www.riesgastronomie.de/burgschenke-harburg/; s €45, d €70-90; meals €7-18; ✕ restaurant closed Mon; P).

Charming rooms are hidden high in the towers with unfolding valley views. All are enchantingly furnished, with private bathrooms, TVs and telephones. But since this is the Romantic Road, after all, consider ensconcing yourself in the whimsical honeymoon suite, with its sublime sunken bedroom, canopied in soft apricot satin.

Beneath the winding red-carpeted staircase, there's a superb restaurant serving internationally influenced regional cuisine prepared by chefs dedicated to producing truly fine fare. Best of all, both the restaurant and hotel are eminently affordable. Who said you can't put a price on romance?

when you're climbing uphill. For a great panorama of the village and the castle, seek out the **Stone Bridge** (1702) spanning the Wörnitz. The **tourist office** (☎ 969 90; www.stadt-harburg-schwaben.de in German; Schlossstrasse; 🕙 8am-noon Mon, Wed & Fri, 2-4pm Tue, 4-6pm Thu) is at the Rathaus. Nearby a handful of guesthouses are squeezed into the Altstadt's miniature streets.

There's an hourly bus service to/from Nördlingen (€3.20, 20 minutes) and trains and buses to/from Donauwörth (€2.60, 13 minutes). Harburg is on the B25.

Donauwörth

☎ 0906 / pop 18,000 / elev 403m

About 15km southeast of Harburg, Donauwörth is at the confluence of the Danube and Wörnitz rivers. From humble beginnings as a fishing village in the 10th century, it reached its zenith as a Free Imperial City in 1301. WWII destroyed much of the medieval town, but plenty of charming buildings still line its central artery, the Reichsstrasse, which is about a 10-minute walk north of the train station. Ried Island lies just to the south of the Altstadt.

The **tourist office** (☎ 789 151; www.donauwoerth.de in German; Rathausgasse 1; 🕙 9am-noon & 1-6pm Mon-Fri, 3-6pm Sat & Sun May-Sep, 9am-noon & 1-5pm Mon-Thu, 9am-1pm Fri Oct-Apr) is at the bottom of Reichsstrasse.

SIGHTS

Donauwörth's landmark is the **Rathaus**, begun in 1236 and altered through the centuries. The carillon on the ornamented step gable plays (at 11am and 4pm daily) a composition by local legend Werner Egk (1901–83) from his opera *Die Zaubergeige* (The Magic Violin).

Just east of the Rathaus, through the Ochsentörl gate, is the pretty-as-a-picture **Promenade**, a linear park and cycleway shaded by trees, through which runs a little canal.

From the Rathaus, Reichsstrasse heads west, flanked by steep-roofed town houses in a rainbow of colours. The two oldest are **Café Engel** (1297) at No 10 and the 14th-century **Tanzhaus** (Dance House) at No 34, now home to an archaeological exhibit, restaurant and concert hall.

Further west, the 15th-century **Liebfrauenkirche** is a Gothic three-nave church decked out with original frescoes; the tabernacle,

choir stalls and baptismal font are also worth a peek. Swabia's largest church bell (6550kg) hangs in the belfry.

Reichsstrasse changes its name to Heilig-Kreuz-Strasse, at the end of which stands its namesake, the **Heilig-Kreuz-Kirche** (1717–20). The faithful have flocked here for centuries to worship a chip of wood said to come from the Holy Cross. The church itself is a baroque confection by Josef Schmuzer of Wessobrunn and part of a Benedictine abbey founded in 1125.

In a former Capuchin monastery is the delightful **Käthe-Kruse-Puppenmuseum** (Doll Museum; ☎ 789 170; Pflegstrasse 21a; adult/concession €2/1; 🕙 11am-5pm Tue-Sun May-Sep, 2-5pm Tue-Sun Apr & Oct, 2-5pm Wed, Sat & Sun Nov-Mar) with lots of dolls and doll houses by world-renowned designer, Käthe Kruse (1901–1983).

South of Reichsstrasse is the **Rieder Tor**, the landmark twin-turreted red gate to picturesque Ried Island.

SLEEPING & EATING

Posthotel Traube (☎ 706 440; www.posthoteltraube.de in German; Kapellenstrasse 14-16; s €38-55, d €75-95; Ⓟ) In a handy location, at the southeastern edge of the Altstadt near Ried Island, rooms here are straightforward but well equipped with hairdryers, telephones and TVs.

Hotel Drei Kronen (☎ 706 170; www.hotel3kronen.com in German; Bahnhofstrasse 25; s/d from 62/92; meals €8-15; Ⓟ ✗ 🖥) Near the train station, the pink-hued Drei Kronen has contemporary, comfortable rooms, and there's a lamp-lit restaurant on the premises.

Café Rafaello (☎ 999 9266; Fischerplatz 1; mains €7.50-18.50) On Ried Island, this trendy Italian eatery with a loftlike Tuscan interior specialises in seafood, and also has good pizza, pasta and gigantic gourmet salads.

Treff Punkt (☎ 213 44; Augsburger Strasse 6; mains 8.50-16.70) Behind the fairy-lit entrance, this unpretentious upmarket restaurant's specialities include pork medallions in homemade butter sauce and variations of turkey. There's a romantic open fire in winter.

GETTING THERE & AWAY

There's direct hourly train service to Nördlingen (€4.20, 30 minutes) via Harburg, and hourly or better trains to Augsburg (€4.20, 30 minutes). The Europabus stops at the Liebfrauenkirche. Donauwörth is at the crossroads of the B2, the B16 and the B25.

South of Augsburg

South of Augsburg, the Romantic Road enters its least-scenic stretch, although there are a few worthwhile stops. About 38km south of town is historic **Landsberg am Lech**, founded by Heinrich der Löwe (Henry the Lion) in 1160. It possesses an especially nice Marktplatz ringed by stately buildings, including the impressive Rathaus. Its awesome façade (1720) is the work of Dominikus Zimmermann, who moonlighted as the town's mayor from 1749 to 1754 while creating the Johanniskirche (1752). Also worth a look is the parish church Maria Himmelfahrt (1458–88), famous for its luminous stained-glass windows.

South of Landsberg, the route enters the **Pfaffenwinkel** (Clerics' Corner), an area with the greatest density of churches and monasteries anywhere in Germany. After the tranquil gateway town of Hohenfurch, the Romantic Road travels to Schongau, which preserves a largely intact medieval appearance and is the Pfaffenwinkel's touristic hub. There's a **tourist office** (☎ 08861-7216; www.schongau.de in German; Münzstrasse 5; ☽ 8am-12.30pm & 2-6pm Mon-Thu, 8am-12.30pm Fri) and sights include the town wall, the Gothic *Ballenhaus* (festival hall), and the baroque Maria Himmelfahrt church (1753), whose choir stucco bears the distinctive Zimmermann touch.

A worthwhile detour is the **Basilika St Michael** (1220) in Altenstadt, about 2km west of Schongau, which ranks as one of the most important Romanesque churches in Bavaria. It has great frescoes, a delicate baptismal font and a 3.5m-high crucifix from around 1200, which is revered as the 'Great God of Altenstadt'.

The route winds south to Peiting, then continues southeast on the B23 to **Rottenbuch** in the romantic Ammertal (Ammer Valley). The town is dominated by an 11th-century Augustinian monastery whose church got its baroque outfit courtesy of Franz Xaver Schmädl and Josef Schmuzer (stucco), and Matthäus Günther (frescoes). Hiking trails lead from the depth of Ammer Gorge back up to elevations reaching 900m. Check with the **tourist office** (☎ 08867-1464; www.rottenbuch .de in German; Klosterhof 36; ☽ 9am-noon Mon-Fri) for maps and directions.

From here, the Romantic Road travels west through Wildsteig before rejoining the B17 in Steingaden, where one of the route's highlights awaits: the Wieskirche.

Wieskirche

Known as 'Wies' for short, the **Wieskirche** (☎ 8862-932 930; www.wieskirche.de; Steingaden; entry by donation; ☽ 8am-7pm Apr-Oct, 8am-5pm Nov-Mar) is one of Bavaria's best-known baroque churches and a Unesco World Heritage site. Every year, about a million visitors – art and spiritual pilgrims alike – flock to what rates as the most accomplished work by the brothers Dominikus and Johann Baptist Zimmermann.

The central object of worship is the rather unassuming statue of the **Scourged Saviour**, now part of the high altar. Originally used in a Good Friday procession in 1730, the statue ended up in the attic of a local innkeeper who revered it greatly. Then, on 14 June 1738, during evening prayers, tears suddenly began weeping from the statue's eyes. Over the next few years, so many pilgrims poured into the town that the local abbot commissioned a new church to house it.

Not even the constant deluge of visitors can detract from the Wies' splendour. Gleaming white pillars are topped by capital stones that seem like leaping flames against the white, gold and pastel stucco. Above it all, the vaulted ceiling fresco celebrates Christ's Resurrection as he is carried on a rainbow.

Free private group tours in German can be arranged by calling the **Schwangau tourist office** (☎ 819 80; www.schwangau.de in German; Münchener Strasse 2; ☽ 8am-12.30pm & 1.30-5pm), which can also discuss rates for group tours in English.

All visitors are asked not to tour through the church during the services.

The Europabus makes a 13-minute stop at the Wieskirche, but only on its south-north route (Füssen–Frankfurt). Local bus No 73 connects the church with Füssen's bus station, next to the train station.

Füssen & Schwangau

☎ 08362 / pop 17,700 / elev 800m

Schwangau and Füssen are the two final stops on the Romantic Road. Nestling at the foot of the Alps, they're actually separate towns, but described here jointly because they form the two anchors of what is

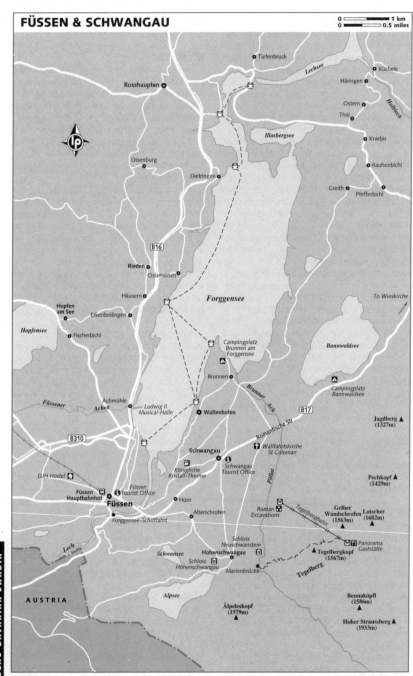

FÜSSEN & SCHWANGAU

0 ━━━━ 1 km
0 ━━━━ 0.5 miles

Tiefenbruck

Lechsee

Küchele

Häringen

Rosshaupten

Ostern

Thal

Hallbach

Illasbergsee

Kniebis

Ussenburg

Rauhenbichl

Dietringen

Greith

Pfefferbichl

B16

Rieden

Osterreinen

Häusern

Forggensee

To Wieskirche

Hopfen
am See

Erkenboilingen

Bannwaldsee

Hopfensee

Fischerbichl

Campingplatz
Brunnen am
Forggensee

Campingplatz
Bannwaldsee

Füssener
Achen

Achmühle

Ludwig II
Musical-Halle

Brunnen

Brunner Ach

B17

Jagdberg ▲
(1327m)

Waltenhofen

Romantische Str

B310

Schwangau

Wallfahrtskirche
St Coloman

Pechkopf ▲
(1429m)

DJH Hostel

Königliche
Kristall-Therme

Schwangau
Tourist Office

Pöllat

Füssen
Tourist Office

Füssen
Hauptbahnhof

Füssen

Horn

Alterschrofen

Roman
Excavations

Tegelbergbahn

Gelber
Wandschrofen
(1563m) ▲

Latscher ▲
(1682m)

Forggensee-Schifffahrt

Panorama
Gaststätte

Lech

Schwansee

Schloss
Neuschwanstein

Hohenschwangau

Schloss
Hohenschwangau

Marienbrücke

▲ Tegelbergkopf
(1567m)

Tegelberg

AUSTRIA

Alpsee

Älpeleskopf
(1579m)
▲

Bennaköpfl
(1586m)
▲

Hoher Straussberg ▲
(1933m)

marketed as the **Königswinkel** (King's Nook). The area gets its name from Ludwig II, the king who built Neuschwanstein, one of Bavaria's biggest tourist attractions. This, as well as his ancestral home the palace of Hohenschwanstein, are actually in tiny Hohenschwangau, the third 'corner' in this triangle of attractive towns, and still owned by the royal family of Bavaria. It basically just exists to cater for castle visitors, which number around 1.3 million a year.

Ludwig's castle Schloss Linderhof (p132) is about 45km northeast of here.

ORIENTATION

The only Bahnhof in the Königswinkel is in Füssen, right in the northern Altstadt, steps away from the tourist office and all the town's sights. The Lech River traverses the town and flows into the Forggensee. Schwangau is about 4km east of Füssen via the B17 (Romantic Road), which, in town, is called Münchener Strasse. Hohenschwangau is more or less in between and south of the two, about 5km from Füssen and 3km from Schwangau. Füssen is the bigger town with better infrastructure. Bus Nos 73 and 78 connect all three.

INFORMATION

Füssen tourist office (☎ 938 50; www.fuessen.de; Kaiser-Maximilian-Platz 1; ☼ 8am-noon & 1.30-5pm Mon-Fri, 10am-1pm Sat May-Oct) This slick office is about three minutes' walk east of the Bahnhof.

Post office (Bahnhofstrasse 10, Füssen)

Schwangau tourist office (☎ 819 80; www .schwangau.de in German; Münchener Strasse 2; ☼ 8am-12.30pm & 1.30-5pm)

Sparkasse (Kaiser-Maximilian-Platz 3, Füssen) This bank is next to the tourist office.

SIGHTS & ACTIVITIES
Schloss Neuschwanstein

Appearing through the mountaintop mist like a dreamy mirage is the world's most famous castle and model for Disneyland's signature citadel: **Schloss Neuschwanstein** (Neuschwanstein Castle; ☎ 930 830; adult/concession €9/8, with Schloss Hohenschwangau €17/15; ☼ 9am-6pm Apr-Sep, 10am-4pm Oct-Mar).

Construction on this idealised romantic Schloss began in 1869 and was never completed. The grey-white granite edifice was an anachronism from the start; by the time Ludwig died in 1886, the first high-

rises had pierced the New York skyline. For all the money spent on it (an estimated €3 million), the king himself was able to enjoy only about 170 days in his dream palace.

Ludwig imagined his palace as a giant stage that would allow him to re-create the world of Germanic mythology immortalised in the operas of Richard Wagner, whom he worshipped. A theatre designer rather than an architect laid out the initial blueprint, which accounts for its dramatic packaging.

The centrepiece is the lavish **Sängersaal** (Minstrels' Hall) with murals depicting scenes from the opera *Tannhäuser*. Though it wasn't used during Ludwig's time, concerts are now held here every September (tickets cost €25 to €70; available from February each year through the Schwangau tourist office).

Other completed sections include **Ludwig's bedroom**, dominated by a huge bed crowned with intricately carved spires like those of a Gothic cathedral, a gaudy **artificial grotto** (another allusion to *Tannhäuser*) and the **Thronsaal** (Throne Room). Built in the style of a Byzantine church, the Thronsaal has a great mosaic floor and a chandelier shaped like a giant crown, though it's actually throneless: Ludwig ordered it shortly before his death but it was never delivered.

Despite his love of the medieval look, Ludwig's fondness for the latest technologies saw the installation of a sophisticated hot-air heating system and running water throughout the castle.

For the postcard view of Neuschwanstein framed by wooded hills, walk 10 minutes up to Marienbrücke (Mary's Bridge), which spans the spectacular Pöllat Gorge over a waterfall just above the castle.

Each of the castles must be seen on 35-minute guided tours (in German or English). Tickets are only available from the **ticket centre** (☎ 930 830; www.ticket-center-hohen schwangau.de; Alpenseestrasse 12, Hohenschwangau). In summer, we recommend that you arrive by 8.30am or earlier to ensure you get a ticket. To avoid disappointment, you can also book tickets in advance by phone or online. You'll need a major credit card to guarantee your booking, but you may cancel as late as two hours before your preassigned tour time. A nonrefundable booking fee of €1.50 per ticket applies.

LUDWIG II MUSICAL

In a case of life imitating art (itself imitating life, imitating art), the grand-scale production of the musical *Ludwig II: Longing for Paradise* – which debuted with much fanfare in its fantastical purpose-built venue on the western shore of the Forggensee in 2000 – closed in late 2004 after financial collapse.

In its place, a completely new musical on Ludwig's life, also titled **Ludwig II** (☎ 01805-131 132; www.ludwig2musical.de; Festspielhaus Neuschwanstein, Im See 1, Füssen; ticket €15-110; ⓨ 7.30pm Thu-Sat, 2.30pm Sat & Sun) is set to have opened in the same extravagant musical hall by the time you're reading this. Two on-site restaurants and a rooftop café intend to provide patrons with dinner-and-show packages.

At the time of writing, plans were also in place to resurrect the original musical in Munich; check with the tourist office there (p63).

When you purchase your ticket, you'll be assigned a tour number and time. Wait by the castle entrance close to the time indicated on your ticket until the digital display shows your tour number. Then put your ticket into the slot next to the turnstiles to meet your tour guide inside.

It is usually possible to visit both castles on the same day. The steep uphill walk from Hohenschwangau to Neuschwanstein takes about 30 to 40 minutes. You can also shell out about €5 per person for a horse-drawn carriage ride.

Schloss Hohenschwangau

Originally built in the 12th century by Schwangau knights, Ludwig spent his childhood at sun-yellow **Schloss Hohenschwangau** (Hohenschwangau Castle; ☎ 930830; adult/concession €9/8, with Schloss Neuschwanstein €17/15; ⓨ 9am-6pm Apr-Sep, 10am-4pm Oct-Mar), down in the village. His father, Max II, had the ruin reconstructed in neo-Gothic fashion in the 1830s. It's less ostentatious than Neuschwanstein, though Ludwig's eccentric taste is still evident, as in the stars painted on his bedroom ceiling.

It was here that Ludwig first met Wagner, and the **Hohenstaufensaal** (High Baptism Hall) features a square piano where the composer would entertain Ludwig with his latest efforts. Some rooms feature murals from German mythology (including the Lohengrin, or Swan Knight).

Purchasing tickets for Schloss Hohenschwangau is the same complicated procedure as for Schloss Neuschwanstein, see p261 for more information.

Altstadt Füssen

Füssen has a distinctly resort feel, with multilanguage street and hotel signs, and upmarket designer boutiques.

The town's tangle of lanes is lorded over by the **Hohe Schloss**, a late-Gothic confection and former summer residence of the bishops of Augsburg. In the inner courtyard you'll do a double take before realising that the gables, oriels and even windows are merely illusionary architecture, done in 1499. The palace's north wing contains the **Staatsgalerie im Hohen Schloss** (Hohen Schloss Art Gallery; ☎ 903 164; Magnusplatz 10; adult/concession with Städtische Gemäldegalerie €2.50/2; ⓨ 11am-4pm Apr-Oct, 2-4pm Nov-Mar, closed Mon), which houses late-Gothic and Renaissance paintings and sculpture by Swabian and Franconian artists. One floor below is the **Städtische Gemäldegalerie** (Municipal Art Gallery) where the emphasis is on 19th-century artists, mostly from Bavaria.

Below the Hohe Schloss is the former **Benediktinerkloster St Mang** (Benedictine Abbey of St Mang), which traces its history back to an 8th-century missionary by the name of Magnus who founded a monk's cell here. He's allegedly buried in the Romanesque crypt of the abbey's baroque basilica, adorned with the oldest extant frescoes in Bavaria (980).

Integrated within the complex is the **Museum Füssen** (☎ 903 145; Lechhalde 3; adult/child under 14/concession €2.50/free/2; ⓨ 10am-5pm Apr-Oct, 1-4pm Nov-Mar, closed Mon), which provides access to the abbey's festive baroque rooms, including the library, festival hall, the Romanesque cloister and the **St Anna Kapelle** (830). A haunting highlight is the **Füssener Totentanz**, a Dance of Death cycle from 1602, created during the dark days of the black plague.

Tegelbergbahn

Views of the Alps and the Forggensee are truly dazzling from the top of the Tegelberg

(1720m), most comfortably reached by **cable car** (☎ 983 60; one-way/round trip €9/15; ☷ 8.30am-5pm Jul-Oct, 9am-5pm Nov-Jun), usually closed for maintenance for six weeks in November and December. The last ascent/descent is 20 minutes before closing. From here, it's a wonderful hike down to the castles (follow the signs to Königsschlösser) in about two to three hours. Call ahead for a weather report (☎ 810 10).

The mountain station is also a prime launch point for hang-gliders and parasailers, while the summer **toboggan track** (adult/child under 14 per ride €2.50/2; ☷ 10am-5pm, closed in bad weather), right next to the valley station, is a winner with kids.

Also here are the ruins of a **Roman bath** (admission free; ☷ 9am-5pm) from the 2nd century AD, uncovered during the construction of the Tegelbergbahn in 1966.

The valley station is about 2km southeast of Schwangau and served by bus Nos 73 and 78 from both the Schwangau village centre and the Füssen train station.

Forggensee

The largest lake in the Allgäu, the Forggensee is actually a reservoir created in the 1950s from the bed of the Lech River. Though a controversial move back then, the lake – which is fully filled from mid-June to October – is now a popular water sports centre, with activities including swimming, sailing, boating, and windsurfing. A 32km-long bike trail hugs its shore, the paved sections of which are also popular with in-line skaters. You can catch a ride on boats operated by **Forggensee-Schifffahrt** (☎ 921 363; Lech-halde 3, Füssen). Check with the tourist offices about current cruise schedules and where to hire sporting equipment.

Königliche Kristall-Therme

Views of the illuminated royal castles make the **Königliche Kristall-Therme** (☎ 819 630; Am Kurpark, Schwangau; admission for 2/4hr €8/11.50, all day €15; ☷ 9am-10pm Sun-Thu, 9am-11pm Fri & Sat) a sensational spot for a swim, hydro-massage, meditation or sauna. Some nights (usually Tuesday and Friday) are for nudists only.

TOURS

If you're in Munich and would like to see the castles on a tight schedule, consider joining an organised tour. Through EurAide in Munich (p63), you can book the **Two Castles**

in a Day tour (adult/under 26 plus castle admission €41/35) to Neuschwanstein and Linderhof with a brief stop in Oberammergau. It operates daily from April to about October and on a more limited schedule for the rest of the year. Rail pass discounts are available.

SLEEPING & EATING
Füssen

Pension Kössler (☎ 7304; fax 399 52; Kemptener Strasse 42; s €30-33, d €60-66; **P**) This pretty pension offers perennially outstanding value with private bathrooms, balconies, TVs and telephones in all rooms.

Hotel Sonne (☎ 9080; www.hotel-sonne.de; Reichenstrasse 37; s €53-63, d €79-89; **P** ✗ ▣) One of the colourful buildings lining the Altstadt, this bright orange hotel has cheerful rooms and friendly service. It's due to undergo a major expansion during 2005, but business should continue as usual.

Altstadt Hotel zum Hechten (☎ 916 00; www .hotel-hechten.com; Ritterstrasse 6, Füssen; s/d €39/78; meals €6.50-11.50; **P**) Set around a quiet inner courtyard, this child-friendly place is one of Füssen's oldest hotels, with traditional public areas and bright, modern bedrooms. The restaurant is stick-to-the-ribs Bavarian.

Luitpoldpark (☎ 9040; fuessen@treff-hotels.de; Luitpoldstrasse 1; s €75-108, d €150-206; **P** ✗ ▣) Dominating the main square, the soaring rose-coloured Luitpoldpark is a major landmark. Grand rooms are complemented by a vast fitness area. Ask about their specials.

DJH hostel (☎ 7754; www.djh.de; Mariahilferstrasse 5; dm €16.45-17.75, s €19.45-20.75, d €38.90-41.50; ☷ closed mid-Nov–late Dec; **P** ✗) The hostel is a five- to 10-minute walk west of the station; breakfast and linen are included.

Franziskaner Stüberl (☎ 371 24; Kemptener Strasse 1, cnr Ritterstrasse; mains €7.50-12.50; ☷ closed Thu) This quaint restaurant specialises in *Schweinshax'n* (pig's trotters) and schnitzel, prepared in infinite varieties. Noncarnivores can indulge in *Kässpätzle* (macaroni and cheese) and other meatless dishes.

Café Bistro Relax (☎ 505 270; Bahnhofstrasse 1; dishes €4.80-7) Spilling onto a large see-and-be-seen terrace, this hip café-bar has good Italian-leaning fare. Local artists' work is on display (and for sale), and there's Internet access (€0.50/€2 per 6/30 minutes).

Snack options include the local **Nordsee** (Reichenstrasse 40) and the butcher-deli **Vinzenzmurr** (Reichenstrasse 35).

Schwangau

Gasthof Bei Weirich (☎ 8412; gasthof.weirich@t-online
.de; Füssener Strasse 108; s €30, d €55-60). In Schwangau's little annex of Horn, 2km towards Füssen and 2km from the castles, this family-run
guesthouse has neat-as-a-pin rooms, and an
excellent restaurant (mains €5 to €17.50) with
specialities such as deer goulash in red wine
with cranberry sauce noodles, calf's liver with
apple rings, and fresh trout.

Hotel Weinbauer (☎ 9860; www.hotel-weinbauer
.de; Füssener Strasse 3; s €33.50-44, d €67-88; mains €6-15)
Easily recognised by its *Lüftlmalerei* (see
the boxed text on p127) façade paintings,
the Weinbauer is a convivial inn with a new
spa area and a good restaurant. The wine
tavern has a vaulted ceiling.

Campingplatz Brunnen am Forggensee (☎ 8273;
www.camping-brunnen.de in German; Seestrasse 81; per
tent €3, per person €5.80-6.80; ☙ closed Nov-20 Dec)
Amenities are upgraded every year at this
five-star camp site at the southern end of
the Forggensee, with a supermarket, laundry, restaurant with beer garden, and children's playground on site.

Campingplatz Bannwaldsee (☎ 930 00; www
.camping-bannwaldsee.de in German; Münchner Strasse
151; per tent €3, per person €5.80-6.80) Lakeside
camping on the Bannwaldsee with boat
and bicycle hire, solar-heated showers, two
restaurants and on-site supermarket.

Pizzeria San Marco (☎ 813 39; Füssener Strasse
6; mains €5-10) Locals congregate at this cosy,
rustic Italian-style place, which serves up
better-than-average pizzas and pastas.

GETTING THERE & AWAY

If you're starting out from Munich and
want to 'do' the royal castles on a day trip,
the best train to catch to beat the crowds departs Munich (€18.20) at the ungodly hour
of 4.58am (5.45am on weekends), getting to
Füssen at 7.23am (7.54am weekends) with a
change in Buchloe.

Direct regional trains to/from Augsburg
(€14.40, two hours) via Kaufbeuren depart
every two hours.

The Europabus stops at the tourist office
in Schwangau, at the foot of the castles in
Hohenschwangau and at Füssen Bahnhof,
its southern terminus.

Several roads lead to the Königswinkel:
the A7 from Memmingen and Kempten,
the B16 from Kaufbeuren and the B17 (Romantic Road) from Augsburg/Munich.

GETTING AROUND

Local bus No 78 connects the castles, Füssen, Schwangau and the Tegelbergbahn.
Taxis to the castles are about €8 to €10, or
it's about a 5km walk from Füssen and 3km
from Schwangau.

In Füssen, **Radsport Zacherl** (☎ 3292; Kemptener Strasse 119; off-peak/peak season per day from €6/7)
hires out two-wheelers. In Schwangau,
bikes can be hired at **Mayr** (☎ 814 58; Mittledorf
3; adult/child €6/4).

KEMPTEN

☎ 0831 / pop 62,000 / elev 646m

Kempten was first mentioned by Greek ge-
ographer Strabonus around AD 18, and as
such lays claim as the oldest recorded German city, though other cities would beg to
differ, notably Trier, which bases its own
claim on the shards and wall remains of the
city of Augusta Treverorum (the paper used
by Strabonus is thought to be older than the
discoveries at Trier).

Derived from Celtic origins, the name
'Kempten' means a fortress or settlement
at the bend of the river. The town was first
founded on the right bank of the Iller River,
but its early-Roman settlement moved to
the foot of Burghalde (Castle Hill) on the
west bank after the Alemanni invaded
around 260. Between 740 and 1525 it
was under monastic rule, before becoming a Free Imperial City and joining the
Reformation in 1527. The long-running
monastic vs Free Imperial hostilities, however, reached a head in 1632–33, when both
engaged in mutual destruction, with Swedish and Imperial forces supplying backup.
The town's 600-year division finally ended
when it became part of Bavaria at the dawn
of the 19th century.

Modern-day Kempten is a progressive,
sophisticated city, and the thriving economic centre of the Allgäu. Every year
in early May the town swings during **Jazz
Spring**, a major jazz festival featuring international artists – check with the tourist
office (opposite) for details.

Orientation & Information

Kempten radiates from the Iller River's western bank. The Burghalde is one
block from St Mang, the main bridge, in
the southwest of the town. The Bahnhof
and central bus station are just outside the

MARTIN MOOS

Hiking (p42), Bavaria

GREG GAWLOWSKI

Rural Bavaria, (p26)

Skiing (p40), Bavaria

CHRISTIAN ASLUND

Christkindlesmarkt (p191), Nuremberg

MARTIN MOOS

DAVID PEEVERS

Traditional bakery, Berchtesgaden (p146)

Lebkuchen (gingerbread) hearts at the Christkindlesmarkt (p191), Nuremberg

MARTIN

Altstadt's southern edge, 1km from the pedestrianised Fischerstrasse, the lively main shopping drag. Just east of Fischerstrasse is Rathausplatz, where you'll find the **tourist office** (☎ 252 5237; www.kempten.de in German; Rathausplatz 24; 9am-5pm Mon-Fri, 10am-1pm Sat May-Oct, 9am-noon & 1.30-5pm Mon-Fri Nov-Apr).

Sights

To see the city's origins from the ground up, head just east of the river (1km from the town centre), to the **Archäologischer Park Cambodunum** (Archaeological Park; ☎ 252 5200; Cambodunumweg 3; adult/concession €3/1.50; 10am-5pm Tue-Sun May-Oct, 10am-4.30pm Nov–mid-Dec & mid-Mar–May, free guided tours 11am Sun). This amazing slice of history incorporates Gallo-Roman temple precincts, reconstructed in part on the city's early foundations; the 'Small Thermae', with undercover ruins; and remnants of the open-air Forum. It's a stark contrast to the humming city shown by the sweeping vistas from here. To get here from the Altstadt, cross St Mang Bridge and turn left onto Kaufbeurer Strasse, then right onto Brodkorbweg.

For more great views of the city, head to **Burghalde**, where there's a **museum** (contact the tourist office for information on exhibits and opening hours), and in summer, an **open-air cinema** (☎ 225 07; Königstrasse 3; tickets around €6; dates vary). From here, **Bäckerstrasse** (Bakers' St) is lined with intact 17th- and 18th-century buildings. Duck down Ankergässele, a little lane featuring the town's only surviving gate, the **Ankertörle**.

At **St Mang-Platz** is the magnificent Gothic **Church of St Mang**. Built in 1426 on Romanesque foundations, highlights are the 66m tower and a 1905 Art Nouveau fountain.

A former market lane lined with patrician houses, the **Rathausplatz** is steeped in rococo, Gothic and baroque influences. The **Rathaus** itself was constructed in 1368 as a half-timbered granary and rebuilt in sturdier stone in 1474.

Dominating the northern end of the Altstadt was the former Benedictine monastery, now the spectacular baroque **Residenz** (☎ 08378-1284; Residenzplatz; admission €3; by tour only every 45min 9am-4pm Tue-San Apr-Sep, 10am-4pm Tue-Sun Oct, 10am-4pm Sat Nov-Mar, extra tours during the Christmas market), once home to the prince-abbot. The ceremonial apartments' rococo interiors especially are a knock-out. The

sprawling **Hofgarten** lies between here and the **Orangerie**, housing the **city library** (☎ 252 5723; 10am-6pm Tue-Fri). The Residenz' **Marstall** (stables; ☎ 252 5200; Landwehrstrasse; adult/child under 16 €2.50/1.25; 10am-4pm Tue-Fri Mar–mid-Nov) now contain both the **Alpinmuseum** (Alpine Museum), an intriguing overview of humankind's relationship with mountains through the ages; and the **Alpinländisches Galerie** (Alpine Gallery), which brings together late-Gothic religious art from the surrounding regions.

It's not hard to miss, but the **Basilica St Lorenz** (☎ 7540 5600; 9.15am-6pm Sun-Thu, 9.15am-1pm Fri) rewards the up-close-and-personal treatment. Beneath its crowning dome and twin towers is an awe-inspiring interior including rare scagliola (imitation marble) panels on the carved choir stalls.

Just west of here is **Grosser Kornhausplatz** (Granary Sq). The granary, which was built in the 1700s, is used for ceremonial purposes; adjoining it is the **Allgäu Museum** (☎ 252 5200; Grosser Kornhausplatz 1; adult/child under 16 €2.50/1.25; 10am-4pm Tue-Sun) with a stunning vaulted gallery displaying regional art.

The southern boundary of the baroque square is **Hildegardplatz**, where vibrant markets are held every Wednesday and Saturday during summer.

Located one block south of Hildegardplatz is Zumsteinhaus. Within this 18th-century neoclassical townhouse, admission covers both the **Roman Museum** and the **Natural History Museum** (☎ 252 5200; Residenzplatz 31; adult/child under 16 €2/1; 10am-noon & 2-4pm Thu & Sun Apr-Oct).

Sleeping & Eating

Hotel Fürstenhof (☎ 253 60; www.fuerstenhof-kempten.de; Rathausplatz 8; s €44-57, d €53-63; P X) Dating back to 1187, this gorgeous rococo confection is the only hotel inside Kempten's pedestrianised Altstadt and has entertained a parade of emperors in its day. Its sprawling rooms have soaring ceilings and are equipped with all mod cons, and the atmospheric vaulted cellar is conducive to quaffing cocktails. Breakfast is an optional extra €8 per person.

Meckatzer Bräu Engel (☎ 565 6489; Prälat-Götz-Strasse 17; mains €7.20-12; closed Mon) Bavarian spirit is in full force at this barrel-lined brewery-pub, whose gleaming copper boiler is right next to the bar with pipes running overhead. Typical regional specials include *Rinderroulade*, thin-sliced beef rolled with bacon and spices, skewered then cooked and served with handmade pasta. There are good vegetarian alternatives. There's an umbrella-shaded deck in summer, and great regular live gigs.

Getting There & Away

Kempten has direct train connections to/from Munich (€18.20, 1½ hours), Memmingen (€5.70, 30 minutes) and Kaufbeuren (€6.90, 30 minutes). It's at the nexus of the A7 and the B12.

MEMMINGEN

☎ 08331 / pop 41,100 / elev 600m

Founded in 1160 by Duke Welf VI, the charming town of Memmingen had its heyday after becoming a Free Imperial City in 1268. In 1525, the *Bauernartikel*, the manifesto that lead to a bloody peasants' revolt the same year, was written here.

Orientation & Information

The Bahnhof and central bus station are on the eastern edge of the Altstadt, about a five-minute walk from Marktplatz, the main square, where you'll find the **tourist office** (☎ 850 172; www.memmingen.de in German; Marktplatz 3; ☻ 9am-5pm Mon-Fri, 9.30am-12.30pm Sat).

Sights

Marktplatz is fringed by restored historical buildings. These include the arcaded **Steuerhaus** (1495), a former tax-collecting office, which got its gaudy façade in 1906; the **Renaissance Rathaus** (1589) with stucco flourishes from the rococo period (1765); and the **Grosszunft** (1719), a former patrician gathering and party house.

Just west of the Marktplatz, the **Stadtmuseum** (☎ 850 134; Zangmeisterstrasse 8; admission €2; ☻ 10am-noon & 2-4pm Tue-Fri & Sun May-Oct) is housed in the Hermannsbau, a pretty patrician private residence from 1766.

Looming further west is the octagonal tower of the Gothic **St Martinskirche** (☎ 856 90; ☻ 10am-4pm Apr, 10am-5pm May-Oct). You can climb it at 3pm from May to October (€2).

A short walk south is the **Antonierhaus**, the former home and hospital run by a religious order called the Antoniter. It incorporates the **Antoniter-Museum** (☎ 850 245; Martin-Luther-Platz 1; adult/concession €1.50/1; ☻ 10am-

noon & 2-4pm Tue-Sat, 10am-12.30pm & 1.30-5pm Sun). In the same building is the more interesting **Strigel-Museum**, dedicated to prominent home-grown Renaissance artist Bernhard Strigel (1461–1528).

On Gerberplatz is the **Siebendächerhaus** (1601), which is so named for its unusual seven overlapping roofs where tanners used to dry their pelts.

Two walking trails around the town have signboard information in English. Red-marked signs on the **Roter Weg** (Red Way) target the town's major points of interest; green-marked signs along the **Grüner Weg** (Green Way) take in the gates and towers of the old town wall. The signs can sometimes be hard to spot; pick up a map from the tourist office that marks out both trails.

Sleeping & Eating

Memmingen's charms are easily assimilated in half a day, but if you want to spend the night, try the Drexel family's **Parkhotel Memmingen** (☎ 9320; www.parkhotel-memmingen .de; Ulmer Strasse 7; s €58-79, d €78-109; mains €8-19.50; ☒ ☒ ⌨). Near the Marktplatz, it has smart, sophisticated rooms, including ones for business travellers, 24-hour reception, and a superior regional and international restaurant. Public parking is right behind the hotel.

There's regular live music at the chandeliered **Café Rau** (☎ 3424; Zangmeisterstrasse 4; mains from €8.50, 4-course menus from €28.50), which spans two glass-walled storeys and also sells speciality confectionery, sumptuous cakes and tiny biscuits.

Getting There & Away

Memmingen has direct train connections with Munich (€16, 1½ hours), Augsburg (€12.90, 1¼ hours), Oberstdorf (€11.10, 1¼ hours), and Kempten (€5.70, 30 minutes). The town's right at the junction of the A7 and the A96.

AROUND MEMMINGEN
Buxheim

About 4km northwest of Memmingen, Buxheim is home to one of the largest and best-preserved Carthusian monasteries in Germany. Founded in 1402 and of Gothic origin, the **monastery** got its splendid stucco decorations and luminous frescoes in the 18th century courtesy of the brothers Do-

---

DETOUR: OTTOBEUREN

No matter from which angle you approach, you'll likely stop momentarily in your tracks at the awe-inspiring sight of the abbey and basilica of **Benediktinerabtei Ottobeuren**, appearing like a celestial mirage above this enchanting little spa village and hometown of Sebastian Kneipp (see the boxed text on p252).

The monastery complex stretches for nearly half a kilometre from the main church portal to the utility buildings at the back. Inside and out, it's such an exuberant celebration of rococo art and architecture that even an atheist may find religion.

Founded in 764 the abbey still has about two dozen active friars today. It took scores of top-ranked architects and artists nearly two generations to create the extraordinary **basilica** (admission incl tours & concerts by donation; 8am-6pm, half-hourly tours 2pm Sat Apr-Oct, organ recitals 4pm Sat late Feb-late Nov), which was built between 1737 and 1766. The richness of the décor hits you from all directions: gilded altars, delicate stucco, vivid frescoes, marble pillars, and a cacophony of angels, but stand-outs are a Romanesque crucifix and the choir stalls, carved with scenes from the Old Testament and the life of St Benedict. If you're able to catch a recital, the organs are some of Bavaria's finest.

In the former abbot's residence, the **museum** (admission €2.50; 10am-noon & 2-5pm Mon-Fri, 10am-noon & 2-4pm Sat & Sun Apr-Oct, 2-4pm Mon-Fri, 10am-noon & 2-4pm Sat & Sun Nov-Mar) has sculptures and paintings, and old pharmacy and baroque theatre displays. Peek into the ballroom-sized library with 15,000 volumes and the majestic **Kaisersaal** (Imperial Hall), site of the illustrious **Ottobeurer Konzerte** (tickets €13 to €31) concert series held annually from May to September. Check with the **tourist office** (08332-921 950; www.ottobeuren.de in German; Marktplatz 14; 9am-noon & 2-5pm Mon-Thu, 9am-noon & 2-4pm Fri), right at the foot of the basilica, for ticket availability. In the abbey is the **Kloster-Café** (08332-925 929; snacks from €1.50; closed Thu Nov-Apr), which has divine cakes.

Bus No 955 travels to Ottobeuren from Memmingen's central bus station several times daily (€2.40, 15 minutes). Ottobeuren is roughly about 11km southeast of Memmingen and 50km northwest of Kaufbeuren via minor roads well signposted from both towns. Take care if you're driving in winter, as the roads can get icy.

---

minikus and Johann Baptist Zimmermann. The dizzyingly ornate choir stalls by Ignaz Waibel are from the same period. The **Deutsches Kartausenmuseum** (618 04; adult/concession €2.50/1.50; 10am-noon & 2-5pm Mon-Sat, 1-5pm Sun Apr-Oct) provides access to restored monk's cells, the cloisters, the refectory, library and historical exhibits. The nearby Parish Church of St Peter and the Chapel of St Anna also sport the Zimmermann touch. Most of the complex is now a boarding school.

Bus No 964 departs hourly Monday to Saturday from the central bus station in Memmingen just by the Bahnhof (€2.40, 12 minutes).

KAUFBEUREN

 08341 / pop 41,000 / elev 678m

Like many Swabian towns, Kaufbeuren began as a Carolingian royal residence, became a Free Imperial City in the Middle Ages and was absorbed into the Bavarian

kingdom in 1802. Behind its largely intact town wall is a web of cobbled lanes and quiet alleys interspersed with churches and proud town houses.

Kaufbeuren's contemporary flair is due in large part to its nearby jewellerymaking community, the suburb of Neugablonz, formed after WWII.

In late July, the **Tänzlfest**, during which about 1600 colourfully costumed kids recreate their town's history, draws thousands of locals and visitors.

Orientation & Information

Kaufbeuren's Altstadt is easily explored on foot. The **tourist office** (404 05; www.kaufbeuren.de in German; Kaiser-Max-Strasse; 9.30am-5pm Mon & Tue, Thu & Fri, 9.30am-2pm Wed year-round, 9.30am-noon Sat May-Oct) is in the Rathaus, at the end of the main commercial artery. The bus station is a short walk north of here, while the Bahnhof is about 500m southeast, outside of the Altstadt.

ALLGÄU-BAVARIAN SWABIA

Sights

Start your exploration at the **Rathaus** (1879–81), a neo-Renaissance edifice designed by Georg Hauberrisser. The meeting halls are covered in paintings by Wilhelm Lindenschmidt, a friend of King Ludwig II. The wedding room features a painting of Prussian Emperor Kaiser Wilhelm I.

Walking west along Kaiser-Max-Strasse will take you straight to the **Fünfknopfturm**, a (so-named) five-spired fortified tower and city landmark.

Built right into the fortifications, **St-Blasius-Kirche** (10-11am & 2-4pm Tue-Sun) has a late-Gothic carved altar (1518) by Jörg Lederer and 64 wall panels documenting the lives and deaths of the 12 apostles and other saints. You'll have good views of the town from up here.

On the site of the former Carolingian palace, the **Crescentia chapel** holds the remains of a local nun who was canonised in 2001. The newly renamed street, Crescentiagässchen (formerly Zitronengasse), which may still appear on older city maps), leads you to the **St-Martins-Kirche**, a Romanesque-turned-Gothic-turned-baroque-turned-neo-Gothic church.

To get to **Neugablonz**, take bus Nos 11, 12 or 13. It was here where an entire town called Gablonz – originally located in the Sudetenland region in today's Czech Republic – resettled once expelled after WWII. They continue to make their world-famous glass and costume jewellery today. For an insight into the community's history, drop into the **Isergebirgs-Museum** (965 018; Marktgasse 8; adult/concession €3/2; 1-5pm Tue-Sun), inside the Gablonzer Haus, which also showcases their jewellery.

Sleeping & Eating

Hotel Goldener Hirsch (430 30; www.goldener-hirsch-kaufbeuren.de in German; Kaiser-Max-Strasse 39-41; s/d from €42/72; meals €8.80-14.70;) This elegant, central hotel is exceptional value and has a fitness room and sauna, as well as a lovely restaurant with contemporary cuisine.

Hotel Hasen (966 190; www.hotel-hasen.com in German; Ganghoferstrasse 7 & 8; s €33.50-54, d €50-75; meals €7.50-12.80;) Occupying two buildings on opposite sides of the street (reception is in the older of the two), Hasen is about a five-minute walk from the Altstadt, close to the train station. Rooms in the newer building are a bit more spacious but it's hard to justify the added cost. The restaurant is classic Bavarian.

Café Smile (955 9688; Kaiser-Max-Strasse 4; mains €7.50-14.80; closed Sun) Perpetually grinning owner-chef Felix Steinert turns out terrific mix-and-match pastas and sauces, plus fish and vegetarian dishes at this gem. At night it's a great place for cocktails.

Getting There & Away

Trains to Munich depart about every half hour (€12.90, one hour), as do those to Augsburg (€9.40, 50 minutes), although this sometimes requires a change in Buchloe. Kaufbeuren is on the B16.

LINDAU

 08382 / pop 24,000 (3500 on the island) / elev 400m

Lindau occupies the only snippet of Bavarian shore on Lake Constance, a giant bulge in the otherwise sinewy course of the Rhine River. More than half of the lake's 272km circumference lies in the German state of Baden-Württemberg with the remainder in Austria and Switzerland. The snow-capped Swiss Alps provide a breathtaking backdrop.

From a 9th-century nunnery, Lindau blossomed into a prosperous town thanks primarily to its spot on a major north–south trading route. In the early 13th century it became a Free Imperial City, a status kept until 1802. After secularisation, it briefly became Austrian, then Bavarian in 1805.

Like something out of an F Scott Fitzgerald novel, Lindau exudes old-world wealth and romance. The French occupied the place for 10 years after WWII, a period that saw the founding of the casino in 1950 and, a year later, the first annual gathering of Nobel prize winners. To this day, every year in late June or early July, scores of scientists descend upon Lindau to exchange ideas and promote research. Rooms are scarce midyear, when holidaymakers invade by the tens of thousands. But even under iron-grey winter skies, Lindau still manages to have the feel of a sophisticated summer playground.

Orientation

Lindau's historic Altstadt lies on a petite island (3.3 hectares) reached by a causeway. The train and bus stations are in the island's southwestern corner, while the harbour and its gorgeous promenade are just to the south. The largely car-free historic core extends east of the station; its main artery is Maximilianstrasse. Impossible to miss, the striking new circular casino (on the same site as the original) is just before the bridge on Chelles Allee.

Information

HypoVereinsbank (Zeppelinstrasse 2)

Post office (Bahnhofsplatz) Just north of the train and bus stations.

Tourist office (☎ 260 030; www.prolindau.de; Ludwigstrasse 68; ⏰ 9am-1pm & 2-6pm Mon-Fri, 10am-2pm Sat Apr–mid-Jun, 9am-6pm Mon-Fri, 10am-2pm Sat & Sun mid-Jun–mid-Sep, 9am-noon & 2-5pm Mon-Fri mid-Oct–Mar) Opposite the Bahnhof, staff here sell the *BodenseeErlebniskarte* (adult/child under 15 €54/€29), available April to October, which entitles you to three days' travel on boats and mountain cableways on and around Lake Constance, including its Austrian and Swiss shores, as well as entry to around 150 tourist attractions and museums. There are also seven-day (€69/€39) and 14-day (€98/€49) versions.

Volksbank (Maximilianstrasse)

Sights

The Bahnhof is only steps away from Lindau's little harbour, which is guarded by a lighthouse and a pillar bearing the Bavarian lion. Both date to the middle of the 19th century and thus are historic youngsters compared to the dignified 13th-century **Mangturm**, which once did double duty as a lighthouse and as part of the fortification. The tower, which can be climbed (€1), anchors Lindau's elegant lakeside **promenade** where you'll find an almost Mediterranean scene, with well-heeled tourists sipping cappuccinos.

Inland, just past the Mangturm, is the Reichsplatz, dominated by the **Altes Rathaus** (1422–36) where the Imperial Diet met in 1496. Murals of rather gaudy intensity cover its façade; added in 1975, they're based on 19th-century designs. The current town hall – **Neues Rathaus** – is in the adjacent baroque edifice.

East on Ludwigstrasse you'll find Barfüsserplatz, site of the city theatre in a 700-year-old church.

The attractive baroque **Haus zum Cavazzen** with trompe l'oeil murals lords over Markt-

platz. Inside is the **Stadtmuseum** (☎ 944 073; adult/concession €2.50/2; ⏰ 11am-5pm Tue, 2-5pm Sat, 11am-5pm Sun Apr-Oct), which has period furniture, paintings, crafts and some fun historical musical instruments.

Magnificent **Maximilianstrasse** is lined with many Gothic and Renaissance town houses, as well as classy boutiques and cafés. On Schrannenplatz are both the **Diebsturm** (Brigand's Tower; 1380), a tiny former jail adjoining the town fortifications, and the **Peterskirche**, Lindau's oldest church (11th century) and now a war memorial. It contains impressive frescoes of the Passion of Christ by Hans Holbein the Elder.

Activities

Lindau is a paradise for sailing and windsurfing; the tourist office has a list of sports clubs and shops offering equipment hire and instruction.

Lake Constance is also ideal cycling territory; **Fahrrad Station** (☎ 212 61; Hauptbahnhof; per day €7-9) hires out a range of bikes.

For an easy tootle around the lake, you can hire row and paddle boats at **Grahneis** (☎ 5514) and **Hodrius** (☎ 297 771; per hr €5-10), both located on the northern shore.

Swimming is possible at several public pools. The largest of which is the **Strandbad Eichwald** (☎ 5539; adult/child €3/2; ⏰ check with the tourist office).

An excellent place for hiking is the Pfänderberg, a 1064m-high mountain just across the Austrian border, with views of Lake Constance and three countries: Germany, Austria and Switzerland. The Pfänderbahn cable car (one-way/return November to March €4.80/€8.30, one-way/return April to October €5.50/€9.50) travels up the mountain every 30 minutes from 9am to 7pm daily from its station near the boat landing in Bregenz.

Tours

You can hire a *Stadthörer,* a self-guided audio tour (in English or German) with commentary on about 15 island sites for €7.50 from the tourist office.

Weisse Flotte (☎ 275 8410) runs round-trip boat tours (€7, one hour) several times daily from Lindau harbour to Bregenz (Austria) and the mouth of the Rhine. Boats leave from the island's eastern shore, just south of the casino.

ALLGÄU-BAVARIAN SWABIA

Sleeping

Hotel Seerose (☎ 838 21; www.seerose-lindau.de; Auf der Mauer 3; s €39-58, d €68-120; P 🍴) The best value on the island, Seerose is located on the old town wall (turn right 200m after the bridge and it's on the left). Airy rooms are furnished with elegant simplicity, there's a sauna and solarium, and – rare for Bavaria – staff will let late arrivals ring the night bell if they're expecting you.

Lindauer Hof (☎ 4064; www.lindauer-hof.de; Seepromenade; s €92-105, d €142-215; meals €13-20; P 🍴 💻) This lavish waterfront hotel has a number of double-storey rooms with sitting areas on the upper levels. Rooms with lake views cost a little extra or you can gaze out from the outstanding 1st-floor restaurant, Atrium, specialising in lake fish.

DJH hostel (☎ 967 10; jhlindau@djh-bayern.de; Herbergsweg 11; B&B with linen €18.15-21.40; s €21.15-24.40, d €32.30-48.80) Lindau's modern hostel is on the mainland, about 2km from the Bahnhof. Take bus Nos 1 or 2 to the ZUP (central transfer station), then change to bus No 3 direction Zech and get off at 'Jugendherberge'.

Hotel Helvetia (☎ 9130; www.hotel-helvetia.com in German; Seepromenade 3; s €58-120, d €98-210; P 🍴 ♿) Behind a citrus-coloured façade right, by the Mangturm, awaits this dedicated wellness hotel. It has wheelchair access and pretty rooms decked out in English-style floral décor.

On the lakeshore at the Austrian border, the ecocamp site **Park-Camping Lindau am See** (☎ 722 36; www.park-camping.de in German; Fraunhoferstrasse 20; per person/tent/car €6/3/3; 🍴 closed Nov; 💻) has a beach, grocery store and restaurant.

Eating

Gasthaus zum Sünfzen (☎ 5865; Maximilianstrasse 1; sausages €5.50-8.50, mains €14-19) This ancient tavern is an island institution and has its own sausage kitchen. A local speciality sausage is the *Lindauer Doppelschröbling*.

Alte Post (☎ 934 60; Fischergasse 3; mains €8-15) At this atmospheric restaurant where every nook and cranny tells a story, you'll find good regional food and a lively beer garden frequented by locals.

Nana (☎ 934 70; Bahnhofplatz 1; mains €14.90-22.90; 🍴 from 5pm Nov-Mar) The timber outdoor deck overlooking the lake is the perfect place to savour the Mediterranean menu here, which includes couscous salad, mozzarella plates and fish platters.

Café-Bistro Wintergarten (☎ 946 172; Salzgasse 5; mains €6.90-9.40; 🍴 to 7.30pm) This glass-roofed, vine-festooned café hosts readings and rotating art exhibits. Crepes are a speciality, and there are at least eight excellent vegetarian dishes.

Insel-Bar (☎ 5017; Maximilianstrasse 42; mains €5.10-8.10; 🍴 to 7pm) Lindau's French heritage is evident at this chic creperie in the cosmopolitan town centre. Sweet and savoury crepes come with an assortment of toppings. Rooms at the upstairs hotel (singles €49 and doubles €97) are equally stylish.

For snack food, drop by the butcher-deli **Vinzenzmurr** (Maximilianstrasse 27). Schafgasse has several international eateries, including **Turkiyem** (Schafgasse 8), which makes good doner kebabs.

Getting There & Away

BOAT

Bodensee Schiffsbetriebe (BSB; ☎ 275 8410; www.bsb-online.com) operates a year-round scheduled boat service between lake communities. Stops (one-way) include Wasserburg (€4.40, 20 minutes), Friedrichshafen (€8.20, 1¼ hours), Meersburg (€10.20, 2¾ hours) and Bregenz (€4, 22 minutes).

CAR & MOTORCYCLE

Lindau is on the B31 and also connected to Munich by the A96. It's the western terminus of the scenic Deutsche Alpenstrasse (German Alpine Road) to Berchtesgaden.

TRAIN

Regional trains from Memmingen (€12.40, 1½ hours) with onward service to Augsburg (€24, three hours) run several times daily. The trip between Lindau and Oberstdorf requires a change in Immenstadt (€13.50, 1½ hours). Bregenz in Austria is just 10 minutes away (€1.90).

Getting Around

As Lindau is a tiny island it is ideal for walking or cycling – you can hire bicycles from **Unger's Fahrradverleih** (☎ 943 688; Inselgraben 14; per day from €8; 🍴 9am-1pm & 3-6pm Mon-Fri, 9am-1pm Sat & Sun). Buses to/from the mainland run every half-hour, singles cost €1.50 and a day pass is €3.50. All buses converge at the ZUP, about 800m north of the bridge on the mainland. Bus Nos 1 and 2 serve the island.

Island parking is limited and potentially frustrating as the causeway backs up quickly in peak months. At the island's northwest edge, P5 charges €5 all day, as does P3, just to the left of the bridge on the mainland; the others are more expensive. A free shuttle bus (June to early September) services mainland parking lots.

AROUND LINDAU
Wasserburg
☎ 08382 / pop 2800

About 6km west of Lindau, tiny Wasserburg is charmingly located and a tranquil alternative for lake explorations. The sites mentioned below are squeezed onto a peninsula, which is also where boats from Lindau and elsewhere dock. The **tourist office** (☎ 887 474; www.wasserburg-bodensee.de in German; Lindenplatz 1) is near the train station, a five-minute walk north via Halbinselstrasse.

Schloss Wasserburg, first mentioned in 784 and rebuilt in 1592 by a branch of the Fugger family from Augsburg, is now a fancy hotel. Nearby is the **Church of St Georg**, where several artists did some fine work, most notably the putti on the altar, the statues of saints and the pietà by Franz Ferdinand Ertinger of Kempten. To learn more about local culture and curiosities, check out the medieval courthouse, which is now the **Museum im Mahlhaus** (Museum in the Mill; ☎ 750 457; admission €2; ☺ 10am-noon Tue-Sun & 3-5pm Wed & Sat May-Oct).

Wasserburg is connected to Lindau by train, infrequent buses, or best of all, by boat (see opposite). It's on the B31.

OBERSTDORF
☎ 08322 / pop 10,500 / elev 843m

Tucked away at the foot of the towering Allgäu Alps, right on the Austrian border, Oberstdorf is Germany's southernmost resort. Quintessentially Alpine, the storybook village itself is almost entirely pedestrianised, with most traffic kept on the perimeter. The setting is nothing but glorious and the options for outdoor pursuits plentiful.

Especially in high season, large crowds can make the place feel claustrophobic. The nicest time to visit is in autumn when you'll find clear skies, colourful forests and thinning throngs.

Oberstdorf is a training centre for athletes in the fields of figure skating (the National

Championships take place here every year in the first week of January), downhill and cross-country skiing, and is the first stop on the Vierschanzen-Tournee, a prestigious international ski-jumping competition held the week after Christmas.

Orientation
The Bahnhof and central bus station are just north of the town centre. The Nebelhorn cable car ferries you directly up the mountain from the southwestern edge of town; other lifts are in valleys away from the village. At night, the dramatically floodlit Heini-Klopfer ski jump dominating the mountainscape makes it easy to orient yourself.

Information
EMERGENCY
Hospital (☎ 7030; Trettachstrasse 16) Just east of the Bahnhof.

INTERNET ACCESS
Kurhaus (☎ 977 0521; Prinzenstrasse 4; per 15min €1)

MONEY
Sparkasse (Bahnhofsplatz 2)

POST
Post office (Bahnhofsplatz 3)

TOURIST INFORMATION
Both offices are well signposted and have extended hours during the ski season.
Tourist office (www.oberstdorf.de) Bahnhof (☎ 700 217; ☺ 8.30am-8pm Mon-Fri, 9.30am-6pm Sat); Marktplatz (☎ 7000; Marktplatz 7; ☺ 8.30am-noon & 2-6pm Mon-Fri, 9.30am-noon Sat)

Sights
For a culture fix, check out the eclectic **Heimatmuseum** (Local History Museum; ☎ 5470; Oststrasse 13; admission free; ☺ 10am-noon & 2-5.30pm Tue-Sat, closed May, Nov & Dec), in a 17th-century town house. Learn how the holes get into the famous Allgäu cheese or how gentian schnapps is distilled, and check out the world's largest shoe.

Activities
SKIING & SNOW SPORTS
Oberstdorf has about 71km of groomed cross-country tracks, but it's really the downhill terrain that people crave. There

are three ski areas – **Nebelhorn**, **Fellhorn** and **Söllereck** – plus the adjacent Kanzelwand area in the Kleinwalsertal on the Austrian side. Thirty lifts ferry skiers up the mountains where they can enjoy around 44km of downhill runs of all degrees of difficulty. There's also a competition-quality half pipe and a snowboarding park. The ski season generally runs from mid-December to early April.

Ski passes good for all four areas cost €33/€64/€88 for one/two/three days (for children under 15 the cost is €15/€30/€41) all season (mid-December to mid-April). Day passes for the Nebelhorn area only are €29.50/€25 for one/two days (for children under 15 the cost is €14/€12) and for the Fellhorn-Kanzelwand area €31/€26.50 (children under 15 €14.50/€12.50).

Numerous ski and snowboarding schools compete for customers. Check with the tourist office for a complete list. Ski gear can be hired all over town, with downhill equipment costing around €11 per day, including boots.

Adrenaline junkies can get a rush at two brand-new **fun parks** (Nebelhorn ☎ 960 00, Fellhorn ☎ 960 0380) at the first stop on the Nebelhornand and Fellhorn slopes. Airboarding (horizontally) on an inflatable yellow toboggan, rolling downhill in a giant ball, snow tubing in tyres, ski foxing (a combination of tobogganing and skiing with ultrashort skis), unmotorised snow scooters and snow cycles, and snow skating on a small skateboardlike board are some of the thrills to be sought. Packages that also include ski passes start at €43.50.

HIKING

Oberstdorf has nearly 200km of hiking trails, 140km of which are open year-round. The tourist office has maps and can make recommendations. For an exhilarating day walk (six hours' hiking time), ride the Nebelhorn cable car to the upper station, then trek down via the Gaisalpseen, two stunning alpine lakes. Sturdy footwear is essential. On a good day, you'll have sweeping views of some 400 peaks.

An easy and fun hike is one travelling through the **Breitachklamm** (☎ 4887; admission €2; ✆ 8am-5pm Apr-Oct, 9am-4pm mid-Dec–Mar), which is mainly a paved trail through a narrow gorge carved by the Breitach Creek. In

winter, frozen icicles, often forming entire curtains, create a magical setting. It takes about 45 minutes to hike through the gorge to the 'Walserschanze' and 2½ hours to the Gasthaus Waldhaus in the Kleinwalsertal; the trail is closed during snow melt. There's an hourly bus service to the mouth of the gorge from the central bus station.

Nordic walking (hiking with stocks) has become hugely popular in recent years, with 12 specially marked tracks, open year-round, graded according to difficulty. Contact the tourist office about stock hire (about €3).

ICE-SKATING

The vast **Eislaufzentrum** (☎ 915 130; Rossbichlstrasse 2-6; skating adult/concession €3/2, visit only €1/0.75, skate hire €2.50; ✆ hr vary, call ahead or check with the tourist office), behind the Nebelhorn cable-car station, has three rinks and is the training centre for top figure skaters.

Sleeping

Oberstdorf teems with private guesthouses. Note that some owners may be reluctant to rent rooms for just one night, especially during high season.

Schüle's Gesundheitsresort & Spa (☎ 7010; www .schueles.com in German; Ludwigstrasse 37-41a; s/d from €111/222; P ✗ ☐ ♨) For sheer indulgence, this spa resort is hard to surpass. From the vast indoor pool framed by arched windows to the sumptuous rooms and near-endless range of wellness treatments available on site, you just may not find a reason to step out the front door.

Gästehaus Geiger (☎ 988 470; www.oberstdorf .net/geiger in German; Frohmarkt 5; s €18-25, with bathroom €20-30, d €30-46; P) This clean, cosy guesthouse has cute-as-a-button timber-floored rooms, and a decent buffet breakfast. The owners are happy to whip up a sandwich or small meal on request.

Hotel Sonnenheim (☎ 809 980; www.sonnenheim .oberstdorf.com; Waltenbergerstrasse 6; s €39-45, d €74-92; P ☐) The décor is refreshingly uncluttered in this well-positioned place, just a few moments east of the centre. Pricier rooms come with balconies or terraces with sun umbrellas, and facilities include a solarium.

Hotel Oberstdorf (☎ 940 770; www.hotel-oberst dorf.de in German; Reute 20; s €35-96, d €70-192; P ✗ ☐ ♨) Individual high-speed Internet terminals are in every room at this

TILL THE COWS COME HOME

One of the great delights of hiking in the Bavarian Alps is to break for a *Brotzeit* (literally, 'bread time') at one of the many *Almen*, simple huts in the mountain pastures where the cattle are brought to graze in the summer. The shepherds who live here in these months often make their own cheese and other products, which they serve, along with drinks, to hungry trekkers.

An important event in the farming year is the Almabtrieb (sort of an Alpine cattle drive) in September, when the animals are brought back down to the valley. Provided none of the cows and shepherds have suffered injuries or sickness, the animals are decorated with magnificent wreaths and garlands. While in Upper Bavaria all cattle are thus adorned, in the Allgäu this is a privilege reserved to the lead cow. Sometimes the animals also wear bells, intended to keep the bad spirits at bay. A successful Almabtrieb is usually an excuse for a big festival and market, which brings together the farmers, locals and visitors. The cattle, meanwhile, head back to their farms where they spend the winter in the stable before trudging back uphill in late spring.

newly renovated, supersleek hotel, about eight minutes' drive west of the town centre. There's also a restaurant, bar, wellness facilities and a panoramic terrace on the premises.

Campingplatz Oberstdorf (☎ 6525; www.camping -oberstdorf.de; Rubinger Strasse 16; per person/tent/car Apr-Oct €4.60/3.60/2.60, Nov-Mar €5.10/4.60/2.60) The local all-seasons camp site is about 1.5km north of the Bahnhof beside the tracks. Facilities include a coin-operated laundry.

Eating

Zum Wilde Männle (☎ 4829; Oststrasse 15; mains €10-12; ☒ closed Thu) Filling, inexpensive regional favourites such as veal goulash make this place immensely popular with locals; menus are available in English.

Mohren (☎ 9120; Marktplatz 6; mains €7-21.50) Right in the town's heart, this upscale restaurant has elegant striped chairs and curved booths beneath a mirrored ceiling. The house speciality is mountain hay, innovatively used in dishes from cream of hay soup to boiled beef in hayflower and hayflower sorbet with lemon balm, plums and sliced apple. If that doesn't appeal, other offerings include fish and game.

Kühberg (☎ 3323; Oytalstrasse 2; mains €7-15; ☒ closed Wed) With breathtaking views over the town, this Bavarian restaurant is a 45-minute scenic walk southeast of town,

but it's easily accessed by car. The menu is honed to a quality-not-quantity list of around a dozen traditional favourites, and local artists' work is on display.

Vinzenzmurr (Hauptstrasse 1; dishes €1.50-4.50) This self-service butcher-deli has terrific sandwiches, sausages and salads; there's also a bakery.

Getting There & Away

Direct trains run from Munich (€24, 2½ hours) via Kempten and there are more requiring a change in Immenstadt. RVA buses shuttle several times daily between Oberstdorf, Füssen and Garmisch-Partenkirchen.

The B19 runs due south to Oberstdorf from Kempten. Parking in the centre is sparse, expensive and comes with strict time limits. Inexpensive parking lots (free to overnight visitors) are at the village entrance at the north of the town, from where you can either walk (between five to 15 minutes) or take the electric shuttle (see below).

Getting Around

Electric shuttle buses plough through town at 30-minute intervals from around 7am to 6pm. Prices start from €0.50 per ride, free with the *Gästekarte* (guest card) handed out by hotels. In winter, a ski bus serves all areas (free with skiing equipment).

Directory

ACCOMMODATION

Accommodation in Bavaria is comfortable, well organised and plentiful. If you're arriving without a reservation, local tourist-office staff can usually help you find suitable lodging (sometimes for a small fee).

The majority of our recommendations in this guide are midrange properties (between €70 and €130 per double), which generally offer the best value for money. You can expect clean, comfortable and decent-sized rooms with at least a modicum of style and a private bathroom, TV and telephone. Top-end hotels (over €130 per double) have an international standard of amenities and perhaps a scenic location, special décor or historical ambience. Hotels in this category are also most likely to have air-con and wheelchair-accessible rooms. Budget places (under €70 per double) are generally hostels and other simple establishments where bathrooms may be shared with other guests. Nonsmoking rooms are becoming increasingly common in midrange and top-end properties. Unless noted, rates quoted include breakfast, which is usually an all-you-can-eat buffet.

Prices listed in this book do not – and in fact cannot – reflect seasonal or promotional discounts. Always ask or check a hotel's website (listed throughout this book) for special deals or packages. At hotels, you can sometimes get lower rates if business is slow.

Properties with on-site parking are identified in this book with the parking icon (P). City hotels often charge extra for parking.

Most resorts and spa towns charge their overnight guests a compulsory, nightly *Kurtaxe* (resort tax). The charge may range from €0.50 to €3.50 and is collected by your lodging establishment. In return you'll be issued a *Kurkarte* (resort card), which entitles you to various benefits, such as free or discounted concerts, bus transportation, museum admission or guided hikes.

Camping

Camp sites are ubiquitous and usually quite well maintained in Bavaria, although they may get jam-packed in summer. The core holiday season runs from May to September, although some camp sites remain open year-round. Expect to pay about €3 to €4.50 for tent sites, plus €4 to €6 per person and €2 to €3 per car. Some farmers may allow you to pitch your tent on their property, but always be sure to ask permission first.

Farm Stays

A holiday on a working farm is a great way for city slickers to get close to nature while being relatively comfortable. This type of vacation is usually a big hit with families. Kids get to meet their favourite farmyard animals up close and maybe even get to help with everyday chores. Accommodation options can range from bare-bones rooms with shared facilities to fully-furnished holiday flats. Minimum stays are common with farm-stay accommodation. Contact the regional tourist associations (p282) for details.

Hostels

Bavaria has over 80 hostels affiliated with Hostelling International (HI), some of which are located in unique and atmospheric settings such as converted monasteries, mills, castles or hospitals. They're run by the Deutsches Jugendherbergswerk (DJH) and cater primarily for people under 27 (rambunctious school groups in particular). Some hostels also admit older people on a space-available basis. Families and single parents travelling with at least one underage child are exempt from the age restriction.

Staying at a DJH hostel requires membership in your home country's HI association. Nonmembers either need to buy a Hostelling International Card for €15.50 (valid for one year) or individual stamps costing €3.10 per night. Both are available at any DJH hostel.

Overnight rates in dorms may range from €13 to €25 and usually include linen and breakfast; lunch and supper cost around €5 extra each. Dorms are gender-segregated, although smaller rooms may be available for families or groups.

About 30 Bavarian hostels can now be booked online either at www.djh.de in German or www.iyhf.org. Alternatively, just contact the hostel directly by phone, fax or email.

A small crop of independent hostels is also finally springing up in Bavaria. Geared toward backpackers, they welcome travellers of all ages and generally attract a more convivial, international crowd. Most have mixed dorms available as well as private rooms. Look out for them in Munich, Nuremberg and Regensburg. New ones are being planned for Bamberg, Würzburg and Plankenfels in Franconian Switzerland. For details, see the Sleeping sections of these destinations. For bookings, contact the hostels directly or try www.hostels.com or www.hostels.net.

Hotels

Hotels range from small family-run establishments to comfortable mid-size proper-

ties to luxurious international chains. Those serving breakfast only are called *Hotel Garni*. This being Germany, you can generally expect even the cheapest places to be spotlessly clean, comfortable and well run.

In most hotels rooms vary (often dramatically) in terms of size, décor and amenities. The cheapest share facilities, while others may come with a shower cubicle installed but no private toilet; only the priciest have ensuite bathrooms. If possible, ask to see several rooms before committing.

Pensions, Inns & Private Rooms

Pensionen (pensions) and *Gasthöfe* or *Gasthäuser* (inns) are usually family run and quite a bit less formal than hotels. Generally they are also cheaper and smaller and often have a restaurant attached. You can expect clean rooms but only minimal amenities; maybe a radio, sometimes a TV, almost never a phone. Facilities may be shared. What rooms lack in amenities, they usually make up for in charm and authenticity, often augmented by friendly and helpful hosts.

Renting a *Privatzimmer* (private room) in someone's home is a popular budget option, especially in the more rural areas. You probably won't have much privacy, but you will get a glimpse of how local people live. The tourist offices keep lists of available rooms or you can simply look for signs saying '*Zimmer Frei*' ('rooms available') in houses or shop windows. If a landlord is reluctant to rent for a single night offer to pay a little extra.

Rental Accommodation

Renting a furnished *Ferienwohnungen* (holiday flat) for a week or longer is a popular form of holiday accommodation in Bavaria. Tourist offices have lists of *Ferienwohnungen* and some pensions, inns and hotels also rent out apartments. Most owners impose a minimum rental period of three days to a week, especially in summer and around holidays. Shorter stays may be possible by paying a surcharge.

BUSINESS HOURS

In Bavaria most shops are open from 9am to 8pm Monday to Saturday, banks are open from 8.30am to 4pm Monday to Friday and restaurants are generally open for lunch from 11.30am to 2pm and dinner from 5.30pm to 9pm. In rural and suburban areas most shops and offices observe a two- to three-hour lunch break and shops generally close at 6pm. Major variations to the above are listed in reviews.

After hours and on Sundays, you can stock up on basic goods at petrol stations and major train-station stores, albeit at inflated prices. Some bakeries open for a few hours on Sundays. Most museums are closed on Mondays, and many restaurants observe a *Ruhetag* (day of rest), usually Monday or Tuesday. Bars generally open between 5pm and 7pm and clubs at 10pm; both close whenever business dies down (there's no curfew). All shops, banks and government offices are closed on public holidays.

Always call ahead to confirm the hours if you've got your eye on a particular place.

CHILDREN
Practicalities

Travelling to Bavaria with tots can be child's play, especially if you don't overly pack your schedule and involve the kids in the day-to-day planning. Lonely Planet's *Travel with Children* has a wealth of tips and tricks on the subject.

Children enjoy a wide range of discounts for everything from museum admissions to bus fares and hotel stays, although the cut-off age can be anything from six to 18. Most hotels have family rooms with three or four beds or can provide rollaway beds or cots. Car-rental firms rent children's safety seats (which are compulsory; see p290) for about €5 per day. Airlines usually allow infants (up to two years old) to fly for free, while older children requiring a seat of their own qualify for reduced fares.

Baby food, infant formulas (both soy and cow's milk), disposable nappies and the like are widely available in supermarkets and pharmacies. Breast-feeding in public is practised, especially in the cities, although most women are discreet about it. If you need a babysitter, ask staff at your hotel for a referral.

Kids are welcome in casual restaurants, where highchairs are standard, but taking them to upmarket ones might raise eyebrows, especially at dinnertime. See p47 for more information.

Sights & Activities

It's easy to keep kids entertained no matter where you travel in Bavaria. The countryside, of course, beckons with all sorts of outdoor pursuits – from swimming and cycling to horseback riding and canoeing – that are sure to leave the little ones exhausted by day's end. Farm holidays (p274) are an excellent way for kids to get a full nature immersion. Bavaria is also packed with legend-shrouded castles, including the medieval Schloss Harburg (p257) and the fantastic Schloss Neuschwanstein (p260), that are sure to fuel the imagination of many a Harry Potter fan. For movie fans there's Bavaria Filmstadt (p83) in Munich.

Even in the cities possibilities abound for keeping those tiny tots occupied. Take them to parks, playgrounds, public pools or kid-friendly museums such as the Deutsches Museum (p79) in Munich or the Spielzeugmuseum (Toy Museum; p189) in Nuremberg. For more Munich-specific ideas, see p85.

CLIMATE CHARTS

For general advice on climate and when to travel in Bavaria, see p9. The climate charts below provide a snapshot of local weather patterns.

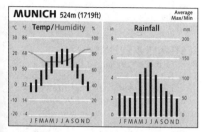

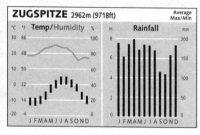

CUSTOMS

Most articles that you take to Germany for your personal use may be imported free of duty and tax. The following allowances apply to duty-free goods purchased in a non-EU country and you can bring in additional products up to a value of €175:

Alcohol 1L of strong liquor or 2L of less than 22% alcohol by volume and 2L of wine (if over age 17)

Coffee and tea 500g of coffee or 200g of coffee extracts and 100g of tea or 40g of tea extracts (if over age 15)

Perfume 50g of perfume or scent and 0.25L of eau de toilette

Tobacco 200 cigarettes or 100 cigarillos or 50 cigars or 250g of loose tobacco (if over age 17)

DANGERS & ANNOYANCES

Bavaria has one of the lowest crime rates in Germany and is a remarkably safe place to live and travel in. Of course, to be on the safe side, you should still take all the usual precautions, such as locking hotel rooms and cars, not leaving valuables unattended and not taking midnight strolls in city parks.

Keep your distance from groups of intoxicated soccer fans, who tend to roam around cities on game days (usually Saturday), and from skinheads, called *Glatzen* (literally 'baldies'). These people are unpredictable, potentially violent and sometimes provoked by as little as a stare.

In Munich and the Bavarian Alps, the Föhn (warm, dry wind) is a local weather-related annoyance most common in autumn. It seems to give some people headaches or make them cranky but also brings exquisite clear views of the mountains.

DISABLED TRAVELLERS

Overall, Bavaria caters well for the needs of the *Behinderte* (disabled), especially the wheelchair-bound. You'll find access ramps and/or lifts in many public buildings, including train stations, museums, theatres and cinemas. Newer hotels have lifts and rooms with extra-wide doors and spacious bathrooms. Nearly all trains are accessible, and local buses and U-Bahns are becoming increasingly so as well. Guide dogs are allowed on all trains.

Good resources include the following:

All Go Here (www.everybody.co.uk) Directory that provides information on disabled services offered by most major airlines.

Deutsche Bahn Mobility Service Center (☎ 01805-512 512, €0.12 per min; www.bahn.de; ☺ 8am-8pm Mon-Fri, 8am-2pm Sat) Telephone operators provide train access information and help with route planning. The website has useful information in English; follow the link to 'International Guests'.

German National Tourism Office (www.germany-tourism.de) Has an entire section (under Travel Tips) about barrier-free travel in Germany.

Natko (☎ 06131-250 410; www.natko.de in German) Central clearinghouse for inquiries about travelling in Germany as a disabled person.

DISCOUNT CARDS

If you're a full-time student, the **International Student Identity Card** (ISIC; www.isic.org) is your ticket to savings on airline fares, travel insurance and many local attractions. Nonstudents under 26 should get the International Youth Travel Card, which grants many of the same benefits. Both cards are issued by student unions, hostelling organisations and youth-oriented travel agencies such as STA Travel.

Discounts are also widely available for seniors, children, families and the disabled, although no special discount cards are needed. In some cases you may be asked to show ID to prove your age.

Some cities offer Welcome Cards entitling visitors to discounts on museums, sights and tours, plus unlimited trips on local public transport. They can be good value, especially if you take advantage of most of the benefits and don't qualify for any of the standard discounts.

EMBASSIES & CONSULATES

For German missions around the world, as well as foreign missions in Germany, see the website of the German **Federal Foreign Office** (www.auswaertiges-amt.de).

German Embassies

Germany has diplomatic representation in almost every country in the world. The embassy is always located in the capital city but consulates, which handle visas and other travel-related services, are usually found in other major cities as well. Contact the embassies listed here for a referral to the consulate nearest you.

Australia (☎ 02-6270 1911; www.germanembassy.org.au; 119 Empire Circuit, Yarralumla, ACT, 2600)
Canada (☎ 613-232 1101; www.ottawa.diplio.de; 1 Waverley St, Ottawa, Ont K2P 0T8)
France (☎ 01 5383 4500; www.amb-allemagne.fr; 13-15 Ave Franklin Roosevelt, Paris, 75008)
Ireland (☎ 01-269 3011; www.germanembassy.ie; 31 Trimleston Ave, Booterstown, Dublin)
Japan (☎ 03-5791 7700; www.tokyo.diplio.de; 4-5-10 Minato-ku, Tokyo, 106-0047)
New Zealand (☎ 04-473 6063; www.wellington.diplio.de; 90-92 Hobson St, Wellington)
UK (☎ 020-7824 1300; www.german-embassy.org.uk; 23 Belgrave Sq, London, SW1X 8PZ)
USA (☎ 202-298 8140; www.germany-info.org; 4645 Reservoir Rd NW, Washington DC, 20007-1998)

Consulates in Germany

Most countries now have their embassies in Berlin but many also have consulates in Munich. Where they don't, we've listed the nearest office.

Australia (☎ 069-905 580; fax 9055 8119; Grüneburgweg 58-62, Frankfurt-am-Main)
Canada (☎ 089-219 9570; fax 2199 5757; Im Tal 29, Munich)
France (☎ 089-419 4110; fax 4191 1141; Möhlstrasse 5, Munich)
Ireland (☎ 089-2080 5990; fax 2080 5989; Denninger Strasse 15, Munich)

Japan (☎ 089-417 6040; fax 470 5710; Karl-Scharnagl-Ring 7, Munich)
New Zealand (☎ 030-206 210; fax 2062 1114; Friedrichstrasse 60, Berlin)
UK (☎ 089-211 090; fax 2110 9144; Bürkleinstrasse 10, Munich) Also for Australian nationals during Oktoberfest.
USA (☎ 089-288 80; fax 283 047; Königinstrasse 5, Munich)

FESTIVALS & EVENTS

Bavaria has a very active festival schedule. This list includes only events celebrated throughout the state or that draw visitors from the entire region and beyond. Many are described in greater detail in the destination chapters, which also list festivals of local importance.

January & February

Fasching (Carnival) The pre-Lent season is celebrated with costumed street partying, parades, satirical shows and general revelry, especially in Munich.
Hornschlittenrennen Locals race downhill on historical sleds once used for bringing hay and wood to the valleys.

May & June

Maifest (May Festival) Villagers celebrate the end of winter by chopping down a *Maibaum* (tree), painting, carving and decorating it, and staging a merry revelry, usually on the eve of 1 May.
Pfingsten (Whitsuntide/Pentecost) Many villages stage elaborate horse parades, some featuring hundreds of riders in traditional outfits, during this religious holiday. Specific celebrations include the Nördlinger Pfingstmesse (p257), the Erlanger Bergkirchweih (p195) and the Historisches Festspiel 'Der Meistertrunk' (p232) in Rothenburg ob der Tauber.
Fronleichnam (Corpus Christi) Ten days after Whitsuntide and Pentecost, this day is celebrated with major processions.
Sonnwendfeier (summer solstice; eve of 21 June) Summer is greeted with big bonfires lit on mountaintops throughout Bavaria.
Munich Film Festival (late June; p87) Important film festival brings the stars to Munich.

June & July

Festspiele Europäische Wochen (mid-June to late July; p172) Major music festival held in Passau, Upper Austria and the Czech Republic.
Landshuter Hochzeit (four weekends in July; p180) Costumed Landshut locals re-enact a historical wedding; held every four years.
Christopher Street Day (second weekend in July; p87) Gay parade and partying in Munich.

Kinderzeche (third week of July; p236) Features children from Dinkelsbühl in re-enactments of their town's history.

July & August
St Annafest (late July to early August; p196) Huge beer party held in an 'enchanted' forest near Forchheim.
Richard Wagner Festival (late July to August; p209) Bayreuth's prestigious social and music event.
Salzburger Festspiele (late July to end August; p121) Among the most important classical music festivals in Europe.
Further Drachenstich (August; p169) Historic dragon slaying is one of the largest folk festivals in Bavaria.
Gäubodenfest (August; p167) Major Oktoberfest-style drink-up and revelry in Straubing from the second Friday in August.
Sandkerwa (fourth weekend in August; p202) Bamberg's big folk festival.

September & October
Reichsstadt-Feststage (early September; p233) Rothenburg ob der Tauber re-enacts its medieval history.
Oktoberfest (mid-September to the first Sunday in October; p87) Millions people can't be wrong. *Prost!*

November & December
Leonhardifahrt (6 November) Major procession, the most famous being in Bad Tölz (p134).
Christkindlesmarkt (Christmas markets; late November to 24 December) Celebrate the holidays with mulled wine, gingerbread cookies and shimmering ornaments. The markets in Munich and Nuremberg are the most famous.
Nikolaustag (eve of 5 December) Children put their boots out hoping that St Nick will fill them with sweets overnight.
Silvester (New Year's Eve; 31 December) After a night of partying amateur pyromaniacs greet the new year with fireworks.

FOOD
The eating recommendations in this guide match all tastes and travel budgets. Budget eateries include takeaways, delis, cafés, snack bars, markets and basic restaurants where you can fill up for under €10. At midrange establishments you usually get tablecloths, full menus, beer and wine lists, and main courses ranging from €10 to €20. Top-end places tend to be full gourmet affairs, with expert service and mains from €20. For more on cuisine and eating customs, see p44.

Nearly all restaurants allow smoking, although some have nonsmoking sections. Only a few have air-conditioning.

GAY & LESBIAN TRAVELLERS
Homosexuality is legal, but Bavaria does not have much of a scene. One major exception is Munich, which has a thriving community of *Schwule* (gays) and *Lesben* (lesbians), although it's nothing like other German cities, such as Cologne or Berlin. Nuremberg and Regensburg are also minor hubs of activity. In rural areas, some landlords may be reluctant to rent double rooms to gay couples.

HOLIDAYS
Germans are huge fans of mini-vacations built in around public holiday periods (especially those in spring such as Ascension Day, Labour Day, Corpus Christi and Whitsuntide and Pentecost), and Bavaria is a favourite getaway destination. Expect heavy crowds on the roads, in the towns, on boats, in beer gardens and almost everywhere else.

The following are *gesetzliche Feiertage* (public holidays) observed in Bavaria.
Neujahrstag (New Year's Day) 1 January
Heilige Drei Könige (Epiphany) 6 January
Ostern (Easter) March/April – Good Friday, Easter Sunday and Easter Monday
Maifeiertag (Labour Day) 1 May
Christi Himmelfahrt (Ascension Day) 40 days after Easter
Pfingsten (Whitsun/Pentecost) mid-May to mid-June – Whit Sunday and Whit Monday
Fronleichnam (Corpus Christi) 10 days after Pentecost
Mariä Himmelfahrt (Assumption Day) 15 August
Tag der Deutschen Einheit (Day of German Unity) 3 October
Allerheiligen (All Saints Day) 1 November 1
Weihnachtstag (Christmas Day) 25 December
2. Weihnachtstag (Boxing/St Stephen's Day) 26 December

INSURANCE
Always make sure you have a comprehensive travel insurance policy that covers you for any medical expenses, for luggage theft or loss, and against cancellations or delays of your travel arrangements. Check your existing insurance policies at home (medical, renters, homeowners etc), since some policies may already provide worldwide coverage. For more information about medical insurance, see p292. For information about what kind of coverage you need while driving in Bavaria, see p290.

Agencies offering comprehensive travel insurance include the following:

Insure.com (in the US ☎ 800-556-9393; www.insure .com) An independent website that compares quotes from 200 US-based insurance companies.

Quoteline Direct (in the UK ☎ 0870-444 0870; www .quotelinedirect.co.uk) Compares quotes from 30 UK-based insurance companies.

Travel Guard (in the US ☎ 800-826-4919; www .travelguard.com)

Travelex (in the US ☎ 800-228-9792; www.travelex .com) Has offices worldwide.

INTERNET ACCESS

Internet cafés are listed in the Information sections of many destinations featured in this guide and charge between €3 to €6 per hour.

Many newer or recently renovated hotels have technology that gets you online in your own room using your laptop. High-speed access is becoming increasingly common in hotels courting a business clientele, as is wireless LAN. Properties offering guest terminals with Internet access are identified in this book with an Internet icon (🖳). To find wireless 'hot spots' anywhere, try the directories at www.jiwire.com and www .hotspot-locations.com.

Beware of digital phones without built-in data ports, which may fry your modem unless you're using a digital-to-analogue converter. Depending on where you bought your laptop, you may also need adapters for German electrical outlets and telephone sockets. Both are available in larger electronics stores.

For a full run-down on Germany-specific connectivity issues see www.german-way .com/german/inet.html. Other good general resources are http://kropla.com/phones.htm and www.teleadapt.com.

LEGAL MATTERS

By law, you must carry photo identification such as your passport, national identity card or driving licence. The permissible

---

THE LEGAL AGE FOR...

- Drinking alcohol – 16
- Driving a car – 18
- Having sex – 14 (with restrictions)
- Voting in an election – 18

---

blood-alcohol limit is 0.05%; drivers caught exceeding this amount are subject to stiff fines, a confiscated licence and even jail time. For general road rules, see p290.

If arrested, you have the right to make a phone call and are presumed innocent until proven guilty. For a referral to a lawyer, contact your embassy (p278).

MAPS

Most tourist offices distribute free (but often very basic) city maps, but for driving around Bavaria you'll need a detailed road map or atlas such as those published by Falkplan, Hallwag, RV Verlag or ADAC. Look for them at bookshops, tourist offices, newsagents and petrol stations. **Map 24** (www.map24 .de) has downloadable driving directions.

MONEY

Euros come in seven notes (five, 10, 20, 50, 100, 200 and 500 euros) and eight coins (one and two euro coins and one, two, five, 10, 20 and 50 cent coins). Cash is king in Bavaria, so you can't really avoid having at least some notes and coins, say €100 or so, on you at all times. At the time of writing, the euro was a very strong currency, certainly compared to the US dollar, although fluctuations are common. See the exchange-rate table on the inside front cover for some guidelines.

Money can be exchanged at most banks and post offices as well as at all foreign-exchange offices (Reisebank is recommended) and American Express branches. Some Sparkasse branches have convenient 24-hour automated foreign-exchange machines, though rates may not be the best.

For an overview of how much things cost in Bavaria, see p9.

ATMs

Usually the best and quickest way to obtain cash is by making a withdrawal from your home bank account via an ATM. Most are linked to international networks such as Cirrus, Plus, Star and Maestro.

Many ATMs also spit out cash if you use your credit card but this method tends to be more expensive because, in addition to a service fee, you'll be charged interest immediately (in other words, there's no grace period as with purchases).

For exact fees, check with your bank or credit-card company.

Credit Cards

Germany is still largely a cash-based society and it's best not to assume that you'll be able to use credit cards – inquire first. Even so, a piece of plastic is vital in emergencies and also useful for phone or Internet bookings. Report lost or stolen cards to the following:

American Express (☎ 01805-840 840)
MasterCard (☎ 0800-819 1040)
Visa (☎ 0800-811 8440)

Tipping

Restaurant bills always include a *Bedienung* (service charge) but most customers usually add about 5% or 10% unless the service was truly abhorrent. At hotels, porters generally get about €1 per bag and it's also nice to leave some cash for the room cleaners. Tip bartenders about 5% and taxi drivers around 10%.

Travellers Cheques

Travellers cheques, which can be replaced if lost or stolen, are rarely accepted in Bavaria, even if denominated in euros. They usually must be cashed at a bank or exchange outlet (bring a passport). Cheques issued by American Express can be cashed free of charge at their offices. Always keep a record of the cheque numbers separate from the cheques themselves.

POST

Main post offices, which are often near train stations, are usually open from 8am to 6pm Monday to Friday and till 2pm on Saturday. Expect suburban and rural branches to be closed at lunchtime and from 5pm or 5.30pm weekdays and noon on Saturday.

Within Germany and the EU, standard-sized postcards cost €0.45 to post, a 20g letter costs €0.55 and a 50g letter costs €1. Postcards to North America and Australasia cost €1, a 20g airmail letter costs €1.55 and a 50g airmail letter costs €2. A surcharge applies to oversized mail. The website of **Deutsche Post** (www.deutsche-post.de) has full details.

Letters sent within Germany take one to two days for delivery; those addressed to destinations within Europe or to North America take four to six days and those to Australasia five to seven days.

SHOPPING

Bavaria is a fun place to shop with a big selection of everyday and unique items. Regional products include traditional Bavarian outfits, including dirndls, lederhosen and Loden jackets. Complete the look with accessories such as felt hats, embroidered shawls or decorated leather belts. Beer mugs are the classic souvenir, no matter whether made of glass or stoneware, plain or decorated, with or without pewter lid – the choices are endless.

Good-quality woodcarvings are widely available in the Alpine regions (Oberammergau's are especially famous). Fans of fragile things could pick up exquisite porcelain made by the Nymphenburger Porzellan Manufaktur or beautiful vases, bowls or ornaments handmade by the glass artisans in the Bavarian Forest.

Nuremberg, with its long tradition in toy making, is still a good place to pick up quality playthings. The city is, of course, famous for its Christkindlesmarkt, although you'll find many other equally lovely Christmas markets throughout Bavaria.

Bargaining almost never occurs in Bavaria, except at flea markets.

SOLO TRAVELLERS

Germans are generally friendly but also tend to be rather reserved and not likely to initiate a conversation with strangers. This shouldn't stop you from approaching them, though, since most will quite happily respond and even be extra helpful once they find out you're a traveller. Women don't need to be afraid of taking the first step either, not even with men. Unless you're overtly coquettish, this most likely won't be interpreted as a sexual advance. Also see Women Travellers, p283.

TELEPHONE & FAX
Fax

You can receive and send faxes at most hotels as well as from copy shops and Internet cafés.

Mobile Phones

Germany uses GSM 900/1800, which is compatible with the standards used in the rest of Europe, Australia and parts of Asia, but not in North America or Japan. Multiband GSM mobile (cell) phones that work practically everywhere are becoming increasingly common.

If yours isn't one of them, the simplest solution, if you find you need a mobile phone, may be to buy a GSM prepaid phone at a German telecom store, such as T-Online or Debitel. For less than €100 you get the phone, some prepaid minutes and a rechargeable SIM chip for buying additional airtime. On the downside, per minute rates are rather high. Mobile phone rentals are also available, for instance from **V2 Connect** (☎ 089-973 5110; ✆ 9am-6pm Mon-Fri) at Munich International Airport.

Note that in Germany calls made to phones are more expensive than those to a stationary number.

Phone Codes

German phone numbers consist of an area code, which starts with ☎ 0 and can be anything from three to six digits long. This is followed by a local number, which can be three to eight digits long. Numbers within the same city don't require dialling the area code.

If calling Germany from abroad, first dial your country's international access code, then ☎ 49 (Germany's country code), the area code (dropping the initial 0) and the local number. Germany's international access code is ☎ 00. For directory assistance in English, dial ☎ 11837 (€0.20 connecting fee, plus €1 per minute).

Numbers starting with ☎ 0800 are toll free, while those starting with ☎ 0190 cost €0.62 per minute. Direct-dialled calls made from hotel rooms are often charged at a premium.

If you have access to a private phone, you can benefit from cheap rates by using a call-by-call access code offered by a bewildering number of providers. An excellent website for wading through the tariff jungle is www.billigertelefonieren.de (in German, but pretty easy to figure out).

Phonecards

Most public payphones only work with Deutsche Telecom (DT) phonecards, which are sold at post offices, newsagents and tourist offices in denominations of €5, €10 and €20.

For long-distance or international calls, prepaid calling cards issued by other comp-

anies tend to offer better rates than standard phonecards. Look for them at newsagents and discount telephone call shops. Most cards also work with payphones but usually at a surcharge. Those sold at Reisebank outlets offer some of the best prices around (eg €0.08 per minute for calls within Germany or to the UK and US).

TIME

Clocks in Germany are set to central European time (GMT/UTC plus one hour). Daylight-saving time comes into effect at 2am on the last Sunday in March and ends on the last Sunday in October. The use of the 24-hour clock (eg 6.30pm is 18.30) is common.

TOURIST INFORMATION

Just about every community in Bavaria has a walk-in tourist office where you can pick up information, maps and sometimes book accommodation. Contact details for these offices are listed throughout this book in the Information section of each town.

Good websites for your pretrip research are those maintained by **Bavaria Tourism** (www .bayern.by) and the **German National Tourist Office** (GNTO; www.germany-tourism.de).

In addition, each Bavarian region operates its own tourist office:

Eastern Bavarian Tourism Association (☎ 0941-585 390; www.ostbayern-tourismus.de in German; info@ostbayern-tourismus.de)

Franconian Tourism Association (☎ 0911-941 510; www.frankentourismus.org in German; info@frankentourismus.de)

Tourism Association Allgäu-Bavarian Swabia (☎ 01805-127 000; www.bavarian-alps.info or www .allgaeu.de in German; info@allgaeu.de)

Upper Bavarian Tourism Association (☎ 089-829 2180; www.oberbayern-tourismus.de in German; touristinfo@oberbayern.de)

TOURS

For information on touring the Romantic Road, see p227.

Bicycle & Walking Tours

Active types might want to consider a self-guided tour offered by the following companies. Rates typically include bicycle rental, lodging and luggage transfer between hotels. The Romantic Road and King Ludwig's castles are popular destinations.

Bents Tour (in the UK ☎ 01568 780 800; www.bents
tours.com)
Euro Bike & Walking (in the US ☎ 800-321-6060;
www.eurobike.com)
Sherpa Expeditions (in the UK ☎ 020-8577 2717;
www.sherpa-walking-holidays.co.uk)

River Cruises
Cruising the Danube and Rhine-Main-
Danube Canal aboard a 'floating hotel' is
a relaxing way of seeing parts of Bavaria.
The following US-based companies offer
all-inclusive tours with English-speaking
guides:
Amadeus Waterways (☎ 800-380-3865; www.ama
deuswaterways.com)
Peter Deilmann Cruises (☎ 800-348-8287; www.deil
mann-cruises.com)
Uniworld (☎ 800-360-9550; www.uniworld.com)

Skiing Vacations
A number of operators offer package tours
to Garmisch-Partenkirchen, which has the
largest ski area in Germany and the most
reliable snow conditions.
Adventure on Skis (in the US ☎ 800-628-9655, 413-
568-2855; www.advonskis.com)
Ski Europe (in the US ☎ 800-333-5533, 713-960-0900;
www.ski-europe.com)

VISAS
Most EU nationals are required to have
their national identity card or passport to
enter, stay and work in Germany. Citizens
of Australia, Canada, Israel, Japan, New
Zealand, Poland, Switzerland and the US
are among those countries that need only a
valid passport (no visa) if entering as tourists for up to three months within a six-
month period. Passports should be valid
for at least another four months from the
planned date of departure from Germany.

Nationals from other countries need a
so-called Schengen Visa, named after the
1995 Schengen Agreement that abolished
passport controls between Austria, Belgium, Denmark, Finland, France, Germany, Iceland, Italy, Greece, Luxembourg,
Netherlands, Norway, Portugal, Spain and
Sweden. For full details, see www.auswaer
tiges-amt.de or check with a German consulate in your country.

WOMEN TRAVELLERS
Bavaria is generally a safe place to travel
for women, but naturally this doesn't mean
you can let your guard down and entrust
your life to every stranger. Simply use the
same common sense as you would at home.
Getting hassled in the streets does happen
but is usually limited to wolf whistles and
unwanted stares. In crowded situations
groping is a rare possibility.

If you've been assaulted, call the **police**
(☎ 110) immediately and contact a women's
or rape crisis centre such as the Munich-
based **Frauennotruf** (☎ 089-763 737; ☺ 10am-
11pm Mon-Fri, 6pm-2am Sat & Sun).

Transport

CONTENTS

GETTING THERE & AWAY

ENTERING THE COUNTRY

Entering Germany is usually a straightforward procedure. Citizens of most Western countries are exempt from visa requirements, but other nationals most likely need a so-called Schengen Visa. If you're arriving in Germany from any of the 15 Schengen countries, such as France or Italy, you no longer have to show your passport or go through customs in Germany, no matter which nationality you are. For a list of Schengen countries as well as an overview of all the passport and visa requirements, see p283.

AIR
Airports

Bavaria's central location within Europe makes it easily accessible from several airports. The main hub, of course, is **Flughafen München** (Munich International Airport; MUC; ☎ 089-975 00; www.munich-airport.de), although most transcontinental flights land at **Frankfurt International Airport** (FRA; ☎ 01805-372 4636; www.frankfurt-airport.de), which is convenient to destinations in northern Bavaria, including the Romantic Road. Some budget airlines, most notably Ryanair, fly into **Frankfurt-Hahn Airport** (HNN; ☎ 06543-509 200; www.hahn

-airport.de), which is about 110km northwest of Frankfurt proper and connected to the city's main train station by bus (1¾ hours, €12). For destinations in Eastern Bavaria or the Bavarian Alps, **Salzburg Airport** (SZG; ☎ +43-662-8580-251; www.salzburg-airport.com) is another alternative. **Nuremberg** (NUE; ☎ 0911-937 00; www.flughafen-nuernberg.de) and **Augsburg** (AGB; ☎ 0821-270 810; www.augsburg-airport.de in German) also have small airports with mostly domestic departures.

Airlines

The main airline serving Germany is the national flagship carrier and Star Alliance member **Lufthansa** (LH; ☎ 01803-803 803; www.lufthansa.de; hub Frankfurt), which operates a huge network of domestic and international flights and has one of the world's best safety records. It also just upped the competitive ante by introducing wireless LAN Internet access in all classes on many of its Munich-bound flights, especially those originating in the US. Of the many other national carriers and budget airlines also serving the region, the main ones are listed below along with their telephone numbers in Germany for reservations, flight changes and information. For contact information in your home country, see the airline's website.

Air Berlin (AB; ☎ 01805-737 800; www.airberlin.com) Hub Berlin-Tegel.

Air Canada (AC; ☎ 01805-0247 226; www.aircanada.ca) Hub Pearson, Toronto.

Air France (AF; ☎ 01805-830 830; www.airfrance.com) Hub Paris Charles-De-Gaulle.

Air New Zealand (NZ; ☎ 0800-5494 5494; www.airnz
.co.nz) Hub Auckland International.

Alitalia (AZ; ☎ 01805-074 747; www.alitalia.com) Main
hubs Rome-Fiumicino, Milan-Malpensa.

American Airlines (AA; ☎ 0180-324 2324; www.aa
.com) Main hubs Dallas/Fort Worth.

British Airways (BA; ☎ 01805-266 522; www
.britishairways.com) Hub London-Heathrow.

Cirrus Airlines (C9; ☎ 0180-444 4888; www.cirrus
-airlines.de) Hub Saarbrücken.

Delta Air Lines (DL; ☎ 0180-333 7880; www.delta
.com) Main hub Hartsfield-Jackson Atlanta International.

Deutsche BA (DI; ☎ 01805-359 3222; www.flydba
.com) Hub Munich.

easyJet (EZY/EZS; ☎ 01803-654 321; www.easyjet.com)
Main hub London-Luton.

El Al (LY; ☎ 089-210 6920; www.elal.co.il) Hub Ben
-Gurion Airport, Tel Aviv.

Germania Express (ST; ☎ 01805-737 100; www.gexx
.com) Hub Berlin-Tegel.

Iberia (IB; ☎ 01803-000 613; www.iberia.com) Hub
Madrid Barajas.

Qantas Airways (QF; ☎ 01805-250 620; www.qantas
.com.au) Hub Kingsford-Smith, Sydney.

Ryanair (FR; ☎ 0190-170 100 - €0.62 per min; www
.ryanair.com) Hub London-Stansted.

Scandinavian Airlines/SAS (SK; ☎ 01803-234 023;
www.scandinavian.net) Main hub Copenhagen.

Singapore Airlines (SQ; ☎ 069-719 5200; www
.singaporeair.com) Hub Changi International.

United Airlines (UA; ☎ 069-5007 0387; www.ual.com)
Main hub Chicago O'Hare.

Tickets

Everybody loves a bargain and timing is
key when it comes to snapping up cheap
airfares. You can generally save a bundle by
booking early or travelling midweek (Tuesday to Thursday). Some airlines offer lower
fares if you stay over a Saturday.

Your best friend in ferreting out deals
is the Internet. Online agencies are good
places to start, but they are best when used
in conjunction with other search engines,
such as ITA Software (www.itasoftware
.com). This search matrix finds the cheapest
fare for a particular day or within a 30-day

DEPARTURE TAX

A departure tax of around €4 to €6 per person and airport security fees are included in
the price of all airline tickets. You shouldn't
have to pay any more fees at the airport.

---

period, sorts results by price and alerts you
to potential downsides such as long layo-
vers, tight connections or overnight travel.

Also check the airlines' own websites for
promotional fares, which may have to be
booked online. This is especially important
with most of the budget carriers, which only
sell to travellers directly and don't even show
up in the computerised systems used by
travel agencies. A good way to learn about
late-breaking bargain fares is by signing
up for airlines' free weekly email newsletters. Even the old-fashioned newspaper can
yield deals, particularly in times of fare wars.
And don't forget about travel agents, who
can be especially helpful when planning a
complex itinerary. STA Travel and Flight
Centre, both with worldwide branches, are
recommended.

Australia & New Zealand

Many airlines compete for business between Australia and New Zealand and Europe, with fares in high/low season starting
at about A$2300/2000. Depending on the
airline, you'll fly via Asia or the Middle
East, with possible stopovers in such cities
as Singapore or Bahrain, or across Canada
or the US, with possible stopovers in Hono-
lulu, Los Angeles or Vancouver. Definitely
look into a round-the-world (RTW) ticket,
which may work out cheaper than regular
return fares. Some local agents:

Flight Centre Australia (☎ 133 133; www.flightcentre
.com.au) New Zealand (☎ 0800 243 544; www.flight
centre.co.nz)

STA Travel Australia (☎ 1300 733 035; www.statravel
.com.au) New Zealand (☎ 0508 782 872; www.statravel
.co.nz)

Travel.com Australia (www.travel.com.au) New Zealand
(www.travel.co.nz)

Canada

Lufthansa and Air Canada fly to Frankfurt and Munich from all major Canadian
airports, with prices in high/low season
starting at C$1400/1200. Some flights may
involve a stopover. **Travel Cuts** (☎ 800-667-2887;
www.travelcuts.com) is Canada's national student travel agency. For online bookings, try
www.expedia.ca and www.travelocity.ca.

Continental Europe

Lufthansa and other national carriers connect all major European cities with Frankfurt

TRANSPORT

and Munich. Ryanair flies to Frankfurt-Hahn from such places as Rome and Oslo, while Air Berlin serves Munich, Frankfurt and Salzburg from Rome, Budapest and many Spanish and Greek cities. Munich is also served by Germania Express from Moscow, Lisbon, Rome, Athens and Stockholm and by Hapag Lloyd Express from Palermo.

Recommended travel agents include **CTS Viaggi** (☎ 06 462 0431; www.cts.it in Italian) in Italy and **Barcelo Viajes** (☎ 902 116 226; www.barcelo viajes.com in Spanish) in Spain. In France, try **Anyway** (☎ 0892 893 892; www.anyway.fr in French), **Nouvelles Frontières** (☎ 0825 000 747; www.nouvelles -frontieres.fr in French), **OTU Voyages** (☎ 0820 817 817; www.otu.fr in French) or **Voyageurs du Monde** (☎ 01 4015 1115; www.vdm.com in French).

Other Parts of Germany

Unless you're travelling to Bavaria from northern Germany, say Hamburg or Berlin, planes are only marginally faster than trains if you factor in the time it takes to travel to and from the airports. Aside from Lufthansa, Air Berlin, Deutsche BA, Cirrus Airlines and Germanwings (www24.germanwings.com) are among the airlines flying domestically.

UK & Ireland

Lufthansa and British Airways both have umpteen flights connecting all major airports in Germany, the UK and Ireland. Of the budget airlines, Ryanair flies to Frankfurt-Hahn from London-Stansted, Glasgow and Shannon and to Salzburg from Stansted. Munich is served by **Hapag Lloyd Express** (www.hlx.com) from Newcastle, easyJet from Stansted and Cirrus Airlines from London City Airport.

Recommended travel agencies:

Bridge the World (☎ 0870 444 7474; www.b-t-w.co.uk)
Expedia (☎ 0870 050 0808; www.expedia.co.uk)
Flightbookers (☎ 0870 010 7000; www.ebookers.com)
Flight Centre (☎ 0870 890 8099; www.flightcentre.co.uk)
North-South Travel (☎ 01245 608 291; www.north southtravel.co.uk) Donates part of its profit to projects in the developing world.
Quest Travel (☎ 0870 442 3542; www.questtravel.com)
STA Travel (☎ 0870 160 0599; www.statravel.co.uk)
Trailfinders (☎ 0845 058 58 58; www.trailfinders.co.uk)
Travel Bag (☎ 0870 890 1456; www.travelbag.co.uk)

USA

Flights to Germany from major US cities abound and bargains are often available.

Lufthansa has non-stop services to Munich from Atlanta, Chicago, Los Angeles, New York, Philadelphia, San Francisco and Washington DC. It also flies directly to Frankfurt from 14 US cities, including Boston, Houston and Miami. Many of its flights now feature wireless LAN Internet access in all classes and, for those who can afford it, ultra-comfortable sleeper seats in business class. Major US carriers serving Frankfurt are Delta, US Airways, American, United, **Northwest** (www.nwa.com) with KLM and Continental. Fares in high/low season start at US$700/US$400 return from New York, US$800/US$450 from Chicago and US$1200/US$600 from Los Angeles.

STA Travel (☎ 800-777 0112; www.sta-travel.com) has offices in major cities around the country, or try the following online agencies:
CheapTickets (www.cheaptickets.com)
Expedia (www.expedia.com)
Lowestfare.com (www.lowestfare.com)
Orbitz (www.orbitz.com)
Travelocity (www.travelocity.com)

LAND
Border Crossings

Germany is bordered anticlockwise by Denmark, the Netherlands, Belgium, Luxembourg, France, Switzerland, Austria, the Czech Republic and Poland. The Schengen Agreement (p283) abolished passport and customs formalities between Germany and all bordering countries except Poland, the Czech Republic and Switzerland.

Bus

Eurolines (www.eurolines.com) is the umbrella organisation of 30 European coach operators serving 500 destinations in 34 countries across Europe. Its website has links to each national company's site with detailed fare and route information, promotional offers, contact numbers and, in many cases, an online booking system. Children ages four to 12 pay half price, while teens, students and seniors get 10% off regular fares.

In Germany, Eurolines is represented by **Deutsche Touring** (☎ 089-8898 9513; www.deutsche -touring.com) with an office at Munich Hauptbahnhof (p104).

If Bavaria is part of your European-wide itinerary, a Eurolines Pass may be a ticket to savings. It allows for unlimited travel between 35 European cities within a 15, 30 or 60 day period and costs €285/€425/€490 respectively, from June to mid-September. During the rest of the year, rates drop to €220/€310/€390.

Backpacker-geared **Busabout** (☎ 020 7950 1661 in the UK; www.busabout.com) also offers passes of varying duration. These allow you to use their hop-on hop-off bus network serving 41 cities, including Munich and Salzburg, in 11 countries between May and October.

Car & Motorcycle

When bringing your own vehicle to Bavaria all you need is a valid driving licence, your registration certificate and proof of insurance. Foreign cars must display a nationality sticker unless they have official Euro-plates (showing a circle of 12 stars above the national identifier). You also need to carry a warning (hazard) triangle and first-aid kit. For information on driving within Germany, see p290.

Coming from the UK, the fastest way to the continent is on the high-speed **Eurotunnel** (☎ 08705 35 35 35 in the UK; www.eurotunnel .com) shuttle trains that whisk cars, motorbikes, bicycles and coaches from Folkestone through the Channel Tunnel to Coquelles (near Calais) in about 35 minutes. From there, you can be in Munich in about nine or 10 hours. Shuttles run daily around the clock, with up to five departures hourly during peak periods. Fares are calculated per vehicle and depend on such factors as time of day, season and length of stay. Expect to pay about £250 return per car for a week-long trip in summer. The website and travel agents have full details.

Train

Long-distance trains connecting major German cities with those in other countries are called EuroCity (EC) trains. Seat reservations are highly recommended, especially during the peak summer season and around major holidays (p279).

For overnight travel you can choose between *Schlafwagen* (sleepers), which are comfortable compartments for up to three people; *Liegewagen* (couchettes), which sleep four to six people; and *Sitzwagen* (seat carriage), which have roomy, reclining seats. For full details, contact Deutsche Bahn's night train specialists (☎ 01805-141

514 in Germany; www.nachtzugreise.de in German).

Linking the UK with continental Europe, the **Eurostar** (www.eurostar.com) needs only two hours and 20 minutes to travel from London to Brussels, where you can change to regular or other high-speed trains taking you to destinations within Bavaria. Eurostar fares depend on class, time of day and season. For the latest fare information, including promotions and special packages, check the website or contact Rail Europe (p291).

SEA

Hoverspeed (☎ 0870-240-8070; www.hoverspeed.co .uk) operates high-speed car ferries that make the trip from Dover to Calais in about one hour. Return tickets start at £98 per car, including all passengers. Standard foot passenger fares are about £30 return. Driving to Munich from Calais should take about nine or 10 hours. Travelling by train, while doable, requires multiple changes. Check www.bahn.de. For other ferry options, consult with a travel agent or check www.cross -channel-ferries-france.co.uk.

GETTING AROUND

The Germans are whizzes at moving people around, and the public transport network is one of the best in Europe. The two best ways of getting around Bavaria are by car and by train. Regional bus services fill the gaps in areas not well served by the rail network.

AIR

Although it is possible to fly, say, from Frankfurt to Munich, the time and cost involved don't make air travel a sensible way to get around Bavaria.

BICYCLE

Bicycling is allowed on all roads and highways but not on the autobahns (motorways). Cyclists must follow the same rules of the road as vehicles. Helmets are not compulsory, not even for children.

Bicycles may be taken on most trains but need a separate *Fahrradkarte* (ticket). These are €8 on long-distance trains (reservations required) and €3 on regional trains. Bicycles are not allowed on high-speed InterCity Express (ICE) trains. If bought in combination with the Bayern-Ticket (see p291), the €3 fee is good for all trips you take while the ticket is valid. There is no charge at all on some trains; for specifics enquire at a local station or call the **DB Radfahrer-Hotline** (bicycle hotline; ☎ 01805-151 415). Free lines are also listed in DB's complimentary *Bahn & Bike* brochure, as are the almost 50 stations where you can hire bikes. It's also available for downloading from www.bahn.de in German.

With three-day advance notice, you can take bicycles on the Europabus travelling along the Romantic Road (see the boxed text on p227). Many regional companies use buses with special bike racks. Bicycles are also allowed on practically all boat services on Bavaria's lakes and rivers.

For additional cycling information, including bicycle hire, see p39.

BUS

Basically, wherever there is a train, take it. Buses are generally slower and less dependable than trains, but in some rural areas they may be your only option for getting around without your own vehicle. This is especially true of the Bavarian Forest, sections of the Alpine foothills and the Alpine region. In this book, we only list bus services if they're a viable and sensible option.

Separate bus companies, each with its own tariffs and schedules, operate in the different regions. The most popular tourist-geared route is the Europabus, which travels along the Romantic Road (see the boxed text on p227).

In cities, buses generally converge at the *Busbahnhof* or *Zentraler Omnibus Bahnhof/ ZOB* (central bus station), which is often close or adjacent to the Hauptbahnhof (train station). The frequency of service varies from 'rarely' to 'constantly' with many routes offering limited or no service in the evenings and on weekends. If you depend on buses to get around, always keep this in mind or risk finding yourself stuck in a remote place on a Saturday. Special fare deals, such as *Tageskarten* (day passes), *Wochenkarten* (weekly passes) or *Touristen-Sondertarife* (special tourist tickets) are quite common, so make it a habit to ask about them.

CAR & MOTORCYCLE

Most German roads are excellent and motoring around Bavaria can be a lot of fun.

Major autobahns traversing Bavaria include the A3 (Passau–Düsseldorf), A7 (Allgäu–Hamburg), A8 (Munich–Stuttgart and Munich–Salzburg), A9 (Munich–Berlin, via Nuremberg), A95 (Munich–Garmisch-Partenkirchen), and A96 (Munich–Lindau). These are supplemented by an extensive network of *Bundesstrassen* (secondary 'B' roads, highways). No tolls are charged on any public roads.

Along each autobahn, you'll find elaborate service areas every 40km to 60km with petrol stations, toilet facilities and restaurants; some are open 24 hours. In between are *Rastplätze* (rest stops), which usually have picnic tables and toilet facilities. Emergency call boxes are spaced about 2km apart.

Seat belts are mandatory for all passengers and there's a €30 fine per person if you get caught not wearing one. Children need a child seat if under four years old and a seat cushion if under 12; children may not ride in the front until age 13. Motorcyclists must wear helmets. Using hand-held mobile phones while driving is very much *verboten* (forbidden).

Automobile Associations

Germany's main motoring organisation, the **Allgemeiner Deutscher Automobil-Club** (ADAC; ☎ 0180-222 2222 for roadside assistance; www.adac.de in German) has offices in all major cities and many smaller ones. Its excellent roadside assistance programme is also available to members of its affiliates, including British AA, American and Australian AAA and Canadian CAA.

Driving Licence

Drivers need a valid driving licence. International Driving Permits (IDP) are not compulsory but having one may help Germans make sense of your home licence (always carry that one too) and may simplify the car or motorcycle hire process. IDPs are inexpensive, valid for one year and issued by your local automobile association – bring a passport photo and your home licence.

Fuel & Spare Parts

Petrol stations, which are mostly self-service, are generally ubiquitous except in sparsely populated rural areas. Petrol is sold in litres. In February 2005, the average cost for mid-grade fuel was around €1.09 per litre.

ROAD DISTANCES (KM)

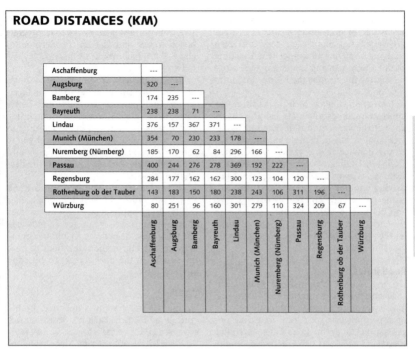

	Aschaffenburg	Augsburg	Bamberg	Bayreuth	Lindau	Munich (München)	Nuremberg (Nürnberg)	Passau	Regensburg	Rothenburg ob der Tauber	Würzburg
Aschaffenburg	---										
Augsburg	320	---									
Bamberg	174	235	---								
Bayreuth	238	238	71	---							
Lindau	376	157	367	371	---						
Munich (München)	354	70	230	233	178	---					
Nuremberg (Nürnberg)	185	170	62	84	296	166	---				
Passau	400	244	276	278	369	192	222	---			
Regensburg	284	177	162	162	300	123	104	120	---		
Rothenburg ob der Tauber	143	183	150	180	238	243	106	311	196	---	
Würzburg	80	251	96	160	301	279	110	324	209	67	---

TRANSPORT

Finding spare parts should not be a problem, especially in the cities, although availability of course depends on the age and model of your car. Be sure to have some sort of roadside emergency assistance plan (see p288) in case your car breaks down.

Hire

As anywhere, rates for car hire vary quite considerably by model, pick-up date and location, but you should be able to get an economy-size vehicle from about €35 per day, plus insurance and taxes. Expect surcharges for hire cars originating at airports and train stations, additional drivers and one-way hire. Child or infant safety seats may be hired for about €5 per day and should be reserved at the time of booking.

In order to hire your own wheels you generally need to be at least 25 years old and hold a valid driving licence and a major credit card. Some companies hire out to drivers between the ages of 21 and 24 for an additional charge (about €15 to €25 per day). Those under age 21 or not in possession of a credit card are usually out of luck,

although some local car hire outfits may accept cash or travellers cheque deposits. Taking your hire car into an Eastern European country, such as the Czech Republic or Poland, is often a no-no, so check in advance if that's where you're headed.

All the main international companies operate in Bavaria, including **Avis** (☎ 01805-557 755; www.avis.com), **Europcar** (☎ 01805-8000; www.europcar.com), **Hertz** (☎ 01805-333 535; www.hertz.com) and Sixt or **Budget** (☎ 01805-260 250; www.budget.com), each with offices or affiliates from Aschaffenburg to Zwiesel.

Prebooked and prepaid packages, arranged from your home country, usually work out much cheaper than on-the-spot hire. The same is true of fly-drive packages. Check for deals with online agencies (eg www.expedia.com), travel agents or car-hire brokers such as the US company **Auto Europe** (☎ 888-223-5555 in the US; www.autoeurope.com) or UK-based **Holiday Autos** (www.holidayautos.co.uk).

Insurance

German law requires that all registered vehicles carry third-party liability insurance.

You could get seriously screwed by driving uninsured or even underinsured. Germans are very fussy about their cars, and even nudging someone's bumper when jostling out of a tight parking space may well result in you having to foot the bill for an entire new one.

If you're hiring a vehicle, make sure your contract includes adequate liability insurance at the very minimum. Car-hire agencies almost never include insurance that covers damage to the vehicle itself, called Collision Damage Waiver (CDW) or Loss Damage Waiver (LDW). It's optional but driving without one is not recommended. Some credit card companies cover CDW and LDW for a certain period if you charge the entire cost to your card. Always confirm with your card issuer what coverage it provides in Germany.

Road Rules

Driving is on the right-hand side of the road and standard international signs are in use. If you're unfamiliar with these, pick up a pamphlet at your local motoring organisation. Obey the road rules carefully: speed and red-light cameras are common and German police are very efficient when it comes to issuing stiff on-the-spot fines. Notices are sent to the car's registration address wherever that may be.

Usual speed limits are 50km/h in cities and towns and 100km/h on highways unless otherwise marked. There is no speed limit on autobahns but stretches where slower speeds must be observed are quite common.

The highest permissible blood-alcohol level for drivers is 0.05%, which for most people equates to roughly one glass of wine or two small beers.

Pedestrians at crossings have the absolute right of way over all motor vehicles. Similarly, you must give right of way to cyclists in bicycle lanes when you're turning.

LOCAL TRANSPORT

Most towns have efficient, frequent and punctual public transportation systems. Buses are the most ubiquitous form of public transportation and practically all towns and rural areas have their own system. Some routes are commuter-oriented and offer only limited or no service in the evenings and at weekends. Bigger cities, such as Munich and Nuremberg, have comprehensive transportation networks that integrate buses, trams, and U-Bahn (underground) and S-Bahn (suburban) trains.

Fares are either determined by zones or time travelled, or sometimes by both. *Streifenkarten* (multi-ticket strips) or *Tageskarten* (day passes) generally offer better value than single-ride tickets. Sometimes, tickets must be stamped upon boarding in order to be valid. Fines are levied if you're caught without a valid ticket. For details, see the Getting Around entries in the destination chapters.

Taxis are metered and cost up to €2.50 at flag fall and €1.30 per kilometre; higher tariffs might apply at night. Some cabbies charge extra for heavy luggage. In most cities, taxis must be ordered by phone (numbers are listed throughout this book or look up *Taxiruf* in the phonebook) or boarded at a taxi rank.

TRAIN

Germany's rail system is operated almost entirely by **Deutsche Bahn** (DB; ☎ reservations & information 118 61, toll-free automated timetable 0800-150 7090; www.bahn.de) with an 'alphabet soup' of train types serving just about every corner of the country. Long-distance trains are either called ICE (InterCity Express), which travel at speeds of up to 280km/h, or the only slightly slower IC (InterCity) or EC (EuroCity) trains. Both run at hourly or bi-hourly intervals. Regional service is provided by the IRE (InterRegio Express), the RB (RegionalBahn), the SE (StadtExpress) and the S-Bahn.

Many city train stations will have a *Reisezentrum* (travel centre) where staff sell tickets and can help you plan an itinerary (ask for an English-speaking agent). Smaller stations may only have a few ticket windows and the smallest ones aren't staffed at all. In this case, you must buy tickets from vending machines. These are also plentiful at staffed stations and convenient if you don't want to queue at a ticket counter. English instructions are normally provided. Both agents and machines accept major credit cards. Tickets sold onboard (cash only) incur a service fee (€2 to €7) unless the station where you boarded was unstaffed or had a broken vending machine. Tickets for trips over 101km are also available online.

Most train stations have coin-operated lockers (small/large lockers cost €1/€2 for 24 hours). *Gepäckaufbewahrung* (left-luggage offices) charge similar rates.

See p287 for more details on taking your bicycle on the train.

Classes

German trains have 1st and 2nd class cars, both of them comfortable. Seating is usually in compartments of up to six people or in newer open-plan carriages with panoramic windows. All trains have smoking and non-smoking cars. ICE, IC and EC trains are fully air-conditioned and have a restaurant or self-service bistro.

For details about sleeper cars, see p287.

Costs

Standard, non-discounted train tickets tend to be quite expensive, but promotions, discount tickets and special offers become available all the time. Check the website or ask at the train station.

One of the best rail deals is the Bayern-Ticket (Bavaria Ticket). For €24 up to five passengers travelling together get unlimited rides within Bavaria from 9am until 3am of the following day from Monday to Friday. On weekends, the ticket is valid from midnight until 3am the following day. It's good for 2nd-class travel on all IRE, SE, RB and S-Bahn trains, as well as all public transportation in greater Munich and Nuremberg. If you're a solo traveller, get the Bayern-Ticket Single for €17. There's a €2 surcharge for tickets bought from agents instead of vending machines.

Reservations

Seat reservations (€3) for long-distance travel are highly recommended, especially if you're travelling on a Friday or Sunday afternoon, around holidays or in summer. They can be made as late as a few minutes before departure by phone, online or at the station.

Train Passes

If your permanent residence is outside Europe, you qualify for the German Rail Pass, which entitles you to unlimited 1st- or 2nd-class travel for four to 10 days within a one-month period. Sample prices for four/seven/10 days of travel are US$180/US$252/US$324 in 2nd class and US$260/US$362/US$464 in 1st (half-price for children ages six to 11). The pass is valid on all trains within Germany as well as some river services. The German Rail Youth Pass for people between 12 and 25 and the German Rail Twin Pass for two adults travelling together are variations on the scheme. If Bavaria is part of a wider European itinerary, look into a **Eurail Pass** (www.eurail.com).

In the US, Canada and the UK, a great resource for rail passes is **Rail Europe** (www.raileurope.com; US ☎ 888-382-7245; Canada ☎ 800-361-7245; UK ☎ 08705-848 848), a major agency specialising in train travel around Europe. The website also lists affiliated agents in other countries, including Australia, New Zealand and Japan.

TRANSPORT

Health

BEFORE YOU GO

While Germany has excellent health care, prevention is the key to staying healthy while abroad. Planning before departure, particularly for pre-existing illnesses, will be beneficial. Bring medications in their original, labelled, containers. A signed and dated letter from your physician describing your conditions and medications, including generic names, is a good idea. If carrying syringes or needles, be sure to have a physician's letter documenting their medical necessity. Carry a spare pair of contact lenses and glasses, and take your optical prescription with you.

INSURANCE

If you're an EU citizen, an E111 form, available from health centres or, in the UK, post offices, covers you for most medical care. E111 will not cover you for nonemergencies, or emergency repatriation. Citizens from other countries should find out if there is a reciprocal arrangement for free medical care between their country and Germany. If you do need health insurance, make sure you get a policy that covers you for the worst possible case, such as an accident requiring an emergency flight home. Find out in advance if your insurance plan will make payments directly to providers or reimburse you later for overseas health expenditures.

MEDICAL CHECKLIST

All the following are readily available in Germany. If you are hiking out of town, these items may come in handy.

- antibiotics
- antidiarrhoeal drugs (eg loperamide)
- acetaminophen (Tylenol) or aspirin
- anti-inflammatory drugs (eg ibuprofen)
- antihistamines (for hay fever and allergic reactions)
- antibacterial ointment (eg Bactroban; for cuts and abrasions)
- steroid cream or cortisone (for poison ivy and other allergic rashes)
- bandages, gauze, gauze rolls
- adhesive or paper tape
- scissors, safety pins, tweezers
- thermometer
- pocketknife
- DEET-containing insect repellent for the skin
- pyrethrin-containing insect spray for clothing, tents and bed nets
- sun block
- oral rehydration salts
- acetazolamide (Diamox; for altitude sickness)

RECOMMENDED VACCINATIONS

No jabs are required to travel to Germany. The World Health Organization (WHO), however, recommends that all travellers should be covered for diphtheria, tetanus, measles, mumps, rubella and polio, regardless of their destination.

IN TRANSIT

DEEP VEIN THROMBOSIS (DVT)

Blood clots may form in the legs during flights, chiefly because of prolonged immobility. The longer the flight, the greater the risk. The chief symptom of DVT is swelling or pain of the foot, ankle or calf, usually but not always on just one side. When a blood clot travels to the lungs, it may cause chest pain and difficulty breathing. Travellers with any of these symptoms should immediately seek medical attention.

To prevent the development of DVT on long flights walk about the cabin, contract the leg muscles while sitting, drink plenty of fluids and avoid alcohol and tobacco.

JET LAG & MOTION SICKNESS

To avoid jet lag (common when crossing more than five time zones) try to drink plenty of nonalchoholic fluids and eat light meals. Upon arrival, get exposure to natural sunlight and readjust your schedule (for meals, sleep etc) as soon as possible.

The first choices for treating motion sickness are usually antihistamines such as dimenhydrinate (Dramamine) and meclizine (Antivert, Bonine). A herbal alternative is ginger.

IN MUNICH & BAVARIA

AVAILABILITY & COST OF HEALTH CARE

Excellent health care is readily available and for minor illnesses such as colds pharmacists can give valuable advice and sell over-the-counter medication. They can also advise when more specialised help is required and point you in the right direction.

TRAVELLER'S DIARRHOEA

If you develop diarrhoea, be sure to drink plenty of fluids, preferably in the form of an oral rehydration solution such as Dioralyte. If diarrhoea is bloody, persists for more than 72 hours or is accompanied by fever, shaking, chills or severe abdominal pain you should seek medical attention.

ENVIRONMENTAL HAZARDS
Heatstroke

Heat exhaustion occurs as a result of excessive fluid loss with inadequate replacement of fluids and salt. Symptoms include headache, dizziness and tiredness. Dehydration is happening by the time you feel thirsty – aim to drink sufficient water to produce pale, diluted urine. To treat heat exhaustion

drink water and/or fruit juice, and cool the body with cold water and fans.

Hypothermia

Hypothermia occurs when the body loses heat faster than it can produce it. As ever, proper preparation will reduce the risks of getting it. Even on a hot day in the mountains, the weather can change rapidly, so carry waterproof garments, warm layers and a hat, and leave details of your route with a responsible person.

Hypothermia starts with shivering, loss of judgment and clumsiness. Unless rewarming occurs, the sufferer deteriorates into apathy, confusion and coma. Prevent further heat loss by seeking shelter, warm dry clothing, hot sweet drinks and shared bodily warmth.

SEXUAL HEALTH

Emergency contraception is available with a doctor's prescription in Germany. It is most effective if taken within 24 hours of unprotected sex. Condoms are readily available throughout Germany.

TRAVELLING WITH CHILDREN

Make sure children are up to date with routine vaccinations, and discuss possible travel vaccines well before departure as some vaccines are not suitable for children under one year old.

If your child has been vomiting or has diarrhoea, lost fluid and salts must be replaced. It may be helpful to take rehydration powders with water that has been boiled.

WOMEN'S HEALTH

Emotional stress, exhaustion and travelling through different time zones can all contribute to an upset in the menstrual pattern.

If using oral contraceptives, remember some antibiotics, diarrhoea and vomiting can stop the pill from working. Time zones, gastrointestinal upsets and antibiotics do not affect injectable contraception.

Travelling during pregnancy is usually possible but always consult your doctor before planning your trip. The most risky times for travel are during the first 12 weeks of pregnancy and after 30 weeks.

HEALTH

Language

CONTENTS

German belongs to the Indo-European language group and is spoken by over 100 million people in countries throughout the world, including Austria and part of Switzerland. Regional dialects still thrive throughout Germany, especially in Cologne, rural Bavaria, Swabia and parts of Saxony. The Sorb minority in eastern Germany has its own language. In northern Germany it is common to hear Plattdeutsch (Low German) and Frisian spoken. Both are distant relatives of English, and the fact that many German words survive in the English vocabulary today makes things a lot easier for native English speakers.

All German school children learn a foreign language – usually English – which means most can speak it to a certain degree.

The words and phrases included in this language guide should help you through the most common travel situations. For language that will be of help when dining see p48. If you're keen to delve a little further into the language, pick up a copy of Lonely Planet's *German Phrasebook*.

GRAMMAR

German grammar can be a nightmare for English speakers. Nouns come in three genders: masculine, feminine and neuter. The corresponding forms of the definite article ('the' in English) are *der*, *die* and *das*, with the universal plural form, *die*. Nouns and articles will alter according to complex grammatical rules relating to the noun's function within a phrase – known as 'case'. In German there are four cases: nominative, accusative, dative and genitive. We haven't allowed for all possible permutations of case in this language guide – it's simply too complex to cover here. However, bad German is better than no German at all, so even if you muddle your cases, you'll find that you'll still be understood – and your efforts will be appreciated regardless.

If you've noticed that written German seems to be full of capital letters, the reason is that German nouns always begin with a capital letter.

PRONUNCIATION

The pronunciation of words and phrases throughout this chapter is based on High German, which is understood throughout the country.

Regional Variation

The German dialect spoken around Munich only differs from High German in pronunciation. In the Munich dialect, when the pairs of letters **p/b**, **k/g**, and **t/d** occur at the start of the word, there's no audible difference between them. In the sentences *Ich backe* (I bake) and *Ich packe* (I pack), the **p** and **b** are pronounced the same, sounding like a combination of both letters. Also, the combinations **st** and **sp** are pronounced 'sht' and 'shp', so the girl's name Astrid would be pronounced 'ashtrid'.

Vowels

German Example	Pronunciation Guide
hat	**a** (eg the 'u' in 'run')
habe	**ah** (eg 'father')
mein	**ai** (eg 'aisle')
Bär	**air** (eg 'hair', with no 'r' sound)
Boot	**aw** (eg 'saw')
leben	**ay** (eg 'say')
Bett/Männer/kaufen	**e** (eg 'bed')
fliegen	**ee** (eg 'thief')
schön	**er** (eg 'her', with no 'r' sound)
mit	**i** (eg 'bit')
Koffer	**o** (eg 'pot')

Leute/Häuser	**oy** (eg 'toy')	
Schuhe	**oo** (eg 'moon')	
Haus	**ow** (eg 'how')	
züruck	**ü** ('ee' said with rounded lips)	
unter	**u** (eg 'put')	

Consonants

The only two tricky consonant sounds in German are **ch** and **r**. All other consonants are pronounced much the same as their English counterparts (except **sch**, which is always as the 'sh' in 'shoe').

The **ch** sound is generally like the 'ch' in the Scottish *loch* – like a hiss from the back of the throat. When **ch** occurs after the vowels **e** and **i** it's more like 'sh', produced with the tongue more forward in the mouth. In this book we've simplified things by using the one symbol **kh** for both sounds.

The **r** sound is different from English, and it isn't rolled like in Italian or Spanish. It's pronounced at the back of the throat, almost like saying 'g' as in 'get' with some friction – a bit like gargling.

Word Stress

As a general rule, word stress in German mostly falls on the first syllable. In the pronunciation guides in the following words and phrases, the stressed syllable is shown in italics.

ACCOMMODATION

Where's a ...?
Wo ist ...? — vaw ist ...
  bed and breakfast
  eine Pension — *ai*·ne pahng·*zyawn*
  camp site
  ein Campingplatz — ain *kem*·ping·plats
  guesthouse
  eine Pension — *ai*·ne pahng·*zyawn*
  hotel
  ein Hotel — ain ho·*tel*
  youth hostel
  eine Jugendherberge — *ai*·ne *yoo*·gent·her·ber·ge

What's the address?
Wie ist die Adresse? — vee ist dee a·*dre*·se
I'd like to book a room, please.
Ich möchte bitte ein — ikh *merkh*·te *bi*·te ain
  Zimmer reservieren. — *tsi*·mer re·zer·*vee*·ren
For (three) nights/weeks.
Für (drei) Nächte/ — für (drai) *nekh*·te/
  Wochen. — *vo*·khen

Do you have a ... room?
Haben Sie ein ...? — *hah*·ben zee ain ...
  single
  Einzelzimmer — *ain*·tsel·tsi·mer
  double
  Doppelzimmer mit — *do*·pel·tsi·mer mit
    einem Doppelbett — *ai*·nem *do*·pel·bet
  twin
  Doppelzimmer mit zwei — *do*·pel·tsi·mer mit tsvai
    Einzelbetten — *ain*·tsel·be·ten

How much is it per ...?
Wie viel kostet es pro ...? — vee feel *kos*·tet es praw ...
  night
  Nacht — nakht
  person
  Person — per·*zawn*

May I see it?
Kann ich es sehen? — kan ikh es *zay*·en
Can I get another room?
Kann ich noch ein — kan ikh nokh ain
  Zimmer bekommen? — *tsi*·mer be·*ko*·men
It's fine. I'll take it.
Es ist gut, ich nehme es. — es ist goot ikh *nay*·me es
I'm leaving now.
Ich reise jetzt ab. — ikh *rai*·ze yetst ap

CONVERSATION & ESSENTIALS

German uses polite and informal forms for 'you' (*Sie* and *Du* respectively). When addressing people you don't know well always use the polite form (though younger people will be less inclined to expect it). In this language guide we use the polite form unless indicated by 'inf' (informal) in brackets.

If you need to ask for assistance from a stranger, remember to always introduce your request with a simple *Entschuldigung* (Excuse me, ...).

Hello.	*Grüss Gott.*	grüs got
Hi.	*Hallo.*	ha·lo/ha·*law*
Good ...	*Guten ...*	*goo*·ten ...
day	*Tag*	tahk
morning	*Morgen*	*mor*·gen
afternoon	*Tag*	tahk
evening	*Abend*	*ah*·bent

Goodbye.		
Auf Wiedersehen.		owf *vee*·der·zay·en
See you later.		
Bis später.		bis *shpay*·ter
Bye.		
Tschüss/Tschau.		chüs/chow

LANGUAGE

How are you?

Wie geht es Ihnen? (pol)   vee gayt es *ee*·nen

Wie geht es dir? (inf)   vee gayt es deer

Fine.

Danke, gut.   *dang*·ke goot

And you?

Und Ihnen? (pol)   unt *ee*·nen

Und dir? (inf)   unt deer

What's your name?

Wie ist Ihr Name? (pol)   vee ist eer *nah*·me

Wie heisst du? (inf)   vee haist doo

My name is ...

Mein Name ist .../   main *nah*·me ist .../

Ich heisse ...   ikh *hai*·se ...

Yes.

Ja.   yah

No.

Nein.   nain

Please.

Bitte.   *bi*·te

Thank you (very much).

Danke/Vielen Dank.   *dang*·ke/*fee*·len dangk

You're welcome.

Bitte (sehr).   *bi*·te (zair)

Excuse me, ... (before asking for help or directions)

Entschuldigung, ...   ent·*shul*·di·gung ...

Sorry.

Entschuldigung.   ent·*shul*·di·gung

DIRECTIONS

Could you help me, please?

Können Sie mir bitte helfen?

ker·nen zee meer *bi*·te *hel*·fen

Where's (a bank)?

Wo ist (eine Bank)?

vaw ist (*ai*·ne bangk)

I'm looking for (the cathedral).

Ich suche (den Dom).

ikh *zoo*·khe (dayn dawm)

Which way's (a public toilet)?

In welcher Richtung ist eine öffentliche toilette?

in *vel*·kher *rikh*·tung ist (*ai*·ne er·*fent*·li·khe to·a·*le*·te)

How far is it?

Wie weit ist es?

vee *vait* ist es

Can you show me (on the map)?

Können Sie es mir (auf der Karte) zeigen?

ker·nen zee es meer (owf dair *kar*·te) *tsai*·gen

near	nahe	*nah*·e
far away	*weit weg*	vait vek
here	*hier*	heer
there	*dort*	dort
straight ahead	*geradeaus*	ge·rah·de·*ows*

SIGNS

Polizei	Police
Eingang	Entrance
Ausgang	Exit
Offen	Open
Geschlossen	Closed
Kein Zutritt	No Entry
Rauchen Verboten	No Smoking
Verboten	Prohibited
Toiletten (WC)	Toilets
Herren	Men
Damen	Women

north	*Norden*	*nor*·den
south	*Süden*	*zü*·den
east	*Osten*	*os*·ten
west	*Westen*	*ves*·ten

Turn ...

Biegen Sie ... ab.   *bee*·gen zee ... ap

  left/right

  links/rechts   lingks/rekhts

  at the next corner

  an der nächsten Ecke   an dair *naykhs*·ten *e*·ke

  at the traffic lights

  bei der Ampel   bai dair *am*·pel

EMERGENCIES

Help!

Hilfe!   *hil*·fe

It's an emergency!

Es ist ein Notfall!   es ist ain *nawt*·fal

Call the police!

Rufen Sie die Polizei!   *roo*·fen zee dee po·li·*tsai*

Call a doctor!

Rufen Sie einen Arzt!   *roo*·fen zee *ai*·nen artst

Call an ambulance!

Rufen Sie einen   *roo*·fen zee *ai*·nen

  Krankenwagen!   *krang*·ken·vah·gen

Leave me alone!

Lassen Sie mich in Ruhe!   *la*·sen zee mikh in *roo*·e

Go away!

Gehen Sie weg!   *gay*·en zee vek

I'm lost.

Ich habe mich verirrt.   ikh *hah*·be mikh fer·*irt*

HEALTH

Where's the nearest ...?

Wo ist der/die/das nächste ...? (m/f/n)

vaw ist dair/dee/das *naykhs*·te ...

  chemist

  Apotheke (f)   a·po·*tay*·ke

dentist
Zahnarzt/ — *tsahn·artst/*
Zahnärztin (m/f) — *tsahn·erts·tin*
doctor
Arzt/Ärztin (m/f) — *artst/erts·tin*
hospital
Krankenhaus (n) — *krang·ken·hows*

I need a doctor (who speaks English).
Ich brauche einen Arzt (, der Englisch spricht).
ikh *brow·*khe *ai·*nen artst (dair *eng·*lish shprikht)

I'm allergic to ...
Ich bin allergisch gegen ... ikh bin a·*lair·*gish *gay·*gen ...
antibiotics
Antibiotika — an·ti·bi·*aw·*ti·ka
aspirin
Aspirin — as·pi·*reen*
penicillin
Penizillin — pe·ni·tsi·*leen*

I'm sick.
Ich bin krank.
ikh bin krangk

LANGUAGE DIFFICULTIES
Do you speak English?
Sprechen Sie Englisch?
shpre·khen zee *eng·*lish
Does anyone here speak English?
Spricht hier jemand Englisch?
shprikht heer *yay·*mant *eng·*lish
I (don't) understand.
Ich verstehe (nicht).
ikh fer·*shtay·*e (nikht)
Could you please write it down?
Könnten Sie das bitte aufschreiben?
*kern·*ten zee das *bi·*te *owf·*shrai·ben

NUMBERS
1	*ains*	aints
2	*zwei*	tsvai
3	*drei*	drai
4	*vier*	feer
5	*fünf*	fünf
6	*sechs*	zeks
7	*sieben*	*zee·*ben
8	*acht*	akht
9	*neun*	noyn
10	*zehn*	tsayn
11	*elf*	elf
12	*zwölf*	zverlf
13	*dreizehn*	drai·tsayn
14	*vierzehn*	feer·tsayn
15	*fünfzehn*	fünf·tsayn
16	*sechzehn*	zeks·tsayn
17	*siebzehn*	zeep·tsayn
18	*achtzehn*	akh·tsayn
19	*neunzehn*	noyn·tsayn
20	*zwanzig*	tsvan·tsikh
21	*einundzwanzig*	ain·unt·tsvan·tsikh
22	*zweiundzwanig*	tsvai·unt·tsvan·tsikh
30	*dreizig*	drai·tsikh
31	*einunddreizig*	ain·und·drai·tsikh
40	*vierzig*	feer·tsikh
50	*fünfzig*	fünf·tsikh
60	*sechzig*	zekh·tsikh
70	*siebzig*	zeep·tsikh
80	*achtzig*	akh·tsikh
90	*neunzig*	noyn·tsikh
100	*hundert*	hun·dert
1000	*tausend*	tow·sent
2000	*zwei tausend*	tsvai tow·sent

SHOPPING & SERVICES
I'm looking for ...
Ich suche ...
ikh *zoo·*khe ...
Where's the (nearest) ...?
Wo ist der/die/das (nächste) ...? (m/f/n)
vaw ist dair/dee/das (*naykhs·*te) ...
How much (is this)?
Wie viel (kostet das)?
vee feel (*kos·*tet das)
I'm just looking.
Ich schaue mich nur um.
ikh *show·*e mikh noor um
Can you write down the price?
Können Sie den Preis aufschreiben?
*ker·*nen zee dayn prais *owf·*shrai·ben

I'd like to ...
Ich möchte ... ikh *merkh·*te ...
change money (cash)
Geld umtauschen gelt *um·*tow·shen
cash a cheque
einen Scheck einlösen *ai·*nen shek *ain·*ler·zen
change some travellers cheques
Reiseschecks einlösen *rai·*ze·sheks *ain·*ler·zen

Do you accept ...?
Nehmen Sie ...? *nay·*men zee ...
credit cards
Kreditkarten kre·*deet·*kar·ten
travellers cheques
Reiseschecks *rai·*ze·sheks

What time does it open/close?
Wann macht er/sie/es auf/zu? (m/f/n)
van makht air/zee/es owf/tsoo

I want to buy a phonecard.
Ich möchte eine Telefonkarte kaufen.
ikh *merkh*·te ai·ne te·le·*fawn*·kar·te *kow*·fen
Where's the local Internet cafe?
Wo ist hier ein Internet-Café?
vaw ist heer ain *in*·ter·net·ka·fay

an ATM	*ein Geldautomat*	ain *gelt*·ow·to·maht
an exchange	*eine Geldwechsel-*	ai·ne *gelt*·vek·sel·
office	*stube*	shtoo·be
a bank	*eine Bank*	ai·ne bangk
the ... embassy	*die ... Botschaft*	dee *bot*·shaft
the hospital	*das Krankenhaus*	das *krang*·ken·hows
the market	*der Markt*	dair markt
the police	*die Polizei*	dee po·li·*tsai*
the post office	*das Postamt*	das *post*·amt
a public phone	*ein öffentliches*	ain er·fent·li·khes
	Telefon	te·le·*fawn*
a public toilet	*eine öffentliche*	ain er·fent·li·khe
	Toilette	to·a·*le*·te

I'd like to ...
Ich möchte ...   ikh *merkh*·te ...
  get Internet access
  Internetzugang haben   *in*·ter·net·tsoo·gang *hah*·ben
  check my email
  meine E-Mails checken   *mai*·ne ee·mayls *che*·ken

TIME & DATES
What time is it?
Wie spät ist es?   vee shpayt ist es
It's (one) o'clock.
Es ist (ein) Uhr.   es ist (ain) oor
Twenty past one.
Zwanzig nach eins.   tsvan·tsikh nahkh ains
Half past one.
Halb zwei. ('half two')   halp tsvai
Quarter to one.
Viertel vor eins.   *fir*·tel fawr ains
am
  morgens/vormittags   *mor*·gens/*fawr*·mi·tahks
pm
  nachmittags/abends   *nahkh*·mi·tahks/*ah*·bents

now	*jetzt*	yetst
today	*heute*	*hoy*·te
tonight	*heute Abend*	*hoy*·te *ah*·bent
tomorrow	*morgen*	*mor*·gen

Monday	*Montag*	*mawn*·tahk
Tuesday	*Dienstag*	*deens*·tahk
Wednesday	*Mittwoch*	*mit*·vokh
Thursday	*Donnerstag*	*do*·ners·tahk
Friday	*Freitag*	*frai*·tahk
Saturday	*Samstag*	*zams*·tahk
Sunday	*Sonntag*	*zon*·tahk

January	*Januar*	yan·u·ahr
February	*Februar*	fay·bru·ahr
March	*März*	merts
April	*April*	a·*pril*
May	*Mai*	mai
June	*Juni*	yoo·ni
July	*Juli*	yoo·li
August	*August*	ow·*gust*
September	*September*	zep·*tem*·ber
October	*Oktober*	ok·*taw*·ber
November	*November*	no·*vem*·ber
December	*Dezember*	de·*tsem*·ber

TRANSPORT
Public Transport
What time does the ... leave?
Wann fährt ... ab?   van fairt ... ap

bus	*der Bus*	dair bus
train	*der Zug*	dair tsook

first	*erste*	*ers*·te
last	*letzte*	*lets*·te
next	*nächste*	*naykhs*·te

Where's the nearest metro station?
Wo ist der nächste U-Bahnhof?
vaw ist dair *naykhs*·te oo·bahn·hawf
Which (bus) goes to ...?
Welcher Bus fährt ...?
vel·kher bus fairt ...

metro	
U-Bahn	oo·bahn
(metro) station	
(U-)Bahnhof	(oo·)bahn·hawf
tram	
Strassenbahn	*shtrah*·sen·bahn
tram stop	
Strassenbahnhalte-	*shtrah*·sen·bahn·*hal*·te·
stelle	shte·le
urban railway	
S-Bahn	es·bahn

A ... ticket to (Munich).
Einen ... nach (München). ai·nen ... nahkh (moon·*khyen*)
  one-way
  einfache Fahrkarte   ain·fa·khe *fahr*·kar·te
  return
  Rückfahrkarte   *rük*·fahr·kar·te

Is this seat free?
Ist dieser Platz frei?   ist *dee*·zer plats frai
Do I need to change trains?
Muss ich umsteigen?   mus ikh *um*·shtai·gen
Is this taxi available? ('Are you free?' – taxi)
Sind Sie frei?   zint zee frai

How much is it to ...?
Was kostet es bis ...?   vas kos·tet es bis ...
Please take me to (this address).
Bitte bringen Sie mich   bi·te bring·en zee mikh
zu (dieser Adresse).   tsoo (dee·zer a·dre·se)

Private Transport

Where can I hire a ...?
Wo kann ich ... mieten?   vaw kan ikh ... mee·ten
I'd like to hire a/an ...
Ich möchte ... mieten.   ikh merkh·te ... mee·ten
  bicycle
  ein Fahrrad   ain fahr·raht
  car
  ein Auto   ain ow·to
  motorbike
  ein Motorrad   ain maw·tor·raht

ROAD SIGNS

Gefahr	Danger
Einfahrt Verboten	No Entry
Einbahnstrasse	One-way
Einfahrt	Entrance
Ausfahrt	Exit
Ausfahrt Freihalten	Keep Clear
Parkverbot	No Parking
Mautstelle	Toll
Radweg	Cycle Path

---

diesel
  Diesel   dee·zel
LPG
  Autogas (n)   ow·to·gahs
petrol (gas)
  Benzin (n)   ben·tseen

Where's a petrol station?
Wo ist eine Tankstelle?
vaw ist ai·ne tangk·shte·le
Does this road go to ...?
Führt diese Strasse nach ...?
fürt dee·ze shtrah·se nahkh ...
(How long) Can I park here?
(Wie lange) Kann ich hier parken?
(vee lang·e) kan ikh heer par·ken
Where do I pay?
Wo muss ich bezahlen?
vaw mus ikh be·tsah·len
I need a mechanic.
Ich brauche einen Mechaniker.
ikh brow·khe ai·nen me·khah·ni·ker
I've run out of petrol.
Ich habe kein Benzin mehr.
ikh hah·be kain ben·tseen mair

TRAVEL WITH CHILDREN

I need a ...
Ich brauche ...   ikh brow·khe ...
Is there a/an ...?
Gibt es ...?   gipt es ...
  baby change room
  einen Wickelraum   ai·nen vi·kel·rowm
  baby seat
  einen Babysitz   ai·nen bay·bi·zits
  booster seat
  einen Kindersitz   ai·nen kin·der·zits
  child-minding service
  einen Babysitter-Service   ai·nen bay·bi·si·ter·ser·vis
  highchair
  einen Kinderstuhl   ai·nen kin·der·shtool
  infant formula (milk)
  Trockenmilch für   tro·ken·milkh für
  Säuglinge   soyg·ling·e
  potty
  ein Kindertöpfchen   ain kin·der·terpf·khen
  stroller
  einen Kinderwagen   ai·nen kin·der·vah·gen

Do you mind if I breastfeed here?
Kann ich meinem Kind hier die Brust geben?
kan ikh mai·nem kint heer dee brust gay·ben
Are children allowed?
Sind Kinder erlaubt?
zint kin·der er·lowpt

Also available from Lonely Planet:
German Phrasebook

Glossary

(pl) indicates plural

Abfahrt – departure
Abtei – abbey
ADAC – Allgemeiner Deutscher Automobil Club (German Automobile Association)
Allee – avenue
Altstadt – old town
Ankunft – arrival
Apotheke – pharmacy
Arzt – doctor
Ärztlicher Notdienst – emergency medical service
Ausfahrt – exit
Ausgang – exit

Bad – spa, bath
Bahnhof – train station
Bahnsteig – train station platform
Basilika – basilica
Bau – building
Bedienung – service; service charge
Behinderte – disabled
Berg – mountain
Bezirk – district
Bibliothek – library
Bierkeller – cellar pub
Bierstube – traditional beer pub
BRD – Bundesrepublik Deutschland or, in English, FRG (Federal Republic of Germany); the name for Germany today, before reunification it applied to West Germany
Brotzeit – literally 'bread time', typically an afternoon snack featuring bread with cold cuts, cheeses or a pair of sausages
Brücke – bridge
Brunnen – fountain, well
Bundesland – federal state
Burg – castle
Busbahnhof – bus station

CDU – Christian Democratic Union
Christkindlmarkt – Christmas food and craft market; sometimes spelt Christkindlesmarkt; see also *Weihnachts-markt*
CSU – Christian Social Union; Bavarian offshoot of *CDU*

DB – Deutsche Bahn (German national railway)
DDR – Deutsche Demokratische Republik or, in English, GDR (German Democratic Republic); the name for the former East Germany
Denkmal – memorial

Deutsche Reich – German empire; refers to the period 1871–1918
DJH – Deutsches Jugendherbergswerk (German youth hostels association)
Dom – cathedral
Dorf – village

Eingang – entrance
Eintritt – admission

Fahrplan – timetable
Fahrrad – bicycle
Fasching – pre-Lenten carnival
FDP – Free Democratic Party
Ferienwohnung, Ferienwohnungen (pl) – holiday flat or apartment
Fest – festival
FKK – nude bathing area
Flohmarkt – flea market
Flughafen – airport
Föhn – an intense autumn wind in the Agerman Alps and Alpine Foothills
Forstweg – forestry track
Franken – 'Franks', Germanic people influential in Europe between the 3rd and 8th centuries
Fremdenverkehrsamt – tourist office
Fremdenverkehrsverein – tourist office
Fremdenzimmer – tourist room
FRG – Federal Republic of Germany; see also *BRD*
Fussball – football, soccer

Garten – garden
Gasse – lane, alley
Gastarbeiter – literally 'guest worker'; labourer from primarily Mediterranean countries who arrived in Germany during the 1950s and 1960s in order to fill a labour shortage
Gästehaus – guesthouse
Gaststätte, Gasthaus – informal restaurant, inn
GDR – German Democratic Republic (the former East Germany); see also *DDR*
Gedenkstätte – memorial site
Gemütlichkeit – a particularly convivial, cosy ambience and setting, for instance in a pub, restaurant or living room
Gepäckaufbewahrung – left-luggage office
Gesamtkunstwerk – literally 'total artwork'; integrates painting, sculpture and architecture
Gestapo – Nazi secret police
Gründerzeit – literally 'foundation time'; the period of industrial expansion in Germany following the founding of the German empire in 1871

Hauptbahnhof – central train station
Herzog – duke
Hitler Jugend – Hitler Youth organisation
Hochdeutsch – literally 'High German'; standard spoken and written German, developed from a regional Saxon dialect
Hochkultur – literally 'high culture'; advanced civilisation
Hof, Höfe (pl) – courtyard
Höhle – cave
Hotel Garni – a hotel without a restaurant where you are only served breakfast

Imbiss – stand-up food stall; see also *Schnellimbiss*
Insel – island

Jugendgästehaus – youth guesthouse of a higher standard than a youth hostel
Jugendherberge – youth hostel
Jugendstil – Art Nouveau

Kabarett – cabaret
Kaffee und Kuchen – literally 'coffee and cake'; traditional afternoon coffee break in Germany
Kanal – canal
Kantine – cafeteria, canteen
Kapelle – chapel
Karte – ticket
Kartenvorverkauf – ticket booking office
Kino – cinema
Kirche – church
Kloster – monastery, convent
Kneipe – pub
Kommunales Kino – alternative or studio cinema
Konditorei – cake shop
König – king
Konsulat – consulate
Konzentrationslager – a concentration camp; abbreviated to KZ
Krankenhaus – hospital
Kreuzgang – monastery
Kunst – art
Kurfürst – prince-elector
Kurhaus – literally 'spa house', but usually a spa town's central building, used for social gatherings and events and often housing the town's casino
Kurort – spa resort
Kurtaxe – resort tax
Kurverwaltung – spa resort administration
Kurzentrum – spa centre

Land, Länder (pl) – state
Landtag – state parliament
Lesbe, Lesben (pl) – lesbian (n)
lesbisch – lesbian (adj)
lieblich – sweet (adj)
Lied – song

Markgraf – margrave; German nobleman ranking above a count
Markt – market; often used instead of *Marktplatz*
Marktplatz – marketplace or square; often abbreviated to *Markt*
Mass – 1L tankard or stein of beer
Mehrwertsteuer – value-added tax; abbreviated to MwST
Meistersinger – literally 'master singer'; highest level in medieval troubadour guilds
Mensa – university cafeteria
Milchcafé – coffee with milk
Münster – minster, large church, cathedral
Münzwäscherei – coin-operated laundrette

Nord – north
Notdienst – emergency service
NSDAP – National Socialist German Workers' Party

Ost – east

Palast – palace, residential quarters of a castle
Pannenhilfe – roadside breakdown assistance for motorists
Parkhaus – car park
Parkschein – parking voucher
Parkscheinautomat – vending machine selling parking vouchers
Passage – shopping arcade
Pension, Pensionen (pl) – inexpensive boarding house
Pfand – deposit for bottles and sometimes glasses (in beer gardens)
Pfarrkirche – parish church
Platz – square
Postamt – post office
Postlagernd – poste restante

Radwandern – bicycle touring
Rathaus – town hall
Ratskeller – town hall restaurant
Reisezentrum – travel centre in train or bus stations
Rezept – medical prescription
R-Gespräch – reverse-charge call
Ruhetag – literally 'rest day'; closing day at a shop or restaurant
Rundgang – tour, route

Saal, Säle (pl) – hall, room
Sammlung – collection
Säule – column, pillar
S-Bahn – Schnellbahn; suburban-metropolitan shuttle lines
Schatzkammer – treasury
Schicki-mickis – yuppies
Schiff – ship
Schifffahrt – shipping, navigation
Schloss – palace, castle
Schnellimbiss – stand-up food stall; see also *Imbiss*

schwul – gay (adj)
Schwuler, Schwule (pl) – gay (n)
See – lake
Selbstbedienung (SB) – self-service (restaurants, laundrettes etc)
SPD – Sozialdemokratische Partei Deutschlands (Social Democratic Party)
Speisekarte – menu
Sportverein – sports association
Stadt – city, town
Stadtbad, Stadtbäder (pl) – public pool
Stadtwald – city or town forest
Stau – traffic jam
Staudamm, Staumauer – dam
Stehcafé – stand-up café
Strand – beach
Strasse – street; often abbreviated to Str
Süd – south
Szene – scene (ie where the action is)

Tageskarte – daily menu or day ticket on public transport
Tal – valley
Tor – gate
Trödel – junk
Turm – tower

U-Bahn – underground train system
Übergang – transit or transfer point
Ufer – bank
Verboten – forbidden

Verkehr – traffic
Verkehrsamt – tourist office
Verkehrsverein – tourist office
Viertel – quarter, district
Volkslied – folk song
Volksmusik – folk music

Wald – forest
Wäscherei – laundry
Wechselstube – currency exchange office
Weg – way, path
Weihnachtsmarkt – Christmas market; see also *Christkindlmarkt*
Weingut – wine-growing estate
Weinkeller – wine cellar
Weinprobe – wine tasting
Weinstube – traditional wine bar or tavern
White skins – skinheads wearing jackboots with white laces
Wiese – meadow
Wirtschaftswunder – Germany's post-WWII 'economic miracle'

Zahnradbahn – cog-wheel railway
Zeitung – newspaper
Zentraler Omnibusbahnhof – central bus station; commonly called the ZOB
Zimmer Frei – room available (for accommodation purposes)
Zimmervermittlung – a room-finding service, primarily for short-term stays

Behind the Scenes

THIS BOOK

Andrea Schulte-Peevers wrote the 1st edition of this book (then entitled *Bavaria*) and was joined by Jeremy Gray and Catherine Le Nevez on this 2nd edition. The Health chapter was written by Dr Caroline Evans.

THANKS from the Authors

Andrea Schulte-Peevers Victoria Larson, Ulrike Eberl-Walter and Alfred Helbrich all deserve gold medals for their generous and tireless help. A great big thank you also goes to Judith Bamber for entrusting me with this gig, and my co-authors Jeremy Gray and Catherine Le Nevez for being both meticulously professional and fun to work with. Of the many people along the way who've shared their knowledge and fed me tips and good advice, the following deserve a special mention: Claudia Bracht, Ursula Bosl, Frau Hertl, Kurt Joachimsthaler, Karl Kollmaier, Frau Meininger, Pia Olligschläger, Irene Peringer, Rainer Uhl, Eva Rossberger, Frau Rühl, Christine Schopf and Kurt Weinzierl. Back on the home front, deep heartfelt thanks to David for once again keeping me sane, fed and loved through long hours at the desk.

Jeremy Gray A warm *danke schön* to all those who made my life easier during research, including Henna Manhard and Robert Leckel at the Munich Tourist Authority; Maxine Ryder and Michael Flossmann, my lovely hosts in Munich; Ann Elbling and Grit Watson, connoisseurs of dining and nightlife; Ursula Karbacher at the Berchtesgaden Tourist Office; and Helga Precht of the Salzburg Tourist Office. Fellow authors Andrea and Catherine were a joy to work with. And thank you, dearest Petra, for your loving support – I couldn't have done it without you.

Catherine Le Nevez Monumental thanks to (Saint) Dirk Marky who from day one provided me with a treasure trove of information, insight and Franconian hospitality. Thanks also to Susanne Bütter, for the same. Karin Mannhardt's and Julia Vogel's insider tips and good company in Nuremberg were much appreciated. In Würzburg, Holger Siefert, Marco Hein and Louisa-Verena Wein showed me around like only locals can, and were generous with their time and hospitality. Experts extraordinaire Harry Ernst and Daniel Weber went above and beyond to guide me through Rothenburg and the Romantic Road – cheers guys. Thanks also to my colleagues Andrea, for endless patience answering questions and for the beers, and Jeremy, for the witty and enlightening anecdotes, as well as Judith Bamber for giving me the gig, and everyone at LP. I'm grateful to all the tourist office staff along the way for their fantastic assistance, and to Erwin Marschall for salient Allgäu background. And to the kindly farmer who rescued me as my hire car slid brakeless down a snowy mountainside and comically explained that it only had 'summer tyres'. Most of all, heartfelt thanks to my family for their unfailing support.

CREDITS

Commissioning Editor Judith Bamber
Coordinating Editor Kate McLeod

THE LONELY PLANET STORY

The story begins with a classic travel adventure: Tony and Maureen Wheeler's 1972 journey across Europe and Asia to Australia. There was no useful information about the overland trail then, so Tony and Maureen published the first Lonely Planet guidebook to meet a growing need.

From a kitchen table, Lonely Planet has grown to become the largest independent travel publisher in the world, with offices in Melbourne (Australia), Oakland (USA) and London (UK). Today Lonely Planet guidebooks cover the globe. There is an ever-growing list of books and information in a variety of media. Some things haven't changed. The main aim is still to make it possible for adventurous travellers to get out there – to explore and better understand the world.

At Lonely Planet we believe travellers can make a positive contribution to the countries they visit – if they respect their host communities and spend their money wisely. Every year 5% of company profit is donated to charities around the world.

Coordinating Cartographer Natasha Velleley
Coordinating Layout Designer Michael Ruff
Managing Cartographer Mark Griffiths
Assisting Editors Helen Christinis, Brooke Lyons, Lucy Monie, Gabbi Wilson
Assisting Cartographers Corey Hutchinson, James Ellis, Emma McNicol, Lachlan Ross
Assisting Layout Designers Laura Jane
Colour Designer Pablo Gastar
Cover Designer Gerilyn Attebery
Project Manager Glenn van der Knijff
Language Content Coordinator Quentin Frayne

Thanks to: Melanie Dankel, Sally Darmody, Brigitte Ellemor, Emma Koch

THANKS from Lonely Planet

Many thanks to the following travellers who used the last edition and wrote to us with helpful hints, useful advice and interesting anecdotes.

B William Ballantine, Paul Beach, Jochen Beier, Mariska Belyea, Maria & Tony Benfield, Fletcher Benton, Astrid Bergner, Guillermo Boughton, Ben Brehmer **C** Romelle Castle, Tara Castle, Lisa Cipelli **D** Mathew Dolenac, Marilyn & Oswald Drews **E** Katie Elder, Jakob Engblom **F** Rainer F, Olivia Faul, Grahame Foster, Rob Francis, **G** S Greenwood **H** Jarrod Hepburn, Mindy Huixing **J** Jimmy & Anja Johnson **K** Anil Kanji, Christoph Kessel, Stephen Kinsella **L** AM Lepper, John Longsworth, Simon Looi **M** Alex MacKenzie, Conor McNamara, Dick Murphy **N** Jonas Nahm **O** Ian Older, Elka (Alice) Olsen **P** Marj & Roger Pemberton, Steve Penny, Eric Philpott, Ed Piekara, Scott Plimpton **R** Tori Robson **S** Karl Scharbert, Petra Schneider, Byron Scott, Elizabeth Sercombe, James A Silverglad, Alistair Staton, Julie Stenberg **T** Eric Thomsen **V** Joyce Vermeer **W** Duncan Waters, Karin Weber

ACKNOWLEDGMENTS

Many thanks to the following for the use of their content:
Globe on back cover © Mountain High Maps 1993 Digital Wisdom, Inc.

Thanks to Münchner Verkehrs- und Tarifverbund GmbH (MVV) for permission to use the Munich Transport map.

SEND US YOUR FEEDBACK

We love to hear from travellers – your comments keep us on our toes and help make our books better. Our well-travelled team reads every word on what you loved or loathed about this book. Although we cannot reply individually to postal submissions, we always guarantee that your feedback goes straight to the appropriate authors, in time for the next edition. Each person who sends us information is thanked in the next edition – and the most useful submissions are rewarded with a free book.

To send us your updates – and find out about Lonely Planet events, newsletters and travel news – visit our award-winning website: **www.lonelyplanet.com/feedback**.

Note: We may edit, reproduce and incorporate your comments in Lonely Planet products such as guidebooks, websites and digital products, so let us know if you don't want your comments reproduced or your name acknowledged. For a copy of our privacy policy visit www.lonelyplanet.com/privacy.

Index

INDEX

INDEX

INDEX

000 Map pages
000 Location of colour photographs

INDEX

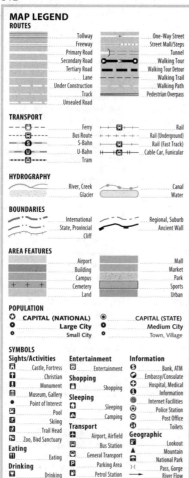

MAP LEGEND
ROUTES
Tollway
Freeway
Primary Road
Secondary Road
Tertiary Road
Lane
Under Construction
Track
Unsealed Road
One-Way Street
Street Mall/Steps
Tunnel
Walking Tour
Walking Tour Detour
Walking Trail
Walking Path
Pedestrian Overpass

TRANSPORT
Ferry
Bus Route
S-Bahn
U-Bahn
Tram
Rail
Rail (Underground)
Rail (Fast Track)
Cable Car, Funicular

HYDROGRAPHY
River, Creek
Glacier
Canal
Water

BOUNDARIES
International
State, Provincial
Cliff
Regional, Suburb
Ancient Wall

AREA FEATURES
Airport
Building
Campus
Cemetery
Land
Mall
Market
Park
Sports
Urban

POPULATION
CAPITAL (NATIONAL)
Large City
Small City
CAPITAL (STATE)
Medium City
Town, Village

SYMBOLS
Sights/Activities
Castle, Fortress
Christian
Monument
Museum, Gallery
Point of Interest
Pool
Skiing
Trail Head
Zoo, Bird Sanctuary
Eating
Eating
Drinking
Drinking
Café

Entertainment
Entertainment
Shopping
Shopping
Sleeping
Sleeping
Camping
Transport
Airport, Airfield
Bus Station
General Transport
Parking Area
Petrol Station
Taxi Rank

Information
Bank, ATM
Embassy/Consulate
Hospital, Medical
Information
Internet Facilities
Police Station
Post Office
Toilets
Geographic
Lookout
Mountain
National Park
Pass, Gorge
River Flow
Waterfall

LONELY PLANET OFFICES

Australia
Head Office
Locked Bag 1, Footscray, Victoria 3011
☎ 03 8379 8000, fax 03 8379 8111
talk2us@lonelyplanet.com.au

USA
150 Linden St, Oakland, CA 94607
☎ 510 893 8555, toll free 800 275 8555
fax 510 893 8572, info@lonelyplanet.com

UK
72–82 Rosebery Ave,
Clerkenwell, London EC1R 4RW
☎ 020 7841 9000, fax 020 7841 9001
go@lonelyplanet.co.uk

Published by Lonely Planet Publications Pty Ltd
ABN 36 005 607 983

2nd Edition – July 2005
First Published – July 2002

© Lonely Planet 2005

© photographers as indicated 2005

Cover photographs by Lonely Planet Images: Neuschwanstein castle, Füssen, Chris Mellor (front); Rides at Oktoberfest, Munich, David Peevers (back). Many of the images in this guide are available for licensing from Lonely Planet Images: www.lonelyplanetimages.com